ANDROID™ FOR PROGRAMMERS

AN APP-DRIVEN APPROACH

DEITEL® DEVELOPER SERIES

The publisher offers excellent discounts on this book when ordered in quantity for bulk purchases or special sales, which may include electronic versions and/or custom covers and content particular to your business, training goals, marketing focus, and branding interests. For more information, please contact:

U. S. Corporate and Government Sales
(800) 382-3419
corpsales@pearsontechgroup.com

For sales outside the U. S., please contact:

International Sales
international@pearsoned.com

Visit us on the Web: informit.com/ph

Library of Congress Cataloging-in-Publication Data

On file

ISBN-13: 978-0-13-212136-1
ISBN-10: 0-13-212136-0

Text printed in the United States on recycled paper at RR Donnelley in Crawfordsville, Indiana.
Second printing, January 2012

ANDROID™ FOR PROGRAMMERS

AN APP-DRIVEN APPROACH

DEITEL® DEVELOPER SERIES

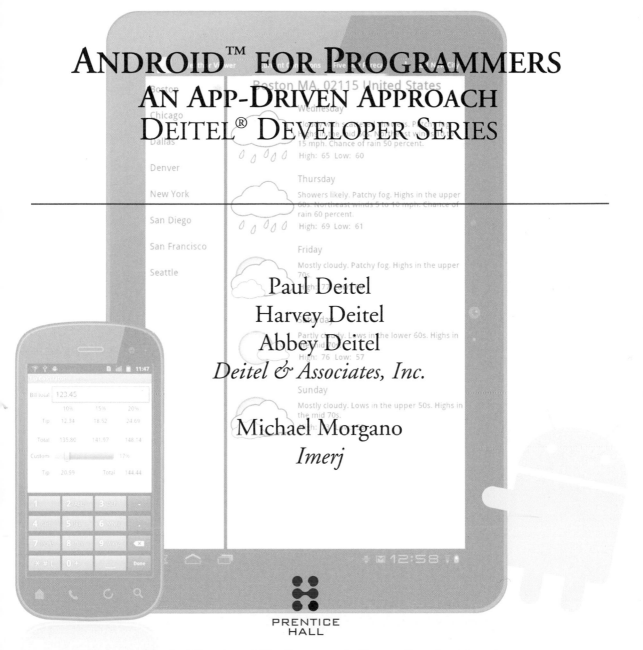

Paul Deitel
Harvey Deitel
Abbey Deitel
Deitel & Associates, Inc.

Michael Morgano
Imerj

PRENTICE HALL

Upper Saddle River, NJ • Boston • Indianapolis • San Francisco
New York • Toronto • Montreal • London • Munich • Paris • Madrid
Capetown • Sydney • Tokyo • Singapore • Mexico City

Trademarks

DEITEL, the double-thumbs-up bug and DIVE INTO are registered trademarks of Deitel and Associates, Inc.

Java is a registered trademark of Oracle and/or its affiliates. Other names may be trademarks of their respective owners.

Microsoft, Internet Explorer and the Windows logo are either registered trademarks or trademarks of Microsoft Corporation in the United States and/or other countries.

Google is a trademark of Google, Inc.

Throughout this book, trademarks are used. Rather than put a trademark symbol in every occurrence of a trademarked name, we state that we are using the names in an editorial fashion only and to the benefit of the trademark owner, with no intention of infringement of the trademark.

In memory of Daniel McCracken.
Computer science has lost one of its greatest educators.

Paul, Harvey, Abbey and Michael

Contents

Chapters on the Web

See the Online Chapters *section of the Preface for information on downloading these chapters.*

Preface

Welcome to the dynamic world of Android smartphone and tablet app development with the Android Software Development Kit (SDK) 2.3.x and 3.x, the Java™ programming language and the Eclipse™ integrated development environment (IDE).

This book presents leading-edge mobile computing technologies for professional software developers. At the heart of the book is our *app-driven approach.* We present concepts in the context of *17 complete working Android apps*—16 developed in the native Android environment and one developed in HTML5 for the portable world of the web—rather than using code snippets. Chapters 3–19 each present one app. We begin each of these chapters with an introduction to the app, an app test-drive showing one or more sample executions and a technologies overview. Then we proceed with a detailed code walk-through of the app's source code. The source code for all the apps is available at `www.deitel.com/books/AndroidFP/`.

Sales of Android devices and app downloads have been growing exponentially. The first-generation Android phones were released in October 2008. A study by comScore® showed that by July 2011, Android had 41.8% of the U.S. smartphone market share, compared to 27% for Apple's iPhone and 21.7% for Blackberry.[1] Billions of apps have been downloaded from Android Market. More than 500,000 Android devices are being activated daily. The opportunities for Android app developers are enormous.

The demand for mobile devices is increasing as more people rely on smartphones and tablets to stay connected and be productive while away from their personal computers. According to comScore, 234 million Americans used mobile devices in a three-month period ending in July 2011. Of those subscribers, 40.6% used apps.[2]

Fierce competition among popular mobile platforms (Android, BlackBerry, iPhone, Palm, Symbian, Windows Phone 7 and others) and among mobile carriers is leading to rapid innovation and falling prices. Competition among the dozens of Android device manufacturers is driving hardware and software innovation within the Android community. There are now over 300 different Android devices.

Android for Programmers: An App-Driven Approach was fun to write! We got to know and love Android, many of its most popular apps and the diversity of Android-based devices. We developed lots of Android apps. The book's apps were carefully designed to introduce you to a broad range of Android features and technologies, including audio, video, animation, telephony, Bluetooth®, speech recognition, the accelerometer, GPS, the compass, widgets, App Widgets, 3D graphics and more. You'll quickly learn everything you'll need to start building Android apps—beginning with a test-drive of the **Doodlz** app

1. `www.comscore.com/Press_Events/Press_Releases/2011/8/comScore_Reports_July_2011_U.S._Mobile_Subscriber_Market_Share`.
2. `www.comscore.com/Press_Events/Press_Releases/2011/8/comScore_Reports_July_2011_U.S._Mobile_Subscriber_Market_Share`.

in Chapter 1, then creating your first app in Chapter 3. Chapter 2, Android Market and App Business Issues walks you through designing great apps, uploading your apps to Google's Android Market and other online app stores, what to expect in the process, deciding whether to sell your apps or offer them for free, and marketing them using the Internet and word-of-mouth, and more.

Copyright Notice and Code License

Intended Audience

We assume that you're a Java programmer with object-oriented programming experience and that you're familiar with XML. We use only complete, working apps, so if you don't know Java and XML but have object-oriented programming experience in C#/.NET, Objective-C/Cocoa or C++ (with class libraries), you should be able to master the material quickly, learning a good amount of Java, Java-style object-oriented programming and XML along the way.

This book is *neither* a Java *nor* an XML tutorial, but it presents a significant amount of Java and XML technology in the context of Android app development. If you're interested in learning Java, check out our publications:

- *Java for Programmers* (`www.deitel.com/books/javafp/`)
- *Java Fundamentals: Parts I and II* LiveLessons videos (`www.deitel.com/books/LiveLessons/`).
- *Java How to Program, 9/e* (`www.deitel.com/books/jhtp9/`)

Key Features

App-Driven Approach. Each of the apps chapters (3–19) presents one app—we discuss what the app does, show screen shots of the app in action, test-drive it and overview the technologies and architecture we'll use to build it. Then we build the app, present the complete code and do a detailed code walkthrough. We discuss the programming concepts and demonstrate the functionality of the Android APIs used in the app. Figure 1 lists the book's apps and the key technologies we used to build each.

Apps	Technologies
Chapter 3, **Welcome** App	Dive-Into® Eclipse and the ADT
Chapter 4, **Tip Calculator** App	Building an Android App with Java

Fig. 1 | *Android for Programmers* apps and the technologies they introduce.

Apps	Technologies
Chapter 5, Favorite Twitter® Searches App	Collections, Widgets and Views
Chapter 6, Flag Quiz App	Intents and Menus
Chapter 7, Cannon Game App	Frame-By-Frame Animation and Handling User Events
Chapter 8, Spot-On Game App	Tweened Animation and Listening for Touches
Chapter 9, Doodlz App	Graphics and Accelerometer
Chapter 10, Address Book App	`AdapterViews` and `Adapters`
Chapter 11, Route Tracker App	Maps API and Compass
Chapter 12, Slideshow App	Photos and Audio Library Access
Chapter 13, Enhanced Slideshow App	Serializing Objects and Playing Video
Chapter 14, Weather Viewer App	Internet Enabled Applications, Web Services and App Widgets
Chapter 15, Pizza Ordering App	Android Telephony and Speech APIs
Chapter 16, Voice Recorder App	Audio Recording and Playback
Chapter 17, Enhanced Address Book App	Managing Persistent Data with SQLite 3 and Transferring Data Via Bluetooth
Chapter 18, 3D Art App	3D Graphics and Animation with OpenGL ES
Chapter 19, Favorite Twitter® Searches App using HTML5 Technologies	Online Bonus Chapter: HTML5, CSS3 and JavaScript for Experienced Web Developers

Fig. 1 | *Android for Programmers* apps and the technologies they introduce.

Android SDK 2.x. We cover many of the new features included in the Android Software Development Kit (SDK) 2.x, including Bluetooth, Google Maps, the Camera APIs, graphics APIs and support for multiple screen sizes and resolutions.

Android SDK 3.x for Tablet Apps. We cover many of the features of the new Android SDK 3.x for developing tablet apps, including property animation, action bar, fragments, status bar notifications and drag-and-drop.

Android Maps APIs. The Route Tracker App uses the Android Maps APIs which allow you to incorporate Google™ Maps in your app. Before developing any app using the Maps APIs, you *must* agree to the Android Maps APIs *Terms of Service* (including the related Legal Notices and Privacy Policy) at `code.google.com/android/maps-api-tos.pdf`.

Eclipse. The free Eclipse integrated development environment (IDE) combined with the free Android SDK and the free Java Development Kit (JDK), provide everything you need to develop and test Android apps.

Multimedia. The apps use a broad range of Android multimedia capabilities, including graphics, images, frame-by-frame animation, property animation, audio, video, speech synthesis and speech recognition.

Android Best Practices. We adhere to accepted Android best practices, pointing them out in the detailed code walkthroughs. Check out our Android Best Practices Resource Center at `www.deitel.com/AndroidBestPractices/`.

Web Services. Web services allow you to use the web as a rich library of services—many of which are free. Chapter 11's **Route Tracker** app uses the built-in Android Maps APIs to interact with the Google Maps web services. Chapter 14's **Weather Viewer** app uses WeatherBug's web services.[3]

Features

Syntax Shading. For readability, we syntax shade the code, similar to Eclipse's use of syntax coloring. Our syntax-shading conventions are as follows:

```
comments appear in gray
constants and literal values appear in bold darker gray
keywords appear in bold black
all other code appears in non-bold black
```

Code Highlighting. We emphasize the key code segments in each program by enclosing them in light gray rectangles.

Using Fonts for Emphasis. We place defining occurrences of key terms in ***bold italic*** text for easy reference. We identify on-screen components in the **bold Helvetica** font (e.g., the **File** menu) and Java and Android program text in the `Lucida` font (e.g., `int x = 5;`).

In this book you'll create GUIs using a combination of visual programming (drag and drop) and writing code. We use different fonts when we refer to GUI elements in program code versus GUI elements displayed in the IDE:

- When we refer to a GUI component that we create in a program, we place its variable name and class name in a `Lucida` font—e.g., "`Button`" or "`myEditText`."
- When we refer to a GUI component that's part of the IDE, we place the component's text in a **bold Helvetica** font and use a plain text font for the component's type—e.g., "the **File** menu" or "the **Run** button."

Using the > Character. We use the > character to indicate selecting a menu item from a menu. For example, we use the notation **File > New** to indicate that you should select the **New** menu item from the **File** menu.

Source Code. All of the book's source code is available for download from:

```
www.deitel.com/books/AndroidFP/
www.informit.com/title/9780132121361
```

Documentation. All the Android and Java documentation you'll need to develop Android apps is available free at `developer.android.com`. The documentation for Eclipse is available at `www.eclipse.org/documentation`.

Chapter Objectives. Each chapter begins with a list of objectives.

Figures. Hundreds of tables, source code listings and Android screen shots are included.

---

3. `apireg.weatherbug.com/defaultAPI.aspx`.

Index. We include an extensive index for reference. The page number of the defining occurrence of each key term in the book is highlighted in the index in **bold maroon**.

Online Chapters

Chapter 1–14 are in the print book. Chapters 15–19 will be posted online as we complete them. We'll make draft versions of the chapters available first, and we'll update these drafts to the final versions once we incorporate all of the reviewers' comments. To access the online chapters, go to:

```
www.informit.com/register
```

You must register for an an InformIT account and then login. After you've logged into your account, you'll see the **Register a Product** box. Enter the book's ISBN to access the page with the online chapters.

Slides for Instructors

PDF slides containing all of the code, tables and art in the text are available *to qualified instructors only* through Pearson Education's Instructor Resource Center at:

```
www.pearsonhighered.com/irc
```

The Deitel Online Android Resource Centers

Our Android Resource Centers include links to tutorials, documentation, software downloads, articles, blogs, podcasts, videos, code samples, books, e-books and more—most of these are free. Check out the growing list of Android-related Resource Centers, including:

- Android (`www.deitel.com/android/`)
- Android Best Practices (`www.deitel.com/androidbestpractices/`)
- Java (`www.deitel.com/java/`)
- Eclipse (`www.deitel.com/Eclipse/`)
- SQLite 3 (`www.deitel.com/SQLite3/`)

We announce our latest Resource Centers in our newsletter, the *Deitel® Buzz Online* and on Twitter® and Facebook®—see below.

Follow Deitel & Associates, Inc. Online

To receive updates on this and other Deitel publications, new and updated apps, Resource Centers, instructor-led onsite training courses, partner offers and more, register for the free *Deitel® Buzz Online* e-mail newsletter at:

```
www.deitel.com/newsletter/subscribe.html
```

follow us on Twitter

```
@deitel
```

and Facebook

```
www.deitel.com/deitelfan/
```

Contacting the Authors

As you read the book, we'd sincerely appreciate your comments, criticisms, corrections and suggestions for improvement. Please address all correspondence to:

```
deitel@deitel.com
```

We'll respond promptly, and post corrections and clarifications on:

```
www.deitel.com/books/AndroidFP/
```

and on Facebook and Twitter.

Acknowledgments

We're fortunate to have worked on this project with the dedicated publishing professionals at Prentice Hall/Pearson. We appreciate the extraordinary efforts and 16-year mentorship of our friend and professional colleague Mark L. Taub, Editor-in-Chief of Pearson Technology Group. Olivia Basegio did a great job recruiting distinguished members of the Android community and managing the review process. Chuti Prasertsith designed the cover with creativity and precision—we gave him our vision for the cover and he made it happen. John Fuller does a superb job managing the production of all of our Deitel Developer Series books.

We'd like to thank our friend, Rich Wong (Partner, Accel Partners), who provided us with valuable contacts in the Android and mobile app development communities.

We'd like to thank AWS Convergence Technologies, Inc., owners of WeatherBug (`weather.weatherbug.com/`), for giving us permission to use their web services in Chapter 14's **Weather Viewer** app.

We'd also like to thank our colleague, Eric Kern, co-author of our related book, *iPhone for Programmers: An App-Driven Approach*, on which many of the apps in *Android for Programmers: An App-Driven Approach* are based.

Reviewers

We wish to acknowledge the efforts of our reviewers. Adhering to a tight time schedule, the reviewers scrutinized the manuscript, providing constructive suggestions for improving the accuracy and completeness of the presentation:

- Paul Beusterien, Principal, Mobile Developer Solutions
- Eric J. Bowden, COO, Safe Driving Systems, LLC
- Ian G. Clifton, Independent Contractor and Android App Developer
- Daniel Galpin, Android Advocate and author of *Intro to Android Application Development*
- Douglas Jones, Senior Software Engineer, Fullpower Technologies
- Sebastian Nykopp, Chief Architect, Reaktor
- Ronan "Zero" Schwarz, CIO, OpenIntents

Well, there you have it! *Android for Programmers: An App-Driven Approach* will quickly get you developing Android apps. We hope you enjoy reading the book as much as we enjoyed writing it!

Paul, Harvey and Abbey Deitel, and Michael Morgano, October 2011

About the Authors

Paul J. Deitel, CEO and Chief Technical Officer of Deitel & Associates, Inc., is a graduate of MIT, where he studied Information Technology. Through Deitel & Associates, Inc., he has delivered hundreds of Java, C++, C, C#, Visual Basic and Internet programming courses to industry clients, including Cisco, IBM, Siemens, Sun Microsystems, Dell, Lucent Technologies, Fidelity, NASA at the Kennedy Space Center, the National Severe Storm Laboratory, White Sands Missile Range, Rogue Wave Software, Boeing, SunGard Higher Education, Stratus, Cambridge Technology Partners, One Wave, Hyperion Software, Adra Systems, Entergy, CableData Systems, Nortel Networks, Puma, iRobot, Invensys and many more. He and his co-author, Dr. Harvey M. Deitel, are the world's best-selling programming-language textbook and professional book authors.

Dr. Harvey M. Deitel, Chairman and Chief Strategy Officer of Deitel & Associates, Inc., has 50 years of experience in the computer field. Dr. Deitel earned B.S. and M.S. degrees from MIT and a Ph.D. from Boston University. He has extensive college teaching experience, including earning tenure and serving as the Chairman of the Computer Science Department at Boston College before founding Deitel & Associates, Inc., with his son, Paul J. Deitel. He and Paul are the co-authors of dozens of books and LiveLessons video packages and they are writing many more. The Deitels' texts have earned international recognition, with translations published in Japanese, German, Russian, Chinese, Spanish, Korean, French, Polish, Italian, Portuguese, Greek, Urdu and Turkish. Dr. Deitel has delivered hundreds of professional programming seminars to major corporations, academic institutions, government organizations and the military.

Abbey Deitel, President of Deitel & Associates, Inc., is a graduate of Carnegie Mellon University's Tepper School of Management where she received a B.S. in Industrial Management. Abbey has been managing the business operations of Deitel & Associates, Inc. for 14 years. She has contributed to numerous Deitel & Associates publications and, together with Paul and Harvey, is the co-author of *iPhone for Programmers: An App-Driven Approach* and *Internet & World Wide Web How to Program, 5/e*.

Michael Morgano, Android Developer at Imerj™, is a graduate of Northeastern University where he received a B.S. and M.S. degrees in Computer Science. Michael is the co-author of *iPhone for Programmers: An App-Driven Approach.*

Corporate Training from Deitel & Associates, Inc.

Deitel & Associates, Inc., founded by Paul Deitel and Harvey Deitel, is an internationally recognized authoring, corporate training and software development organization specializing in Android and iPhone app development, computer programming languages, object technology and Internet and web software technology. The company offers instructor-led training courses delivered at client sites worldwide on major programming languages and platforms, such as Android app development, Objective-C and iPhone app development, Java™, C, C++, Visual C++®, Visual C#®, Visual Basic®, XML®, Python®, object technology, Internet and web programming, and a growing list of additional programming and software development courses. The company's clients include many of the world's largest companies, government agencies, branches of the military, and academic institutions.

Through its 36-year publishing partnership with Prentice Hall/Pearson, Deitel & Associates, Inc., publishes leading-edge programming professional books, college textbooks, and *LiveLessons* DVD- and web-based video courses. Deitel & Associates, Inc. and the authors can be reached at:

```
deitel@deitel.com
```

To learn more about Deitel's *Dive Into*® *Series* Corporate Training curriculum, visit:

```
www.deitel.com/training/
```

To request a proposal for on-site, instructor-led training at your company or organization, e-mail `deitel@deitel.com`.

Individuals wishing to purchase Deitel books and *LiveLessons* DVD- and web-based training courses can do so through `www.deitel.com`. Bulk orders by corporations, the government, the military and academic institutions should be placed directly with Pearson. For more information, visit `www.pearsoned.com/professional/index.htm`.

Before You Begin

This section contains information and instructions you should review to ensure that your computer is set up properly for use with this book. We'll post updates (if any) to the Before You Begin section on the book's website:

```
www.deitel.com/books/AndroidFP/
```

Font and Naming Conventions

We use fonts to distinguish between on-screen components (such as menu names and menu items) and Java code or commands. Our convention is to show on-screen components in a sans-serif bold **Helvetica** font (for example, **Project** menu) and to show file names, Java code and commands in a sans-serif `Lucida` font (for example, the keyword `public` or class `Activity`).

Software and Hardware System Requirements

To develop Android apps you need a Windows®, Linux or Mac OS X system. To view the latest operating-system requirements visit:

```
developer.android.com/sdk/requirements.html
```

We developed the apps in this book using the following software:

- Java SE 6 Software Development Kit
- Eclipse 3.6.2 (Helios) IDE for Java Developers
- Android SDK versions 2.2, 2.3.3 and 3.x
- ADT (Android Development Tools) Plugin for Eclipse

We tell you where to get each of these in the next section.

Installing the Java Development Kit (JDK)

Android requires the *Java Development Kit (JDK)* version 5 or 6 (JDK 5 or JDK 6). *We used JDK 6.* To download the JDK for Linux or Windows, go to

```
www.oracle.com/technetwork/java/javase/downloads/index.html
```

You need only the JDK. Be sure to follow the installation instructions at

```
www.oracle.com/technetwork/java/javase/index-137561.html
```

Recent versions of Mac OS X come with Java SE 6. Be sure to get the latest version by using the Apple menu feature to check for software updates.

Installing the Eclipse IDE

Eclipse is the recommended integrated development environment (IDE) for Android development, though it's possible to use other IDEs, text editors and command-line tools. To download the *Eclipse IDE for Java Developers*, go to

```
www.eclipse.org/downloads/
```

This page will allow you to download the latest version of Eclipse—3.7.1 at the time of this writing. To use the same version we used when developing this book (3.6.2), click the **Older Versions** link above the list of downloads. Select the appropriate version for your operating system (Windows, Mac or Linux). To install Eclipse, you simply extract the archive's contents to your hard drive. On our Windows 7 system, we extracted the contents to `C:\Eclipse`. For more Eclipse installation information, see

```
bit.ly/InstallingEclipse
```

Important: To ensure that the book's examples compile correctly, configure Eclipse to use JDK 6 by performing the following steps:

1. Locate the Eclipse folder on your system and double click the Eclipse ( ) icon to open Eclipse.
2. When the **Workspace Launcher** window appears, click **OK**.
3. Select **Window > Preferences** to display the **Preferences** window.
4. Expand the **Java** node and select the **Compiler** node. Under **JDK Compliance**, set **Compiler compliance level** to 1.6.
5. Close Eclipse.

Installing the Android SDK

The ***Android Software Development Kit (SDK)*** provides the tools you need to develop, test and debug Android apps. You can download the Android SDK from

```
developer.android.com/sdk/index.html
```

Click the link for your platform—Windows, Mac OS X or Linux—to download the SDK's archive file. Once you've downloaded the archive, simply extract its contents to a directory of your choice on your computer. The SDK *does not* include the Android platform—you'll download this separately using the tools in the Android SDK.

Installing the ADT Plugin for Eclipse

The ***Android Development Tools (ADT) Plugin*** for Eclipse enables you to use the Android SDK tools to develop Android applications in the Eclipse IDE. To install the ADT Plugin, go to

```
developer.android.com/sdk/eclipse-adt.html
```

and *carefully* follow the instructions for downloading and installing the ADT Plugin. If you have any trouble with the installation, be sure to read the troubleshooting tips further down the web page.

Installing the Android Platform(s)

You must now install the Android platform(s) that you wish to use for app development. In this book, we used Android 2.2, 2.3.3 and 3.x. Perform the following steps to install the Android platform(s) and additional SDK tools:

1. Open Eclipse ( ).
2. When the **Workspace Launcher** window appears, specify where you'd like your apps to be stored, then click **OK**.
3. Select **Window > Preferences** to display the **Preferences** window. In the window, select the Android node, then specify the location where you placed the Android SDK on your system in the **SDK Location** field. On our Windows system, we extracted it at `c:\android-sdk-windows`. Click **OK**.
4. Select **Window > Android SDK Manager** to display the **Android SDK Manager** window (Fig. 1).

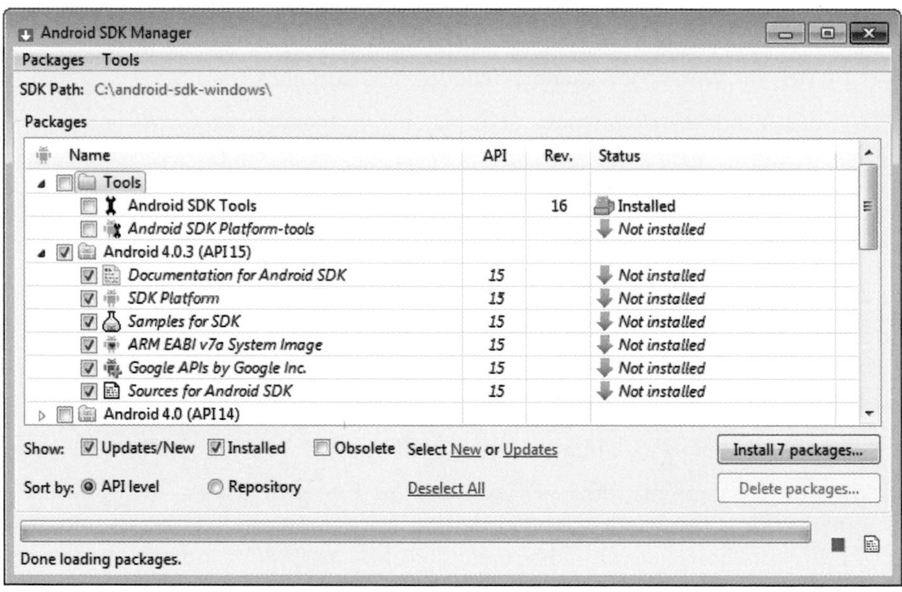

Fig. 1 | **Android SDK Manager** window.

5. The **Name** column of the window shows all of the tools, Android platform versions and extras that you can install. For use with this book, you need the items that are checked in Fig. 2. [*Note:* Most items in the **Extras** node are optional. The **Google USB Driver package** is necessary only for testing Android apps on actual devices using Windows. The **Google Market Licensing package** is necessary only if you intend to develop apps that query the Android Market to determine if a user has a proper license for an app before allowing the app to be used. The **Google Market Billing package** is necessary only if you intend to sell digital content through your app.]

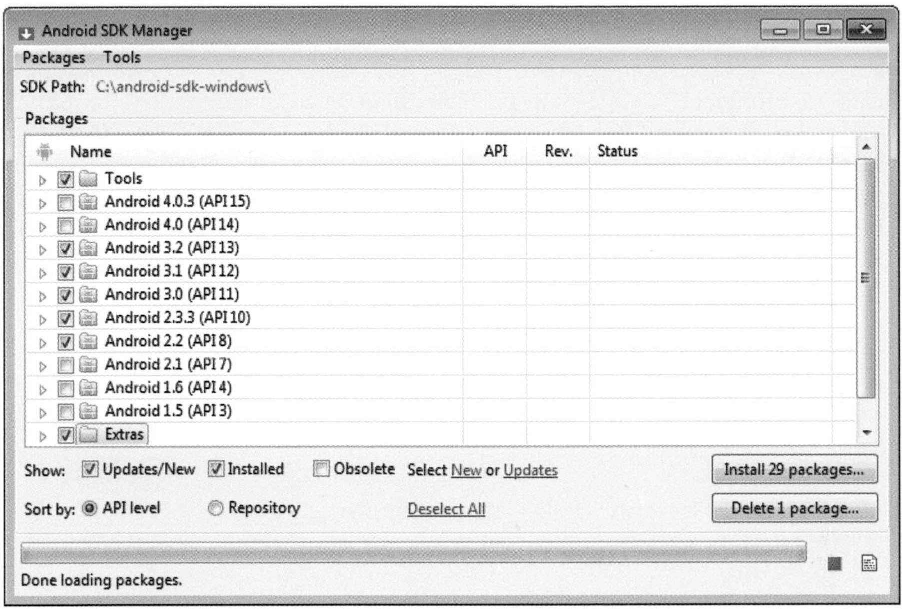

Fig. 2 | Selecting items to install.

6. Click the **Install** button to display the **Choose Packages to Install** window (Fig. 3). In this window, you can read the license agreements for each item. When you're done, click the **Accept All** radio button, then click the **Install** button. The status of the installation process will be displayed in the **Android SDK Manager** window. When the installation is complete, you should close and reopen Eclipse.

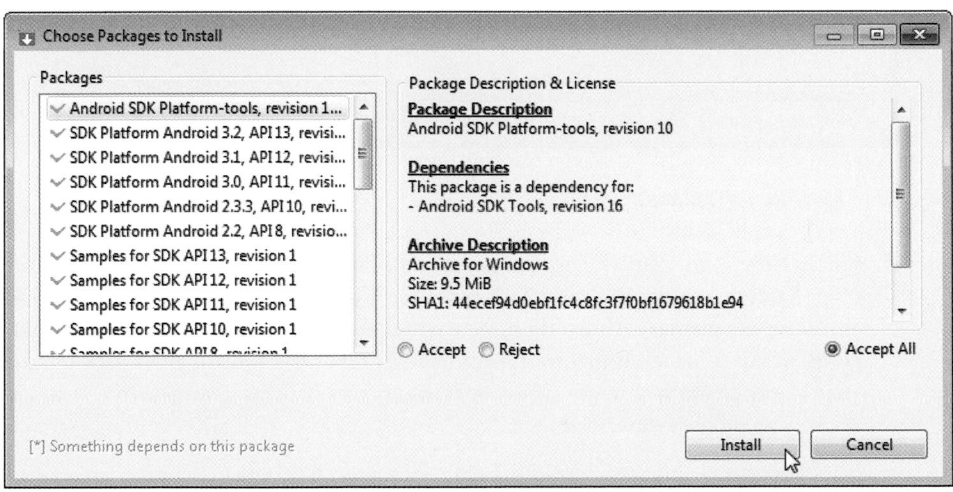

Fig. 3 | **Choose Packages to Install** window.

Creating Android Virtual Devices (AVDs) for Use in the Android Emulator

The ***Android emulator***, included in the Android SDK, allows you to run Android apps in a simulated environment on your computer rather than on an actual Android device. Before running an app in the emulator, you must create an ***Android Virtual Device (AVD)*** which defines the characteristics of the device on which you want to test, including the screen size in pixels, the pixel density, the physical size of the screen, size of the SD card for data storage and more. If you want to test your apps for multiple Android devices, you can create separate AVDs that emulate each unique device. To do so, perform the following steps:

1. Open Eclipse.
2. Select **Window > AVD Manager** to display the **Android Virtual Device Manager** window (Fig. 4).

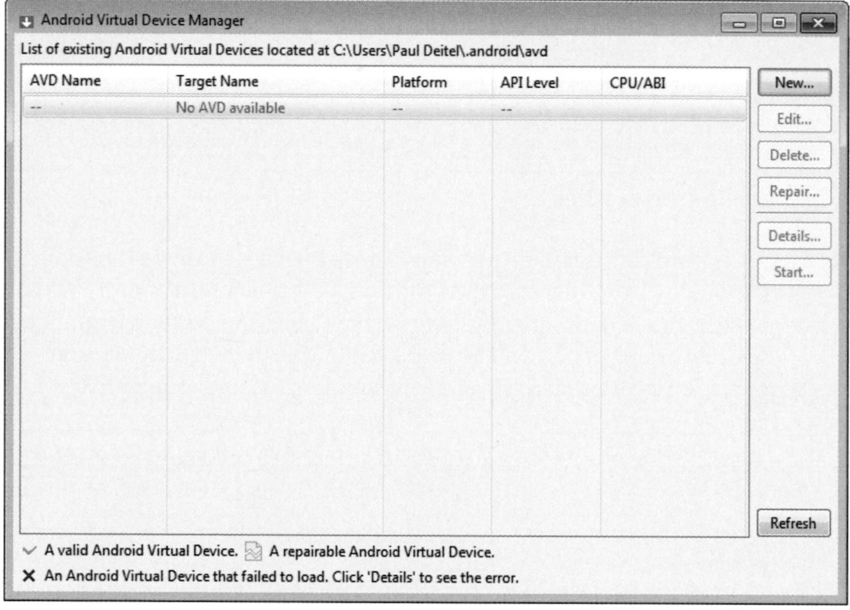

Fig. 4 | **Android AVD Manager** window.

3. Click **New...** to display the **Create new Android Virtual Device (AVD)** window (Fig. 5), then configure the options as shown and click **Create AVD**. These settings simulate the primary Android phone that we used for testing—the original Samsung Nexus S, which was running Android 2.3.3 at the time of this writing. Each AVD you create has many other options specified in its `config.ini`. You can modify this file as described at

```
developer.android.com/guide/developing/devices/
   managing-avds.html
```

to more precisely match the hardware configuration of your device.

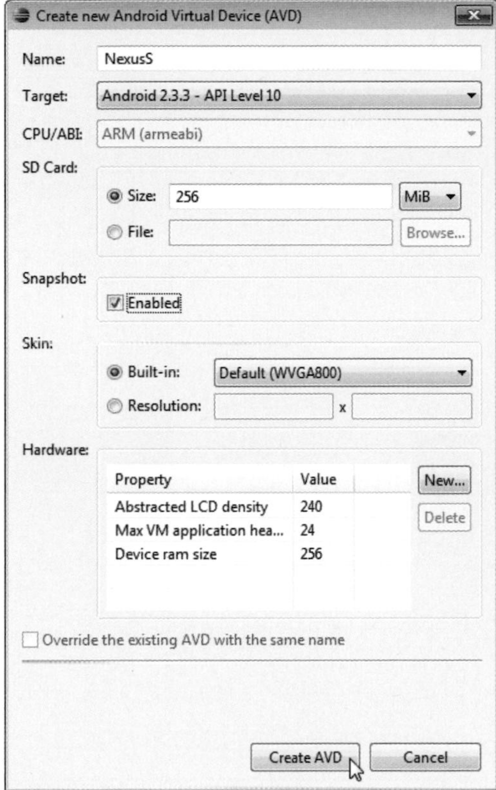

Fig. 5 | **Create new Android Virtual Device (AVD)** window.

4. We also configured an AVD that represents the Motorola Xoom tablet running Android 3.1 so we could test our tablet apps. Its settings are shown in Fig. 6.

AVD Performance

At the time of this writing, AVD performance was quite slow. To improve AVD load time, ensure that the **Enabled** checkbox in the Snapshot section is checked.

(Optional) Setting Up an Android Device for Development

Eventually, you might want to execute your apps on actual Android devices. To do so, follow the instructions at

```
developer.android.com/guide/developing/device.html
```

If you're developing on Microsoft Windows, you'll also need the Windows USB driver for Android devices, which we included as one of the checked items in Fig. 2. In some cases, you may also need device-specific USB drivers. For a list of USB driver sites for various device brands, visit:

```
developer.android.com/sdk/oem-usb.html
```

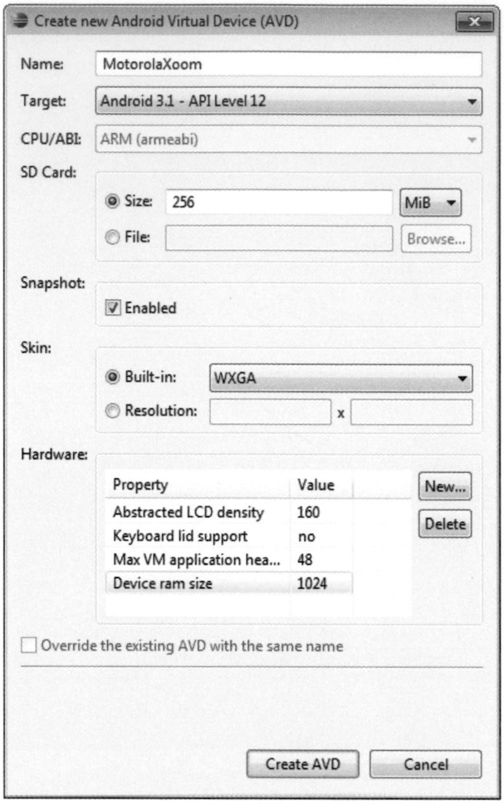

Fig. 6 | **Create new Android Virtual Device (AVD)** window.

(Optional) Other IDEs for Developing Android Apps

We developed all the apps in this book using the Eclipse IDE. Though this is the most popular IDE for Android development, there are other IDEs and tools available. Many early Android developers prefered to work with the command-line tools and some phone vendors (such as Motorola) provide their own Android development tools. The site

```
developer.android.com/guide/developing/projects/
    projects-cmdline.html
```

includes information you'd need to develop Android apps using the command-line tools. Some of the tools for command-line development are summarized in (Fig. 7).

Tool	URL	Description
`android`	`developer.android.com/guide/developing/tools/index.html`	Used to create, view and delete AVDs; create and update Android projects; and update your Android SDK.

Fig. 7 | Tools for developing Android apps in IDEs other than Eclipse.

Tool	URL	Description
Android Emulator	developer.android.com/guide/developing/tools/emulator.html	Allows you to develop and test Android apps on a computer.
Android Debug Bridge (adb)	developer.android.com/guide/developing/tools/adb.html	Allows you to manage the state of a device or the emulator.
Apache Ant	ant.apache.org/	Application build tool.
Keytool and Jarsigner (or similar signing tool)	developer.android.com/guide/publishing/app-signing.html	Included in the JDK. Keytool generates a private key for digitally signing your Android apps. Jarsigner is used to sign the apps.

Fig. 7 | Tools for developing Android apps in IDEs other than Eclipse.

Obtaining the Code Examples

The examples for *Android for Programmers* are available for download at

```
www.deitel.com/books/androidFP/
```

If you're not already registered at our website, go to `www.deitel.com` and click the **Register** link below our logo in the upper-left corner of the page. Fill in your information. There's no charge to register, and we do not share your information with anyone. We send you only account-management e-mails unless you register separately for our free, double-opt-in *Deitel® Buzz Online* e-mail newsletter at

```
www.deitel.com/newsletter/subscribe.html
```

After registering for our website, you'll receive a confirmation e-mail with your verification code—please verify that you entered your email address correctly. *You'll need to click the verification link in the email to sign in at* `www.deitel.com` *for the first time.* Configure your e-mail client to allow e-mails from `deitel.com` to ensure that the verification e-mail is not filtered as junk mail.

Next, visit `www.deitel.com` and sign in using the **Login** link below our logo in the upper-left corner of the page. Go to `www.deitel.com/books/androidFP/`. Click the **Examples** link to download the `Examples.zip` file to your computer. Double click `Examples.zip` to unzip the archive.

You're now ready to begin developing Android apps with *Android for Programmers: An App-Driven Approach*. Enjoy!

Introduction to Android

Objectives

In this chapter you'll be introduced to:

- The history of Android and the Android SDK.
- The Android Market for apps.
- A review of basic object-technology concepts.
- Key software for Android app development, including the Android SDK, the Java SDK and Eclipse integrated development environment (IDE).
- Important Android documentation.
- Test-driving an Android app that enables you to draw on the screen.
- The Deitel online Android Resource Centers.

Outline

1.1 Introduction

Welcome to Android app development! We hope that you'll find working with *Android for Programmers: An App-Driven Approach* to be an informative, challenging, entertaining and rewarding experience. This book is geared toward Java programmers. We use only complete working apps, so if you don't know Java but have object-oriented programming experience in another language, such as C#, Objective-C/Cocoa or C++ (with class libraries), you should be able to master the material quickly, learning Java and Java-style object-oriented programming as you learn Android app development.

The book uses an **app-driven approach**—we discuss each new technology in the context of complete working Android apps, with one app per chapter. We describe the app and test-drive it. Next, we briefly overview the key **Eclipse** (integrated development environment), Java and **Android SDK (Software Development Kit)** technologies we'll use to implement the app. For apps that require it, we walk through designing the GUI visually using Eclipse. Then we provide the complete source-code listing, using line numbers, syntax shading (to mimic the syntax coloring used in the Eclipse IDE) and code highlighting to emphasize the key portions of the code. We also show one or more screen shots of the running app. Then we do a detailed code walkthrough, emphasizing the new programming concepts introduced in the app. The source code for all of the book's apps can be downloaded from `www.deitel.com/books/AndroidFP/`. Figure 1.1 lists key online Android documentation.

Title	URL
Android Developer Guide	`developer.android.com/guide/index.html`
Using the Android Emulator	`developer.android.com/guide/developing/devices/emulator.html`
Android Package Index	`developer.android.com/reference/packages.html`
Android Class Index	`developer.android.com/reference/classes.html`
User Interface Guidelines	`developer.android.com/guide/practices/ui_guidelines/index.html`
Data Backup	`developer.android.com/guide/topics/data/backup.html`

Fig. 1.1 | Key online documentation for Android developers. (Part 1 of 2.)

Title	URL
Security and Permissions	developer.android.com/guide/topics/security/security.html
Managing Projects from Eclipse with ADT	developer.android.com/guide/developing/projects/projects-eclipse.html
Debugging Tasks	developer.android.com/guide/developing/debug-tasks.html
Tools Overview	developer.android.com/guide/developing/tools/index.html
Publishing Your Apps	developer.android.com/guide/publishing/publishing.html
Android Market Getting Started	market.android.com/support/bin/topic.py?hl=en&topic=15866
Android Market Developer Distribution Agreement	www.android.com/us/developer-distribution-agreement.html

Fig. 1.1 | Key online documentation for Android developers. (Part 2 of 2.)

Read the Before You Begin section following the Preface for information on downloading the software you'll need to build Android apps. The Android Developer site provides free downloads plus documentation, how-to videos (Fig. 1.37), coding guidelines and more. To publish your apps to Google's app marketplace—**Android Market**—you'll need to create a developer profile at `market.android.com/publish/signup`. There's a registration fee and you must agree to the Android Market Developer Distribution Agreement. We discuss publishing your apps in more detail in Chapter 2, Android Market and App Business Issues.

As you dive into Android app development, you may have questions about the tools, design issues, security and more. There are several Android developer newsgroups and forums where you can get the latest announcements or ask questions (Fig. 1.2).

Title	Subscribe	Description
Android Discuss	*Subscribe using Google Groups:* android-discuss *Subscribe via e-mail:* android-discuss-subscribe@googlegroups.com	A general Android discussion group where you can get answers to your app-development questions.
Stack Overflow	stackoverflow.com/questions/tagged/android	Use this list for beginner-level Android app-development questions, including getting started with Java and Eclipse, and questions about best practices.

Fig. 1.2 | Android newsgroups and forums. (Part 1 of 2.)

Title	Subscribe	Description
Android Developers	*Subscribe using Google Groups:* android-developers *Subscribe via e-mail:* android-developers-subscribe@googlegroups.com	Experienced Android developers use this list for troubleshooting apps, GUI design issues, performance issues and more.
Android Market Help Forum	www.google.com/support/forum/p/Android+market	Ask questions and find answers regarding Android Market.
Android Forums	www.androidforums.com/	Ask questions, share tips with other developers and find forums targeting specific Android devices.

Fig. 1.2 | Android newsgroups and forums. (Part 2 of 2.)

1.2 Android Overview

The first-generation Android phones were released in October 2008. According to Gartner, North American sales of Android-based phones increased 707% in the first quarter of 2010 over the previous year.[1] By March 2011, a Nielsen study showed that Android had 37% of the U.S. smartphone market share, compared to 27% for Apple's iPhone and 22% for Blackberry.[2] In August 2010, more than 200,000 Android smartphones were being activated each day, up from 100,000 per day only two months earlier.[3] As of June 2011, more than 500,000 Android devices were being activated daily. There are now over 300 different Android devices worldwide.

The Android operating system was developed by Android, Inc., which was acquired by Google in July 2005. In November 2007, the Open Handset Alliance™—a 34-company consortium initially and 81 now (www.openhandsetalliance.com/oha_members.html)—was formed to develop Android, driving innovation in mobile technology and improving the user experience while reducing costs. Android is used in numerous smartphones, e-reader devices and tablet computers.

Openness and Open Source

One benefit of developing Android apps is the openness of the platform. The operating system is *open source* and free. This allows you to view Android's source code and see how its features are implemented. You can also contribute to Android by reporting bugs (see source.android.com/source/report-bugs.html) or by participating in the Open Source Project discussion groups (source.android.com/community/index.html). Numerous open-source Android apps from Google and others are available on the Internet (Fig. 1.3). Figure 1.4 shows you where you can get the Android source code, learn about the philosophy behind the open-source operating system and get licensing information.

---

1. www.gartner.com/it/page.jsp?id=1372013.
2. blog.nielsen.com/nielsenwire/online_mobile/u-s-smartphone-market-whos-the-most-wanted/.
3. www.wired.com/gadgetlab/2010/08/google-200000-android-phones/.

Description	URL
Extensive list of open-source apps, organized by category (e.g., games, utilities, etc.).	en.wikipedia.org/wiki/List_of_open_source_Android_applications
Google's sample apps for the Android platform.	code.google.com/p/apps-for-android/
Thirty sample apps demonstrating several Android features.	developer.android.com/resources/browser.html?tag=sample
Lists 12 open-source Android apps.	www.techdrivein.com/2010/11/12-open-source-android-applications.html
Provides links to a selection of open-source Android games.	www.techdrivein.com/2010/12/15-nice-and-simple-open-source-android.html

Fig. 1.3 | Open-source Android apps resource sites.

Title	URL
Get Android Source Code	source.android.com/source/download.html
Philosophy and Goals	source.android.com/about/philosophy.html
Licenses	source.android.com/source/licenses.html
FAQs	source.android.com/faqs.html#aosp

Fig. 1.4 | Android source code and documentation resources.

Java

Android apps are developed with Java—the world's most widely used programming language. Java was a logical choice for the Android platform, because it's powerful, free and open source. Java is used to develop large-scale enterprise applications, to enhance the functionality of web servers, to provide applications for consumer devices (e.g., cell phones, pagers and personal digital assistants) and for many other purposes.

Java enables you to develop apps that will run on a variety of devices without any platform-specific code. Experienced Java programmers can quickly dive into Android development, using the Android APIs (Application Programming Interfaces) and others available from third parties.

The openness of the platform spurs rapid innovation. Android is available on devices from dozens of original equipment manufacturers (OEMs) in 48 countries through 59 carriers.[4] The intense competition among OEMs and carriers benefits customers.

Java is object oriented and has access to powerful class libraries that help you develop apps quickly. GUI programming in Java is event driven—in this book, you'll write apps that respond to various user-initiated events such as screen touches and keystrokes. In addition to directly programming portions of your apps, you'll also use Eclipse to conve-

4. code.google.com/events/io/2010/.

niently drag and drop predefined objects such as buttons and textboxes into place on your screen, and label and resize them. Using Eclipse with the Android Development Tools (ADT) Plugin, you can create, run, test and debug Android apps quickly and conveniently, and you can visually design your user interfaces.

Multitouch Screen

Many Android smartphones wrap the functionality of a mobile phone, Internet client, MP3 player, gaming console, digital camera and more into a handheld device with full-color ***multitouch screens***. These allow you to control the device with ***gestures*** involving one touch or multiple simultaneous touches (Fig. 1.5).

Gesture name	Physical action	Used to
Touch	Tap the screen once.	Open an app, "press" a button or a menu item.
Double tap	Tap the screen twice.	Zoom in and then back out on pictures, Google Maps and web pages.
Long press	Touch the screen and hold finger in position.	Open a context menu or grab app icons or objects to move by dragging.
Drag	Touch and drag your finger across the screen.	Move objects or icons, or scroll precisely on a web page or list.
Fling	Touch and quickly flick your finger across the screen in the direction you'd like to move.	Scroll through a **List View** (e.g., **Contacts**) or a **DatePicker View** and **TimePicker View** (e.g., dates and times in the **Calendar**).
Pinch zoom	Using two fingers, touch and pinch your fingers together, or spread them apart.	Zoom in and then back out on the screen (e.g., enlarging text and pictures).

Fig. 1.5 | Android gestures.

Using the multitouch screen, you can navigate easily between your phone, apps, music library, web browsing, and so on. The screen can display a keyboard for typing e-mails and text messages and entering data in apps (some Android devices also have physical keyboards). Using two fingers, you can zoom in (moving your fingers apart) and out (pinching your fingers together) on photos, videos and web pages. You can scroll up and down or side to side by just swiping your finger across the screen.

Built-in Apps

Android devices come with several built-in apps, which may vary depending on the device. These typically include **Phone**, **Contacts**, **Mail**, **Browser** and more. Many manufacturers customize the default apps; we'll show you how to interact with the apps regardless of how they've been changed.

Android Naming Convention

Each new version of Android is named after a dessert, going in alphabetical order:

- Android 1.6 (Donut)

- Android 2.0–2.1 (Eclair)
- Android 2.2 (Froyo)
- Android 2.3 (Gingerbread)
- Android 3.0 (Honeycomb)

1.3 Android 2.2 (Froyo)

Android 2.2 (also called **Froyo**, released in May 2010) included several new features and enhancements (Fig. 1.6). In subsequent sections we'll discuss Android 2.3 (Gingerbread) and Android 3.0 (Honeycomb).

Feature	Description
Improved memory and performance	Upgrades include: • Dalvik Virtual Machine enhancements made it two to five times faster than in Android 2.1. • Chrome V8 engine quickly loads JavaScript web pages. • Kernel memory-management boost improves device performance.
Auto-discovery	Allows Exchange users to enter a username and password to quickly sync their Exchange accounts with their Android devices.
Calendar	Users can sync their Exchange Calendar with the **Calendar** app.
Global Address Lists (GAL) look-up	Accesses addresses for e-mail users and distribution lists in the user's Microsoft Exchange e-mail system, enabling auto-complete of recipients' contact names when creating a new e-mail.
Passwords	Users can add alphanumeric passwords to unlock a device. This enhances data security by preventing anyone from accessing information on the locked device.
Remote Wipe	If you're unable to find your Android device, the Remote Wipe feature restores it to the factory settings (removing all personal data), thus protecting the privacy of your information. Once you Remote Wipe the phone, any data that you haven't backed up will be lost. [*Note:* Availability of Remote Wipe varies by manufacturer and device policy managers.]
Contacts and accounts	The **Quick Contact** for Android gives users easy access to contact information and modes for communicating with their contacts, such as e-mail, SMS or phone. A user can tap a contact's photo (e.g., in the contacts list, image gallery, e-mail or calendar), bringing up the **Quick Contact** widget with the various communication modes. As a developer, you can incorporate **Quick Contact** into your apps.

Fig. 1.6 | Android 2.2 user features (`developer.android.com/sdk/android-2.2-highlights.html`). (Part 1 of 2.)

Feature	Description
Camera	The camera controls in Android 2.2 include camera flash support and digital zoom. Users can adjust the camera settings to account for their environment (e.g., night, sunset, action), add effects (e.g., sepia, red tint, blue tint) and more. You can program the camera's preview and capture settings and retrieve and encode video.
Android virtual keyboard	The keyboard layout has been improved, making typing on the multitouch screen easier, and ensuring that keyboard touches aren't missed when typing with two fingers.
Improved dictionary	The more sophisticated dictionary learns from the user's word usage and includes the user's contacts in the suggested spellings.
Browser	The browser's improved user interface features a new address bar that the user can tap for search and navigation, and double-tap to zoom in and back out on a web page. It also supports HTML5, which includes features such as video playback and drag and drop that were previously available only through third-party plugins, such as Adobe Flash. [*Note:* The Browser also supports Flash.]
Multiple-languages keyboard	Users can add keyboards in other languages and easily switch among them by "flinging" from right to left across the space bar on the keyboard. To add keyboards, either on a device or in the emulator, go to **Settings > Language & keyboard > Android keyboard > Input languages**.
Media framework	Android's ***Stagefright media framework*** enables video playback and HTTP progressive streaming—i.e., sending video over the Internet using the HyperText Transfer Protocol to a browser and playing the video even while it's still downloading. The previous media framework, OpenCORE, is still supported in Android.
Bluetooth	Users can now wirelessly connect their Android devices to other Bluetooth-enabled devices such as headsets and car docks (for connecting the phone to a car's hands-free phone system), share contact information with Bluetooth-enabled phones and voice dial.
Tethering and Wi-Fi hotspot support	Android 2.x included built-in tethering and Wi-Fi hotspot support, enabling users to connect their phone to their Windows or Linux computer with a USB cable to use the phone's 3G service to connect to the Internet `www.engadget.com/2010/05/13/android-2-2-froyo-to-include-usb-tethering-wifi-hotspot-funct/`

Fig. 1.6 | Android 2.2 user features (`developer.android.com/sdk/android-2.2-highlights.html`). (Part 2 of 2.)

New Developer Features in Android 2.2

The **Android Cloud to Device Messaging (C2DM)** service allows app developers to send data from their servers to their apps installed on Android devices, even when the apps are not currently running. The server notifies the apps to contact the server directly to receive updated app or user data.[5] **Android Application Error Reports**, which can be accessed by logging into your Android Market publisher account, enable you to receive app-crash and app-freeze reports from your apps' users.

Android 2.2 also includes several new APIs that allow you to easily add functionality into your apps (Fig. 1.7). We use some of these new frameworks in this book. We also use **web services.** With these, you can create **mashups**, which enable you to rapidly develop apps by combining the complementary web services of several organizations, possibly with information feeds of various types (such as RSS, Atom, XML, JSON and others) (Fig. 1.8). For example, `www.housingmaps.com` uses web services to combine Craigslist (`www.craigslist.org`) real-estate listings with the capabilities of Google Maps—the most widely used API for mashups—to show the locations of apartments for rent in a given area. We use WeatherBug web services in Chapter 14.

API	Description
Apps on external storage	Apps can be stored on an external memory device rather than just the Android device's internal memory.
Camera and camcorder	New features include the Camera Preview API which doubles the frame rate (now 20 frames per-second), portrait orientation, zoom controls, exposure data and a thumbnail utility. The new **CamcorderProfile** classes can be used in apps to determine the camcorder hardware capabilities of the user's device.
Data backup	Back up data to the cloud and restore data after a user resets the device to the original factory settings or switches devices.
Device policy management	Create administrator apps to control device security features (e.g., password strength).
Graphics	Access to the OpenGL ES 2.0 graphics APIs which were previously available only through the Android NDK—a toolset that allows you to use native code for performance-critical app components (`developer.android.com/sdk/ndk/overview.html`).
Media framework	APIs for audio focus, auto-scanning files to the media database (e.g., audio and video files), detecting sound loading completion, auto-pause and auto-resume of audio playback, and more.
UI framework	The `UiModeManager` car mode, desk mode and night mode controls enable you to adjust an app's user interface, the scale gesture detector API improves multi-touch events, and the bottom strip of a **TabWidget** is now customizable.

Fig. 1.7 | Android 2.2 APIs (`developer.android.com/sdk/android-2.2-highlights.html`).

5. `code.google.com/android/c2dm/`.

Web services source	How it's used
Google Maps	Mapping services
Facebook	Social networking
Foursquare	Mobile check-in
LinkedIn	Social networking for business
YouTube	Video search
Twitter	Microblogging
Groupon	Social commerce
Netflix	Movie rentals
eBay	Internet auctions
Wikipedia	Collaborative encyclopedia
PayPal	Payments
Last.fm	Internet radio
Amazon eCommerce	Shopping for books and more
Salesforce.com	Customer Relationship Management (CRM)
Skype	Internet telephony
Microsoft Bing	Search
Flickr	Photo sharing
Zillow	Real-estate pricing
Yahoo Search	Search
WeatherBug	Weather

Fig. 1.8 | Some popular web services (`www.programmableweb.com/apis/directory/1?sort=mashups`).

Figure 1.9 lists directories where you'll find information about many of the most popular web services.

Directory	URL
ProgrammableWeb	`www.programmableweb.com`
Webmashup.com	`www.webmashup.com/`
Webapi.org	`www.webapi.org/webapi-directory/`
Google Code API Directory	`code.google.com/apis/gdata/docs/directory.html`
APIfinder	`www.apifinder.com/`

Fig. 1.9 | Web-services directories.

1.4 Android 2.3 (Gingerbread)

Android 2.3 (Gingerbread), released in December 2010 (with Android 2.3.3—a minor update—released in February 2011), added more user refinements, such as a redesigned keyboard, improved navigation capabilities, increased power efficiency and more. Figure 1.10 describes some of the key new user features and updates.

Feature	Description
Power management	Apps that consume processor power while running in the background, or are awake longer than normal, can be closed by Android (if appropriate) to save battery power and improve performance. Users can also view the apps and system components consuming battery power.
Manage Applications shortcut	The **Manage Applications** shortcut in the **Options** menu on the Home screen allows users to view all apps that are running. For each app, you can view the amount of storage and memory it's using, permissions the app has been granted (whether it can read the user's contact data, create Bluetooth connections, etc.) and more. Users can also "force-stop" the app.
Near-field communications	**Near-field communication (NFC)** is a short-range wireless connectivity standard that enables communication between two devices, or a device and a tag (which stores data that can be read by NFC-enabled devices), within a few centimeters. NFC-enabled devices can operate in three modes—reader/writer (e.g., reading data from a tag), peer to peer (e.g., exchanging data between two devices) and card emulation (e.g., acting like a smart card for contactless payments). NFC-enabled Android devices can be used in reader/writer and peer-to-peer modes. NFC support and features vary by Android device.
Improved **Copy** and **Paste** functionality	You can touch a word to select it, drag the markers to adjust the selection, copy the text by touching the highlighted area, then paste the text. You can also move the cursor by dragging the cursor arrow.
Camera	Apps can access both rear-facing and front-facing cameras.
Internet calling	Android includes Session Initiation Protocol (SIP) support—an Internet Engineering Task Force (IETF) standard protocol for initiating and terminating voice calls over the Internet. Users with SIP accounts (available through third parties) can make Internet voice calls to other contacts with SIP accounts. Not all Android devices or carriers support SIP and Internet calling. For a list of SIP providers, see `www.cs.columbia.edu/sip/service-providers.html`.
Downloads app	Users can access files downloaded from e-mail, the browser, etc. through the **Downloads** app.

Fig. 1.10 | Android 2.3 user features (`developer.android.com/sdk/android-2.3-highlights.html`).

The platform also added several new developer features for enhanced communications, game development and multimedia (Figure 1.11). For further details about each of these features, go to `developer.android.com/sdk/android-2.3-highlights.html`.

Feature	Description
Internet telephony	The new SIP support allows you to build Internet telephony functionality into your apps—namely, making and receiving voice calls.
Near-field communications API	Build apps that read and respond to data from NFC tags or devices. Android 2.3.3 apps can also write to tags and work in peer-to-peer mode with other devices. Note that NFC support varies by Android device.
Audio effects API	Add equalization (for adjusting bass or treble), bass boost (increasing the volume of bass sounds), headphone virtualization (simulated surround sound), and reverb (echo effects) to an audio track or across multiple tracks.
New audio formats	Built-in support for Advanced Audio Coding (AAC—a successor to MP3) and Adaptive Multi-Rate Wideband encoding (AMR-WB) for capturing high-quality audio.
New video formats	Built-in support for VP8 open video compression with the WebM open-container format.
Camera API	Use the enhanced Camera API to access rear- and front-facing cameras on a device, determine their features and open the appropriate camera.

Fig. 1.11 | Android 2.3 developer features (`developer.android.com/sdk/android-2.3-highlights.html`).

1.5 Android 3.0 (Honeycomb)

Tablet sales will account for over 20% of all personal-computer sales by 2015.[6] Interest in Android tablets is increasing rapidly. At the 2011 Consumer Electronic Show, 85 new Android tablets were announced.[7] **Android 3.0 (Honeycomb)** includes user-interface improvements specifically for large-screen devices (e.g., tablets), such as a redesigned keyboard for more efficient typing, a visually appealing 3D user interface, System and Action Bars for easier navigation and more (Fig. 1.12). It also gives developers new tools to optimize apps for larger-screen devices (Fig. 1.13).

Feature	Description
Holographic UI	Attractive 3D-looking user interface.
Customizable home screen	Organize widgets, app shortcuts and more.

Fig. 1.12 | New Android 3 features (`developer.android.com/sdk/android-3.0-highlights.html`). (Part 1 of 2.)

6. `www.forrester.com/ER/Press/Release/0,1769,1340,00.html`.
7. `www.computerworld.com/s/article/9206219/Google_Android_tablets_gain_traction_with_developers?source=CTWNLE_nlt_dailyam_2011-01-25`.

Feature	Description
Redesigned keyboard	Enables improved typing accuracy and efficiency.
Improved editing	New user interface makes it easier to select, copy and paste text.
System Bar	Quickly access navigation buttons, notifications and system status from the System Bar at the bottom of the screen.
Action Bar	Provides app-specific controls (such as navigation) from the Action Bar at the top of each app's screen.
Improved multitasking	The **Recent Apps** list in the System Bar allows you to see the tasks that are running simultaneously and switch between apps.
Connectivity options	Connect your Android device to a keyboard using either USB or Bluetooth.
Photo Transfer Protocol (PTP) and Media Transfer Protocol (MTP) support	Developed by Microsoft, these protocols enable you to transfer photos, videos and music files to your computer. You can create apps that allow users to create and manage media files and share them on multiple devices.
Bluetooth tethering	Connect to a Wi-Fi or 3G network on your computer or other devices using your Android device as a modem.
Browser	Features tabs instead of multiple windows, easier browsing of non-mobile sites (using improved zoom, scrolling, etc.), "incognito" mode for browsing sites anonymously, multitouch support for JavaScript and plugins and more. You can also automatically sign into Google sites and sync your bookmarks with Google Chrome.
Camera	Redesigned for larger-screen devices, you can easily access camera features such as the front-facing camera, flash, auto-focus and more. The time-lapse video recording capabilities allow you to capture "frames" at a slower-than-normal rate, then play the video back at normal speed, making it appear as though time is moving faster.
Contacts	The two-pane user interface makes it easier to read, edit and organize contacts. Fast scroll helps you find contacts quickly.
Email	Use the Action Bar to organize e-mail in folders and sync attachments. You can also use the e-mail widget on your home screen to easily monitor your messages.
Gallery	View albums in full-screen mode, with thumbnail images to view other photos in the album.

Fig. 1.12 | New Android 3 features (`developer.android.com/sdk/android-3.0-highlights.html`). (Part 2 of 2.)

Feature	Description
Backward compatibility	Android 3.x is compatible with apps developed using previous versions of Android.

Fig. 1.13 | New developer features in Android 3 (`developer.android.com/sdk/android-3.0-highlights.html`). (Part 1 of 3.)

Feature	Description
Holographic UI	Give your new and existing apps the new Android 3 holographic look and feel by adding an attribute in the app's manifest file.
Add layouts for large-screen devices to existing apps	Add new layouts and assets for large-screen devices to your existing apps designed for small-screen devices.
Activity fragments	Divide an app's activities into modularized fragments, which can be used in a variety of combinations. Google is enhancing this API so it can be used on Android 1.6 and later.
New and updated UI and Home-screen widgets	Include a search box, calendar, 3D stack, a date/time picker, number picker and more. Home-screen widgets can now be controlled with touch gestures to scroll and flip through the content.
Action Bar	Each app now has its own persistent Action Bar, providing users with options for navigation, etc.
Enhancements for gaming	Enhancements for gaming include: • Performance enhancements such as a concurrent garbage collector, faster event distribution and updated video drivers. • Native input and sensor events. • New sensors—gyroscope, barometer, gravity sensor and more—for better 3D motion processing. • Khronos OpenSL ES API for native audio. • Khronos EGL library for native graphics management. • Native access to the Activity Lifecycle, and APIs for managing windows. • Native Asset Manager API and Storage Manager API.
Additional notifications capabilities	Add large and small icons, titles and priority flags to your apps' notifications using the builder class.
Clipboard	Allows users to copy and paste data across multiple apps.
Drag and drop	Use the `DragEvent` framework to add drag-and-drop capabilities in an app.
Multiselect	Allow users to select *multiple* items from a list or grid.
Media/Picture Transfer Protocol (MTP/PTP)	Allows users to easily transfer any type of media files between devices and to a host computer.
Multicore processor architecture support	Run Android 3.x on single-core or multicore processor architectures for enhanced performance.
HTTP Live Streaming (HLS)	Apps can provide a URL for a multimedia playlist to the media framework to launch an HTTP Live Streaming session. This provides higher quality support for adaptive video.
Renderscript 3D graphics engine	Create high-performance 3D graphics for apps, widgets, etc. and offloading calculations to the Graphics Processing Unit (GPU).

Fig. 1.13 | New developer features in Android 3 (`developer.android.com/sdk/android-3.0-highlights.html`). (Part 2 of 3.)

Feature	Description
Hardware-accelerated 2D graphics	The new OpenGL renderer improves performance of common graphics operations.
New animation framework	Easily animate user-interface elements or objects.
Bluetooth A2DP and HSP	APIs for Bluetooth Advanced Audio Distribution Profile (A2DP) and Headset Profile (HSP) allow your apps to check for connected Bluetooth devices, battery level and more.
Digital Rights Management (DRM) framework	API that enables you to manage protected content in your apps.
New policies for device administration apps	Enterprise device-administration apps can now support policies such as password expiration and more.

Fig. 1.13 | New developer features in Android 3 (`developer.android.com/sdk/android-3.0-highlights.html`). (Part 3 of 3.)

1.6 Android Ice Cream Sandwich

Android Ice Cream Sandwich, scheduled to be released in late 2011, will merge Android 2.3 (Gingerbread) and Android 3.0 (Honeycomb) into one operating system for use on all Android devices. This will allow you to incorporate Honeycomb's features such as the holographic user interface, new launcher and more (previously available only on tablets) into your smartphone apps, and easily scale your apps to work on different devices. Ice Cream Sandwich will also add new functionality (Fig. 1.14).

Feature	Description
0-click NFC Peer-to-Peer Sharing	Users with compatible Android devices will be able to share content (e.g., contacts, videos) just by placing the devices near each other.
Head tracking	Using the camera, compatible devices will determine the positioning of the user's eyes, nose and mouth. The camera will also be able to track where the user is looking, allowing you to create apps that change perspective based on where the user is looking (e.g., 3D game landscapes).
Virtual camera operator	When taking video, the camera will automatically focus on the person speaking. For example, if two people are participating in one side of a video chat, the camera will determine which of the two is speaking and focus the camera on that person.
Android@Home framework	Will enable you to create Android apps to control appliances in the user's home, such as turning lights on and off (with special light bulbs from Lighting Science), adjusting the thermostat, controlling the irrigation system and more.

Fig. 1.14 | Some Android Ice Cream Sandwich features.

1.7 Downloading Apps from the Android Market

At the time of this printing, there were hundreds of thousands of apps in Google's **Android Market**, and the number continues to grow quickly. Figure 1.15 lists some popular Android apps. You can download additional apps directly onto your Android device through Android Market. Android Market notifies you when updates to your downloaded apps are available.

Android Market Category	Sample apps
Comics	Marvel Superheroes, Dilbert Calendar, Jerry Seinfeld Jokes
Communication	Google Voice, Skype mobile™, Wi-Fi Locator, Easy
Entertainment	Face Melter, Fingerprint Scanner, Fandango® Movies
Finance	Mint.com Personal Finance, PayPal, Debt Payoff Planner
Games: Arcade & Action	NESoid, Droid Breakout, Raging Thunder 2 Lite, Whac 'em!
Games: Brain & Puzzle	Enjoy Sudoku, Spin Cube Lite, Ultimate Simpson Puzzle
Games: Cards & Casino	Texas Hold'em Poker, Tarot Cards, Chessmaster™
Games: Casual	City Mayor, LOL Libs, Paper Toss, SuperYatzy Free Edition
Health	Fast Food Calorie Counter, CardioTrainer, StopSmoking
Lifestyle	Zillow Real Estate, Epicurious Recipe App, Family Locator
Multimedia	Pandora Radio, Shazam, Last.fm, iSyncr, Camera Illusion
News & Weather	The Weather Channel, CNN, NYTimes, FeedR News Reader
Productivity	Adobe® Reader®, Documents To Go 2.0 Main App
Reference	Google Sky Map, Dictionary.com, Wikidroid for Wikipedia
Shopping	Gluten Free, Amazon.com, Barcode Scanner, Pkt Auctions eBay
Social	Facebook®, Twitter for Android, MySpace, Bump, AIM
Sports	NFL Mobile, Nascar Mobile, Google Scoreboard
Themes	Pixel Zombies Live Wallpaper, Aquarium Live Wallpaper
Tools	Compass, Droidlight LED Flashlight, AppAlarm Pro
Travel	Google Earth, Yelp®, Urbanspoon, WHERE, XE Currency
Demo	Screen Crack, Bubbles, CouponMap, SnowGlobe
Software libraries	Translate Tool, Security Guarder, Car Locator Bluetooth Plugin

Fig. 1.15 | Some popular Android apps in Android Market.

Visit `market.android.com` to check out the featured apps, or check out some of the other Android app review and recommendation sites (Fig. 1.16). Some are free and some are fee based. Developers set the prices for their apps sold through Android Market and receive 70% of the revenue. As a marketing strategy, many app developers offer basic versions of their apps for free so users can determine whether they like them, then purchase more feature-rich versions. We discuss this so-called "lite" strategy in more detail in Section 2.10.

Name	URL
AppBrain	`www.appbrain.com/`
AndroidLib	`www.androlib.com/`
Android Tapp™	`www.androidtapp.com/`
Appolicious™	`www.androidapps.com/`
AndroidZoom	`www.androidzoom.com/`
doubleTwist®	`www.doubletwist.com/apps/`
mplayit™	`mplayit.com/#homepage`

Fig. 1.16 | Android app review and recommendation sites.

1.8 Packages

Android uses a collection of packages, which are named groups of related, predefined classes. Some of the packages are Android specific, while others are Java and Google packages. These packages allow you to conveniently access Android OS features and incorporate them into your apps. They're written mainly in Java and are accessible to Java programs. The Android packages help you create apps that adhere to Android's unique look-and-feel conventions. Figure 1.17 lists the packages we discuss in this book. For a complete list of Android packages, see `developer.android.com/reference/packages.html`.

Package	Description
`android.app`	Includes high-level classes in the Android app model. (Chapter 4's **Tip Calculator** app.)
`android.os`	Operating-systems services. (Chapter 4's **Tip Calculator** app.)
`android.text`	Rendering and tracking text on the device. (Chapter 4's **Tip Calculator** app.)
`android.widget`	User-interface classes for widgets. (Chapter 4's **Tip Calculator** app.)
`android.net`	Network access classes. (Chapter 5's **Favorite Twitter® Searches** app.)
`android.view`	User interface classes for layout and user interactions. (Chapter 5's **Favorite Twitter® Searches** app.)
`java.io`	Streaming, serialization and file-system access of input and output facilities. (Chapter 6's **Flag Quiz** app.)
`java.util`	Utility classes. (Chapter 5's **Favorite Twitter® Searches** app.)
`android.content.res`	Classes for accessing app resources (e.g., media, colors, drawables, etc.), and device-configuration information affecting app behavior. (Chapter 6's **Flag Quiz Game** app.)

Fig. 1.17 | Android, Java and Google packages used in this book, listed with the chapter in which they *first* appear. (Part 1 of 2.)

Package	Description
`android.graphics.drawable`	Classes for display-only elements (e.g., gradients, etc.). (Chapter 6's **Flag Quiz Game** app.)
`android.media`	Classes for handling audio and video media interfaces. (Chapter 8's **Spotz Game** app.)
`android.util`	Utility methods and XML utilities. (Chapter 7's **Cannon Game** app.)
`android.content`	Access and publish data on a device. (Chapter 9's **Doodlz** app.)
`android.hardware`	Device hardware support. (Chapter 9's **Doodlz** App and Chapter 13's **Enhanced Slideshow** app.)
`android.provider`	Access to Android content providers. (Chapter 9's **Doodlz** app.)
`android.database`	Handling data returned by the content provider. (Chapter 10's **Address Book** app.)
`android.database.sqlite`	SQLite database management for private databases. (Chapter 10's **Address Book** app.)
`android.graphics`	Graphics tools used for drawing to the screen. (Chapter 11's **Route Tracker** app.)
`android.location`	Location-based services. (Chapter 11's **Route Tracker** app.)
`com.google.android.maps`	Used in Chapter 11's **Route Tracker** app.
`android.appwidget`	Used in Chapter 14's **Weather Viewer** app.
`java.net`	Networking classes (e.g., handling Internet addresses and HTTP requests). (Chapter 14's **Weather Viewer** app.)
`javax.xml.parsers`	Processing XML documents. (Chapter 14's **Weather Viewer** app.)
`org.xml.sax`	Simple API for XML (SAX API) for reading data from XML documents. (Chapter 14's **Weather Viewer** app.)
`android.speech`	Speech recognition classes. (Chapter 15's **Pizza Ordering** app.)
`android.speech.tts`	Text-to-speech classes. (Chapter 15's **Pizza Ordering** app.)
`android.telephony`	Phone APIs for monitoring network information, connection state and more. We'll use these APIs to send SMS messages. (Chapter 15's **Pizza Ordering** app.)
`android.opengl`	OpenGL graphics tools. (Chapter 18's **3D Art** app.)
`java.nio`	Buffers for handling data. (Chapter 18's **3D Art** app.)
`javax.microedition.khronos.egl`	Khronos EGL APIs for 3D graphics. (Chapter 18's **3D Art** app.)
`javax.microedition.khronos.opengles`	Khronos OpenGL® ES interfaces. (Chapter 18's **3D Art** app.)

Fig. 1.17 | Android, Java and Google packages used in this book, listed with the chapter in which they *first* appear. (Part 2 of 2.)

1.9 Android Software Development Kit (SDK)

The Android SDK provides the tools you'll need to build Android apps. It's available at no charge through the Android Developers site. See the Before You Begin section after the Preface for complete details on downloading the tools you need to develop Android apps, including the Java SE, the Eclipse IDE, the Android SDK 3.x and the ADT Plugin for Eclipse.

Eclipse Integrated Development Environment (IDE)

Eclipse is the recommended integrated development environment for Android development, though developers may also use a text editor and command-line tools to create Android apps. Eclipse supports many programming languages, including Java, C++, C, Python, Perl, Ruby on Rails and more. The vast majority of Android development is done in Java. The Eclipse IDE includes:

- Code editor with support for syntax coloring and line numbering
- Auto-indenting and auto-complete (i.e., type hinting)
- Debugger
- Version control system
- Refactoring support

You'll use Eclipse in Section 1.11 to test-drive the **Doodlz** app. Starting in Chapter 3, **Welcome** App, you'll use Eclipse to build apps.

Android Development Tools (ADT) Plugin for Eclipse

The **Android Development Tools (ADT) Plugin for Eclipse**—an extension to the Eclipse IDE—allows you to create, run and debug Android apps, export them for distribution (e.g., upload them to Android Market), and more. ADT also includes a visual GUI design tool. GUI components can be dragged and dropped into place to form GUIs without any coding. You'll learn more about ADT in Chapter 3, **Welcome** App.

The Android Emulator

The Android emulator, included in the Android SDK, allows you to run Android apps in a simulated environment within Windows, Mac OS X or Linux. The emulator displays a realistic Android user-interface window. Before running an app in the emulator, you'll need to create an **Android Virtual Device (AVD)**, which defines the characteristics of the device on which you want to test, including the hardware, system image, screen size, data storage and more. If you want to test your apps for multiple Android devices, you'll need to create separate AVDs to emulate each unique device.

We used the emulator (not an actual Android device) to take most of the Android screen shots for this book. You can reproduce on the emulator most of the Android gestures (Fig. 1.18) and controls (Fig. 1.19) using your computer's keyboard and mouse. The gestures on the emulator are a bit limited, since your computer probably cannot simulate all the Android hardware features. For example, to test GPS apps in the emulator, you'll need to create files that simulate GPS readings. Also, although you can simulate orientation changes (to portrait or landscape mode), there's no way to simulate particular ***accelerometer*** readings (the accelerometer measures the orientation and tilting of the device). You can, however, upload your app to an Android device to test these features. You'll see how to do this in Chapter 11, **Route Tracker** app. You'll start creating AVDs and using the emulator to develop Android apps in Chapter 3's **Welcome** app.

Gesture	Emulator action
Tap	Click the mouse once. Introduced in Chapter 4's **Tip Calculator** app.
Double tap	Double-click the mouse. Introduced in Chapter 7's **Cannon Game** app.
Long press	Click and hold the mouse.
Drag	Click, hold and drag the mouse. Introduced in Chapter 7's **Cannon Game** app.
Swipe	Click and hold the mouse, move the pointer in the swipe direction and release the mouse. Introduced in Chapter 10's **Address Book** app.
Fling	Click and hold the mouse, move the pointer in the flick direction and quickly release. Introduced in Chapter 10's **Address Book** app.
Pinch	Press and hold the *Ctrl* (*Control*) key. Two circles that simulate the two touches will appear. Move the circles to the start position, click and hold the mouse and drag the circles to the end position. Introduced in Chapter 11's **Route Tracker** app.

Fig. 1.18 | Android gestures on the emulator (`developer.android.com/guide/developing/tools/emulator.html`).

Control	Emulator action
Back	*Esc*
Call/dial button	*F3*
Camera	*Ctrl-KEYPAD_5*, *Ctrl-F3*
End call button	*F4*
Home	*Home* button
Menu (left softkey)	*F2* or *Page Up* button
Power button	*F7*
Search	*F5*
* (right softkey)	*Shift-F2* or *Page Down* button
Rotate left	*KEYPAD_7*, *Ctrl-F11*
Rotate right	*KEYPAD_9*, *Ctrl-F12*
Toggle cell networking on/off	*F8*
Volume up button	*KEYPAD_PLUS*, *Ctrl-F5*
Volume down button	*KEYPAD_MINUS*, *Ctrl-F6*

Fig. 1.19 | Android hardware controls on the emulator (for additional controls, go to `developer.android.com/guide/developing/tools/emulator.html`).

1.10 Object Technology: A Quick Refresher

Building software quickly, correctly and economically remains an elusive goal at a time when demands for new and more powerful software are soaring. *Objects*, or more precisely—as we'll see in Chapter 3—the *classes* objects come from, are essentially *reusable* software components. There are date objects, time objects, audio objects, video objects, automobile objects, people objects, etc. Almost any *noun* can be reasonably represented as a software object in terms of *attributes* (e.g., name, color and size) and *behaviors* (e.g., calculating, moving and communicating). Software developers are discovering that using a modular, object-oriented design and implementation approach can make software development groups much more productive than was possible with earlier popular techniques like "structured programming"—object-oriented programs are often easier to understand, correct and modify.

The Automobile as an Object

To help you understand objects and their contents, let's begin with a simple analogy. Suppose you want to *drive a car and make it go faster by pressing its accelerator pedal.* What must happen before you can do this? Well, before you can drive a car, someone has to *design* it. A car typically begins as engineering drawings, similar to the *blueprints* that describe the design of a house. These drawings include the design for an accelerator pedal. The pedal *hides* from the driver the complex mechanisms that actually make the car go faster, just as the brake pedal hides the mechanisms that slow the car, and the steering wheel "hides" the mechanisms that turn the car. This enables people with little or no knowledge of how engines, braking and steering mechanisms work to drive a car easily.

Just as you cannot cook meals in the kitchen of a blueprint, you cannot drive a car's engineering drawings. Before you can drive a car, it must be *built* from the engineering drawings that describe it. A completed car has an *actual* accelerator pedal to make the car go faster, but even that's not enough—the car won't accelerate on its own (hopefully!), so the driver must *press* the pedal to accelerate the car.

Methods and Classes

Let's use our car example to introduce some key object-oriented programming concepts. Performing a task in a program requires a **method**. The method houses the program statements that actually perform its tasks. The method hides these statements from its user, just as the accelerator pedal of a car hides from the driver the mechanisms of making the car go faster. A program unit called a **class** houses the methods that perform the class's tasks. For example, a class that represents a bank account might contain one method to *deposit* money to an account, another to *withdraw* money from an account and a third to *inquire* what the account's current balance is. A class is similar in concept to a car's engineering drawings, which house the design of an accelerator pedal, steering wheel, and so on.

Instantiation

Just as someone has to *build a car* from its engineering drawings before you can actually drive a car, you must *build an object* of a class before a program can perform the tasks that the class's methods define. The process of doing this is called *instantiation.* An object is then referred to as an **instance** of its class.

Reuse

Just as a car's engineering drawings can be *reused* many times to build many cars, you can *reuse* a class many times to build many objects. Reuse of existing classes when building new classes and programs saves time and effort. Reuse also helps you build more reliable and effective systems, because existing classes and components often have gone through extensive *testing*, *debugging* and *performance* tuning. Just as the notion of *interchangeable parts* was crucial to the Industrial Revolution, reusable classes are crucial to the software revolution that has been spurred by object technology.

Messages and Methods Calls

When you drive a car, pressing its gas pedal sends a *message* to the car to perform a task—that is, to go faster. Similarly, you *send messages to an object*. Each message is a **method call** that tells a method of the object to perform its task. For example, a program might call a particular bank-account object's *deposit* method to increase the account's balance.

Attributes and Instance Variables

A car, besides having capabilities to accomplish tasks, also has *attributes*, such as its color, its number of doors, the amount of gas in its tank, its current speed and its record of total miles driven (i.e., its odometer reading). Like its capabilities, the car's attributes are represented as part of its design in its engineering diagrams (which, for example, include an odometer and a fuel gauge). As you drive an actual car, these attributes are carried along with the car. Every car maintains its *own* attributes. For example, each car knows how much gas is in its own gas tank, but *not* how much is in the tanks of *other* cars.

An object, similarly, has attributes that it carries along as it's used in a program. These attributes are specified as part of the object's class. For example, a bank-account object has a *balance attribute* that represents the amount of money in the account. Each bank-account object knows the balance in the account it represents, but *not* the balances of the *other* accounts in the bank. Attributes are specified by the class's **instance variables**.

Encapsulation

Classes **encapsulate** (i.e., wrap) attributes and methods into objects—an object's attributes and methods are intimately related. Objects may communicate with one another, but they're normally not allowed to know how other objects are implemented—implementation details are *hidden* within the objects themselves. This **information hiding** is crucial to good software engineering.

Inheritance

A new class of objects can be created quickly and conveniently by **inheritance**—the new class absorbs the characteristics of an existing one, possibly customizing them and adding unique characteristics of its own. In our car analogy, a "convertible" certainly *is an* object of the more *general* class "automobile," but more *specifically*, the roof can be raised or lowered.

Object-Oriented Analysis and Design (OOAD)

How will you create the code for your programs? Perhaps, like many programmers, you'll simply turn on your computer and start typing. This approach may work for small programs, but what if you were asked to create a software system to control thousands of automated teller machines for a major bank? Or suppose you were asked to work on a team of 1,000 software developers building the next U.S. air traffic control system? For projects so large and complex, you should not simply sit down and start writing programs.

To create the best solutions, you should follow a detailed **analysis** process for determining your project's **requirements** (i.e., defining *what* the system is supposed to do) and developing a **design** that satisfies them (i.e., deciding *how* the system should do it). Ideally, you'd go through this process and carefully review the design (and have your design reviewed by other software professionals) before writing any code. If this process involves analyzing and designing your system from an object-oriented point of view, it's called an **object-oriented analysis and design (OOAD) process**. Languages like Java are object oriented. Programming in such a language, called **object-oriented programming** (OOP), allows you to implement an object-oriented design as a working system.

1.11 Test-Driving the Doodlz App in an Android Virtual Device (AVD)

In this section, you'll run and interact with your first Android app. The **Doodlz** app allows the user to "paint" on the screen using different brush sizes and colors. You'll build this app in Chapter 9. The following steps show how to import the app's project into Eclipse and how to test-drive the app in the Android Virtual Device (AVD) that you set up in the Before You Begin section following the Preface. Later in this section, we'll also discuss how to run the app on an actual Android device.

The screen captures in the following steps (and throughout this book) were taken on a computer running Windows 7, Java SE 6, Eclipse 3.6.1, Android 2.2/2.3/3.0 and the ADT Plugin for Eclipse.

1. ***Checking your setup.*** Confirm that you've set up your computer properly to develop Android apps by reading the Before You Begin section located after the Preface.
2. ***Opening Eclipse.*** To start Eclipse, open the folder containing Eclipse on your system and double-click the Eclipse (●) icon. If this is your first time opening Eclipse, the **Welcome** tab (Fig. 1.20) will open. Click the **Workbench** button to close this tab and switch to the program development view—this is formally called the **Java perspective** in Eclipse.

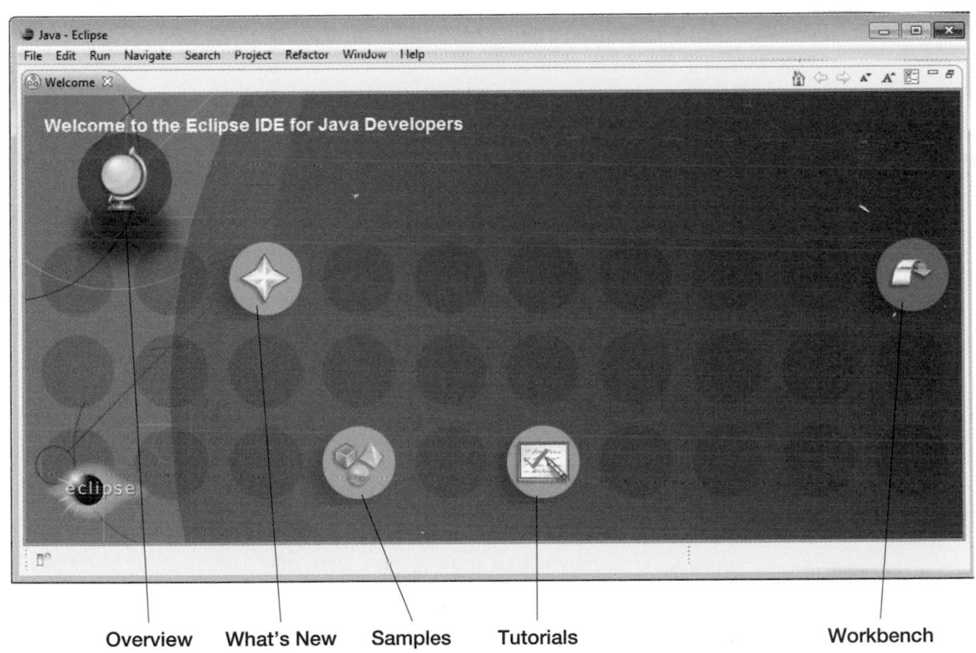

Fig. 1.20 | **Welcome to Eclipse** tab in Eclipse.

3. ***Opening the* Import *Dialog.*** Select **File > Import...** to open the **Import** dialog (Fig. 1.21).

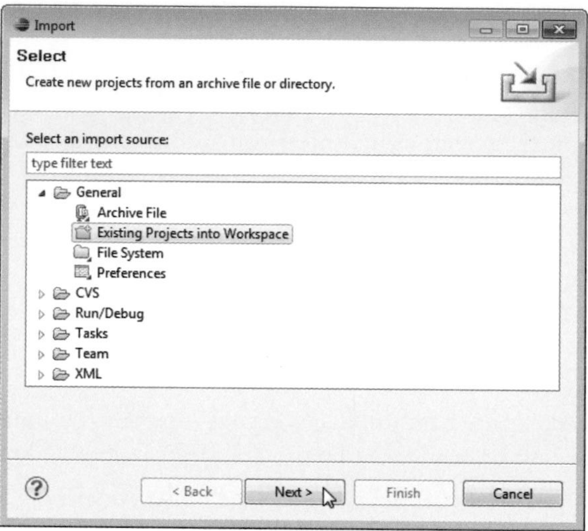

Fig. 1.21 | **Import** dialog.

4. ***Importing the* Doodlz *app's project.*** In the **Import** dialog, expand the **General** node and select **Existing Projects into Workspace**, then click **Next >** to proceed to the **Import Projects** step (Fig. 1.22). Ensure that **Select root directory** is selected, then

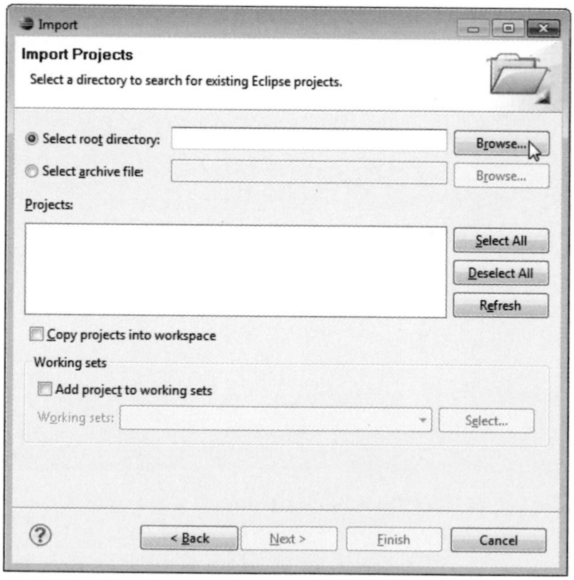

Fig. 1.22 | **Import** dialog's **Import Projects** step.

click the **Browse...** button. In the **Browse For Folder** dialog (Fig. 1.23), locate the **Doodlz** folder in the book's examples folder, select it and click **OK.** Click **Finish** to import the project into Eclipse. The project now appears in the **Package Explorer** window (Fig. 1.24) at the left side of the Eclipse window.

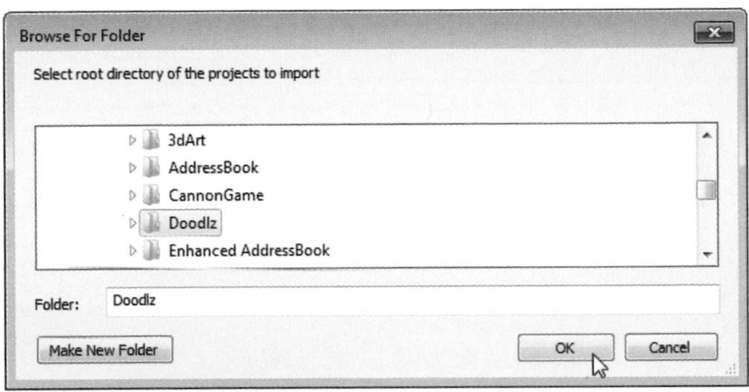

Fig. 1.23 | **Browser For Folder** dialog.

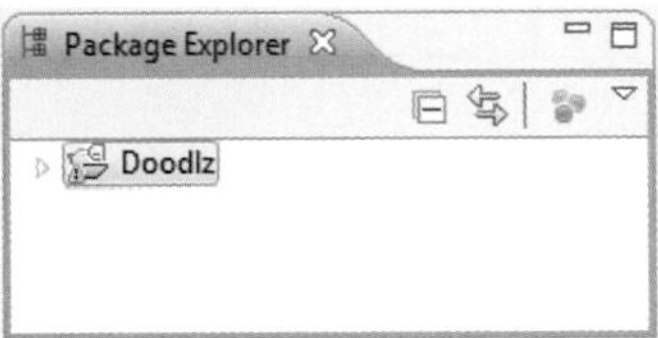

Fig. 1.24 | **Package Explorer** window in Eclipse.

5. ***Launching the* Doodlz *app.*** In Eclipse, select the **Doodlz** project in the **Package Explorer** window (Fig. 1.24), then select **Run As > Android Application** from the **Run As** button (▶ ▾) drop-down menu on the IDE's toolbar (Fig. 1.25). This will execute **Doodlz** in the NexusS Android Virtual Device (AVD) (Fig. 1.26) that you created in the Before You Begin section. If you prefer to test the app in a different AVD, you select **Window > Android SDK and AVD Manager**, then select the AVD you wish to use and click **Start....** If multiple AVDs are running when you launch an app, the **Android Device Chooser** dialog will appear to allow you to choose the AVD on which to execute the app. We'll discuss the **Android Device Chooser** dialog later in this section.
6. ***Exploring the AVD.*** The left side of the AVD displays the running app. The right side (Fig. 1.27) contains various buttons that simulate the hard and soft buttons on an actual Android device and a keyboard that simulates the device's hard or soft keyboard. **Hard buttons** are actual buttons on a device. **Soft buttons** are buttons that appear on the device's touch screen. You use the AVD's buttons to interact with apps and the Android OS in the AVD. When the app is installed on an Android device, you can create a new painting by dragging your finger anywhere on the canvas. In the AVD, you "touch" the screen by using the mouse.

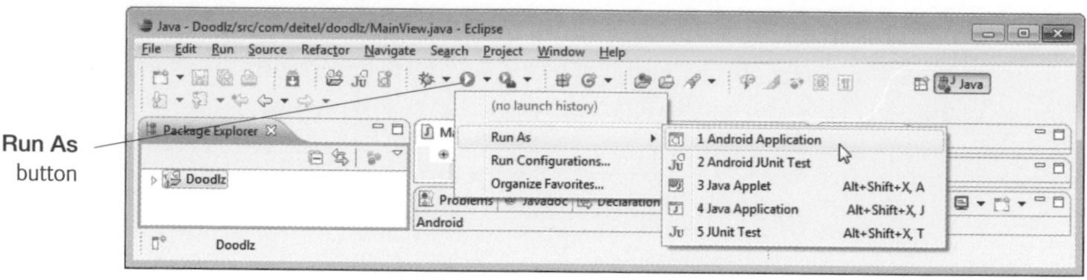

Fig. 1.25 | Launching the **Doodlz** app.

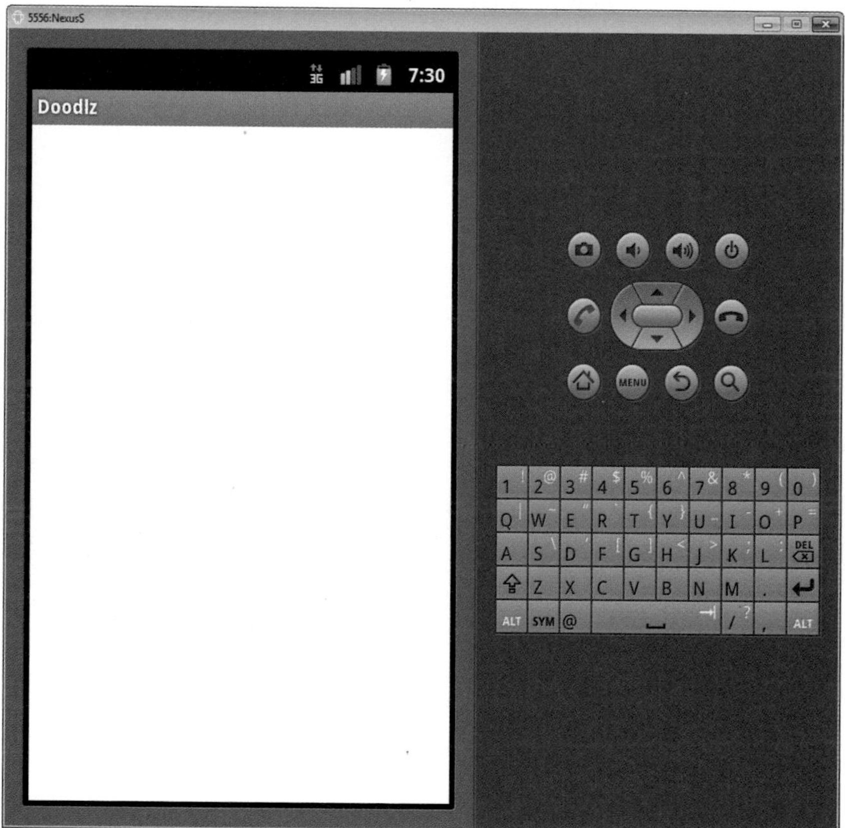

Fig. 1.26 | Android Virtual Device (AVD) with the running **Doodlz** app.

7. ***Displaying the app's options.*** To display the app's options, touch the **Menu** (MENU) button—on some actual devices this button appears as parallel horizontal bars (☰). The app now appears as shown in Fig. 1.28. The options include **Color**, **Line Width**, **Erase**, **Clear** and **Save Image**. Touching **Color** displays a GUI for changing the line color. Touching **Line Width** displays a GUI for changing the thickness of the line that will be drawn. Touching **Erase** sets the drawing color to

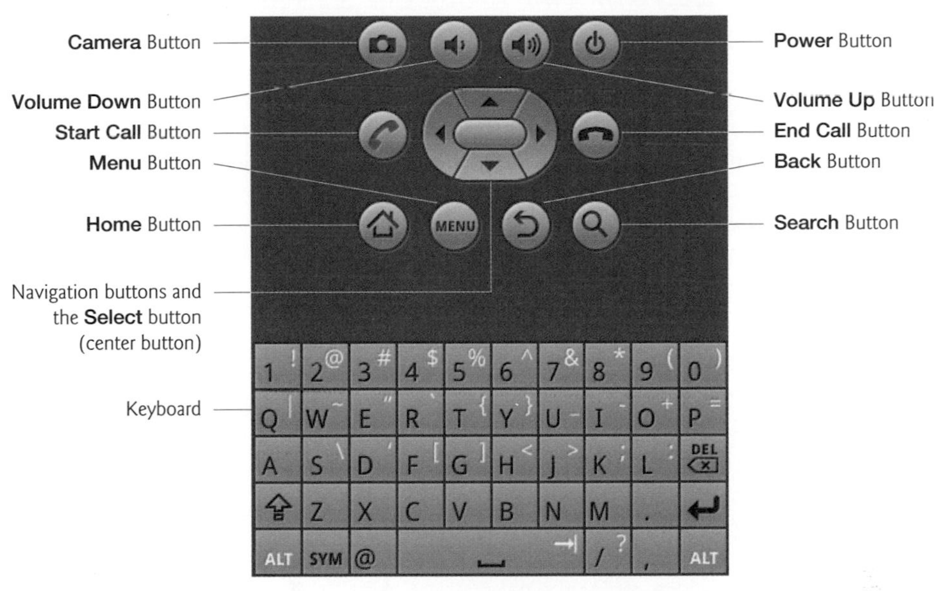

Fig. 1.27 | Android Virtual Device (AVD) with the running **Doodlz** app.

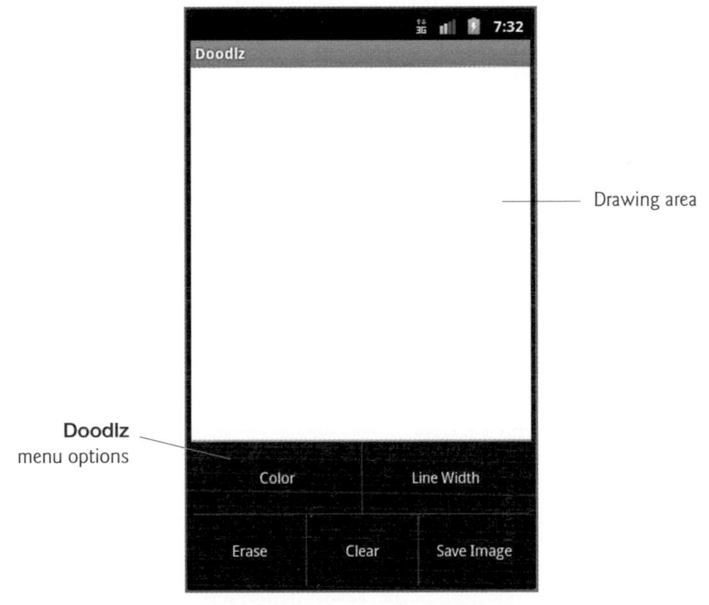

Fig. 1.28 | **Doodlz** menu options.

white so that as you draw over colored areas, the color is erased. Touching **Clear** clears the entire drawing. Touching **Save Image** saves the image into the device's **Gallery** of images. You'll explore each of these options momentarily.

8. ***Changing the brush color to red.*** To change the brush color, first touch the **Color** menu item to display the GUI for changing the color (Fig. 1.29(a)). Colors are defined using the RGBA color scheme in which the red, green, blue and alpha components are specified by integers in the range 0–255. The GUI consists of **Red**, **Green**, **Blue** and **Alpha** `SeekBar`s that allow you to select the amount of red, green, blue and transparency in the drawing color. You drag the `SeekBar`s to change the color. As you do, the app displays the new color. Select a red color now by dragging the **Red** `SeekBar` to the right as in Fig. 1.29(a). Touch the **Done** button to return to the drawing area. Drag your "finger" (that is, the mouse) on the screen to draw flower petals (Fig. 1.29(b)).

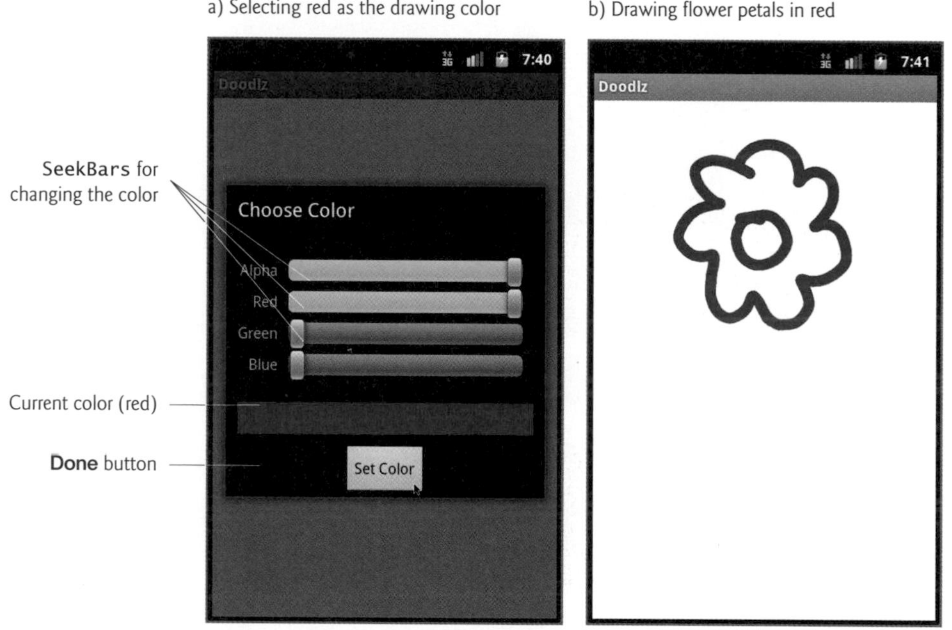

Fig. 1.29 | Changing the drawing color to red and drawing flower petals.

9. ***Changing the brush color to dark green.*** Change the drawing color again by touching the AVD's **Menu** (MENU) button, then touching **Color**. Select a dark green color by dragging the **Green** `SeekBar` to the right and ensuring that the **Red** and **Blue** `SeekBar`s are at the far left (Fig. 1.30(a)).

10. ***Changing the line width.*** To change the line width, touch the **Menu** (MENU) button, then touch **Line Width**. Drag the `SeekBar` for the line width to the right to thicken the line (Fig. 1.30(b)). Touch the **Done** button to return to the drawing area. Draw the flower stem and leaves. Repeat Steps 9 and 10 for a lighter green color and thinner line, then draw the grass. (Fig. 1.31).

11. ***Finishing the drawing.*** Use the instructions in Steps 9–10 to change the drawing color to blue (Fig. 1.32(a)) and select a narrower line (Fig. 1.32(b)). Switch back to the drawing area and draw the raindrops (Fig. 1.33).

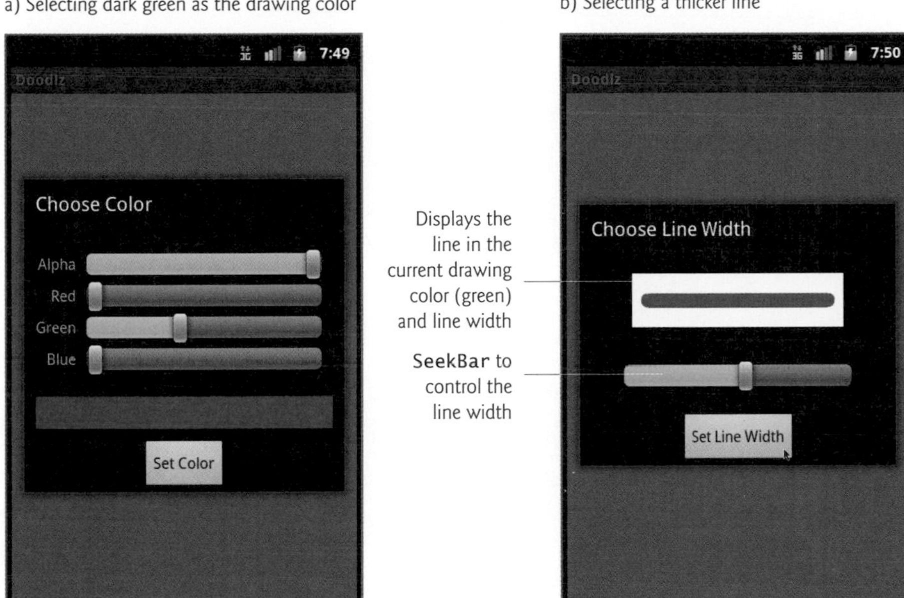

Fig. 1.30 | Changing the line color and line width.

Fig. 1.31 | Drawing the stem and grass in the new line color and line width.

a) Selecting blue as the drawing color

b) Selecting a thinner line

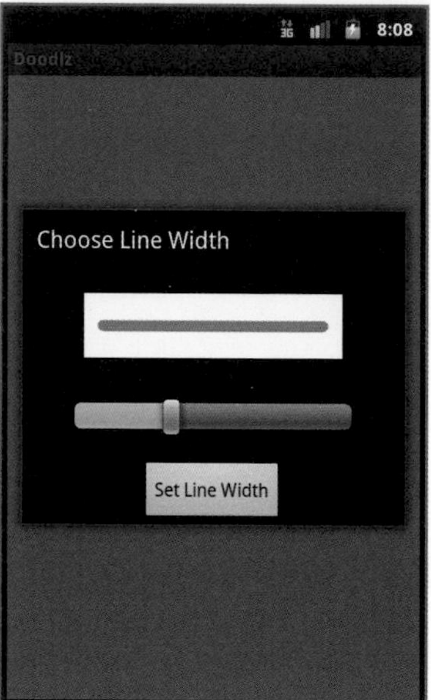

Fig. 1.32 | Changing the line color and width.

c)

Fig. 1.33 | Drawing the rain in the new line color and line width.

12. ***Saving the image.*** If you'd like, you can save the image to the **Gallery** by touching the **Menu** (MENU) button, then touching **Save Image.** You can then view this image and others stored on the device by opening the **Gallery** app.
13. ***Returning to the home screen.*** You can return to the AVD's home screen by clicking the home ( ) button on the AVD.

Running the **Doodlz** *App on an Android Device*

If you have an Android device, you can easily execute an app on the device for testing purposes.

1. First, you must enable debugging on the device. To do so, go to the device's **Settings** app, then select **Applications > Development** and ensure that **USB debugging** is checked.
2. Next, connect the device to your computer via a USB cable—typically this comes with the device when you purchase it.
3. In Eclipse, select the **Doodlz** project in the **Package Explorer** window, then select **Run As > Android Application** from the **Run As** button ( ) drop-down menu on the IDE's toolbar (Fig. 1.25).

If you do not have any AVDs open, but do have an Android device connected, the IDE will automatically install the app on your device and execute it. If you have one or more AVDs open and/or devices connected, the **Android Device Chooser** dialog (Fig. 1.34) is displayed so that you can select the AVD or device on which to install and execute the app. In this case, we first started two AVDs and connected one actual device, so there are three "devices" on which we could possibly run the app. We set up several AVDs so that we could simulate real Android devices with different versions of the Android OS and different screen sizes.

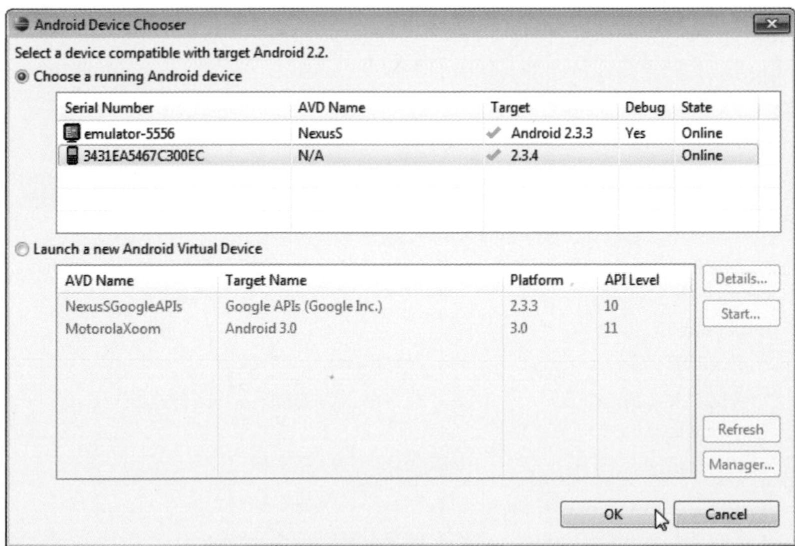

Fig. 1.34 | **Android Device Chooser** dialog.

In the **Choose a running Android device** section of Fig. 1.34, the dialog shows that we have one actual device connected to the computer (represented by the second line in the device list) and three AVDs. Each AVD has an **AVD Name** that we chose (`NexusS` and `MotorolaXoom`). Select the device or AVD you wish to use, then click **OK** to install and execute the app on that device or AVD. If you have other AVDs that you've defined and they're not currently executing, you can use the bottom half of this dialog to select and launch one of those AVDs.

When you build apps for distribution via the Android Market, you should test the apps on as many actual devices as you can. Remember that some features can be tested *only* on real devices. If you don't have many actual devices available to you, consider creating AVDs that simulate the various devices on which you'd like your app to execute. When you configure each AVD to simulate a specific real device, look up the real device's specifications online and configure the AVD accordingly. In addition, you can modify the AVD's `config.ini` file as described in the section **Setting hardware emulation options** at

```
developer.android.com/guide/developing/tools/avd.html
```

This file contains options that are not configurable via the ADT Plugin in Eclipse. Modifying these options allows you to more precisely match the hardware configuration of a real device.

1.12 Deitel Resources

Our website (`www.deitel.com`) provides more than 100 Resource Centers on various topics including programming languages, software development, Web 2.0, Internet business and open-source projects. The Resource Centers evolve out of the research we do to support our publications and business endeavors. We've found many exceptional resources online, including tutorials, documentation, software downloads, articles, blogs, podcasts, videos, code samples, books, e-books and more—most of them are free. We announce our latest Resource Centers in our newsletter, the *Deitel® Buzz Online*, and on Facebook and Twitter. Figure 1.35 provides a list of the Deitel resources to help you get started with Android app development.

Deitel Android resource	URL
Android for Programmers: An App-Driven Approach book page	`www.deitel.com/books/AndroidFP/`
Android Resource Center	`www.deitel.com/android/`
Android Best Practices Resource Center	`www.deitel.com/androidbestpractices/`
Java Resource Center	`www.deitel.com/java/`
Eclipse Resource Center	`www.deitel.com/Eclipse/`
SQLite 3 Resource Center	`www.deitel.com/SQLite3/`

Fig. 1.35 | Deitel Android resources. (Part 1 of 2.)

Deitel Android resource	URL
Deitel Resource Centers homepage	www.deitel.com/ResourceCenters.html
Deitel on Facebook	www.deitel.com/DeitelFan/
Deitel on Twitter	@deitel
Deitel® Buzz Online e-mail newsletter	www.deitel.com/newsletter/subscribe.html

Fig. 1.35 | Deitel Android resources. (Part 2 of 2.)

1.13 Android Development Resources

Figure 1.36 is a list of Android development resources. Figure 1.37 lists several of the Android developer videos available on `developer.android.com`. For additional resources, visit our Android Resource Center at `www.deitel.com/android`.

Android development tips and resources	URL
Android Developers' Channel on YouTube	www.youtube.com/user/androiddevelopers
Sample Android apps from Google	code.google.com/p/apps-for-android/
O'Reilly article, "Ten Tips for Android Application Development"	answers.oreilly.com/topic/862-ten-tips-for-android-application-development/
Bright Hub™ website for Android programming tips and how-to guides	www.brighthub.com/mobile/google-android.aspx
The article, "10 User Experience Tips for Successful Android Apps"	www.androidtapp.com/10-user-experience-tips-for-successful-android-apps/
Rapid Android development tips	www.droidnova.com/
The tutorial, "Working with XML on Android: Build Java applications for mobile devices," by Michael Galpin, software architect at eBay	www.ibm.com/developerworks/opensource/library/x-android/index.html
The Android Developers blog	android-developers.blogspot.com/
The Sprint Application Developers Program	developer.sprint.com/site/global/develop/mobile_platforms/android/android.jsp
The T-Mobile Android developer website	developer.t-mobile.com/site/global/resources/partner_hubs/android/p_android.jsp
HTC's Developer Center for Android and Windows Mobile development	developer.htc.com/
The Motorola Android development site	developer.motorola.com/

Fig. 1.36 | Android development tips and resources.

Video	URL
Androidology, Part 1 of 3: Architecture Overview	developer.android.com/videos/index.html#v=QBGfUs9mQYY
Androidology, Part 2 of 3: Application Lifecycle	developer.android.com/videos/index.html#v=fL6gSd4ugSI
Androidology, Part 3 of 3: APIs	developer.android.com/videos/index.html#v=MPukbH6D-lY
Android Developer Soapbox: Easy for Java Developers, Build Desktop Widgets	developer.android.com/videos/index.html#v=FTAxE6SIWeI
A Beginner's Guide to Android	developer.android.com/videos/index.html#v=yqCj83leYRE
The World of List View	developer.android.com/videos/index.html#v=wDBM6wVEO70
Android UI Design Patterns	developer.android.com/videos/index.html#v=M1ZBjlCRfz0
Writing Zippy Android Apps	developer.android.com/videos/index.html#v=c4znvD-7VDA
Casting a Wide Net for All Android Devices	developer.android.com/videos/index.html#v=zNmohaZYvPw
Building Push Applications for Android	developer.android.com/videos/index.html#v=PLM4LajwDVc

Fig. 1.37 | Android developer videos.

1.14 Wrap-Up

This chapter presented a brief history of Android and discussed its functionality. We discussed features of the Android 2.2, 2.3 and 3.0 operating system. We provided links to some of the key online documentation and to the newgroups and forums you can use to connect with the developer community. We discussed Android Market and provided links to some popular app review and recommendation sites. You learned the Android gestures and how to perform each on an Android device and on the emulator. We introduced the Java, Android and Google packages that enable you to use the hardware and software functionality you'll need to build your Android apps. You'll use many of these packages in this book. We also discussed Java programming and the Android SDK. We provided a quick refresher on basic object-technology concepts, including classes, objects, attributes and behaviors. You test-drove the **Doodlz** app on the Android emulator.

In Chapter 2, we discuss the business side of Android app development. You'll see how to prepare your apps for submission to the Android Market. We provide tips for pricing and marketing your app. We also show how to use Android Market capabilities for tracking app sales, payments and more.

2

Android Market and App Business Issues

Objectives

In this chapter you'll be introduced to:

- Characteristics of great Android apps.
- User interface guidelines for designing your apps.
- Registering for Android Market.
- Submitting your apps to Android Market.
- Pricing your apps and the benefits of free vs. paid apps.
- In-app billing.
- Launching Android Market from within an app.
- Marketing and monetizing your apps.
- Other Android app stores.
- Other popular mobile and Internet app platforms to which you can port your apps.
- Android humor.

Outline

2.1 Introduction

In Chapters 3–18, we'll develop a wide variety of Android apps. Once you've developed and tested your own apps—both in the emulator and on Android devices—the next step is to submit them to Android Market—or other app marketplaces—for distribution. In this chapter, we'll discuss the *User Interface Guidelines* and *Best Practices* to follow when designing apps, and provide characteristics of great apps. You'll learn how to register for Android Market and set up a Google Checkout account so that you can sell apps. You'll learn how to prepare your apps for publication and how to upload them to Android Market. We'll discuss some considerations for making your apps free or selling them for a fee, and mention key resources for monetizing apps. We'll provide resources for marketing your apps, and mention other popular app platforms to which you may want to port your Android apps. And, we'll point you to online Android developer documentation for additional information.

2.2 Building Great Android Apps

With over 200,000 apps in Android Market[1], how do you create an Android app that people will find, download, use and recommend to others? Consider what makes an app fun, useful, interesting, appealing and enduring. A clever app name, an attractive icon and an engaging description might lure people to your app on Android Market or one of the many other Android app marketplaces. But once users download the app, what will make them use it regularly and recommend it to others? Figure 2.1 shows some characteristics of great apps.

1. `googleblog.blogspot.com/2011/05/android-momentum-mobile-and-more-at.html`.

Characteristics of great apps

General Characteristics

- *Future proofed* for subsequent versions of Android (`developer.android.com/sdk/1.5_r3/upgrading.html#FutureProofYourApps`).
- *Updated frequently* with new features.
- *Work properly* (and bugs are fixed promptly).
- Follow standard Android app GUI *conventions*.
- *Responsive* and don't require too much memory, bandwidth or battery power.
- *Novel* and *creative*—possess a "wow" factor.
- *Enduring*—something that you'll use regularly.
- Use quality graphics, images, animations, audio and video.
- *Intuitive* and easy to use (don't require extensive help documentation).
- *Accessible* to people with disabilities (`www.google.com/accessibility/`).
- Give users reasons and a means to *tell others about your app* (e.g., you can give users the option to post their game scores to Facebook).
- *Provide additional content* for content-driven apps (e.g., additional game levels, puzzles, articles).
- *Do not request excessive permissions.*
- Built for *broad distribution*.

Great Games

- *Entertaining.*
- *Challenging.*
- *Progressive levels of difficulty.*
- Show your scores and *record high scores*.
- Provide *audio and visual feedback*.
- Offer *single-player*, *multiplayer* and *networked* games.
- Have high quality *animations*.
- Support *control schemes* that work on a variety of devices.

Useful Utilities

- Provide *useful* functionality and accurate information.
- Make tasks more *convenient* (e.g., maintaining a to-do list, managing expenses).
- Make the user *better informed*.
- *Topical*—provide information on current subjects of interest (e.g., stock prices, news, severe storm warnings, movie reviews, epidemics).
- Provide access on-the-go to your *favorite websites* (e.g., stores, banks).
- Increase your personal and business *productivity*.

Fig. 2.1 | Characteristics of great apps.

2.3 Android Best Practices

The *Android Developer's Guide* (called the *Dev Guide*) *Best Practices* section discusses compatibility, supporting multiple screens, user interface guidelines, and designing for performance, responsiveness and seamlessness. You should also check out the general mobile app design guidelines available from other online resources (Fig. 2.2).

Mobile app design resource	URL
Android Developer Guide: Best Practices	
Compatibility	`developer.android.com/guide/practices/compatibility.html`
Supporting Multiple Screens	`developer.android.com/guide/practices/screens_support.html`
User Interface Guidelines	`developer.android.com/guide/practices/ui_guidelines/index.html`
Designing for Performance	`developer.android.com/guide/practices/design/performance.html`
Designing for Responsiveness	`developer.android.com/guide/practices/design/responsiveness.html`
Designing for Seamlessness	`developer.android.com/guide/practices/design/seamlessness.html`

Fig. 2.2 | Online resources for mobile app design.

2.3.1 Compatibility

When developing an Android app, you need to determine which devices and versions of the operating system it will target. The `<uses-feature>` elements listed in your app's manifest file describe the app's feature needs (Fig. 2.3), allowing Android Market to filter the app so that only users with *compatible devices* can view and download it.

Feature	Descriptor
Hardware	
Audio	`android.hardware.audio.low_latency`
Bluetooth	`android.hardware.bluetooth`
Camera	`android.hardware.camera`
Camera auto-focus	`android.hardware.camera.autofocus`
Camera flash	`android.hardware.camera.flash`
Front-facing camera	`android.hardware.camera.front`
Location	`android.hardware.location`

Fig. 2.3 | Feature descriptors for specifying hardware and software requirements in the manifest file (`developer.android.com/guide/topics/manifest/uses-feature-element.html`). (Part 1 of 2.)

Feature	Descriptor
Network-based geolocation	`android.hardware.location.network`
GPS	`android.hardware.location.gps`
Microphone	`android.hardware.microphone`
Near-field communications	`android.hardware.nfc`
Accelerometer sensor	`android.hardware.sensor.accelerometer`
Barometer sensor	`android.hardware.sensor.barometer`
Compass sensor	`android.hardware.sensor.compass`
Gyroscope sensor	`android.hardware.sensor.gyroscope`
Light sensor	`android.hardware.sensor.light`
Proximity sensor	`android.hardware.sensor.proximity`
Telephony	`android.hardware.telephony`
CDMA telephony	`android.hardware.telephony.cdma`
GSM telephony	`android.hardware.telephony.gsm`
Emulated touchscreen	`android.hardware.faketouch`
Touchscreen	`android.hardware.touchscreen`
Multitouch screen (two or more fingers)	`android.hardware.touchscreen.multitouch`
Multitouch distinct (unique tracking of two points for two fingers, used for rotate gestures)	`android.hardware.touchscreen.multitouch.distinct`
Multitouch Jazzhand (touch from up to five fingers)	`android.hardware.touchscreen.multitouch.jazzhand`
Wi-Fi	`android.hardware.wifi`
Software	
Live Wallpaper	`android.software.live_wallpaper`
SIP	`android.software.sip`
SIP/VoIP	`android.software.sip.voip`

Fig. 2.3 | Feature descriptors for specifying hardware and software requirements in the manifest file (`developer.android.com/guide/topics/manifest/uses-feature-element.html`). (Part 2 of 2.)

You also can filter sales and downloads of your app by country and wireless carrier. For example, your app might be relevant to only Verizon customers or to users located in the United Kingdom. These Market filters can be added when you log into Android Market to publish the app. Apps can also dynamically query the device to determine its capabilities. For example, if your app includes features that use the camera but does not *require* the camera, the app can query the device to determine if a camera is available.

For information about *designing for multiple devices* and ensuring that your app will continue to work after *new versions of Android* are released, see `developer.android.com/guide/practices/compatibility.html`. For information about Market filters for restricting app distribution, see `developer.android.com/guide/appendix/market-filters.html`.

2.3.2 Supporting Multiple Screens

Android SDK 1.6 and higher support *multiple screen sizes* (the diagonal measurement) and *screen densities* (the distribution of pixels across the screen). But you do not need (nor would you want to try) to design your app for every possible screen size and density.

Android provides four generalized screen sizes (*small*, *normal*, *large* and *extra large*) and densities (*low*, *medium*, *high* and *extra high*), making it easier for you to design apps that work on multiple screens. You can use these screen sizes and densities when developing your app, even though the exact sizes of the devices might vary. You may need to create multiple resources (e.g., layouts, icons, graphics) to ensure that they scale properly to the appropriate screens. When the user runs the app, Android automatically renders it at the device's actual screen size and density and chooses the appropriate resources if you've specified separate ones for different screen sizes. You can set the `<supports-screens>` element in the `AndroidManifest.xml` file to specify the screen sizes your app supports. For additional information, see *Supporting Multiple Screens* at

```
developer.android.com/guide/practices/screens_support.html.
```

2.3.3 Android User Interface Guidelines

It's important when creating Android apps to follow the *Android User Interface Guidelines* for designing icons, widgets, activities, tasks and menus:

```
developer.android.com/guide/practices/ui_guidelines/index.html
```

Icon Design Guidelines

The *Icon Design Guidelines* provide information about each of the icons you'll need to provide (e.g., *launcher*, *menu*, *status bar*, *tab*, *dialog* and *list view icons*) and the design specifications for each (size, color, positioning, effects, etc.). It also includes a downloadable **Android Icon Templates Pack**, where you'll find templates for creating your own app icons in Adobe Photoshop and Adobe Illustrator.

Widget Design Guidelines

The *Widget Design Guidelines* provide specifications for designing **widgets**—displays of timely information on the user's **Home** screen, such as the current weather, stock prices and news (Fig. 2.4). Widgets can be stand-alone (as demonstrated in Chapter 14, **Weather Viewer** App), but they're typically included as an optional feature of an app to engage the user. For example, ESPN's ScoreCenter app includes a widget for tracking your favorite sports teams on your **Home** screen rather than launching your app each time you want to check the scores. The user can choose whether or not to display an app's widget on their **Home** screen.

Widget	Functionality
ESPN® ScoreCenter	Track scores of your favorite sports teams.
Pandora Radio	Control your personalized Pandora Internet radio station (e.g., pause or skip).

Fig. 2.4 | Popular Android widgets. (Part 1 of 2.)

Widget	Functionality
WeatherBug Elite	Three-day forecast and a weather-map widget.
Twidroyd PRO	Follow your favorite Twitterers.
Shazam Encore	Easily tag, share and buy music.
Weather & Toggle Widget	A clock, weather widgets and toggle widgets that allow you to easily change phone settings (e.g., brightness, Wi-Fi, etc.).
BatteryLife	Customizable widget for monitoring the device's battery life.
System Info Widget	Monitor system information such as battery life, memory availability (RAM, internal and SD card) and more.
Stock Alert	Track stock prices, currencies, commodities and futures.
The Coupons App	Real-time coupons for local restaurants, shops and gas stations.
Favorite Quotes	Daily quote and random quote widgets.
ecoTips	Ecological tips from the Wildlife Fund site.
Difficult Logic Riddles Pro	Math and logic riddles (hints and answers are included).
App Protector Pro	Lock any app on your phone (e.g., SMS, Market, etc.).
Android Agenda Widget	Displays your calendar events from the calendar on the device, Google Calendar and more.

Fig. 2.4 | Popular Android widgets. (Part 2 of 2.)

Activity and Task Design Guidelines

The *Activity and Task Design Guidelines* discuss:

- **Activities**—reusable components used to build an app's user interface. Activities perform actions such as searching, viewing information and dialing a phone number. *A separate activity is often associated with each different screen of an app.* We discuss activities in Chapter 4.
- **The activity stack**—a reverse chronological history of all of the activities, allowing the user to navigate to the previous activity using the **Back** button.
- **Tasks**—a series of activities that enable the user to complete an objective within an app or across multiple apps.

Menu Design Guidelines

The *Menu Design Guidelines* discuss **Options** and **Context** menus. The **Options** menu—accessed through the device's **Menu** button—provides actions and operations for the app's current screen. For example, selecting the **Options** menu in the **Messaging** app brings up a menu of icons including **Compose**, **Delete Threads**, **Search** and **Settings.** Selecting the **Context** menu from within a message in the **Messaging** app (by touching and holding—also called *long pressing*—within the message on a touchscreen) brings up a menu of options specific to that message, including **Select all**, **Select text**, **Cut all**, **Copy all**, **Paste** and **Input method.**

Figures 2.5 and 2.6 provide suggestions for designing user interfaces for your apps, including tips to ensure that your apps are responsive to user interactions and will perform *efficiently* and *seamlessly* on mobile devices. We'll introduce additional best practices in the code walkthroughs throughout the book.

Points and suggestions when designing the user interface

General Guidelines

- Most important, read the *Dev Guide*'s *Best Practices* (including the *User Interface Guidelines*).
- Keep in mind *why* the user is using your app.
- Keep your app's *goals* in mind as you design it.
- Model your app after the way things work in the *real world.*
- Provide *feedback* to user actions—for example, use indicators such as *progress bars* to show that an app is working on a task.
- Support the standard Android *gestures* (Fig. 1.5).
- *Read user feedback* for suggestions, to learn about bugs and to adjust your app accordingly.
- Support interaction between apps (see `developer.motorola.com/docstools/library/Best_Practices_for_User_Interfaces/`).

User Interface Design

- Apps should be *intuitive*—the user should be able to figure out what to do with minimal help.
- Make your apps *aesthetically pleasing*—use attractive colors, high-quality graphics, etc.
- *Avoid cluttering the screen.*
- Provide *lists of choices* that the user can touch (or select) rather than requiring key stroking, if possible.
- *Use standard buttons and icons* provided by Android, when possible.
- If you use *custom icons*, make them easily *distinguishable* from the Android system icons.
- Make each user interface element large enough for a user to easily touch it.
- All font sizes should be scale-independent pixels (SP); use density-independent pixels (DIP or DP) for everything else (see `stackoverflow.com/questions/2025282/difference-of-px-dp-dip-and-sp-in-android`).
- Support screen orientation changes between *portrait* (when the device is held upright) and *landscape* when the device is held sideways or a physical keyboard is open).
- Design your app to run on *multiple devices* with *varying screen sizes* (see `developer.android.com/guide/practices/screens_support.html`) and devices.

Fig. 2.5 | Points and suggestions when designing the user interface.

Designing for performance, responsiveness and seamlessness

Performance (`developer.android.com/guide/practices/design/performance.html`)

- Apps should be *efficient*—the device has limited battery life, computing power and memory.
- *Never perform long tasks (for example, loading large files or accessing a database) in the UI thread,* as they could make the app unresponsive.
- *Remove cached files* when they're no longer needed.

Fig. 2.6 | Designing for performance, responsiveness and seamlessness. (Part 1 of 2.)

Designing for performance, responsiveness and seamlessness

- Consider how the app will handle a *lost or unavailable network connection* (for example, it might display a message to the user).
- The app should notify the user of any actions that may result in *charges from their provider* (e.g., additional data services, SMS and MMS).
- Many devices have limited storage space for apps and data. If the app does not need secure data, consider writing to the SD card, if available.

Responsiveness (`developer.android.com/guide/practices/design/responsiveness.html`)

- Your code must be *efficient* so the apps are *fast* and *responsive.*
- If your app takes a while to load, use a ***splash screen***—an image that will be displayed when the icon is tapped on the screen so that the user sees an immediate response while waiting for the app to load. A splash screen usually resembles the app's user interface—often just an image of the background elements of the GUI. You could also show a progress bar.

Seamlessness (`developer.android.com/guide/practices/design/seamlessness.html`)

- Design your app to handle configuration changes properly, such as changing orientation and sliding a hardware keyboard in and out.
- *Save user data* before the app switches from running in the foreground to the background.
- Use a `ContentProvider` to easily *share data* from your app with other apps on the device.
- Use the `NotificationManager` for notifications to the user.
- Don't launch an `Activity` UI from the background.
- Design for multiple devices—your app should support touchscreen and keyboard input, and multiple screen sizes and resolutions.

Fig. 2.6 | Designing for performance, responsiveness and seamlessness. (Part 2 of 2.)

Designing for Accessibility

Android includes built-in tools to help you design apps that are *accessible* to people with disabilities such as low vision or blindness. The **Text-to-Speech (TTS)** speech synthesis capability (available in English, Spanish, French, German and Italian) allows apps to "speak" text strings. We'll use the text-to-speech (speech synthesis) and speech-to-text (speech recognition) input to create a talking app in Chapter 15, **Pizza Ordering** App. You can also incorporate responses to user input such as making sounds (for the visually impaired) and vibrating (for the hearing impaired).

Localization

If you intend to make your app available in multiple countries, you should consider localizing it for each. For example, if you intend to offer your app in France, you should translate its resources (e.g., text, audio files) into French. You might also choose to use different colors, graphics and sounds based on the *locale*. For each locale, you'll have a separate, customized set of resources for your app. When the user launches the app, Android automatically finds and loads the resources that match the locale of the device.To learn about how to set up multiple resource directories to localize your apps, see `developer.android.com/guide/topics/resources/localization.html`.

2.4 Registering at Android Market

To publish your apps on Android Market, you must register for an account at

```
market.android.com/publish/
```

There's a one-time registration fee. Unlike with other popular mobile platforms, *Android Market has no approval process for uploading apps*. You must, however, adhere to the *Android Market Content Policy for Developers*. If your app is in violation of this policy, it can be removed at any time; serious or repeated violations may result in account termination (Fig. 2.7).

Violations of the *Android Market Content Policy for Developers*

- Infringing on others' intellectual property rights (e.g., trademarks, patents and copyrights).
- Promoting hate or violence.
- Providing pornographic or obscene content, or anything unsuitable for children under age 18.
- Breaching the carrier's terms of service for usage.
- Illegal content.
- Invading personal privacy.
- Interfering with the services of other parties.
- Harming the user's device or personal data.
- Adversely impacting a user's service charges or a wireless carrier's network.
- Creating a "spammy" user experience (e.g., misleading the user about the app's purpose).
- Impersonation or deception.
- Gambling.

Fig. 2.7 | Violations of the *Android Market Content Policy for Developers* (`www.android.com/market/terms/developer-content-policy.html`).

2.5 Setting Up a Google Checkout Merchant Account

To sell your apps on Android Market, you'll need a ***Google Checkout merchant account***, available to Android Market developers located in 29 countries at the time of this writing (Fig. 2.8).[2] Once you've registered and logged into Android Market at `market.android.com/publish/`, click the **Setup Merchant Account** link. You'll need to

- provide private information by which Google can contact you.
- provide customer-support contact information where users can contact you.
- provide financial information so that Google may perform a credit check.
- agree to the Terms of Service, which describe the features of the service, permissible transactions, prohibited actions, service fees, payment terms and more.

2. `checkout.google.com/support/sell/bin/answer.py?answer=150324&cbid=-eqo3objy740w&src=cb&lev=%20index`.

Locations				
Argentina	Denmark	Israel	Norway	Sweden
Australia	Finland	Italy	Portugal	Switzerland
Austria	France	Japan	Russia	Taiwan
Belgium	Germany	Mexico	Singapore	United Kingdom
Brazil	Hong Kong	Netherlands	Spain	United States
Canada	Ireland	New Zealand	South Korea	

Fig. 2.8 | Supported locations for Google Checkout merchants.

Google Checkout processes payments and helps protect you from fraudulent purchases. The standard payment processing rates are waived for your Android Market sales,[3] but you do pay a transaction fee of 30% of the app price, charged by Android Market. Note that once you set up a Google Checkout account, you'll be able to use it for much more than just selling your apps. Similar to PayPal, Google Checkout is used as a payment service for online transactions. Android Market may add other payment services such as PayPal in the future.

2.6 AndroidManifest.xml File

The ***AndroidManifest.xml*** ***file***, referred to as the ***manifest***, provides information needed to run your app in Android and to filter it properly in Android Market. This allows you to hide your app from users who are browsing Android Market on devices that are not compatible with your app. For example, a user whose device does not have a camera will not see apps that require a camera per the app's manifest. The manifest is automatically generated by the ADT Plugin for Eclipse, but you'll need to manually add information to the file before you upload the app to Android Market. The ADT Plugin for Eclipse includes an **Android Manifest Editor**, which enables you to easily edit the manifest file rather than updating the code directly in the XML file.

To access the Android Manifest Editor in Eclipse, go to the **Packages Explorer** tab and double-click the AndroidManifest.xml file in the app's folder. The file will open in the Eclipse workspace. Select the **Manifest** tab at the bottom of the workspace page to display the **Manifest General Attributes** page, where you'll provide basic information about your app, including package names, version numbers and elements. Figure 2.9 lists some of the common elements included in the manifest. You can find a complete list of elements at

developer.android.com/guide/topics/manifest/manifest-intro.html

When your app is ready, you'll come back to the **Manifest General Attributes** page to prepare it for distribution (which we discuss in Section 2.8).

3. checkout.google.com/termsOfService?type=SELLER.

Element	Description
Uses Feature	Specifies features required by the app. See Section 2.3.1, Compatibility.
Protected Broadcast	Specifies the name of the protected broadcast, which allows an app to declare that only it can send the broadcasted Intent.
Supports Screens	Specifies physical screen sizes (**Small, Normal, Large, XLarge, Resizeable**) and densities—the concentration of pixels on the screen—supported by the app. For each option, select **true** or **false**.
Uses Configuration	Declares the app's hardware requirements. Options include **Touch screen, Keyboard type, Hard keyboard, Navigation** (such as trackball or wheel) and **Five way nav** key (i.e., a trackball or key that allows you to navigate up, down, right and left, and select an item on the screen).
Uses SDK	SDK features required for the app to run properly (e.g., features specific to Android 2.3, 3.0, etc.). Note that you can develop against the current Android SDK but allow the app to run on a device with an earlier SDK using this flag and being careful not to call unsupported APIs.

Fig. 2.9 | Some common elements to add to your app's manifest.

On the **Application** tab at the bottom of the editor you'll define the attributes specific to the app, including the icon, description, permission, debugging and more. On the **Permissions** tab you'll specify if the app must use protected features on the device (that is, features that require permission to be accessed), such as writing SMS messages, setting the wallpaper or accessing location. Before installing an app, Android Market displays a list of permissions the app requires. You should request only the permissions that your app needs to execute correctly. For a list of permissions, see `developer.android.com/reference/android/Manifest.permission.html`. We discuss editing the manifest file in more detail in Section 2.7.

2.7 Preparing Your Apps for Publication

Preparing to Publish: A Checklist in the *Dev Guide* at `developer.android.com/guide/publishing/preparing.html` lists items to consider before publishing your app on Android Market, including:

- *Testing* your app on Android devices
- Considering including an *End User License Agreement* with your app (optional)
- Adding an *icon* and label to the app's manifest
- Turning off *logging* and *debugging*
- *Versioning* your app (e.g., 1.0, 1.1, 2.0, 2.3, 3.0)
- Getting a *cryptographic key* for *digitally signing* your app
- *Compiling* your app
- *Signing* your app

We discuss some of these next.

Testing Your App

Before submitting your app to Android Market, test it thoroughly to make sure it works properly on a variety of devices. Although the app might work perfectly using the emulator on your computer, problems could arise when running it on a particular Android device. Figure 2.10 lists Android functionality that's *not* available on the emulator.

Android functionality not available on the emulator
• Making or receiving real phone calls (the emulator allows simulated calls only) • USB connections • Camera and video capture • Device-attached headphones • Determining connected state of the phone • Determining battery charge or power charging state • Determining SD card insert/eject • Bluetooth • Near-field communications • Sensors (accelerometer, barometer, compass, light sensor, proximity sensor) • OpenGL ES 2.0 (and non-software rendered OpenGL)

Fig. 2.10 | Android functionality not available on the emulator (`developer.android.com/guide/developing/devices/emulator.html`).

To enable an Android device for testing and debugging apps, go to **Settings > Applications > Development** on the device and select the checkbox for **USB (Universal Serial Bus) Debugging.**

End User License Agreement

You have the option to include an ***End User License Agreement (EULA)*** with your app. An EULA is an agreement through which you license your software to the user. It typically stipulates terms of use, limitations on redistribution and reverse engineering, product liability, compliance with applicable laws and more. You might want to consult an attorney when drafting an EULA for your app. To view a sample EULA, see

```
www.developer-resource.com/sample-eula.htm.
```

Icons and Labels

Design an icon for your app and provide a text label (a name) that will appear in Android Market and on the user's device. The icon could be your company logo, an image from the app or a custom image. Create the icon for multiple screen densities:

- High-density screens: 72 x 72 pixels
- Medium-density screens: 48 x 48 pixels
- Low-density screens: 36 x 36 pixels

You'll also need a high-resolution app icon for use in Android Market.[4] This icon should be:

- 512 x 512 pixels
- 32-bit PNG with alpha
- 1,024 KB maximum

For further specifications and best practices, see the *Icon Design Guidelines* at `developer.android.com/guide/practices/ui_guidelines/icon_design.html`. Consider hiring an experienced graphic designer to help you create a compelling, professional icon (Fig. 2.11). We've found custom app icon design services ranging from $65 to $400 or more. Once you've created the icon and label, you'll need to specify them in the app's manifest. Go to the Android Manifest Editor and click on the **Application** tab at the bottom of the editor.

Company	URL	Services
glyFX	`www.glyfx.com/index.html`	Custom icon design and some free downloadable icons.
Androidicons	`www.androidicons.com/`	Custom icon design and several free downloadable menu icons.
Iconiza	`www.iconiza.com/portfolio/appicon.html`	Designs custom icons for a flat fee.
Aha-Soft	`www.aha-soft.com/icon-design.htm`	Designs custom icons for a flat fee.
Elance®	`www.elance.com`	Search for freelance icon designers.

Fig. 2.11 | Custom app icon design firms.

Turning Off Logging and Debugging

Before publishing your app you must turn off debugging. Click on the **Application** tab in the **Android Manifest Editor** and set the **Debuggable** attribute to **false**. Remove extraneous files such as log or backup files.

Versioning Your App

It's important to include a version name (shown to the users) and a version code (an integer used by Android Market) for your app, and to consider your strategy for numbering updates. For example, the first version code of your app might be 1.0, minor updates might be 1.1 and 1.2, and the next major update might be 2.0. For additional guidelines, see *Versioning Your Applications* at

```
developer.android.com/guide/publishing/versioning.html
```

Shrinking, Optimizing and Obfuscating Your App Code

The Android Market ***licensing service*** allows you to create licensing policies to control access to your paid apps. For example, you might use a licensing policy to limit how often

4. `market.android.com/support/bin/answer.py?answer=1078870`.

the app checks in with the server, how many simultaneous device installs are allowed, and what happens when an unlicensed app is identified. To learn more about the licensing service, visit

```
developer.android.com/guide/publishing/licensing.html
```

In addition to creating a licensing policy, you should "obfuscate" any apps you upload to Android Market to prevent reverse engineering of your code and further protect your apps. The ***ProGuard*** tool—which runs when you build your app in release mode—shrinks the size of your .apk file and optimizes and obfuscates the code. To learn how to set up and use the ProGuard tool, go to

```
developer.android.com/guide/developing/tools/proguard.html
```

For additional information about protecting your apps from piracy using code obfuscation and other techniques, visit

```
android-developers.blogspot.com/2010/09/securing-android-lvl-
applications.html
```

Getting a Private Key for Digitally Signing Your App

Before uploading your app to a device, to Android Market or to other app marketplaces, you must *digitally sign* the ***.apk file*** (Android app package file) using a ***digital certificate*** that identifies you as the author of the app. A digital certificate includes your name or company name, contact information, etc. It can be self-signed using a ***private key*** (i.e., a secure password used to *encrypt* the certificate); you do not need to purchase a certificate from a third-party certificate authority (though it's an option). During development, Eclipse automatically digitally signs your app so that you can run it on test devices. That digital certificate is not valid for use with the Android Market. The Java Development Kit (JDK) includes the tools you'll need to sign your apps. The ***Keytool*** generates a private key and ***Jarsigner*** is used to sign the `.apk` file. When running your app from Eclipse, the build tools included in the ADT Plugin automatically use the Keytool to sign the `.apk` file—you won't be asked for a password. They then run the ***zipalign*** tool to optimize the app's memory usage.

If you're using Eclipse with the ADT Plugin, you can use the **Export Wizard** to compile the app, generate a private key and sign the `.apk` file in release mode:

1. Select the project in the **Package Explorer**, then select **File > Export**.
2. Double click to open the **Android** folder, select **Export Android Application**, then click **Next**.
3. Select the project (i.e., your app) to export, then click **Next**.
4. Select the **Create new keystore** radio button. Enter a **Location** for your keystore where your digital certificate and private key will be stored (e.g., `c:\android\keystore`). Create a secure **Password**, **Confirm** the password, then click **Next** to go to the **Key Creation** GUI.
5. In the **Alias** field, enter a unique name for your key (e.g., "`releasekey`"). Note that only the first eight characters of the alias will be used. In the **Password** field, enter a secure password for your key, then re-enter the password in the **Confirm**

field. In the **Validity** field, enter the number of years that the key will be valid. Android Market requires that the private key be valid beyond October 22, 2033, and Google suggests that it should be valid for more than 25 years (longer than the anticipated life of the app), so that all updated versions of the app are signed with the same key. *If you sign updated versions with a different key, users will not be able to seamlessly upgrade to the new version of your app.* In the next several fields enter your personal information, including your **First and Last Name**, **Organizational Unit**, **Organization**, **City or Locality**, **State or Province** and two-letter **Country Code** (e.g., US). Click **Next**.

For additional information, see *Signing Your Applications* at:

```
developer.android.com/guide/publishing/app-signing.html
```

Screenshot(s)

Take at least two screenshots of your app that will be included with your app description in Android Market (Fig. 2.12). These provide a preview, since users can't test the app before downloading it. Choose attractive screenshots that show the app's functionality. Also, take screenshots from an emulator that does not have any extra icons in the status bar or that use custom skins that can be confusing or distracting for users. When you upload your app to Android Market, you'll have the option to include a URL for a promotional video.

Specification	Description
Size	320w x 480h pixels or 480w x 854h pixels (landscape images must be cropped accordingly).
Format	24-bit PNG or JPEG format with no alpha (transparency) effects.
Image	Full bleed to the edge with no borders.

Fig. 2.12 | Screenshot specifications.

The Dalvik Debug Monitor Service (DDMS), which is installed with the ADT Plugin for Eclipse, helps you debug your apps running on actual devices. The DDMS also enables you to capture screenshots on your device. To do so, perform the following steps:

1. Run the app on your device as described at the end of Section 1.11.
2. In Eclipse, select **Window > Open Perspective > DDMS**, which allows you to use the DDMS tools.
3. In the **Devices** window (Fig. 2.13), select the device from which you'd like to obtain a screen capture.
4. Click the **Screen Capture** button to display the **Device Screen Capture** window (Fig. 2.14).
5. After you've ensured that the screen is showing what you'd like to capture, you can click the **Save** button to save the image.

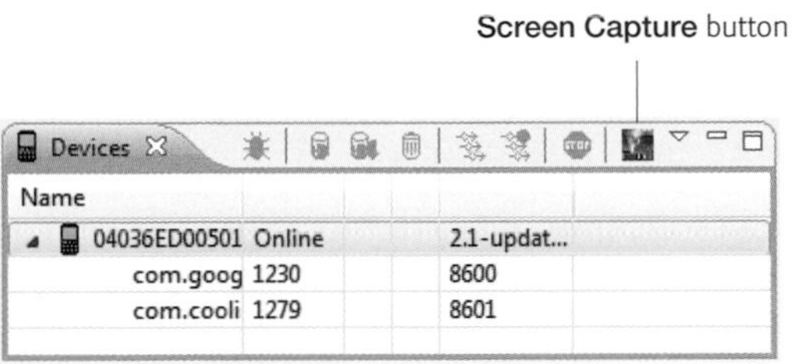

Fig. 2.13 | **Devices** window in the DDMS perspective.

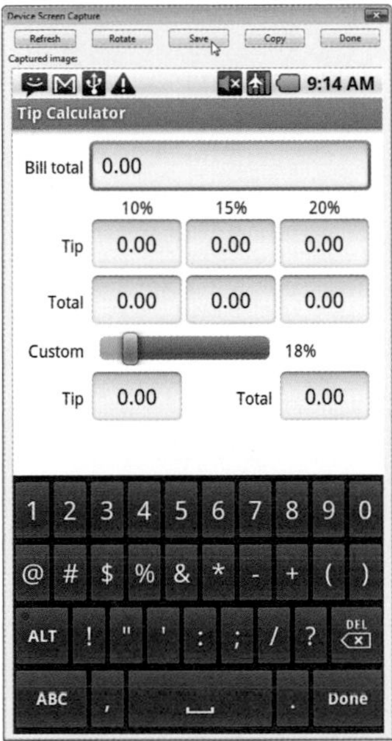

Fig. 2.14 | **Device Screen Capture** window showing a capture of the **Tip Calculator** app from Chapter 4.

If you wish to change what's on your device's screen before saving the image, make the change on the device, then press the **Refresh** button in the **Device Screen Capture** window to recapture the device's screen.

2.8 Uploading Your Apps to Android Market

Once you've prepared all of your files and you're ready to upload your app, read the steps at:

```
developer.android.com/guide/publishing/publishing.html
```

Then log into Android Market at `market.android.com/publish` (Section 2.4) and click the **Upload Application** button to begin the upload process. The remainder of this section discusses some of the steps you'll encounter.

Uploading Assets

1. *App .apk file.* Click the **Choose File** button to select the Android app package (`.apk`) file, which includes the app's code files (`.dex` files), assets, resources and the manifest file. Then click **Upload**.
2. *Screenshots.* Click the **Choose File** button to select at least two screenshots of your app to be included in Android Market. Click **Upload** after you've selected each screenshot.
3. *High-resolution app icon.* Click the **Choose File** button to select the 512 x 512 pixels app icon to be included in Android Market. Then click **Upload.**
4. *Promotional graphic (optional).* You may upload a promotional graphic for Android Market to be used by Google if they decide to promote your app (for examples, check out some of the graphics for featured apps on Android Market). The graphic must be 180w x 120h pixels in 24-bit PNG or JPEG format with *no alpha transparency effects*. It must also have a full bleed (i.e., go to the edge of the screen with no border in the graphic). Click the **Choose File** button to select the image, then click **Upload.**
5. *Feature Graphic (optional).* This graphic is used in the **Featured** section on Android Market. The graphic must be 1024w x 500h pixels in 24-bit PNG or JPEG format with no alpha transparency effects.[5] Click the **Choose File** button to select the image, then click **Upload.**
6. *Promotional video (optional).* You may include a URL for a promotional video for your app (e.g., a YouTube link to a video that demonstrates how your app works).
7. *Marketing opt-out.* Select the checkbox if you do not want Google to promote your app outside Android Market or other Google owned sites.

Listing Details

1. *Language.* By default, your app will be listed in English. If you'd like to list it in additional languages, click the **add language** hyperlink and select the checkboxes for the appropriate languages (Fig. 2.15), then click **OK.** Each language you select will appear as a hyperlink next to **Language** in the **Listing Details.** Click on each language to add the translated title, description and promotional text.

Language					
French	Spanish	Czech	Japanese	Swedish	Hindi
German	Dutch	Portuguese	Korean	Norwegian	Hebrew
Italian	Polish	Taiwanese	Russian	Danish	Finnish

Fig. 2.15 | Languages for listing apps in Android Market.

2. *Title.* The title of your app as it will appear in Android Market (30 characters maximum). *It does not need to be unique among all Android apps.*

5. `market.android.com/support/bin/answer.py?hl=en&answer=1078870`.

3. ***Description.*** A description of your app and its features (4,000 characters maximum). It's recommended that you use the last portion of the description to explain why each permission is required and how it's used.
4. ***Recent changes.*** A walkthrough of any changes specific to the latest version of your app (500 characters maximum).
5. ***Promo text.*** The promotional text for marketing your app (80 characters maximum).
6. ***App type.*** Choose **Applications** or **Games.**
7. ***Category.*** Select the category (Fig. 1.15) that best suits your game or app.
8. ***Price.*** This defaults to **Free**. To sell your app for a fee, click the **Setup a Merchant Account at Google Checkout** link to apply.

Publishing Options

1. ***Content rating.*** You may select **Mature**, **Teen**, **Pre-teen** or **All**. For more information, read the *Android Market Developer Program Policies* and the *Content Rating Guidelines* at `market.android.com/support/bin/answer.py?answer=188189`.
2. ***Locations.*** By default, **All Locations** is selected, which means that the app will be listed in all current and future Android Market locations. To pick and choose specific Android Markets where you'd like your app to be listed, uncheck the **All Locations** checkbox to display the list of countries. Then select each country you wish to support.

Contact Information

1. ***Website.*** Your website will be listed in Android Market. If possible, include a direct link to the page for the app, so that users interested in downloading your app can find more information, including marketing copy, feature listings, additional screenshots, instructions, etc.
2. ***E-mail.*** Your e-mail address will also be included in Android Market, so that customers can contact you with questions, report errors, etc.
3. ***Phone number.*** Sometimes your phone number is included in Android Market, therefore it's recommended that you leave this field blank unless you provide phone support. You may also want to provide a phone number for customer service on your website.

Consent

1. Read the *Android Content Guidelines* at `www.android.com/market/terms/developer-content-policy.html` (see Section 2.4), then check the **This application meets Android Content Guidelines** checkbox.
2. Next, you must acknowledge that your app may be subject to United States export laws (which generally deal with software that uses *encryption*), that you've complied with such laws and you certify that your app is authorized for export from the U.S. If you agree, check the checkbox. For more information about export laws, click **Learn More**, where you'll find some helpful links.

If you're ready to publish your app, click the **Publish** button. Otherwise, click the **Save** button to save your information to be published at a later date.

2.9 Other Android App Marketplaces

In addition to Android Market, you may choose to make your apps available through other Android app marketplaces (Fig. 2.16), or even through your own website using services such as AndroidLicenser (`www.androidlicenser.com`). However, according to the Android Market *Terms of Service*, you cannot use customer information obtained through Android Market to sell or distribute your apps elsewhere.

Marketplace	URL
Amazon Appstore	`developer.amazon.com/welcome.html`
AndAppStore	`www.andappstore.com`
Androidguys	`store.androidguys.com/home.asp`
Andspot Market	`www.andspot.com`
GetJar	`www.getjar.com`
Handango	`www.handango.com`
Mplayit™	`www.mplayit.com`
PocketGear	`www.pocketgear.com`
Shop4Apps™	`developer.motorola.com/shop4apps/`
SlideMe	`www.slideme.org`
Youpark	`www.youpark.com`
Zeewe	`www.zeewe.com`

Fig. 2.16 | Other Android app marketplaces.

2.10 Pricing Your App: Free or Fee

You set the price for the apps that you distribute through Android Market. Developers often offer their apps for free as a marketing and publicity tool, earning revenue through increased sales of products and services, sales of more *feature-rich versions* of the same app, or *in-app advertising*. Figure 2.17 lists ways to *monetize* your apps.

Ways to monetize apps
• *Sell the app* on Android Market or other Android app marketplaces.
• *Sell paid upgrades* to the app.
• *Sell virtual goods* (see Section 2.12).
• Use *mobile advertising* services for in-app ads (see Section 2.14).
• Sell *in-app advertising space* directly to your customers.
• Use it to *drive sales of a more feature-rich version* of the app.

Fig. 2.17 | Ways to monetize apps.

Paid Apps

According to a study by app store analytics firm Distimo (`www.distimo.com/`), the average price of paid Android apps is around $3.62[6] (the median is $2.72[7]). Although these prices may seem low, keep in mind that successful apps could sell tens of thousands, hundreds of thousands or even millions of copies! According to AdMob (`www.admob.com/`), Android users who purchase apps download an average of five apps per month.[8] When setting a price for your app, start by researching your competition. How much do their apps cost? Do theirs have similar functionality? Is yours more feature-rich? Will offering your app at a lower price than the competition attract users? Is your goal is to recoup development costs and generate additional revenue?

Financial transactions for paid apps in Android Market are handled by Google Checkout (`checkout.google.com`), though customers of some mobile carriers (such as AT&T, Sprint and T-Mobile) can opt to use carrier billing to charge paid apps to their wireless bill. Google retains 30% of the purchase price and distributes 70% to you. Earnings are paid to Google Checkout merchants monthly.[9] It may take your bank a few business days to deposit the payout in your account. You're responsible for paying taxes on the revenue you earn through Android Market.

Free Apps

There are now more free apps for Android than iPhone.[10] Approximately 57% of apps on Android Market are free, and they comprise the vast majority of downloads.[11] Given that users are more likely to download an app if it's free, consider offering a free "lite" version of your app to encourage users to download and try it. For example, if your app is a game, you might offer a free lite version with just the first few levels. When the users finished playing any of the free levels, the app would display a message encouraging them to buy your more robust app with numerous game levels through Android Market, or a message that they can purchase additional levels using in-app billing (for a more seamless upgrade). According to a recent study by AdMob, *upgrading from the "lite" version is the number one reason why users purchase a paid app.*[12]

Many companies use free apps to build brand awareness and drive sales of other products and services (Fig. 2.18).

Free app	Functionality
Amazon® Mobile	Browse and purchase items on Amazon.

Fig. 2.18 | Free Android apps that build brand awareness. (Part 1 of 2.)

6. `gizmodo.com/5479298/android-app-store-is-57-free-compared-to-apples-25`.
7. `android-apps.com/tag/median-price/`.
8. `metrics.admob.com/2010/06/may-2010-mobile-metrics-report/`.
9. `checkout.google.com/support/sell/bin/answer.py?hl=en&answer=25400`.
10. `techcrunch.com/2011/04/27/there-are-now-more-free-apps-for-android-than-for-the-ios-platform-distimo/?utm_source=feedburner&utm_medium=email&utm_campaign=Feed%3A+Techcrunch+%28TechCrunch%29`.
11. `gizmodo.com/5479298/android-app-store-is-57-free-compared-to-apples-25`.
12. `metrics.admob.com/wp-content/uploads/2009/08/AdMob-Mobile-Metrics-July-09.pdf`.

Free app	Functionality
Bank of America	Locate ATMs and bank branches in your area, check balances and pay bills.
Best Buy®	Browse and purchase items on Best Buy.
Epicurious Recipe	View thousands of recipes from several Condé Nast magazines including *Gourmet* and *Bon Appetit.*
ESPN® ScoreCenter	Set up personalized scoreboards to track your favorite college and professional sports teams.
Men's Health Workouts	View numerous workouts from the leading men's magazine.
NFL Mobile	Get the latest NFL news and updates, live programming, NFL Replay and more.
UPS® Mobile	Track shipments, find drop-off locations, get estimated shipping costs and more.
NYTimes	Read articles from the *New York Times*, free of charge.
Pocket Agent™	State Farm Insurance's app enables you contact an agent, file claims, find local repair centers, check your State Farm bank and mutual fund accounts and more.
ING Direct ATM Finder	Find fee-free ATMs by GPS or address.
Progressive® Insurance	Report a claim and submit photos from the scene of a car accident, find a local agent, get car safety information when you're shopping for a new car and more.
USA Today®	Read articles from *USA Today* and get the latest sports scores.
Wells Fargo® Mobile	Locate ATMs and bank branches in your area, check balances, make transfers and pay bills.

Fig. 2.18 | Free Android apps that build brand awareness. (Part 2 of 2.)

2.11 Monetizing Apps with In-App Advertising

Some developers offer free apps monetized with ***in-app advertising***—often banner ads similar to those you find on websites. Mobile advertising networks such as AdMob (`www.admob.com/`) and Google AdSense for Mobile (`www.google.com/mobileads/publisher_home.html`) aggregate advertisers for you and serve the ads to your app (see Section 2.15). You earn advertising revenue based on the number of views. The top 100 free apps might earn anywhere from a few hundred dollars to a few thousand dollars per day from in-app advertising. In-app advertising does not generate significant revenue for most apps, so if your goal is to recoup development costs and generate profits, you should consider charging a fee for your app. According to a study by Pinch Media, 20% of people who download a free iPhone app will use it within the first day after they download it, but only 5% will continue to use it after 30 days[13]—we haven't seen a comparable study for Android yet, but the results are probably similar. *Unless your app is widely downloaded and used, it will generate minimal advertising revenue.*

13. `www.techcrunch.com/2009/02/19/pinch-media-data-shows-the-average-shelf-life-of-an-iphone-app-is-less-than-30-days/`.

2.12 Monetizing Apps: Using In-App Billing to Sell Virtual Goods in Your Apps

The Android Market **In-app Billing** service enables you to sell **virtual goods** (e.g., digital content) through apps on devices running Android 2.3 or higher (Fig. 2.19). According to Google, apps that use in-app billing earn profoundly more revenue than paid apps alone. Of the top 10 revenue-generating games on Android Market, the top nine use in-app billing.[14] The In-app Billing Service is available only for apps purchased through Android Market; it may not be used in apps sold through third-party app stores. To use in-app billing, you'll need an Android Market publisher account (see Section 2.4) and a Google Checkout merchant account (see Section 2.5). Google collects 5% of the price of all in-app purchases—other app stores charge up to 30%.

Selling virtual goods can generate higher revenue per user than advertising.[15] Virtual goods generated $1.6 billion in the United States in 2010 ($10 billion globally[16]), and U.S. sales are expected to grow to $2.1 billion in 2011.[17] A few websites that have been successful selling virtual goods include Second Life®, World of Warcraft®, Farmville™ and Stardoll™. Virtual goods are particularly popular in mobile games. According to a report by the research company Frank N. Magid Associates, over 70 million Americans own smartphones, of whom 16% spend an average of $41 per year on in-game virtual goods.[18]

Virtual goods		
Magazine subscriptions	Localized guides	Avatars
Virtual apparel	Game levels	Game scenery
Add-on features	Ringtones	Icons
E-cards	E-gifts	Virtual currency
Wallpapers	Images	Virtual pets
Audios	Videos	E-books

Fig. 2.19 | Virtual goods.

To implement in-app billing, follow these steps:

1. In your app's manifest file, add the `com.android.vending.BILLING` permission. Then, upload your app per the steps in Section 2.8.
2. Log into your Android Market publisher account at `market.android.com/publish`.

---

14. `www.youtube.com/watch?v=GxU8N21wfrM`.
15. `www.virtualgoodsnews.com/2009/04/super-rewards-brings-virtual-currency-platform-to-social-web.html`.
16. `www.internetretailer.com/2010/05/28/consumers-are-buying-digital-goods-new-ways`.
17. `www.bloomberg.com/news/2010-09-28/u-s-virtual-goods-sales-to-top-2-billion-in-2011-report-says.html`.
18. `www.webwire.com/ViewPressRel.asp?aId=118878`.

3. Go to **All Android Market Listings**. You'll see a list of your uploaded apps. Under the appropriate app, click **In-app Products**. This page lists all in-app products for the app.
4. Click **Add in-app product**. This takes you to the **Create New In-app Product** page, where you can enter the details about each product.
5. *In-app product ID*. Enter an identifying code (up to 100 characters) you'll use for each separate in-app product. The ID must start with a number or a lowercase letter and may use only numbers, lowercase letters, underscores (_) and dots (.).
6. *Purchase type.* If you select the **Managed per user account** radio button, the item may be purchased only once per user account. If you select the **Unmanaged** radio button, users can purchase the item multiple times.
7. *Publishing state.* To make your products available to users, the publishing state must be set to **Published**.
8. *Language.* The default language for the product is the same as the language you selected when uploading and publishing the app.
9. *Title.* Provide a unique title (up to 25 characters) for the product that will be visible to users.
10. *Description.* Provide a brief description (up to 80 characters) of the item that will be visible to users.
11. *Price.* Provide a price for the item in U.S. dollars.
12. Click **Publish** to make the items available or **Save** if you want to leave the item to be published at a later date.

For additional information about in-app billing, including sample apps, security best practices and more, visit `developer.android.com/guide/market/billing/index.html`.

In-app Purchase for Apps Sold Through Other App Marketplaces

If you choose to sell your apps through other app marketplaces (see Section 2.9), several third-party mobile payment providers can enable you to build *in-app purchase* into your apps using APIs from mobile payment providers (Fig. 2.20). Start by building the additional *locked functionality* (e.g., game levels, avatars) into your app. When the user opts to make a purchase, the in-app purchasing tool handles the financial transaction and returns a message to the app verifying payment. The app then unlocks the additional functionality. According to the mobile payment company Boku, mobile carriers collect between 25% and 45% of the price.[19]

Provider	URL	Description
PayPal Mobile Payments Library	`www.x.com/community/ppx/xspaces/mobile/mep`	Users click the **Pay with PayPal** button, log into their PayPal account, then click **Pay**.

Fig. 2.20 | Mobile payment providers for in-app purchase. (Part 1 of 2.)

Provider	URL	Description
Zong	`www.zong.com/android`	Provides **Buy** button for one-click payment. Payments appear on the user's phone bill.
Boku	`www.boku.com`	Users click **Pay by Mobile**, enter their mobile phone number, then complete the transaction by replying to a text message sent to their phone.

Fig. 2.20 | Mobile payment providers for in-app purchase. (Part 2 of 2.)

2.13 Launching the Market App from Within Your App

To drive additional sales of your apps, you can launch the **Market** app (Android Market) from within your app (typically by including a button that users can touch) so that the user can download other apps you've published or purchase a related app with functionality beyond that of the previously downloaded version. You can also launch the **Market** app to enable users to download the latest updates.

There are two ways to launch the **Market** app. First, you can bring up Android Market search results for apps with a specific developer name, package name or a string of characters. For example, if you want to encourage users to download other apps you've published, you could include a button in your app that, when touched, launches the **Market** app and initiates a search for apps containing your name or company name. The second option is to bring the user to the details page in the **Market** app for a specific app.

To learn about launching **Market** from within an app, see *Publishing Your Applications: Using Intents to Launch the Market Application on a Device* at `developer.android.com/guide/publishing/publishing.html#marketintent`.

2.14 Managing Your Apps in Android Market

The Android Market Developer Console allows you to manage your account and your apps, check users' star ratings for your apps (0 to 5 stars), track the overall number of installs of each app and the number of active installs (installs minus uninstalls). You can view installation trends and the distribution of app downloads across Android versions, devices, and more. Android Application Error Reports list any crash and freeze information from users. If you've made upgrades to your app, you can easily publish the new version. You may remove the app from Market, but users who downloaded it previously may keep it on their devices. Users who uninstalled the app will be able to reinstall it even after it's been removed (it will remain on Google's servers unless it's removed for violating the Terms of Service).

2.15 Marketing Your App

Once your app has been published, you'll want to market it to your audience.[20] Viral marketing (i.e., word-of-mouth) through social media sites such as Facebook, Twitter and

19. `www.boku.com/help/faq/publisher/`.
20. To learn more about marketing your Android apps, check out the book *Android Apps Marketing: Secrets to Selling Your Android App* by Jeffrey Hughes.

YouTube, can help you get your message out. These sites have tremendous visibility. According to comScore, YouTube accounts for 10% of all time spent online worldwide and Facebook accounts for a remarkable 17%.[21] Figure 2.21 lists some of the most popular social media sites. Also, e-mail and electronic newsletters are still effective and often inexpensive marketing tools.

Social media site	URL	Description
Facebook	`www.facebook.com`	Social networking
Twitter	`www.twitter.com`	Micro blogging, social networking
Groupon	`www.groupon.com`	Social commerce
Foursquare	`www.foursquare.com`	Check-in
Gowalla	`www.gowalla.com`	Check-in
YouTube	`www.youtube.com`	Video sharing
LinkedIn	`www.linkedin.com`	Social networking for business
Flickr	`www.flickr.com`	Photo sharing
Digg	`www.digg.com`	Content sharing and discovery
StumbleUpon	`www.stumbleupon.com`	Social bookmarking
Delicious	`www.delicious.com`	Social bookmarking
Bebo	`www.bebo.com`	Social networking
Tip'd	`www.tipd.com`	Social news for finance and business
Blogger	`www.blogger.com`	Blogging sites
Wordpress	`www.wordpress.com`	Blogging sites
Squidoo	`www.squidoo.com`	Publishing platform and community

Fig. 2.21 | Popular social media sites.

Facebook

Facebook, the premier social networking site, has more than 600 million active users (up from 200 million in early 2009[22]), each with an average of 130 friends,[23] and it's growing at about 5% per month! It's an excellent resource for viral (word-of-mouth) marketing. Start by setting up an official Facebook page for your app. Use the page to post:

- App information
- News
- Updates
- Reviews
- Tips

---

21. `tech.fortune.cnn.com/2010/07/29/google-the-search-party-is-over/`.
22. `topics.nytimes.com/top/news/business/companies/facebook_inc/index.html`.
23. `techcrunch.com/2010/07/15/facebook-500-million-users/?utm_source=feedburner&utm_medium=email&utm_campaign=Feed:+Techcrunch+(TechCrunch)`.

- Videos
- Screenshots
- High scores for games
- User feedback
- Links to Android Market where users can download your app

Next, you need to spread the word. Encourage your co-workers and friends to "like" your Facebook page and tell their friends to do so as well. As people interact with your page, stories will appear in their friends' news feeds, building awareness to a growing audience.

Twitter

Twitter is a micro blogging, social networking site that attracts over 190 million visitors per month.[24] You post **tweets**—messages of 140 characters or less. Twitter then distributes your tweets to all your followers (at the time of this writing, one famous rock star had over 8.5 million followers). Many people use Twitter to track news and trends. Tweet about your app—include announcements about new releases, tips, facts, comments from users, etc. Also encourage your colleagues and friends to tweet about your app. Use a **hashtag** (#) to reference your app. For example, when tweeting about this book on our Twitter feed, `@deitel`, we use the hashtag `#AndroidFP`. Others may use this hashtag as well to write comments about the book. This enables you to easily search tweets for messages related to *Android for Programmers*.

Viral Video

Viral video—shared on video sites (e.g., YouTube, Dailymotion, Bing Videos, Yahoo! Video), on social networking sites (e.g., Facebook, Twitter, MySpace), through e-mail, etc.—is another great way to spread the word about your app. If you create a compelling video, which is often something humorous or even outrageous, it may quickly rise in popularity and may be tagged by users across multiple social networks.

E-Mail Newsletters

If you have an e-mail newsletter, use it to promote your app. Include links to Android Market, where users can download the app. Also include links to your social networking pages, such as your Facebook page and Twitter feed, where users can stay up-to-date with the latest news about your app.

App Reviews

Contact influential bloggers and app review sites (Fig. 2.22) and tell them about your app. Provide them with a promotional code to download your app for free (see Section 2.10). Influential bloggers and reviewers receive many requests, so keep yours concise and informative without too much marketing hype. Many app reviewers post video app reviews on YouTube and other sites (Fig. 2.23).

---

24. `techcrunch.com/2010/06/08/twitter-190-million-users/`.

Android app review site	URL
Android Tapp™	www.androidtapp.com/
Appolicious™	www.androidapps.com
AppBrain	www.appbrain.com
Best Android Apps Review	www.bestandroidappsreview.com
AppStoreHQ	android.appstorehq.com
Android App Review Source	www.androidappreviewsource.com
Androinica	www.androinica.com
AndroidZoom	www.androidzoom.com
AndroidLib	www.androlib.com
Android and Me	www.androidandme.com
AndroidGuys	www.androidguys.com/category/reviews/
Android Police	www.androidpolice.com/
Phandroid	www.phandroid.com

Fig. 2.22 | Android app review sites.

Android app review videos	URL
ADW Launcher	www.youtube.com/watch?v=u5gRgpuQE_k
Daily App Show	dailyappshow.com
Timeriffic	androidandme.com/2010/03/news/android-app-video-rse-view-timeriffic/
Frackulous	frackulous.com/141-glympse-android-app-review/
Moto X Mayhem	www.appvee.com/games/articles/6968-android-app-video-review-moto-x-mayhem

Fig. 2.23 | Sample Android app review videos.

Internet Public Relations

The public relations industry uses media outlets to help companies get their message out to consumers. With the phenomenon known as Web 2.0, public relations practitioners are incorporating blogs, podcasts, RSS feeds and social media into their PR campaigns. Figure 2.24 lists some free and fee-based Internet public relations resources, including press-release distribution sites, press-release writing services and more. For additional resources, check out our Internet Public Relations Resource Center at `www.deitel.com/InternetPR/`.

Mobile Advertising Networks

Purchasing advertising spots (e.g., in other apps, online, in newspapers and magazines or on radio and television) is another way to market your app. Mobile advertising networks (Fig. 2.25) specialize in advertising Android (and other) mobile apps on mobile platforms. You can pay these networks to market your Android apps. Keep in mind that most apps don't make much money, so be careful how much you spend on advertising. You can also

Internet public relations resource	URL	Description
Free Services		
PRWeb®	www.prweb.com	Online press-release distribution service with free and fee-based services.
ClickPress™	www.clickpress.com	Submit your news stories for approval (free of charge). If approved, they'll be available on the ClickPress site and to news search engines.
PRLog	www.prlog.org/pub/	Free press-release submission and distribution.
i-Newswire	www.i-newswire.com	Free press-release submission and distribution.
openPR®	www.openpr.com	Free press-release publication.
Fee-Based Services		
PR Leap	www.prleap.com	Fee-based online press-release distribution service.
Marketwire	www.marketwire.com	Fee-based press-release distribution service allows you to target your audience by geography, industry, etc.
InternetNewsBureau.com®	www.internetnewsbureau.com	Online press-release services for businesses and journalists.
PRX Builder	www.prxbuilder.com/x2/	Tool for creating social media press releases.
Mobility PR	www.mobilitypr.com	Public relations services for companies in the mobile industry.
Press Release Writing	www.press-release-writing.com	Press-release distribution and services including press-release writing, proofreading and editing. Check out the tips for writing effective press releases.

Fig. 2.24 | Internet public relations resources.

use these advertising networks to monetize your free apps by including banner ads within the apps. Many of these mobile advertising networks can target audiences by location, carrier, device (e.g., Android, iPhone, BlackBerry, etc.) and more.

Mobile ad networks	URL	Description
AdMob	www.admob.com/	Advertise your app online and in other apps, or incorporate ads in your app for monetization.

Fig. 2.25 | Mobile advertising networks. (Part 1 of 2.)

Mobile ad networks	URL	Description
Google AdSense for Mobile	www.google.com/mobileads/	Display Google ads (targeted to mobile platforms) within your mobile apps or mobile web pages. Advertisers can also place ads on YouTube mobile.
AdWhirl (by AdMob)	www.adwhirl.com	Open source service that aggregates multiple mobile ad networks, allowing you to increase your advertising fill rate (the frequency with which ads will appear in your app).
Medialets	www.medialets.com	Mobile advertising SDK allows you to incorporate ads into your app. The analytics SDK enables you to track usage of the app and ad clickthroughs.
Nexage	www.nexage.com	Mobile advertising SDK allows you to incorporate ads from numerous advertising networks into your app, then manage all of them through a single reporting dashboard.
Smaato®	www.smaato.net	Smaato's SOMA (Smaato Open Mobile Advertising) ad optimization platform aggregates over 50 mobile ad networks.
Decktrade™	www.decktrade.com	Advertise your app on mobile sites, or incorporate ads in your app for monetization.
Flurry™	www.flurry.com/	Analytics tools for tracking downloads, usage and revenue for your Android apps.

Fig. 2.25 | Mobile advertising networks. (Part 2 of 2.)

Advertising Costs

The eCPM (effective cost per 1000 impressions) for ads in Android apps ranges from \$0.09 to \$4, depending on the ad network and the ad.[25] Most ads on the Android pay based on clickthrough rate (CTR) of the ads rather than the number of impressions generated. If the CTRs of the ads in your app are high, your ad network may serve you higher-paying ads, thus increasing your earnings. CTRs are generally 1 to 2% on ads in apps (though this varies based on the app).

2.16 Other Popular App Platforms

By porting your Android apps to other platforms such as iPhone and BlackBerry, you could reach an enormous audience (Fig. 2.26). According to a study by AdMob, over 70% of iPhone developers planned to develop for Android over the subsequent six months and 48% of Android developers planned to develop for the iPhone.[26] The disparity occurs because

25. seoamit.wordpress.com/2010/02/06/monetizing-mobile-apps-android-and-iphone/.
26. metrics.admob.com/wp-content/uploads/2010/03/AdMob-Mobile-Metrics-Mar-10-Publisher-Survey.pdf.

iPhone apps must be developed on Macs, which can be costly, and with the Objective-C programming language, which only a small percentage of developers know. Android, however, can be developed on Windows, Linux or Mac computers with Java—the world's most widely used programming language. The new BlackBerry Playbook tablet is able to run Android apps (which will soon be available for sale in BlackBerry's App World store).

Platform	URL
Mobile App Platforms	
BlackBerry (RIM)	`na.blackberry.com/eng/services/appworld/?`
iOS (Apple)	`developer.apple.com/iphone/`
webOS (Palm)	`developer.palm.com`
Windows Phone 7	`developer.windowsphone.com`
Symbian	`developer.symbian.org`
Internet App Platforms	
Facebook	`developers.facebook.com`
Twitter	`apiwiki.twitter.com`
Foursquare	`developer.foursquare.com`
Gowalla	`gowalla.com/api/docs`
Google	`code.google.com`
Yahoo!	`developer.yahoo.com`
Bing	`www.bing.com/developers`
Chrome	`code.google.com/chromium/`
LinkedIn	`developer.linkedin.com/index.jspa`

Fig. 2.26 | Other popular app platforms besides Android.

2.17 Android Developer Documentation

Figure 2.27 lists some of the key Android developer documentation. For additional documentation, go to `developer.android.com/`.

Document	URL
Application Fundamentals	`developer.android.com/guide/topics/fundamentals.html`
`Manifest.permission` *Summary*	`developer.android.com/reference/android/Manifest.permission.html`
`AndroidManifest.xml` *File* `<uses-feature>` *Element*	`developer.android.com/guide/topics/manifest/uses-feature-element.html`
Android Compatibility	`developer.android.com/guide/practices/compatibility.html`

Fig. 2.27 | Android developer documentation. (Part 1 of 2.)

Document	URL
Supporting Multiple Screens	developer.android.com/guide/practices/screens_support.html
Designing for Performance	developer.android.com/guide/practices/design/performance.html
Designing for Responsiveness	developer.android.com/guide/practices/design/responsiveness.html
Designing for Seamlessness	developer.android.com/guide/practices/design/seamlessness.html
Android User Interface Guidelines	developer.android.com/guide/practices/ui_guidelines/index.html
Icon Design Guidelines	developer.android.com/guide/practices/ui_guidelines/icon_design.html
Android Market Content Policy for Developers	www.android.com/market/terms/developer-content-policy.html
In-app Billing	developer.android.com/guide/market/billing/index.html
Android Emulator	developer.android.com/guide/developing/tools/emulator.html
Versioning Your Applications	developer.android.com/guide/publishing/versioning.html
Preparing to Publish: A Checklist	developer.android.com/guide/publishing/preparing.html
Market Filters	developer.android.com/guide/appendix/market-filters.html
Localization	developer.android.com/guide/topics/resources/localization.html
Technical Articles	developer.android.com/resources/articles/index.html
Sample Apps	developer.android.com/resources/samples/index.html
Android FAQs	developer.android.com/resources/faq/index.html
Common Tasks and How to Do Them in Android	developer.android.com/resources/faq/commontasks.html
Using Text-to-Speech	developer.android.com/resources/articles/tts.html
Speech Input	developer.android.com/resources/articles/speech-input.html

Fig. 2.27 | Android developer documentation. (Part 2 of 2.)

2.18 Android Humor

Figure 2.28 lists sites where you'll find Android-related humor.

Humor site	Description
crenk.com/android-vs-iphone-humor/	A funny image that emphasizes one of the key differences between Android and iPhone.
www.collegehumor.com/video:1925037	A humorous video by CollegeHumor that tries to encourage you to buy an Android phone.
www.youtube.com/watch?v=MAHwDx0lI-M	Humorous video, "Samsung Behold II Man Adventures—Part 1."
www.theonion.com/video/new-google-phone-service-whispers-targeted-ads-dir,17470/	The Onion video, "New Google Phone Service Whispers Targeted Ads Directly in Users' Ears."
www.collegehumor.com/article:1762453	"A Few Problems with the New Google Phone," from CollegeHumor, making fun of the "Did-You-Mean" feature from Google Search.

Fig. 2.28 | Android humor.

2.19 Wrap-Up

In this chapter, we walked through the registration process for Android Market and setting up a Google Checkout account so you can sell your apps. We showed you how to prepare apps for submission to Android Market, including testing them on the emulator and on Android devices, creating icons and splash screens, following the *Android User Interface Guidelines* and best practices, and editing the `AndroidManifest.xml` file. We walked through the steps for uploading your apps to Android Market. We provided alternative Android app marketplaces where you can sell your apps. We also provided tips for pricing your apps, and resources for monetizing them with in-app advertising and in-app sales of virtual goods. And we included resources for marketing your apps, once they're available through Android Market.

Chapters 3–18 present 16 complete working Android apps that exercise a broad range of functionality, including the latest Android 2.3 and 3.0 features. In Chapter 3, you'll use the Eclipse IDE to create your first Android app, using visual programming without writing any code, and you'll become familiar with Eclipse's extensive help features. In Chapter 4, you'll begin programming Android apps in Java.

Welcome App

Dive-Into® Eclipse and the ADT Plugin

Objectives

In this chapter you'll:

- Learn the basics of the Eclipse IDE for writing, running and debugging your Android apps.
- Create an Eclipse project to develop a new app.
- Design a GUI visually (without programming) using the ADT (Android Development Tools) visual layout editor.
- Edit the properties of GUI components.
- Build a simple Android app and execute it on an Android Virtual Device (AVD).

Outline

3.1 Introduction

In this chapter, you'll build the **Welcome** app—a simple app that displays a welcome message and two images—*without writing any code.* You'll use the Eclipse IDE with the ADT (Android Development Tools) Plugin—the most popular tools for creating and testing Android apps. We'll overview Eclipse and show you how to create a simple Android app (Fig. 3.1) using the ADT's Visual Layout Editor, which allows you to build GUIs using drag-and-drop techniques. Finally, you'll execute your app on an Android Virtual Device (AVD).

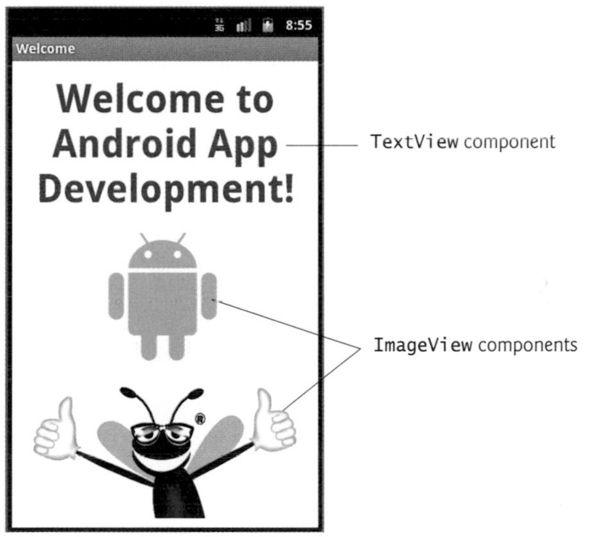

Fig. 3.1 | **Welcome** app.

3.2 Technologies Overview

This chapter introduces the Eclipse IDE and ADT Plugin. You'll learn how to navigate Eclipse and create a new project. With the ADT Visual Layout Editor, you'll display pictures in **`ImageView`s** and display text in a **`TextView`**. You'll see how to edit GUI component properties (e.g., the `Text` property of a `TextView` and the `Src` property of an `ImageView`) in Eclipse's **Properties** tab and you'll run your app on an Android Virtual Device (AVD).

3.3 Eclipse IDE

This book's examples were developed using the versions of the Android SDK that were most current at the time of this writing (versions 2.3.3 and 3.0), and the Eclipse IDE with the ADT (Android Development Tools) Plugin. In this chapter, we assume that you've already set up the Java SE Development Kit (JDK), the Android SDK and the Eclipse IDE, as discussed in the Before You Begin section that follows the Preface.

Introduction to Eclipse

Eclipse enables you to manage, edit, compile, run and debug applications. The ADT Plugin for Eclipse gives you the additional tools you'll need to develop Android apps. You can also use the ADT Plugin to manage multiple Android platform versions, which is important if you're developing apps for many devices with different Android versions installed. When you start Eclipse for the first time, the **Welcome** tab (Fig. 3.2) is displayed. This contains several icon links, which are described in Fig. 3.3. Click the **Workbench** button to display the Java **development perspective**, in which you can begin developing Android apps. Eclipse supports development in many programming languages. Each set of Eclipse tools you install is represented by a separate development perspective. Changing perspectives reconfigures the IDE to use the tools for the corresponding language.

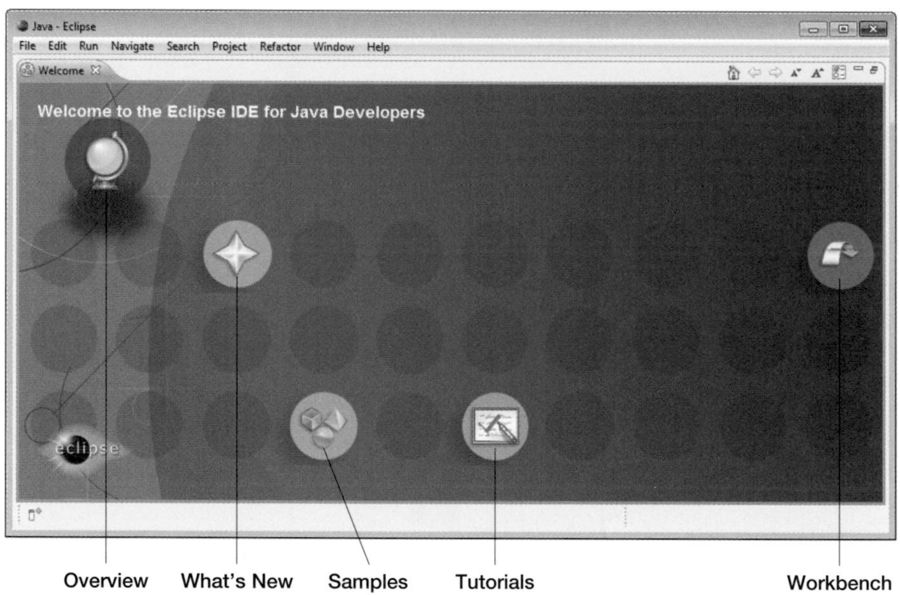

Fig. 3.2 | **Welcome to the Eclipse IDE for Java Developers** tab in the **Eclipse** window.

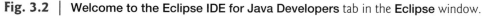

Link	Description
Overview	Provides an overview of the IDE and its features.

Fig. 3.3 | Links on the Eclipse IDE's **Welcome** tab. (Part 1 of 2.)

Link	Description
What's New	Provides information about what's new in the installed version of Eclipse as well as links to the online Eclipse community and updates for the IDE.
Samples	Provides links to samples for the Eclipse configuration you downloaded.
Tutorials	Provides tutorials to help you get started with Java development in Eclipse and to help you use various Eclipse capabilities.
Workbench	Takes you to the development perspective.

Fig. 3.3 | Links on the Eclipse IDE's **Welcome** tab. (Part 2 of 2.)

3.4 Creating a New Project

To begin programming with Android in Eclipse, select **File > New > Project...** to display the **New Project** dialog. Expand the **Android** node, select **Android Project** and click **Next >** to display the **New Android Project dialog** (Fig. 3.4). You can also do this with the **New** ( ) toolbar buttons's drop-down list. After you create your first project, the **Android Project** option will appear in the **File > New** menu and in the **New** ( ) button's drop-down list.

A **project** is a group of related files, such as the code files and any images that make up an app. Using the **New Android Project** dialog, you can create a project from scratch or you can use existing source code—such as the code examples from this book.

In this dialog, specify the following information:

1. In the **Project name:** field, enter `Welcome`. This will be the name of the project's root node in Eclipse's **Package Explorer** tab.
2. In the **Contents** section, ensure that **Create new project in workspace** is selected to create a new project from scratch. The **Create project from existing source** option allows you to create a new project and incorporate existing Java source-code files.
3. In the **Build Target** section, select the Android version you wish to use. For most of this book's examples, we use version 2.3.3; however, it's recommended that you select the minimum version that your app requires so that it can run on the widest variety of devices.

In the **Properties** section of the dialog, specify the following information:

1. In the **Application name:** field, enter `Welcome`. We typically give our applications the same name as their projects, but this is not required. This name appears in a bar at the top of the app, if that bar is not *explicitly* hidden by the app.
2. Android uses conventional Java package-naming conventions and requires a minimum of two parts in the package name (e.g., `com.deitel`). In the **Package name:** field, enter `com.deitel.welcome`. We use our domain `deitel.com` in reverse followed by the app's name. All the classes and interfaces that are created as part of your app will be placed in this Java package. Android and the Android Market use the package name as the app's unique identifier.
3. In the **Create Activity:** field, enter `Welcome`. This will become the name of a class that controls the app's execution. Starting in the next chapter, we'll modify this class to implement an app's functionality.

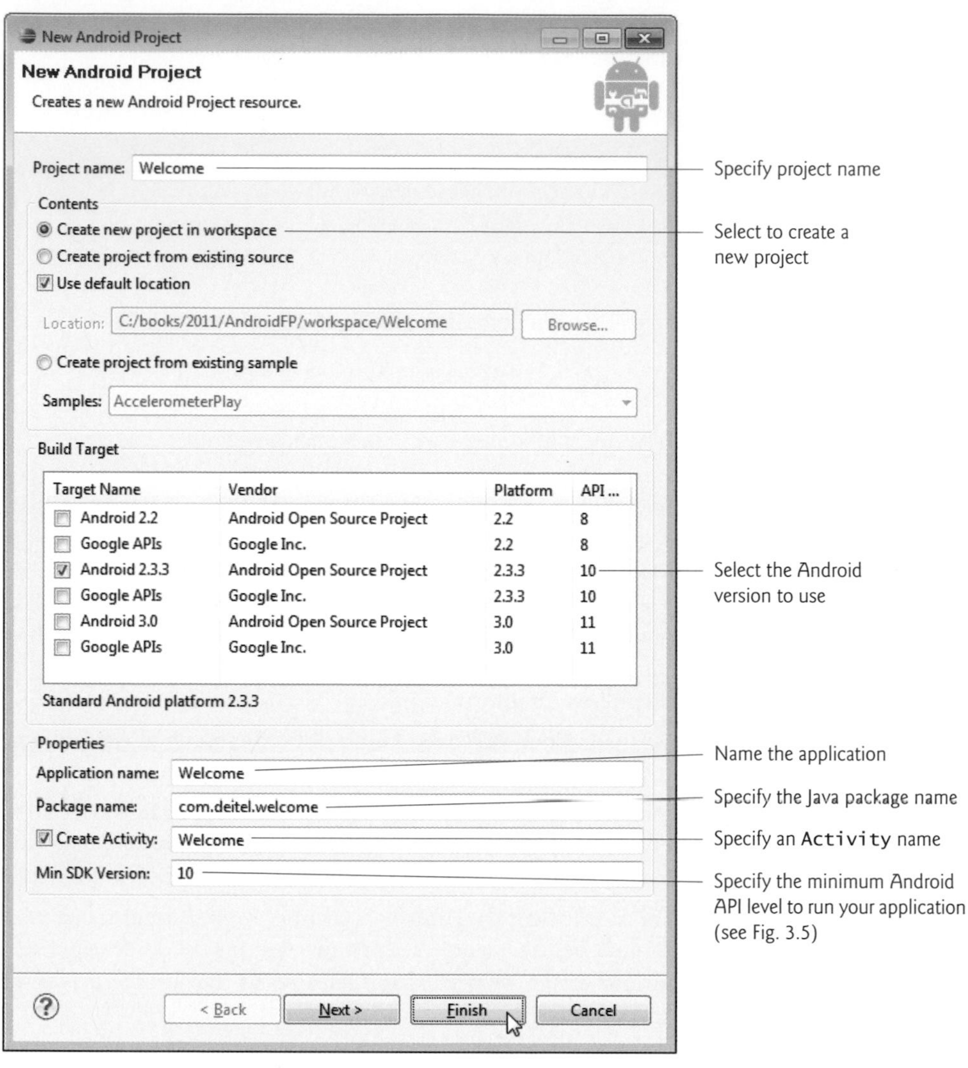

Fig. 3.4 | **New Android Project** dialog.

4. In the **Min SDK Version:** field, enter the minimum API level that's required to run your app. This allows your app to execute on devices at that API level and higher. In this book, we typically use the API level 10, which corresponds to Android 2.3.3, or API level 11, which corresponds to Android 3.0. To run your app on Android 2.2 and higher, select API level 8. *In this case, you must ensure that your app does not use features that are specific to more recent versions of Android.* Figure 3.5 shows the Android SDK versions and API levels. *Other versions of the SDK are now deprecated and should not be used.* The following webpage shows the current percentage of Android devices running each platform version:

```
developer.android.com/resources/dashboard/platform-versions.html
```

Android SDK version	API level
3.0	11
2.3.3	10
2.2	8
2.1	7
1.6	4
1.5	3

Fig. 3.5 | Android SDK versions and API levels. (`developer.android.com/sdk/index.html`)

5. Click **Finish** to create the project. [*Note:* You might see project errors while Eclipse loads the Android SDK.]

Package Explorer Window

Once you create (or open) a project, the **Package Explorer** window at the left of the IDE provides access to all of the project's files. Figure 3.6 shows the project contents for the **Welcome** app. The **Welcome** node represents the project. You can have many projects open in the IDE at once—each will have its own top-level node.

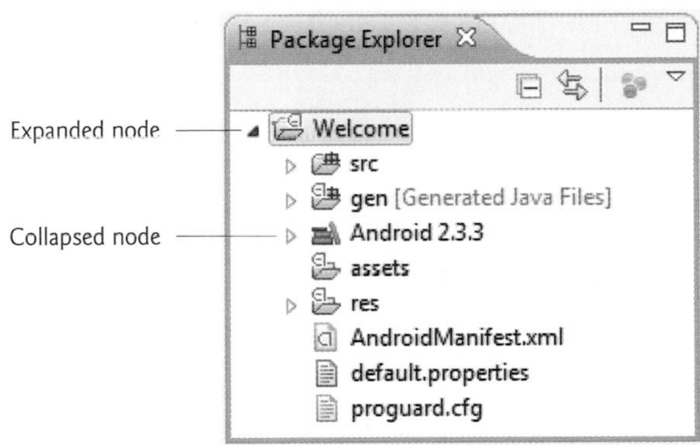

Fig. 3.6 | **Package Explorer** window.

Within a project's node the project's contents are organized into various files and folders, including:

- **src**—A folder containing the project's Java source files.
- **gen**—A folder containing the Java files generated by the IDE.
- **Android 2.3.3**—A folder containing the Android framework version you selected when you created the app.
- **res**—A folder containing the **resource files** associated with your app, such as GUI layouts and images used in your app.

We discuss the other files and folders as necessary throughout the book.

3.5 Building the Welcome App's GUI with the ADT's Visual Layout Editor

Next, you'll create the GUI for the **Welcome** app. The ADT's **Visual Layout Editor** allows you to build your GUI by dragging and dropping GUI components, such as `Buttons`, `TextViews`, `ImageViews` and more, onto an app. For an Android app that you create with Eclipse, the *GUI layout is stored in an XML file called* **`main.xml`**, by default. Defining the GUI in XML allows you to easily separate your app's logic from its presentation. Layout files are considered app *resources* and are stored in the project's **`res`** folder. GUI layouts are placed within that folder's `layout` subfolder. When you double click the `main.xml` file in your app's `/res/layout` folder, the Visual Layout Editor view is displayed by default (Fig. 3.7). To view the XML contents of the file (Fig. 3.8), click the tab with the name of the layout file (**main.xml** in this case). You can switch back to the Visual Layout Editor by clicking the **Graphical Layout** tab. We'll present the layout's XML in Section 3.6.

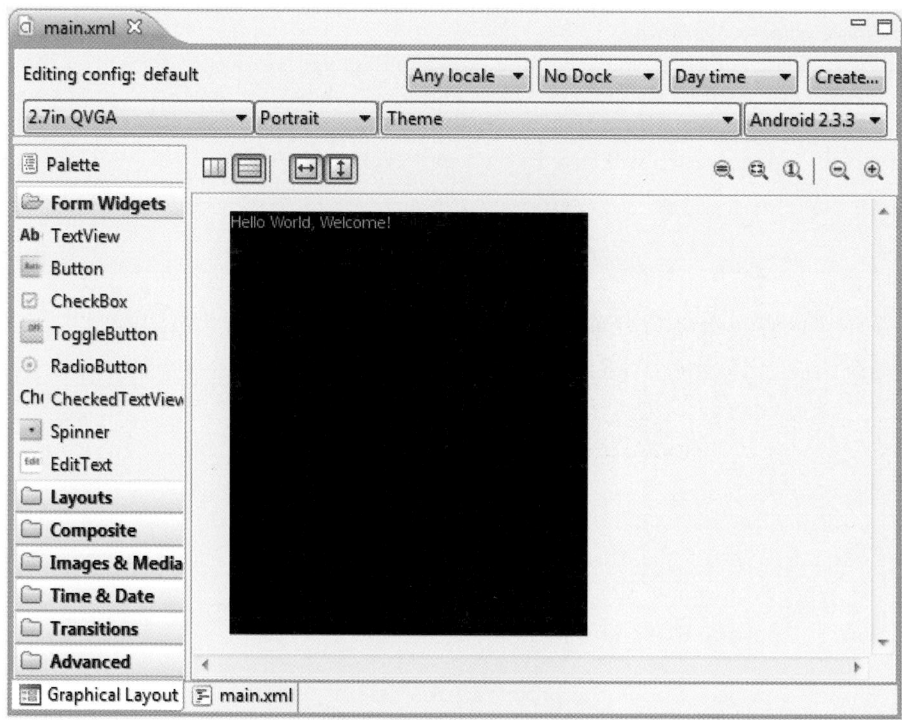

Fig. 3.7 | Visual Layout Editor view of the app's default GUI.

The Default GUI

The default GUI for a new Android app consists of a `LinearLayout` with a black background and contains a `TextView` with the text `"Hello World, Welcome!"` (Fig. 3.7). A **`LinearLayout`** arranges GUI components in a line horizontally or vertically. A **`TextView`** allows you to display text. If you were to execute this app in an AVD or on a device, you'd see the default black background and text.

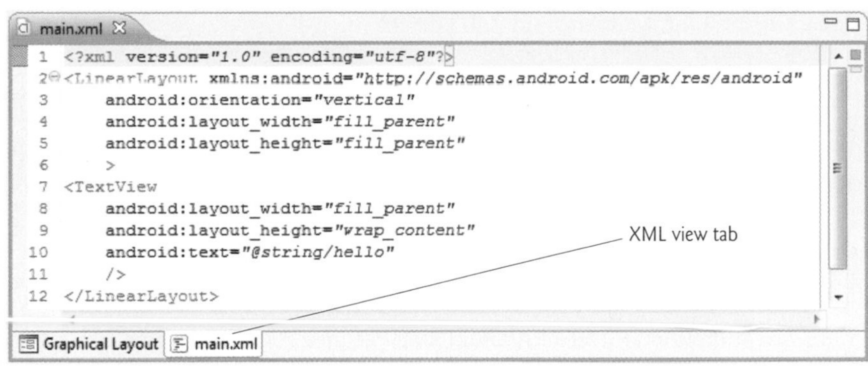

Fig. 3.8 | XML view of the app's default GUI.

Figure 3.9 lists some of the layouts from the **android.widget** package.[1] We'll cover many more GUI components that can be placed in layouts—for a complete list, visit:

```
developer.android.com/reference/android/widget/package-summary.html
```

Look-and-Feel Observation 3.1

To support devices of varying screen sizes and densities, it's recommended that you use `RelativeLayout` *and* `TableLayout` *in your GUI designs.*

Layout	Description
`FrameLayout`	Allocates space for a single component. You can add more than one component to this layout, but each will be displayed from the layout's upper-left corner. The last component added will appear on top.
`LinearLayout`	Arranges components horizontally in one row or vertically in one column.
`RelativeLayout`	Arranges components relative to one another or relative to their parent container.
`TableLayout`	Arranges components into a table of rows. You can then use the `TableRow` layout (a subclass of `LinearLayout`) to organize the columns.

Fig. 3.9 | Android layouts (package `android.widget`).

Configuring the Visual Layout Editor to use the Appropriate Android SDK

If you've installed multiple Android SDKs, the ADT Plugin selects the most recent one as the default for design purposes in the **Graphical Layout** tab—regardless of the SDK you selected when you created the project. In Fig. 3.7, we selected Android 2.3.3 from the

1. Earlier Android SDKs also have an `AbsoluteLayout` in which each component specifies its exact position. This layout is now deprecated. According to `developer.android.com/reference/android/widget/AbsoluteLayout.html`, you should use `FrameLayout`, `RelativeLayout` or a custom layout instead.

SDK selector drop-down list at the top-right side of the **Graphic Layout** tab to indicate that we're designing a GUI for an Android 2.3.3 device.

Deleting and Recreating the `main.xml` File

For this application, you'll replace the default `main.xml` file with a new one that uses a `RelativeLayout`, in which components are arranged relative to one another. Perform the following steps to replace the default `main.xml` file:

1. Make sure `main.xml` is closed, then right click it in the project's `/res/layout` folder and select **Delete** to delete the file.
2. Right click the layout folder and select **New > Other...** to display the **New** dialog.
3. In the **Android** node, select **Android XML File** and click **Next >** to display the **New Android XML File** dialog.
4. Configure the file name, location and root layout for the new `main.xml` file as shown in Fig. 3.10, then click **Finish**.

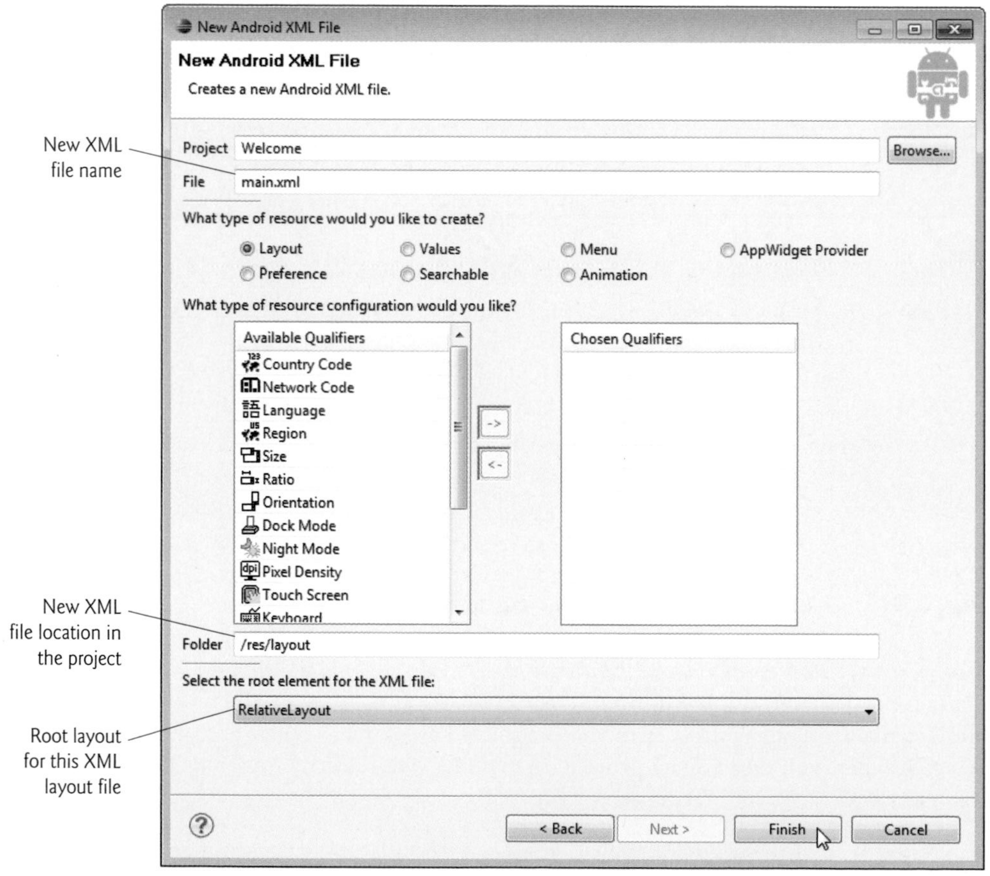

Fig. 3.10 | Creating a new `main.xml` file in the **New Android XML File** dialog.

Configuring the Visual Layout Editor's Size and Resolution

Figure 3.11 shows the new `main.xml` file in the Visual Layout Editor. Android runs on a wide variety of devices, so the Visual Layout Editor comes with several device configurations that represent various screen sizes and resolutions. These can be selected from the Device Configurations drop-down list at the top-left side of the **Graphic Layout** tab (Fig. 3.11). If these predefined configurations do not match the device you wish to target, you can create your own device configurations from scratch, or by copying and modifying the existing ones.

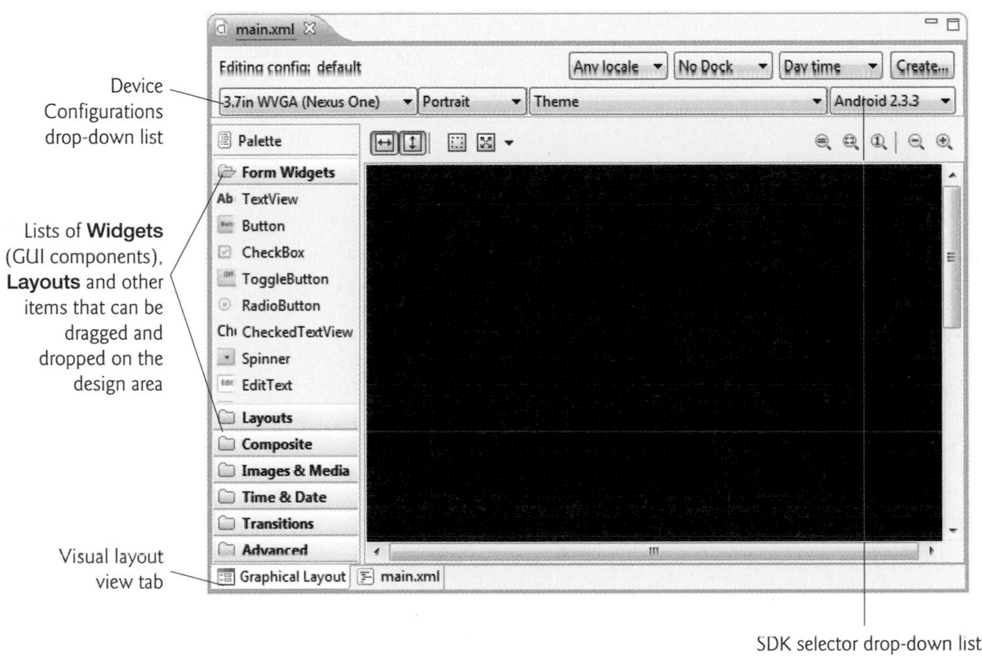

Fig. 3.11 | Visual Layout Editor view of the app's default GUI.

Our primary testing device for this book was the Samsung Nexus S, which has a 4-inch screen with 480-by-800 (WVGA) resolution. When designing an Android GUI, you typically want it to be *scalable* so that it displays properly on various devices. For this reason, the Visual Layout Editor's design area does not need to precisely match your actual device's. Instead, you can choose a similar device configuration. In Fig. 3.11, we selected the **3.7in WVGA (Nexus One)** option—this device has the same WVGA resolution as the Nexus S, but a slightly smaller screen size. Many of today's smartphones have 480-by-800 or 480-by-854 resolution.

Images and Screen Sizes/Resolutions

Because Android devices have various screen sizes, resolutions and pixel densities (that is, dots per inch or DPI), Android allows you to provide separate images (and other resources) that the operating system chooses based on the actual device's pixel density. For this reason your project's `res` folder contains three subfolders for images—`drawable-hdpi` (high density), `drawable-mdpi` (medium density) and `drawable-ldpi` (low density). These folders store images with different pixel densities (Fig. 3.12).

Density	Description
`ldpi`	Low density—approximately 120 dots-per-inch.
`mdpi`	Medium density—approximately 160 dots-per-inch.
`hdpi`	High density—approximately 240 dots-per-inch.
`xhdpi`	Extra high density—approximately 320 dots-per-inch.
`nodpi`	Indicates that a resource should not be scaled regardless of screen density.

Fig. 3.12 | Android pixel densities.

Images for devices that are similar in pixel density to our testing device are placed in the folder `drawable-hdpi`. Images for medium- and low-density screens are placed in the folders `drawable-mdpi` and `drawable-ldpi`, respectively. As of Android 2.2, you can also add a `drawable-xhdpi` subfolder to the app's `res` folder to represent screens with extra high pixel densities. Android will scale images up and down to different densities as necessary.

Look-and-Feel Observation 3.2

For detailed information on supporting multiple screens and screen sizes in Android, visit `developer.android.com/guide/practices/screens_support.html`.

Look-and-Feel Observation 3.3

For images to render nicely, a high-pixel-density device needs higher-resolution images than a low-pixel-density device. Low-resolution images do not scale well.

Step 1: Adding Images to the Project

You'll now begin designing the **Welcome** app. In this chapter, we'll use the Visual Layout Editor and the **Outline** window to build the app, then we'll explain the generated XML in detail. In subsequent chapters, we'll also edit the XML directly.

Look-and-Feel Observation 3.4

Many Android professionals prefer to create their GUIs directly in XML and use the Visual Layout Editor to preview the results. As you type in the XML view, Eclipse provides auto-complete capabilities showing you component names, attribute names and values that match what you've typed so far. These help you write the XML quickly and correctly.

For this app, you'll need to add the Deitel bug image (`bug.png`) and the Android logo image (`android.png`) to the project—we've provided these in the `images` folder with the book's examples. Perform the following steps to add the images to this project:

1. In the **Package Explorer** window, expand the project's `res` folder.
2. Locate and open the `images` folder provided with the book's examples, then drag the images in the folder onto the `res` folder's `drawable-hdpi` subfolder.

These images can now be used in the app.

Step 2: Changing the `Id` *Property of the* `RelativeLayout`

You can use the **Properties** window to configure the properties of the selected layout or component without editing the XML directly. If the **Properties** window is not displayed, you can display it by double clicking the `RelativeLayout` in the **Outline** window. You can also select **Window > Show View > Other...**, then select **Properties** from the **General** node in the **Show View** dialog. To select a layout or component, you can either click it in the Visual Layout Editor or select its node in the **Outline** window (Fig. 3.13). The **Properties** window cannot be used when the layout is displayed in XML view.

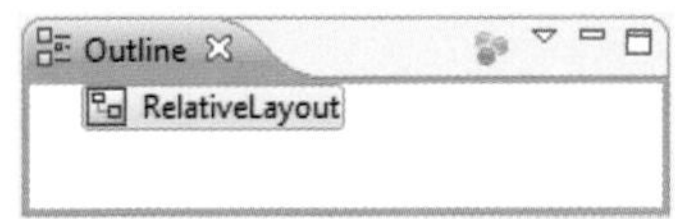

Fig. 3.13 | Hierarchical GUI view in the **Outline** window.

You should rename each layout and component with a relevant name, especially if the the layout or component will be manipulated programmatically (as we'll do in later apps). Each object's name is specified via its **Id property**. The `Id` can be used to access and modify component without knowing its exact location in the XML. As you'll see shortly, the `id` can also be used to specify the relative positioning of components in a `RelativeLayout`.

Select the `RelativeLayout`, then scroll to the **Id property** in the **Properties** window and set its value to

```
@+id/welcomeRelativeLayout
```

The + in the syntax `@+id` indicates that a new `id` (that is, a variable name) should be created with the identifier to the right of the `/`. The **Properties** and **Outline** windows should now appear as in Fig. 3.14.

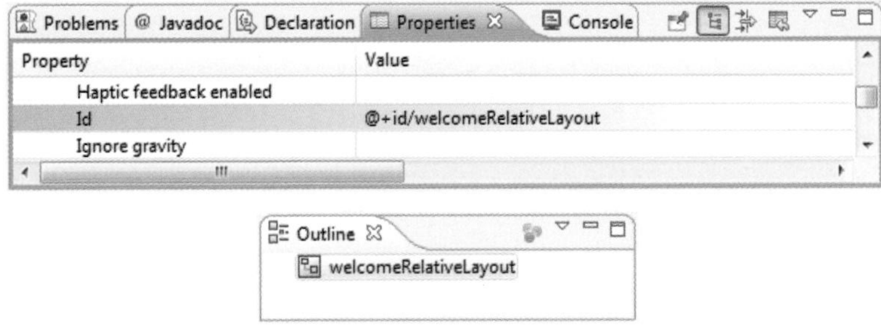

Fig. 3.14 | **Properties** window after changing the `RelativeLayout`'s **Id** property.

Step 3: Changing the **Background** *Property of the* `RelativeLayout`

The layout's default background color is black, but we'd like it to be white. Every color can be created from a combination of red, green and blue components called **RGB values**—each is an integer in the range 0–255. The first value defines the amount of red in the color, the second the amount of green and the third the amount of blue. When using the IDE to specify a color you typically use hexadecimal format. In this case, the RGB components are represented as values in the range 00–FF.

To change the background color, locate the **Background property** in the **Properties** window and set its value to #FFFFFF (Fig. 3.15). This represents white in the hexadecimal format #RRGGBB—the pairs of hexadecimal digits represent the red, green and blue color components, respectively. Android also supports alpha (transparency) values in the range 0–255, where 0 represents completely transparent and 255 represents completely opaque. If you wish to use alpha values, you can specify the color in the format #AARRGGBB, where the first two hexadecimal digits represent the alpha value. For cases in which both digits of each component of the color are the same, you can use the formats #RGB or #ARGB. For example, #FFF will be treated as #FFFFFF.

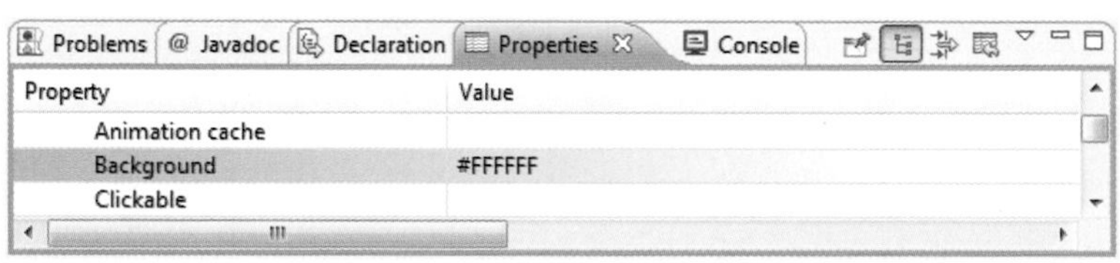

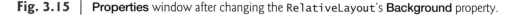

Fig. 3.15 | **Properties** window after changing the `RelativeLayout`'s **Background** property.

Step 4: Adding a `TextView`

Next, we'll add a `TextView` to the user interface. In the **Form Widgets** list at the left of the Visual Layout Editor window, locate `TextView` and drag it onto the design area (Fig. 3.16). When you add a new component to the user interface, it's automatically selected and its properties are displayed in the **Properties** window.

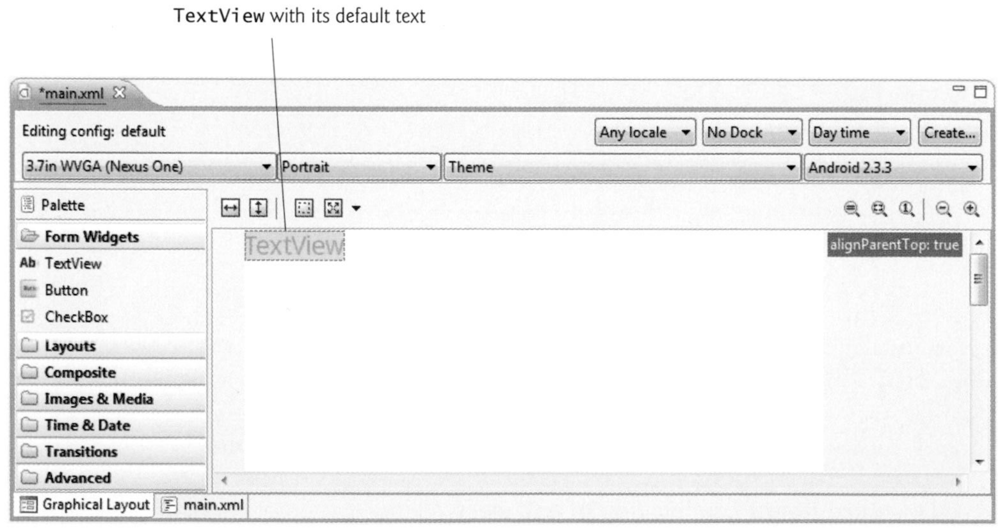

Fig. 3.16 | `TextView` with its default text.

Step 5: Configuring the `TextView`'s Text Property Using a String Resource

According to the Android documentation for application resources

```
developer.android.com/guide/topics/resources/index.html
```

it's considered a good practice to "externalize" strings, string arrays, images, colors, font sizes, dimensions and other app resources so that you, or someone else on your team, can manage them separately from your application's code. For example, if you externalize color values, all components that use the same color can be updated to a new color simply by changing the color value in a central resource file.

If you wish to localize your app in several different languages, storing the strings separately from the app's code allows you to change them easily. In your project's `res` folder, the subfolder `values` contains a `strings.xml` file that's used to store strings. To provide localized strings for other languages, you can create separate `values` folders for each language. For example, the folder `values-fr` would contain a `strings.xml` file for French and `values-es` would contain a `strings.xml` file for Spanish. You can also name these folders with region information. For example, `values-en-rUS` would contain a `strings.xml` file for U.S. English and `values-en-rGB` would contain a `strings.xml` file for United Kingdom English. For more information on localization, see

```
developer.android.com/guide/topics/resources/
   providing-resources.html#AlternativeResources
developer.android.com/guide/topics/resources/localization.html
```

To set the `TextView`'s **Text property**, we'll create a new string resource in the `strings.xml` file.

1. Ensure that the `TextView` is selected.
2. Locate its **Text** property in the **Properties** window, click its default value, then click the ellipsis button (...) at the right size of the property's value field to display the **Resource Chooser** dialog.
3. In the **Resource Chooser** dialog, click the **New String...** button to display the **Create New Android String** dialog (Fig. 3.17).
4. Fill the **String** and **New R.string** fields as shown in Fig. 3.17, then click **OK** to dismiss the **Create New Android String** dialog and return to the **Resource Chooser** dialog.
5. The new string resource named `welcome` is automatically selected. Click **OK** to select this resource.

In the **Properties** window, the **Text** property should now appear as shown in Fig. 3.18. The syntax `@string` indicates that an existing string resource will be selected from the `strings.xml` file, and the name `welcome` indicates which string resource to select.

A key benefit of defining your string values this way is that you can easily *localize* your app by creating additional XML resource files for string resources in other languages. In each file, you use the same name in the **New R.string** field and provide the internationalized string in the **String** field. Android can then choose the appropriate resource file based on the device user's preferred language. For more information on localization, visit

```
developer.android.com/guide/topics/resources/localization.html
```

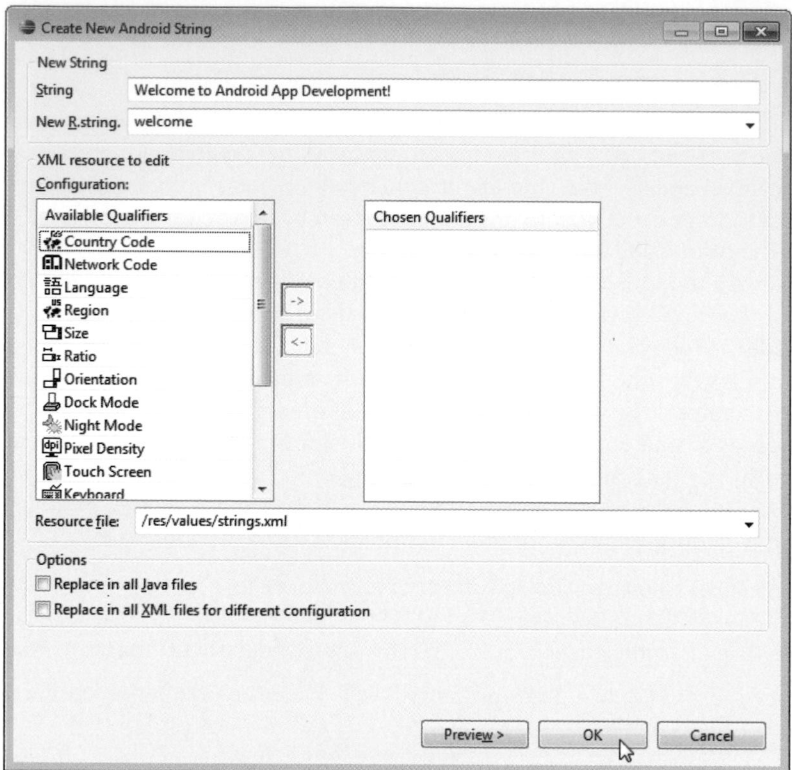

Fig. 3.17 | **Create New Android String** window.

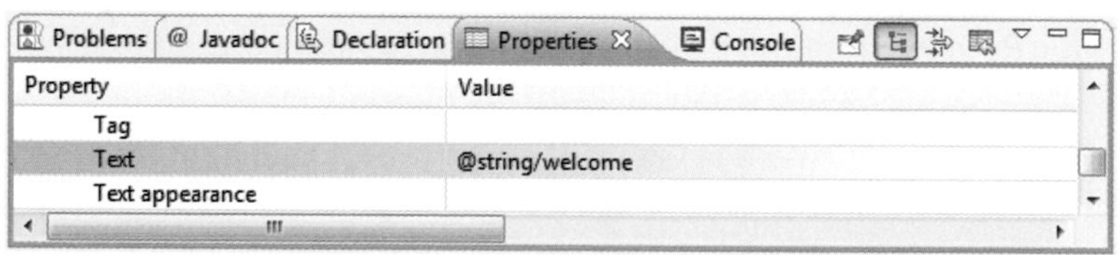

Fig. 3.18 | **Properties** window after changing the `TextView`'s **Text** property.

Step 6: Configuring the `TextView`*'s* **Text size** *and* **Padding top** *Properties—Scaled Pixels and Density-Independent Pixels*

The sizes of GUI components and text in Android can be specified in several different units (Fig. 3.19). The documentation for supporting multiple screen sizes

```
developer.android.com/guide/practices/screens_support.html
```

recommends that you use density-independent pixels for the dimensions of GUI components and other screen elements and scale-independent pixels for font sizes.

Defining your GUIs with **density-independent pixels** enables the Android platform to automatically scale the GUI, based on the pixel density of the actual device's screen.

Unit	Description
`px`	pixel
`dp` or `dip`	density-independent pixel
`sp`	scale-independent pixel
`in`	inches
`mm`	millimeters

Fig. 3.19 | Measurement units.

One density-independent pixel is equivalent to one pixel on a screen with 160 dpi (dots per inch). On a screen with 240 dpi, each density-independent pixel will be scaled by a factor of 240/160 (i.e., 1.5). So, a component that's 100 density-independent pixels wide will be scaled to 150 actual pixels wide. On a screen with 120 dpi, each density-independent pixel is scaled by a factor of 120/160 (i.e., .75). So, the same component that's 100 density-independent pixels wide will be 75 actual pixels wide. ***Scale-independent pixels*** are scaled like density-independent pixels, and they're also scaled by the user's preferred font size specified on the device. [*Note:* At the time of this writing, users cannot yet change the preferred font size on Android devices, but this feature is expected in the future.]

You'll now increase the size of the `TextView`'s font and add some padding above the `TextView` to separate the text from the edge of the device's screen.

1. To change the font size, ensure that the **TextView** is selected, then change its **Text size property** to `40sp`.
2. To add some space between the top edge of the layout and the `TextView`, set the **Layout margin top property** in the **Misc** section of the **Properties** window to `10dp`.

Step 7: Configuring Additional `TextView` Properties

Configure the following additional `TextView`'s properties as well:

1. Set its **Id** property to `@+id/welcomeTextView`.
2. Set its **Text color property** to `#00F` (blue).
3. Set its **Text style property** to `bold`. To do so, click the **Value** field for this property, then click the ellipsis button (…) to display the dialog for selecting the font style. Click the **bold** checkbox, then click **OK** to set the text style.
4. To center the text in the `TextView` if it wraps to multiple lines, set its **Gravity property** to `center`. To do so, click the **Value** field for this property, then click the ellipsis button to display a dialog with the **Gravity** property's options (Fig. 3.20). Click the **center** checkbox, then click **OK** to set the value.

The Visual Layout Editor window should now appear as shown in Fig. 3.21.

Step 8: Adding `ImageView`s to Display the Android Logo and the Deitel Bug Logo

Next, you'll add two `ImageView`s to the GUI to display the images that you added to the project in *Step 1*. When you first drag an `ImageView` onto the Visual Layout Editor, nothing appears. For this reason, we'll use the **Outline** window to add the `ImageView`s. Perform the following steps:

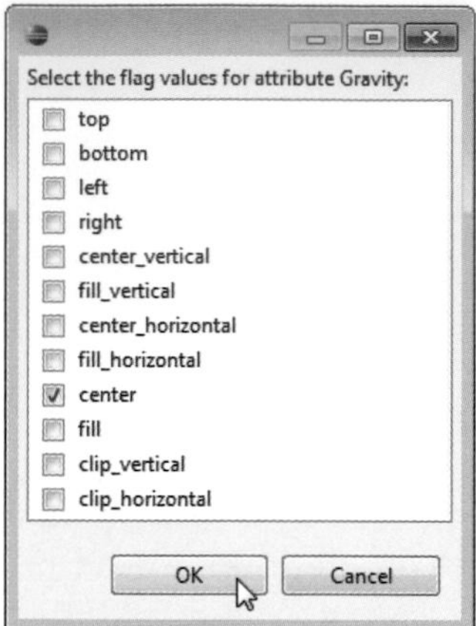

Fig. 3.20 | Options for the `gravity` attribute of an object.

Fig. 3.21 | Visual Layout Editor window after completing the `TextView`'s configuration.

1. Drag an `ImageView` from the **Images & Media** category in the Visual Layout Editor's **Palette** and drop it onto the **Outline** window as shown in Fig. 3.22. The new `ImageView` appears below the `welcomeTextView` node. This *does not* indicate that this component will appear below the `TextView` in the GUI. This requires setting the **Layout below** property, which we'll do in a moment. [*Note:* If you drag the `ImageView` over the `welcomeTextView` and hover for a moment, a green rectangle with sections will appear around the `welcomeTextView`. If you then drag the `ImageView` over one of those sections and drop it, the Visual Layout Editor can set the relative positioning for you.]

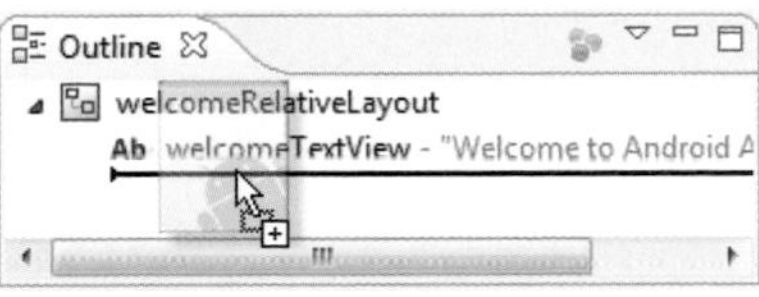

Fig. 3.22 | Dragging and dropping an `ImageView` onto the **Outline** window.

2. Set the `ImageView`'s **Id** property to `@+id/droidImageView`. The **Outline** window now shows the object's name as `droidImageView`.
3. Set the `droidImageView`'s **Layout below** property to `@id/welcomeTextView` to position the `ImageView` below the `welcomeTextView`. To do so, click the **Value** field for this property, then click the ellipsis button to display the **Reference Chooser** dialog (Fig. 3.23). The **ID** node contains the names of the objects in the GUI. Expand the **ID** node and select `welcomeTextView`.

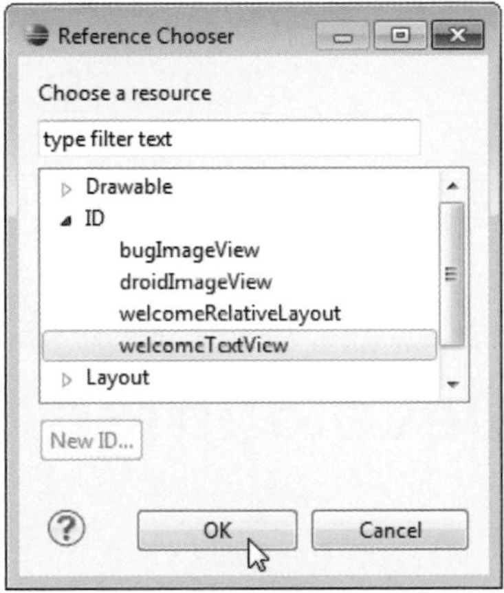

Fig. 3.23 | Selecting the value for the `droidImageView`'s **Layout below** property.

4. Set the `droidImageView`'s **Layout center horizontal** property to `true` to center the `ImageView` in the layout.
5. Set the `droidImageView`'s **Src property** to the image that should be displayed. To do so, click the **Value** field for this property, then click the ellipsis button to display the **Reference Chooser** dialog (Fig. 3.24). The **Drawable** node contains the resources in your app's `drawable` folders within the `res` folder. In the dialog, expand the **Drawable** node and select `android`, which represents the `android.png` image.
6. Repeat items 1–5 above to create the `bugImageView`. For this component, set its **Id** property to `@+id/bugImageView`, its **Src** property to `bug` and its Layout below property to `droidImageView`.

The Visual Layout Editor window should now appear as shown in Fig. 3.25.

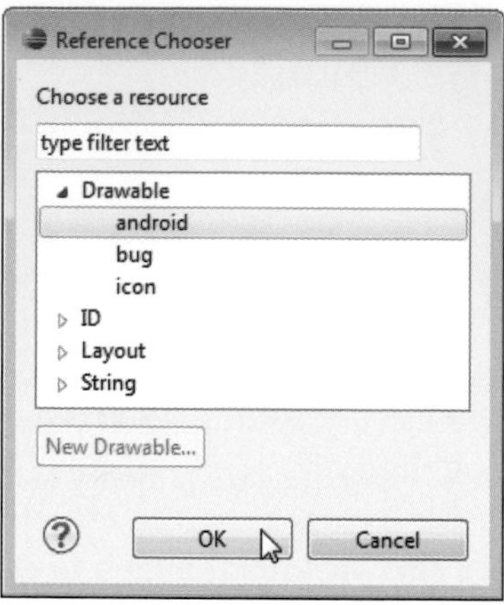

Fig. 3.24 | Selecting the value for the `droidImageView`'s **Src** property.

Fig. 3.25 | Visual Layout Editor window after completing the GUI configuration.

3.6 Examining the main.xml File

XML is a natural way to express a GUI's contents. It allows you, in a human- and computer-readable form, to say which layouts and components you wish to use, and to specify their attributes, such as size, position and color. The ADT Plugin can then parse the XML and generate the code that produces the actual GUI. Figure 3.26 shows the final `main.xml` file after you perform the steps in Section 3.5. We reformatted the XML and added some comments to make the XML more readable. (Eclipse's **Source > Format** command can help you with this.) As you read the XML, notice that each XML attribute name that contains multiple words does not contain spaces, whereas the corresponding properties in the **Properties** window do. For example, the XML attribute `android:paddingTop` corresponds to the property **Padding top** in the **Properties** window. When the IDE displays property names, it displays the multiword names as separate words for readability.

```
<?xml version="1.0" encoding="utf-8"?>
<!-- main.xml -->
<!-- Welcome App's XML layout. -->

<!-- RelativeLayout that contains the App's GUI components. -->
<RelativeLayout xmlns:android="http://schemas.android.com/apk/res/android"
   android:layout_width="match_parent"
   android:layout_height="match_parent"
   android:id="@+id/welcomeRelativeLayout" android:background="#FFFFFF">

   <!-- TextView that displays "Welcome to Android App Development!" -->
   <TextView android:layout_width="wrap_content"
      android:layout_height="wrap_content"
      android:text="@string/welcome"
      android:textSize="40sp" android:id="@+id/welcomeTextView"
      android:textColor="#00F" android:textStyle="bold"
      android:layout_centerHorizontal="true" android:gravity="center"
      android:layout_marginTop="10dp"></TextView>

   <!-- ImageView that displays the Android logo -->
   <ImageView android:layout_height="wrap_content"
      android:layout_width="wrap_content" android:id="@+id/droidImageView"
      android:layout_centerHorizontal="true"
      android:src="@drawable/android"
      android:layout_below="@id/welcomeTextView"></ImageView>

   <!-- ImageView that displays the Deitel bug logo -->
   <ImageView android:layout_height="wrap_content"
      android:layout_width="wrap_content" android:id="@+id/bugImageView"
      android:src="@drawable/bug"
      android:layout_below="@id/droidImageView"
      android:layout_centerHorizontal="true"></ImageView>
</RelativeLayout>
```

Fig. 3.26 | **Welcome** App's XML layout.

`welcomeRelativeLayout`

The `welcomeRelativeLayout` (lines 6–33) contains all of the app's GUI components.

- Its opening XML tag (lines 6–9) sets various `RelativeLayout` attributes.
- Line 6 uses the `xmlns` attribute to indicate that the elements in the document are all part of the `android` XML namespace. This is required and auto-generated by the IDE when you create any layout XML file.
- Lines 7–8 specify the value `match_parent` for both the `android:layout_width` and `android:layout_height` attributes, so the layout occupies the entire width and height of layout's parent element—that is, the one in which this layout is nested. In this case, the `RelativeLayout` is the *root node* of the XML document, so the layout occupies the *entire screen* (excluding the status bar).
- Line 9 specifies the values for the `welcomeRelativeLayout`'s `android:id` and `android:background` attributes.

`welcomeTextView`

The first element in the `welcomeRelativeLayout` is the `welcomeTextView` (lines 12–18).

- Lines 12 and 13 set the `android:layout_width` and `android:layout_height` attributes to `wrap_content`. This value indicates that the view should be just large enough to fit its content, including its padding values that specify the spacing around the content.
- Line 14 sets the `android:text` attribute to the string resource named `welcome` that you created in Section 3.5, Step 5.
- Line 15 sets the `android:textSize` attribute to `40sp` and the `android:id` attribute to `"@+id/welcomeTextView"`.
- Line 16 sets the `android:textColor` attribute to `"#00F"` (for blue text) and the `android:textStyle` attribute to `"bold"`.
- Line 17 sets the `android:layout_centerHorizontal` attribute to `"true"`, which centers the component horizontally in the layout, and sets the `android:gravity` attribute to `"center"` to center the text in the `TextView`. The `android:gravity` attribute specifies how the text should be positioned with respect to the width and height of the `TextView` if the text is smaller than the `TextView`.
- Line 18 sets the `android:marginTop` attribute to `10dp` so that there's some space between the top of the `TextView` and the top of the screen.

`droidImageView`

The last two elements nested in the `welcomeRelativeLayout` are the `droidImageView` (lines 21–25) and the `bugImageView` (lines 28–32). We set the same attributes for both `ImageViews`, so we discuss only the `droidImageView`'s attributes here.

- Lines 21 and 22 set the `android:layout_width` and `android:layout_height` attributes to `wrap_content`. Line 22 also sets the `android:id` attribute to `"@+id/droidImageView"`.
- Line 23 sets the `android:layout_centerHorizontal` attribute to `"true"` to centers the component in the layout.

- Line 24 sets the `android:src` attribute to the drawable resource named `android`, which represents the `android.png` image.
- Line 25 sets the `android:layout_below` attribute to `"@id/welcomeTextView"`. The `RelativeLayout` specifies each component's position relative to other components. In this case, the `ImageView` follows the `welcomeTextView`.

3.7 Running the Welcome App

To run the app in an Android Virtual Device (AVD), right click the app's root node in the **Package Explorer** window and select **Run As > Android Application**. Figure 3.27 shows the running app.

Fig. 3.27 | **Welcome** app running in an AVD.

3.8 Wrap-Up

This chapter introduced key features of the Eclipse IDE and the ADT Visual Layout Editor. You used the Visual Layout Editor to create a working Android app without writing any code. You used the `TextView` and `ImageView` GUI components to display text and images, respectively, and you arranged these components in a `RelativeLayout`. You edited the properties of GUI components to customize them for your app. You then tested the app in an Android Virtual Device (AVD). Finally, we presented a detailed walkthrough of the XML markup that generates the GUI.

In the next chapter we introduce how to program Android apps using Java. Android development is a combination of GUI design, and Java and XML coding. Java allows you to specify the behavior of your apps. You'll develop the **Tip Calculator** app, which calculates a range of tip possibilities when given a restaurant bill amount. You'll design the GUI and add Java code to specify how the app should process user inputs and display the results of its calculations.

4

Tip Calculator App

Building an Android App with Java

Objectives

In this chapter you'll:

- Design a GUI using a `TableLayout`.
- Use the ADT Plugin's **Outline** window in Eclipse to add GUI components to a `TableLayout`.
- Directly edit the XML of a GUI layout to customize properties that are not available through the Visual Layout Editor and **Properties** window in Eclipse.
- Use `TextView`, `EditText` and `SeekBar` GUI components.
- Use Java object-oriented programming capabilities, including classes, anonymous inner classes, objects, interfaces and inheritance to create an Android app.
- Programmatically interact with GUI components to change the text that they display.
- Use event handling to respond to user interactions with an `EditText` and a `SeekBar`.

Outline

4.1 Introduction

The **Tip Calculator** app (Fig. 4.1) calculates and displays tips for a restaurant bill. As the user enters a bill total, the app calculates and displays the tip amount and total bill for three common tipping percentages—10%, 15% and 20%. The user can also specify a custom tip percentage by moving the thumb of a `Seekbar`—this updates the percentage shown to the right of the `Seekbar`. We chose 18% as the default custom percentage in this app because many restaurants add this tip percentage for parties of six people or more. The suggested tips and bill totals are updated in response to each user interaction. [*Note:* The keypad in Fig. 4.1 may differ based on your AVD's or device's Android version.]

a) Initial GUI after user touches the **Bill total** `EditText` and the numeric keyboard is displayed

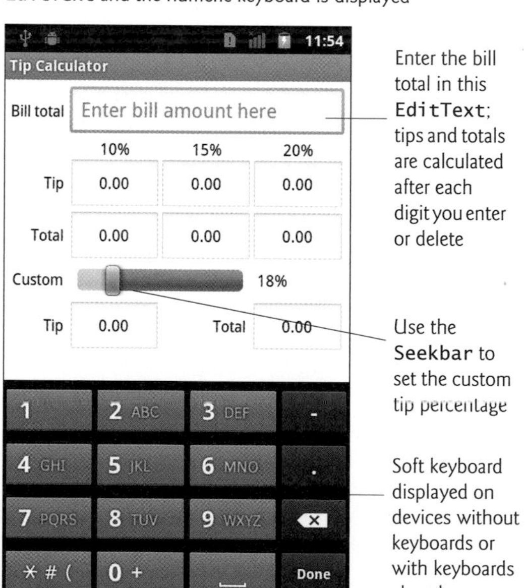

b) GUI after user enters the bill total 123.45 and changes the **Custom** tip percentage to 17%

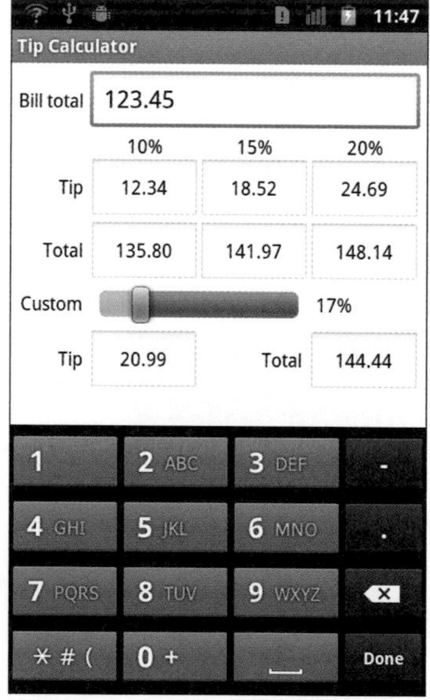

Fig. 4.1 | Entering the bill total and calculating the tip.

You'll begin by testing the app—you'll use it to calculate standard and custom tips. Then we'll overview the technologies we used to build the app. Next you'll build the app's GUI using the **Outline** window in Eclipse to add the GUI components, and you'll use the Visual Layout Editor to see what the GUI looks like. Most of the XML for this GUI will be generated for you by the ADT Plugin tools, but you'll also directly edit the XML to customize properties that aren't available through the **Properties** window. Finally, we'll present the complete code for the app and do a detailed code walkthrough.

4.2 Test-Driving the Tip Calculator App

Open and Run the App

Open Eclipse and import the **Tip Calculator** app project. Perform the following steps:

1. *Open the* **Import** *Dialog.* Select **File > Import...** to open the **Import** dialog.
2. *Import the* **Tip Calculator** *app's project.* In the **Import** dialog, expand the **General** node and select **Existing Projects into Workspace**, then click **Next >** to proceed to the **Import Projects** step. Ensure that **Select root directory** is selected, then click the **Browse...** button. In the **Browse For Folder** dialog, locate the `TipCalculator` folder in the book's examples folder, select it and click **OK**. Click **Finish** to import the project into Eclipse. The project now appears in the **Package Explorer** window at the left side of the Eclipse window.
3. *Launch the* **Tip Calculator** *app.* In Eclipse, right click the `TipCalculator` project in the **Package Explorer** window, then select **Run As > Android Application** from the menu that appears. This will execute **Tip Calculator** in the AVD that you created in the Before You Begin section. [*Note*: If you have multiple AVDs or any Android devices connected to your computer, you may need to select one of them on which to execute the app.]

Enter a Bill Total

Touch the **Bill Total** `EditText` to display the keypad, then enter **123.45** into it using the keypad. [*Note:* If the keyboard displays Japanese text, long press the **Bill Total** `EditText`—that is, touch it for a couple of seconds—then select **Input method** from the list of options. Next, select **Android keyboard** from the second list of options.]

If you make a mistake, press the delete (⌫) button to erase the last digit you entered. The `EditTexts` under **10%**, **15%** and **20%** display the tip and the total bill for the pre-specified tip percentages (Fig. 4.1(b)), and the `EditTexts` for the custom tip and total display the tip and total bill, respectively, for the default **18%** custom tip percentage. All the **Tip** and **Total** `EditTexts` update each time you enter or delete a digit.

Select a Custom Tip Percentage

Use the `Seekbar` to specify a custom tip percentage. Drag the `Seekbar`'s thumb until the custom percentage reads **17%**. The tip and bill total for this custom tip percentage now appear in the `EditTexts` below the `Seekbar`. By default, the `Seekbar` allows you to select values from 0 to 100.

4.3 Technologies Overview

This chapter uses many Java object-oriented programming capabilities, including classes, anonymous inner classes, objects, methods, interfaces and inheritance. You'll create a subclass of Android's `Activity` class to specify what should happen when the app starts executing and to define the logic of the **Tip Calculator**. You'll programmatically interact with `EditText`s, a `TextView` and a `SeekBar`. You'll create these components using the Visual Layout Editor and **Outline** window in Eclipse, and some direct manipulation of the GUI layout's XML. An ***EditText***—often called a text box or text field in other GUI technologies—is a subclass of `TextView` (presented in Chapter 3) that can display text and accept text input from the user. A ***SeekBar***—often called a slider in other GUI technologies—represents an integer in the range 0–100 by default and allows the user to select a number in that range. You'll use event handling and anonymous inner classes to process the user's GUI interactions.

4.4 Building the App's GUI

In this section, you'll build the GUI for the **Tip Calculator** using the ADT Plugin tools. At the end of this section, we'll present the XML that the ADT Plugin generates for this app's layout. We'll show the precise steps for building the GUI. In later chapters, we'll focus primarily on new features in each app's GUI and present the final XML layouts, highlighting the portions of the XML we modified. [*Note:* As you work your way through this section, keep in mind that the GUI will not look like the one shown in Fig. 4.1 until you've completed the majority of the steps in Sections 4.4.2–4.4.4.]

4.4.1 TableLayout Introduction

In this app, you'll use a ***TableLayout*** (Fig. 4.2) to arrange GUI components into six rows and four columns. Each cell in a `TableLayout` can be empty or can hold one component, which can be a layout that *contains* other components. As you can see in rows 0 and 4 of Fig. 4.2, a component can span *multiple* columns. To create the rows, you'll use ***TableRow*** objects. The number of columns in the `TableLayout` is defined by the `TableRow` that contains the *most* components. Each row's height is determined by the *tallest* component in that row—in Fig. 4.2, you can see that rows 1 and 4 are shorter than the other rows. Similarly, the width of a column is defined by the *widest* element in that column—unless you allow the table's columns to stretch to fill the width of the screen, in which case the columns could be wider. By default, components are added to a row from left to right. You can specify the exact location of a component—rows and columns are numbered from 0 by default. You can learn more about class `TableLayout` at:

```
developer.android.com/reference/android/widget/TableLayout.html
```

and class `TableRow` at

```
developer.android.com/reference/android/widget/TableRow.html
```

Figure 4.3 shows the names of all the GUI components in the app's GUI. For clarity, our naming convention is to use the GUI component's class name in each component's **Id** property in the XML layout and in each component's variable name in the Java code.

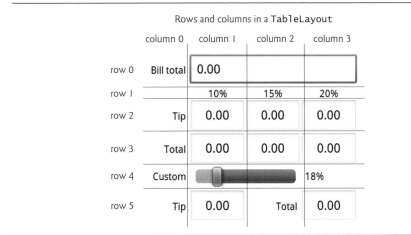

Rows and columns in a `TableLayout`

	column 0	column 1	column 2	column 3
row 0	Bill total	0.00		
row 1		10%	15%	20%
row 2	Tip	0.00	0.00	0.00
row 3	Total	0.00	0.00	0.00
row 4	Custom			18%
row 5	Tip	0.00	Total	0.00

Fig. 4.2 | **Tip Calculator** GUI's `TableLayout` labeled by its rows and columns.

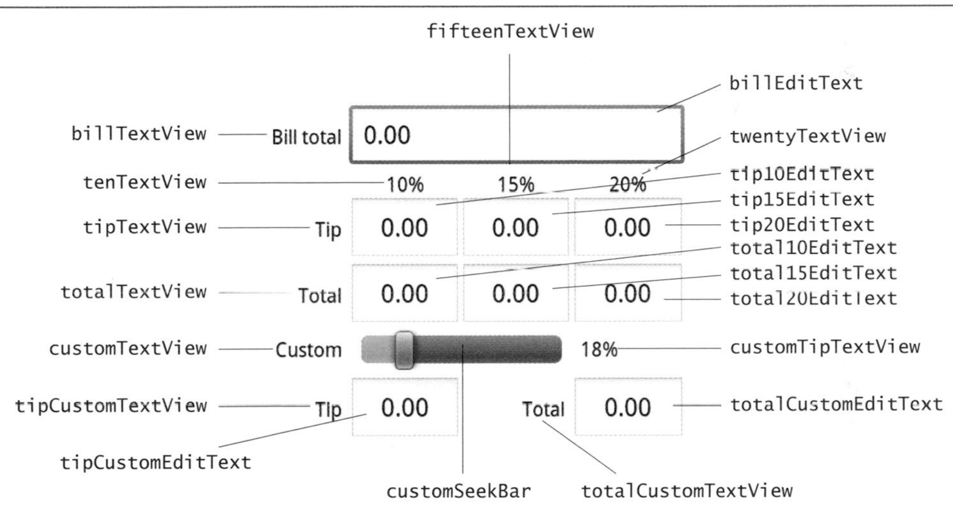

Fig. 4.3 | **Tip Calculator** GUI's components labeled with their **Id** property values.

4.4.2 Creating the Project and Adding the `TableLayout` and Components

You'll now build the GUI in Fig. 4.2. You'll start with the basic layout and controls, then customize the controls' properties to complete the design. As you add components to each row of the `TableLayout`, set the **Id** and **Text** properties of the components as shown in Fig. 4.3. As you learned in Section 3.5, literal string values should be placed in the `strings.xml` file in the app's `res/values` folder—especially if you intend to localize your app for use with multiple languages. For the **10%**, **15%** and **20%** `TextViews`, we chose not to use string resources. Be sure to perform the steps for building the GUI in the exact order specified—otherwise, the components will *not* appear in the correct order in each row. If this happens, you can rearrange the components in the **Outline** window or in the `main.xml` file.

In the following steps, you'll use the **Outline** window to add components to the proper `TableRows` of the `TableLayout`. When working with more complex layouts like `TableLayouts`, it's difficult to see the *nested structure of the layout* and to place components in the correct nested locations using the Visual Layout Editor. The **Outline** window makes these tasks easier because it shows the nested structure of the GUI. So, in a `TableLayout`, you can select the appropriate row and add a GUI component to it.

Step 1: Creating the `TipCalculator` Project

Eclipse allows only one project with a given name per workspace, so before you perform this step, delete from the workspace the existing **Tip Calculator** app that you executed in the test drive. To do so, right click it and select **Delete**. In the dialog that appears, ensure that **Delete project contents on disk** is not selected, then click **OK**. This removes the project from the workspace, but leaves the project's folder on disk. Next, create a new Android project named `TipCalculator`. Specify the following values in the **New Android Project** dialog, then press **Finish**:

- **Build Target:** Ensure that **Android 2.3.3** is checked
- **Application name:** `Tip Calculator`
- **Package name:** `com.deitel.tipcalculator`
- **Create Activity:** `TipCalculator`
- **Min SDK Version:** `10`. [*Note:* This SDK version corresponds to Android 2.3.3; however, we do not use any Android 2.3.3-specific functionality in this app. If you'd like this app to execute on AVDs or devices running an earlier Android version, you can set the **Min SDK Version** to a lower value. For example, you could specify 8 to indicate that the app can execute on Android 2.2 or higher.]

Step 2: Deleting and Recreating the `main.xml` File

For this application, you'll replace the default `main.xml` file with a new one that uses a `TableLayout` in which components are arranged relative to one another. Perform the following steps to replace the default `main.xml` file:

1. Right click the `main.xml` file in the projects `/res/layout` folder and select **Delete** to delete the file.
2. Right click the layout folder and select **New > Other...** to display the **New** dialog.
3. In the **Android** node, select **Android XML File** and click **Next >** to display the **New Android XML File** dialog.
4. Specify the file name `main.xml` and select `TableLayout`, then click **Finish**.

Step 3: Configuring the Visual Layout Editor to Use the Appropriate Android SDK

After completing the previous step, the new `main.xml` file opens in the Visual Layout Editor. Recall that if you've installed multiple Android SDKs, the ADT Plugin selects the most recent one as the default for design purposes in the **Graphical Layout** tab—regardless of the SDK you selected when you created the project. As you did in Fig. 3.7, select Android 2.3.3 from the SDK selector drop-down list at the top-right side of the **Graphical Layout** tab to indicate that we're designing a GUI for an Android 2.3.3 device.

Step 4: Configuring the Visual Layout Editor's Size and Resolution

As you did in Fig. 3.11, select **3.7in WVGA (Nexus One)** from the Device Configurations drop-down list at the top-left side of the **Graphical Layout** tab. This configures the design area for devices with 480-by-800 (WVGA) resolution.

Step 5: Configuring the `TableLayout`

Select the `TableLayout` the **Outline** window to display its properties in the **Properties** window, then set the following properties:

- **Background:** `#FFF`
- **Id:** `@+id/tableLayout`
- **Padding:** `5dp`
- **Stretch columns:** `1,2,3`

By default, the **Layout width** and **Layout height** properties are set to `match_parent` so that the layout fills the entire screen. Setting the ***Padding** property* to `5dp` ensures that there will be 5 density-independent pixels around the border of the entire layout. The ***Stretch columns*** property—represented in the XML with the attribute ***`android:stretchColumns`*** (Fig. 4.5, line 8)—indicates that columns 1, 2 and 3 should stretch horizontally to fill the layout's width. Column 0 will be as wide as its widest element plus any padding specified for that element.

Step 6: Adding the `TableRows`

Next, you'll use the **Outline** window to add six `TableRows` to the `TableLayout`. To do so:

1. Right click `tableLayout` in the **Outline** window and select **Add Row** to add a `TableRow`.
2. Repeat this process five more times.

Be sure to right click `tableLayout` each time so that the `TableRows` are properly nested in the `TableLayout`. The **Id** properties of the `TableRows` are automatically specified as `tableRow1` through `tableRow6`, respectively. Since columns are numbered from 0, for consistency, we changed the `TableRows`' **Id** properties to `tableRow0` through `tableRow5`, respectively. Also, select each `TableRow` and set its **Layout width** property to `match_parent` so that the rows are the full width of the layout. To do this for all six `TableRows` at once, click the first `TableRow` in the **Outline** window, then hold the *Shift* key and click the last `TableRow` in the **Outline** window to select all six. Then, you can set the property value.

Step 7: Adding the Components for `tableRow0`

Next, you'll add a `TextView` and `EditText` to `tableRow0`. To do so:

1. Drag a `TextView` (`billTextView`) from the **Palette**'s **Form Widgets** section onto `tableRow0` in the **Outline** window.
2. Drag an `EditText` (`billEditText`) from the **Palette**'s **Form Widgets** section onto `tableRow0` in the **Outline** window.
3. Set the **Id** and **Text** property values for each component. For quick access to these properties, you can right click the component in the **Outline** window and select **Edit ID...** and **Edit Text...**, respectively.

It's important to drop these items onto the proper TableRow in the **Outline** window to ensure that the elements are nested in the proper TableRow object.

Step 8: Adding the Components for **tableRow1**
Add three TextViews to tableRow1. To do so:

1. Drag a TextView (tenTextView) onto tableRow1 in the **Outline** window.
2. Repeat this process to add the fifteenTextView and twentyTextView.
3. Set the **Id** and **Text** property values for each component.

Step 9: Adding the Components for **tableRow2**
Add a TextView and three EditTexts to tableRow2. To do so:

1. Drag a TextView (tipTextView) onto tableRow2 in the **Outline** window.
2. Drag three EditTexts onto tableRow2 in the **Outline** window—tip10EditText, tip15EditText and tip20EditText.
3. Set the **Id** and **Text** property values for each component.

Step 10: Adding the Components for **tableRow3**
Add a TextView and three EditTexts to tableRow3. To do so:

1. Drag a TextView (totalTextView) onto tableRow3 in the **Outline** window.
2. Drag three EditTexts onto tableRow3 in the **Outline** window—total10EditText, total15EditText and total20EditText.
3. Set the **Id** and **Text** property values for each component.

Step 11: Adding the Components for **tableRow4**
Add a TextView, a SeekBar and another TextView tableRow4. To do so:

1. Drag a TextView (customTextView) onto tableRow4 in the **Outline** window.
2. Drag a SeekBar (customSeekBar) onto tableRow4 in the **Outline** window.
3. Drag a TextView (customTipTextView) onto tableRow4 in the **Outline** window.
4. Set the **Id** and **Text** property values for the TextViews.

Step 12: Adding the Components for **tableRow5**
Add a TextView, an EditText, another TextView and another EditText to tableRow5. To do so:

1. Drag a TextView (tipCustomTextView) onto tableRow5 in the **Outline** window.
2. Drag an EditText (tipCustomEditText) onto tableRow5 in the **Outline** window.
3. Drag a TextView (totalCustomTextView) onto tableRow5 in the **Outline** window.
4. Drag an EditText (totalCustomEditText) onto tableRow5 in the **Outline** window.
5. Set the **Id** and **Text** property values for each component.

4.4.3 Reviewing the Layout So Far

At this point, the GUI should appear as shown in Fig. 4.4. As you compare this to Fig. 4.2, notice that:

- The `billEditText` and `customSeekBar` do not yet span multiple columns.
- The text of all the `TextViews` is light gray and hard to read.
- Some of the components are in the *wrong* columns—in particular, the **10%, 15%** and **20%** `TextViews` in `tableRow1` and the **18%** `TextView` in `tableRow4`. The last of these will self-correct after we make the `customSeekBar` span two columns.
- Most of the text in Fig. 4.2 is either *center aligned* or *right aligned*, whereas all the text in Fig. 4.4 is *left aligned.*

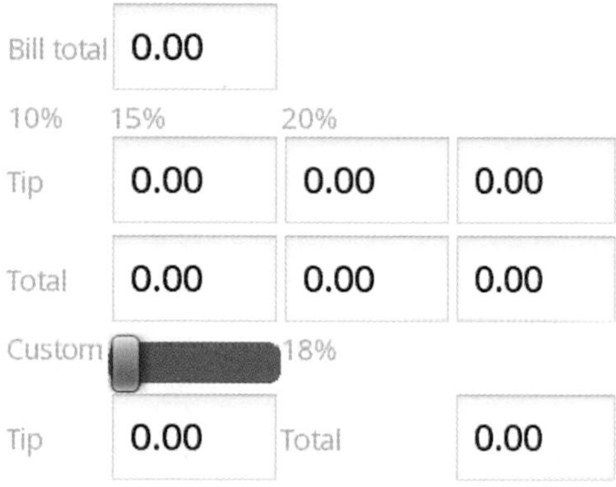

Fig. 4.4 | **Tip Calculator** GUI before customizing properties other than the **Id** and **Text** of each component.

4.4.4 Customizing the Components to Complete the Design

In the next steps, you'll complete the app's design by customizing the components' properties.

Step 13: Change the Text color *Property of All the* `TextViews`

In the **Outline** window, you can select multiple components at the same time by holding the *Ctrl* (or *Control*) key as you click each component that you wish to select. When you do this, the **Properties** window shows you *only* the properties that the selected components have in common. If you change a property value with multiple components selected, that property's value is changed for *every* selected component. We'd like all of the `TextViews` to use *black text* to make them more readable. To change the **Text color** property for all of the `TextViews` at once:

1. Hold the *Ctrl* (or *Control*) key and click each `TextView` until they're all selected.
2. Locate the **Text color** property in the **Properties** window and set it to `#000`.

Step 14: Moving the 10%, 15% and 20% `TextView`s to the Correct Columns

In Fig. 4.2, the **10%**, **15%** and **20%** column heads are in the second, third and fourth columns, respectively. By default, when you add components to a `TableRow`, the first component is placed in the first column, the second component is placed in the second column and so on. To start in a different column, you must specify the component's *column number*. Unfortunately, this property is not displayed in the **Properties** window by default. To specify a component's column, you must edit the component's XML directly.

1. Switch to the **main.xml** tab in the Visual Layout Editor to view the layout's XML markup.
2. Locate the `<TextView>` element with the `android:id` attribute that has the value `"@+id/tenTextView"`.
3. In the `TextView`'s opening XML tag, add the following attribute/value pair:

```
android:layout_column="1"
```

This moves the **10%** `TextView` to the second column—columns are numbered from 0. All other components in the row are placed in the subsequent columns automatically. If you wish to skip other columns, you can set the `android:layout_column` attribute on each component in a row to specify the exact column in which the component should appear. Once you manually add an attribute to the XML, the attribute and its value are displayed in the **Properties** window under the **Misc** section.

Step 15: Centering the Text in the `TextView`s of `tableRow1` and the `EditText`s of `tableRow2`, `tableRow3` and `tableRow5` and Setting the `EditText`s' Font Size

In Fig. 4.2, the text of many components is centered. Here you'll set the **Gravity** property of these components to center their text. Switch back to the **Graphical Layout** tab in the Visual Layout Editor, then perform the following steps:

1. In the **Outline** window, select the three `TextView`s in `tableRow1`.
2. Set the **Gravity** property to `center` in the **Properties** window.
3. Select all the `EditText`s in `tableRow2`, `tableRow3` and `tableRow5`.
4. Set the **Gravity** property to `center` in the **Properties** window.
5. Set the **Text size** property to `14sp`—this reduces the default font size in the `EditText`s so more digits can be displayed without wrapping the text.

Step 16: Setting `billEditText` and the `customSeekBar` to Span Multiple Columns

In Fig. 4.2, the `billEditText` spans columns 1–3 and the `customSeekBar` spans columns 1–2. You must add the spanning attribute directly in the XML.

1. Click the **main.xml** tab in the Visual Layout Editor to view the layout's markup.
2. Locate the `<EditText>` element with the `android:id` attribute that has the value `"@+id/billEditText"`.
3. In the `EditText`'s opening XML tag, add the following attribute/value pair:

```
android:layout_span="3"
```

4. Locate the `<SeekBar>` element.

5. In the `SeekBar`'s opening XML tag, add the following attribute/value pair:

```
android:layout_span="2"
```

The `billEditText` now spans columns 1–3 and `customSeekBar` now spans columns 1–2.

Step 17: Right Aligning the `TextViews`

The `TextViews` in column 0 are all right aligned as is the `TextView` in `tableRow5`'s third column. Also, each of these `TextViews` has `5dp` of padding at its right side to separate it from the control immediately to its right.

1. Switch back to the **Graphical Layout** tab in the Visual Layout Editor.
2. In the **Outline** window, select all the `TextViews` in column 0 and the second `TextView` in the last row.
3. Set the **Gravity** property to `right`, then set the **Padding right** to `5dp`.

Step 18: Vertically Centering the `TextViews` *in* `tableRow4`

We'd like the `TextViews` in `tableRow4` to align better vertically with the `SeekBar`, so we'll now adjust the **Gravity** property.

1. In the **Outline** window, select the `customTextView` in `tableRow4`.
2. Locate the **Gravity** property and click the ellipsis (...) button to the right of the property's value to display the list of possible **Gravity** values.
3. Check the `center_vertical` value. Now both `right` and `center_vertical` should be checked.
4. Click **OK** to apply the value.
5. In the **Outline** window, select the `customTipTextView` in `tableRow4`.
6. Set the **Gravity** property to `center_vertical`.
7. Click **OK** to apply the value.
8. In the **Outline** window, select both `TextViews` in `tableRow4` and set their **Layout height** properties to `match_parent` and the **Padding bottom** property to `5dp`. This makes the two `TextViews` the same height as the `SeekBar` and enables the **Gravity** property to align the text vertically with the **SeekBar**. We'll also be setting the **Padding bottom** property of the `SeekBar` momentarily, so setting this property on the `TextViews` helps keep their text aligned with the `SeekBar`.
9. Finally, set the `customTipTextView`'s **Padding left** property to `5dp` to separate the `TextView` from the `SeekBar`.

Step 19: Setting the `customSeekBar`*'s* Progress *Property and Padding*

To complete the GUI design, you'll set the ***Progress***, **Padding left** and **Padding right** properties of the `SeekBar`. Initially, we'd like the `SeekBar`'s thumb position to represent 18%, since that's what we're displaying in the `TextView` to the `SeekBar`'s right. Also, we need to add some padding to the left and right side of the `SeekBar`. When you move the thumb to the far left or far right of the `SeekBar` (representing 0 and 100, respectively), the thumb becomes hard for the user to grab if there is not enough space between the `SeekBar` and the components to its left and right.

1. In the **Outline** window, select the `customSeekBar`.
2. Set the **Progress** property to `18`.
3. Set the **Padding left** and **Padding right** properties to `8dp`.
4. Set the **Padding bottom** property to `5dp` to separate it from the last row of components.
5. Set the ***Focusable property*** to `false` so that when the user changes the `SeekBar`'s value, the `billEditText` still maintains the focus—this helps keep the keyboard on the screen on a device that displays the soft keyboard.

Step 20: Preventing the User from Manipulating Text in the `EditText`s That Show Calculation Results

With the exception of the `billEditText` at the top of the GUI, all the other `EditText`s in this app are used simply to show the results of calculations. For this reason, the user should not be allowed to manipulate their text. You can control whether or not the user can give the focus to an `EditText` by setting its **Focusable** property. You can also prevent the user from long clicking an `EditText` and prevent an `EditText` from displaying a cursor so that the user can't manipulate the text. To configure these options:

1. In the **Outline** window, select all the `EditText`s except the `billEditText`.
2. Set the **Focusable, Long clickable** and **Cursor visible** properties to `false`.

Step 21: Specifying `billEditText`'s Keypad Type

The user should be allowed to enter only floating-point numbers in `billEditText`. To configure this options:

1. In the **Outline** window, select the `billEditText`.
2. Set the **Input type** property to `numberDecimal`.

Step 22: Set the Layout Weights of Various Components

A component's **Layout weight** specifies its relative importance with respect to other components. By default, all components have a **Layout weight** of `0`. Each component's **Layout weight** determines how it should be sized relative to other components. In this layout, we set **Layout weight** to `1` for all the components except the `TextView`s in the left column. When the layout is stretched to fill the width of the screen, the `TextView`s in the left column will occupy only the width required by the widest `TextView` in that column. The other components with **Layout weight** set to `1` will stretch to fill the remaining space and will share that space equally. If a component in a row had **Layout weight** set to `2`, it would occupy twice as much space as the components with **Layout weight** set to `1` in that row.

This completes the GUI design. The next section presents the XML markup that was generated by the Visual Layout Editor, then Section 4.5 presents the app's code.

4.4.5 Final XML Markup for the Tip Calculator GUI

Your GUI should now appear as shown in Fig. 4.2. Figure 4.5 presents the completed XML markup for the **Tip Calculator**'s GUI. We've reformatted the XML and added comments for readability. We've also highlighted some of the key new GUI features that were discussed in Sections 4.4.2 and 4.4.4.

```
<?xml version="1.0" encoding="utf-8"?>
<!-- main.xml -->
<!-- Tip Calculator's XML Layout -->

<TableLayout xmlns:android="http://schemas.android.com/apk/res/android"
   android:layout_width="match_parent" android:layout_height="match_parent"
   android:background="#FFF" android:id="@+id/tableLayout"
   android:stretchColumns="1,2,3" android:padding="5dp">

   <!-- tableRow0 -->
   <TableRow android:layout_height="wrap_content"
      android:layout_width="match_parent" android:id="@+id/tableRow0">
      <TextView android:id="@+id/billTextView"
         android:layout_width="wrap_content"
         android:layout_height="wrap_content"
         android:text="@string/billTotal" android:textColor="#000"
         android:gravity="right" android:paddingRight="5dp"></TextView>
      <EditText android:layout_width="wrap_content"
         android:id="@+id/billEditText"
         android:layout_height="wrap_content" android:layout_span="3"
         android:inputType="numberDecimal" android:layout_weight="1">
      </EditText>
   </TableRow>

   <!-- tableRow1 -->
   <TableRow android:layout_height="wrap_content"
      android:layout_width="match_parent" android:id="@+id/tableRow1">
      <TextView android:id="@+id/tenTextView"
         android:layout_width="wrap_content"
         android:layout_height="wrap_content" android:text="10%"
         android:textColor="#000" android:layout_column="1"
         android:gravity="center" android:layout_weight="1"></TextView>
      <TextView android:id="@+id/fifteenTextView"
         android:layout_width="wrap_content"
         android:layout_height="wrap_content" android:text="15%"
         android:textColor="#000" android:gravity="center"
         android:layout_weight="1"></TextView>
      <TextView android:id="@+id/twentyTextView"
         android:layout_width="wrap_content"
         android:layout_height="wrap_content" android:text="20%"
         android:textColor="#000" android:gravity="center"
         android:layout_weight="1"></TextView>
   </TableRow>

   <!-- tableRow2 -->
   <TableRow android:layout_height="wrap_content"
      android:layout_width="match_parent" android:id="@+id/tableRow2">
      <TextView android:id="@+id/tipTextView"
         android:layout_width="wrap_content"
         android:layout_height="wrap_content"
         android:text="@string/tip" android:textColor="#000"
         android:gravity="right" android:paddingRight="5dp"></TextView>
```

Fig. 4.5 | **Tip Calculator** app's XML layout. (Part 1 of 3.)

```
         <EditText android:layout_width="wrap_content"
            android:id="@+id/tip10EditText"
            android:layout_height="wrap_content" android:text="@string/zero"
            android:gravity="center" android:focusable="false"
            android:layout_weight="1" android:textSize="14sp"
            android:cursorVisible="false" android:longClickable="false">
         </EditText>
         <EditText android:layout_width="wrap_content"
            android:id="@+id/tip15EditText"
            android:layout_height="wrap_content" android:text="@string/zero"
            android:gravity="center" android:focusable="false"
            android:layout_weight="1" android:textSize="14sp"
            android:cursorVisible="false" android:longClickable="false">
         </EditText>
         <EditText android:layout_height="wrap_content"
            android:layout_width="wrap_content"
            android:id="@+id/tip20EditText" android:text="@string/zero"
            android:gravity="center" android:focusable="false"
            android:layout_weight="1" android:textSize="14sp"
            android:cursorVisible="false" android:longClickable="false">
         </EditText>
      </TableRow>

      <!-- tableRow3 -->
      <TableRow android:layout_height="wrap_content"
         android:layout_width="match_parent" android:id="@+id/tableRow3">
         <TextView android:layout_width="wrap_content"
            android:layout_height="wrap_content"
            android:id="@+id/totalTextView" android:text="@string/total"
            android:textColor="#000" android:gravity="right"
            android:paddingRight="5dp"></TextView>
         <EditText android:layout_width="wrap_content"
            android:text="@string/zero" android:layout_height="wrap_content"
            android:id="@+id/total10EditText" android:gravity="center"
            android:focusable="false" android:layout_weight="1"
            android:textSize="14sp" android:cursorVisible="false"
            android:longClickable="false"></EditText>
         <EditText android:layout_width="wrap_content"
            android:text="@string/zero" android:layout_height="wrap_content"
            android:id="@+id/total15EditText" android:gravity="center"
            android:focusable="false" android:layout_weight="1"
            android:textSize="14sp" android:cursorVisible="false"
            android:longClickable="false"></EditText>
         <EditText android:layout_width="wrap_content"
            android:text="@string/zero" android:layout_height="wrap_content"
            android:id="@+id/total20EditText" android:gravity="center"
            android:focusable="false" android:layout_weight="1"
            android:textSize="14sp" android:cursorVisible="false"
            android:longClickable="false"></EditText>
      </TableRow>

```

Fig. 4.5 | **Tip Calculator** app's XML layout. (Part 2 of 3.)

```
   <!-- tableRow4 -->
   <TableRow android:layout_height="wrap_content"
      android:layout_width="match_parent" android:id="@+id/tableRow4">
      <TextView android:id="@+id/customTextView"
         android:layout_width="wrap_content" android:text="@string/custom"
         android:textColor="#000" android:paddingRight="5dp"
         android:gravity="right|center_vertical"
         android:layout_height="match_parent" android:paddingBottom="5dp"
         android:focusable="false"></TextView>
      <SeekBar android:layout_height="wrap_content"
         android:layout_width="match_parent"
         android:id="@+id/customSeekBar" android:layout_span="2"
         android:progress="18" android:paddingLeft="8dp"
         android:paddingRight="8dp" android:paddingBottom="5dp"
         android:layout_weight="1"></SeekBar>
      <TextView android:id="@+id/customTipTextView"
         android:layout_width="wrap_content" android:text="18%"
         android:textColor="#000" android:gravity="center_vertical"
         android:layout_height="match_parent" android:paddingLeft="5dp"
         android:paddingBottom="5dp" android:focusable="false"
         android:layout_weight="1"></TextView>
   </TableRow>

   <!-- tableRow5 -->
   <TableRow android:layout_height="wrap_content"
      android:layout_width="match_parent" android:id="@+id/tableRow5">
      <TextView android:layout_width="wrap_content"
         android:layout_height="wrap_content"
         android:id="@+id/tipCustomTextView" android:text="@string/tip"
         android:textColor="#000" android:gravity="right"
         android:paddingRight="5dp"></TextView>
      <EditText android:layout_width="wrap_content"
         android:layout_height="wrap_content"
         android:id="@+id/tipCustomEditText" android:text="@string/zero"
         android:gravity="center" android:focusable="false"
         android:layout_weight="1" android:textSize="14sp"
         android:cursorVisible="false" android:longClickable="false">
      </EditText>
      <TextView android:id="@+id/totalCustomTextView"
         android:layout_width="wrap_content"
         android:layout_height="wrap_content" android:text="@string/total"
         android:textColor="#000" android:gravity="right"
         android:paddingRight="5dp" android:layout_weight="1"></TextView>
      <EditText android:layout_height="wrap_content"
         android:layout_width="wrap_content"
         android:id="@+id/totalCustomEditText" android:text="@string/zero"
         android:gravity="center" android:focusable="false"
         android:layout_weight="1" android:textSize="14sp"
         android:cursorVisible="false" android:longClickable="false">
      </EditText>
   </TableRow>
</TableLayout>
```

Fig. 4.5 | **Tip Calculator** app's XML layout. (Part 3 of 3.)

4.4.6 `strings.xml`

Figure 4.6 contains the string resources that are used in Fig. 4.5.

```
<?xml version="1.0" encoding="utf-8"?>
<resources>
   <string name="app_name">Tip Calculator</string>
   <string name="billTotal">Bill total</string>
   <string name="tip">Tip</string>
   <string name="total">Total</string>
   <string name="custom">Custom</string>
   <string name="zero">0.00</string>
</resources>
```

Fig. 4.6 | String resources in `strings.xml`.

4.5 Adding Functionality to the App

Figures 4.7–4.15 implement the **Tip Calculator** app in the single class `TipCalculator` that calculates 10%, 15%, 20% and custom percentage tips on a bill amount, then adds the tip to the bill amount to calculate the total bill.

The `package` *and* `import` *Statements*

Figure 4.7 shows the `package` statement and `import` statements in `TipCalculator.java`. The `package` statement in line 3 indicates that the class in this file is part of the package `com.deitel.tipcalculator`. This line was inserted when you created the project in *Step 1* of Section 4.4.

```
1  // TipCalculator.java
2  // Calculates bills using 5, 10, 15 and custom percentage tips.
3  package com.deitel.tipcalculator;
4
5  import android.app.Activity;
6  import android.os.Bundle;
7  import android.text.Editable;
8  import android.text.TextWatcher;
9  import android.widget.EditText;
10 import android.widget.SeekBar;
11 import android.widget.SeekBar.OnSeekBarChangeListener;
12 import android.widget.TextView;
13
```

Fig. 4.7 | `TipCalculator`'s `package` and `import` statements.

The `import` statements in lines 5–14 import the various classes and interfaces the app uses:

- Class `Activity` of package `android.app` (line 5) provides the basic *lifecycle methods* of an app—we'll discuss these shortly.
- Class `Bundle` of package `android.os` (line 6) represents an app's state information. An app can save its state when it's sent to the background by the operating

system—for example, when the user launches another app or a phone call is received.

- Interface `Editable` of package `android.text` (line 7) allows you to change the content and markup of text in a GUI.
- You implement interface `TextWatcher` of package `android.text` (line 8) to respond to events when the user interacts with an `EditText` component.
- Package `android.widget` (lines 9–12) contains the widgets (i.e., GUI components) and layouts that are used in Android GUIs, such as `EditText` (line 9), `SeekBar` (line 10) and `TextView` (line 12).
- You implement interface `SeekBar.OnSeekBarChangeListener` of package `android.widget` (line 11) to respond to the user moving the `SeekBar`'s thumb.

Tip Calculator App `Activity` *and the Activity Lifecycle*

Android apps *don't have a* `main` *method*. Instead, they have four types of components—*activities, services, content providers* and *broadcast receivers*—we'll show how these are initiated. In this chapter, we'll discuss only activities. Users interact with activities through views—that is, GUI components. A separate activity is typically associated with each screen of an app.

Class `TipCalculator` (Figs. 4.8–4.15) is the **Tip Calculator** app's only `Activity` class. In later chapters, we'll create apps that have several activities—typically each activity represents a different screen in the app. The `TipCalculator` class extends (inherits from) class `Activity` (line 15). When you created the `TipCalculator` project, the ADT Plugin generated this class as a subclass of `Activity` and provided the shell of an overridden `onCreate` method, which every `Activity` subclass *must* override. We'll discuss this method shortly.

```
14  // main Activity class for the TipCalculator
15  public class TipCalculator extends Activity
16  {
```

Fig. 4.8 | Class `TipCalculator` is a subclass of `Activity`.

Throughout its life an activity can be in one of several *states*—*active* (or *running*), *paused* or *stopped*. The activity transitions between these states in response to various *events*.

- An *active* (or *running*) activity is visible on the screen and "has the focus"—that is, it's in the foreground. This is the activity the user is interacting with.
- A *paused* activity is *visible* on the screen but doesn't have the focus. A *paused* activity can be killed when its memory is needed by the operating system (perhaps to run another app), but *stopped* activities are killed first.
- A *stopped* activity is *not visible* on the screen and is likely to be killed by the system when its memory is needed.

As an activity transitions among these states, it receives calls to various *lifecycle methods*—all of which are defined in the `Activity` class (`developer.android.com/reference/android/app/Activity.html`). Two lifecycle methods that we implement in the **Tip Calculator** app are `onCreate` and `onSaveInstanceState`. Some other key methods are onStart, onPause, onRestart, onResume, onStop and onDestroy. We'll discuss most of these methods in later chapters.

- **onCreate** is called by the system when an Activity is starting—that is, when its GUI is about to be displayed so that the user can interact with the Activity.
- **onSaveInstanceState** is called by the system when the configuration of the device changes during the app's execution—for example, when the user rotates the device or slides out a keyboard on a device with a hard keyboard (like the original Motorola Droid). This method can be used to save state information that you'd like to restore when the app's onCreate method is called as part of the configuration change. When an app is simply placed into the background, perhaps so the user can answer a phone call or when the user starts another app, the app's GUI components will automatically save their contents for when the app is brought back to the foreground (provided that the system does not kill the app).

Each activity lifecycle method you override must call the superclass's version of that method first; otherwise, an exception will be thrown when that method is called.

Class Variables and Instance Variables

Lines 18–32 of Fig. 4.9 declare class TipCalculator's variables, many of which are the EditTexts into which the user types the bill amount, and in which the app displays the possible tip amounts and total bills with the tip amounts included. The static Strings (lines 18–19) are used as the keys in key/value pairs for the current bill total and custom tip percentage. These key/value pairs are stored and retrieved in onSaveInstanceState and onCreate, respectively, when the app's configuration changes.

```
17    // constants used when saving/restoring state
18    private static final String BILL_TOTAL = "BILL_TOTAL";
19    private static final String CUSTOM_PERCENT = "CUSTOM_PERCENT";
20
21    private double currentBillTotal; // bill amount entered by the user
22    private int currentCustomPercent; // tip % set with the SeekBar
23    private EditText tip10EditText; // displays 10% tip
24    private EditText total10EditText; // displays total with 10% tip
25    private EditText tip15EditText; // displays 15% tip
26    private EditText total15EditText; // displays total with 15% tip
27    private EditText billEditText; // accepts user input for bill total
28    private EditText tip20EditText; // displays 20% tip
29    private EditText total20EditText;  // displays total with 20% tip
30    private TextView customTipTextView; // displays custom tip percentage
31    private EditText tipCustomEditText; // displays custom tip amount
32    private EditText totalCustomEditText; // displays total with custom tip
33
```

Fig. 4.9 | TipCalculator class's instance variables.

The bill amount entered by the user into EditText billEditText is read and stored as a String in currentBillTotal—this requires a conversion that we'll explain in a moment. The custom tip percentage that the user sets by moving the Seekbar thumb (an Integer in the range 0–100) will be stored in currentCustomPercent—this value will eventually be multiplied by .01 to create a `double` for use in calculations. The amount of the custom tip and the total bill including the custom tip are stored in `tipCustomEditText` and `totalCustomEditText`, respectively. Line 30 declares the `TextView` in which the custom tip percentage that corresponds to the `SeekBar` thumb's position is displayed (see the 18% in Fig. 4.1(a)).

The fixed percentage tips of 10%, 15% and 20% and the total bills with these tips included are displayed in `EditText`s. The amount of the 10% tip and the total bill including a 10% tip are stored in `tip10EditText` and `total10EditText`, respectively. The amount of the 15% tip and the total bill including a 15% tip are stored in `tip15EditText` and `total15EditText`, respectively. The amount of the 20% tip and the total bill including a 20% tip are stored in `tip20EditText` and `total20EditText`, respectively.

Overriding Method `onCreate` *of Class* `Activity`

The `onCreate` method (Fig. 4.10)—which is auto-generated when you create the app's project—is called by the system when an `Activity` is *started*. Method `onCreate` typically initializes the `Activity`'s instance variables and GUI components. This method should be as simple as possible so that the app loads quickly. In fact, if the app takes longer than five seconds to load, the operating system will display an ***ANR (Application Not Responding) dialog***—giving the user the option to forcibly terminate the app. Time-consuming initializations should be done in a background process instead of the `onCreate` method.

```
34     // Called when the activity is first created.
35     @Override
36     public void onCreate(Bundle savedInstanceState)
37     {
38        super.onCreate(savedInstanceState); // call superclass's version
39        setContentView(R.layout.main); // inflate the GUI
40
41        // check if app just started or is being restored from memory
42        if ( savedInstanceState == null ) // the app just started running
43        {
44           currentBillTotal = 0.0; // initialize the bill amount to zero
45           currentCustomPercent = 18; // initialize the custom tip to 18%
46        } // end if
47        else // app is being restored from memory, not executed from scratch
48        {
49           // initialize the bill amount to saved amount
50           currentBillTotal = savedInstanceState.getDouble(BILL_TOTAL);
51
52           // initialize the custom tip to saved tip percent
53           currentCustomPercent =
54              savedInstanceState.getInt(CUSTOM_PERCENT);
55        } // end else
56
57        // get references to the 10%, 15% and 20% tip and total EditTexts
58        tip10EditText = (EditText) findViewById(R.id.tip10EditText);
59        total10EditText = (EditText) findViewById(R.id.total10EditText);
60        tip15EditText = (EditText) findViewById(R.id.tip15EditText);
61        total15EditText = (EditText) findViewById(R.id.total15EditText);
```

Fig. 4.10 | Overriding `Activity` method `onCreate`. (Part 1 of 2.)

```
62          tip20EditText = (EditText) findViewById(R.id.tip20EditText);
63          total20EditText = (EditText) findViewById(R.id.total20EditText);
64
65          // get the TextView displaying the custom tip percentage
66          customTipTextView = (TextView) findViewById(R.id.customTipTextView);
67
68          // get the custom tip and total EditTexts
69          tipCustomEditText = (EditText) findViewById(R.id.tipCustomEditText);
70          totalCustomEditText =
71             (EditText) findViewById(R.id.totalCustomEditText);
72
73          // get the billEditText
74          billEditText = (EditText) findViewById(R.id.billEditText);
75
76          // billEditTextWatcher handles billEditText's onTextChanged event
77          billEditText.addTextChangedListener(billEditTextWatcher);
78
79          // get the SeekBar used to set the custom tip amount
80          SeekBar customSeekBar = (SeekBar) findViewById(R.id.customSeekBar);
81          customSeekBar.setOnSeekBarChangeListener(customSeekBarListener);
82       } // end method onCreate
83
```

Fig. 4.10 | Overriding `Activity` method `onCreate`. (Part 2 of 2.)

During the app's execution, the user could change the device's configuration by rotating the device or sliding out a hard keyboard. The user wants the app to continue operating smoothly through such configuration changes. When the system calls `onCreate`, it passes a ***`Bundle`*** to parameter `savedInstanceState`. This contains the activity's saved state, if any. Typically, this state information is saved by the `Activity`'s `onSaveInstanceState` method (Fig. 4.13). (We use `savedInstanceState` in lines 42–55.) Line 38 calls the superclass's `onCreate` method, which is essential when overriding *any* `Activity` method.

As you build your app's GUI and add resources (such as `strings` in the `strings.xml` file or GUI components in the `main.xml` file) to your app, the ADT Plugin tools generate a class named ***`R`*** that contains nested `static` classes representing each type of resource in your project's `res` folder. You can find this class in your project's ***gen folder***, which contains generated source-code files. Within class `R`'s nested classes, the tools create `static final int` constants that enable you to refer to these resources programmatically from your app's code (as we'll discuss momentarily). Some of the nested classes in class `R` include:

- Class ***`drawable`***—contains constants for any `drawable` items, such as images, that you put in the various `drawable` folders in your app's `res` folder
- Class ***`id`***—contains constants for the GUI components in your XML layout files
- Class ***`layout`***—contains constants that represent each layout file in your project (such as, `main.xml`)
- Class ***`string`***—contains constants for each `String` in the `strings.xml` file

The call to ***`setContentView`*** (line 39) receives the constant ***`R.layout.main`*** to indicate which XML file represents the activity's GUI—in this case, the constant represents the `main.xml` file. Method `setContentView` uses this constant to load the corresponding XML document, which is then parsed and converted into the app's GUI. This process is known as ***inflating*** the GUI.

Lines 42–55 determine whether the app has just started executing or is being restored from a configuration change. If savedInstanceState is null (line 42), the app just started executing, so lines 44–45 initialize currentBillTotal and currentCustomPercent with the values that are required when the app first loads. If the app is being restored, line 50 calls the savedInstanceState object's ***getString method*** to get the saved bill total as a double value, and lines 53–54 call the savedInstanceState object's ***getInt method*** to get the saved custom tip percentage as an int value.

Once the layout is inflated, you can get references to the individual widgets using Activity's findViewById method. This method takes an int constant for a specific view (that is, a GUI component) and returns a reference to it. The name of each GUI component's constant in the ***R.id*** class is determined by the GUI component's android:id attribute in the main.xml file. For example, billEditText's constant is R.id.billEditText.

Lines 58–63 obtain references to the six EditTexts that hold the 10%, 15% and 20% calculated tips and total bills including these tips. Line 66 obtains a reference to the TextView that will be updated when the user changes the custom tip percentage. Lines 69–71 obtain references to the EditTexts where the custom tip and total amounts will be displayed.

Line 74 gets a reference to the billEditText, and line 77 calls its addTextChangedListener method to register the TextChangedListener that will respond to events generated when the user changes the text in the billEditText. We define this listener object in Fig. 4.15.

Line 80 gets a reference to the customSeekBar and line 81 calls its setOnSeekBarChangeListener method to register the OnSeekBarChangeListener that will respond to events generated when the user moves the customSeekBar's thumb to change the custom tip percentage. We define this listener object in Fig. 4.14.

Method updateStandard *of Class* TipCalculator

Method updateStandard (Fig. 4.11) updates the 10%, 15% and 20% tip and total EditTexts each time the user changes the bill total. The method uses the currentBillTotal value to calculate tip amounts and bill totals for tips of 10% (lines 88–95), 15% (lines 98–106) and 20% (lines 109–116) tips. Class String's static format method is used to convert the tip amounts and bill amounts to Strings that are displayed in the corresponding EditTexts.

```
84     // updates 10, 15 and 20 percent tip EditTexts
85     private void updateStandard()
86     {
87        // calculate bill total with a ten percent tip
88        double tenPercentTip = currentBillTotal * .1;
89        double tenPercentTotal = currentBillTotal + tenPercentTip;
90
91        // set tipTenEditText's text to tenPercentTip
92        tip10EditText.setText(String.format("%.02f", tenPercentTip));
93
```

Fig. 4.11 | TipCalculator method updateStandard calculates and displays the tips and totals for the standard tip percentages—10%, 15% and 20%. (Part 1 of 2.)

```
        // set totalTenEditText's text to tenPercentTotal
        total10EditText.setText(String.format("%.02f", tenPercentTotal));

        // calculate bill total with a fifteen percent tip
        double fifteenPercentTip = currentBillTotal * .15;
        double fifteenPercentTotal = currentBillTotal + fifteenPercentTip;

        // set tipFifteenEditText's text to fifteenPercentTip
        tip15EditText.setText(String.format("%.02f", fifteenPercentTip));

        // set totalFifteenEditText's text to fifteenPercentTotal
        total15EditText.setText(
           String.format("%.02f", fifteenPercentTotal));

        // calculate bill total with a twenty percent tip
        double twentyPercentTip = currentBillTotal * .20;
        double twentyPercentTotal = currentBillTotal + twentyPercentTip;

        // set tipTwentyEditText's text to twentyPercentTip
        tip20EditText.setText(String.format("%.02f", twentyPercentTip));

        // set totalTwentyEditText's text to twentyPercentTotal
        total20EditText.setText(String.format("%.02f", twentyPercentTotal));
     } // end method updateStandard

```

Fig. 4.11 | `TipCalculator` method `updateStandard` calculates and displays the tips and totals for the standard tip percentages—10%, 15% and 20%. (Part 2 of 2.)

Method **updateCustom** *of Class* **TipCalculator**

Method `updateCustom` (Fig. 4.12) updates the custom tip and total `EditText`s based on the tip percentage the user selected with the `customSeekBar`. Line 123 sets the `customTipTextView`'s text to match the position of the `SeekBar`. Lines 126–127 calculate the `customTipAmount`. Line 130 calculates the `customTotalAmount`. Lines 133–135 convert the `customTipAmount` and the `customTotalAmount` to `String`s and display them in the `tipCustomEditText` and `totalCustomEditText`, respectively.

```
119     // updates the custom tip and total EditTexts
120     private void updateCustom()
121     {
122        // set customTipTextView's text to match the position of the SeekBar
123        customTipTextView.setText(currentCustomPercent + "%");
124
125        // calculate the custom tip amount
126        double customTipAmount =
127           currentBillTotal * currentCustomPercent * .01;
128
129        // calculate the total bill, including the custom tip
130        double customTotalAmount = currentBillTotal + customTipAmount;
```

Fig. 4.12 | `TipCalculator` method `updateCustom` calculates and displays the tip and total for the custom tip percentage that the user selects with the `customSeekBar`. (Part 1 of 2.)

```

        // display the tip and total bill amounts
        tipCustomEditText.setText(String.format("%.02f", customTipAmount));
        totalCustomEditText.setText(
           String.format("%.02f", customTotalAmount));
     } // end method updateCustom

```

Fig. 4.12 | `TipCalculator` method `updateCustom` calculates and displays the tip and total for the custom tip percentage that the user selects with the `customSeekBar`. (Part 2 of 2.)

Overriding Method `onSaveInstanceState` *of Class* `Activity`

Lines 139–146 of Fig. 4.13 override class `Activity`'s `onSaveInstanceState` method, which the system calls when the configuration of the device changes during the app's execution—for example, when the user rotates the device or slides out a keyboard on a device with a hard keyboard. In Eclipse, you can generate this method by right clicking in the source code, then selecting **Source > Override/Implement Methods....** The dialog that appears shows you every method that can be overridden or implemented in the class. Simply select the checkbox for `onSaveInstanceState`, specify where in your class you'd like the IDE to insert the code and click **OK** to create the method's shell.

```
138     // save values of billEditText and customSeekBar
139     @Override
140     protected void onSaveInstanceState(Bundle outState)
141     {
142        super.onSaveInstanceState(outState);
143
144        outState.putDouble( BILL_TOTAL, currentBillTotal );
145        outState.putInt( CUSTOM_PERCENT, currentCustomPercent );
146     } // end method onSaveInstanceState
147
```

Fig. 4.13 | Overriding `Activity` method `onSaveInstanceState` to save state when the app's configuration changes.

In this app we first call the superclass's `onSaveInstanceState` method, then we store key/value pairs in the `Bundle` that was passed to the method. Line 144 saves the current bill total and line 145 saves the custom tip percentage (that is, the current position of the `SeekBar`'s thumb). These values are used in `onCreate` when it's called to restore the app after the configuration change. In upcoming apps, we'll explore several other `Activity` lifecycle methods, which are documented in detail at:

```
bit.ly/ActivityLifeCycle
```

Anonymous Inner Class That Implements Interface `OnSeekBarChangeListener`

Lines 149–171 of Fig. 4.14 create the anonymous inner-class object `customSeekBarListener` that responds to `customSeekBar`'s events. If you're not familiar with anonymous inner classes, visit the following page from Oracle's Java Tutorial

```
bit.ly/AnonymousInnerClasses
```

Line 81 registered `customSeekBarListener` as `customSeekBar`'s event-handling object. Lines 153–170 implement the methods of interface `OnSeekBarChangeListener`.

```
148    // called when the user changes the position of SeekBar
149    private OnSeekBarChangeListener customSeekBarListener =
150       new OnSeekBarChangeListener()
151    {
152       // update currentCustomPercent, then call updateCustom
153       @Override
154       public void onProgressChanged(SeekBar seekBar, int progress,
155          boolean fromUser)
156       {
157          // sets currentCustomPercent to position of the SeekBar's thumb
158          currentCustomPercent = seekBar.getProgress();
159          updateCustom(); // update EditTexts for custom tip and total
160       } // end method onProgressChanged
161
162       @Override
163       public void onStartTrackingTouch(SeekBar seekBar)
164       {
165       } // end method onStartTrackingTouch
166
167       @Override
168       public void onStopTrackingTouch(SeekBar seekBar)
169       {
170       } // end method onStopTrackingTouch
171    }; // end OnSeekBarChangeListener
172
```

Fig. 4.14 | Anonymous inner class that implements interface `OnSeekBarChangeListener` to respond to the events of the `customSeekBar`.

Overriding Method `onProgressChanged` *of Interface* `OnSeekBarChangeListener`

Lines 153–160 override method `onProgressChanged`. In line 158, `SeekBar` method `getProgress` returns an `Integer` in the range 0–100 representing the position of the `SeekBar`'s thumb and assigns this value to `currentCustomPercent`. Line 159 calls method `updateCustom`, which uses the `customCurrentPercent` to calculate and display the custom tip and total bill.

Overriding Methods `onStartTrackingTouch` *and* `onStopTrackingTouch` *of Interface* `OnSeekBarChangeListener`

Java requires that we override *every* method of an interface that we implement. We don't use either of these interface methods in our app, so we simply provide an empty shell for each (lines 162–170) to fulfill the interface contract.

Anonymous Inner Class That Implements Interface `TextWatcher`

Lines 174–206 of Fig. 4.15 create the anonymous inner-class object `billEditTextWatcher` that responds to `billEditText`'s events. Line 77 registered `billEditTextWatcher` to listen for `billEditText`'s events. Lines 177–205 implement the methods of interface `TextWatcher`.

```
173    // event-handling object that responds to billEditText's events
174    private TextWatcher billEditTextWatcher = new TextWatcher()
175    {
176       // called when the user enters a number
177       @Override
178       public void onTextChanged(CharSequence s, int start,
179          int before, int count)
180       {
181          // convert billEditText's text to a double
182          try
183          {
184             currentBillTotal = Double.parseDouble(s.toString());
185          } // end try
186          catch (NumberFormatException e)
187          {
188             currentBillTotal = 0.0; // default if an exception occurs
189          } // end catch
190
191          // update the standard and custom tip EditTexts
192          updateStandard(); // update the 10, 15 and 20% EditTexts
193          updateCustom(); // update the custom tip EditTexts
194       } // end method onTextChanged
195
196       @Override
197       public void afterTextChanged(Editable s)
198       {
199       } // end method afterTextChanged
200
201       @Override
202       public void beforeTextChanged(CharSequence s, int start, int count,
203          int after)
204       {
205       } // end method beforeTextChanged
206    }; // end billEditTextWatcher
207 } // end class TipCalculator
```

Fig. 4.15 | Anonymous inner class that implements interface `TextWatcher` to respond to the events of the `billEditText`.

Overriding Method `onTextChanged` *of Interface* `TextWatcher`

The onTextChanged method (lines 177–194) is called whenever the text in the `billEditText` is modified. The method receives four parameters (lines 178–179). In this example, we use only `CharSequence s`, which contains a copy of `billEditText`'s text. The other parameters indicate that the `count` characters starting at `start` replaced previous text of length `before`.

Line 184 converts the text the user entered in `billEditText` to a `double`. Line 192 calls `updateStandard` to update the 10%, 15% and 20% `EditTexts` for both the tip amounts and the total bills including the tip amounts. Line 193 calls `updateCustom` to update the custom tip and total bill `EditTexts`, based on the custom tip percentage obtained from the `SeekBar`.

Methods `beforeTextChanged` *and* `afterTextChanged` *of the* `billEditTextWatcher TextWatcher`

We don't use these `TextWatcher` interface methods in our app, so we simply override each with an empty method (lines 196–205) to fulfill the interface contract.

4.6 Wrap-Up

In this chapter, you created your first interactive Android app—the **Tip Calculator.** We overviewed the app's capabilities, then you test-drove it to calculate standard and custom tips based on the bill amount entered. You followed detailed step-by-step instructions to build the app's GUI using the ADT Plugin's tools in Eclipse, including the Visual Layout Editor, the **Outline** window and the **Properties** window. In subsequent chapters, we'll discuss only the new GUI capabilities as we introduce them. Finally, we did a detailed code walkthrough of the `Activity` class `TipCalculator`, which specifies what happens when the app starts executing and defines the app's logic.

In the app's GUI, you used a `TableLayout` to arrange the GUI components into rows and columns. You learned that each cell in a `TableLayout` can be empty or can hold one component, and each cell can be a layout that contains other components. You used `TableRows` to create the rows in the layout and learned that the number of columns is defined by the `TableRow` that contains the most components. You also learned that each row's height is determined by the tallest component in that row and the width of a column is defined by the widest element in that column (unless the columns are set to stretch). You used `TextViews` to label the GUI's components, an `EditText` to receive the bill total from the user, non-`focusable` `EditTexts` to display the various tips and totals for different tip percentages, and a `SeekBar` to allow the user to specify a custom tip percentage. Most of the XML for the GUI was generated for you by the ADT Plugin's tools, but you also directly edited the XML to customize several properties that were not available through the **Properties** window.

You used many Java object-oriented programming capabilities, including classes, anonymous inner classes, objects, methods, interfaces and inheritance. We explained the notion of inflating the GUI from its XML file into its screen representation. You learned about Android's `Activity` class and part of the `Activity` lifecycle. In particular, you overrode the `onCreate` method to initialize the app when it's launched and the `onSaveInstanceState` method save app state when the device's configuration changes. In the `onCreate` method, you used `Activity` method `findViewById` to get references to each of the GUI components that the app interacts with programmatically. For the `billEditText`, you defined an anonymous inner class that implements the `TextWatcher` interface so the app can calculate new tips and totals as the user changes the text in the `EditText`. For the `customSeekBar`, you defined an anonymous inner class that implements the `OnSeekBarChangeListener` interface so the app can calculate a new custom tip and total as the user changes the custom tip percentage by moving the `SeekBar`'s thumb.

In the next chapter, we introduce collections while building the **Favorite Twitter Searches** app. You'll lay out a GUI programmatically—allowing you to add and remove components dynamically in response to user interactions.

5

Favorite Twitter® Searches App

SharedPreferences, Buttons, Nested Layouts, Intents AlertDialogs, Inflating XML Layouts and the Manifest File

Objectives

In this chapter you'll:

- Enable users to interact with an app via `Button`s.
- Use a `ScrollView` to display objects that do not fit on the screen.
- Create GUI components dynamically in response to user interactions by inflating an XML layout.
- Store key/value pairs of data associated with an app using `SharedPreferences`.
- Modify key/value pairs of data associated with an app using `SharedPreferences.Editor`.
- Use an `AlertDialog.Builder` object to create `AlertDialog`s.
- Programmatically open a website in a web browser by using an `Intent`.
- Programmatically hide the soft keyboard.

Outline

5.1 Introduction

The **Favorite Twitter Searches** app allows users to save their favorite (possibly lengthy) Twitter search strings with easy-to-remember, user-chosen, short tag names. Users can then conveniently follow the tweets on their favorite topics. Twitter search queries can be finely tuned using Twitter's search operators (`dev.twitter.com/docs/using-search`)—but more complex queries are lengthy, time consuming and error prone to type on a mobile device. The user's favorite searches are saved on the device, so they're immediately available each time the app launches. Figure 5.1(a) shows the app with several saved

a) App with several saved searches

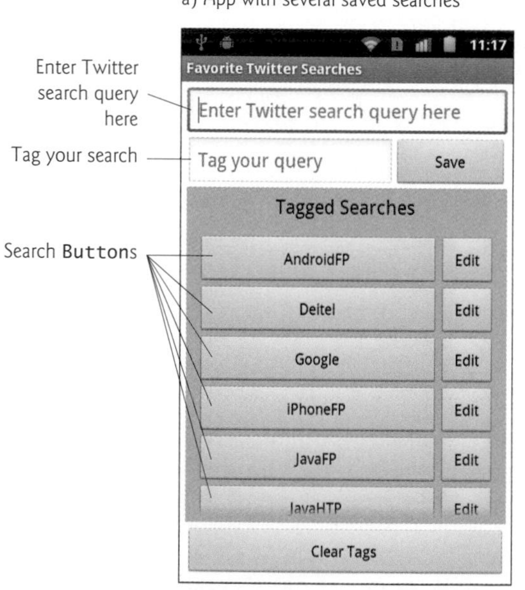

b) Results of touching the **Google** `Button`

Fig. 5.1 | **Favorite Twitter Searches** app.

searches—the user can save many searches and scroll through them in alphabetical order. Search queries and their corresponding tags are entered in the `EditTexts` at the top of the screen, and the **Save** `Button` adds each search to the favorites list. Touching a search `Button` sends that search to Twitter and displays the search results in the device's web browser. Figure 5.1(b) shows the result of touching the **Google** `Button`, which searches for tweets from Google—specified by the Twitter search `from:Google`. You can edit the searches using the **Edit** `Buttons` to the right of each search `Button`. This enables you to tweak your searches for better results after you save them as favorites. Touching the **Clear Tags** `Button` at the bottom of the screen removes all the searches from the favorites list—a dialog asks the user to confirm this first.

5.2 Test-Driving the Favorite Twitter Searches App

Opening and Running the App

Open Eclipse, then import the **Favorite Twitter Searches** app project. Perform the following steps:

1. *Open the* **Import** *Dialog.* Select **File > Import...** to open the **Import** dialog.
2. *Import the* **Favorite Twitter Searches** *app project.* In the **Import** dialog, expand the **General** node and select **Existing Projects into Workspace**, then click **Next >** to proceed to the **Import Projects** step. Ensure that **Select root directory** is selected, then click the **Browse...** button. In the **Browse For Folder** dialog, locate the `FavoriteTwitterSearches` folder in the book's examples folder, select it and click **OK**. Click **Finish** to import the project into Eclipse. The project now appears in the **Package Explorer** window at the left side of the Eclipse window.
3. *Launch the* **Favorite Twitter Searches** *app.* In Eclipse, right click the `FavoriteTwitterSearches` project in the **Package Explorer** window, then select **Run As > Android Application** from the menu that appears. This will execute **Favorite Twitter Searches** in the AVD that you created in the Before You Begin section (Fig. 5.2).

The top two `EditTexts` allow you to enter new searches, and the **Tagged Searches** section displays previously saved searches (in this case, none yet).

Adding a New Favorite Search

Enter `from:Google` into the top `EditText` specifying your search subject. Enter `Google` into the bottom `EditText` (Fig. 5.3(a)). This will be the short name displayed in the **Tagged Searches** section. Press the **Save** `Button` to save the search and hide the keyboard—a **Google** `Button` appears under the **Tagged Searches** heading (Fig. 5.3(b)). Also, notice that the soft keyboard is dismissed—this app hides the soft keyboard programmatically.

Editing a Search

To the right of each search `Button` is an **Edit** `Button`. Touch this to reload your query and tag into the `EditTexts` at the top of the app for editing. Let's restrict our search to tweets since April 1, 2011. Add `since:2011-04-01` to the end of the query (Fig. 5.4). Touching **Save** updates the saved search. [*Note:* If you change the tag name, this will create a new search `Button`—this is useful if you want to base a new query on a previously saved query.]

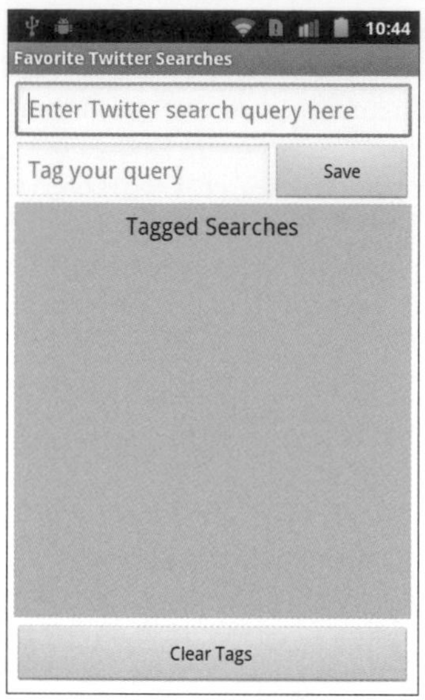

Fig. 5.2 | Running the **Favorite Twitter Searches** app.

a) Entering a Twitter search and search tag

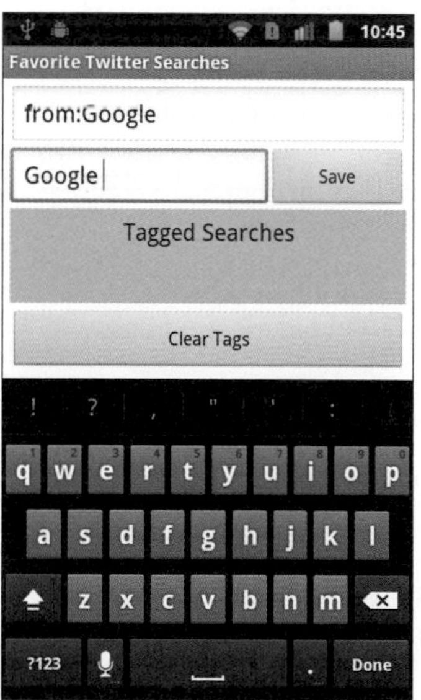

b) App after saving the search and search tag

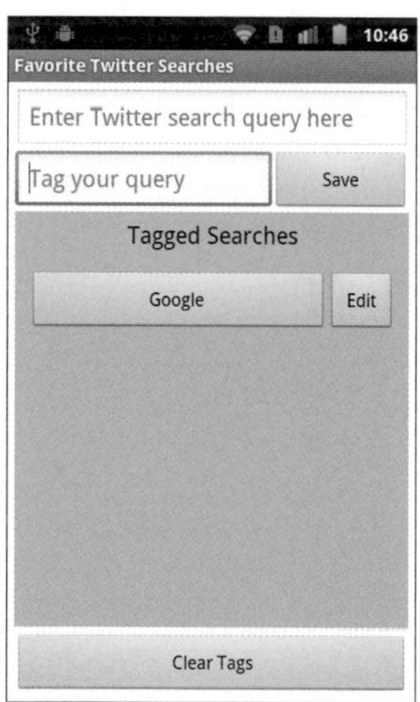

Fig. 5.3 | Entering a Twitter search.

Viewing Twitter Search Results

To see the search results touch the **Google** search query `Button`. This opens the web browser and accesses the Twitter website to obtain and display the search results (Fig. 5.5).

Fig. 5.4 | Editing a Twitter search.

Fig. 5.5 | Viewing search results.

5.3 Technologies Overview

This app uses `EditText`, `ScrollView` and `Button` GUI components. A **`ScrollView`** is a **`ViewGroup`** that can contain other `Views` (like a layout) and that lets users *scroll* through content too large to display on the screen. We use a `ScrollView` to display an arbitrarily large list of saved searches, because the user may have more favorite searches than can fit on the screen. Each search is associated with a **Button**, which the user can tap to pass the search to the browser.

SharedPreferences

You can have one or more files containing key/value pairs associated with each app. We use this capability to manipulate a file called searches in which we store the pairs of tags and Twitter search queries that the user creates. To read the key/value pairs from this file we'll use **SharedPreferences** objects (package **android.content**). To modify the file's contents, we'll use **SharedPreferences.Editor** objects (package android.content). The keys in the file must be Strings, and the values can be Strings or primitive-type values.

We read in the saved searches in our refreshButtons method, which is called from the Activity's onCreate method—this is acceptable because the amount of data being loaded is small. When an app is launched, Android creates a main thread called the UI thread which handles the GUI—*extensive input/output should not be performed on the UI thread, since that would affect your app's responsiveness.* We'll show how to deal with this in Chapter 10.

Intents

Intents are typically used to launch activities—they indicate an *action* to be performed and the *data* on which that action is to be performed. When the user touches a Button representing a search, we create a URL that contains the Twitter search query. We load the URL into a web browser by creating a new Intent for viewing a URL, then passing that Intent to the **startActivity method,** which our Activity inherits indirectly from class Context. To view a URL, startActivity launches the device's web browser to display the content—in this app, the results of a Twitter search.

LayoutInflater

Each new search that the user enters adds another row of Buttons to the user interface—one Button that represents the search and one that allows you to edit that search. We use a **LayoutInflater** to programmatically create these GUI components from a predefined XML layout. The LayoutInflater inflates an XML layout file, thus creating the components specified in the XML. Then we set the search Button's text, register event handlers for each Button and attach the new GUI components to the user interface.

AlertDialog

We want the user to enter both a query and a tag before storing a new search—if either EditText is empty, we display a message to the user. We also want the user to confirm that all searches should be deleted when the **Clear Tags** button is touched. You can display messages and confirmations like these with an **AlertDialog**. While the dialog is displayed, the user cannot interact with the app—this is known as a **modal dialog**. As you'll see, you specify the settings for the dialog with an **AlertDialog.Builder** object, then use it to create the AlertDialog.

AndroidManifest.xml

The **AndroidManifest.xml** file is created for you when you create an app using the ADT Plugin in Eclipse. This file specifies settings such as the app's name, the package name, the target and minimum SDKs, the app's Activity name(s) and more. We'll introduce this file at the end of the chapter and show you how to add a new setting to the manifest that prevents the soft keyboard from displaying when the app first loads.

5.4 Building the App's GUI and Resource Files

In this section, we'll build the GUI for the **Favorite Twitter Searches** app. We'll present the XML that the ADT Plugin generates for the app's layout. We'll focus primarily on new GUI features and present the final XML layout, highlighting the key portions of the XML. We'll also create a second XML layout that will be dynamically inflated to create the tag and **Edit** `Buttons` for each search. This will allow the app to load the previously stored searches and adapt at runtime as the user adds or deletes searches.

5.4.1 `main.xml` `TableLayout`

As in Chapter 4, this app's main layout uses a `TableLayout` (Fig. 5.6)—here we use five rows and two columns. All of the GUI components in row 0 and rows 2–4 span both columns. The `TableLayout`'s `android:stretchColumns` attribute is set to `"*"`, which indicates that all of the table's columns are stretchable—the elements in each column can expand to the screen's full width.

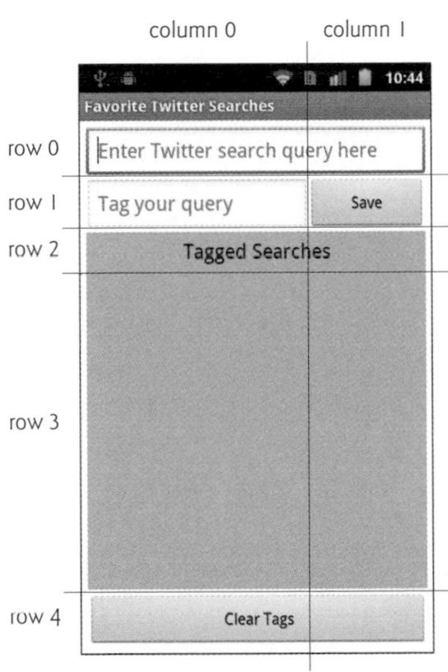

Fig. 5.6 | Rows and columns in the **Favorite Twitter Searches** app's `TableLayout`.

Figure 5.7 shows the names of all the app's GUI components. Recall that, for clarity, our naming convention is to use the GUI component's class name in each component's **Id** property in the XML layout and in each variable name in the Java code.

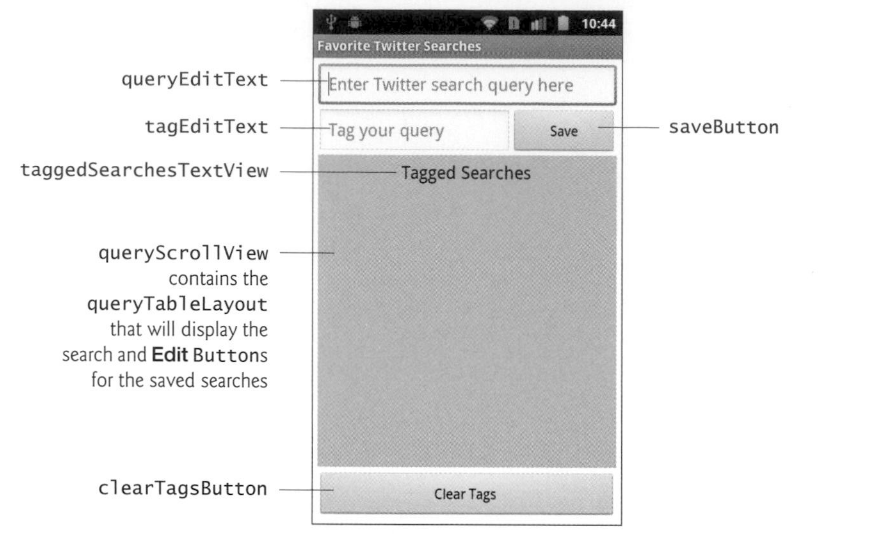

Fig. 5.7 | **Favorite Twitter Searches** GUI's components labeled with their **Id** property values.

5.4.2 Creating the Project

Begin by creating a new Android project named `FavoriteTwitterSearches`. Specify the following values in the **New Android Project** dialog, then press **Finish**:

- **Build Target:** Ensure that **Android 2.3.3** is checked
- **Application name:** `Favorite Twitter Searches`
- **Package name:** `com.deitel.favoritetwittersearches`
- **Create Activity:** `FavoriteTwitterSearches`
- **Min SDK Version:** `10`. [*Note:* This SDK version corresponds to Android 2.3.3; however, we do not use any Android 2.3.3-specific functionality in this app. If you'd like this app to execute on AVDs or devices running an earlier Android version, you can set the **Min SDK Version** to a lower value. For example, you could specify 8 to indicate that the app can execute on Android 2.2 or higher.]

5.4.3 Creating the Resource Files

In this app, we stored a literal color value and a few literal dimension values in the files `colors.xml` and `dimen.xml`, respectively. These file names are used by convention, and the files are placed in the app's `res/values` folder. Each color and dimension you create in these files will be represented in the auto-generated `R.java` file by a constant that you can use to reference the specified value. To create each file:

1. Right click the project name in the **Package Explorer** window and select **New > Other...**, then select **Android XML File** from the **Android** node in the **New** dialog. This displays the **New Android XML File** dialog.
2. In the **File** text field, enter the name `colors.xml`.

3. Under **What type of resource would you like to create?**, select the **Values** radio button. This will cause the new file to be placed into the project's `res/values` folder.
4. Click **Finish** to create the file.
5. Repeat this process to create the `dimen.xml` file.

The contents of these two files are shown in Figs. 5.8–5.9. As you'll see, we use the color and dimensions in these files in our XML layouts. We'll also use several Android predefined colors from the class `R.color`. As in previous apps, we also defined various string resources in the `strings.xml` file.

colors.xml

Each XML document that represents resources must contain a ***resources element*** in which you specify the resources. Within that element in Fig. 5.8, we define the one color value that we use in this app (`light_orange`). The ***color element*** (line 3) specifies a `name` attribute that's used to reference the color and a hexadecimal value specifying the color.

```
1  <?xml version="1.0" encoding="UTF-8"?>
2  <resources>
3     <color name="light_orange">#8f90</color>
4  </resources>
```

Fig. 5.8 | Colors defined in `colors.xml`.

dimen.xml

In Fig. 5.9, we define ***dimen elements*** that represent the widths search tag and **Edit** `Buttons`. A benefit of defining dimensions as resources is that you can use density-independent pixel (`dp` or `dip`) and scale-independent pixel (`sp`) values, which Android automatically converts to the appropriate pixel values for a given device. In code, you can set only fixed pixel sizes, so you'd have to manually calculate the proper pixel values for each device.

```
<?xml version="1.0" encoding="UTF-8"?>
<resources>
   <dimen name="tagButtonWidth">230dp</dimen>
   <dimen name="editButtonWidth">50dp</dimen>
</resources>
```

Fig. 5.9 | Dimensions defined in `dimen.xml`.

strings.xml

In Fig. 5.10, we define the `String` literal values we use throughout this app. Line 4 defines the `searchURL`. The user's search queries are appended to this URL before the twitter search is displayed in the device's web browser.

```
1  <?xml version="1.0" encoding="UTF-8"?>
2  <resources>
3     <string name="app_name">Favorite Twitter Searches</string>
```

Fig. 5.10 | Strings defined in `strings.xml`. (Part 1 of 2.)

```
    <string name="searchURL">http://search.twitter.com/search?q=</string>
    <string name="tagPrompt">Tag your query</string>
    <string name="queryPrompt">Enter Twitter search query here</string>
    <string name="taggedSearches">Tagged Searches</string>
    <string name="edit">Edit</string>
    <string name="clearTags">Clear Tags</string>
    <string name="save">Save</string>
    <string name="erase">Erase</string>
    <string name="cancel">Cancel</string>
    <string name="OK">OK</string>
    <string name="missingTitle">Missing Text</string>
    <string name="missingMessage">
       Please enter a search query and tag it.</string>
    <string name="confirmTitle">Are You Sure?</string>
    <string name="confirmMessage">
       This will delete all saved searches</string>
</resources>
```

Fig. 5.10 | Strings defined in `strings.xml`. (Part 2 of 2.)

5.4.4 Adding the `TableLayout` and Components

Using the techniques you learned in Chapter 4, you'll build the GUI in Figs. 5.6–5.7. You'll start with the basic layout and controls, then customize the controls' properties to complete the design. As you add components to each row of the `TableLayout`, set the **Id** and **Text** properties of the components as shown in Fig. 5.7. When building the GUI, place your literal string values in the `strings.xml` file in the app's `res/values` folder. Use the **Outline** window to add components to the proper `TableRow`s of the `TableLayout`.

Step 1: Deleting and Recreating the `main.xml` File

For this application, once again you'll replace the default `main.xml` file with a new one that uses a `TableLayout` in which components are arranged relative to one another. Perform the following steps to replace the default `main.xml` file:

1. Right click the `main.xml` file in the projects `/res/layout` folder and select **Delete** to delete the file.
2. Right click the layout folder and select **New > Other...** to display the **New** dialog.
3. In the **Android** node, select **Android XML File** and click **Next >** to display the **New Android XML File** dialog.
4. Specify the file name `main.xml` and select `TableLayout`, then click **Finish**.

Step 2: Configuring the Visual Layout Editor to Use the Appropriate Android SDK

As you did in Fig. 3.7, select Android 2.3.3 from the SDK selector drop-down list at the top-right side of the **Graphical Layout** tab to indicate that we're designing a GUI for an Android 2.3.3 device.

Step 3: Configuring the Visual Layout Editor's Size and Resolution

As you did in Fig. 3.11, select **3.7in WVGA (Nexus One)** from the Device Configurations drop-down list at the top-left side of the **Graphical Layout** tab. This configures the design area for devices with 480-by-800 (WVGA) resolution.

Step 4: Configuring the **`TableLayout`**

In the **Outline** window, select the `TableLayout` and set the following properties:

- **Background:** `@android:color/white`
- **Id:** `@+id/tableLayout`
- **Padding:** `5dp`
- **Stretch columns:** `*`

We've specified the **Background** color using one of Android's predefined color values (`white`) from the ***`R.color`* *class***—you can find the names of the predefined colors at

`developer.android.com/reference/android/R.color.html`

To access a predefined color resource, you specify `@android:color/` followed by the name of the resource.

By default, the layout fills the entire screen, because the **Layout width** and **Layout height** properties have the value `match_parent`. Setting the **Padding** property to `5dp` ensures that there will be 5 density-independent pixels around the border of the entire GUI. The **Stretch columns** property indicates that the columns should stretch horizontally to fill the layout's width.

Step 5: Adding the **`TableRows`**

Next, use the **Outline** window as you did in Chapter 4 to add five `TableRows` to the `TableLayout`. Select the `TableLayout` each time before adding the next `TableRow`, so that the `TableRows` are properly nested in the `TableLayout`. Change the **Id** properties of the five `TableRows` to `tableRow0`, `tableRow1`, `tableRow2`, `tableRow3` and `tableRow4`, respectively. Also, select each `TableRow` and set its **Layout width** property to `match_parent` so that the rows are the full width of the layout.

Step 6: Adding the Components to the **`TableRows`**

Using Figs. 5.6–5.7 as your guide, add the `EditTexts`, `Buttons`, `TextView` and `ScrollView` to the layout. Also, place a `TableLayout` inside the `ScrollView`. Name the elements as shown in Fig. 5.7. Study the XML elements in `main.xml` (Fig. 5.11) to see the values specified for the attributes of each GUI component. We've highlighted the new features and key features for this example.

```
<?xml version="1.0" encoding="utf-8"?>
<TableLayout xmlns:android="http://schemas.android.com/apk/res/android"
   android:id="@+id/tableLayout" android:layout_width="match_parent"
   android:layout_height="match_parent" android:padding="5dp"
   android:stretchColumns="*" android:background="@android:color/white">

   <!-- tableRow0 -->
   <TableRow android:id="@+id/tableRow0"
      android:layout_height="wrap_content"
      android:layout_width="match_parent">
      <EditText android:layout_width="match_parent"
         android:layout_height="wrap_content" android:layout_span="2"
```

Fig. 5.11 | **Favorite Twitter Search** app's XML layout. (Part 1 of 3.)

```
         android:inputType="text" android:id="@+id/queryEditText"
         android:hint="@string/queryPrompt"
         android:imeOptions="actionNext">
      </EditText>
   </TableRow>

   <!-- tableRow1 -->
   <TableRow android:id="@+id/tableRow1"
      android:layout_height="wrap_content"
      android:layout_width="match_parent">
      <EditText android:layout_height="wrap_content"
         android:hint="@string/tagPrompt" android:inputType="text"
         android:id="@+id/tagEditText" android:imeOptions="actionDone"
         android:layout_gravity="center_vertical"></EditText>
      <Button android:id="@+id/saveButton"
         android:layout_height="wrap_content"
         android:layout_width="wrap_content"
         android:layout_gravity="center_vertical"
         android:text="@string/save"></Button>
   </TableRow>

   <!-- tableRow2 -->
   <TableRow android:id="@+id/tableRow2"
      android:layout_height="wrap_content"
      android:layout_width="match_parent"
      android:background="@color/light_orange">

      <TextView android:layout_height="wrap_content"
         android:id="@+id/taggedSearchesTextView"
         android:text="@string/taggedSearches"
         android:layout_width="match_parent"
         android:layout_gravity="center_horizontal"
         android:layout_span="2" android:textSize="18sp"
         android:textColor="@android:color/black"
         android:padding="5dp"></TextView>
   </TableRow>

   <!-- tableRow3 -->
   <TableRow android:id="@+id/tableRow3"
      android:background="@color/light_orange"
      android:layout_height="wrap_content"
      android:layout_width="match_parent" android:layout_weight="1">

      <ScrollView android:id="@+id/queryScrollView"
         android:layout_width="match_parent"
         android:layout_span="2" android:padding-"5dp">
         <TableLayout android:id="@+id/queryTableLayout"
            android:layout_width="match_parent"
            android:layout_height="match_parent" android:padding="5dp"
            android:stretchColumns="*"></TableLayout>
      </ScrollView>
   </TableRow>

```

Fig. 5.11 | **Favorite Twitter Search** app's XML layout. (Part 2 of 3.)

```
66     <!-- tableRow4 -->
67     <TableRow android:id="@+id/tableRow4"
68        android:layout_height="wrap_content"
69        android:layout_width="match_parent">
70
71        <Button android:layout_width="wrap_content"
72           android:layout_height="wrap_content"
73           android:text="@string/clearTags"
74           android:id="@+id/clearTagsButton"
75           android:layout_span="2" android:layout_marginTop="5dp"></Button>
76     </TableRow>
77  </TableLayout>
```

Fig. 5.11 | **Favorite Twitter Search** app's XML layout. (Part 3 of 3.)

Key Features in `main.xml`

Recall from Chapter 4 that the `android:layout_span` attribute (lines 12, 45, 58 and 75) *must* be specified directly in the XML, as it does *not* display in the **Properties** window in design view. We've highlighted the resources from the `colors.xml`, `dimen.xml` and `strings.xml` files that were used to set various properties of the GUI components. You can access the various resource values in XML as follows:

- Strings: Specify `@string/` followed by the name of the resource—for example, lines 14 and 31 specify string resource values for the ***`android:hint`*** attribute of the each `EditText`. This attribute displays inside an `EditText` a hint that helps the user understand the `EditText`'s purpose. We use other string resources to represent the text on various GUI components, such as the `Buttons` (lines 31 and 73) and the `TextView` (line 41).
- Colors: Specify `@color/` followed by the name of the resource—for example, lines 38 and 52 specify a color resource for the background color of `tableRow2` and the `ScrollView`, respectively.

Lines 15 and 25 introduce the `EditText` attribute **`android:imeOptions`**, which enables you to configure options for the current input method. For example, when `queryEditText` has the focus and the soft keyboard is displayed, the keyboard contains a **Next** button—specified with the `android:imeOptions` attribute value `actionNext` (line 15). If the user touches this button, the focus is transfered to the next component that can accept text input—`tagEditText`. When `tagEditText` has the focus, the soft keyboard contains a **Done** button—specified with the `android:imeOptions` attribute value `actionDone` (line 25). If the user touches this button, the system hides the soft keyboard.

Lines 27–31 and 71–75 define the `Buttons` for saving a search and clearing all previously saved searches, respectively. Lines 56–63 define a `ScrollView` that contains a `TableLayout` (lines 59–62) in which the search `Buttons` will be displayed programmatically. The `TableLayout`'s `android:stretchColumns` attribute is set to `"*"` so that the contents of each `TableRow` we programmatically place in this `TableLayout` can stretch to fill the layout's width. If there are more search `Buttons` than can be displayed on the screen, you can drag your finger up or down the `ScrollView` to scroll through the `Buttons` in the `TableLayout`. As you'll see in Section 5.5, this `TableLayout` will contain `TableRows` that each contain a search `Button` and an **Edit** `Button`.

You'll notice in line 54 that we set `tableRow3`'s `android:layout_weight` attribute to `1`. This value makes `tableRow3` more important than the other rows when the main table layout is resized based on the available space. Because `tableRow3` is the only component to that specifies a `android:layout_weight` attribute, it stretches vertically to occupy all remaining vertical space that is not occupied by the other rows.

5.4.5 Creating a `TableRow` That Displays a Search and an Edit `Button`

Next, you'll define a `TableRow` that will be programmatically inflated to create each search `Button` and corresponding **Edit** `Button`. In Section 5.5, you'll configure these `Buttons` and add this `TableRow` to the `queryTableLayout` (Fig. 5.11, lines 59–62) to display the `Buttons`. To create another layout XML file:

1. Right click the layout folder and select **New > Other...** to display the **New** dialog.
2. In the **Android** node, select **Android XML File** and click **Next >** to display the **New Android XML File** dialog.
3. In the **File** text field, enter the name `new_tag_view.xml`.
4. Under **What type of resource would you like to create?**, select the **Layout** radio button. This places the new file `new_tag_view.xml` into the project's `res/layout` folder.
5. At the bottom of the dialog, you can select the *root element* for the new layout. Choose `TableRow`.
6. Click **Finish** to create the file. The file opens immediately in **XML** view.
7. Switch to **Graphical Layout** tab in the Visual Layout Editor, then select Android 2.3.3 from the SDK selector drop-down list at the top-right side of the **Graphical Layout** tab and **3.7in WVGA (Nexus One)** from the Device Configurations drop-down list at the top-left side of the **Graphical Layout** tab.

Add two `Buttons` to the layout. Configure the `Buttons`' and the layout's properties as shown in (Fig. 5.12). We didn't specify the `android:text` attribute for the `newTagButton` because we'll set this text to a particular search tag when the `Buttons` are created programmatically. We set the `TableLayout`'s `android:background` attribute to the predefined color ***`transparent`*** (line 6), so that the background color of the `ScrollView` will show through when we attach the `TableRow` to the `ScrollView`. By default, the `ScrollView` has the same background color as its parent—that is, `tableRow3`. In lines 9 and 12, notice that we use `@dimen/` followed by the name of a dimension resource to specify the `Buttons`' widths.

```
1  <?xml version="1.0" encoding="UTF-8"?>
2  <TableRow xmlns:android="http://schemas.android.com/apk/res/android"
3     android:id="@+id/newTagTableRow"
4     android:layout_width="match_parent"
5     android:layout_height="wrap_content"
6     android:background="@android:color/transparent">
7
```

Fig. 5.12 | The `newTagTableRow` that will be programmatically inflated. (Part 1 of 2.)

```
   <Button android:id="@+id/newTagButton"
      android:layout_width="@dimen/tagButtonWidth"
      android:layout_height="wrap_content"></Button>
   <Button android:id="@+id/newEditButton"
      android:layout_width="@dimen/editButtonWidth"
      android:layout_height="wrap_content"
      android:text="@string/edit"></Button>
</TableRow>
```

Fig. 5.12 | The `newTagTableRow` that will be programmatically inflated. (Part 2 of 2.)

5.5 Building the App

Figures 5.13–5.23 implement the **Favorite Twitter Searches** app in the single class `FavoriteTwitterSearches`, which extends `Activity`.

The `package` *and* `import` *Statements*

Figure 5.13 shows the app's `package` and `import` statements. The `package` statement (line 4) indicates that the class in this file is part of the `com.deitel.favoritetwittersearches` package. This line was inserted by the IDE when you created the project. The `import` statements in lines 6–23 import the various classes and interfaces the app uses.

```
1  // FavoriteTwitterSearches.java
2  // Stores Twitter search queries and tags for easily opening them
3  // in a browser.
4  package com.deitel.favoritetwittersearches;
5
6  import java.util.Arrays;
7
8  import android.app.Activity;
9  import android.app.AlertDialog;
10 import android.content.Context;
11 import android.content.DialogInterface;
12 import android.content.Intent;
13 import android.content.SharedPreferences;
14 import android.net.Uri;
15 import android.os.Bundle;
16 import android.view.LayoutInflater;
17 import android.view.View;
18 import android.view.View.OnClickListener;
19 import android.view.inputmethod.InputMethodManager;
20 import android.widget.Button;
21 import android.widget.EditText;
22 import android.widget.TableLayout;
23 import android.widget.TableRow;
24
```

Fig. 5.13 | `FavoriteTwitterSearches`' `package` and `import` statements.

Line 6 imports the `Arrays` class from the `java.util` package. We'll use this class's `sort` method to sort the tags that represent each search so they appear in alphabetical order. Of the remaining `import` statements, we consider only those for the classes being introduced in this chapter.

- **Class `AlertDialog` of package `android.app`** (line 9) is used to display dialogs.
- **Class `Context` of package `android.content`** (line 10) provides access to information about the environment in which the app is running and allows you to access various Android services. We'll be using a constant from this class with a `LayoutInflater` (discussed below) to help load new GUI components dynamically.
- **Class `DialogInterface` of package `android.content`** (line 11) contains the nested interface ***`OnClickListener`***. We implement this interface to handle the events that occur when the user touches a button on an `AlertDialog`.
- **Class `Intent` of package `android.content`** (line 12) enables us to work with `Intents`. An `Intent` specifies an *action* to be performed and the *data* to be acted upon—Android uses `Intents` to launch the appropriate activities.
- **Class `SharedPreferences` of package `android.content`** (line 13) is used to manipulate persistent key/value pairs that are stored in files associated with the app.
- **Class `Uri` of package `android.net`** (line 14) enables us to convert an Internet URL into the format required by an `Intent` that launches the device's web browser. We'll say more about URIs and URLs in Section 5.5.
- **Class `LayoutInflater` of package `android.view`** (line 16) enables us to inflate an XML layout file dynamically to create the layout's GUI components.
- **Class `InputMethodManager` of package `android.view.inputmethod`** (line 19) enables us to hide the soft keyboard when the user saves a search.
- **Package `android.widget`** (lines 20–23) contains the widgets (i.e., GUI components) and layouts that are used in Android GUIs. **Class `Button` of package `android.widget`** (line 20) represents a simple push button that the user touches to get the app to perform a specific action. You implement **interface `View.OnClickListener` of package `android.view`** (line 18) to specify the code that should execute when the user touches a `Button`.

Favorite Twitter Searches App `Activity`

`FavoriteTwitterSearches` (Figs. 5.14–5.23) is the **Favorite Twitter Searches** app's only `Activity` class. When you created the `FavoriteTwitterSearches` project, the ADT Plugin generated this class as a subclass of `Activity` (Fig. 5.14, line 26) and provided the shell of an overridden `onCreate` method, which every `Activity` subclass *must* override.

```
25 // main (and only) Activity class for the Favorite Twitter Searches app
26 public class FavoriteTwitterSearches extends Activity
27 {
28    private SharedPreferences savedSearches; // user's favorite searches
29    private TableLayout queryTableLayout; // shows the search buttons
30    private EditText queryEditText; // where the user enters queries
31    private EditText tagEditText; // where the user enters a query's tag
32
```

Fig. 5.14 | Class `FavoriteTwitterSearches` is a subclass of `Activity`.

Line 28 declares the `SharedPreferences` instance variable `savedSearches`. `SharedPreferences` objects store *key/value pairs* in which the keys are `String`s and the values are primitive types or `String`s. We use the `SharedPreferences` object to store the user's saved searches. Line 29 declares the `TableLayout` that will be used to access the part of the GUI in which we programmatically display new buttons. Lines 30–31 declare two `EditText`s that we'll use to access the queries and tags the user enters at the top of the app.

Overridden Method `OnCreate` *of Class* `Activity`

The `onCreate` method (Fig. 5.15) is called by the system

- when the app loads
- if the app's process was killed by the operating system while the app was in the background, and the app is then restored
- each time the configuration changes, such as when the user rotates the device or opens/closes a physical keyboard.

The method initializes the `Activity`'s instance variables and GUI components—we keep it simple so the app loads quickly. Line 37 makes the required call to the superclass's `onCreate` method. As in the previous app, the call to `setContentView` (line 38) passes the constant `R.layout.main` to inflate the GUI from `main.xml`. Method `setContentView` uses this constant to load the corresponding XML document, then inflates the GUI.

```
33     // called when the activity is first created
34     @Override
35     public void onCreate(Bundle savedInstanceState)
36     {
37        super.onCreate(savedInstanceState); // call the superclass version
38        setContentView(R.layout.main); // set the layout
39
40        // get the SharedPreferences that contains the user's saved searches
41        savedSearches = getSharedPreferences("searches", MODE_PRIVATE);
42
43        // get a reference to the queryTableLayout
44        queryTableLayout =
45           (TableLayout) findViewById(R.id.queryTableLayout);
46
47        // get references to the two EditTexts and the Save Button
48        queryEditText = (EditText) findViewById(R.id.queryEditText);
49        tagEditText = (EditText) findViewById(R.id.tagEditText);
50
51        // register listeners for the Save and Clear Tags Buttons
52        Button saveButton = (Button) findViewById(R.id.saveButton);
53        saveButton.setOnClickListener(saveButtonListener);
54        Button clearTagsButton =
55          (Button) findViewById(R.id.clearTagsButton);
56        clearTagsButton.setOnClickListener(clearTagsButtonListener);
57
58        refreshButtons(null); // add previously saved searches to GUI
59     } // end method onCreate
60
```

Fig. 5.15 | Overriding `Activity` method `onCreate`.

Line 41 uses the method **getSharedPreferences** (inherited indirectly from class Context) to get a SharedPreferences object that can read *tag/query pairs* stored previously (if any) from the "searches" file. The first argument indicates the name of the file that contains the data. The second argument specifies the accessibility of the file and can be set to one of the following options:

- **MODE_PRIVATE**—The file is accessible *only* to this app. In most cases, you'll use this constant as the second argument to getSharedPreferences.
- **MODE_WORLD_READABLE**—Any app on the device can *read* from the file.
- **MODE_WORLD_WRITABLE**—Any app on the device can *write* to the file.

These constants can be combined with the bitwise OR operator (|).

We aren't reading a lot of data in this app, so it's fast enough to load the searches in onCreate—*lengthy data access should never be done in the UI thread; otherwise, the app will display an Application Not Responding (ANR) dialog—typically after five seconds of inactivity.* For more information about ANR dialogs and designing responsive apps, see

```
developer.android.com/guide/practices/design/responsiveness.html
```

Lines 44–49 obtain references to the queryTableLayout, queryEditText and tagEditText to initialize the corresponding instance variables. Lines 52–56 obtain references to the saveButton and clearTagsButton and register their listeners. Finally, line 58 calls refreshButtons (discussed in Fig. 5.16) to create Buttons for the previously saved searches and their corresponding **Edit** buttons that allow the user to edit each search.

refreshButtons Method of Class FavoriteTwitterSearches

Method refreshButtons of class FavoriteTwitterSearches (Fig. 5.16) creates and displays new query tag and edit Buttons either for a newly saved search (when its argument is not null) or for all saved searches (when its argument is null).

We'd like to display the Buttons in *alphabetical order* so the user can easily scan them to find a search to perform. First, lines 66–67 get an array of Strings representing the keys in the SharedPreferences object. SharedPreferences method **getAll** returns a Map containing all the key/value pairs. We then call **keySet** on that object to get a Set of all the keys. Finally, we call **toArray** (with an empty String array as an argument) on the Set object to convert the Set into an array of Strings, which we then sort in line 68. **Arrays.sort** (a static method of class Arrays from package java.util) sorts the array in its first argument. Since the user could enter tags using mixtures of uppercase and lowercase letters, we chose to perform a *case-insensitive sort* by passing the predefined Comparator<String> object **String.CASE_INSENSITIVE_ORDER** as the second argument to Arrays.sort.

```
61    // recreate search tag and edit Buttons for all saved searches;
62    // pass null to create all the tag and edit Buttons.
63    private void refreshButtons(String newTag)
64    {
```

Fig. 5.16 | refreshButtons method of class FavoriteTwitterSearches recreates and displays new search tag and edit Buttons for all saved searches. (Part 1 of 2.)

```
65         // store saved tags in the tags array
66         String[] tags =
67            savedSearches.getAll().keySet().toArray(new String[0]);
68         Arrays.sort(tags, String.CASE_INSENSITIVE_ORDER); // sort by tag
69
70         // if a new tag was added, insert in GUI at the appropriate location
71         if (newTag != null)
72         {
73            makeTagGUI(newTag, Arrays.binarySearch(tags, newTag));
74         } // end if
75         else // display GUI for all tags
76         {
77            // display all saved searches
78            for (int index = 0; index < tags.length; ++index)
79               makeTagGUI(tags[index], index);
80         } // end else
81      } // end method refreshButtons
82
```

Fig. 5.16 | `refreshButtons` method of class `FavoriteTwitterSearches` recreates and displays new search tag and edit `Buttons` for all saved searches. (Part 2 of 2.)

Lines 71–80 determine whether the method was called to create the GUI for one new search or for all the saved searches. Line 73 calls `makeTagGUI` (Fig. 5.18) to insert the GUI for one new tag. The call to **`Arrays.binarySearch`** in the second argument locates the insertion point that enables us to maintain the tag buttons in alphabetical order. When `refreshButtons` is called with a null argument, lines 78–79 call `makeTagGUI` for every saved search.

`makeTag` Method of Class `FavoriteTwitterSearches`

Method `makeTag` of class `FavoriteTwitterSearches` (Fig. 5.17) adds a new search to `savedSearches` or modifies an existing search. Line 87 uses `SharedPreferences` method **`getString`** to look up the previous value, if any, associated with `tag`. If the `tag` does not already exist in the file, the second argument (`null` in this case) is returned. In this case, the method also calls `refreshButtons` (line 96) to add the GUI for the new search.

```
83      // add new search to the save file, then refresh all Buttons
84      private void makeTag(String query, String tag)
85      {
86         // originalQuery will be null if we're modifying an existing search
87         String originalQuery = savedSearches.getString(tag, null);
88
89         // get a SharedPreferences.Editor to store new tag/query pair
90         SharedPreferences.Editor preferencesEditor = savedSearches.edit();
91         preferencesEditor.putString(tag, query); // store current search
92         preferencesEditor.apply(); // store the updated preferences
93
```

Fig. 5.17 | `makeTag` method of class `FavoriteTwitterSearches` adds a new search to the save file, then resets the `Buttons`. (Part 1 of 2.)

```
94         // if this is a new query, add its GUI
95         if (originalQuery == null)
96            refreshButtons(tag); // adds a new button for this tag
97      } // end method makeTag
98
```

Fig. 5.17 | `makeTag` method of class `FavoriteTwitterSearches` adds a new search to the save file, then resets the `Buttons`. (Part 2 of 2.)

Lines 90–92 add the new `tag` or modify the existing `tag`'s corresponding value. To modify the file associated with a `SharedPreferences` object, you must first call its ***edit* method** to obtain a `SharedPreferences.Editor` object (line 90). This object provides methods for adding key/value pairs to, removing key/value pairs from, and modifying the value associated with a particular key in a `SharedPreferences` file. Line 91 calls its ***putString* method** to save the new search's tag (the key) and query (the corresponding value). Line 92 *commits* the changes to the `"searches"` file by calling `SharedPreferences.Editor` method ***apply*** to make the changes to the file.

makeTagGUI Method of Class FavoriteTwitterSearches

Method `makeTagGUI` of class `FavoriteTwitterSearches` (Fig. 5.18) adds to the `queryTableLayout` one new row containing a tag and an **Edit** button. To do this, we first inflate the `new_tag_view.xml` layout that you created in Section 5.4.5. Recall that this layout consists of a `TableRow` with a `newTagButton` and a `newEditButton`.

Android provides a *service* that enables you to *inflate a layout*. To use this service, you obtain a reference to it (lines 103–104) by calling the `Activity`'s inherited ***getSystemService* method** with the argument ***Context.LAYOUT_INFLATER_SERVICE***. Since `getSystemService` can return references to various system services, you must *cast* the result to type `LayoutInflater`. Line 107 calls the `LayoutInflater`'s ***inflate* method** with the `R.layout.new_tag_view` constant that represents the `new_tag_view.xml` layout. This returns a reference to a `View`, which is actually the `TableRow` containing the `Buttons`. Lines 110–113 get a reference to the `newTagButton`, set its text to the value of `tag` and register its `OnClickListener`. Lines 116–118 get a reference to the `newEditButton` and register its `OnClickListener`. Line 121 adds the `newTagView` to the `queryTableLayout` at the specified `index`.

```
99      // add a new tag button and corresponding edit button to the GUI
100     private void makeTagGUI(String tag, int index)
101     {
102        // get a reference to the LayoutInflater service
103        LayoutInflater inflater = (LayoutInflater) getSystemService(
104           Context.LAYOUT_INFLATER_SERVICE);
105
106        // inflate new_tag_view.xml to create new tag and edit Buttons
107        View newTagView = inflater.inflate(R.layout.new_tag_view, null);
108
```

Fig. 5.18 | `makeTagGUI` method of class `FavoriteTwitterSearches` creates the tag and **Edit** `Button`'s for one search and adds them to the `queryTableLayout` at the specified index. (Part 1 of 2.)

```
      // get newTagButton, set its text and register its listener
      Button newTagButton =
         (Button) newTagView.findViewById(R.id.newTagButton);
      newTagButton.setText(tag);
      newTagButton.setOnClickListener(queryButtonListener);

      // get newEditButton and register its listener
      Button newEditButton =
         (Button) newTagView.findViewById(R.id.newEditButton);
      newEditButton.setOnClickListener(editButtonListener);

      // add new tag and edit buttons to queryTableLayout
      queryTableLayout.addView(newTagView, index);
   } // end makeTagGUI

```

Fig. 5.18 | `makeTagGUI` method of class `FavoriteTwitterSearches` creates the tag and **Edit** `Button`'s for one search and adds them to the `queryTableLayout` at the specified index. (Part 2 of 2.)

`clearButtons` Method of Class `FavoriteTwitterSearches`

Method `clearButtons` (Fig. 5.19) removes all of the saved search `Buttons` from the app. Line 128 calls the `queryTableLayout`'s **`removeAllViews` method** to remove all of the nested `TableRows` containing the `Buttons`.

```
124    // remove all saved search Buttons from the app
125    private void clearButtons()
126    {
127       // remove all saved search Buttons
128       queryTableLayout.removeAllViews();
129    } // end method clearButtons
130
```

Fig. 5.19 | method `clearButtons` of class `FavoriteTwitterSearches` removes all the `Buttons` representing the saved searches from the app.

Anonymous Inner Class That Implements Interface `OnClickListener` to Respond to the Events of the `saveButton`

Lines 132–170 (Fig. 5.20) create the anonymous inner-class object `saveButtonListener` that implements interface `OnClickListener`. Line 53 registered `saveButtonListener` as `saveButtons`'s event-handling object. Lines 134–169 implement the `OnClickListener` interface's `onClick` method. If the user entered both a query and a tag (lines 138–139), the method calls `makeTag` (Fig. 5.17) to store the tag/query pair (lines 141–142), then clears the two `EditTexts` (lines 143–144) and hides the soft keyboard (lines 147–149).

If the user did not enter both a query and a tag, the method displays an `AlertDialog` (lines 151–168) indicating that the user must enter both a query and a tag. You use an `AlertDialog.Builder` object (created at lines 154–155) to configure and create an `AlertDialog`. The argument to the constructor is the `Context` in which the dialog will be displayed—in this case, the `FavoriteTwitterSearches Activity`, which we refer to via its `this` reference. Because we're accessing `this` from an anonymous inner class, we must

```
131      // create a new Button and add it to the ScrollView
132      public OnClickListener saveButtonListener = new OnClickListener()
133      {
134         @Override
135         public void onClick(View v)
136         {
137            // create tag if both queryEditText and tagEditText are not empty
138            if (queryEditText.getText().length() > 0 &&
139               tagEditText.getText().length() > 0)
140            {
141               makeTag(queryEditText.getText().toString(),
142                  tagEditText.getText().toString());
143               queryEditText.setText(""); // clear queryEditText
144               tagEditText.setText(""); // clear tagEditText
145
146               // hide the soft keyboard
147               ((InputMethodManager) getSystemService(
148                  Context.INPUT_METHOD_SERVICE)).hideSoftInputFromWindow(
149                  tagEditText.getWindowToken(), 0);
150            } // end if
151            else // display message asking user to provide a query and a tag
152            {
153               // create a new AlertDialog Builder
154               AlertDialog.Builder builder =
155                  new AlertDialog.Builder(FavoriteTwitterSearches.this);
156
157               builder.setTitle(R.string.missingTitle); // title bar string
158
159               // provide an OK button that simply dismisses the dialog
160               builder.setPositiveButton(R.string.OK, null);
161
162               // set the message to display
163               builder.setMessage(R.string.missingMessage);
164
165               // create AlertDialog from the AlertDialog.Builder
166               AlertDialog errorDialog = builder.create();
167               errorDialog.show(); // display the Dialog
168            } // end else
169         } // end method onClick
170      }; // end OnClickListener anonymous inner class
171
```

Fig. 5.20 | Anonymous inner class that implements interface `OnClickListener` to respond to the events of the `saveButton`.

fully qualify it with the class name. Line 157 sets the `AlertDialog`'s title with the `String` resource `R.string.missingTitle`. This will appear at the top of the dialog.

Dialogs often have multiple buttons. In this case, we need only one button that allows the user to acknowledge the message. We specify this as the dialog's positive button (line 160). Method `setPositiveButton` receives the button's label (specified with the `String` resource `R.string.OK`) and a reference to the button's event handler. For this dialog, we don't need to respond to the event, so we specify `null` for the event handler. When the user touches the button, the dialog is simply dismissed from the screen.

Line 163 sets the message that appears in the dialog (specified with the `String` resource `R.string.missingMessage`). Line 166 creates the `AlertDialog` by calling the `AlertDialog.Builder`'s `create` method. Line 167 displays the modal dialog by calling `AlertDialog`'s `show` method.

Anonymous Inner Class That Implements Interface `OnClickListener` *to Respond to the Events of the* `clearTagsButton`

Lines 173–213 of Fig. 5.21 create the anonymous inner-class object `clearTagsButton-Listener` that implements interface `OnClickListener`. Line 56 registered this object as `clearTagsButtons`'s event handler. Lines 175–212 implement the `OnClickListener` interface's `onClick` method, which displays an `AlertDialog` asking the user to confirm that all the stored searches should be removed.

```
172     // clears all saved searches
173     public OnClickListener clearTagsButtonListener = new OnClickListener()
174     {
175        @Override
176        public void onClick(View v)
177        {
178           // create a new AlertDialog Builder
179           AlertDialog.Builder builder =
180              new AlertDialog.Builder(FavoriteTwitterSearches.this);
181
182           builder.setTitle(R.string.confirmTitle); // title bar string
183
184           // provide an OK button that simply dismisses the dialog
185           builder.setPositiveButton(R.string.erase,
186              new DialogInterface.OnClickListener()
187              {
188                 @Override
189                 public void onClick(DialogInterface dialog, int button)
190                 {
191                    clearButtons(); // clear all saved searches from the map
192
193                    // get a SharedPreferences.Editor to clear searches
194                    SharedPreferences.Editor preferencesEditor =
195                       savedSearches.edit();
196
197                    preferencesEditor.clear(); // remove all tag/query pairs
198                    preferencesEditor.apply(); // commit the changes
199                 } // end method onClick
200              } // end anonymous inner class
201           ); // end call to method setPositiveButton
202
203           builder.setCancelable(true);
204           builder.setNegativeButton(R.string.cancel, null);
205
206           // set the message to display
207           builder.setMessage(R.string.confirmMessage);
```

Fig. 5.21 | Anonymous inner class that implements interface `OnClickListener` to respond to the events of the `clearTagsButton`. (Part 1 of 2.)

```
208
209          // create AlertDialog from the AlertDialog.Builder
210          AlertDialog confirmDialog = builder.create();
211          confirmDialog.show(); // display the Dialog
212       } // end method onClick
213    }; // end OnClickListener anonymous inner class
214
```

Fig. 5.21 | Anonymous inner class that implements interface `OnClickListener` to respond to the events of the `clearTagsButton`. (Part 2 of 2.)

Lines 185–201 define the `AlertDialog`'s positive button and its event handler. When the user clicks this button, its event handler executes. Line 191 calls `clearButtons` (Fig. 5.19) to remove all the `Buttons` representing the saved searches. Then, we get a `SharedPreferences.Editor` object for `savedSearches` (lines 194–195), clear all the *key/value pairs* by calling the `SharedPreferences.Editor` object's ***`clear`* method** (line 192) and *commit* the changes to the file (line 198). Line 203 indicates that the dialog is cancelable, so the user can press the back button on the device to dismiss the dialog. Line 204 sets the dialog's negative button and event handler. Like the positive button in Fig. 5.20, this button simply dismisses the dialog. Lines 207–211 set the dialog's message, create the dialog and display it.

Anonymous Inner Class That Implements Interface `OnClickListener` *to Respond to the Events of each of the* `newTagButtons`

Lines 216–234 of Fig. 5.22 create the anonymous inner-class object `queryButtonListener` that implements interface `OnClickListener`. Line 113 registers this object as the event-handling object for each of the `newTagButtons` as they're created.

Lines 218–233 implement the `OnClickListener` interface's `onClick` method. Line 222 gets the text of the `Button` that was clicked, and line 223 retrieves the corresponding search query from `savedSearches`. Line 226 call `Activity`'s inherited method **`getString`** to get the `String` resource named `searchURL`, which contains the Twitter search page's URL. We then append the `query` to the end of the URL.

```
215    // load selected search in a web browser
216    public OnClickListener queryButtonListener = new OnClickListener()
217    {
218       @Override
219       public void onClick(View v)
220       {
221          // get the query
222          String buttonText = ((Button)v).getText().toString();
223          String query = savedSearches.getString(buttonText, null);
224
225          // create the URL corresponding to the touched Button's query
226          String urlString = getString(R.string.searchURL) + query;
227
```

Fig. 5.22 | Anonymous inner class that implements interface `OnClickListener` to respond to the events of the `queryButton`. (Part 1 of 2.)

```
228            // create an Intent to launch a web browser
229            Intent getURL = new Intent(Intent.ACTION_VIEW,
230               Uri.parse(urlString));
231
232            startActivity(getURL); // execute the Intent
233         } // end method onClick
234      }; // end OnClickListener anonymous inner class
235
```

Fig. 5.22 | Anonymous inner class that implements interface `OnClickListener` to respond to the events of the `queryButton`. (Part 2 of 2.)

Lines 229–230 create a new `Intent`, which we'll use to launch the device's web browser and display the Twitter search results. An `Intent` is a description of an *action* to be performed with associated *data*. The first argument passed to `Intent`'s constructor is a constant describing the *action* we wish to perform. Here we use **`Intent.ACTION_VIEW`** because we wish to display a representation of the data. Many constants are defined in the `Intent` class describing actions such as *searching*, *choosing*, *sending* and *playing*. The second argument (line 230) is a **`Uri`** (uniform resource identifier) to the *data* on which we want to perform the action. Class `Uri`'s **parse method** converts a `String` representing a URL (uniform resource locator) to a `Uri`.

Line 232 passes the `Intent` to the `startActivity` method (inherited indirectly from class `Context`) which starts the correct `Activity` to perform the specified action on the given data. In this case, because we've said to view a URI, the `Intent` launches the device's web browser to display the corresponding web page. This page shows the results of the supplied Twitter search. This is an example of an **implicit `Intent`**—*we did not specify a component to display the web page but instead allowed the system to launch the most appropriate `Activity` based on the type of data.* If multiple activities can handle the action and data passed to `startActivity`, the system displays a dialog in which the user can select which activity to use. If the system cannot find an activity to handle the action, then method `startActivity` throws an `ActivityNotFoundException`. In general, it's a good practice to handle this exception. We chose not to here, because Android devices on which this app is likely to be installed will have a browser capable of displaying a web page.

In future apps, we'll also use **explicit `Intents`**, which specify an exact `Activity` class to run in the same app. For a list of apps and the intents they support, visit

```
openintents.org
developer.android.com/guide/appendix/g-app-intents.html
```

Anonymous Inner Class That Implements Interface `OnClickListener` to Respond to the Events of the `editButton`

Lines 237–253 of Fig. 5.23 create the anonymous inner-class object `editButtonListener` that implements interface `OnClickListener`. Line 118 registers this object as each `newEditButtons`'s event-handling object. Lines 239–252 implement the `onClick` method of interface `OnClickListener`. To determine which search `Button`'s query to edit, we first get the `editButton`'s *parent layout* (line 243)—the one that contains the `editButton`—then use it to get the `Button` with the ID `R.id.newTagButton` in that layout (lines 244–245)—this is the corresponding search `Button`. Line 247 gets the `searchButton`'s text, then uses it in line 250 to set the `tagEditText`'s value. Finally, line 251 gets the corresponding query from the `savedSearches` object and displays that value in the `queryEditText`.

```
236      // edit selected search
237      public OnClickListener editButtonListener = new OnClickListener()
238      {
239         @Override
240         public void onClick(View v)
241         {
242            // get all necessary GUI components
243            TableRow buttonTableRow = (TableRow) v.getParent();
244            Button searchButton =
245               (Button) buttonTableRow.findViewById(R.id.newTagButton);
246
247            String tag = searchButton.getText().toString();
248
249            // set EditTexts to match the chosen tag and query
250            tagEditText.setText(tag);
251            queryEditText.setText(savedSearches.getString(tag, null));
252         } // end method onClick
253      }; // end OnClickListener anonymous inner class
254   } // end class FavoriteTwitterSearches
```

Fig. 5.23 | Anonymous inner class that implements interface `OnClickListener` to respond to the events of the `editButton`.

5.6 AndroidManifest.xml

When you create the project for each Android app in Eclipse, the ADT Plugin creates and configures the `AndroidManifest.xml` file (also known as the app's *manifest*), which describes information about the app. Here, we introduce the contents of this file (Fig. 5.24) and discuss one new feature we added to it. We'll discuss other manifest features file as they're needed in later apps. For complete details of the manifest, visit:

```
developer.android.com/guide/topics/manifest/manifest-intro.html
```

The **`manifest` element** (lines 2–17) is the root element of `AndroidManifest.xml`. This element's `package` attribute (line 3) specifies the package that's used to manage the code. The element's `android:versionCode` attribute (line 4) specifies an internal integer version number for your app that's used to determine whether one version of the app is newer than another. The element's `android:versionName` attribute (line 4) specifies the version number that is displayed to users when they're managing apps on a device.

Within the `manifest` element are the nested `application` (lines 5–15) and `uses-sdk` (line 16) elements. The **`application` element** is required. The element's **`android:icon` attribute** specifies a drawable resource which is used as the app's icon. If you don't provide your own icon, the app uses the icon that is supplied by the ADT Plugin when you create the app's project. Versions of this icon are stored in app's `res/drawable` folders. The element's **`android:label` attribute** specifies the app's name. The **`uses-sdk` element** specifies the app's target SDK (10 represents Android SDK version 2.3.3) and its minimum SDK (8 represents version 2.2). These settings allow this app to execute on devices running Android versions 2.2 and higher.

```
1  <?xml version="1.0" encoding="utf-8"?>
2  <manifest xmlns:android="http://schemas.android.com/apk/res/android"
3     package="com.deitel.favoritetwittersearches"
4     android:versionCode="1" android:versionName="1.0">
5     <application android:icon="@drawable/icon"
6        android:label="@string/app_name">
7        <activity android:name=".FavoriteTwitterSearches"
8           android:label="@string/app_name"
9           android:windowSoftInputMode="stateAlwaysHidden">
10          <intent-filter>
11             <action android:name="android.intent.action.MAIN" />
12             <category android:name="android.intent.category.LAUNCHER" />
13          </intent-filter>
14       </activity>
15    </application>
16    <uses-sdk android:targetSdkVersion="10" android:minSdkVersion="8"/>
17 </manifest>
```

Fig. 5.24 | `AndroidManifest.xml` file for the **Favorite Twitter Searches** app.

Within the application element is the **`activity` element** (lines 7–14), which specifies information about this app's `Activity`. If the app has more than one `Activity`, each will have its own `activity` element. The **`android:name` attribute** (line 7) specifies the `Activity`'s fully qualified class name. If you precede the class name with just a dot (`.`), the class name is automatically appended to the package name specified in the `manifest` element. The **`android:label` attribute** (line 8) specifies a string that is displayed with the `Activity`. By default, the manifest was configured with the app's name for this attribute. We added the **`android:windowSoftInputMode` attribute** in line 9. The value `stateAlwaysHidden` indicates that the soft keyboard should not be displayed when this `Activity` is launched. To add this attribute, you can either edit the XML directly, or you can double click the `AndroidManifest.xml` file in your project to open the manifest editor. Figure 5.25 shows the **Application** tab of the manifest editor. The tab names are at the bottom of the editor window. To set the `android:windowSoftInputMode` attribute, select `.FavoriteTwitterSearches` in the **Application Nodes** section of the window (at the bottom-left side). This displays the activity elements attributes at the bottom-right of the editor. Scroll to **Window soft input mode** and click the **Select...** button to see the available options, then select `stateAlwaysHidden` and click **OK**.

Within the `activity` element is the ***`intent-filter` element*** (lines 10–13), which specifies the types of intents the `Activity` can respond to. This element must contain one or more ***`action` elements***. The one at line 11 indicates that this is the app's main activity—that is, the one that is displayed when the app is launched. The ***`category` element*** (line 12) specifies the kind of Android component that handles the event. In this case, the value `"android.intent.category.LAUNCHER"` indicates that this activity should be listed in the application launcher with other apps on the device.

5.7 Wrap-Up

In this chapter, we created the **Favorite Twitter Searches** app. First we designed the GUI. We introduced the `ScrollView` component—a `ViewGroup` that lets users *scroll* through

Fig. 5.25 | **Application** tab in the manifest editor.

content too large to display in the space available—and used it to display the arbitrarily large list of saved searches. Each search was associated with a `Button` that the user could touch to pass the search to the device's web browser. You also learned how to create resource files by using the **New Android XML File** dialog. In particular, you created a `colors.xml` file to store color resources, a `dimen.xml` file to store dimensions and a second layout file that the app inflated dynamically. We discussed how to reference colors and dimensions in XML layouts and how to use predefined colors from Android's `R.color` class.

We stored the search tag/query pairs in a `SharedPreferences` file associated with the app and showed how to programmatically hide the soft keyboard. We also used a `SharedPreferences.Editor` object to store values in, modify values in and remove values from a `SharedPreferences` file. In response to the user touching a search `Button`, we loaded a `Uri` into the device's web browser by creating a new `Intent` and passing it to `Context`'s `startActivity` method.

You used `AlertDialog.Builder` objects to configure and create `AlertDialogs` for displaying messages to the user. You created GUI components programmatically by manually inflating an XML layout file, which enabled the app to modify the GUI dynamically in response to user interactions. You used this technique to create a `TableRow` containing two new `Buttons` for each search—one to perform the search and one to edit the search. These `TableRows` were added to a `TableLayout` in a `ScrollView`, so that all the tagged searches could be displayed in a scrollable region on the screen.

Finally, we discussed the `AndroidManifest.xml` file and showed you how to configure the app so that the soft keyboard is not displayed when the app is launched.

In Chapter 6, you'll build the **Flag Quiz Game** app in which the user is shown a graphic of a country's flag and must guess the country from 3, 6 or 9 choices. You'll use a menu and checkboxes to customize the quiz, limiting the flags and countries chosen to specific regions of the world.

Flag Quiz Game App

Assets, AssetManager, Tweened Animations, Handler, Menus and Logging Error Messages

Objectives

In this chapter you'll:

- Store `String` arrays in `strings.xml`.
- Use the assets folder to store a set of images in subfolders.
- Use an `AssetManager` to get a list of all assets in an app.
- Use random-number generation to vary flag choices.
- Use a `Drawable` to display a flag image in an `ImageView`.
- Use a `Handler` to schedule a future action.
- Use an `ArrayList` to hold collections of items and a `HashMap` to hold name–value pairs.
- Override `Activity`'s `onCreateOptionsMenu` method to create a `Menu` and `MenuItem`s that enable the user to configure the app's options.
- Use Android's logging mechanism to log error messages.

Outline

6.1 Introduction

The **Flag Quiz Game** app tests the user's ability to correctly identify country flags (Fig. 6.1). Initially, the app presents the user with a flag image and three possible answers—one *matches* the flag and the others are *randomly* selected, nonduplicated *incorrect* answers. The app displays the user's progress throughout the quiz, showing the question number (out of 10) in a `TextView` above the current flag image.

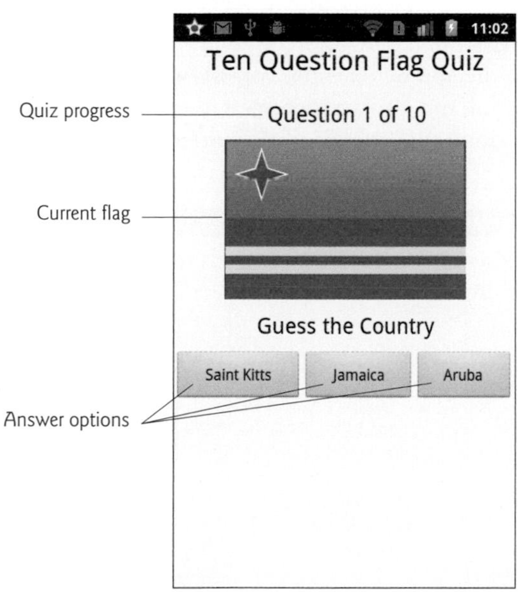

Fig. 6.1 | **Flag Quiz Game** app.

User Making a Correct Selection

The user chooses the country by touching the corresponding `Button`. If the choice is correct, the app disables all the answer `Buttons` and displays the country name in green followed by an exclamation point at the bottom of the screen (Fig. 6.2). After a one-second delay, the app loads the next flag and displays a new set of answer `Buttons`.

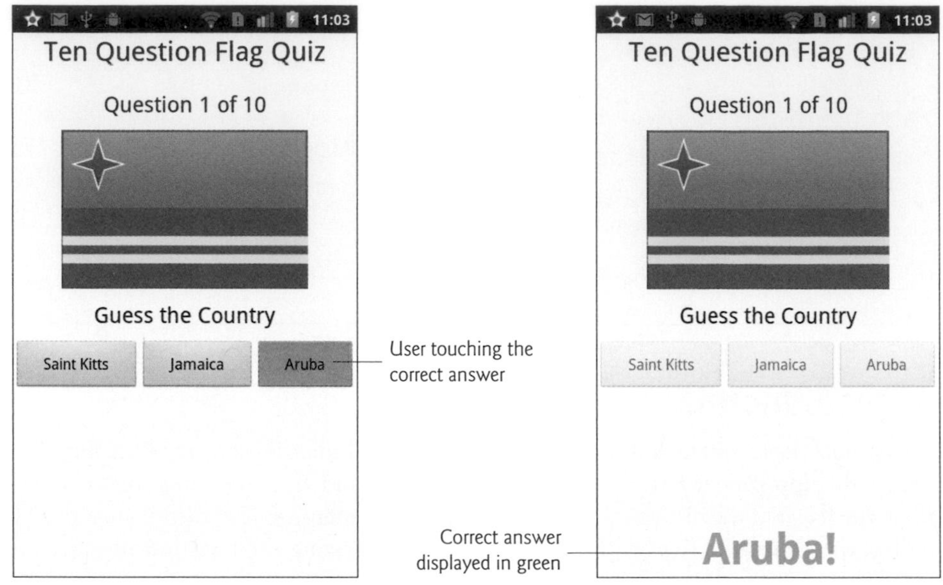

Fig. 6.2 | User choosing the correct answer and the correct answer displayed.

User Making an Incorrect Selection

If the user selects incorrectly, the app disables the corresponding country name `Button`, uses an animation to *shake* the flag and displays **Incorrect!** in red at the bottom of the screen (Fig. 6.3). The user keeps choosing countries until the correct one is picked.

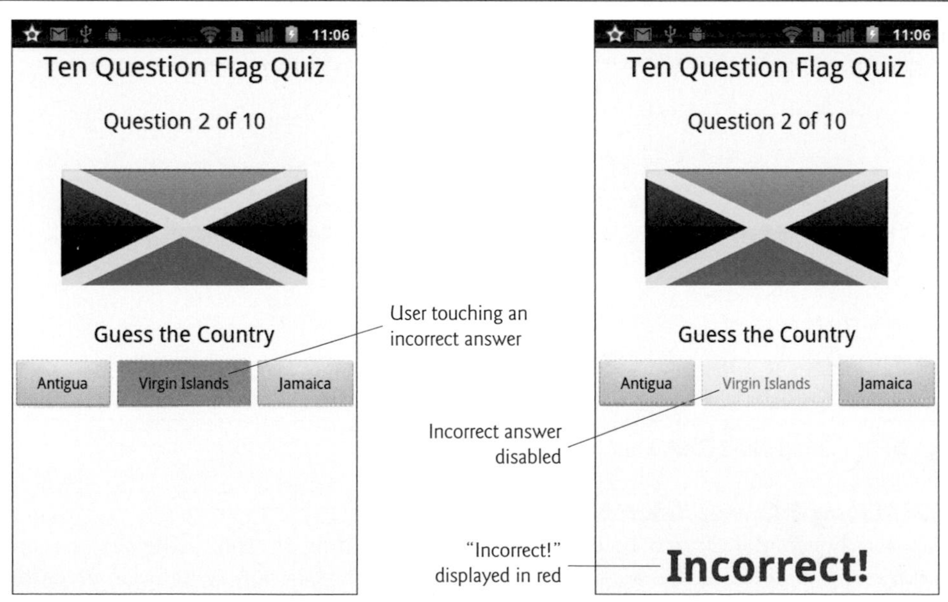

Fig. 6.3 | Disabled incorrect answer in the **Flag Quiz Game** app.

Completing the 10 Questions

After the user selects the 10 correct country names, a popup `AlertDialog` displays over the app and shows the user's total number of guesses and the percentage of correct answers (Fig. 6.4). When the user touches the dialog's **Reset Quiz** `Button`, a new quiz begins based on the current quiz options.

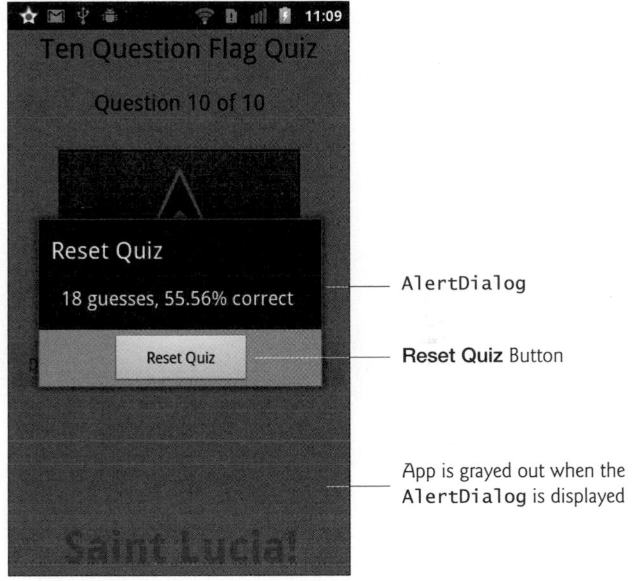

Fig. 6.4 | **Results** alert after quiz completion.

Customizing the Number of Answers Displayed with Each Flag

The user can customize the quiz by using the app's menu. When the user touches the device's menu button, the menu options **Select Number of Choices** and **Select Regions** are displayed. When the user touches **Select Number of Choices**, the app displays an `AlertDialog` from which the user can select **3**, **6** or **9** as the number of answers to display below each flag (Fig. 6.5). When the user touches an option, the game restarts with the specified number of answers for each flag (and the currently enabled world regions).

Customizing the Regions from Which Flags Are Selected

When the user touches **Select Regions** in the app's menu, the app displays an `AlertDialog` containing a checkbox for each world region (Fig. 6.6)—five of the major continents and Oceania, which consists of Australia, New Zealand and various South Pacific islands. If a region's checkbox is checked, flags from that region can be used in the quiz. When the user touches the **Reset Quiz** `Button`, the game restarts with flags selected from the current enabled regions.

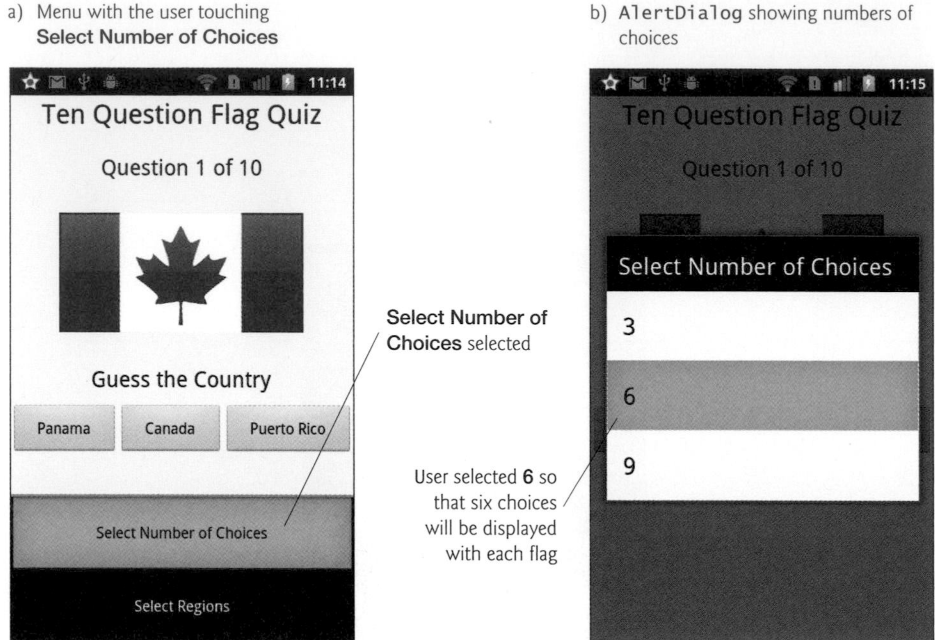
a) Menu with the user touching **Select Number of Choices**
b) AlertDialog showing numbers of choices
11:14
Ten Question Flag Quiz
Question 1 of 10
Guess the Country
Panama
Canada
Puerto Rico
Select Number of Choices
Select Regions
Select Number of Choices selected
11:15
Ten Question Flag Quiz
Question 1 of 10
Select Number of Choices
3
6
9
User selected **6** so that six choices will be displayed with each flag

Fig. 6.5 | Menu of the **Flag Quiz Game** app.

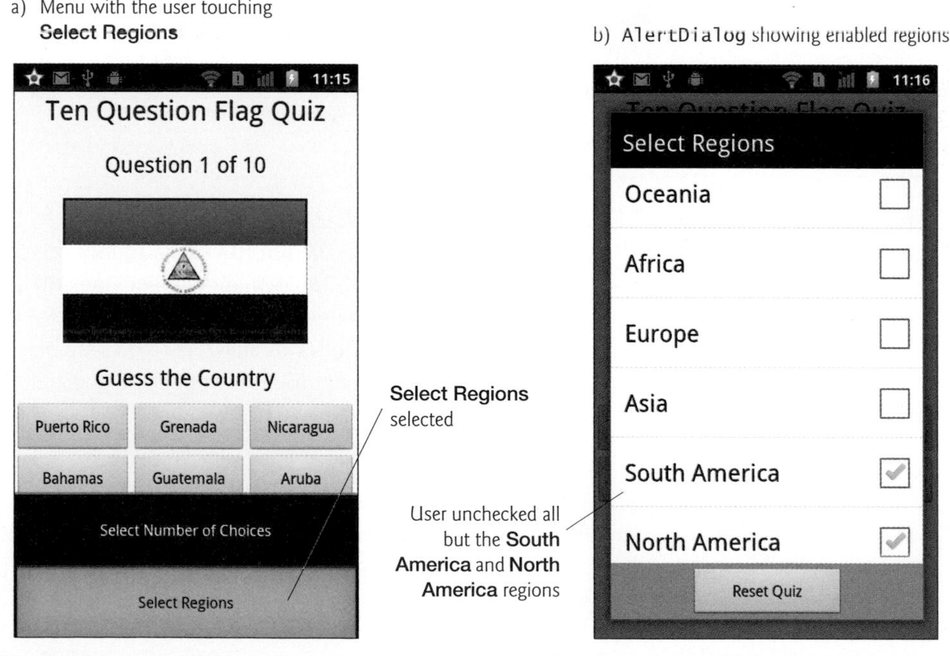
a) Menu with the user touching **Select Regions**
b) AlertDialog showing enabled regions
11:15
Ten Question Flag Quiz
Question 1 of 10
Guess the Country
Puerto Rico
Grenada
Nicaragua
Bahamas
Guatemala
Aruba
Select Number of Choices
Select Regions
Select Regions selected
11:16
Select Regions
Oceania
Africa
Europe
Asia
South America
North America
Reset Quiz
User unchecked all but the **South America** and **North America** regions

Fig. 6.6 | Choices `Dialog` of the **Flag Quiz Game** app.

6.2 Test-Driving the Flag Quiz Game App

Opening and Running the App

Open Eclipse and import the **Flag Quiz Game** app project. Perform the following steps:

1. *Open the* **Import** *Dialog.* Select **File > Import...** to open the **Import** dialog.
2. *Import the* **FlagQuiz Game** *app's project.* In the **Import** dialog, expand the **General** node and select **Existing Projects into Workspace**, then click **Next >** to proceed to the **Import Projects** step. Ensure that **Select root directory** is selected, then click the **Browse...** button. In the **Browse For Folder** dialog, locate the `FlagQuizGame` folder in the book's examples folder, select it and click **OK**. Click **Finish** to import the project into Eclipse. The project now appears in the **Package Explorer** window at the left side of the Eclipse window.
3. *Launch the* **FlagQuiz Game** *app.* In Eclipse, right click the `FlagQuizGame` project in the **Package Explorer** window, then from the menu that appears select **Run As > Android Application**.

Configuring the Quiz

Touch the **Menu** `Button` (or your device's menu button) to access the menu so you can view the app's options. Touch **Select Number of Choices** to specify the number of answers that should be displayed with each flag (as in Fig. 6.5). By default, three choices are displayed with each flag when the app is first executed. Touch **6** to display six answers with each flag.

Touch **Select Regions** to display the checkboxes representing the world regions (as in Fig. 6.6). By default, all regions are enabled when the app is first executed, so any of the world's flags can be selected randomly for the quiz. Touch the checkboxes next to **Africa** and **Oceania** to uncheck them—this excludes the countries of those regions from the quiz. Touch **Reset Quiz** to start a new game with the updated settings.

Completing the Quiz

A new quiz starts with six answer choices and no flags from either Africa or Oceania. Work through the quiz by touching the country that you think matches each flag. If you guess incorrectly, keep guessing until you get the correct answer for that flag. After you've successfully matched 10 flags, the quiz is grayed out and an `AlertDialog` displays the number of guesses you made and your accuracy percentage (as in Fig. 6.4). Touch the **Reset Quiz** `Button` to take another quiz.

6.3 Technologies Overview

Using the App's `assets` *Folder*

The app contains one image for each flag.[1] These images are loaded into the app only when needed. The images are located in the app's **`assets` folder**—we dragged each region's folder from our file system onto the assets folder. These folders are located with the book's examples in the `images/FlagQuizGameImages` folder. Unlike an app's `drawable`

1. We obtained the images from `www.free-country-flags.com`.

folders, which require their image contents to be at the root level in each folder, the `assets` folder may contain files of any type that can be organized in subfolders—we maintain the flag images for each region in a separate subfolder. Files in the `assets` folders are accessed via an **`AssetManager`** (package `android.content.res`), which can provide a list of all of the file names in a specified subfolder of `assets` and can be used to access each asset.

When the app needs to display a quiz question's flag, we use the `AssetManager` to open an `InputStream` (package `java.io`) to read from the flag image's file. Next, we use that stream as an argument to class **`Drawable`**'s `static` method **`createFromStream`**, which creates a `Drawable` object. That `Drawable` (package `android.graphics.drawable`) is then set as an `ImageView`'s item to display with `ImageView`'s **`setImageDrawable`** method.

Using a `Menu` *to Provide App Options*

The number of answer choices displayed and the regions from which flags can be selected can each be set by the user via the app's **`Menu`** (package `android.view`). To specify the `Menu` options, you override `Activity`'s **`onCreateOptionsMenu` method** and add the options to the `Menu` that the method receives as an argument. When the user selects an item from the `Menu`, `Activity` method **`onOptionsItemSelected`** is called to respond to the selection. We override this method to display the corresponding options in `AlertDialog`s.

Using a `Handler` *to Execute a* `Runnable` *in the Future*

To delay displaying the next flag after a correct guess, we use a **`Handler`** (package `android.os`) object to execute a `Runnable` after a 1,000-millisecond delay. `Handler` method **`postDelayed`** receives as arguments a `Runnable` to execute and a delay in milliseconds.

Animating the Flag When an Incorrect Choice Is Touched

When the user makes an incorrect choice, the app shakes the flag by applying an **`Animation`** (package `android.view.animation`) to the `ImageView`. We use **`AnimationUtils`** `static` method **`loadAnimation`** to load the animation from an XML file that specifies the animation's options. We also specify the number of times the animation should repeat with `Animation` method **`setRepeatCount`** and perform the animation by calling `View` method **`startAnimation`** (with the `Animation` as an argument) on the `ImageView`.

Logging Exception Messages with `Log.e`

When exceptions occur, you can *log* them for debugging purposes with Android's built-in logging mechanism, which uses a circular buffer to store the messages for a short time. Android provides class **`Log`** (package `android.util`) with several `static` methods that represent messages of varying detail. Logged messages can be viewed with the **Android `logcat` tool**. These messages are also displayed in the Android DDMS (Dalvik Debug Monitor Server) perspective's **LogCat** tab in Eclipse. For more details on logging messages, visit

```
developer.android.com/reference/android/util/Log.html
```

Java Data Structures

This app uses various data structures from the `java.util` package. The app dynamically loads the image file names for the enabled regions and stores them in an `ArrayList<String>`. We use `Collections` method `shuffle` to randomize the order of the image file names in the `ArrayList<String>` for each new game. We use a second `ArrayList<String>` to hold the image file names of the 10 countries in the current quiz. We also use a HashMap<String, Boolean> to store the region names and corresponding Boolean values, indicating whether each region is enabled or disabled. We refer to the ArrayList<String> and HashMap<String, Boolean> objects with variables of interface types List<String> and Map<String, Boolean>, respectively—this is a good Java programming practice that enables you to change data structures easily without affecting the rest of your app's code. In addition, we use interface Set<String> when referring to the keys in the HashMap.

6.4 Building the App's GUI and Resource Files

In this section, you'll build the GUI for the **Flag Quiz Game** app. You'll create a second XML layout that will be dynamically inflated to create the country-name Buttons that represent each quiz question's possible answers. You'll also create an XML representation of the *shake animation* that's applied to the flag image when the user guesses incorrectly.

6.4.1 main.xml LinearLayout

In this app, we use main.xml's default vertical LinearLayout. Figure 6.7 shows the app's GUI component names. Recall that, for clarity, our naming convention is to use the GUI component's class name in each component's **Id** property in the XML layout and in each variable name in the Java code.

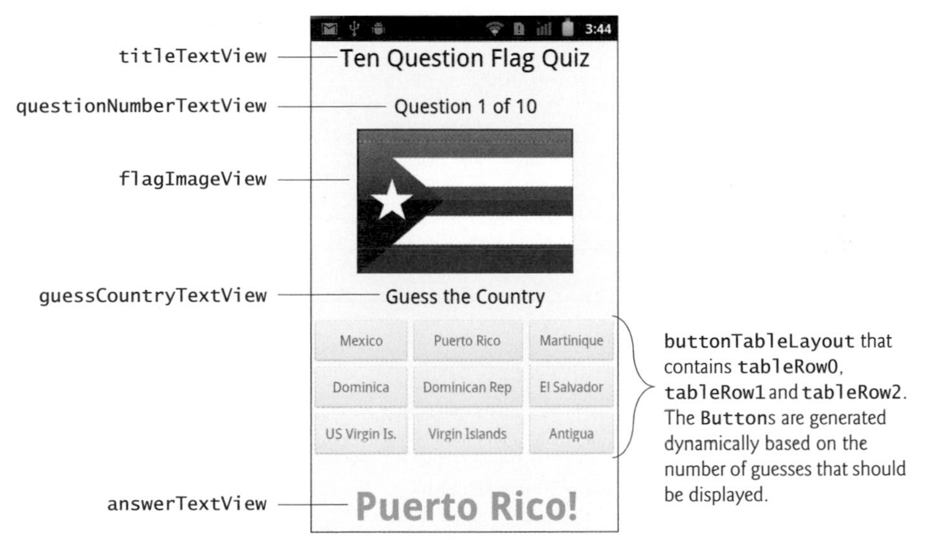

Fig. 6.7 | **Flag Quiz Game** GUI's components labeled with their **Id** property values.

6.4.2 Creating the Project

Begin by creating a new Android project named FlagQuizGame. Specify the following values in the **New Android Project** dialog, then press **Finish**:

- **Build Target:** Ensure that **Android 2.3.3** is checked
- **Application name:** FlagQuizGame

- **Package name:** `com.deitel.flagquizgame`
- **Create Activity:** `FlagQuizGame`
- **Min SDK Version:** 8.

6.4.3 Creating and Editing the Resource Files

As in the previous app, create the files `colors.xml` and `dimen.xml` to store literal color and dimension values, respectively. To create each file:

1. Right click the project name in the **Package Explorer** window and select **New > Other...**, then select **Android XML File** from the **Android** node in the **New** dialog. This displays the **New Android XML File** dialog.
2. In the **File** text field, enter the name `colors.xml`.
3. Under **What type of resource would you like to create?**, select the **Values** radio button to place the new file in the project's `res/values` folder.
4. Click **Finish** to create the file.
5. Repeat this process to create the `dimen.xml` file.

The contents of these two files are shown in Figs. 6.8–6.9. We use these colors and dimensions in `main.xml`. You should add these resources to these files in your project.

```
<?xml version="1.0" encoding="UTF-8"?>
<resources>
   <color name="text_color">#000000</color>
   <color name="background_color">#FFFFCC</color>
   <color name="correct_answer">#00CC00</color>
   <color name="incorrect_answer">#FF0000</color>
</resources>
```

Fig. 6.8 | Colors defined in `colors.xml`.

```
<?xml version="1.0" encoding="UTF-8"?>
<resources>
   <dimen name="title_size">25sp</dimen>
   <dimen name="flag_width">227dp</dimen>
   <dimen name="flag_height">150dp</dimen>
   <dimen name="answer_size">40sp</dimen>
   <dimen name="text_size">20sp</dimen>
</resources>
```

Fig. 6.9 | Dimensions defined in `dimen.xml`.

strings.xml

As in previous apps, we defined `String` resources in `strings.xml` (Fig. 6.10). For the first time, we also defined two `String` arrays in `strings.xml`. These arrays represent the region names (lines 18–25) and the number of answer `Buttons` displayed with each question (lines 26–30), respectively. You can enter these directly in the XML using the elements **`string-array`** and **`item`** as shown in Fig. 6.10.

```
<?xml version="1.0" encoding="UTF-8"?>
<resources>
   <string name="app_name">FlagQuizGame</string>
   <string name="choices">Select Number of Choices</string>
   <string name="correct">correct</string>
   <string name="guess_country">Guess the Country</string>
   <string name="guesses">guesses</string>
   <string name="incorrect_answer">Incorrect!</string>
   <string name="more_regions_title">More Regions Required</string>
   <string name="more_regions_message">There are not enough countries in
      the selected regions. Please select more regions.</string>
   <string name="of">of</string>
   <string name="ok">OK</string>
   <string name="question">Question</string>
   <string name="quiz_title">Ten Question Flag Quiz</string>
   <string name="regions">Select Regions</string>
   <string name="reset_quiz">Reset Quiz</string>
   <string-array name="regionsList">
      <item>Africa</item>
      <item>Asia</item>
      <item>Europe</item>
      <item>North_America</item>
      <item>Oceania</item>
      <item>South_America</item>
   </string-array>
   <string-array name="guessesList">
      <item>3</item>
      <item>6</item>
      <item>9</item>
   </string-array>
</resources>
```

Fig. 6.10 | Strings defined in `strings.xml`.

You can also use the resource-file editor to create these arrays as follows:

1. Click the **Add...** button in the editor, then select **String Array** from the dialog that appears and click **OK**.
2. Specify the array name in the **Name** field on the editor window's right side.
3. Next, right click the array name in the resource list and select **Add...** from the popup menu, then click **OK** to add a new **Item** to the array.
4. Repeat *Step 3* for the required number of array elements.
5. Select each **Item** in the resource list and specify its value in the **Value** field on the editor window's right side

6.4.4 Adding the Components to the `LinearLayout`

Using the techniques you learned in earlier chapters, build the GUI in Fig. 6.7. You'll start with the basic layout and controls, then customize the controls' properties to complete the design. Use the resources in `strings.xml` (Fig. 6.10), `colors.xml` (Fig. 6.8) and dimen.xml (Fig. 6.9) as necessary. We summarize building this app's GUI here. In subsequent apps, we'll focus only on the new GUI features, but still provide the final XML layout so you can see the attributes we set for each component.

Step 1: Configuring the LinearLayout

In the **Outline** window, select the LinearLayout and set the following properties:

- **Background:** @color/background_color
- **Gravity:** center_horizontal
- **Id:** @+id/linearLayout

Also change the **Layout width** and **Layout height** property values from fill_parent (which is deprecated) to match_parent.

Step 2: Adding the Components and Configuring Their Properties

Using Fig. 6.7 as your guide, add the TextViews, ImageView and TableLayout to the app's linearLayout. As you add these components, set their **Id** and **Text** properties. Study the XML elements in the final main.xml file (Fig. 6.11) to see each component's attribute values. We've highlighted important features and the resources we used. Don't create any Buttons in the TableRows—the Buttons are generated dynamically during the quiz.

```
<?xml version="1.0" encoding="utf-8"?>

<LinearLayout xmlns:android="http://schemas.android.com/apk/res/android"
   android:id="@+id/linearLayout" android:orientation="vertical"
   android:layout_width="match_parent"
   android:layout_height="match_parent"
   android:gravity="center_horizontal"
   android:background="@color/background_color">

   <TextView android:id="@+id/titleTextView"
      android:layout_width="match_parent"
      android:layout_height="wrap_content"
      android:text="@string/quiz_title" android:layout_marginBottom="10dp"
      android:textSize="@dimen/title_size"
      android:textColor="@color/text_color" android:gravity="center">
   </TextView>

   <TextView android:id="@+id/questionNumberTextView"
      android:layout_width="match_parent"
      android:layout_height="wrap_content"
      android:layout_marginBottom="10dp" android:layout_marginTop="10dp"
      android:textColor="@color/text_color"
      android:textSize="@dimen/text_size" android:layout_gravity="center"
      android:gravity="center"></TextView>

   <ImageView android:id="@+id/flagImageView"
      android:adjustViewBounds="false"
```

Fig. 6.11 | **FlagQuizGame** app's XML layout (main.xml). (Part 1 of 2.)

```
28          android:layout_width="@dimen/flag_width"
29          android:layout_height="@dimen/flag_height"></ImageView>
30
31       <TextView android:id="@+id/guessCountryTextView"
32          android:layout_width="wrap_content"
33          android:layout_height="wrap_content"
34          android:layout_marginBottom="10dp" android:layout_marginTop="10dp"
35          android:text="@string/guess_country"
36          android:textColor="@color/text_color"
37          android:textSize="@dimen/text_size"></TextView>
38
39       <TableLayout android:id="@+id/buttonTableLayout"
40          android:layout_width="match_parent"
41          android:layout_height="wrap_content"
42          android:layout_weight="1" android:stretchColumns="0,1,2">
43          <TableRow android:id="@+id/tableRow0"
44             android:layout_width="match_parent"
45             android:layout_height="wrap_content"
46             android:orientation="horizontal"></TableRow>
47          <TableRow android:id="@+id/tableRow1"
48             android:layout_width="match_parent"
49             android:layout_height="wrap_content"
50             android:orientation="horizontal"></TableRow>
51          <TableRow android:id="@+id/tableRow2"
52             android:layout_width="match_parent"
53             android:layout_height="wrap_content"
54             android:orientation="horizontal"></TableRow>
55       </TableLayout>
56
57       <TextView android:id="@+id/answerTextView"
58          android:layout_width="match_parent"
59          android:layout_height="wrap_content"
60          android:textSize="@dimen/answer_size"
61          android:layout_gravity="center" android:textStyle="bold"
62          android:gravity="center"></TextView>
63    </LinearLayout>
```

Fig. 6.11 | **FlagQuizGame** app's XML layout (`main.xml`). (Part 2 of 2.)

Notes on `main.xml`

Line 27 introduces the `ImageView` attribute **`android:adjustViewBounds`**, which specifies whether or not the `ImageView` maintains the aspect ratio of its `Drawable`. In this case we set it to `false` so we can size the flag images.

You'll notice in line 42 that we set `buttonTableLayout`'s `android:layout_weight` attribute to `1`. This value makes `buttonTableLayout` more important than the other components when the main `linearLayout` is resized based on the available space. Because `buttonTableLayout` is the only component that specifies an `android:layout_weight`, it stretches vertically to occupy all remaining vertical space that's not occupied by the other components. Also, the `buttonTableLayout`'s `android:stretchColumns` attribute is set to `0,1,2` to ensure that all three columns in a given `TableRow` stretch to fill the available horizontal space.

6.4.5 Creating a Button That Can Be Dynamically Inflated

Next, you'll define an XML representation of a `Button`. The app inflates this XML file to create each answer `Button`. In Section 6.5, you'll configure these `Buttons` and attach them to the appropriate `TableRow`. To create another layout XML layout file:

1. Right click the layout folder and select **New > Other...** to display the **New** dialog.
2. In the **Android** node, select **Android XML File** and click **Next >** to display the **New Android XML File** dialog.
3. In the **File** text field, enter the name `guess_button.xml`.
4. Under **What type of resource would you like to create?**, select the **Layout** radio button. This places the new file `guess_button.xml` into the project's `res/layout` folder.
5. At the bottom of the dialog, you can select the *root element* for the new layout. Choose `Button`.
6. Click **Finish** to create the file. The file opens immediately in **XML** view.
7. Configure the `Button`'s attributes as shown in Fig. 6.12.

```
<?xml version="1.0" encoding="UTF-8"?>
<Button xmlns:android="http://schemas.android.com/apk/res/android"
   android:id="@+id/newGuessButton" android:layout_weight="1"
   android:layout_width="wrap_content"
   android:layout_height="wrap_content"></Button>
```

Fig. 6.12 | The `newGuessButton` that will be dynamically inflated (`guess_button.xml`).

6.4.6 Creating the Flag Shake Animation

The XML in Fig. 6.13 defines the *flag shake animation* that we use when the user makes an incorrect guess. We'll show how this XML-defined animation is used by the app in Section 6.5.

```
<?xml version="1.0" encoding="utf-8"?>

<set xmlns:android="http://schemas.android.com/apk/res/android"
   android:interpolator="@android:anim/decelerate_interpolator">

   <translate android:fromXDelta="0" android:toXDelta="-5%p"
      android:duration="100"/>

   <translate android:fromXDelta="-5%p" android:toXDelta="5%p"
      android:duration="100" android:startOffset="100"/>

   <translate android:fromXDelta="5%p" android:toXDelta="-5%p"
      android:duration="100" android:startOffset="200"/>
</set>
```

Fig. 6.13 | Shake animation (`incorrect_shake.xml`) that's applied to the flag when the user guesses incorrectly.

To create this animation file:

1. Right click the layout folder and select **New > Other...** to display the **New** dialog.
2. In the **Android** node, select **Android XML File** and click **Next >** to display the **New Android XML File** dialog.
3. In the **File** text field, enter the name `incorrect_shake.xml`.
4. Under **What type of resource would you like to create?**, select the **Animation** radio button. This places the new file `incorrect_shake.xml` into the project's `res/anim` folder.
5. At the bottom of the dialog, you can select `set` as the animation's *root element*.
6. Click **Finish** to create the file. The file opens immediately in **XML** view.
7. Configure the animation as shown in Fig. 6.13.

In this example, we use **`View` animations** to create a *shake effect* that consists of three animations in an **animation set** (lines 3–14)—a collection of animations which make up a larger animation. Animation `set`s may contain any combination of **tweened animations—`alpha`** (transparency), **`scale`** (resize), **`translate`** (move) and **`rotate`**. Our shake animation consists of a series of three `translate` animations. A `translate` animation moves a `View` within its parent. As of version 3.0, Android now supports *property animations* in which you can animate any property of any object. We use property animations in our **SpotOn Game** app in Chapter 8.

The first `translate` animation (lines 6–7) moves a `View` from a starting location to an ending position over a specified period of time. The **`android:fromXDelta` attribute** is the `View`'s offset when the animation starts and the **`android:toXDelta` attribute** is the `View`'s offset when the animation ends. These attributes can have

- absolute values (in pixels)
- a percentage of the animated `View`'s size
- a percentage of the animated `View`'s *parent's* size

For the `android:fromXDelta` attribute, we specified an absolute value of 0. For the `android:toXDelta` attribute, we specified the value `-5%p`, which indicates that the `View` should move to the *left* (due to the minus sign) by 5% of the parent's width (indicated by the `p`). If we wanted to move by 5% of the `View`'s width, we would leave out the `p`. The **`android:duration` attribute** specifies how long the animation lasts in milliseconds. So the animation in lines 6–7 will move the `View` to the left by `5%` of its parent's width in 100 milliseconds.

The second animation (lines 9–10) continues from where the first finished, moving the `View` from the `-5%p` offset to a `%5p` offset in 100 milliseconds. By default, animations in an animation `set` are applied *in parallel*, but you can use the **`android:startOffset` attribute** to specify the number of milliseconds into the future at which an animation should begin. This can be used to sequence the animations in a `set`. In this case, the second animation starts 100 milliseconds after the first. The third animation (lines 12–13) is the same as the second but in the reverse direction, and it starts 200 milliseconds after the first animation.

6.5 Building the App

Figures 6.14–6.22 implement the **Flag Quiz Game** app in the single class `FlagQuizGame`, which extends `Activity`.

The `package` *and* `import` *Statements*

Figure 6.14 shows the `package` statement and `import` statements in `FlagQuizGame.java`. The `package` statement in line 3 indicates that the class in this file is part of the package `com.deitel.flagquizgame`—this line was inserted when you created the project. Lines 5–35 `import` the various Java and Android classes and interfaces the app uses. We discussed those that are new in this app in Section 6.3.

```
1  // FlagQuizGame.java
2  // Main Activity for the Flag Quiz Game App
3  package com.deitel.flagquizgame;
4
5  import java.io.IOException;
6  import java.io.InputStream;
7  import java.util.ArrayList;
8  import java.util.Collections;
9  import java.util.HashMap;
10 import java.util.List;
11 import java.util.Map;
12 import java.util.Random;
13 import java.util.Set;
14
15 import android.app.Activity;
16 import android.app.AlertDialog;
17 import android.content.Context;
18 import android.content.DialogInterface;
19 import android.content.res.AssetManager;
20 import android.graphics.drawable.Drawable;
21 import android.os.Bundle;
22 import android.os.Handler;
23 import android.util.Log;
24 import android.view.LayoutInflater;
25 import android.view.Menu;
26 import android.view.MenuItem;
27 import android.view.View;
28 import android.view.View.OnClickListener;
29 import android.view.animation.Animation;
30 import android.view.animation.AnimationUtils;
31 import android.widget.Button;
32 import android.widget.ImageView;
33 import android.widget.TableLayout;
34 import android.widget.TableRow;
35 import android.widget.TextView;
36
```

Fig. 6.14 | `FlagQuizGames`'s `package` and `import` statements.

Instance Variables

Figure 6.15 lists class `FlagQuizGame`'s variables. Line 40 declares the `static final String` `TAG`, which is used when we log error messages using class `Log` (Fig. 6.17) to distinguish this `Activity`'s error messages from others that are being written to the device's log.

The `List<String>` object `fileNameList` holds the flag image file names for the currently enabled geographic regions. The `List<String>` object `quizCountriesList` holds the 10 flag file names for the countries in the quiz. The `Map<String, Boolean>` object `regionsMap` stores the geographic regions that are enabled.

The `String correctAnswer` holds the flag file name for the current flag's correct answer. The `int totalGuesses` stores the total number of correct and incorrect guesses the player has made so far. The `int correctAnswers` is the number of correct guesses so far; this will eventually be 10 if the user completes the quiz. The `int guessRows` is the number of three-`Button` rows displaying the flag answer choices.

The `Random` object `random` is the pseudorandom-number generator that we use to randomly pick the flags that will be included in the quiz and to randomly select the row and column where the correct answer's `Button` will be placed. We use the `Handler` object `handler` to delay by one second the loading of the next flag to be tested.

The `Animation shakeAnimation` holds the dynamically inflated *shake animation* that's applied to the flag image when an incorrect guess is made. Lines 53–56 contain variables that we use to manipulate various GUI components programatically.

```
37 public class FlagQuizGame extends Activity
38 {
39    // String used when logging error messages
40    private static final String TAG = "FlagQuizGame Activity";
41
42    private List<String> fileNameList; // flag file names
43    private List<String> quizCountriesList; // names of countries in quiz
44    private Map<String, Boolean> regionsMap; // which regions are enabled
45    private String correctAnswer; // correct country for the current flag
46    private int totalGuesses; // number of guesses made
47    private int correctAnswers; // number of correct guesses
48    private int guessRows; // number of rows displaying choices
49    private Random random; // random number generator
50    private Handler handler; // used to delay loading next flag
51    private Animation shakeAnimation; // animation for incorrect guess
52
53    private TextView answerTextView; // displays Correct! or Incorrect!
54    private TextView questionNumberTextView; // shows current question #
55    private ImageView flagImageView; // displays a flag
56    private TableLayout buttonTableLayout; // table of answer Buttons
57
```

Fig. 6.15 | `FlagQuizGame` class's instance variables.

Overriding Method **`OnCreate`** *of Class* **`Activity`**

Method `onCreate` (Fig. 6.16) inflates the GUI and initializes the `Activity`'s instance variables. As in prior apps, we first call the superclass's `onCreate` method (line 62), then inflate the `Activity`'s GUI (line 63).

```
58      // called when the activity is first created
59      @Override
60      public void onCreate(Bundle savedInstanceState)
61      {
62         super.onCreate(savedInstanceState); // call the superclass's method
63         setContentView(R.layout.main); // inflate the GUI
64
65         fileNameList = new ArrayList<String>(); // list of image file names
66         quizCountriesList = new ArrayList<String>(); // flags in this quiz
67         regionsMap = new HashMap<String, Boolean>(); // HashMap of regions
68         guessRows = 1; // default to one row of choices
69         random = new Random(); // initialize the random number generator
70         handler = new Handler(); // used to perform delayed operations
71
72         // load the shake animation that's used for incorrect answers
73         shakeAnimation =
74            AnimationUtils.loadAnimation(this, R.anim.incorrect_shake);
75         shakeAnimation.setRepeatCount(3); // animation repeats 3 times
76
77         // get array of world regions from strings.xml
78         String[] regionNames =
79            getResources().getStringArray(R.array.regionsList);
80
81         // by default, countries are chosen from all regions
82         for (String region : regionNames)
83            regionsMap.put(region, true);
84
85         // get references to GUI components
86         questionNumberTextView =
87            (TextView) findViewById(R.id.questionNumberTextView);
88         flagImageView = (ImageView) findViewById(R.id.flagImageView);
89         buttonTableLayout =
90            (TableLayout) findViewById(R.id.buttonTableLayout);
91         answerTextView = (TextView) findViewById(R.id.answerTextView);
92
93         // set questionNumberTextView's text
94         questionNumberTextView.setText(
95            getResources().getString(R.string.question) + " 1 " +
96            getResources().getString(R.string.of) + " 10");
97
98         resetQuiz(); // start a new quiz
99      } // end method onCreate
100
```

Fig. 6.16 | Overriding method `onCreate` of class `Activity`.

Lines 65–66 create `ArrayList<String>` objects that will store the flag image file names for the currently enabled geographical regions and the 10 countries in the current quiz, respectively. Line 67 creates the `HashMap<String, Boolean>` that stores whether each geographical region is enabled.

We set `guessRows` to 1 so that the game initiallys displays only one row of `Buttons` containing three possible answers. The user has the option to make the game more challenging by displaying two rows (with six possible answers) or three rows (with nine possible answers).

Line 69 creates the Random object random that we use to randomly pick the flags that will be included in the quiz and to randomly select the row and column where the correct answer's Button will be placed. Line 70 creates the Handler object handler, which we'll use to delay by one second the appearance of the next flag after the user correctly guesses the current flag.

Lines 73–74 dynamically load the *shake animation* that will be applied to the flag when an incorrect guess is made. AnimationUtils static method loadAnimation loads the animation from the XML file represented by the constant R.anim.incorrect_shake. The first argument indicates the Context (this FlagQuizGame instance) containing the resources that will be animated. Line 75 specifies the number of times the animation should repeat with Animation method setRepeatCount.

Lines 78–79 *dynamically load* the contents of the String array regionNames. Method **getResources** (inherited indirectly from class ContextWrapper) returns a **Resources** object (package android.content.res) that can be used to load the Activity's resources. We then call that object's **getStringArray** method to load the array associated with the resource constant R.array.regionsList from the file strings.xml.

Lines 82–83 use method put to add each of the six regions to the regions HashMap. Each region is set initially to true (i.e., enabled). The user can enable and disable the regions as desired via the app's options menu (Figs. 6.20–6.21).

Lines 86–91 get references to various GUI components that we'll programmatically manipulate. Lines 94–96 set the text in questionNumberTextView. Here, we could have used String formatting to create questionNumberTextView's text. In Section 7.4.3, we demonstrate how to create String resources for format Strings. Line 98 calls the FlagQuizGame class's resetQuiz method to set up the next quiz.

resetQuiz Method of Class FlagQuizGame (Our App)

Method resetQuiz (Fig. 6.17) sets up and starts the next quiz. Recall that the images for the game are stored in the app's assets folder. To access this folder's contents, the method gets the app's AssetManager (line 106) by calling method **getAssets** (inherited indirectly from class ContextWrapper). Next, line 107 clears the fileNameList to prepare to load image file names for only the enabled geographical regions. We use HashMap method keySet (line 111) to form a set of the six region names from regionsMap and assign it to the Set<String> object regions. Then we iterate through all the regions (lines 114–124). For each region we use the AssetManager's list method (line 119) to get an array of all the flag image file names, which we store in the String array paths. Lines 121–122 remove the .png extension from each flag image file name and place the names in the fileNameList.

```
101    // set up and start the next quiz
102    private void resetQuiz()
103    {
104       // use the AssetManager to get the image flag
105       // file names for only the enabled regions
106       AssetManager assets = getAssets(); // get the app's AssetManager
107       fileNameList.clear(); // empty the list
108
```

Fig. 6.17 | resetQuiz method of class FlagQuizGame. (Part 1 of 2.)

```
109       try
110       {
111          Set<String> regions = regionsMap.keySet(); // get Set of regions
112
113          // loop through each region
114          for (String region : regions)
115          {
116             if (regionsMap.get(region)) // if region is enabled
117             {
118                // get a list of all flag image files in this region
119                String[] paths = assets.list(region);
120
121                for (String path : paths)
122                   fileNameList.add(path.replace(".png", ""));
123             } // end if
124          } // end for
125       } // end try
126       catch (IOException e)
127       {
128          Log.e(TAG, "Error loading image file names", e);
129       } // end catch
130
131       correctAnswers = 0; // reset the number of correct answers made
132       totalGuesses = 0; // reset the total number of guesses the user made
133       quizCountriesList.clear(); // clear prior list of quiz countries
134
135       // add 10 random file names to the quizCountriesList
136       int flagCounter = 1;
137       int numberOfFlags = fileNameList.size(); // get number of flags
138
139       while (flagCounter <= 10)
140       {
141          int randomIndex = random.nextInt(numberOfFlags); // random index
142
143          // get the random file name
144          String fileName = fileNameList.get(randomIndex);
145
146          // if the region is enabled and it hasn't already been chosen
147          if (!quizCountriesList.contains(fileName))
148          {
149             quizCountriesList.add(fileName); // add the file to the list
150             ++flagCounter;
151          } // end if
152       } // end while
153
154       loadNextFlag(); // start the quiz by loading the first flag
155    } // end method resetQuiz
156
```

Fig. 6.17 | resetQuiz method of class FlagQuizGame. (Part 2 of 2.)

Next, lines 131–133 reset the counters for the number of correct guesses the user has made (correctAnswers) and the total number of guesses the user has made (totalGuesses) to 0 and clear the quizCountriesList.

Lines 136–152 add 10 randomly selected file names to the `quizCountriesList`. We get the total number of flags, then randomly generate the index in the range 0 to one less than the number of flags. We use this index to select one image file name from `fileNamesList`. If the `quizCountriesList` does not already contain that file name, we add it to `quizCountriesList` and increment the `flagCounter`. We repeat this process until 10 unique file names have been selected. Then line 154 calls `loadNextFlag` (Fig. 6.18) to load the quiz's first flag.

`loadNextFlag`, `getTableRow` and `getCountryName` Methods of Class `FlagQuizGame`

Method `loadNextFlag` (Fig. 6.18) loads and displays the next flag and the corresponding set of answer `Buttons`. The image file names in `quizCountriesList` have the format

regionName-countryName

without the `.png` extension. If a *regionName* or *countryName* contains multiple words, they're separated by underscores (_).

```
   // after the user guesses a correct flag, load the next flag
   private void loadNextFlag()
   {
      // get file name of the next flag and remove it from the list
      String nextImageName = quizCountriesList.remove(0);
      correctAnswer = nextImageName; // update the correct answer

      answerTextView.setText(""); // clear answerTextView

      // display the number of the current question in the quiz
      questionNumberTextView.setText(
         getResources().getString(R.string.question) + " " +
         (correctAnswers + 1) + " " +
         getResources().getString(R.string.of) + " 10");

      // extract the region from the next image's name
      String region =
         nextImageName.substring(0, nextImageName.indexOf('-'));

      // use AssetManager to load next image from assets folder
      AssetManager assets = getAssets(); // get app's AssetManager
      InputStream stream; // used to read in flag images

      try
      {
         // get an InputStream to the asset representing the next flag
         stream = assets.open(region + "/" + nextImageName + ".png");

         // load the asset as a Drawable and display on the flagImageView
         Drawable flag = Drawable.createFromStream(stream, nextImageName);
         flagImageView.setImageDrawable(flag);
      } // end try
      catch (IOException e)
      {
```

Fig. 6.18 | `loadNextFlag` method of `FlagQuizGame`. (Part 1 of 3.)

```
            Log.e(TAG, "Error loading " + nextImageName, e);
         } // end catch

         // clear prior answer Buttons from TableRows
         for (int row = 0; row < buttonTableLayout.getChildCount(); ++row)
            ((TableRow) buttonTableLayout.getChildAt(row)).removeAllViews();

         Collections.shuffle(fileNameList); // shuffle file names

         // put the correct answer at the end of fileNameList
         int correct = fileNameList.indexOf(correctAnswer);
         fileNameList.add(fileNameList.remove(correct));

         // get a reference to the LayoutInflater service
         LayoutInflater inflater = (LayoutInflater) getSystemService(
            Context.LAYOUT_INFLATER_SERVICE);

         // add 3, 6, or 9 answer Buttons based on the value of guessRows
         for (int row = 0; row < guessRows; row++)
         {
            TableRow currentTableRow = getTableRow(row);

            // place Buttons in currentTableRow
            for (int column = 0; column < 3; column++)
            {
               // inflate guess_button.xml to create new Button
               Button newGuessButton =
                  (Button) inflater.inflate(R.layout.guess_button, null);

               // get country name and set it as newGuessButton's text
               String fileName = fileNameList.get((row * 3) + column);
               newGuessButton.setText(getCountryName(fileName));

               // register answerButtonListener to respond to button clicks
               newGuessButton.setOnClickListener(guessButtonListener);
               currentTableRow.addView(newGuessButton);
            } // end for
         } // end for

         // randomly replace one Button with the correct answer
         int row = random.nextInt(guessRows); // pick random row
         int column = random.nextInt(3); // pick random column
         TableRow randomTableRow = getTableRow(row); // get the TableRow
         String countryName = getCountryName(correctAnswer);
         ((Button)randomTableRow.getChildAt(column)).setText(countryName);
      } // end method loadNextFlag

      // returns the specified TableRow
      private TableRow getTableRow(int row)
      {
         return (TableRow) buttonTableLayout.getChildAt(row);
      } // end method getTableRow

```

Fig. 6.18 | loadNextFlag method of FlagQuizGame. (Part 2 of 3.)

```
244    // parses the country flag file name and returns the country name
245    private String getCountryName(String name)
246    {
247       return name.substring(name.indexOf('-') + 1).replace('_', ' ');
248    } // end method getCountryName
249
```

Fig. 6.18 | `loadNextFlag` method of `FlagQuizGame`. (Part 3 of 3.)

Line 161 removes the first name from `quizCountriesList` and stores it in `nextImageName`. We also save this in `correctAnswer` so it can be used later to determine whether the user made a correct guess. Next, we clear the `answerTextView` and display the current question number in the `questionNumerTextView` (lines 164–170)—again, here we could have used a formatted `String` resource as we'll show in Chapter 7.

Lines 173–174 extract from `nextImageName` the region to be used as the `assets` subfolder name from which we'll load the image. Next we get the `AssetManager`, then use it in the `try` statement to open an `InputStream` for reading from the flag image's file. We use that stream as an argument to `Drawable`'s `static` method `createFromStream`, which creates a `Drawable` object. That `Drawable` is set as `flagImageView`'s item to display with its `setImageDrawable` method. If an exception occurs in the `try` block (lines 180–188), we *log* it for debugging purposes with Android's built-in logging mechanism, which provides `static` methods that provide varying detail in the log messages. `Log` `static` method **`e`** is used to log errors and is the least verbose in terms of the generated error message. If you require more detail in your log messages, see the complete list of `Log` methods at

```
developer.android.com/reference/android/util/Log.html
```

Lines 195–196 remove all previous answer `Buttons` from the `buttonTableLayout`'s three `TableRows`. Next, line 198 shuffles the `fileNameList`, and lines 201–202 locate the `correctAnswer` and move it to the end of the `fileNameList`—later we'll insert this answer randomly into the answer `Buttons`.

Lines 205–206 get a `LayoutInflater` for inflating the answer `Button` objects from the layout file `guess_button.xml`. Lines 209–228 iterate through the rows and columns of the `buttonTableLayout` (for the current number of `guessRows`). For each new Button:

- lines 217–218 inflate the `Button` from `guess_button.xml`
- line 221 gets the flag file name
- line 222 sets `Button`'s text with the country name
- line 225 sets the new `Button`'s `OnClickListener`, and
- line 226 adds the new `Button` to the appropriate `TableRow`.

Lines 231–235 pick a random row (based on the current number of `guessRows`) and column in the `buttonTableLayout`, then set the text of the `Button` in that row and column to the correct answer.

Lines 211 and 233 in method `loadNextFlag` use utility method `getTableRow` (lines 239–242) to obtain the `TableRow` at a specific index in the `buttonTableLayout`. Lines 222 and 234 use utility method `getCountryName` (lines 245–248) to parse the country name from the image file name.

submitGuess and disableButtons Methods of Class FlagQuizGame

Method submitGuess (Fig. 6.19) is called when the user clicks a country Button to select an answer. The method receives the clicked Button as parameter guessButton. We get the Button's text (line 253) and the parsed country name (line 254), then increment totalGuesses.

```
250    // called when the user selects an answer
251    private void submitGuess(Button guessButton)
252    {
253       String guess = guessButton.getText().toString();
254       String answer = getCountryName(correctAnswer);
255       ++totalGuesses; // increment the number of guesses the user has made
256
257       // if the guess is correct
258       if (guess.equals(answer))
259       {
260          ++correctAnswers; // increment the number of correct answers
261
262          // display "Correct!" in green text
263          answerTextView.setText(answer + "!");
264          answerTextView.setTextColor(
265             getResources().getColor(R.color.correct_answer));
266
267          disableButtons(); // disable all answer Buttons
268
269          // if the user has correctly identified 10 flags
270          if (correctAnswers == 10)
271          {
272             // create a new AlertDialog Builder
273             AlertDialog.Builder builder = new AlertDialog.Builder(this);
274
275             builder.setTitle(R.string.reset_quiz); // title bar string
276
277             // set the AlertDialog's message to display game results
278             builder.setMessage(String.format("%d %s, %.02f%% %s",
279                totalGuesses, getResources().getString(R.string.guesses),
280                (1000 / (double) totalGuesses),
281                getResources().getString(R.string.correct)));
282
283             builder.setCancelable(false);
284
285             // add "Reset Quiz" Button
286             builder.setPositiveButton(R.string.reset_quiz,
287                new DialogInterface.OnClickListener()
288                {
289                   public void onClick(DialogInterface dialog, int id)
290                   {
291                      resetQuiz();
292                   } // end method onClick
293                } // end anonymous inner class
294             ); // end call to setPositiveButton
295
```

Fig. 6.19 | submitGuess method of FlagQuizGame. (Part 1 of 2.)

```
296             // create AlertDialog from the Builder
297             AlertDialog resetDialog = builder.create();
298             resetDialog.show(); // display the Dialog
299          } // end if
300          else // answer is correct but quiz is not over
301          {
302             // load the next flag after a 1-second delay
303             handler.postDelayed(
304                new Runnable()
305                {
306                   @Override
307                   public void run()
308                   {
309                      loadNextFlag();
310                   }
311                }, 1000); // 1000 milliseconds for 1-second delay
312          } // end else
313       } // end if
314       else // guess was incorrect
315       {
316          // play the animation
317          flagImageView.startAnimation(shakeAnimation);
318
319          // display "Incorrect!" in red
320          answerTextView.setText(R.string.incorrect_answer);
321          answerTextView.setTextColor(
322             getResources().getColor(R.color.incorrect_answer));
323          guessButton.setEnabled(false); // disable the incorrect answer
324       } // end else
325    } // end method submitGuess
326
327    // utility method that disables all answer Buttons
328    private void disableButtons()
329    {
330       for (int row = 0; row < buttonTableLayout.getChildCount(); ++row)
331       {
332          TableRow tableRow = (TableRow) buttonTableLayout.getChildAt(row);
333          for (int i = 0; i < tableRow.getChildCount(); ++i)
334             tableRow.getChildAt(i).setEnabled(false);
335       } // end outer for
336    } // end method disableButtons
337
```

Fig. 6.19 | `submitGuess` method of `FlagQuizGame`. (Part 2 of 2.)

If the guess is correct (line 258), we increment `correctAnswers`. Next, we set the `answerTextView`'s text to the country name and change its color to the color represented by the constant `R.color.correct_answer`, and we call our utility method `disableButtons` (defined in lines 328–336) to iterate through the `buttonTableLayout`'s rows and columns and disable all the answer `Buttons`.

If `correctAnswers` is 10 (line 270), the quiz is over. Lines 273–299 create a new `AlertDialog.Builder`, use it to configure the dialog that shows the quiz results, create the

AlertDialog and show it on the screen. When the user touches the dialog's **Reset Quiz** **Button**, method resetQuiz is called to start a new game.

If correctAnswers is less than 10, then lines 303–311 call the postDelayed method of Handler object handler. The first argument defines an anonymous inner class that implements the Runnable interface—this represents the task to perform (loadNextFlag) some number of milliseconds into the future. The second argument is the delay in milliseconds (1000).

If the guess is incorrect, line 317 invokes flagImageView's startAnimation method to play the shakeAnimation that was loaded in method onCreate. We also set the text on answerTextView to display "Incorrect!" in red (lines 320–322), then call the guessButton's setEnabled method with false (line 323) to *disable* the Button that corresponds to the incorrect answer.

Overriding Method onCreateOptionsMenu *of Class* Activity

We override Activity method OnCreateOptionsMenu (Fig. 6.20) to initialize Activity's standard options menu. The system passes in the Menu object where the options will appear. The app has its own built-in options menu from which the user can select one of two menus by touching either **Select Number of Choices** or **Select Regions.** The **Select Number of Choices** option enables the user to specify whether 3, 6 or 9 flags should be shown for each quiz. The **Select Regions** option enables the user to enable and disable the geographical regions from which the flags can be selected for a quiz.

```
338    // create constants for each menu id
339    private final int CHOICES_MENU_ID = Menu.FIRST;
340    private final int REGIONS_MENU_ID = Menu.FIRST + 1;
341
342    // called when the user accesses the options menu
343    @Override
344    public boolean onCreateOptionsMenu(Menu menu)
345    {
346       super.onCreateOptionsMenu(menu);
347
348       // add two options to the menu - "Choices" and "Regions"
349       menu.add(Menu.NONE, CHOICES_MENU_ID, Menu.NONE, R.string.choices);
350       menu.add(Menu.NONE, REGIONS_MENU_ID, Menu.NONE, R.string.regions);
351
352       return true; // display the menu
353    } // end method onCreateOptionsMenu
354
```

Fig. 6.20 | Overriding method onCreateOptionsMenu of class Activity.

Lines 349–340 create constants for two menu IDs. The constant Menu.FIRST represents the option that will appear first in the Menu. Each option should have a unique ID. Method onCreateOptionsMenu first calls call super's onCreateOptionsMenu. Then we call Menu's add method to add MenuItems to the Menu (lines 333–334). The first argument represents the MenuItem's group ID, which is used to group MenuItems that share state (such as whether they're currently enabled or visible on the screen). This argument should be Menu.NONE if the MenuItem does *not* need to be part of a group. The second argument is the MenuItem's unique item ID. The third argument is the order in which the MenuItem should appear—use Menu.NONE if the order of your MenuItems does not matter. The last argument is the resource identifier for the String that will be displayed. We return true to display the menu (line 352).

Overriding Method onOptionsItemSelected *of class* Activity

Method onOptionsItemSelected (Fig. 6.21) is called when the user selects an item in the app's options menu and receives the selected MenuItem (item). A switch statement distinguishes between the two cases. The controlling expression of the switch invokes item's getItemId method to return this menu item's unique identifier (line 360) so we can determine which MenuItem was selected.

```
355    // called when the user selects an option from the menu
356    @Override
357    public boolean onOptionsItemSelected(MenuItem item)
358    {
359       // switch the menu id of the user-selected option
360       switch (item.getItemId())
361       {
362          case CHOICES_MENU_ID:
363             // create a list of the possible numbers of answer choices
364             final String[] possibleChoices =
365                getResources().getStringArray(R.array.guessesList);
366
367             // create a new AlertDialog Builder and set its title
368             AlertDialog.Builder choicesBuilder =
369                new AlertDialog.Builder(this);
370             choicesBuilder.setTitle(R.string.choices);
371
372             // add possibleChoices items to the Dialog and set the
373             // behavior when one of the items is clicked
374             choicesBuilder.setItems(R.array.guessesList,
375                new DialogInterface.OnClickListener()
376                {
377                   public void onClick(DialogInterface dialog, int item)
378                   {
379                      // update guessRows to match the user's choice
380                      guessRows = Integer.parseInt(
381                         possibleChoices[item].toString()) / 3;
382                      resetQuiz(); // reset the quiz
383                   } // end method onClick
384                } // end anonymous inner class
385             );  // end call to setItems
386
387             // create an AlertDialog from the Builder
388             AlertDialog choicesDialog = choicesBuilder.create();
389             choicesDialog.show(); // show the Dialog
390             return true;
391
```

Fig. 6.21 | Overriding method onOptionsItemSelected of class Activity. (Part 1 of 3.)

```
         case REGIONS_MENU_ID:
            // get array of world regions
            final String[] regionNames =
               regionsMap.keySet().toArray(new String[regionsMap.size()]);

            // boolean array representing whether each region is enabled
            boolean[] regionsEnabled = new boolean[regionsMap.size()];
            for (int i = 0; i < regionsEnabled.length; ++i)
               regionsEnabled[i] = regionsMap.get(regionNames[i]);

            // create an AlertDialog Builder and set the dialog's title
            AlertDialog.Builder regionsBuilder =
               new AlertDialog.Builder(this);
            regionsBuilder.setTitle(R.string.regions);

            // replace _ with space in region names for display purposes
            String[] displayNames = new String[regionNames.length];
            for (int i = 0; i < regionNames.length; ++i)
               displayNames[i] = regionNames[i].replace('_', ' ');

            // add displayNames to the Dialog and set the behavior
            // when one of the items is clicked
            regionsBuilder.setMultiChoiceItems(
               displayNames, regionsEnabled,
               new DialogInterface.OnMultiChoiceClickListener()
               {
                  @Override
                  public void onClick(DialogInterface dialog, int which,
                     boolean isChecked)
                  {
                     // include or exclude the clicked region
                     // depending on whether or not it's checked
                     regionsMap.put(
                        regionNames[which].toString(), isChecked);
                  } // end method onClick
               } // end anonymous inner class
            ); // end call to setMultiChoiceItems

            // resets quiz when user presses the "Reset Quiz" Button
            regionsBuilder.setPositiveButton(R.string.reset_quiz,
               new DialogInterface.OnClickListener()
               {
                  @Override
                  public void onClick(DialogInterface dialog, int button)
                  {
                     resetQuiz(); // reset the quiz
                  } // end method onClick
               } // end anonymous inner class
            ); // end call to method setPositiveButton

            // create a dialog from the Builder
            AlertDialog regionsDialog = regionsBuilder.create();
            regionsDialog.show(); // display the Dialog
```

Fig. 6.21 | Overriding method `onOptionsItemSelected` of class `Activity`. (Part 2 of 3.)

```
445             return true;
446       } // end switch
447
448       return super.onOptionsItemSelected(item);
449    } // end method onOptionsItemSelected
450
```

Fig. 6.21 | Overriding method `onOptionsItemSelected` of class `Activity`. (Part 3 of 3.)

If the user touched **Select Number of Choices** the `case` in lines 362–390 executes. Lines 364–365 obtain the `String` array `guessesList` from the app's resources and assign it to variable `possibleChoices`. Next, we create a new `AlertDialog.Builder` and set the dialog's title (lines 368–370).

Each of the `AlertDialogs` we've created previously has displayed a simple text message and one or two `Buttons`. In this case, we'd like to display the `possibleChoice`'s items in the `Dialog` and specify what to do when the user touches one of the items. To do this, we call `AlertDialog.Builder` method **`setItems`** (lines 374–385). The first argument is an array of `Strings` or a resource constant representing an array of `Strings`—these represent a set of mutually exclusive options. The second argument is the `DialogInterface.OnClickListener` that responds to the user touching one of the items. The listener's `onClick` method receives as its second argument the zero-based index of the item the user touched. We use that index to select the appropriate element from `possibleChoices`, then convert that `String` to an `int` and divide it by 3 to determine the number of `guessRows`. Then, we call `resetQuiz` to start a new quiz with the specified number of answer `Buttons`. Lines 388–389 create and display the dialog.

If the user touched **Select Regions**, the `case` in lines 392–445 executes to display an `AlertDialog` containing a list of region names in which multiple items can be enabled. First, we assign `regionNames` the array of `Strings` containing the keys in `regionsMap` (lines 394–395). Next, lines 398–400 create an array of `booleans` representing whether each region is enabled. Lines 403–405 create an `AlertDialog.Builder` and set the dialog's title. Lines 408–410 create the `displayNames` `String` array and store in it the region names with underscores replaced by spaces.

Next, we call `AlertDialog.Builder` method **`setMultiChoiceItems`** to display the list of regions. Each region that's currently enabled displays a check mark in its corresponding checkbox (as in Fig. 6.6). The first two arguments are the array of items to display and a corresponding array of `booleans` indicating which items should be enabled. The first argument can be either an array of `Strings` or a resource constant representing an array of `Strings`. The third argument is the `DialogInterface.OnMultiChoiceClickListener` that responds to each touch of an item in the dialog. The anonymous inner class (lines 416–427) implements the listener's `onClick` method to include or exclude the clicked region, depending on whether or not it's checked. The method's second argument represents the index of the item the user touched and the third argument represents its checked state. We use these to put the appropriate updated state information into `regionsMap`.

Lines 431–440 define the dialog's positive `Button`. If the user touches this button, the `resetQuiz` method is called to start a new game, based on the current game settings. If the user simply touches the device's back button, the new settings will *not* take effect until the next quiz begins. Finally, lines 443–444 create the dialog and display it.

Anonymous Inner Class That Implements Interface `OnClickListener` *to Respond to the Events of the Guess Buttons*

The anonymous inner class object `guessButtonListener` implements interface `OnClickListener` to respond to `Button`'s events. Line 225 registered `guessButtonListener` as the event-handling object for each `newGuessButton`. Method `onClick` simply passes the selected `Button` to method `submitGuess`.

```
451    // called when a guess Button is touched
452    private OnClickListener guessButtonListener = new OnClickListener()
453    {
454       @Override
455       public void onClick(View v)
456       {
457          submitGuess((Button) v); // pass selected Button to submitGuess
458       } // end method onClick
459    }; // end answerButtonListener
460 } // end FlagQuizGame
```

Fig. 6.22 | Anonymous inner class that implements interface `OnClickListener` to respond to the events of the `answerButton`.

6.6 AndroidManifest.xml

In Section 5.6, we introduced the contents of the manifest file. For this app, we explain only the new features (Fig. 6.23). In line 7, we use the **`android:theme` attribute** of the `application` element to apply a theme to the application's GUI. A theme is a set of styles that specify the appearance of a GUI's components. In this case, the attribute's value indicates that the application's title bar—where the app's name is normally displayed—should be hidden. For a complete list of predefined styles and themes, see

```
developer.android.com/reference/android/R.style.html
```

and for more details on applying styles and themes, see

```
developer.android.com/guide/topics/ui/themes.html
```

You can set the application's theme on the **Application** tab in the manifest editor. Simply enter the attribute value shown in line 7 into the **Theme** field.

In the `activity` element, line 10 uses **`android:screenOrientation` attribute** to specify that this app should always appear in *portrait mode* (that is, a vertical orientation). To set this attribute's value, select the activity in the bottom left corner of the **Application** tab in the manifest editor. The manifest options for the activity are displayed at the bottom right side of the **Application** tab. In the **Screen** orientation drop down list, select **portrait**. After making your changes to the manifest, be sure to save your changes.

```
1  <?xml version="1.0" encoding="utf-8"?>
2  <manifest xmlns:android="http://schemas.android.com/apk/res/android"
3     package="com.deitel.flagquizgame" android:versionCode="1"
4     android:versionName="1.0">
```

Fig. 6.23 | `AndroidManifest.xml` file for the **Flag Quiz Game** app. (Part 1 of 2.)

```
    <application android:icon="@drawable/icon"
       android:label="@string/app_name"
       android:theme="@android:style/Theme.NoTitleBar">
       <activity android:name=".FlagQuizGame"
          android:label="@string/app_name"
          android:screenOrientation="portrait">
          <intent-filter>
             <action android:name="android.intent.action.MAIN" />
             <category android:name="android.intent.category.LAUNCHER" />
          </intent-filter>
       </activity>
    </application>
    <uses-sdk android:targetSdkVersion="10" android:minSdkVersion="8"/>
</manifest>
```

Fig. 6.23 | AndroidManifest.xml file for the **Flag Quiz Game** app. (Part 2 of 2.)

6.7 Wrap-Up

In this chapter, we built a **Flag Quiz Game** app that tests the user's ability to correctly identify country flags. You learned how to define String arrays in the strings.xml file. You also learned how to load color and String array resources from the colors.xml and strings.xml files into memory by using the Activity's Resources object.

When the app needed to display a quiz question's flag, you used the AssetManager to open an InputStream to read from the flag image's file. Then, you used that stream with class Drawable's static method createFromStream to create a Drawable object that could be displayed on an ImageView with ImageView's setImageDrawable method.

You learned how to use the app's Menu to allow the user to configure the app's options To specify the Menu options, you overrode Activity's onCreateOptionsMenu method. To respond to the user's menu selections, you overrode Activity method onOptionsItemSelected.

To delay displaying the next flag after a correct guess, you used a Handler object postDelayed to execute a Runnable after a 1,000-millisecond delay. When the user made an incorrect choice, the app shook the flag by applying an Animation to the ImageView. You used AnimationUtils static method loadAnimation to load the animation from an XML file that specified the animation's options. You also specified the number of times the animation should repeat with Animation method setRepeatCount and performed the animation by calling View method startAnimation (with the Animation as an argument) on the ImageView.

You learned how to log exceptions for debugging purposes with Android's built-in logging mechanism, which uses a circular buffer to store the messages for a short time. You also used various collection classes and interfaces from the java.util package to manage data in the app.

In Chapter 7, you'll create a **Cannon Game app** using multithreading and frame-by-frame animation. You'll handle touch gestures and use a timer to generate events and update the display in response to those events. We also show how to perform simple collision detection.

Cannon Game App

Listening for Touches and Gestures, Manual Frame-By-Frame Animation, Graphics, Sound, Threading, `SurfaceView` and `SurfaceHolder`

Objectives

In this chapter you'll:

- Create a simple game app that's easy to code and fun to play.
- Create a custom `SurfaceView` subclass and use it to display the game's graphics from a separate thread of execution.
- Draw graphics using `Paints` and a `Canvas`.
- Override `Activity`'s `onTouchEvent` to process touch events when the user touches the screen or drags a finger on the screen.
- Use a `GestureDetector` to recognize more sophisticated user touch motions, such as double taps.
- Perform simple collision detection.
- Add sound to your app using a `SoundPool` and the `AudioManager`.
- Override three additional `Activity` lifecycle methods.

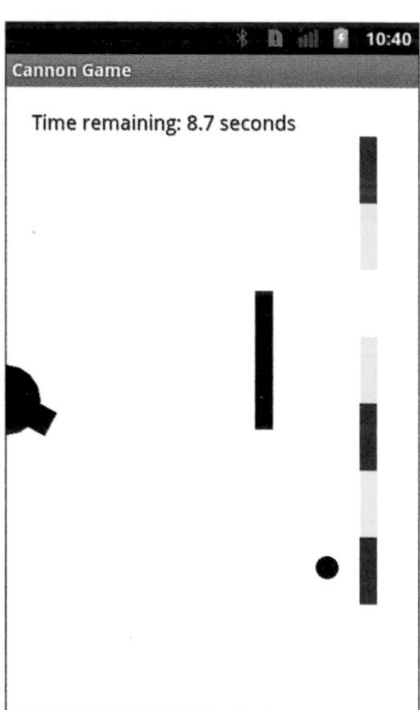

Outline

7.1 Introduction

The **Cannon Game** app challenges you to destroy a seven-piece target before a ten-second time limit expires (Fig. 7.1). The game consists of four visual components—a *cannon* that you control, a *cannonball*, the *target* and a *blocker* that defends the target. You aim the cannon by *touching* the screen—the cannon then aims at the touched point. The cannon fires a cannonball when you *double-tap* the screen. At the end of the game, the app displays an `AlertDialog` indicating whether you won or lost, and showing the number of shots fired and the elapsed time (Fig. 7.2).

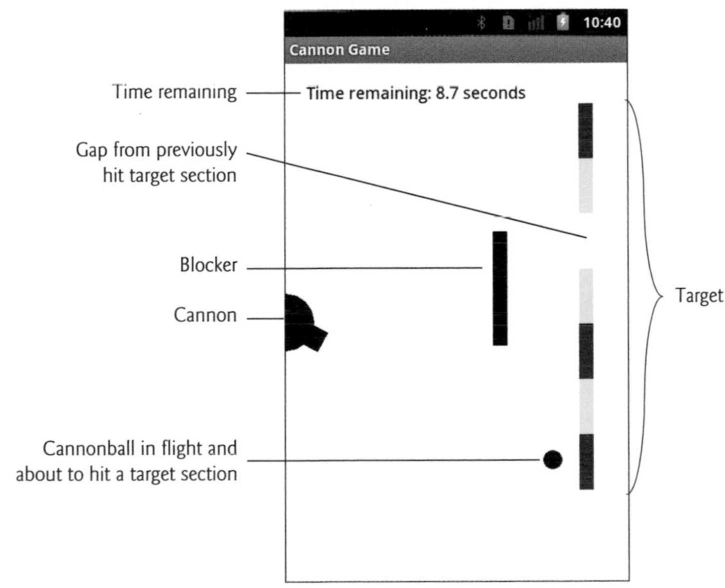

Fig. 7.1 | Completed **Cannon Game** app.

The game begins with a *10-second time limit*. Each time you hit a target section, three seconds are *added* to the time limit, and each time you hit the blocker, two seconds are *subtracted*. You win by destroying all seven target sections before time runs out. If the timer reaches zero, you lose.

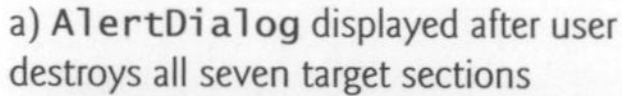

a) `AlertDialog` displayed after user destroys all seven target sections

b) `AlertDialog` displayed when game ends before user destroys all seven target sections

Fig. 7.2 | **Cannon Game** app `AlertDialog`s showing a win and a loss.

When you fire the cannon, the game plays a *firing sound.* The target consists of seven pieces. When a cannonball hits the target, a *glass-breaking sound* plays and that piece of the target disappears from the screen. When the cannonball hits the blocker, a *hit sound* plays and the cannonball bounces back. The blocker cannot be destroyed. The target and blocker move *vertically* at different speeds, changing direction when they hit the top or bottom of the screen.

7.2 Test-Driving the Cannon Game App

Opening and Running the App

Open Eclipse and import the **Cannon Game** app project. Perform the following steps:

1. *Open the* **Import** *Dialog.* Select **File > Import...** to open the **Import** dialog.
2. *Import the* **Cannon Game** *app's project.* In the **Import** dialog, expand the **General** node and select **Existing Projects into Workspace**, then click **Next >** to proceed to the **Import Projects** step. Ensure that **Select root directory** is selected, then click the **Browse...** button. In the **Browse for Folder** dialog, locate the `CannonGame` folder in the book's examples folder, select it and click **OK**. Click **Finish** to import the project into Eclipse. The project now appears in the **Package Explorer** window at the left side of the Eclipse window.
3. *Launch the* **Cannon Game** *app.* In Eclipse, right click the `CannonGame` project in the **Package Explorer** window, then select **Run As > Android Application** from the menu that appears.

Playing the Game
Drag your finger on the screen or tap it to aim the cannon. Double tap the screen to fire a shot. You can fire a cannonball only if there is not another cannonball on the screen. If you're running this in an AVD, your "finger" is the mouse. Try to destroy the target as fast as you can—if the timer runs out, the game ends.

7.3 Technologies Overview

This section presents the many new technologies that we use in the **Cannon Game** app in the order they're encountered throughout the chapter.

Defining `String` *Formatting Resources in* `strings.xml`
In this app, we define `String` resources to represent the format `Strings` that are used in calls to class `Resource`'s method `getString` (or to class `String`'s `static` method `format`). When format `Strings` contain multiple format specifiers, you're *required* to number them (from 1) to indicate the order in which the corresponding values will be substituted into the format `String`. In some spoken languages, a `String`'s phrasing might result in the values being placed at different locations in the localized `String` resources. In such cases, the localized versions of `strings.xml` can use the original format-specifier numbers, but place the format specifiers at appropriate locations in the localized `Strings`. The syntax for numbering format specifiers is shown in Section 7.4.3.

Attaching a Custom `View` *to a Layout*
You can create a *custom view* by extending class `View` or one of its subclasses, as we do with class `CannonView` (Section 7.5.3), which extends `SurfaceView` (discussed shortly). To add a custom component to a layout's XML file, you must *fully qualify* its class name in the XML element that represents the component. This is demonstrated in Section 7.4.4.

Using the Resource Folder `raw`
Media files, such as the sounds used in the **Cannon Game** app are placed in the app's resource folder **`res/raw`**. Section 7.4.5 discusses how to create this folder. You'll then drag the app's sound files into it.

`Activity` *Lifecycle Methods* `onPause` *and* `onDestroy`
This app uses additional `Activity` lifecycle methods. Method **`onPause`** is called for the *current* `Activity` when *another* activity receives the focus, which sends the current activity to the background. We use `onPause` to suspend game play so that the game does not continue executing when the user cannot interact with it.

When an `Activity` is shut down, its **`onDestroy`** method is called. We use this method to release the app's sound resources. These lifecycle methods are used in Section 7.5.2.

Overriding `Activity` *Method* `onTouchEvent`
As you know, users interact with this app by touching the device's screen. A *touch* or *single tap* aligns the cannon to face the touch or single tap point on the screen. To process simple touch events for an `Activity`, you can override class `Activity`'s **`onTouchEvent`** method (Section 7.5.2) then use constants from class **`MotionEvent`** (package `android.view`) to test which type of event occurred and process it accordingly.

`GestureDetector` and `SimpleOnGestureListener`

For more complex gestures, like the *double taps* that fire the cannon, you'll use a **`GestureDetector`** (package `android.view`), which can recognize user actions that represent a *series* of `MotionEvents`. A `GestureDetector` allows an app to react to more sophisticated user interactions such as *flings*, *double-taps*, *long presses* and *scrolls*. Your apps can respond to such events by implementing the methods of the **`GestureDetector.OnGestureListener`** and **`GestureDetector.OnDoubleTapListener`** interfaces. Class **`GestureDetector.SimpleOnGestureListener`** is an *adapter class* that implements all the methods of these two interfaces, so you can extend this class and override just the method(s) you need from these interfaces. In Section 7.5.2, we initialize a `GestureDetector` with a `SimpleOnGestureListener`, which will handle the *double tap* event that fires the cannon.

Adding Sound with `SoundPool` and `AudioManager`

An app's sound effects are managed with a **`SoundPool`** (package `android.media`), which can be used to *load*, *play* and *unload* sounds. Sounds are played using one of Android's several audio streams, which include streams for alarms, DTMF tones, music, notifications, phone rings, system sounds and phone calls. The Android documentation recommends that games use the *music audio stream* to play sounds. We use the `Activity`'s **`setVolumeControlStream`** method to specify that the game's volume can be controlled with the device's volume keys and should be the same as the device's music playback volume. The method receives a constant from class **`AudioManager`** (package `android.media`).

Frame-by-Frame Animation with `Threads`, `SurfaceView` and `SurfaceHolder`

This app *performs its animations manually* by updating the game elements from a separate thread of execuion. To do this, we use a subclass of `Thread` with a `run` method that directs our custom `CannonView` to update the positions of all the game's elements, then draws the elements. Normally, all updates to an app's user interface must be performed in the GUI thread of execution. However, in Android, it's important to minimize the amount of work you do in the GUI thread to ensure that the GUI remains responsive and does not display ANR (Application Not Responding) dialogs.

Games often require complex logic that should be performed in separate threads of execution and those threads often need to draw to the screen. For such cases, Android provides class **`SurfaceView`**—a subclass of `View` to which any thread can draw. You manipulate a `SurfaceView` via an object of class **`SurfaceHolder`**, which enables you to obtain a `Canvas` on which you can draw graphics. Class `SurfaceHolder` also provides methods that give a thread exclusive access to the `Canvas` for drawing, because only one thread at a time can draw to a `SurfaceView`. Each `SurfaceView` subclass should implement the interface **`SurfaceHolder.Callback`**, which contains methods that are called when the `SurfaceView` is created, changed (e.g., its size or orientation changes) or destroyed.

Simple Collision Detection

The `CannonView` performs simple collision detection to determine whether the cannonball has collided with any of the `CannonView`'s edges, with the blocker or with a section of the target. These techniques are presented in Section 7.5.3. [*Note:* Many game-development frameworks provide more sophisticated collision detection capabilities.]

Drawing Graphics Using **Paint** *and* **Canvas**

We use methods of class **Canvas** (package `android.graphics`) to draw text, lines and circles. A `Canvas` draws on a `View`'s **Bitmap**. Each drawing method in class `Canvas` uses an object of class **Paint** (package `android.graphics`) to specify drawing characteristics, including color, line thickness, font size and more. These capabilities are presented with the `drawGameElements` method in Section 7.5.3. For more details on the drawing characteristics you can specify with a `Paint` object, visit

```
developer.android.com/reference/android/graphics/Paint.html
```

7.4 Building the App's GUI and Resource Files

In this section, you'll create the app's resource files and `main.xml` layout file.

7.4.1 Creating the Project

Begin by creating a new Android project named `CannonGame`. Specify the following values in the **New Android Project** dialog, then press **Finish**:

- **Build Target:** Ensure that **Android 2.3.3** is checked
- **Application name:** `Cannon Game`
- **Package name:** `com.deitel.cannongame`
- **Create Activity:** `CannonGame`
- **Min SDK Version:** 8.

7.4.2 `AndroidManifest.xml`

Figure 7.3 shows this app's `AndroidManifest.xml` file. As in Section 6.6, we set the `activity` element's `android:screenOrientation` attribute to `"portrait"` (line 9) so that the app always displays in portrait mode.

```
1  <?xml version="1.0" encoding="utf-8"?>
2  <manifest xmlns:android="http://schemas.android.com/apk/res/android"
3     package="com.deitel.cannongame" android:versionCode="1"
4     android:versionName="1.0">
5     <application android:icon="@drawable/icon"
6        android:label="@string/app_name" android:debuggable="true">
7        <activity android:name=".CannonGame"
8           android:label="@string/app_name"
9           android:screenOrientation="portrait">
10          <intent-filter>
11             <action android:name="android.intent.action.MAIN" />
12             <category android:name="android.intent.category.LAUNCHER" />
13          </intent-filter>
14       </activity>
15    </application>
16    <uses-sdk android:minSdkVersion="8" android:targetSdkVersion="10"/>
17 </manifest>
```

Fig. 7.3 | `AndroidManifest.xml`.

7.4.3 strings.xml

We've specified format Strings (Fig. 7.4. lines 4–5 and 9–10) in this app's strings.xml file. As mentioned in Section 7.3, format Strings that contain multiple format specifiers must number the format specifiers for localization purposes. The notation 1$ in %1$.1f (line 5) indicates that the *first* argument after the format String should replace the format specifier %1$d. Similarly, %2$.1f indicates that the *second* argument after the format String should replace the format specifier %2$.1f. The d in the first format specifier indicates that we're formatting a decimal integer and the f in the second one indicates that we're formatting a floating-point value. In localized versions of strings.xml, the format specifiers %1$d and %2$.1f can be reordered as necessary—the *first* argument after the format String in a call to Resourcesmethod getString or String method format will replace %1$d—regardless of where it appears in the format String—and the *second* argument will replace %2$.1f *regardless* of where they appear in the format String.

```
1  <?xml version="1.0" encoding="UTF-8"?>
2  <resources>
3     <string name="app_name">Cannon Game</string>
4     <string name="results_format">
5        Shots fired: %1$d\nTotal time: %2$.1f</string>
6     <string name="reset_game">Reset Game</string>
7     <string name="win">You win!</string>
8     <string name="lose">You lose!</string>
9     <string name="time_remaining_format">
10       Time remaining: %.1f seconds</string>
11 </resources>
```

Fig. 7.4 | Strings defined in strings.xml.

7.4.4 main.xml

In this app, we deleted the default main.xml file and replaced it with one containing a FrameLayout. The only component in this app's layout is an instance of our custom View subclass, CannonView, which you'll add to the project in Section 7.5.3. Figure 7.5 shows the completed main.xml in which we manually entered the XML element shown in lines 2–7. That element indicates that the CannonView should occupy the entire width and height of the parent layout and should have a white background. Recall from Section 7.3 that you must fully qualify a custom View's class name in the layout XML, so line 2 refers to the CannonView as com.deitel.cannongame.CannonView.

```
1  <?xml version="1.0" encoding="utf-8"?>
2  <com.deitel.cannongame.CannonView
3     xmlns:android="http://schemas.android.com/apk/res/android"
4     android:id="@+id/cannonView"
5     android:layout_width="match_parent"
6     android:layout_height="match_parent"
7     android:background="@android:color/white"/>
```

Fig. 7.5 | **Cannon Game** app's XML layout (main.xml).

7.4.5 Adding the Sounds to the App

As we mentioned previously, sound files are stored in the app's `res/raw` folder. This app uses three sound files—`blocker_hit.wav`, `target_hit.wav` and `cannon_fire.wav`—which are located with the book's examples in the `sounds` folder. To add these files to your project:

1. Right click the app's `res` folder then select **New > Folder.**
2. Specify the folder name `raw` and click **Finish** to create the folder.
3. Drag the sound files into the `res/raw` folder.

7.5 Building the App

This app consists of three classes—`Line` (Fig. 7.6), `CannonGame` (the `Activity` subclass; Figs. 7.7–7.10) and `CannonView` (Figs. 7.11–7.23).

7.5.1 `Line` Class Maintains a Line's Endpoints

Class `Line` (Fig. 7.6) simply groups two `Points` that represent a line's starting `Point` and ending `Point`. We use objects of this class to define the blocker and target. To add class `Line` to the project:

1. Expand the project's `src` node in the **Package Explorer.**
2. Right click the package (`com.deitel.cannongame`) and select **New > Class** to display the **New Java Class** dialog.
3. In the dialog's **Name** field, enter `Line` and click **Finish.**
4. Enter the code in Fig. 7.6 into the `Line.java` file.

```
// Line.java
// Class Line represents a line with two endpoints.
package com.deitel.cannongame;

import android.graphics.Point;

public class Line
{
   public Point start; // starting Point
   public Point end; // ending Point

   // default constructor initializes Points to the origin (0, 0)
   public Line()
   {
      start = new Point(0, 0); // start Point
      end = new Point(0, 0); // end Point
   } // end method Line
} // end class Line
```

Fig. 7.6 | Class `Line` represents a line with two endpoints.

7.5.2 `CannonGame` Subclass of `Activity`

Class `CannonGame` (Figs. 7.7–7.10) is the **Cannon Game** app's main `Activity`.

`package` *Statement,* **`import`** *Statements and Instance Variables*

Section 7.3 discussed the key new classes and interfaces that class `CannonGame` uses. We've highlighted these classes and interfaces in Fig. 7.7. Line 15 declares variable `cannonView`, which will enable class `CannonGame` to interact with the `CannonView`.

```
1  // CannonGame.java
2  // Main Activity for the Cannon Game app.
3  package com.deitel.cannongame;
4
5  import android.app.Activity;
6  import android.os.Bundle;
7  import android.media.AudioManager;
8  import android.view.GestureDetector;
9  import android.view.MotionEvent;
10 import android.view.GestureDetector.SimpleOnGestureListener;
11
12 public class CannonGame extends Activity
13 {
14    private GestureDetector gestureDetector; // listens for double taps
15    private CannonView cannonView; // custom view to display the game
16
```

Fig. 7.7 | `CannonGame` `package` statement, `import` statements and instance variables.

Overriding **`Activity`** *Methods* **`onCreate`***,* **`onPause`** *and* **`onDestroy`**

Figure 7.8 presents overridden `Activity` methods `onCreate` (lines 18–32), `onPause` (lines 35–40) and `onDestroy` (lines 43–48). Method `onCreate` inflates the activity's `main.xml` layout, then gets a reference to the `CannonView` object (line 25). Line 28 creates the `GestureDetector` that detects double taps for this activity using the `gestureListener`, which is defined in Fig. 7.10. Line 31 allows the game's audio volume to be controlled by the device's volume keys.

```
17    // called when the app first launches
18    @Override
19    public void onCreate(Bundle savedInstanceState)
20    {
21       super.onCreate(savedInstanceState); // call super's onCreate method
22       setContentView(R.layout.main); // inflate the layout
23
24       // get the CannonView
25       cannonView = (CannonView) findViewById(R.id.cannonView);
26
27       // initialize the GestureDetector
28       gestureDetector = new GestureDetector(this, gestureListener);
29
30       // allow volume keys to set game volume
31       setVolumeControlStream(AudioManager.STREAM_MUSIC);
32    } // end method onCreate
33
```

Fig. 7.8 | Overriding `Activity` methods `onCreate`, `onPause` and `onDestroy`. (Part 1 of 2.)

```
34      // when the app is pushed to the background, pause it
35      @Override
36      public void onPause()
37      {
38         super.onPause(); // call the super method
39         cannonView.stopGame(); // terminates the game
40      } // end method onPause
41
42      // release resources
43      @Override
44      protected void onDestroy()
45      {
46         super.onDestroy();
47         cannonView.releaseResources();
48      } // end method onDestroy
49
```

Fig. 7.8 | Overriding `Activity` methods `onCreate`, `onPause` and `onDestroy`. (Part 2 of 2.)

Method `onPause` (lines 35–40) ensures that the `CannonGame` activity does not continue executing when it's sent to the background. If the game did continue executing, not only would the user not be able to interact with the game because another activity has the focus, but the app would also continue consuming battery power—a precious resource for mobile devices. When `onPause` is called, line 39 calls the `cannonView`'s `stopGame` method (Fig. 7.21) to terminate the game's thread—we don't save the game's state in this example.

When the activity is shut down, method `onDestroy` (lines 43–46) calls the `cannonView`'s `releaseResources` method (Fig. 7.21), which releases the app's sound resources.

Overriding `Activity` *Method* `onTouchEvent`

In this example, we override method `onTouchEvent` (Fig. 7.9) to determine when the user touches the screen or moves a finger across the screen. The `MotionEvent` parameter contains information about the event that occurred. Line 55 uses the `MotionEvent`'s `getAction` method to determine which type of event occurred. Then, lines 58–59 determine whether the user touched the screen (`MotionEvent.ACTION_DOWN`) or moved a finger across the screen (`MotionEvent.ACTION_MOVE`). In either case, line 61 calls the `cannonView`'s `alignCannon` method (Fig. 7.18) to aim the cannon towards that touch point. Line 65 then passes the `MotionEvent` object to the `gestureDetector`'s `onTouchEvent` method to check whether a double tap occurred.

```
50      // called when the user touches the screen in this Activity
51      @Override
52      public boolean onTouchEvent(MotionEvent event)
53      {
54         // get int representing the type of action which caused this event
55         int action = event.getAction();
56
```

Fig. 7.9 | Overriding `Activity` method `onTouchEvent`. (Part 1 of 2.)

```
      // the user user touched the screen or dragged along the screen
      if (action == MotionEvent.ACTION_DOWN ||
         action == MotionEvent.ACTION_MOVE)
      {
         cannonView.alignCannon(event); // align the cannon
      } // end if

      // call the GestureDetector's onTouchEvent method
      return gestureDetector.onTouchEvent(event);
   } // end method onTouchEvent
```

Fig. 7.9 | Overriding `Activity` method `onTouchEvent`. (Part 2 of 2.)

Anonymous Inner Class That Extends `SimpleOnGestureListener`

Figure 7.10 creates the `SimpleOnGestureListener` named `gestureListener` which was registered at line 28 with the `GestureDetector`. Recall that `SimpleOnGestureListener` is an adapter class that implements all the methods of interfaces `OnGestureListener` and `OnDoubleTapListener`. The methods simply return `false`—indicating that the events were not handled. We override only the **`onDoubleTap` method** (lines 71–76), which is called when the user double taps the screen. Line 74 calls `CannonView`'s `fireCannonBall` method (Fig. 7.17) to fire a cannonball. Method `fireCannonBall` obtains the *screen location of the double-tap* from its `MotionEvent` argument—this is used to aim the shot at the correct angle. Line 75 returns `true` indicating that the event was handled.

```
67    // listens for touch events sent to the GestureDetector
68    SimpleOnGestureListener gestureListener = new SimpleOnGestureListener()
69    {
70       // called when the user double taps the screen
71       @Override
72       public boolean onDoubleTap(MotionEvent e)
73       {
74          cannonView.fireCannonball(e); // fire the cannonball
75          return true; // the event was handled
76       } // end method onDoubleTap
77    }; // end gestureListener
78 } // end class CannonGame
```

Fig. 7.10 | Anonymous inner class that extends `SimpleOnGestureListener`.

7.5.3 `CannonView` Subclass of `View`

Class `CannonView` (Figs. 7.11–7.23) is a custom subclass of `View` that implements the **Cannon Game**'s logic and draws game objects on the screen. To add the class to the project:

1. Expand the project's `src` node in the **Package Explorer**.
2. Right click the package (`com.deitel.cannongame`) and select **New > Class** to display the **New Java Class** dialog.
3. In the dialog's **Name** field, enter `CannonView`, in the **Superclass** field enter `android.view.View`, then click **Finish**.
4. Enter the code in Figs. 7.11–7.21 into the `CannonView.java` file.

package and import Statements

Figure 7.11 lists the package statement and the import statements for class CannonView. Section 7.3 discussed the key new classes and interfaces that class CannonView uses. We've highlighted them in Fig. 7.11.

```
// CannonView.java
// Displays the Cannon Game
package com.deitel.cannongame;

import java.util.HashMap;
import java.util.Map;

import android.app.Activity;
import android.app.AlertDialog;
import android.content.Context;
import android.content.DialogInterface;
import android.graphics.Canvas;
import android.graphics.Color;
import android.graphics.Paint;
import android.graphics.Point;
import android.media.AudioManager;
import android.media.SoundPool;
import android.util.AttributeSet;
import android.view.MotionEvent;
import android.view.SurfaceHolder;
import android.view.SurfaceView;

```

Fig. 7.11 | CannonView class's package and import statements.

CannonView Instance Variables and Constants

Figure 7.12 lists the large number of class CannonView's constants and instance variables. Most are self explanatory, but we'll explain each as we encounter it in the discussion.

```
public class CannonView extends SurfaceView
   implements SurfaceHolder.Callback
{
   private CannonThread cannonThread; // controls the game loop
   private Activity activity; // to display Game Over dialog in GUI thread
   private boolean dialogIsDisplayed = false;

   // constants for game play
   public static final int TARGET_PIECES = 7; // sections in the target
   public static final int MISS_PENALTY = 2; // seconds deducted on a miss
   public static final int HIT_REWARD = 3; // seconds added on a hit

   // variables for the game loop and tracking statistics
   private boolean gameOver; // is the game over?
```

Fig. 7.12 | CannonView class's fields. (Part 1 of 2.)

```
    private double timeLeft; // the amount of time left in seconds
    private int shotsFired; // the number of shots the user has fired
    private double totalTimeElapsed; // the number of seconds elapsed

    // variables for the blocker and target
    private Line blocker; // start and end points of the blocker
    private int blockerDistance; // blocker distance from left
    private int blockerBeginning; // blocker distance from top
    private int blockerEnd; // blocker bottom edge distance from top
    private int initialBlockerVelocity; // initial blocker speed multiplier
    private float blockerVelocity; // blocker speed multiplier during game

    private Line target; // start and end points of the target
    private int targetDistance; // target distance from left
    private int targetBeginning; // target distance from top
    private double pieceLength; // length of a target piece
    private int targetEnd; // target bottom's distance from top
    private int initialTargetVelocity; // initial target speed multiplier
    private float targetVelocity; // target speed multiplier during game

    private int lineWidth; // width of the target and blocker
    private boolean[] hitStates; // is each target piece hit?
    private int targetPiecesHit; // number of target pieces hit (out of 7)

    // variables for the cannon and cannonball
    private Point cannonball; // cannonball image's upper-left corner
    private int cannonballVelocityX; // cannonball's x velocity
    private int cannonballVelocityY; // cannonball's y velocity
    private boolean cannonballOnScreen; // is the cannonball on the screen
    private int cannonballRadius; // cannonball radius
    private int cannonballSpeed; // cannonball speed
    private int cannonBaseRadius; // cannon base radius
    private int cannonLength; // cannon barrel length
    private Point barrelEnd; // the endpoint of the cannon's barrel
    private int screenWidth; // width of the screen
    private int screenHeight; // height of the screen

    // constants and variables for managing sounds
    private static final int TARGET_SOUND_ID = 0;
    private static final int CANNON_SOUND_ID = 1;
    private static final int BLOCKER_SOUND_ID = 2;
    private SoundPool soundPool; // plays sound effects
    private Map<Integer, Integer> soundMap; // maps IDs to SoundPool

    // Paint variables used when drawing each item on the screen
    private Paint textPaint; // Paint used to draw text
    private Paint cannonballPaint; // Paint used to draw the cannonball
    private Paint cannonPaint; // Paint used to draw the cannon
    private Paint blockerPaint; // Paint used to draw the blocker
    private Paint targetPaint; // Paint used to draw the target
    private Paint backgroundPaint; // Paint used to clear the drawing area
```

Fig. 7.12 | CannonView class's fields. (Part 2 of 2.)

CannonView Constructor

Figure 7.13 shows class `CannonView`'s constructor. When a `View` is inflated, its constructor is called and passed a `Context` and an `AttributeSet` as arguments. In this case, the `Context` is the `Activity` (`CannonGame`) to which the `CannonView` is attached and the **`AttributeSet`** (package `android.util`) contains the values for any attributes that are set in the layout's XML document. These arguments should be passed to the superclass constructor (line 92) to ensure that the custom `View` object is properly configured with the values of any standard `View` attributes specified in the XML.

Line 93 stores a reference to the parent `Activity` so we can use it at the end of a game to display an `AlertDialog` from the `Activity`'s GUI thread. Line 96 registers `this` (i.e.,

```
89     // public constructor
90     public CannonView(Context context, AttributeSet attrs)
91     {
92        super(context, attrs); // call super's constructor
93        activity = (Activity) context;
94
95        // register SurfaceHolder.Callback listener
96        getHolder().addCallback(this);
97
98        // initialize Lines and points representing game items
99        blocker = new Line(); // create the blocker as a Line
100       target = new Line(); // create the target as a Line
101       cannonball = new Point(); // create the cannonball as a point
102
103       // initialize hitStates as a boolean array
104       hitStates = new boolean[TARGET_PIECES];
105
106       // initialize SoundPool to play the app's three sound effects
107       soundPool = new SoundPool(1, AudioManager.STREAM_MUSIC, 0);
108
109       // create Map of sounds and pre-load sounds
110       soundMap = new HashMap<Integer, Integer>(); // create new HashMap
111       soundMap.put(TARGET_SOUND_ID,
112          soundPool.load(context, R.raw.target_hit, 1));
113       soundMap.put(CANNON_SOUND_ID,
114          soundPool.load(context, R.raw.cannon_fire, 1));
115       soundMap.put(BLOCKER_SOUND_ID,
116          soundPool.load(context, R.raw.blocker_hit, 1));
117
118       // construct Paints for drawing text, cannonball, cannon,
119       // blocker and target; these are configured in method onSizeChanged
120       textPaint = new Paint(); // Paint for drawing text
121       cannonPaint = new Paint(); // Paint for drawing the cannon
122       cannonballPaint = new Paint(); // Paint for drawing a cannonball
123       blockerPaint = new Paint(); // Paint for drawing the blocker
124       targetPaint = new Paint(); // Paint for drawing the target
125       backgroundPaint = new Paint(); // Paint for drawing the target
126    } // end CannonView constructor
127
```

Fig. 7.13 | `CannonView` constructor.

the CannonView) as the object that implements SurfaceHolder.Callback to receive the method calls that indicate when the SurfaceView is created, updated and destroyed. SurfaceView method **getHolder** returns the corresponding SurfaceHolder object for managing the SurfaceView, and SurfaceHolder method **addCallback** stores the object that implements SurfaceHolder.Callback.

Lines 99–101 create the blocker and target as Lines and the cannonball as a Point. Next, we create boolean array hitStates to keep track of which of the target's seven pieces have been hit (and thus should not be drawn).

Lines 107–116 configure the sounds that we use in the app. First, we create the SoundPool that's used to load and play the app's sound effects. The constructor's first argument represents the maximum number of simultaneous sound streams that can play at once. We play only one sound at a time, so we pass 1. The second argument specifies which audio stream will be used to play the sounds. There are seven sound streams identified by constants in class AudioManager, but the documentation for class SoundPool recommends using the stream for playing music (AudioManager.STREAM_MUSIC) for sound in games. The last argument represents the sound quality, but the documentation indicates that this value is not currently used and 0 should be specified as the default value.

Line 110 creates a HashMap (soundMap). Then, lines 111–116 populate it, using the constants at lines 75–77 as keys. The corresponding values are the return values of the SoundPool's **load method**, which returns an ID that can be used to play (or unload) a sound. SoundPool method load receives three arguments—the application's Context, a resource ID representing the sound file to load and the sound's priority. According to the documentation for this method, the last argument is not currently used and should be specified as 1.

Lines 120–125 create the Paint objects that are used when drawing the game's objects. We configure these in method onSizeChanged, because some of the Paint settings depend on scaling the game elements based on the device's screen size.

Overriding View Method onSizeChanged

Figure 7.14 overrides class View's **onSizeChanged method**, which is called whenever the View's size changes, including when the View is first added to the View hierarchy as the layout is inflated. This app always displays in portrait mode, so onSizeChanged is called only once when the activity's onCreate method inflates the GUI. The method receives the View's new width and height and its old width and height—when this method is called the first time, the old width and height are 0. The calculations performed here *scale* the game's on-screen elements based on the device's pixel width and height—we arrived at our scaling factors via trial and error. After the calculations, line 173 calls method newGame (Fig. 7.15).

```
128    // called when the size of this View changes--including when this
129    // view is first added to the view hierarchy
130    @Override
131    protected void onSizeChanged(int w, int h, int oldw, int oldh)
132    {
133       super.onSizeChanged(w, h, oldw, oldh);
134
135       screenWidth = w; // store the width
136       screenHeight = h; // store the height
```

Fig. 7.14 | Overridden onSizeChanged method. (Part 1 of 2.)

```
        cannonBaseRadius = h / 18; // cannon base radius 1/18 screen height
        cannonLength = w / 8; // cannon length 1/8 screen width

        cannonballRadius = w / 36; // cannonball radius 1/36 screen width
        cannonballSpeed = w * 3 / 2; // cannonball speed multiplier

        lineWidth = w / 24; // target and blocker 1/24 screen width

        // configure instance variables related to the blocker
        blockerDistance = w * 5 / 8; // blocker 5/8 screen width from left
        blockerBeginning = h / 8; // distance from top 1/8 screen height
        blockerEnd = h * 3 / 8; // distance from top 3/8 screen height
        initialBlockerVelocity = h / 2; // initial blocker speed multiplier
        blocker.start = new Point(blockerDistance, blockerBeginning);
        blocker.end = new Point(blockerDistance, blockerEnd);

        // configure instance variables related to the target
        targetDistance = w * 7 / 8; // target 7/8 screen width from left
        targetBeginning = h / 8; // distance from top 1/8 screen height
        targetEnd = h * 7 / 8; // distance from top 7/8 screen height
        pieceLength = (targetEnd - targetBeginning) / TARGET_PIECES;
        initialTargetVelocity = -h / 4; // initial target speed multiplier
        target.start = new Point(targetDistance, targetBeginning);
        target.end = new Point(targetDistance, targetEnd);

        // endpoint of the cannon's barrel initially points horizontally
        barrelEnd = new Point(cannonLength, h / 2);

        // configure Paint objects for drawing game elements
        textPaint.setTextSize(w / 20); // text size 1/20 of screen width
        textPaint.setAntiAlias(true); // smoothes the text
        cannonPaint.setStrokeWidth(lineWidth * 1.5f); // set line thickness
        blockerPaint.setStrokeWidth(lineWidth); // set line thickness
        targetPaint.setStrokeWidth(lineWidth); // set line thickness
        backgroundPaint.setColor(Color.WHITE); // set background color

        newGame(); // set up and start a new game
    } // end method onSizeChanged

```

Fig. 7.14 | Overridden onSizeChanged method. (Part 2 of 2.)

CannonView Method newGame

Method newGame (Fig. 7.15) resets the initial values of the instance variables that are used to control the game. If variable gameOver is true, which occurs only after the first game completes, line 197 resets gameOver and lines 198–199 create a new CannonThread and start it to begin the new game.

```
176    // reset all the screen elements and start a new game
177    public void newGame()
178    {
```

Fig. 7.15 | CannonView method newGame. (Part 1 of 2.)

```
      // set every element of hitStates to false--restores target pieces
      for (int i = 0; i < TARGET_PIECES; ++i)
         hitStates[i] = false;

      targetPiecesHit = 0; // no target pieces have been hit
      blockerVelocity = initialBlockerVelocity; // set initial velocity
      targetVelocity = initialTargetVelocity; // set initial velocity
      timeLeft = 10; // start the countdown at 10 seconds
      cannonballOnScreen = false; // the cannonball is not on the screen
      shotsFired = 0; // set the initial number of shots fired
      totalElapsedTime = 0.0; // set the time elapsed to zero
      blocker.start.set(blockerDistance, blockerBeginning);
      blocker.end.set(blockerDistance, blockerEnd);
      target.start.set(targetDistance, targetBeginning);
      target.end.set(targetDistance, targetEnd);

      if (gameOver)
      {
         gameOver = false; // the game is not over
         cannonThread = new CannonThread(getHolder());
         cannonThread.start();
      } // end if
   } // end method newGame

```

Fig. 7.15 | CannonView method newGame. (Part 2 of 2.)

CannonView Method updatePositions

Method updatePositions (Fig. 7.16) is called by the CannonThread's run method (Fig. 7.23) to update the on-screen elements' positions and to perform simple collision detection. The new locations of the game elements are calculated based on the elapsed time in milliseconds between the previous frame of the animation and the current frame of the animation. This enables the game to update the amount by which each game element moves based on the device's refresh rate. We discuss this in more detail when we cover game loops in Fig. 7.23.

```
   // called repeatedly by the CannonThread to update game elements
   private void updatePositions(double elapsedTimeMS)
   {
      double interval = elapsedTimeMS / 1000.0; // convert to seconds

      if (cannonballOnScreen) // if there is currently a shot fired
      {
         // update cannonball position
         cannonball.x += interval * cannonballVelocityX;
         cannonball.y += interval * cannonballVelocityY;

         // check for collision with blocker
         if (cannonball.x + cannonballRadius > blockerDistance &&
            cannonball.x - cannonballRadius < blockerDistance &&
```

Fig. 7.16 | CannonView method updatePositions. (Part 1 of 3.)

```
            cannonball.y + cannonballRadius > blocker.start.y &&
            cannonball.y - cannonballRadius < blocker.end.y)
         {
            cannonballVelocityX *= -1; // reverse cannonball's direction
            timeLeft -= MISS_PENALTY; // penalize the user

            // play blocker sound
            soundPool.play(soundMap.get(BLOCKER_SOUND_ID), 1, 1, 1, 0, 1f)
         } // end if

         // check for collisions with left and right walls
         else if (cannonball.x + cannonballRadius > screenWidth ||
            cannonball.x - cannonballRadius < 0)
            cannonballOnScreen = false; // remove cannonball from screen

         // check for collisions with top and bottom walls
         else if (cannonball.y + cannonballRadius > screenHeight ||
            cannonball.y - cannonballRadius < 0)
            cannonballOnScreen = false; // make the cannonball disappear

         // check for cannonball collision with target
         else if (cannonball.x + cannonballRadius > targetDistance &&
            cannonball.x - cannonballRadius < targetDistance &&
            cannonball.y + cannonballRadius > target.start.y &&
            cannonball.y - cannonballRadius < target.end.y)
         {
            // determine target section number (0 is the top)
            int section =
               (int) ((cannonball.y - target.start.y) / pieceLength);

            // check if the piece hasn't been hit yet
            if ((section >= 0 && section < TARGET_PIECES) &&
               !hitStates[section])
            {
               hitStates[section] = true; // section was hit
               cannonballOnScreen = false; // remove cannonball
               timeLeft += HIT_REWARD; // add reward to remaining time

               // play target hit sound
               soundPool.play(soundMap.get(TARGET_SOUND_ID), 1,
                  1, 1, 0, 1f);

               // if all pieces have been hit
               if (++targetPiecesHit == TARGET_PIECES)
               {
                  cannonThread.setRunning(false);
                  showGameOverDialog(R.string.win); // show winning dialog
                  gameOver = true; // the game is over
               } // end if
            } // end if
         } // end else if
      } // end if

```

Fig. 7.16 | CannonView method updatePositions. (Part 2 of 3.)

```
270       // update the blocker's position
271       double blockerUpdate = interval * blockerVelocity;
272       blocker.start.y += blockerUpdate;
273       blocker.end.y += blockerUpdate;
274
275       // update the target's position
276       double targetUpdate = interval * targetVelocity;
277       target.start.y += targetUpdate;
278       target.end.y += targetUpdate;
279
280       // if the blocker hit the top or bottom, reverse direction
281       if (blocker.start.y < 0 || blocker.end.y > screenHeight)
282          blockerVelocity *= -1;
283
284       // if the target hit the top or bottom, reverse direction
285       if (target.start.y < 0 || target.end.y > screenHeight)
286          targetVelocity *= -1;
287
288       timeLeft -= interval; // subtract from time left
289
290       // if the timer reached zero
291       if (timeLeft <= 0)
292       {
293          timeLeft = 0.0;
294          gameOver = true; // the game is over
295          cannonThread.setRunning(false);
296          showGameOverDialog(R.string.lose); // show the losing dialog
297       } // end if
298    } // end method updatePositions
299
```

Fig. 7.16 | `CannonView` method `updatePositions`. (Part 3 of 3.)

Line 206 converts the elapsed time since the last animation frame from milliseconds to seconds. This value is used to modify the positions of various game elements.

Line 208 checks whether the cannonball is on the screen. If it is, we update its position by adding the distance it should have traveled since the last timer event. This is calculated by multiplying its velocity by the amount of time that passed (lines 211–212). Lines 215–218 check whether the cannonball has collided with the blocker. We perform simple *collision detection*, based on the rectangular boundary of the cannonball. There are four conditions that must be met if the cannonball is in contact with the blocker:

- The cannonball's *x*-coordinate plus the cannon ball's radius must be greater than the blocker's distance from the left edge of the screen (`blockerDistance`) (line 215). This means that the cannonball has reached the blocker's distance from the left edge of the screen.
- The cannonball's *x*-coordinate minus the cannon ball's radius must also be less than the blocker's distance from the left edge of the screen (line 216). This ensures that the cannonball has not yet passed the blocker.
- Part of the cannonball must be lower than the top of the blocker (line 217).
- Part of the cannonball must be higher than the bottom of the blocker (line 218).

If all these conditions are met, we *reverse* the cannonball's direction on the screen (line 220), *penalize* the user by *subtracting* MISS_PENALTY from timeLeft, then call soundPool's **play method** to play the blocker hit sound—BLOCKER_SOUND_ID is used as the soundMap key to locate the sound's ID in the SoundPool.

We remove the cannonball if it reaches any of the screen's edges. Lines 228–230 test whether the cannonball has *collided* with the left or right wall and, if it has, remove the cannonball from the screen. Lines 233–235 remove the cannonball if it collides with the top or bottom of the screen.

We then check whether the cannonball has hit the target (lines 238–241). These conditions are similar to those used to determine whether the cannonball collided with the blocker. If the cannonball hit the target, we determine which *section* of the target was hit. Lines 244–245 determine which section has been hit—dividing the distance between the cannonball and the bottom of the target by the length of a piece. This expression evaluates to 0 for the top-most section and 6 for the bottom-most. We check whether that section was previously hit, using the hitStates array (line 249). If it wasn't, we set the corresponding hitStates element to true and remove the cannonball from the screen. We then add HIT_REWARD to timeLeft, increasing the game's time remaining, and play the target hit sound (TARGET_SOUND_ID). We increment targetPiecesHit, then determine whether it's equal to TARGET_PIECES (line 260). If so, the game is over, so we terminate the CannonThread by calling its setRunning method with the argument false, invoke method showGameOverDialog with the String resource ID representing the winning message and set gameOver to true.

Now that all possible cannonball collisions have been checked, the blocker and target positions must be updated. Lines 271–273 change the blocker's position by multiplying blockerVelocity by the amount of time that has passed since the last update and adding that value to the current *x*- and *y*-coordinates. Lines 276–278 do the same for the target. If the blocker has collided with the top or bottom wall, its direction is *reversed* by multiplying its velocity by -1 (lines 281–282). Lines 285–286 perform the same check and adjustment for the full length of the target, including any sections that have already been hit.

We decrease timeLeft by the time that has passed since the prior animation frame. If timeLeft has reached zero, the game is over—we set timeLeft to 0.0 just in case it was negative; otherwise, we'll sometimes display a negative final time on the screen). Then we set gameOver to true, terminate the CannonThread by calling its setRunning method with the argument false and call method showGameOverDialog with the String resource ID representing the losing message.

CannonView Method fireCannonball

When the user double taps the screen, the event handler for that event (Fig. 7.10) calls method fireCannonball (Fig. 7.17) to fire a cannonball. If there's already a cannonball on the screen, the method returns immediately; otherwise, it fires the cannon. Line 306 calls alignCannon to aim the cannon at the double-tap point and get the cannon's angle. Lines 309–310 "load" the cannon (that is, position the cannonball inside the cannon). Then, lines 313 and 316 calculate the horizontal and vertical components of the cannonball's velocity. Next, we set cannonballOnScreen to true so that the cannonball will be drawn by method drawGameElements (Fig. 7.19) and increment shotsFired. Finally, we play the cannon's firing sound (CANNON_SOUND_ID).

```
   // fires a cannonball
   public void fireCannonball(MotionEvent event)
   {
      if (cannonballOnScreen) // if a cannonball is already on the screen
         return; // do nothing

      double angle = alignCannon(event); // get the cannon barrel's angle

      // move the cannonball to be inside the cannon
      cannonball.x = cannonballRadius; // align x-coordinate with cannon
      cannonball.y = screenHeight / 2; // centers ball vertically

      // get the x component of the total velocity
      cannonballVelocityX = (int) (cannonballSpeed * Math.sin(angle));

      // get the y component of the total velocity
      cannonballVelocityY = (int) (-cannonballSpeed * Math.cos(angle));
      cannonballOnScreen = true; // the cannonball is on the screen
      ++shotsFired; // increment shotsFired

      // play cannon fired sound
      soundPool.play(soundMap.get(CANNON_SOUND_ID), 1, 1, 1, 0, 1f);
   } // end method fireCannonball

```

Fig. 7.17 | CannonView method fireCannonball.

CannonView Method alignCannon

Method alignCannon (Fig. 7.18) aims the cannon at the point where the user double tapped the screen. Line 328 gets the *x*- and *y*-coordinates of the double tap from the MotionEvent argument. We compute the vertical distance of the touch from the center of the screen. If this is not zero, we calculate cannon barrel's angle from the horizontal (line 338). If the touch is on the lower-half of the screen we adjust the angle by Math.PI (line 342). We then use the cannonLength and the angle to determine the *x* and *y* coordinate values for the endpoint of the cannon's barrel—this is used to draw a line from the cannon base's center at the left edge of the screen to the cannon's barrel endpoint.

```
324    // aligns the cannon in response to a user touch
325    public double alignCannon(MotionEvent event)
326    {
327       // get the location of the touch in this view
328       Point touchPoint = new Point((int) event.getX(), (int) event.getY());
329
330       // compute the touch's distance from center of the screen
331       // on the y-axis
332       double centerMinusY = (screenHeight / 2 - touchPoint.y);
333
334       double angle = 0; // initialize angle to 0
335
```

Fig. 7.18 | CannonView method alignCannon. (Part 1 of 2.)

```
      // calculate the angle the barrel makes with the horizontal
      if (centerMinusY != 0) // prevent division by 0
         angle = Math.atan((double) touchPoint.x / centerMinusY);

      // if the touch is on the lower half of the screen
      if (touchPoint.y > screenHeight / 2)
         angle += Math.PI; // adjust the angle

      // calculate the endpoint of the cannon barrel
      barrelEnd.x = (int) (cannonLength * Math.sin(angle));
      barrelEnd.y =
         (int) (-cannonLength * Math.cos(angle) + screenHeight / 2);

      return angle; // return the computed angle
   } // end method alignCannon

```

Fig. 7.18 | CannonView method alignCannon. (Part 2 of 2.)

Drawing the Game Elements

The method drawGameElements (Fig. 7.19) draws the cannon, cannonball, blocker and target on the SurfaceView using the Canvas that the CannonThread obtains from the SurfaceView's SurfaceHolder.

```
   // draws the game to the given Canvas
   public void drawGameElements(Canvas canvas)
   {
      // clear the background
      canvas.drawRect(0, 0, canvas.getWidth(), canvas.getHeight(),
         backgroundPaint);

      // display time remaining
      canvas.drawText(getResources().getString(
         R.string.time_remaining_format, timeLeft), 30, 50, textPaint);

      // if a cannonball is currently on the screen, draw it
      if (cannonballOnScreen)
         canvas.drawCircle(cannonball.x, cannonball.y, cannonballRadius,
            cannonballPaint);

      // draw the cannon barrel
      canvas.drawLine(0, screenHeight / 2, barrelEnd.x, barrelEnd.y,
         cannonPaint);

      // draw the cannon base
      canvas.drawCircle(0, (int) screenHeight / 2,
         (int) cannonBaseRadius, cannonPaint);

      // draw the blocker
      canvas.drawLine(blocker.start.x, blocker.start.y, blocker.end.x,
         blocker.end.y, blockerPaint);
```

Fig. 7.19 | CannonView method drawGameElements. (Part 1 of 2.)

```
379
380         Point currentPoint = new Point(); // start of current target section
381
382         // initialize curPoint to the starting point of the target
383         currentPoint.x = target.start.x;
384         currentPoint.y = target.start.y;
385
386         // draw the target
387         for (int i = 1; i <= TARGET_PIECES; ++i)
388         {
389            // if this target piece is not hit, draw it
390            if (!hitStates[i - 1])
391            {
392               // alternate coloring the pieces yellow and blue
393               if (i % 2 == 0)
394                  targetPaint.setColor(Color.YELLOW);
395               else
396                  targetPaint.setColor(Color.BLUE);
397
398               canvas.drawLine(currentPoint.x, currentPoint.y, target.end.x,
399                  (int) (currentPoint.y + pieceLength), targetPaint);
400            }
401
402            // move curPoint to the start of the next piece
403            currentPoint.y += pieceLength;
404         } // end for
405      } // end method drawGameElements
406
```

Fig. 7.19 | CannonView method drawGameElements. (Part 2 of 2.)

First, we call Canvas's **drawRect method** (lines 356–357) to clear the Canvas so that all the game elements can be displayed in their new positions. The method receives as arguments the rectangle's upper-left *x-y* coordinates, the rectangle's width and height, and the Paint object that specifies the drawing characteristics—recall that backgroundPaint sets the drawing color to white. Next, we call Canvas's **drawText method** (lines 360–361) to display the time remaining in the game. We pass as arguments the String to be displayed, the *x*- and *y*-coordinates at which to display it and the textPaint (configured in lines 166–167) to describe how the text should be rendered (that is, the text's font size, color and other attributes).

If the cannonball is on the screen, lines 365–366 use Canvas's **drawCircle method** to draw the cannonball in its current position. The first two arguments represent the coordinates of the circle's center. The third argument is the circle's radius. The last argument is the Paint object specifying the circle's drawing characteristics.

We use Canvas's **drawLine method** to display the cannon barrel (lines 369–370), the blocker (lines 377–378) and the target pieces (lines 398–399). This method receives five parameters—the first four represent the *x-y* coordinates of the line's start and end, and the last is the Paint object specifying the line's characteristics, such as the line's thickness.

Lines 373–374 use Canvas's drawCircle method to draw the cannon's half-circle base by drawing a circle that's centered at the left edge of the screen—because a circle is displayed based on its center point, half of this circle is drawn off the left side of the SurfaceView.

Lines 380–404 draw the target sections. We iterate through the target's sections, drawing each in the correct color—blue for the odd-numbered pieces and yellow for the others. Only those sections that haven't been hit are displayed.

CannonView Method showGameOverDialog

When the game ends, the `showGameOverDialog` method (Fig. 7.20) displays an `AlertDialog` indicating whether the player won or lost, the number of shots fired and the total time elapsed. Lines 419–430 call the `Builder`'s `setPositiveButton` method to create a reset button. The `onClick` method of the button's listener indicates that the dialog is no longer displayed and calls `newGame` to set up and start a new game. A dialog must be displayed from the GUI thread, so lines 432–440 call `Activity` method **`runOnUiThread`** and pass it an object of an anonymous inner class that implements `Runnable`. The `Runnable`'s `run` method indicates that the dialog is displayed and then displays it.

```
407    // display an AlertDialog when the game ends
408    private void showGameOverDialog(int messageId)
409    {
410       // create a dialog displaying the given String
411       final AlertDialog.Builder dialogBuilder =
412          new AlertDialog.Builder(getContext());
413       dialogBuilder.setTitle(getResources().getString(messageId));
414       dialogBuilder.setCancelable(false);
415
416       // display number of shots fired and total time elapsed
417       dialogBuilder.setMessage(getResources().getString(
418          R.string.results_format, shotsFired, totalElapsedTime));
419       dialogBuilder.setPositiveButton(R.string.reset_game,
420          new DialogInterface.OnClickListener()
421          {
422             // called when "Reset Game" Button is pressed
423             @Override
424             public void onClick(DialogInterface dialog, int which)
425             {
426                dialogIsDisplayed = false;
427                newGame(); // set up and start a new game
428             } // end method onClick
429          } // end anonymous inner class
430       ); // end call to setPositiveButton
431
432       activity.runOnUiThread(
433          new Runnable() {
434             public void run()
435             {
436                dialogIsDisplayed = true;
437                dialogBuilder.show(); // display the dialog
438             } // end method run
439          } // end Runnable
440       ); // end call to runOnUiThread
441    } // end method showGameOverDialog
442
```

Fig. 7.20 | `CannonView` method `showGameOverDialog`.

`CannonView` Methods `stopGame` and `releaseResources`

`Activity` class `CannonGame`'s `onPause` and `onDestroy` methods (Fig. 7.8) call class `CannonView`'s `stopGame` and `releaseResources` methods (Fig. 7.21), respectively. Method `stopGame` (lines 444–448) is called from the main `Activity` to stop the game when the `Activity`'s `onPause` method is called—for simplicity, we don't store the game's state in this example. Method `releaseResources` (lines 451–455) calls the `SoundPool`'s **`release` method** to release the resources associated with the `SoundPool`.

```
443    // pauses the game
444    public void stopGame()
445    {
446       if (cannonThread != null)
447          cannonThread.setRunning(false);
448    } // end method stopGame
449
450    // releases resources; called by CannonGame's onDestroy method
451    public void releaseResources()
452    {
453       soundPool.release(); // release all resources used by the SoundPool
454       soundPool = null;
455    } // end method releaseResources
456
```

Fig. 7.21 | `CannonView` methods `stopGame` and `releaseResources`.

Implementing the `SurfaceHolder.Callback` Methods

Figure 7.22 implements the **`surfaceChanged`**, **`surfaceCreated`** and **`surfaceDestroyed`** methods of interface `SurfaceHolder.Callback`. Method `surfaceChanged` has an empty body in this app because the app is always displayed in portrait view. This method is called when the `SurfaceView`'s size or orientation changes, and would typically be used to redisplay graphics based on those changes. Method `surfaceCreated` (lines 465–471) is called when the `SurfaceView` is created—e.g., when the app first loads or when it resumes from the background. We use `surfaceCreated` to create and start the `CannonThread` to begin the game. Method `surfaceDestroyed` (lines 474–492) is called when the `SurfaceView` is destroyed—e.g., when the app terminates. We use the method to ensure that the `CannonThread` terminates properly. First, line 479 calls `CannonThread`'s `setRunning` method with `false` as an argument to indicate that the thread should stop, then lines 481–491 wait for the thead to terminate. This ensures that no attempt is made to draw to the `SurfaceView` once `surfaceDestroyed` completes execution.

```
457    // called when surface changes size
458    @Override
459    public void surfaceChanged(SurfaceHolder holder, int format,
460       int width, int height)
461    {
462    } // end method surfaceChanged
463
```

Fig. 7.22 | Implementing the `SurfaceHolder.Callback` methods. (Part 1 of 2.)

```
   // called when surface is first created
   @Override
   public void surfaceCreated(SurfaceHolder holder)
   {
      cannonThread = new CannonThread(holder);
      cannonThread.setRunning(true);
      cannonThread.start(); // start the game loop thread
   } // end method surfaceCreated

   // called when the surface is destroyed
   @Override
   public void surfaceDestroyed(SurfaceHolder holder)
   {
      // ensure that thread terminates properly
      boolean retry = true;
      cannonThread.setRunning(false);

      while (retry)
      {
         try
         {
            cannonThread.join();
            retry = false;
         } // end try
         catch (InterruptedException e)
         {
         } // end catch
      } // end while
   } // end method surfaceDestroyed

```

Fig. 7.22 | Implementing the `SurfaceHolder.Callback` methods. (Part 2 of 2.)

`CannonThread`: Using a Thread to Create a Game Loop

Figure 7.23 defines a subclass of `Thread` which updates the game. The thread maintains a reference to the `SurfaceView`'s `SurfaceHolder` (line 497) and a `boolean` indicating whether the thread is running. The class's `run` method (lines 514–543) drives the frame-by-frame animations—this is know as the *game loop*. Each update of the game elements on the screen is performed based on the number of milliseconds that have passed since the last update. Line 518 gets the system's current time in milliseconds when the thread begins running. Lines 520–542 loop until `threadIsRunning` is `false`.

```
494    // Thread subclass to control the game loop
495    private class CannonThread extends Thread
496    {
497       private SurfaceHolder surfaceHolder; // for manipulating canvas
498       private boolean threadIsRunning = true; // running by default
499
```

Fig. 7.23 | `Runnable` that updates the game every `TIME_INTERVAL` milliseconds. (Part 1 of 2.)

```
500       // initializes the surface holder
501       public CannonThread(SurfaceHolder holder)
502       {
503          surfaceHolder = holder;
504          setName("CannonThread");
505       } // end constructor
506 
507       // changes running state
508       public void setRunning(boolean running)
509       {
510          threadIsRunning = running;
511       } // end method setRunning
512 
513       // controls the game loop
514       @Override
515       public void run()
516       {
517          Canvas canvas = null; // used for drawing
518          long previousFrameTime = System.currentTimeMillis();
519 
520          while (threadIsRunning)
521          {
522             try
523             {
524                canvas = surfaceHolder.lockCanvas(null);
525 
526                // lock the surfaceHolder for drawing
527                synchronized(surfaceHolder)
528                {
529                   long currentTime = System.currentTimeMillis();
530                   double elapsedTimeMS = currentTime - previousFrameTime;
531                   totalElapsedTime += elapsedTimeMS / 1000.0;
532                   updatePositions(elapsedTimeMS); // update game state
533                   drawGameElements(canvas); // draw
534                   previousFrameTime = currentTime; // update previous time
535                } // end synchronized block
536             } // end try
537             finally
538             {
539                if (canvas != null)
540                   surfaceHolder.unlockCanvasAndPost(canvas);
541             } // end finally
542          } // end while
543       } // end method run
544    } // end nested class CannonThread
545 } // end class CannonView
```

Fig. 7.23 | `Runnable` that updates the game every `TIME_INTERVAL` milliseconds. (Part 2 of 2.)

First we must obtain the `Canvas` for drawing on the `SurfaceView` by calling `SurfaceHolder` method **`lockCanvas`** (line 524). Only one thread at a time can draw to a `SurfaceView`, so we must first lock the `SurfaceHolder`, which we do with a synchronized block. Next, we get the current time in milliseconds, then calculate the elapsed time and add that to the total time that has elapsed so far—this will be used to help display the amount of time left in the game. Line 532 calls method `updatePositions` with the elapsed time in milliseconds as an argument—this moves all the game elements using the elapsed time to help scale the amount of movement. This helps ensure that the game operates at the same speed regardless of how fast the device is. If the time between frames is larger (i.e, the device is slower), the game elements will move further when each frame of the animation is displayed. If the time between frames is smaller (i.e, the device is faster), the game elements will move less when each frame of the animation is displayed. Finally, line 533 draws the game elements using the `SurfaceView`'s `Canvas` and line 534 stores the `currentTime` as the `previousFrameTime` to prepare to calculate the elapsed time in the next frame of the animation.

7.6 Wrap-Up

In this chapter, you created the **Cannon Game** app, which challenged the player to destroy a seven-piece target before a 10-second time limit expired. The user aimed the cannon by touching the screen. The cannon fired a cannonball when the user double-tapped the screen.

You learned how to define `String` resources to represent the format `Strings` that are used in calls to class `Resource`'s `getString` method and class `String`'s `format` method, and how to number format specifiers for localization purposes. You created a custom view by extending class `SurfaceView` and learned that custom component class names must be fully qualified in the XML layout element that represents the component.

We presented additional `Activity` lifecycle methods. You learned that method `onPause` is called for the current `Activity` when another activity receives the focus and that method `onDestroy` is called when the system shuts down an `Activity`.

You handled touches and single taps by overriding `Activity`'s `onTouchEvent` method. To handle the double taps that fired the cannon, you used a `GestureDetector`. You responded to the double tap event with a `SimpleOnGestureListener` that contained an overridden `onDoubleTap` method.

You added sound effects to the app's `res/raw` folder and managed them with a `SoundPool`. You also used the system's `AudioManager` service to obtain the device's current music volume and use it as the playback volume.

This app manually performed its animations by updating the game elements on a `SurfaceView` from a separate thread of execution. To do this, extended class `Thread` and created a `run` method that displayed graphics with methods of class `Canvas`. You used the `SurfaceView`'s `SurfaceHolder` to obtain the appropriate `Canvas`. You also learned how to build a game loop that controls a game based on the amount of time that has elapsed between animation frames, so that the game will operate at the same overall speed on all devices.

In the next chapter, we create the **SpotOn** game app—our first Android 3.x app. **SpotOn** uses Android 3.x's property animation to animate `Views` that contain images. The app tests the user's reflexes by animating multiple spots that the user must touch before they disappear.

SpotOn Game App

Property Animation, ViewPropertyAnimator, AnimatorListener, Thread-Safe Collections, Default SharedPreferences for an Activity

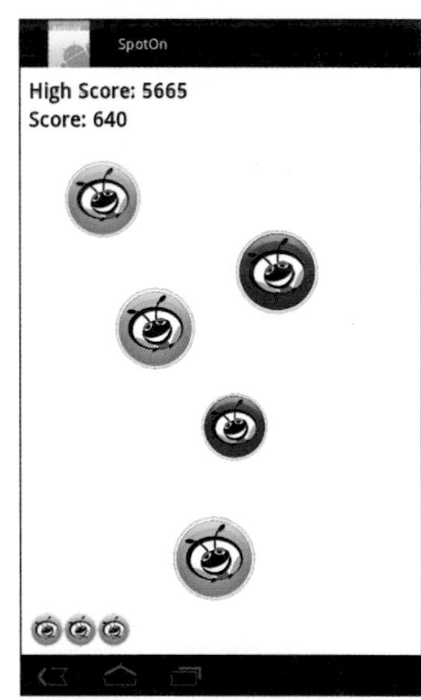

Objectives

In this chapter you'll:

- Create a simple game app that's easy to code and fun to play.
- Use `ViewPropertyAnimator`s to group animations that move and resize `ImageView`s.
- Respond to animation lifecycle events with an `AnimatorListener`.
- Process click events for `ImageView`s and touch events for the screen.
- Use the thread-safe `ConcurrentLinkedQueue` collection from the `java.util.concurrent` package to allow concurrent access to a collection from multiple threads.

Outline

8.1 Introduction

The **SpotOn** game tests a user's reflexes by requiring the user to touch moving spots before they disappear (Fig. 8.1). The spots shrink as they move, making them harder to touch. The game begins on level one, and the user reaches each higher level by touching 10 spots. The higher the level, the faster the spots move—making the game increasingly challenging. When the user touches a spot, the app makes a popping sound and the spot disappears. Points are awarded for each touched spot (10 times the current level). Accuracy is important—any touch that isn't on a spot decreases the score by 15 times the current level. The user begins the game with *three* additional lives, which are displayed in the bottom-left corner of the app. If a spot disappears before the user touches it, a flushing sound plays and the user loses a life. The user gains a life for each new level reached, up to a maximum of *seven* lives. When no additional lives remain and a spot's animation ends without the spot being touched, the game ends (Fig. 8.2).

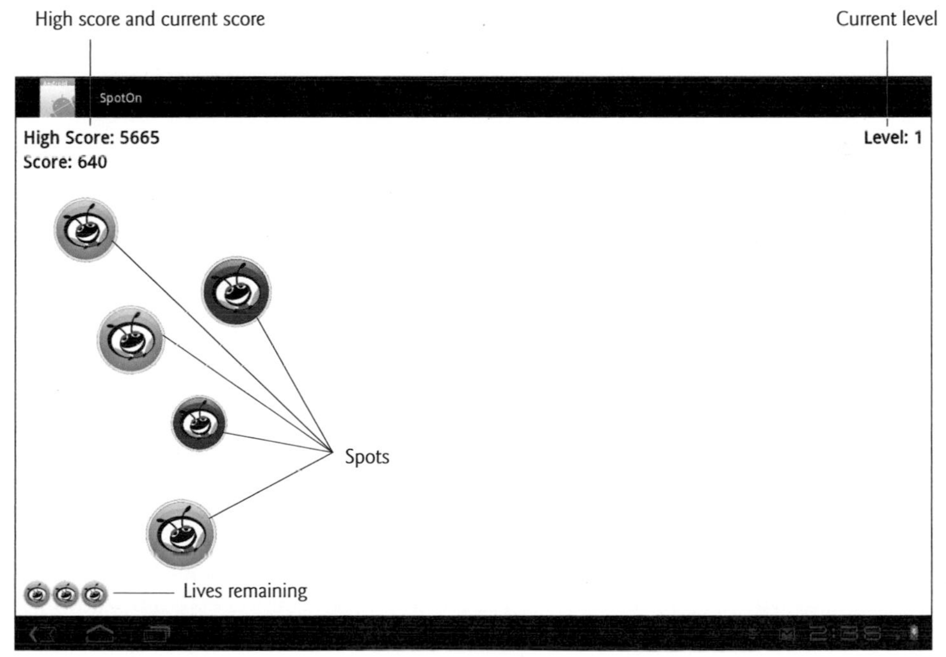

Fig. 8.1 | **SpotOn** game app.

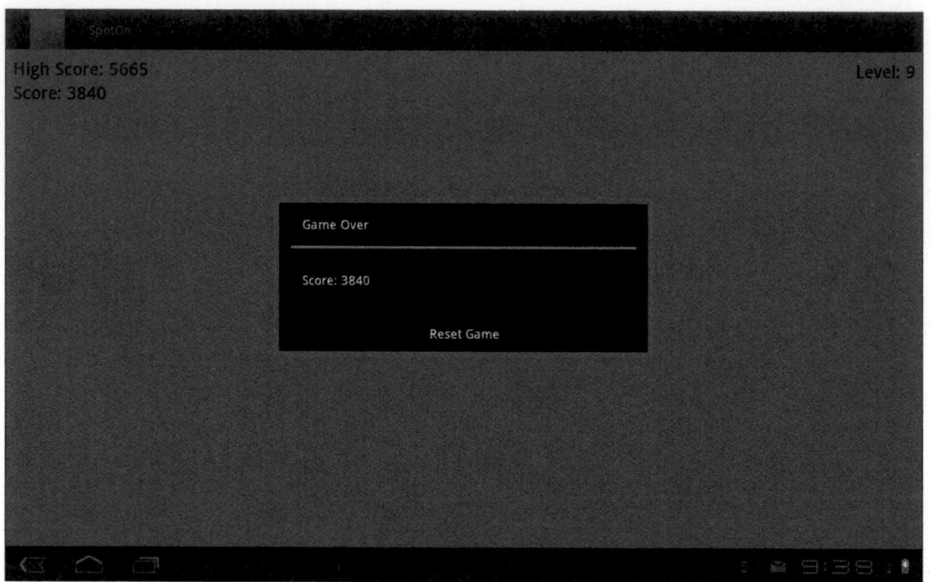

Fig. 8.2 | **Game Over** alert showing final score and **Reset Game** button.

8.2 Test-Driving the SpotOn Game App

Opening and Running the App

Open Eclipse and import the **SpotOn** app project. Perform the following steps:

1. *Open the* **Import** *dialog.* Select **File > Import...** to open the **Import** dialog.
2. *Import the* **SpotOn** *app project.* In the **Import** dialog, expand the **General** node and select **Existing Projects into Workspace**, then click **Next >** to proceed to the **Import Projects** step. Ensure that **Select root directory** is selected, then click the **Browse...** button. In the **Browse for Folder** dialog, locate the `SpotOn` folder in the book's examples folder, select it and click **OK**. Click **Finish** to import the project into Eclipse. The project now appears in the **Package Explorer** window at the left side of the Eclipse window.
3. *Launch the* **SpotOn** *app.* In Eclipse, right click the `SpotOn` project in the **Package Explorer** window, then select **Run As > Android Application** from the menu that appears.

Playing the Game

As spots appear on the screen, tap them with your finger (or the mouse in an AVD). Try not to allow any spot to complete its animation, as you'll lose one of your remaining lives. The game ends when you have no lives remaining and a spot completes its animation without you touching it. [*Note:* This is an Android 3.1 app. At the time of this writing, AVDs for Android 3.0 and higher are *extremely* slow. If possible, you should run this app on an Android 3.1 device.]

8.3 Technologies Overview

Android 3.x and Property Animation

This is our first app that uses features of Android 3.0+. In particular, we use **property animation**—which was added to Android in version 3.0—to move and scale `ImageView`s.

Android versions prior to 3.0 have two primary animation mechanisms:

- *Tweened* `View` *animations* allow you to change limited aspects of a `View`'s *appearance*, such as where it's displayed, its rotation and its size.
- *Frame* `View` *animations* display a sequence of images.

For any other animation requirements, you have to create your own animations, as we did in Chapter 7. Unfortunately, `View` animations affect only how a `View` is *drawn* on the screen. So, if you animate a `Button` from one location to another, the user can initiate the `Button`'s click event only by touching the `Button`'s original screen location.

With property animation (package **`android.animation`**), you can animate *any* property of *any* object—the mechanism is not limited to `View`s. Moving a `Button` with property animation not only draws the `Button` in a different location on the screen, it also ensures that the user can continue to interact with that `Button` in its current location.

Property animations animate *values* over *time*. To create an animation you specify:

- the target object containing the property or properties to animate
- the property or properties to animate
- the animation's duration
- the values to animate between for each property
- how to change the property values over time—known as an *interpolator*

The property animation classes are `ValueAnimator` and `ObjectAnimator`. **`ValueAnimator`** calculates property values over time, but you must specify an **`AnimatorUpdateListener`** in which you programmatically modify the target object's property values. This can be useful if the target object does not have standard *set* methods for changing property values. `ValueAnimator` subclass **`ObjectAnimator`** uses the target object's *set* methods to modify the object's animated properties as their values change over time.

Android 3.1 added the new utility class **`ViewPropertyAnimator`** to simplify property animation for `View`s and to allow multiple properties to be animated in parallel. Each `View` now contains an **`animate` method** that returns a `ViewPropertyAnimator` on which you can *chain* method calls to configure the animation. When the last method call in the chain completes execution, the animation starts. We'll use this technique to animate the spots in the game. For more information on animation in Android, see the following blog posts:

```
android-developers.blogspot.com/2011/02/animation-in-honeycomb.html
android-developers.blogspot.com/2011/05/
   introducing-viewpropertyanimator.html
```

Listening for Animation Lifecycle Events

You can listen for property-animation lifecycle events by implementing the interface **`AnimatorListener`**, which defines methods that are called when an animation starts, ends, repeats or is canceled. If your app does not require all four, you can extend class **`AnimatorListenerAdapter`** and override only the listener method(s) you need.

Touch Handling

Chapter 7 introduced touch handling by overriding `Activity` method `onTouchEvent`. There are two types of touches in the **SpotOn** game—touching a spot and touching elsewhere on the screen. We'll register `OnClickListeners` for each spot (i.e., `ImageView`) to process a touched spot, and we'll use `onTouchEvent` to process all other screen touches.

`ConcurrentLinkedQueue` and `Queue`

We use the **`ConcurrentLinkedQueue`** class (from package **`java.util.concurrent`**) and the **`Queue`** interface to maintain *thread-safe* lists of objects that can be accessed from multiple threads of execution in parallel.

8.4 Building the App's GUI and Resource Files

In this section, you'll build the GUI and resource files for the **SpotOn** game app. To save space, we do not show this app's `strings.xml` resource file. You can view the contents of this file by opening it from the project in Eclipse.

8.4.1 `AndroidManifest.xml`

Figure 8.3 shows this app's `AndroidManifest.xml` file. We set the `uses-sdk` element's `android:minSdkVersion` attribute to `"12"` (line 5), which represents the Android 3.1 SDK. This app will run only on Android 3.1+ devices and AVDs. Line 7 sets the attribute **`android:hardwareAccelerated`** to `"true"`. This allows the app to use *hardware accelerated graphics*, if available, for performance. Line 9 sets the attribute `android:screenOrientation` to specify that this app should always appear in *landscape mode* (that is, a horizontal orientation).

```
1  <?xml version="1.0" encoding="utf-8"?>
2  <manifest xmlns:android="http://schemas.android.com/apk/res/android"
3     android:versionCode="1" android:versionName="1.0"
4     package="com.deitel.spoton">
5     <uses-sdk android:minSdkVersion="12"/>
6     <application android:icon="@drawable/icon"
7        android:hardwareAccelerated="true" android:label="@string/app_name">
8        <activity android:name=".SpotOn" android:label="@string/app_name"
9           android:screenOrientation="landscape">
10          <intent-filter>
11             <action android:name="android.intent.action.MAIN" />
12             <category android:name="android.intent.category.LAUNCHER"/>
13          </intent-filter>
14       </activity>
15    </application>
16 </manifest>
```

Fig. 8.3 | `AndroidManifest.xml`.

8.4.2 `main.xml RelativeLayout`

This app's `main.xml` (Fig. 8.4) layout file contains a `RelativeLayout` that positions the app's `TextViews` for displaying the high score, level and current score, and a `LinearLayout` for displaying the lives remaining. The layouts and GUI components used here have been presented previously, so we've highlighted only the key features in the file. Figure 8.5 shows the app's GUI component names.

```
<?xml version="1.0" encoding="utf-8"?>
<RelativeLayout xmlns:android="http://schemas.android.com/apk/res/android"
   android:id="@+id/relativeLayout" android:layout_width="match_parent"
   android:layout_height="match_parent"
   android:background="@android:color/white">
   <TextView android:id="@+id/highScoreTextView"
      android:layout_width="wrap_content"
      android:layout_height="wrap_content"
      android:layout_marginTop="10dp"
      android:layout_marginLeft="10dp"
      android:textColor="@android:color/black" android:textSize="25sp"
      android:text="@string/high_score"></TextView>
   <TextView android:id="@+id/levelTextView"
      android:layout_toRightOf="@id/highScoreTextView"
      android:layout_width="wrap_content"
      android:layout_height="wrap_content"
      android:layout_marginTop="10dp"
      android:layout_marginRight="10dp"
      android:gravity="right"
      android:layout_alignParentRight="true"
      android:textColor="@android:color/black" android:textSize="25sp"
      android:text="@string/level"></TextView>
   <TextView android:id="@+id/scoreTextView"
      android:layout_below="@id/highScoreTextView"
      android:layout_width="wrap_content"
      android:layout_height="wrap_content"
      android:layout_marginLeft="10dp"
      android:textColor="@android:color/black" android:textSize="25sp"
      android:text="@string/score"></TextView>
   <LinearLayout android:id="@+id/lifeLinearLayout"
      android:layout_alignParentBottom="true"
      android:layout_width="match_parent"
      android:layout_height="wrap_content"
      android:layout_margin="10dp"></LinearLayout>
</RelativeLayout >
```

Fig. 8.4 | **SpotOn**'s `main.xml` layout file.

8.4.3 `untouched.xml` ImageView for an Untouched Spot

This app's `untouched.xml` (Fig. 8.6) layout file contains an `ImageView` that's inflated and configured dynamically as we create each new spot in the game.

8.4.4 `life.xml` ImageView for a Life

This app's `life.xml` (Fig. 8.7) layout file contains an `ImageView` that's inflated and configured dynamically each time a new life is added to the screen during the game.

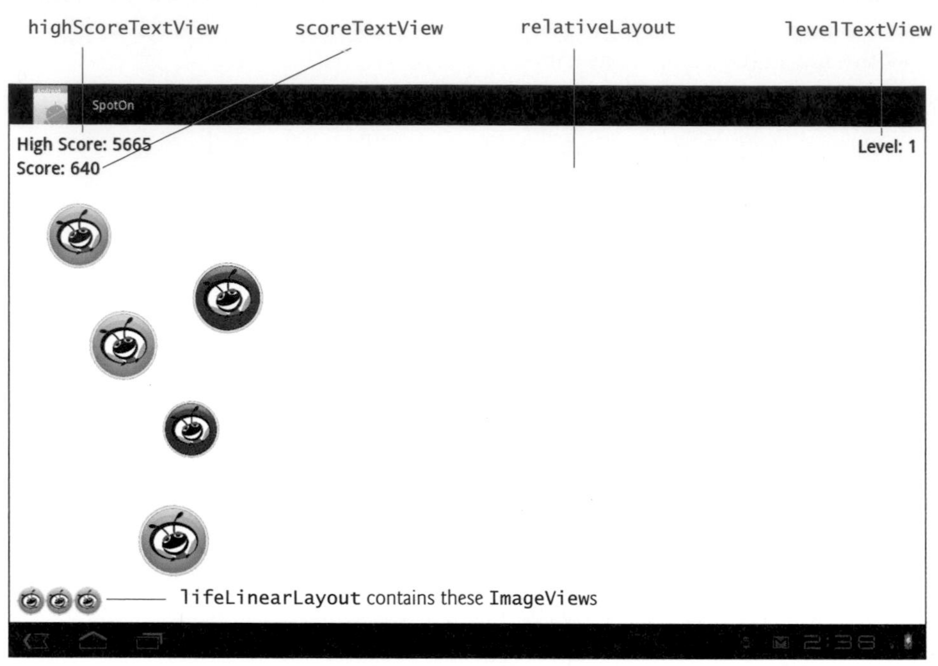

Fig. 8.5 | **SpotOn** GUI component names.

```
<?xml version="1.0" encoding="utf 8"?>
<ImageView xmlns:android="http://schemas.android.com/apk/res/android">
</ImageView>
```

Fig. 8.6 | **SpotOn**'s `untouched.xml` `ImageView` for a new spot.

```
<?xml version="1.0" encoding="utf-8"?>
<ImageView xmlns:android="http://schemas.android.com/apk/res/android"
   android:src="@drawable/life"></ImageView>
```

Fig. 8.7 | **SpotOn**'s `life.xml` layout file.

8.5 Building the App

The **SpotOn** game consists of two classes—`SpotOn` (Section 8.5.1) is the app's main `Activity` and class `SpotOnView` (Section 8.5.1) defines the game logic and spot animations.

8.5.1 SpotOn Subclass of `Activity`

Class `SpotOn` (Fig. 8.8) overrides `onCreate` to configure the GUI. Lines 24–25 create the `SpotOnView` and line 26 adds it to the `RelativeLayout` at position 0—that is, behind all the other elements in the layout. `SpotOnView`'s constructor requires three arguments—the `Context` in which this GUI component is displayed (i.e., this `Activity`), a `SharedPref-`

```
// SpotOn.java
// Activity for the SpotOn app
package com.deitel.spoton;

import android.app.Activity;
import android.content.Context;
import android.os.Bundle;
import android.widget.RelativeLayout;

public class SpotOn extends Activity
{
   private SpotOnView view; // displays and manages the game

   // called when this Activity is first created
   @Override
   public void onCreate(Bundle savedInstanceState)
   {
      super.onCreate(savedInstanceState);
      setContentView(R.layout.main);

      // create a new SpotOnView and add it to the RelativeLayout
      RelativeLayout layout =
         (RelativeLayout) findViewById(R.id.relativeLayout);
      view = new SpotOnView(this, getPreferences(Context.MODE_PRIVATE),
         layout);
      layout.addView(view, 0); // add view to the layout
   } // end method onCreate

   // called when this Activity moves to the background
   @Override
   public void onPause()
   {
      super.onPause();
      view.pause(); // release resources held by the View
   } // end method onPause

   // called when this Activity is brought to the foreground
   @Override
   public void onResume()
   {
      super.onResume();
      view.resume(this); // re-initialize resources released in onPause
   } // end method onResume
} // end class SpotOn
```

Fig. 8.8 | Class `SpotOn` defines the app's main `Activity`.

erences object and the `RelativeLayout` (so that the `SpotOnView` can interact with the other GUI components in the layout). Chapter 5 showed how to read from and write to a named `SharedPreferences` file. In this app, we use the default one that's associated with the `Activity`, which we obtain with a call to `Activity` method **`getPreferences`**.

Overridden `Activity` methods `onPause` and `onResume` call the `SpotOnView`'s `pause` and `resume` methods, respectively. When the `Activity`'s `onPause` method is called, `Spot-`

OnView's pause method releases the SoundPool resources used by the app and cancels any running animations. As you know when an Activity begins executing, its onCreate method is called. This is followed by calls to the Activity's onStart then **onResume** methods. Method onResume is also called when an Activity in the background returns to the foreground. When onResume is called in this app's Activity, SpotOnView's resume method obtains the SoundPool resources again and restarts the game. This app *does not* save the game's state when the app is not on the screen.

8.5.2 SpotOnView Subclass of View

Class SpotOnView (Figs. 8.9–8.21) defines the game logic and spot animations.

package and import Statements

Section 8.3 discussed the key new classes and interfaces that class SpotOnView uses. We've highlighted them in Fig. 8.9.

```
// SpotOnView.java
// View that displays and manages the game
package com.deitel.spoton;

import java.util.HashMap;
import java.util.Map;
import java.util.Random;
import java.util.concurrent.ConcurrentLinkedQueue;
import java.util.Queue;

import android.animation.Animator;
import android.animation.AnimatorListenerAdapter;
import android.app.AlertDialog;
import android.app.AlertDialog.Builder;
import android.content.Context;
import android.content.DialogInterface;
import android.content.SharedPreferences;
import android.content.res.Resources;
import android.media.AudioManager;
import android.media.SoundPool;
import android.os.Handler;
import android.view.LayoutInflater;
import android.view.MotionEvent;
import android.view.View;
import android.widget.ImageView;
import android.widget.LinearLayout;
import android.widget.RelativeLayout;
import android.widget.TextView;

```

Fig. 8.9 | SpotOnView package and import statements.

Constants and Instance Variables

Figure 8.10 begins class SpotOnView's definition and defines the class's constants and instance variables. Lines 33–34 define a constant and a SharedPreferences variable that we use to load and store the game's high score in the Activity's default SharedPreferences file. Lines 37–73 define variables and constants for managing aspects of the game—we discuss these variables as they're used. Lines 76–84 define variables and constants for managing and playing the game's sounds. Chapter 7 demonstrated how to use sounds in an app.

```
30 public class SpotOnView extends View
31 {
32    // constant for accessing the high score in SharedPreference
33    private static final String HIGH_SCORE = "HIGH_SCORE";
34    private SharedPreferences preferences; // stores the high score
35
36    // variables for managing the game
37    private int spotsTouched; // number of spots touched
38    private int score; // current score
39    private int level; // current level
40    private int viewWidth; // stores the width of this View
41    private int viewHeight; // stores the height of this view
42    private long animationTime; // how long each spot remains on the screen
43    private boolean gameOver; // whether the game has ended
44    private boolean gamePaused; // whether the game has ended
45    private boolean dialogDisplayed; // whether the game has ended
46    private int highScore; // the game's all time high score
47
48    // collections of spots (ImageViews) and Animators
49    private final Queue<ImageView> spots =
50       new ConcurrentLinkedQueue<ImageView>();
51    private final Queue<Animator> animators =
52       new ConcurrentLinkedQueue<Animator>();
53
54    private TextView highScoreTextView; // displays high score
55    private TextView currentScoreTextView; // displays current score
56    private TextView levelTextView; // displays current level
57    private LinearLayout livesLinearLayout; // displays lives remaining
58    private RelativeLayout relativeLayout; // displays spots
59    private Resources resources; // used to load resources
60    private LayoutInflater layoutInflater; // used to inflate GUIs
61
62    // time in milliseconds for spot and touched spot animations
63    private static final int INITIAL_ANIMATION_DURATION = 6000;
64    private static final Random random = new Random(); // for random coords
65    private static final int SPOT_DIAMETER = 100; // initial spot size
66    private static final float SCALE_X = 0.25f; // end animation x scale
67    private static final float SCALE_Y = 0.25f; // end animation y scale
68    private static final int INITIAL_SPOTS = 5; // initial # of spots
69    private static final int SPOT_DELAY = 500; // delay in milliseconds
70    private static final int LIVES = 3; // start with 3 lives
71    private static final int MAX_LIVES = 7; // maximum # of total lives
72    private static final int NEW_LEVEL = 10; // spots to reach new level
73    private Handler spotHandler; // adds new spots to the game
74
75    // sound IDs, constants and variables for the game's sounds
76    private static final int HIT_SOUND_ID = 1;
77    private static final int MISS_SOUND_ID = 2;
```

Fig. 8.10 | SpotOnView constants and instance variables. (Part 1 of 2.)

```
   private static final int DISAPPEAR_SOUND_ID = 3;
   private static final int SOUND_PRIORITY = 1;
   private static final int SOUND_QUALITY = 100;
   private static final int MAX_STREAMS = 4;
   private SoundPool soundPool; // plays sound effects
   private int volume; // sound effect volume
   private Map<Integer, Integer> soundMap; // maps ID to soundpool

```

Fig. 8.10 | SpotOnView constants and instance variables. (Part 2 of 2.)

SpotOnView Constructor

Class SpotOnView's constructor (Fig. 8.11) initializes several of the class's instance variables. Line 93 stores the SpotOn Activity's default SharedPreferences object, then line 94 uses it to load the high score. The second argument indicates that getInt should return 0 if the key HIGH_SCORE does not already exist. Line 97 uses the context argument to get and store the Activity's Resources object—we'll use this to load String resources for displaying the current and high scores, the current level and the user's final score. Lines 100–101 store a LayoutInflater for inflating the ImageViews dynamically throughout the game. Line 104 stores the reference to the SpotOn Activity's RelativeLayout, then lines 105–112 use it to get references to the LinearLayout where lives are displayed and the TextViews that display the high score, current score and level. Line 114 creates a Handler that method resetGame (Fig. 8.14) uses to display the game's first several spots.

```
86     // constructs a new SpotOnView
87     public SpotOnView(Context context, SharedPreferences sharedPreferences,
88        RelativeLayout parentLayout)
89     {
90        super(context);
91
92        // load the high score
93        preferences = sharedPreferences;
94        highScore = preferences.getInt(HIGH_SCORE, 0);
95
96        // save Resources for loading external values
97        resources = context.getResources();
98
99        // save LayoutInflater
100       layoutInflater = (LayoutInflater) context.getSystemService(
101          Context.LAYOUT_INFLATER_SERVICE);
102
103       // get references to various GUI components
104       relativeLayout = parentLayout;
105       livesLinearLayout = (LinearLayout) relativeLayout.findViewById(
106          R.id.lifeLinearLayout);
107       highScoreTextView = (TextView) relativeLayout.findViewById(
108          R.id.highScoreTextView);
109       currentScoreTextView = (TextView) relativeLayout.findViewById(
110          R.id.scoreTextView);
```

Fig. 8.11 | SpotOnView constructor. (Part 1 of 2.)

```
      levelTextView = (TextView) relativeLayout.findViewById(
         R.id.levelTextView);

      spotHandler = new Handler(); // used to add spots when game starts
   } // end SpotOnView constructor

```

Fig. 8.11 | `SpotOnView` constructor. (Part 2 of 2.)

Overriding `View` *Method* `onSizeChanged`

We use the `SpotOnView`'s width and height when calculating the random coordinates for each new spot's starting and ending locations. The `SpotOnView` is not sized until it's added to the `View` hierarchy, so we can't get the width and height in its constructor. Instead, we override `View`'s `onSizeChanged` method (Fig. 8.12), which is guaranteed to be called *after* the `View` is added to the `View` hierarchy and sized.

```
   // store SpotOnView's width/height
   @Override
   protected void onSizeChanged(int width, int height, int oldw, int oldh)
   {
      viewWidth = width; // save the new width
      viewHeight = height; // save the new height
   } // end method onSizeChanged

```

Fig. 8.12 | Overriding `View` method `onSizeChanged`.

Methods `pause`*,* `cancelAnimations` *and* `resume`

Methods `pause`, `cancelAnimations` and `resume` (Fig. 8.13) help manage the app's resources and ensure that the animations do not continue executing when the app is not on the screen.

```
   // called by the SpotOn Activity when it receives a call to onPause
   public void pause()
   {
      gamePaused = true;
      soundPool.release(); // release audio resources
      soundPool = null;
      cancelAnimations(); // cancel all outstanding animations
   } // end method pause

   // cancel animations and remove ImageViews representing spots
   private void cancelAnimations()
   {
      // cancel remaining animations
      for (Animator animator : animators)
         animator.cancel();

```

Fig. 8.13 | `SpotOnView` methods `pause`, `cancelAnimations` and `resume`. (Part 1 of 2.)

```
141         // remove remaining spots from the screen
142         for (ImageView view : spots)
143            relativeLayout.removeView(view);
144
145         spotHandler.removeCallbacks(addSpotRunnable);
146         animators.clear();
147         spots.clear();
148      } // end method cancelAnimations
149
150      // called by the SpotOn Activity when it receives a call to onResume
151      public void resume(Context context)
152      {
153         gamePaused = false;
154         initializeSoundEffects(context); // initialize app's SoundPool
155
156         if (!dialogDisplayed)
157            resetGame(); // start the game
158      } // end method resume
159
```

Fig. 8.13 | SpotOnView methods pause, cancelAnimations and resume. (Part 2 of 2.)

When the Activity's onPause method is called, method pause (lines 126–132) releases the SoundPool resources used by the app and calls cancelAnimations. Variable gamePaused is used in Fig. 8.18 to ensure that method missedSpot is not called when an animation ends and the app is not on the screen.

Method cancelAnimations (lines 135–148) iterates through the animators collection and calls method **cancel** on each Animator. This immediately terminates each animation and calls its AnimationListener's onAnimationCancel and onAnimationEnd methods.

When the Activity's onResume method is called, method resume (lines 151–158) obtains the SoundPool resources again by calling initalizeSoundEffects (Fig. 8.15). If dialogDisplayed is true, the end-of-game dialog is still displayed on the screen and the user can click the dialog's **Reset Game** button to start a new game; otherwise, line 157 calls resetGame (Fig. 8.14) to start a new game.

Method resetGame

Method resetGame (Fig. 8.14) restores the game to its initial state, displays the initial extra lives and schedules the display of the initial spots. Lines 163–164 clear the spots and animators collections, and line 165 uses ViewGroup method removeAllViews to remove the life ImageViews from the livesLinearLayout. Lines 167–171 reset instance variables that are used to manage the game:

- animationTime specifies the duration of each animation—for each new level, we decrease the animation time by 5% from the prior level
- spotsTouched helps determine when each new level is reached, which occurs every NEW_LEVEL spots
- score stores the current score
- level stores the current level
- gameOver indicates whether the game has ended

```
160    // start a new game
161    public void resetGame()
162    {
163       spots.clear(); // empty the List of spots
164       animators.clear(); // empty the List of Animators
165       livesLinearLayout.removeAllViews(); // clear old lives from screen
166
167       animationTime = INITIAL_ANIMATION_DURATION; // init animation length
168       spotsTouched = 0; // reset the number of spots touched
169       score = 0; // reset the score
170       level = 1; // reset the level
171       gameOver = false; // the game is not over
172       displayScores(); // display scores and level
173
174       // add lives
175       for (int i = 0; i < LIVES; i++)
176       {
177          // add life indicator to screen
178          livesLinearLayout.addView(
179             (ImageView) layoutInflater.inflate(R.layout.life, null));
180       } // end for
181
182       // add INITIAL_SPOTS new spots at SPOT_DELAY time intervals in ms
183       for (int i = 1; i <= INITIAL_SPOTS; ++i)
184          spotHandler.postDelayed(addSpotRunnable, i * SPOT_DELAY);
185    } // end method resetGame
186
```

Fig. 8.14 | `SpotOnView` method `resetGame`.

Line 172 calls `displayScores` (Fig. 8.16) to reset the game's `TextViews`. Lines 175–180 inflate the `life.xml` file repeatedly and add each new `ImageView` that's created to the `livesLinearLayout`. Finally, lines 183–184 use `spotHandler` to schedule the display of the game's first several spots every `SPOT_DELAY` milliseconds.

Method `initializeSoundEffects`

Method `initializeSoundEffects` (Fig. 8.15) uses the techniques we introduced in the **Cannon Game** app (Section 7.5.3) to prepare the game's sound effects. In this game, we use three sounds represented by the following resources:

- `R.raw.hit` is played when the user touches a spot
- `R.raw.miss` is played when the user touches the screen, but misses a spot
- `R.raw.disappear` is played when a spot completes its animation without having been touched by the user

These MP3 files are provided with the book's examples.

```
   // create the app's SoundPool for playing game audio
   private void initializeSoundEffects(Context context)
   {
```

Fig. 8.15 | `SpotOnView` method `initializeSoundEffects`. (Part 1 of 2.)

```
      // initialize SoundPool to play the app's three sound effects
      soundPool = new SoundPool(MAX_STREAMS, AudioManager.STREAM_MUSIC,
         SOUND_QUALITY);

      // set sound effect volume
      AudioManager manager =
         (AudioManager) context.getSystemService(Context.AUDIO_SERVICE);
      volume = manager.getStreamVolume(AudioManager.STREAM_MUSIC);

      // create sound map
      soundMap = new HashMap<Integer, Integer>(); // create new HashMap

      // add each sound effect to the SoundPool
      soundMap.put(HIT_SOUND_ID,
         soundPool.load(context, R.raw.hit, SOUND_PRIORITY));
      soundMap.put(MISS_SOUND_ID,
         soundPool.load(context, R.raw.miss, SOUND_PRIORITY));
      soundMap.put(DISAPPEAR_SOUND_ID,
         soundPool.load(context, R.raw.disappear, SOUND_PRIORITY));
   } // end method initializeSoundEffect

```

Fig. 8.15 | SpotOnView method initializeSoundEffects. (Part 2 of 2.)

Method displayScores

Method displayScores (Fig. 8.16) simply updates the game's three TextViews with the high score, current score and current level. Parts of each string are loaded from the strings.xml file using the resources object's getString method.

```
   // display scores and level
   private void displayScores()
   {
      // display the high score, current score and level
      highScoreTextView.setText(
         resources.getString(R.string.high_score) + " " + highScore);
      currentScoreTextView.setText(
         resources.getString(R.string.score) + " " + score);
      levelTextView.setText(
         resources.getString(R.string.level) + " " + level);
   } // end function displayScores

```

Fig. 8.16 | SpotOnView method displayScores.

Runnable AddSpotRunnable

When method resetGame (Fig. 8.14) uses spotHandler to schedule the game's initial spots for display, each call to the spotHandler's postDelayed method receives the addSpotRunnable (Fig. 8.17) as an argument. This Runnable's run method simply calls method addNewSpot (Fig. 8.18).

```
   // Runnable used to add new spots to the game at the start
   private Runnable addSpotRunnable = new Runnable()
   {
      public void run()
      {
         addNewSpot(); // add a new spot to the game
      } // end method run
   }; // end Runnable

```

Fig. 8.17 | `Runnable addSpotRunnable` adds a new spot to the game.

Method `addNewSpot`

Method `addNewSpot` (Fig. 8.18) adds one new spot to the game. It's called several times near the beginning of the game to display the initial spots and whenever the user touches a spot or a spots animation ends without the spot being touched.

Lines 236–239 use the `SpotOnView`'s width and height to select the random coordinates where the spot will begin and end its animation. Then lines 242–250 inflate and configure the new spot's `ImageView`. Lines 245–246 specify the `ImageView`'s width and height by calling its **`setLayoutParams` method** with a new **`RelativeLayout.LayoutParams`** object. Next, lines 247–248 randomly select between two image resources and call `ImageView` method **`setImageResource`** to set the spot's image. Lines 249–250 set the spot's initial position. Lines 251–259 configure the `ImageView`'s `OnClickListener` to call `touchedSpot` (Fig. 8.20) when the user touches the `ImageView`. Then we add the spot to the `relativeLayout`, which displays it on the screen.

```
232    // adds a new spot at a random location and starts its animation
233    public void addNewSpot()
234    {
235       // choose two random coordinates for the starting and ending points
236       int x = random.nextInt(viewWidth - SPOT_DIAMETER);
237       int y = random.nextInt(viewHeight - SPOT_DIAMETER);
238       int x2 = random.nextInt(viewWidth - SPOT_DIAMETER);
239       int y2 = random.nextInt(viewHeight - SPOT_DIAMETER);
240
241       // create new spot
242       final ImageView spot =
243          (ImageView) layoutInflater.inflate(R.layout.untouched, null);
244       spots.add(spot); // add the new spot to our list of spots
245       spot.setLayoutParams(new RelativeLayout.LayoutParams(
246          SPOT_DIAMETER, SPOT_DIAMETER));
247       spot.setImageResource(random.nextInt(2) == 0 ?
248          R.drawable.green_spot : R.drawable.red_spot);
249       spot.setX(x); // set spot's starting x location
250       spot.setY(y); // set spot's starting y location
251       spot.setOnClickListener( // listens for spot being clicked
252          new OnClickListener()
253          {
```

Fig. 8.18 | `SpotOnView` method `addNewSpot`. (Part 1 of 2.)

```
254             public void onClick(View v)
255             {
256                touchedSpot(spot); // handle touched spot
257             } // end method onClick
258          } // end OnClickListener
259       ); // end call to setOnClickListener
260       relativeLayout.addView(spot); // add spot to the screen
261
262       // configure and start spot's animation
263       spot.animate().x(x2).y(y2).scaleX(SCALE_X).scaleY(SCALE_Y)
264          .setDuration(animationTime).setListener(
265             new AnimatorListenerAdapter()
266             {
267                @Override
268                public void onAnimationStart(Animator animation)
269                {
270                   animators.add(animation); // save for possible cancel
271                } // end method onAnimationStart
272
273                public void onAnimationEnd(Animator animation)
274                {
275                   animators.remove(animation); // animation done, remove
276
277                   if (!gamePaused && spots.contains(spot)) // not touched
278                   {
279                      missedSpot(spot); // lose a life
280                   } // end if
281                } // end method onAnimationEnd
282             } // end AnimatorListenerAdapter
283          ); // end call to setListener
284    } // end addNewSpot method
285
```

Fig. 8.18 | `SpotOnView` method `addNewSpot`. (Part 2 of 2.)

Lines 263–283 configure the spot's `ViewPropertyAnimator`, which is returned by the `View`'s `animate` method. A `ViewPropertyAnimator` configures animations for commonly animated `View` properties—alpha (transparency), rotation, scale, translation (moving relative to the current location) and location. In addition, a `ViewPropertyAnimator` provides methods for setting an animation's duration, `AnimatorListener` (to respond to animation lifecycle events) and `TimeInterpolator` (to determine how property values are calculated throughout the animation). To configure the animation, you chain `ViewPropertyAnimator` method calls together. In this example, we use the following methods:

- **`x`**—specifies the final value of the `View`'s *x*-coordinate
- **`y`**—specifies the final value of the `View`'s *y*-coordinate
- **`scaleX`**—specifies the `View`'s final width as a percentage of the original width
- **`scaleY`**—specifies the `View`'s final height as a percentage of the original height
- **`setDuration`**—specifies the animation's duration in milliseconds
- **`setListener`**—specifies the animation's `AnimatorListener`

When the last method call in the chain (`setListener` in our case) completes execution, the animation starts. If you don't specify a `TimeInterpolator`, a `LinearInterpolator` is used by default—the change in values for each property over the animation's duration is constant. For a list of the predefined interpolators, visit

```
developer.android.com/reference/android/animation/
   TimeInterpolator.html
```

For our `AnimatorListener`, we create an anonymous class that extends `AnimatorListenerAdapter`, which provides empty method definitions for each of `AnimatorListener`'s four methods. We override only **`onAnimationStart`** and **`onAnimationEnd`** here.

When the animation begins executing, its listener's `onAnimationStart` method is called. The **`Animator`** that the method receives as an argument provides methods for manipulating the animation that just started. We store the `Animator` in our `animators` collection. When the `SpotOn Activity`'s `onPause` method is called, we'll use the `Animators` in this collection to cancel the animations.

When the animation finishes executing, its listener's `onAnimationEnd` method is called. We remove the corresponding `Animator` from our `animators` collection (it's no longer needed). Then, if the game is not paused and the spot is still in the `spots` collection, we call `missedSpot` (Fig. 8.21) to indicate that the user missed this spot and should lose a life. If the user touched the spot, it will no longer be in the `spots` collection.

Overriding View *Method* onTouchEvent

Overridden `View` method `onTouchEvent` (Fig. 8.19) responds to touches in which the user touches the screen but misses a spot. We play the sound for a missed touch, subtract 15 times the level from the score, ensure that the score does not fall below 0 and display the updated score.

```
   // called when the user touches the screen, but not a spot
   @Override
   public boolean onTouchEvent(MotionEvent event)
   {
      // play the missed sound
      if (soundPool != null)
         soundPool.play(MISS_SOUND_ID, volume, volume,
            SOUND_PRIORITY, 0, 1f);

      score -= 15 * level; // remove some points
      score = Math.max(score, 0); // do not let the score go below zero
      displayScores(); // update scores/level on screen
      return true;
   } // end method onTouchEvent

```

Fig. 8.19 | Overriding `View` method `onTouchEvent`.

Method touchedSpot

Method `touchedSpot` (Fig. 8.20) is called each time the user touches an `ImageView` representing a spot. We remove the spot from the game, update the score and play the sound indicating a hit spot. Next, we determine whether the user has reached the next level and whether a new life needs to be added to the screen (only if the user has not reached the maximum number of lives). Finally, we display the updated score and, if the game is not over, add a new spot to the screen.

```
   // called when a spot is touched
   private void touchedSpot(ImageView spot)
   {
      relativeLayout.removeView(spot); // remove touched spot from screen
      spots.remove(spot); // remove old spot from list

      ++spotsTouched; // increment the number of spots touched
      score += 10 * level; // increment the score

      // play the hit sounds
      if (soundPool != null)
         soundPool.play(HIT_SOUND_ID, volume, volume,
            SOUND_PRIORITY, 0, 1f);

      // increment level if player touched 10 spots in the current level
      if (spotsTouched % 10 == 0)
      {
         ++level; // increment the level
         animationTime *= 0.95; // make game 5% faster than prior level

         // if the maximum number of lives has not been reached
         if (livesLinearLayout.getChildCount() < MAX_LIVES)
         {
            ImageView life =
               (ImageView) layoutInflater.inflate(R.layout.life, null);
            livesLinearLayout.addView(life); // add life to screen
         } // end if
      } // end if

      displayScores(); // update score/level on the screen

      if (!gameOver)
         addNewSpot(); // add another untouched spot
   } // end method touchedSpot

```

Fig. 8.20 | SpotOnView method touchedSpot.

Method missedSpot

Method missedSpot (Fig. 8.21) is called each time a spot reaches the end of its animation without having been touched by the user. We remove the spot from the game and, if the game is already over, immediately return from the method. Otherwise, we play the sound for a disappearing spot. Next, we determine whether the game should end. If so, we check whether there is a new high score and store it (lines 356–362). Then we cancel all remaining animations and display a dialog showing the user's final score. If the user still has lives remaining, lines 385–390 remove one life and add a new spot to the game.

```
   // called when a spot finishes its animation without being touched
   public void missedSpot(ImageView spot)
   {
      spots.remove(spot); // remove spot from spots List
      relativeLayout.removeView(spot); // remove spot from screen

      if (gameOver) // if the game is already over, exit
         return;

      // play the disappear sound effect
      if (soundPool != null)
         soundPool.play(DISAPPEAR_SOUND_ID, volume, volume,
            SOUND_PRIORITY, 0, 1f);

      // if the game has been lost
      if (livesLinearLayout.getChildCount() == 0)
      {
         gameOver = true; // the game is over

         // if the last game's score is greater than the high score
         if (score > highScore)
         {
            SharedPreferences.Editor editor = preferences.edit();
            editor.putInt(HIGH_SCORE, score);
            editor.commit(); // store the new high score
            highScore = score;
         } // end if

         cancelAnimations();

         // display a high score dialog
         Builder dialogBuilder = new AlertDialog.Builder(getContext());
         dialogBuilder.setTitle(R.string.game_over);
         dialogBuilder.setMessage(resources.getString(R.string.score) +
            " " + score);
         dialogBuilder.setPositiveButton(R.string.reset_game,
            new DialogInterface.OnClickListener()
            {
               public void onClick(DialogInterface dialog, int which)
               {
                  displayScores(); // ensure that score is up to date
                  dialogDisplayed = false;
                  resetGame(); // start a new game
               } // end method onClick
            } // end DialogInterface
         ); // end call to dialogBuilder.setPositiveButton
         dialogDisplayed = true;
         dialogBuilder.show(); // display the reset game dialog
      } // end if
      else // remove one life
      {
         livesLinearLayout.removeViewAt( // remove life from screen
            livesLinearLayout.getChildCount() - 1);
```

Fig. 8.21 | SpotOnView method missedSpot. (Part 1 of 2.)

```
            addNewSpot(); // add another spot to game
         } // end else
      } // end method missedSpot
   } // end class SpotOnView
```

Fig. 8.21 | SpotOnView method missedSpot. (Part 2 of 2.)

8.6 Wrap-Up

In this chapter, we presented the **SpotOn** game, which tested a user's reflexes by requiring the user to touch moving spots before they disappear. This was our first app that used features specific to Android 3.0 or higher. In particular, we used property animation, which was introduced in Android 3.0, to move and scale `ImageView`s.

You learned that Android versions prior to 3.0 had two animation mechanisms—tweened `View` animations that allow you to change limited aspects of a `View`'s appearance and frame `View` animations that display a sequence of images. You also learned that `View` animations affect only how a `View` is drawn on the screen.

Next, we introduced property animations that can be used to animate any property of any object. You learned that property animations animate values over time and require a target object containing the property or properties to animate, the length of the animation, the values to animate between for each property and how to change the property values over time.

We discussed Android 3.0's `ValueAnimator` and `ObjectAnimator` classes, then focused on Android 3.1's new utility class `ViewPropertyAnimator`, which was added to the animation APIs to simplify property animation for `View`s and to allow animation of multiple properties in parallel.

We used a `View`'s `animate` method to obtain the `View`'s `ViewPropertyAnimator`, then chained method calls to configure the animation. When the last method call in the chain completed execution, the animation started. You listened for property-animation lifecycle events by implementing the interface `AnimatorUpdateListener`, which defines methods that are called when an animation starts, ends, repeats or is canceled. Since we needed only two of the lifecycle events, we implemented our listener by extending class `AnimatorListenerAdapter`.

Finally, you used the `ConcurrentLinkedQueue` class from package `java.util.concurrent` and the `Queue` interface to maintain thread-safe lists of objects that could be accessed from multiple threads of execution in parallel. In Chapter 9, we present the **Doodlz** app, which uses Android's graphics capabilities to turn a device's screen into a *virtual canvas*.

9

Doodlz App

Two-Dimensional Graphics, SensorManager, Multitouch Events and Toasts

Objectives

In this chapter you'll:

- Detect when the user touches the screen, moves a finger across the screen and removes a finger from the screen.
- Process multiple screen touches so the user can draw with multiple fingers at once.
- Use a `SensorManager` to detect accelerometer motion events to clear the screen when the user shakes the device.
- Use an `AtomicBoolean` object to allow multiple threads to access a `boolean` value in a thread-safe manner.
- Use a `Paint` object to specify the color and width of a line.
- Use `Path` objects to store each line's data as the user draws the lines and to draw those lines with a `Canvas`.
- Use a `Toast` to briefly display a message on the screen.

Outline

9.1 Introduction

The **Doodlz** app turns your device's screen into a *virtual canvas* (Fig. 9.1). You paint by dragging one or more fingers across the screen. The app's options enable you to set the *drawing color* and *line width*. The **Choose Color** dialog (Fig. 9.2(a)) provides alpha (transparency), red, green and blue `SeekBar`s (i.e., sliders) that allow you to select the ARGB color. As you move the *thumb* on each `SeekBar`, the color swatch below the `SeekBar`s shows you the current color. The **Choose Line Width** dialog (Fig. 9.2(b)) provides a single `SeekBar` that controls the thickness of the line that you'll draw. Additional menu items (Fig. 9.3) allow you to turn your finger into an eraser (**Erase**), to clear the screen (**Clear**) and to save the current drawing into your device's **Gallery** (**Save Image**). At any point, you can *shake* the device to clear the entire drawing from the screen.

Fig. 9.1 | **Doodlz** app with a finished drawing.

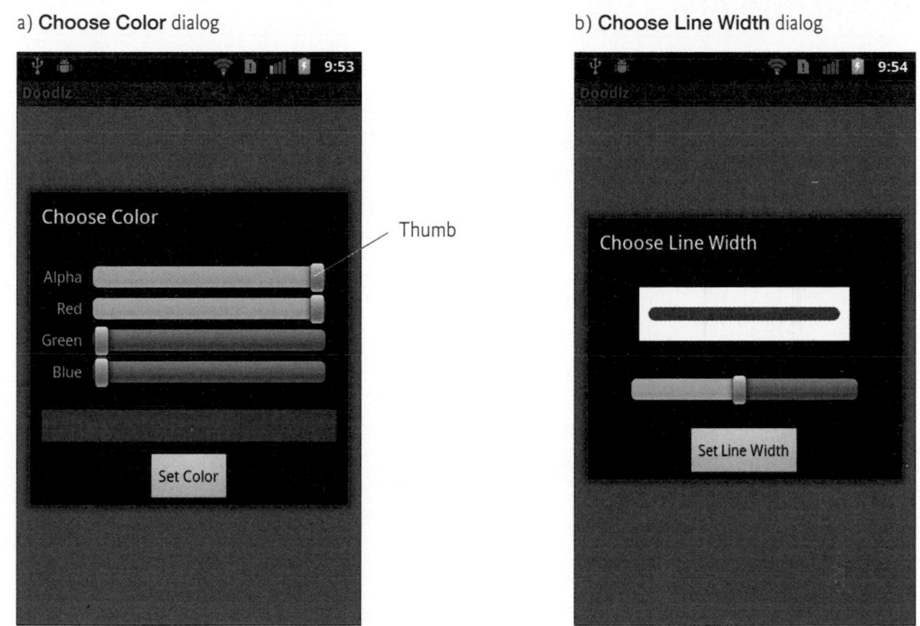

Fig. 9.2 | **Choose Color** and **Choose Line Width** dialogs for the **Doodlz** app.

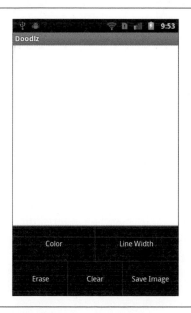

Fig. 9.3 | **Doodlz** app menu options.

9.2 Test-Driving the Doodlz App

You test drove this app in Section 1.11, so we do not present a test drive in this chapter.

9.3 Technologies Overview

This section presents the many new technologies that we use in the **Doodlz** app in the order they're encountered throughout the chapter.

Enabling an App to Integrate Better with Android 3.0 and Higher

Though we don't use any Android-3.0 features in this app, we specify in the app's manifest that we target the Android 3.0 SDK (Section 9.4.2). Doing so allows the app's GUI components to use Android 3.0's look-and-feel—the so-called **holographic theme**—on Android tablet devices. In addition, the app's menu is displayed at the right side of the Android 3.0 **action bar**, which appears at the top of the screen on tablet devices.

Using `SensorManager` *to Listen for Accelerometer Events*

This app allows the user to shake the device to erase the current drawing. Most devices have an **accelerometer** that allows apps to detect movement. Other sensors currently supported by Android include gravity, gyroscope, light, linear acceleration, magnetic field, pressure, proximity, rotation vector and temperature. The list of **`Sensor`** constants representing the sensor types can be found at:

```
developer.android.com/reference/android/hardware/Sensor.html
```

To listen for sensor events, you get a reference to the system's **`SensorManager`** service (Section 9.5.1), which enables the app to receive data from the device's sensors. You use the `SensorManager` to register the sensor changes that your app should receive and to specify the **`SensorEventListener`** that will handle those sensor-change events. The classes and interfaces for processing sensor events are located in package **`android.hardware`**.

Creating Custom `Dialogs`

Several previous apps have used `AlertDialogs` to display information to the user or to ask questions and receive responses from the user in the form of `Button` clicks. `AlertDialogs` can display only simple `Strings` and `Buttons`. For more complex dialogs, you can use objects of class **`Dialog`** (package `android.app`) that display custom GUIs (Section 9.5.1). In this app, we use these to allow the user to select a drawing color or select a line width, and we inflate each `Dialog`'s GUI from an XML layout file (Figs. 9.7–Fig. 9.8).

`AtomicBoolean`

In Android, sensor events are handled in a separate thread of execution from GUI events. Therefore, it's possible that the event handler for the shake event could try to display the confirmation dialog for erasing an image when another dialog is already on the screen. To prevent this, we'll use an **`AtomicBoolean`** (package import **`java.util.concurrent.atomic`**) to indicate when a dialog is currently displayed. An `AtomicBoolean` manages a `boolean` value in a thread-safe manner, so that it can be accessed from multiple threads of execution. When the `AtomicBoolean`'s value is `true`, we will not allow the event handler for the shake event to display a dialog.

Custom `Colors`

The user can set a custom drawing `Color` (Section 9.5.1) in this app by specifying the alpha, red, green and blue components of the `Color` with `SeekBars` in a `Dialog`. Each value is in the range 0 to 255. The alpha component specifies the `Color`'s *transparency* with 0 representing completely transparent and 255 representing completely opaque. Class `Color` provides methods for assembling a `Color` from its component values (which we need to set the custom drawing `Color`) and for obtaining the component values from a `Color` (which we need to set the initial values of the `SeekBars` in the **Choose Color** dialog).

Drawing Lines and `Paths`

This app draws lines onto **`Bitmaps`** (package `android.graphics`). You can associate a `Canvas` with a `Bitmap`, then use the `Canvas` to draw on the `Bitmap`, which can then be displayed on the screen (Sections 9.5.1 and 9.5.2). A `Bitmap` can also be saved into a file—we'll use this capability to store drawings in the device's gallery when the user touches the **Save Image** menu item.

Processing Touch Events

The user can touch the screen with one or more fingers and drag the fingers to draw lines. We store the information for each individual finger as a **`Path`** object (package `android.graphics`), which represents a geometric path consisting of line segments and curves. *Touch events* are processed by overriding the `View` method **`OnTouchEvent`** (Section 9.5.2). This method receives a **`MotionEvent`** (package `android.view`) that contains the type of touch event that occurred and the ID of the finger (i.e., pointer) that generated the event. We use the IDs to distinguish the different fingers and add information to the corresponding `Path` objects. We use the type of the touch event to determine whether the user has *touched* the screen, *dragged* across the screen or *lifted a finger* from the screen.

Saving the Drawing to the Device's Gallery

The app provides a **Save Image** menu item that allows the user to save a drawing into the device's gallery—the default location in which photos taken with the device are stored. A **`ContentResolver`** (package `android.content`) enables the app to read data from and store data on a device. We'll use one (Section 9.5.2) to get an `OutputStream` for writing data into the gallery and save the image in JPEG format.

Using `Toasts` to Display a Message for a Short Time

A **`Toast`** (package `android.widget`) displays a message for a short time, then disappears from the screen. These are often used to display minor error messages or informational messages, such as an indication that an app's data has been refreshed. We use one (Section 9.5.2) to indicate whether or not the user's drawing was successfully saved to the gallery.

9.4 Building the App's GUI and Resource Files

In this section, you'll create the **Doodlz** app's resource files and GUI layout files.

9.4.1 Creating the Project

Begin by creating a new Android project named `Doodlz`. Specify the following values in the **New Android Project** dialog, then press **Finish**:

- **Build Target**: Ensure that **Android 2.3.3** is checked
- **Application name**: `Doodlz`
- **Package name**: `com.deitel.doodlz`

- **Create Activity:** Doodlz
- **Min SDK Version:** 8

9.4.2 AndroidManifest.xml

Figure 9.4 shows this app's `AndroidManifest.xml` file. In this app, we set the `uses-sdk` element's `android:targetSdkVersion` attribute to `"11"` (line 15), which represents the Android 3.0 SDK. If this app is installed on a device running Android 3.0 or higher, Android 3.0's holographic theme will be applied to the app's GUI components, and the menu items will be placed at the right side of the app's action bar, which appears at the top of the screen on tablet devices. Setting the `android:targetSdkVersion` attribute to `"11"` has no effect when the app is installed on a device running an earlier version of Android. Targeting SDK version 11 is recommended for any apps that you'd like users to install on Android tablets, so the apps have the look-and-feel of those that are developed specifically for Android 3.0 and higher.

```
1  <?xml version="1.0" encoding="utf-8"?>
2  <manifest xmlns:android="http://schemas.android.com/apk/res/android"
3     android:versionCode="1" android:versionName="1.0"
4     package="com.deitel.doodlz">
5     <application android:icon="@drawable/icon"
6        android:label="@string/app_name" android:debuggable="true">
7        <activity android:label="@string/app_name" android:name=".Doodlz"
8           android:screenOrientation="portrait">
9           <intent-filter>
10             <action android:name="android.intent.action.MAIN" />
11             <category android:name="android.intent.category.LAUNCHER"/>
12          </intent-filter>
13       </activity>
14    </application>
15    <uses-sdk android:minSdkVersion="8" android:targetSdkVersion="11" />
16 </manifest>
```

Fig. 9.4 | AndroidManifest.xml.

9.4.3 strings.xml

Figure 9.5 defines the `String` resources used in this app.

```
<?xml version="1.0" encoding="utf-8"?>
<resources>
   <string name="app_name">Doodlz</string>
   <string name="button_erase">Erase</string>
   <string name="button_cancel">Cancel</string>
   <string name="button_set_color">Set Color</string>
   <string name="button_set_line_width">Set Line Width</string>
   <string name="label_alpha">Alpha</string>
   <string name="label_red">Red</string>
   <string name="label_green">Green</string>
```

Fig. 9.5 | Strings defined in `strings.xml`. (Part 1 of 2.)

```
    <string name="label_blue">Blue</string>
    <string name="menuitem_clear">Clear</string>
    <string name="menuitem_color">Color</string>
    <string name="menuitem_erase">Erase</string>
    <string name="menuitem_line_width">Line Width</string>
    <string name="menuitem_save_image">Save Image</string>
    <string name="message_erase">Erase the drawing?</string>
    <string name="message_error_saving">
       There was an error saving the image</string>
    <string name="message_saved">
       Your painting has been saved to the Gallery</string>
    <string name="title_color_dialog">Choose Color</string>
    <string name="title_line_width_dialog">Choose Line Width</string>
</resources>
```

Fig. 9.5 | Strings defined in `strings.xml`. (Part 2 of 2.)

9.4.4 `main.xml`

We deleted the default `main.xml` file and replaced it with a new one. In this case, the only component in the layout is an instance of our custom `View` subclass, `DoodleView`, which you'll add to the project in Section 9.5.2. Figure 9.6 shows the completed `main.xml` in which we manually entered the XML element shown in lines 2–5—our custom `DoodleView` is not in the ADT's **Palette**, so it cannot be dragged and dropped onto the layout.

```
1 <?xml version="1.0" encoding="utf-8"?>
2 <com.deitel.doodlz.DoodleView "
3    xmlns:android="http://schemas.android.com/apk/res/android"
4    android:layout_width="match_parent"
5    android:layout_height="match_parent"/>
```

Fig. 9.6 | **Doodlz** app's XML layout (`main.xml`).

9.4.5 `color_dialog.xml`

Figure 9.7 shows the completed `color_dialog.xml`, which defines the GUI for a dialog that allows the user to specify the alpha, red, green and blue components of the drawing color. The `LinearLayout` (lines 61–67) has a white background and contains a `View` (lines 64–66) that we use to display the current drawing color based on the values of the four `SeekBar`s, each allowing the user to select values from 0 (the default minimum) to 255 (the specified maximum). The white background enables the color to display accurately on the `View` when the user makes the color semitransparent with the `alphaSeekBar`. We use the standard `SeekBar` thumb in our apps, but you can customize it by setting the `SeekBar`'s `android:thumb` attribute to a drawable resource, such as an image.

```
1 <?xml version="1.0" encoding="utf-8"?>
2 <LinearLayout xmlns:android="http://schemas.android.com/apk/res/android"
```

Fig. 9.7 | Layout for the **Choose Color** dialog. (Part 1 of 3.)

```
   android:id="@+id/colorDialogLinearLayout"
   android:layout_width="match_parent" android:minWidth="300dp"
   android:layout_height="match_parent" android:orientation="vertical">

   <TableLayout android:id="@+id/tableLayout"
      android:layout_width="match_parent"
      android:layout_height="wrap_content" android:layout_margin="10dp"
      android:stretchColumns="1">
      <TableRow android:orientation="horizontal"
         android:layout_width="match_parent"
         android:layout_height="wrap_content">
         <TextView android:layout_width="wrap_content"
            android:layout_height="wrap_content"
            android:text="@string/label_alpha" android:gravity="right"
            android:layout_gravity="center_vertical"/>
         <SeekBar android:id="@+id/alphaSeekBar"
            android:layout_width="wrap_content"
            android:layout_height="wrap_content" android:max="255"
            android:paddingLeft="10dp" android:paddingRight="10dp"/>
      </TableRow>
      <TableRow android:orientation="horizontal"
         android:layout_width="match_parent"
         android:layout_height="wrap_content">
         <TextView android:layout_width="wrap_content"
            android:layout_height="wrap_content"
            android:text="@string/label_red" android:gravity="right"
            android:layout_gravity="center_vertical"/>
         <SeekBar android:id="@+id/redSeekBar"
            android:layout_width="wrap_content"
            android:layout_height="wrap_content" android:max="255"
            android:paddingLeft="10dp" android:paddingRight="10dp"/>
      </TableRow>
      <TableRow android:orientation="horizontal"
         android:layout_width="match_parent"
         android:layout_height="wrap_content">
         <TextView android:layout_width="wrap_content"
            android:layout_height="wrap_content"
            android:text="@string/label_green" android:gravity="right"
            android:layout_gravity="center_vertical"/>
         <SeekBar android:id="@+id/greenSeekBar"
            android:layout_width="wrap_content"
            android:layout_height="wrap_content" android:max="255"
            android:paddingLeft="10dp" android:paddingRight="10dp"/>
      </TableRow>
      <TableRow android:orientation="horizontal"
         android:layout_width="wrap_content"
         android:layout_height="wrap_content">
         <TextView android:layout_width="match_parent"
            android:layout_height="wrap_content"
            android:text="@string/label_blue" android:gravity="right"
            android:layout_gravity="center_vertical"/>
```

Fig. 9.7 | Layout for the **Choose Color** dialog. (Part 2 of 3.)

```
            <SeekBar android:id="@+id/blueSeekBar"
               android:layout_width="wrap_content"
               android:layout_height="wrap_content" android:max="255"
               android:paddingLeft="10dp" android:paddingRight="10dp"/>
         </TableRow>
      </TableLayout>

      <LinearLayout android:background="@android:color/white"
         android:layout_width="match_parent"
         android:layout_height="wrap_content" android:layout_margin="10dp">
         <View android:id="@+id/colorView"
            android:layout_width="match_parent"
            android:layout_height="30dp"/>
      </LinearLayout>

      <Button android:id="@+id/setColorButton"
         android:layout_width="wrap_content"
         android:layout_height="wrap_content"
         android:layout_gravity="center_horizontal"
         android:text="@string/button_set_color"/>
   </LinearLayout>
```

Fig. 9.7 | Layout for the **Choose Color** dialog. (Part 3 of 3.)

9.4.6 width_dialog.xml

Figure 9.8 shows the completed `width_dialog.xml`, which defines the GUI for a dialog that allows the user to specify the line width for drawing. As the user moves the `widthSeekBar`'s thumb, we use the `ImageView` (lines 6–8) to display a sample line in the current line width and current color.

```
1  <?xml version="1.0" encoding="utf-8"?>
2  <LinearLayout xmlns:android="http://schemas.android.com/apk/res/android"
3     android:id="@+id/widthDialogLinearLayout"
4     android:layout_width="match_parent"  android:minWidth="300dp"
5     android:layout_height="match_parent" android:orientation="vertical">
6     <ImageView android:id="@+id/widthImageView"
7        android:layout_width="match_parent" android:layout_height="50dp"
8        android:layout_margin="10dp"/>
9     <SeekBar android:layout_height="wrap_content" android:max="50"
10       android:id="@+id/widthSeekBar" android:layout_width="match_parent"
11       android:layout_margin="20dp" android:paddingLeft="20dp"
12       android:paddingRight="20dp"
13       android:layout_gravity="center_horizontal"/>
14    <Button android:id="@+id/widthDialogDoneButton"
15       android:layout_width="wrap_content"
16       android:layout_height="wrap_content"
17       android:layout_gravity="center_horizontal"
18       android:text="@string/button_set_line_width"/>
19 </LinearLayout>
```

Fig. 9.8 | Layout for the **Choose Line Width** dialog.

9.5 Building the App

This app consists of two classes—class `Doodlz` (the `Activity` subclass; Figs. 9.9–9.20) and class `DoodleView` (Figs. 9.21–9.29).

9.5.1 Doodlz Subclass of Activity

Class `Doodlz` (Figs. 9.9–9.20) is the **Doodlz** app's main `Activity`. It provides the app's menu, dialogs and accelerometer event handling.

package and import Statements

Section 9.3 discussed the key new classes and interfaces that class `Doodlz` uses. We've highlighted these classes and interfaces in Fig. 9.9.

```
// Doodlz.java
// Draws View which changes color in response to user touches.
package com.deitel.doodlz;

import java.util.concurrent.atomic.AtomicBoolean;

import android.app.Activity;
import android.app.AlertDialog;
import android.app.Dialog;
import android.content.Context;
import android.content.DialogInterface;
import android.graphics.Bitmap;
import android.graphics.Canvas;
import android.graphics.Color;
import android.graphics.Paint;
import android.hardware.Sensor;
import android.hardware.SensorEvent;
import android.hardware.SensorEventListener;
import android.hardware.SensorManager;
import android.os.Bundle;
import android.view.Menu;
import android.view.MenuItem;
import android.view.View;
import android.view.View.OnClickListener;
import android.widget.Button;
import android.widget.ImageView;
import android.widget.SeekBar;
import android.widget.SeekBar.OnSeekBarChangeListener;

```

Fig. 9.9 | `Doodlz` class `package` and `import` statements.

Instance Variables and Constants

Figure 9.10 shows the instance variables and constants of class `Doodlz`. `DoodleView` variable `doodleView` (line 32) represents the drawing area. The `sensorManager` is used to monitor the accelerometer to detect the device movement. The `float` variables declared in lines 34–36 are used to calculate changes in the device's acceleration to determine when a *shake event* occurs (so we can ask whether the user would like to erase the drawing), and the constant in line 47 is used to ensure that small movements are not interpreted as shakes—we picked this constant via trial and error by shaking the app on several devices. Line 37 defines the `AtomicBoolean` object (with the value `false` by default) that will be used throughout this class to specify when there is a dialog displayed on the screen, so we can prevent multiple dialogs from being displaed at the same time. Lines 40–44 declare the `int` constants for the app's five menu items. We use the `Dialog` variable `currentDialog` (line 50) to refer to the **Choose Color** or **Choose Line Width** dialogs that allow the user to change the drawing color and line width, respectively.

```
30   public class Doodlz extends Activity
31   {
32      private DoodleView doodleView; // drawing View
33      private SensorManager sensorManager; // monitors accelerometer
34      private float acceleration; // acceleration
35      private float currentAcceleration; // current acceleration
36      private float lastAcceleration; // last acceleration
37      private AtomicBoolean dialogIsDisplayed = new AtomicBoolean(); // false
38
39      // create menu ids for each menu option
40      private static final int COLOR_MENU_ID = Menu.FIRST;
41      private static final int WIDTH_MENU_ID = Menu.FIRST + 1;
42      private static final int ERASE_MENU_ID = Menu.FIRST + 2;
43      private static final int CLEAR_MENU_ID = Menu.FIRST + 3;
44      private static final int SAVE_MENU_ID = Menu.FIRST + 4;
45
46      // value used to determine whether user shook the device to erase
47      private static final int ACCELERATION_THRESHOLD = 15000;
48
49      // variable that refers to a Choose Color or Choose Line Width dialog
50      private Dialog currentDialog;
51
```

Fig. 9.10 | Fields of class `Doodlz`.

Overriding `Activity` *Methods* `onCreate` *and* `onPause`

Class `Doodlz`'s `onCreate` method (Fig. 9.11) gets a reference to the `DoodleView`, then initializes the instance variables that help calculate acceleration changes to determine whether the user shook the device to erase the drawing. We initially set variables `currentAcceleration` and `lastAcceleration` to `SensorManager`'s `GRAVITY_EARTH` constant, which represents the acceleration due to gravity on earth. `SensorManager` also provides constants for other planets in the solar system, for the moon and for several other entertaining values, which you can see at:

```
developer.android.com/reference/android/hardware/SensorManager.html
```

Next, line 67 calls method `enableAccelerometerListening` (Fig. 9.12) to configure the `SensorManager` to listen for accelerometer events. Class `Doodlz`'s `onPause` method (lines 71–76) calls method `disableAccelerometerListening` (Fig. 9.12) to unregister the accelerometer event handler when the app is sent to the background.

```
    // called when this Activity is loaded
    @Override
    protected void onCreate(Bundle savedInstanceState)
    {
       super.onCreate(savedInstanceState);
       setContentView(R.layout.main); // inflate the layout

       // get reference to the DoodleView
       doodleView = (DoodleView) findViewById(R.id.doodleView);

       // initialize acceleration values
       acceleration = 0.00f;
       currentAcceleration = SensorManager.GRAVITY_EARTH;
       lastAcceleration = SensorManager.GRAVITY_EARTH;

       enableAccelerometerListening(); // listen for shake
    } // end method onCreate

    // when app is sent to the background, stop listening for sensor events
    @Override
    protected void onPause()
    {
       super.onPause();
       disableAccelerometerListening(); // don't listen for shake
    } // end method onPause

```

Fig. 9.11 | Overridden `Activity` methods `onCreate` and `onPause`.

Methods `enableAccelerometerListening` *and* `disableAccelerometerListening`

Method `enableAccelerometerListening` (Fig. 9.12; lines 79–87) configures the `SensorManager`. Lines 82–83 use `Activity`'s `getSystemService` method to retrieve the system's `SensorManager` service, which enables the app to interact with the device's sensors. We then register to receive accelerometer events using `SensorManager`'s **`registerListener`** method, which receives three arguments:

- the `SensorEventListener` object that will respond to the events
- a `Sensor` representing the type of sensor data the app wishes to receive. This is retrieved by calling `SensorManager`'s **`getDefaultSensor`** method and passing a `Sensor`-type constant (`Sensor.TYPE_ACCELEROMETER` in this app).
- a rate at which sensor events should be delivered to the app. We chose `SENSOR_DELAY_NORMAL` to receive sensor events at the default rate—a faster rate can be used to get more accurate data, but this is also more resource intensive.

Method `disableAccelerometerListening` (Fig. 9.12; lines 90–101), which is called from `onPause`, uses class `SensorManager`'s `unregisterListener` method to stop listening for accelerometer events. Since we don't know whether the app will return to the foreground, we also set the `sensorManager` reference to `null`.

```
   // enable listening for accelerometer events
   private void enableAccelerometerListening()
   {
      // initialize the SensorManager
      sensorManager =
         (SensorManager) getSystemService(Context.SENSOR_SERVICE);
      sensorManager.registerListener(sensorEventListener,
         sensorManager.getDefaultSensor(Sensor.TYPE_ACCELEROMETER),
         SensorManager.SENSOR_DELAY_NORMAL);
   } // end method enableAccelerometerListening

   // disable listening for accelerometer events
   private void disableAccelerometerListening()
   {
      // stop listening for sensor events
      if (sensorManager != null)
      {
         sensorManager.unregisterListener(
            sensorEventListener,
            sensorManager.getDefaultSensor(
               SensorManager.SENSOR_ACCELEROMETER));
         sensorManager = null;
      } // end if
   } // end method disableAccelerometerListening

```

Fig. 9.12 | Methods `enableAccelerometerListening` and `disableAccelerometerListening`.

Anonymous Inner Class That Implements Interface `SensorEventListener` *to Process Accelerometer Events*

Figure 9.13 overrides `SensorEventListener` method **onSensorChanged** (lines 108–168) to process accelerometer events. If the user moves the device, this method attempts to determine whether the movement was enough to be considered a shake. If so, lines 133–165 build and display an `AlertDialog` asking the user whether the drawing should be erased. Interface `SensorEventListener` also contains method `onAccuracyChanged` (lines 171–174)—we don't use this method in this app, so we provide an empty body.

```
103    // event handler for accelerometer events
104    private SensorEventListener sensorEventListener =
105       new SensorEventListener()
106       {
107          // use accelerometer to determine whether user shook device
108          @Override
109          public void onSensorChanged(SensorEvent event)
110          {
111             // ensure that other dialogs are not displayed
112             if (!dialogIsVisible.get())
113             {
```

Fig. 9.13 | Anonymous inner class that implements `SensorEventListener`. (Part 1 of 3.)

```
               // get x, y, and z values for the SensorEvent
               float x = event.values[0];
               float y = event.values[1];
               float z = event.values[2];

               // save previous acceleration value
               lastAcceleration = currentAcceleration;

               // calculate the current acceleration
               currentAcceleration = x * x + y * y + z * z;

               // calculate the change in acceleration
               acceleration = currentAcceleration *
                  (currentAcceleration - lastAcceleration);

               // if the acceleration is above a certain threshold
               if (acceleration > ACCELERATION_THRESHOLD)
               {
                  // create a new AlertDialog Builder
                  AlertDialog.Builder builder =
                     new AlertDialog.Builder(Doodlz.this);

                  // set the AlertDialog's message
                  builder.setMessage(R.string.message_erase);
                  builder.setCancelable(true);

                  // add Erase Button
                  builder.setPositiveButton(R.string.button_erase,
                     new DialogInterface.OnClickListener()
                     {
                        public void onClick(DialogInterface dialog, int id)
                        {
                          dialogIsVisible.set(false);
                          doodleView.clear(); // clear the screen
                        } // end method onClick
                     } // end anonymous inner class
                  ); // end call to setPositiveButton

                  // add Cancel Button
                  builder.setNegativeButton(R.string.button_cancel,
                     new DialogInterface.OnClickListener()
                     {
                        public void onClick(DialogInterface dialog, int id)
                        {
                          dialogIsVisible.set(false);
                          dialog.cancel(); // dismiss the dialog
                        } // end method onClick
                     } // end anonymous inner class
                  ); // end call to setNegativeButton

                  dialogIsVisible.set(true); // dialog is on the screen
```

Fig. 9.13 | Anonymous inner class that implements SensorEventListener. (Part 2 of 3.)

```
165                builder.show(); // display the dialog
166             } // end if
167          } // end if
168       } // end method onSensorChanged
169
170       // required method of interface SensorEventListener
171       @Override
172       public void onAccuracyChanged(Sensor sensor, int accuracy)
173       {
174       } // end method onAccuracyChanged
175    }; // end anonymous inner class
176
```

Fig. 9.13 | Anonymous inner class that implements `SensorEventListener`. (Part 3 of 3.)

The user can shake the device even when dialogs are already displayed on the screen. For this reason, `onSensorChanged` first checks whether a dialog is displayed by calling `dialogIsVisible`'s `get` method (line 110). This test ensures that no other dialogs are displayed. This is important because the sensor events occur in a different thread of execution. Without this test, we'd be able to display the confirmation dialog for erasing the image when another dialog is on the screen.

The **`SensorEvent`** parameter contains information about the sensor change that occurred. For accelerometer events, this parameter's `values` array contains three elements representing the acceleration (in *meter/second*^{2}) in the x (left/right), y (up/down) and z (forward/backward) directions. A description and diagram of the coordinate system used by the `SensorEvent` API is available at:

`developer.android.com/reference/android/hardware/SensorEvent.html`

This link also describes the real-world meanings for a `SensorEvent`'s x, y and z values for each different `Sensor`.

We store the acceleration values (lines 115–117), then store the last value of `currentAcceleration` (line 120). Line 123 sums the squares of the `x`, `y` and `z` acceleration values and stores them in `currentAcceleration`. Then, using the `currentAcceleration` and `lastAcceleration` values, we calculate a value (`acceleration`) that can be compared to our `ACCELERATION_THRESHOLD` constant. If the value is greater than the constant, the user moved the device enough for this app to consider the movement a shake. In this case, we set `shakeDetected` to `true`, then configure and display an `AlertDialog` in which the user can confirm that the shake should erase the drawing or cancel the dialog. Setting variable `shakeDetected` to `true` ensures that while the confirmation dialog is displayed, method `onSensorChanged` will not display another dialog if the user shakes the device again. If the user confirms that the drawing should be erased, line 147 calls the `DoodleView`'s `clear` method (Fig. 9.23). [*Note:* It's important to handle sensor events quickly or to copy the event data (as we did) because the array of sensor values is reused for each sensor event.]

Methods `onCreateOptionsMenu` *and* `onOptionsItemSelected`

Figure 9.14 overrides `Activity`'s `onCreateOptionsMenu` method to setup the `Activity`'s menu. We use the `menu`'s `add` method to add menu items (lines 184–193). Recall that the first argument is the group identifier, which can be used to group items together. We do

```
177    // displays configuration options in menu
178    @Override
179    public boolean onCreateOptionsMenu(Menu menu)
180    {
181       super.onCreateOptionsMenu(menu); // call super's method
182
183       // add options to menu
184       menu.add(Menu.NONE, COLOR_MENU_ID, Menu.NONE,
185          R.string.menuitem_color);
186       menu.add(Menu.NONE, WIDTH_MENU_ID, Menu.NONE,
187          R.string.menuitem_line_width);
188       menu.add(Menu.NONE, ERASE_MENU_ID, Menu.NONE,
189          R.string.menuitem_erase);
190       menu.add(Menu.NONE, CLEAR_MENU_ID, Menu.NONE,
191          R.string.menuitem_clear);
192       menu.add(Menu.NONE, SAVE_MENU_ID, Menu.NONE,
193          R.string.menuitem_save_image);
194
195       return true; // options menu creation was handled
196    } // end onCreateOptionsMenu
197
198    // handle choice from options menu
199    @Override
200    public boolean onOptionsItemSelected(MenuItem item)
201    {
202       // switch based on the MenuItem id
203       switch (item.getItemId())
204       {
205          case COLOR_MENU_ID:
206             showColorDialog(); // display color selection dialog
207             return true; // consume the menu event
208          case WIDTH_MENU_ID:
209             showLineWidthDialog(); // display line thickness dialog
210             return true; // consume the menu event
211          case ERASE_MENU_ID:
212             doodleView.setDrawingColor(Color.WHITE); // line color white
213             return true; // consume the menu event
214          case CLEAR_MENU_ID:
215             doodleView.clear(); // clear doodleView
216             return true; // consume the menu event
217          case SAVE_MENU_ID:
218             doodleView.saveImage(); // save the current images
219             return true; // consume the menu event
220       } // end switch
221
222       return super.onOptionsItemSelected(item); // call super's method
223    } // end method onOptionsItemSelected
224
```

Fig. 9.14 | Overridden `Activity` methods `onCreateOptionsMenu` and `onOptionsItemSelected`.

not have any groups, so we use `Menu`'s `NONE` constant for each item. The second argument is the item's unique identifier—one of the constants declared in lines 40–44. The third argument specifies the menu item's order with respect to the other menu items. We use `Menu`'s `NONE` constant, because the order is not important in this app. This value allows the item's sizes to determine how Android lays out the menu items. The final argument is the `String` resource to display on each menu item.

Lines 199–223 override `Activity`'s `onOptionItemSelected` method, which is called when the user touches a menu item. We use the `MenuItem` argument's ID (line 203) to take different actions depending on the item the user selected. The actions are as follows:

- For **Color**, line 206 calls method `showColorDialog` (Fig. 9.15) to allow the user to select a new drawing color.
- For **Width**, line 209 calls method `showLineWidthDialog` (Fig. 9.18) to allow the uset to select a new line width.
- For **Erase**, line 212 sets the `doodleView`'s drawing color to white, which effectively turns the user's fingers into *erasers*.
- For **Clear**, line 215 calls the `doodleView`'s `clear` method to remove all painted lines from the display.
- For **Save**, line 218 calls `doodleView`'s `saveImage` method to save the painting as an image stored in the device's image gallery.

Method `showColorDialog`

The `showColorDialog` method (Fig. 9.15) creates a `Dialog` and sets its GUI by calling **`setContentView`** to inflate `color_dialog.xml` (lines 229–230). We also set the dialog's title and indicate that it's cancelable—the user can press the device's *back button* to dismiss the dialog without making any changes to the current color. Lines 235–242 get references to the dialog's four `SeekBar`s, then lines 256–248 set each `SeekBar`'s `OnSeekBarChangeListener` to the `colorSeekBarChanged` listener (Fig. 9.16). Lines 251–255 get the current drawing color from `doodleView`, then use it to set each `SeekBar`'s current value. `Color`'s `static` methods **`alpha`**, **`red`**, **`green`** and **`blue`** are used to extract the ARGB values from the current color, and `SeekBar`'s `setProgress` method positions the thumbs. Lines 258–260 get a reference to the dialog's `setColorButton` and register `setColorButtonListener` (Fig. 9.17) as its event handler. Line 262 indicates that a dialog is displayed by calling `isDialigVisible`'s `set` method with the value `true`. Finally, line 263 displays the `Dialog` using its **`show`** method. The new color is set only if the user touches the **Set Color** `Button` in the `Dialog`.

```
225    // display a dialog for selecting color
226    private void showColorDialog()
227    {
228       // create the dialog and inflate its content
229       currentDialog = new Dialog(this);
230       currentDialog.setContentView(R.layout.color_dialog);
231       currentDialog.setTitle(R.string.title_color_dialog);
232       currentDialog.setCancelable(true);
```

Fig. 9.15 | Method `showColorDialog` displays a `Dialog` for changing the current drawing color. (Part 1 of 2.)

```
233
234       // get the color SeekBars and set their onChange listeners
235       final SeekBar alphaSeekBar =
236          (SeekBar) currentDialog.findViewById(R.id.alphaSeekBar);
237       final SeekBar redSeekBar =
238          (SeekBar) currentDialog.findViewById(R.id.redSeekBar);
239       final SeekBar greenSeekBar =
240          (SeekBar) currentDialog.findViewById(R.id.greenSeekBar);
241       final SeekBar blueSeekBar =
242          (SeekBar) currentDialog.findViewById(R.id.blueSeekBar);
243
244       // register SeekBar event listeners
245       alphaSeekBar.setOnSeekBarChangeListener(colorSeekBarChanged);
246       redSeekBar.setOnSeekBarChangeListener(colorSeekBarChanged);
247       greenSeekBar.setOnSeekBarChangeListener(colorSeekBarChanged);
248       blueSeekBar.setOnSeekBarChangeListener(colorSeekBarChanged);
249
250       // use current drawing color to set SeekBar values
251       final int color = doodleView.getDrawingColor();
252       alphaSeekBar.setProgress(Color.alpha(color));
253       redSeekBar.setProgress(Color.red(color));
254       greenSeekBar.setProgress(Color.green(color));
255       blueSeekBar.setProgress(Color.blue(color));
256
257       // set the Set Color Button's onClickListener
258       Button setColorButton = (Button) currentDialog.findViewById(
259          R.id.setColorButton);
260       setColorButton.setOnClickListener(setColorButtonListener);
261
262       dialogIsVisible.set(true); // dialog is on the screen
263       currentDialog.show(); // show the dialog
264    } // end method showColorDialog
265
```

Fig. 9.15 | Method showColorDialog displays a Dialog for changing the current drawing color. (Part 2 of 2.)

Anonymous Inner Class That Implements Interface **OnSeekBarChangeListener** *to Respond to the Events of the* **alpha**, **red**, **green** *and* **blue SeekBars**

Figure 9.16 defines an anonymous inner class that implements interface OnSeekBarChangeListener to respond to events when the user adjusts the SeekBars in the **Choose Color** Dialog. This was registered as the SeekBars' event handler in Fig. 9.15 (lines 246–249). Method onProgressChanged (lines 270–290) is called when the position of a SeekBar's thumb changes. We retrieve from the currentDialog each of the SeekBars and the View used to display the color (lines 275–284). We then use class View's **setBackgroundColor** method to update the colorView with a Color that matches the current state of the SeekBars (lines 287–289). Class Color's static method **argb** combines the SeekBars' values into a Color and returns the appropriate Color. [*Note:* Method onProgressChanged is called frequently when the user drags a SeekBar's thumb. For this reason, it's better practice to get the GUI component references once and store them as instance variables in your class, rather than getting the references each time onProgressChanged is called.]

```
// OnSeekBarChangeListener for the SeekBars in the color dialog
private OnSeekBarChangeListener colorSeekBarChanged =
   new OnSeekBarChangeListener()
{
   @Override
   public void onProgressChanged(SeekBar seekBar, int progress,
      boolean fromUser)
   {
      // get the SeekBars and the colorView LinearLayout
      SeekBar alphaSeekBar =
         (SeekBar) currentDialog.findViewById(R.id.alphaSeekBar);
      SeekBar redSeekBar =
         (SeekBar) currentDialog.findViewById(R.id.redSeekBar);
      SeekBar greenSeekBar =
         (SeekBar) currentDialog.findViewById(R.id.greenSeekBar);
      SeekBar blueSeekBar =
         (SeekBar) currentDialog.findViewById(R.id.blueSeekBar);
      View colorView =
         (View) currentDialog.findViewById(R.id.colorView);

      // display the current color
      colorView.setBackgroundColor(Color.argb(
         alphaSeekBar.getProgress(), redSeekBar.getProgress(),
         greenSeekBar.getProgress(), blueSeekBar.getProgress()));
   } // end method onProgressChanged

   // required method of interface OnSeekBarChangeListener
   @Override
   public void onStartTrackingTouch(SeekBar seekBar)
   {
   } // end method onStartTrackingTouch

   // required method of interface OnSeekBarChangeListener
   @Override
   public void onStopTrackingTouch(SeekBar seekBar)
   {
   } // end method onStopTrackingTouch
}; // end colorSeekBarChanged
```

Fig. 9.16 | Anonymous inner class that implements interface `OnSeekbarChangeListener` to respond to `SeekBar` events in the **Choose Color** `Dialog`.

Anonymous Inner Class That Implements Interface `OnClickListener` *to Set the New Drawing Color*

Figure 9.17 defines an anonymous inner class that implements interface `OnClickListener` to set the new drawing color when the user clicks the **Set Color** `Button` in the **Choose Color** `Dialog`. This was registered as the `Button`'s event handler in Fig. 9.15 (line 261). Method `onClick` gets references to the `SeekBar`s, then uses them in lines 322–324 to get the value from each `SeekBar` and set the new drawing color. Line 325 indicates that a dialog is not displayed by calling `isDialigVisible`'s `set` method with the value `false`. Line 326 calls the `Dialog`'s **`dismiss`** method to close the dialog and return to the app.

```
// OnClickListener for the color dialog's Set Color Button
private OnClickListener setColorButtonListener = new OnClickListener()
{
   @Override
   public void onClick(View v)
   {
      // get the color SeekBars
      SeekBar alphaSeekBar =
         (SeekBar) currentDialog.findViewById(R.id.alphaSeekBar);
      SeekBar redSeekBar =
         (SeekBar) currentDialog.findViewById(R.id.redSeekBar);
      SeekBar greenSeekBar =
         (SeekBar) currentDialog.findViewById(R.id.greenSeekBar);
      SeekBar blueSeekBar =
         (SeekBar) currentDialog.findViewById(R.id.blueSeekBar);

      // set the line color
      doodleView.setDrawingColor(Color.argb(
         alphaSeekBar.getProgress(), redSeekBar.getProgress(),
         greenSeekBar.getProgress(), blueSeekBar.getProgress()));
      dialogIsVisible.set(false); // dialog is not on the screen
      currentDialog.dismiss(); // hide the dialog
      currentDialog = null; // dialog no longer needed
   } // end method onClick
}; // end setColorButtonListener

```

Fig. 9.17 | Anonymous inner class that implements interface `OnClickListener` to respond when the user touches the **Set Color** `Button`.

Method `showLineWidthDialog`

The `showLineWidthDialog` method (Fig. 9.18) creates a `Dialog` and sets its GUI by calling `setContentView` to inflate `width_dialog.xml` (lines 335–336). We also set the dialog's title and indicate that it's cancelable. Lines 341–344 get a reference to the dialog's `SeekBar`, set its `OnSeekBarChangeListener` to the `widthSeekBarChanged` listener (Fig. 9.19) and set its current value. Lines 347–349 get a reference to the dialog's `Button` and set its `OnClickListener` to the `setLineWidthButtonListener` (Fig. 9.20). Line 351 indicates that a dialog is displayed by calling `isDialigVisible`'s `set` method with the value `true`. Finally, line 352 displays the dialog. The new line width is set only if the user touches the **Set Line Width** `Button` in the `Dialog`.

```
331    // display a dialog for setting the line width
332    private void showLineWidthDialog()
333    {
334       // create the dialog and inflate its content
335       currentDialog = new Dialog(this);
336       currentDialog.setContentView(R.layout.width_dialog);
337       currentDialog.setTitle(R.string.title_line_width_dialog);
```

Fig. 9.18 | Method `showLineWidthDialog` creates and displays a `Dialog` for changing the line width. (Part 1 of 2.)

```
        currentDialog.setCancelable(true);

        // get widthSeekBar and configure it
        SeekBar widthSeekBar =
           (SeekBar) currentDialog.findViewById(R.id.widthSeekBar);
        widthSeekBar.setOnSeekBarChangeListener(widthSeekBarChanged);
        widthSeekBar.setProgress(doodleView.getLineWidth());

        // set the Set Line Width Button's onClickListener
        Button setLineWidthButton =
           (Button) currentDialog.findViewById(R.id.widthDialogDoneButton);
        setLineWidthButton.setOnClickListener(setLineWidthButtonListener);

        dialogIsVisible.set(true); // dialog is on the screen
        currentDialog.show(); // show the dialog
     } // end method showLineWidthDialog

```

Fig. 9.18 | Method `showLineWidthDialog` creates and displays a `Dialog` for changing the line width. (Part 2 of 2.)

Anonymous Inner Class That Implements Interface **`OnSeekBarChangeListener`** *to Respond to the Events of the* **`widthSeekBar`**

Figure 9.19 defines the `widthSeekBarChanged` `OnSeekBarChangeListener` that responds to events when the user adjusts the `SeekBar` in the **Choose Line Width** `Dialog`. Lines 359–360 create a `Bitmap` on which to display a sample line representing the selected line thickness. Line 361 creates a `Canvas` for drawing on the `Bitmap`. Method `onProgressChanged` (lines 364–381) draws the sample line based on the current drawing color and the `SeekBar`'s value. First, lines 368–369 get a reference to the `ImageView` where the line is displayed. Next, lines 372–375 configure a `Paint` object for drawing the sample line. Class `Paint`'s **`setStrokeCap`** method (line 374) specifies the appearance of the line ends—in this case, they're rounded (`Paint.Cap.ROUND`). Line 378 clears `bitmap`'s background to white with `Bitmap` method **`eraseColor`**. We use canvas to draw the sample line. Finally, line 380 displays `bitmap` in the `widthImageView` by passing it to `ImageView`'s **`setImageBitmap`** method.

```
355    // OnSeekBarChangeListener for the SeekBar in the width dialog
356    private OnSeekBarChangeListener widthSeekBarChanged =
357       new OnSeekBarChangeListener()
358       {
359          Bitmap bitmap = Bitmap.createBitmap( // create Bitmap
360             400, 100, Bitmap.Config.ARGB_8888);
361          Canvas canvas = new Canvas(bitmap); // associate with Canvas
362
363          @Override
364          public void onProgressChanged(SeekBar seekBar, int progress,
365             boolean fromUser)
366          {
```

Fig. 9.19 | Anonymous inner class that implements interface `OnSeekbarChangeListener` to respond to `SeekBar` events in the **Choose Line Width** `Dialog`. (Part 1 of 2.)

```
            // get the ImageView
            ImageView widthImageView = (ImageView)
               currentDialog.findViewById(R.id.widthImageView);

            // configure a Paint object for the current SeekBar value
            Paint p = new Paint();
            p.setColor(doodleView.getDrawingColor());
            p.setStrokeCap(Paint.Cap.ROUND);
            p.setStrokeWidth(progress);

            // erase the bitmap and redraw the line
            bitmap.eraseColor(Color.WHITE);
            canvas.drawLine(30, 50, 370, 50, p);
            widthImageView.setImageBitmap(bitmap);
         } // end method onProgressChanged

         // required method of interface OnSeekBarChangeListener
         @Override
         public void onStartTrackingTouch(SeekBar seekBar)
         {
         } // end method onStartTrackingTouch

         // required method of interface OnSeekBarChangeListener
         @Override
         public void onStopTrackingTouch(SeekBar seekBar)
         {
         } // end method onStopTrackingTouch
      }; // end widthSeekBarChanged

```

Fig. 9.19 | Anonymous inner class that implements interface `OnSeekbarChangeListener` to respond to `SeekBar` events in the **Choose Line Width** `Dialog`. (Part 2 of 2.)

Anonymous Inner Class That Implements Interface `OnClickListener` *to Respond to the Events of the* **Set Line Width** `Button`

Figure 9.20 defines an anonymous inner class that implements interface `OnClickListener` to set the new line width color when the user clicks the **Set Line Width** `Button` in the **Choose Line Width** `Dialog`. This was registered as the `Button`'s event handler in Fig. 9.18 (line 349). Method `onClick` gets a reference to `Dialog`'s `SeekBar`, then uses it to set the new line width based on the `SeekBar`'s value. Line 409 indicates that a dialog is not displayed by calling `isDialigVisible`'s `set` method with the value `false`. Line 410 calls the `Dialog`'s `dismiss` method to close the dialog and return to the app.

```
396    // OnClickListener for the line width dialog's Set Line Width Button
397    private OnClickListener setLineWidthButtonListener =
398       new OnClickListener()
399       {
```

Fig. 9.20 | Anonymous inner class that implements interface `OnClickListener` to respond when the user touches the **Set Line Width** `Button`. (Part 1 of 2.)

```
            @Override
            public void onClick(View v)
            {
               // get the color SeekBars
               SeekBar widthSeekBar =
                  (SeekBar) currentDialog.findViewById(R.id.widthSeekBar);

               // set the line color
               doodleView.setLineWidth(widthSeekBar.getProgress());
               dialogIsVisible.set(false); // dialog is not on the screen
               currentDialog.dismiss(); // hide the dialog
               currentDialog = null; // dialog no longer needed
            } // end method onClick
         }; // end setColorButtonListener
} // end class Doodlz
```

Fig. 9.20 | Anonymous inner class that implements interface `OnClickListener` to respond when the user touches the **Set Line Width** `Button`. (Part 2 of 2.)

9.5.2 `DoodleView` Subclass of `View`

Class `DoodleView` (Figs. 9.21–9.29) processes the user's touches and draws the corresponding lines.

`DoodleView` Class for the `Doodlz` App—The Main Screen That's Painted

Figure 9.21 lists the `package` and `import` statements and the fields for class `DoodleView` of the **Doodlz** app. The new classes and interfaces were discussed in Section 9.3 and are highlighted here.

```
// DoodleView.java
// Main View for the Doodlz app.
package com.deitel.doodlz;

import java.io.IOException;
import java.io.OutputStream;
import java.util.HashMap;

import android.content.ContentValues;
import android.content.Context;
import android.graphics.Bitmap;
import android.graphics.Canvas;
import android.graphics.Color;
import android.graphics.Paint;
import android.graphics.Path;
import android.graphics.Point;
import android.net.Uri;
import android.provider.MediaStore.Images;
import android.util.AttributeSet;
import android.view.Gravity;
import android.view.MotionEvent;
```

Fig. 9.21 | `DoodleView` package and import statements. (Part 1 of 2.)

```
import android.view.View;
import android.widget.Toast;
```

Fig. 9.21 | DoodleView package and import statements. (Part 2 of 2.)

DoodleView Fields, Constructor and onSizeChanged Method

Class DoodleView's fields (Fig. 9.22, lines 29–36) are used to manage the data for the set of lines that the user is currently drawing and to draw those lines. The constructor (lines 39–54) initializes the class's fields. Line 43 creates the Paint object paintScreen that will be used to display the user's drawing on the screen and line 46 creates the Paint object paintLine that specifies the settings for the line(s) the user is currently drawing. Lines 47–51 specify the settings for the paintLine object. We pass true to Paint's **setAntiAlias** method to enable *anti-aliasing* which smooths the edges of the lines. Next, we set the Paint's style to Paint.Style.STROKE with Paint's **setStyle** method. The style can be STROKE, FILL or FILL_AND_STROKE for a line, a filled shape without a border and a filled shape with a border, respectively. The default option is Paint.Style.FILL. We set the line's width using Paint's setStrokeWidth method. This sets the app's *default line width* to five pixels. We also use Paint's setStrokeCap method to round the ends of the lines with Paint.Cap.ROUND. Line 52 creates the pathMap, which maps each finger ID (known as a pointer) to a corresponding Path object for the lines currently being drawn. Line 53 creates the previousPointMap, which maintains the last point for each finger—as each finger moves, we draw a line from its current point to its previous point.

```
25  // the main screen that is painted
26  public class DoodleView extends View
27  {
28     // used to determine whether user moved a finger enough to draw again
29     private static final float TOUCH_TOLERANCE = 10;
30
31     private Bitmap bitmap; // drawing area for display or saving
32     private Canvas bitmapCanvas; // used to draw on bitmap
33     private Paint paintScreen; // use to draw bitmap onto screen
34     private Paint paintLine; // used to draw lines onto bitmap
35     private HashMap<Integer, Path> pathMap; // current Paths being drawn
36     private HashMap<Integer, Point> previousPointMap; // current Points
37
38     // DoodleView constructor initializes the DoodleView
39     public DoodleView(Context context, AttributeSet attrs)
40     {
41        super(context, attrs); // pass context to View's constructor
42
43        paintScreen = new Paint(); // used to display bitmap onto screen
44
45        // set the initial display settings for the painted line
46        paintLine = new Paint();
47        paintLine.setAntiAlias(true); // smooth edges of drawn line
48        paintLine.setColor(Color.BLACK); // default color is black
```

Fig. 9.22 | DoodleView fields, constructor and overridden onSizeChanged method. (Part 1 of 2.)

```
49        paintLine.setStyle(Paint.Style.STROKE); // solid line
50        paintLine.setStrokeWidth(5); // set the default line width
51        paintLine.setStrokeCap(Paint.Cap.ROUND); // rounded line ends
52        pathMap = new HashMap<Integer, Path>();
53        previousPointMap = new HashMap<Integer, Point>();
54     } // end DoodleView constructor
55
56     // Method onSizeChanged creates BitMap and Canvas after app displays
57     @Override
58     public void onSizeChanged(int w, int h, int oldW, int oldH)
59     {
60        bitmap = Bitmap.createBitmap(getWidth(), getHeight(),
61           Bitmap.Config.ARGB_8888);
62        bitmapCanvas = new Canvas(bitmap);
63        bitmap.eraseColor(Color.WHITE); // erase the BitMap with white
64     } // end method onSizeChanged
65
```

Fig. 9.22 | `DoodleView` fields, constructor and overridden `onSizeChanged` method. (Part 2 of 2.)

The `DoodleView`'s size is not determined until it's inflated and added to the `Doodlz Activity`'s `View` hierarchy; therefore, we can't determine the size of the drawing `Bitmap` in `onCreate`. So, lines 58–64 override `View` method `onSizeChanged`, which is called when the `DoodleView`'s size changes—e.g., when it's added to an `Activity`'s `View` hierarchy or when the user device rotates the device. In this app, `onSizeChanged` is called only when the `DoodleView` is added to the `Doodlz Activity`'s `View` hierarchy, because the app always displays in *portrait mode* (Fig. 9.4). `Bitmap`'s `static` **`createBitmap`** method creates a `Bitmap` of the specified width and height—here we use the `DoodleView`'s width and height as the `Bitmap`'s dimensions. The last argument to `createBitmap` is the `Bitmap`'s encoding, which specifies how each pixel in the `Bitmap` is stored. The constant `Bitmap.Config.ARGB_8888` indicates that each pixel's color is stored in four bytes (one byte each for the alpha, red, green and blue values of the pixel's color. Next, we create a new `Canvas` that is used to draw shapes directly to the `Bitmap`. Finally, we use `Bitmap`'s `eraseColor` method to fill the `Bitmap` with white pixels—the default `Bitmap` background is black.

Methods `clear`*,* `setDrawingColor`*,* `getDrawingColor`*,* `setLineWidth` *and* `getLineWidth` *of Class* `DoodleView`

Figure 9.23 defines methods `clear` (lines 67–73), `setDrawingColor` (lines 76–79), `getDrawingColor` (lines 82–85), `setLineWidth` (lines 88–91) and `getLineWidth` (lines 94–97), which are called from the `Doodlz Activity`. Method `clear` empties the `pathMap` and `previousPointMap`, erases the `Bitmap` by setting all of its pixels to white, then calls the inherited `View` method **`invalidate`** to indicate that the `View` needs to be redrawn. Then, the system automatically determines when the `View`'s `onDraw` method should be called. Method `setDrawingColor` changes the current drawing color by setting the color of the `Paint` object `paintLine`. `Paint`'s `setColor` method receives an `int` that represents the new color in ARGB format. Method `getDrawingColor` returns the current color, which we use in the **Choose Color** `Dialog`. Method `setLineWidth` sets `paintLine`'s stroke width to the specified number of pixels. Method `getLineWidth` returns the current stroke width, which we use in the **Choose Line Width** `Dialog`.

```
   // clear the painting
   public void clear()
   {
      pathMap.clear(); // remove all paths
      previousPointMap.clear(); // remove all previous points
      bitmap.eraseColor(Color.WHITE); // clear the bitmap
      invalidate(); // refresh the screen
   } // end method clear

   // set the painted line's color
   public void setDrawingColor(int color)
   {
      paintLine.setColor(color);
   } // end method setDrawingColor

   // return the painted line's color
   public int getDrawingColor()
   {
      return paintLine.getColor();
   } // end method getDrawingColor

   // set the painted line's width
   public void setLineWidth(int width)
   {
      paintLine.setStrokeWidth(width);
   } // end method setLineWidth

   // return the painted line's width
   public int getLineWidth()
   {
      return (int) paintLine.getStrokeWidth();
   } // end method getLineWidth

```

Fig. 9.23 | `DoodleView` `clear`, `setDrawingColor`, `getDrawingColor`, `setLineWidth` and `getLineWidth` methods.

Overriding View *Method* OnDraw

When a `View` needs to be *redrawn*, it's **`onDraw`** method is called. Figure 9.24 overrides `onDraw` to display `bitmap` (the `Bitmap` that contains the drawing) on the `DoodleView` by calling the `Canvas` argument's **`drawBitmap`** method. The first argument is the `Bitmap` to draw, the next two arguments are the *x-y* coordinates where the upper-left corner of the `Bitmap` should be placed on the `View` and the last argument is the `Paint` object that specifies the drawing characteristics. Lines 107–108 then loop through each `Integer` key in the `pathMap` `HashMap`. For each, we pass the corresponding `Path` to `Canvas`'s **`drawPath`** method to draw each `Path` to the screen using the `paintLine` object, which defines the line *width* and *color*.

Overriding View *Method* onTouchEvent

Method `OnTouchEvent` (Fig. 9.25) is called when the `View` receives a touch event. Android supports multitouch—that is, having multiple fingers touching the screen. The user can touch the screen with more fingers or remove fingers from the screen at any time. For this

```
    // called each time this View is drawn
    @Override
    protected void onDraw(Canvas canvas)
    {
       // draw the background screen
       canvas.drawBitmap(bitmap, 0, 0, paintScreen);

       // for each path currently being drawn
       for (Integer key : pathMap.keySet())
          canvas.drawPath(pathMap.get(key), paintLine); // draw line
    } // end method onDraw

```

Fig. 9.24 | DoodleView overridden onDraw method.

reason, each finger—known as a pointer—has a unique ID that identifies it across touch events. We'll use that ID to locate the corresponding Path objects that represent each line currently being drawn. These Paths are stored in pathMap.

MotionEvent's **getActionMasked** method (line 116) returns an int representing the MotionEvent type, which you can use with constants from class MotionEvent to determine

```
111    // handle touch event
112    @Override
113    public boolean onTouchEvent(MotionEvent event)
114    {
115       // get the event type and the ID of the pointer that caused the event
116       int action = event.getActionMasked(); // event type
117       int actionIndex = event.getActionIndex(); // pointer (i.e., finger)
118
119       // determine which type of action the given MotionEvent
120       // represents, then call the corresponding handling method
121       if (action == MotionEvent.ACTION_DOWN ||
122          action == MotionEvent.ACTION_POINTER_DOWN)
123       {
124          touchStarted(event.getX(actionIndex), event.getY(actionIndex),
125             event.getPointerId(actionIndex));
126       } // end if
127       else if (action == MotionEvent.ACTION_UP ||
128          action == MotionEvent.ACTION_POINTER_UP)
129       {
130          touchEnded(event.getPointerId(actionIndex));
131       } // end else if
132       else
133       {
134          touchMoved(event);
135       } // end else
136
137       invalidate(); // redraw
138       return true; // consume the touch event
139    } // end method onTouchEvent
140
```

Fig. 9.25 | DoodleView overridden onTouchEvent method.

how to handle each event. MotionEvent's **getActionIndex** method returns an integer index representing which finger caused the event. This index is *not* the finger's unique ID—it's simply the index at which that finger's information is located in this MotionEvent object. To get the finger's unique ID that persists across MotionEvents until the user removes that finger from the screen, we'll use MotionEvent's **getPointerID** method (lines 125 and 130), passing the finger index as an argument.

If the action is MotionEvent.ACTION_DOWN or MotionEvent.ACTION_POINTER_DOWN (lines 121–122), the user *touched the screen with a new finger*. The first finger to touch the screen generates a MotionEvent.ACTION_DOWN event, and all other fingers generate MotionEvent.ACTION_POINTER_DOWN events. For these cases, we call the touchStarted method (Fig. 9.26) to store the initial coordinates of the touch. If the action is MotionEvent.ACTION_UP or MotionEvent.ACTION_POINTER_UP, the user *removed a finger from the screen*, so we call method touchEnded (Fig. 9.28) to draw the completed Path to the bitmap so that we have a permanent record of that Path. For all other touch events, we call method touchMoved (Fig. 9.27) to draw the lines. After the event is processed, line 137 calls the inherited View method invalidate to redraw the screen, and line 138 returns true to indicate that the event has been processed.

touchStarted Method of Class DoodleView

The utility method touchStarted (Fig. 9.26) is called when a finger first *touches* the screen. The coordinates of the touch and its ID are supplied as arguments. If a Path already exists for the given ID (line 148), we call Path's **reset** method to *clear* any existing points so we can *reuse* the Path for a new stroke. Otherwise, we create a new Path, add it to pathMap, then add a new Point to the previousPointMap. Lines 163–165 call Path's **moveTo** method to set the Path's starting coordinates and specify the new Point's x and y values.

```
141    // called when the user touches the screen
142    private void touchStarted(float x, float y, int lineID)
143    {
144       Path path; // used to store the path for the given touch id
145       Point point; // used to store the last point in path
146
147       // if there is already a path for lineID
148       if (pathMap.containsKey(lineID))
149       {
150          path = pathMap.get(lineID); // get the Path
151          path.reset(); // reset the Path because a new touch has started
152          point = previousPointMap.get(lineID); // get Path's last point
153       } // end if
154       else
155       {
156          path = new Path(); // create a new Path
157          pathMap.put(lineID, path); // add the Path to Map
158          point = new Point(); // create a new Point
159          previousPointMap.put(lineID, point); // add the Point to the Map
160       } // end else
161
```

Fig. 9.26 | DoodleView touchStarted method. (Part 1 of 2.)

```
162        // move to the coordinates of the touch
163        path.moveTo(x, y);
164        point.x = (int) x;
165        point.y = (int) y;
166     } // end method touchStarted
167
```

Fig. 9.26 | DoodleView touchStarted method. (Part 2 of 2.)

touchMoved Method of Class DoodleView

The utility method touchMoved (Fig. 9.27) is called when the user moves one or more fingers across the screen. The system MotionEvent passed from onTouchEvent contains touch information for multiple moves on the screen if they occur at the same time. MotionEvent method **getPointerCount** (line 172) returns the number of touches this MotionEvent describes. For each, we store the finger's ID (line 175) in pointerID, and store the finger's corresponding index in this MotionEvent (line 176) in pointerIndex. Then we check whether there's a corresponding Path in the pathMap HashMap (line 179). If so, we use MotionEvent's getX and getY methods to get the last coordinates for this *drag* event for the specified pointerIndex. We get the corresponding Path and last Point for the pointerID from each respective HashMap, then calculate the difference between the last point and the current point—we want to update the Path *only* if the user has moved a distance that's greater than our TOUCH_TOLERANCE constant. We do this because many devices are sensitive enough to generate MotionEvents indicating small movements when the user is attempting to hold a finger motionless on the screen. If the user moved a finger further than the TOUCH_TOLERANCE, we use Path's **quadTo** method (lines 198–199) to add a geometric curve (specifically a *quadratic bezier curve*) from the previous Point to the new Point. We then update the most recent Point for that finger.

```
168     // called when the user drags along the screen
169     private void touchMoved(MotionEvent event)
170     {
171        // for each of the pointers in the given MotionEvent
172        for (int i = 0; i < event.getPointerCount(); i++)
173        {
174           // get the pointer ID and pointer index
175           int pointerID = event.getPointerId(i);
176           int pointerIndex = event.findPointerIndex(pointerID);
177
178           // if there is a path associated with the pointer
179           if (pathMap.containsKey(pointerID))
180           {
181              // get the new coordinates for the pointer
182              float newX = event.getX(pointerIndex);
183              float newY = event.getY(pointerIndex);
184
185              // get the Path and previous Point associated with
186              // this pointer
187              Path path = pathMap.get(pointerID);
```

Fig. 9.27 | DoodleView touchMoved method. (Part 1 of 2.)

```
            Point point = previousPointMap.get(pointerID);

            // calculate how far the user moved from the last update
            float deltaX = Math.abs(newX - point.x);
            float deltaY = Math.abs(newY - point.y);

            // if the distance is significant enough to matter
            if (deltaX >= TOUCH_TOLERANCE || deltaY >= TOUCH_TOLERANCE)
            {
               // move the path to the new location
               path.quadTo(point.x, point.y, (newX + point.x) / 2,
                  (newY + point.y) / 2);

               // store the new coordinates
               point.x = (int) newX;
               point.y = (int) newY;
            } // end if
         } // end if
      } // end for
   } // end method touchMoved

```

Fig. 9.27 | `DoodleView` `touchMoved` method. (Part 2 of 2.)

`touchEnded` *Method of Class* `DoodleView`

The utility method `touchEnded` (Fig. 9.28) is called when the user lifts a finger from the screen. The method receives the ID of the finger (`lineID`) for which the touch just ended as an argument. Line 212 gets the corresponding `Path`. Line 213 calls the `bitmapCanvas`'s `drawPath` method to draw the `Path` on the `Bitmap` object named `bitmap` before we call `Path`'s `reset` method to clear the `Path`. Resetting the `Path` does not erase its corresponding painted line from the screen, because those lines have already been drawn to the `bitmap` that's displayed to the screen. The lines that are currently being drawn by the user are displayed on top of that `bitmap`.

```
209    // called when the user finishes a touch
210    private void touchEnded(int lineID)
211    {
212       Path path = pathMap.get(lineID); // get the corresponding Path
213       bitmapCanvas.drawPath(path, paintLine); // draw to bitmapCanvas
214       path.reset(); // reset the Path
215    } // end method touchEnded
216
```

Fig. 9.28 | `DoodleView` `touchEnded` method.

`saveImage` *Method*

The `saveImage` method (Fig. 9.29) saves the current drawing to a file in the device's gallery. [*Note:* It's possible that the image will not immediately appear in the gallery. For example, Android scans storage for new media items like images, videos and music when a device is first powered on. Some devices scan for new media in the background. In an AVD, you can run the AVD's **Dev Tools** app and touch its **Media Scanner** option, then the new image will appear in the gallery.]

```
   // save the current image to the Gallery
   public void saveImage()
   {
      // use "Doodlz" followed by current time as the image file name
      String fileName = "Doodlz" + System.currentTimeMillis();

      // create a ContentValues and configure new image's data
      ContentValues values = new ContentValues();
      values.put(Images.Media.TITLE, fileName);
      values.put(Images.Media.DATE_ADDED, System.currentTimeMillis());
      values.put(Images.Media.MIME_TYPE, "image/jpg");

      // get a Uri for the location to save the file
      Uri uri = getContext().getContentResolver().insert(
         Images.Media.EXTERNAL_CONTENT_URI, values);

      try
      {
         // get an OutputStream to uri
         OutputStream outStream =
            getContext().getContentResolver().openOutputStream(uri);

         // copy the bitmap to the OutputStream
         bitmap.compress(Bitmap.CompressFormat.JPEG, 100, outStream);

         // flush and close the OutputStream
         outStream.flush(); // empty the buffer
         outStream.close(); // close the stream

         // display a message indicating that the image was saved
         Toast message = Toast.makeText(getContext(),
            R.string.message_saved, Toast.LENGTH_SHORT);
         message.setGravity(Gravity.CENTER, message.getXOffset() / 2,
            message.getYOffset() / 2);
         message.show(); // display the Toast
      } // end try
      catch (IOException ex)
      {
         // display a message indicating that the image was saved
         Toast message = Toast.makeText(getContext(),
            R.string.message_error_saving, Toast.LENGTH_SHORT);
         message.setGravity(Gravity.CENTER, message.getXOffset() / 2,
            message.getYOffset() / 2);
         message.show(); // display the Toast
      } // end catch
   } // end method saveImage
} // end class DoodleView
```

Fig. 9.29 | `DoodleView saveImage` method.

We use `"Doodlz"` followed by current time as the image's file name. Line 224 creates a new **`ContentValues`** object, which will be used by a `ContentResolver` to specify the image's title (i.e., file name), the date the image was created and the *MIME type* of the image (`"image/jpg"` in this example). For more information on MIME types, visit

```
www.w3schools.com/media/media_mimeref.asp
```

`ContentValues` method `put` adds a key-value pair to a `ContentValues` object. The key `Images.Media.TITLE` (line 225) is used to specify `fileName` as the image file name. The key `Images.Media.DATE_ADDED` (line 226) is used to specify the time when this file was saved to the device. The key `Images.Media.MIME_TYPE` (line 227) is used to specify the file's MIME type as a JPEG image.

Lines 230–231 get this app's `ContentResolver`, then call its **`insert`** method to get a `Uri` where the image will be stored. The constant `Images.Media.EXTERNAL_CONTENT_URI` indicates that we want to store the image on the device's external storage device—typically an SD card if one is available. We pass our `ContentValues` as the second argument to create a file with our supplied file name, creation date and MIME type. Once the file is created we can write the screenshot to the location provided by the returned `Uri`. To do so, we get an `OutputStream` that allows us to write to the specified `Uri` (lines 236–237). Next, we invoke class `Bitmap`'s **`compress`** method, which receives a constant representing the compression format (`Bitmap.CompressFormat.JPEG`), an integer representing the quality (100 indicates the best quality image) and the `OutputStream` where the image's bytes should be written. Then lines 243–244 flush and close the `OutputStream`, respectively.

If the file is saved successfully, we use a `Toast` to indicate that the image was saved (lines 247–251); otherwise, we use a `Toast` to indicate that there was an error when saving the image (lines 256–260). `Toast` method **`makeText`** receives as arguments the `Context` on which the `Toast` is displayed, the message to display and the duration for which the `Toast` will be displayed. `Toast` method **`setGravity`** specifies where the `Toast` will appear. The constant `Gravity.CENTER` indicates that the `Toast` should be centered over the coordinates specified by the method's second and third arguments. `Toast` method `show` displays the `Toast`.

9.6 Wrap-Up

In this app, you learned how to turn a device's screen into a virtual canvas. You set the app's target SDK to `"11"` to enable a pre-Android 3.0 app to use Android 3.0's holographic user interface components and to integrate the app menu into Android 3.0's action bar, when the app runs on an Android 3.0 device. You processed sensor events—such as those generated by a device's accelerometer—by registering a `SensorEventListener` with the system's `SensorManager` service. We displayed dialogs with complex GUIs in objects of class `Dialog`. We also used a thread-safe `AtomicBoolean` to help determine when a dialog was already on the screen so that our sensor event handler would not display another dialog.

You learned how to create custom ARGB `Colors` with alpha, red, green and blue components and how to extract those individual components from an existing `Color`. We drew lines onto `Bitmaps` using associated `Canvas` objects, then displayed those `Bitmaps` on the screen. You also saved a `Bitmap` as an image in the device's gallery.

As the user dragged one or more fingers on the screen, we stored the information for each finger as a `Path`. We processed the touch events by overriding the `View` method `onTouchEvent` and using its `MotionEvent` parameter to get the type of touch event that occurred and the ID of the finger that generated the event.

You learned how to save an image into the device's gallery by getting an `OutputStream` from a `ContentResolver`. Finally, you used a `Toast` to display a message that automatically disappears after a short period of time.

In Chapter 10, we build the **Address Book** app, which provides quick and easy access to stored contact information and the ability to delete contacts, add contacts and edit existing contacts. The user can scroll through an alphabetical contact list, add contacts and view more information about individual contacts. Touching a contact's name displays a screen showing the contact's detailed information.

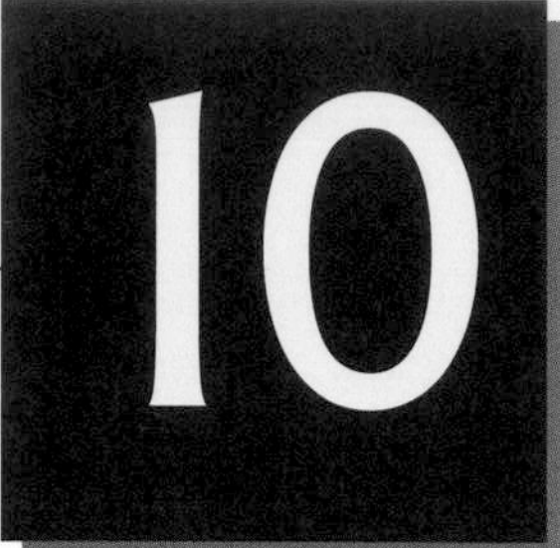

Address Book App

ListActivity, AdapterViews, Adapters, Multiple Activities, SQLite, GUI Styles, Menu Resources and MenuInflater

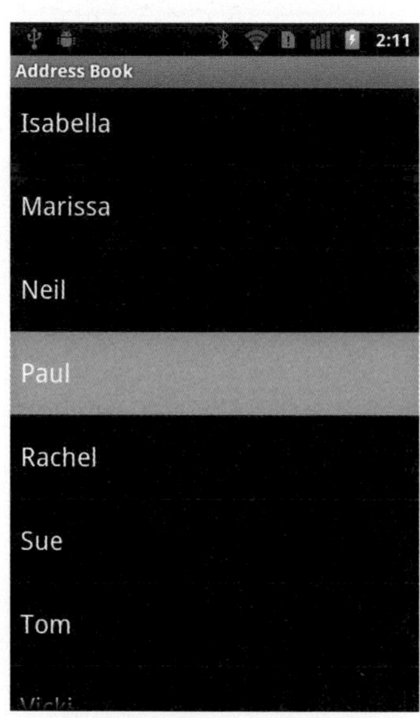

Objectives

In this chapter you'll:

- Extend `ListActivity` to create an `Activity` that consists of a `ListView` by default.
- Create multiple `Activity` subclasses to represent the app's tasks and use explicit `Intent`s to launch them.
- Create and open SQLite databases using a `SQLiteOpenHelper`, and insert, delete and query data in a SQLite database using a `SQLiteDatabase` object
- Use a `SimpleCursorAdapter` to bind database query results to a `ListView`'s items.
- Use a `Cursor` to manipulate database query results.
- Use multithreading to perform database operations outside the GUI thread and maintain application responsiveness.
- Define styles containing common GUI attributes and values, then apply them to multiple GUI components.
- Create XML **menu** resources and inflate them with a `MenuInflater`.

Outline

10.1 Introduction

The **Address Book** app (Fig. 10.1) provides convenient access to stored contact information. On the main screen, the user can *scroll* through an alphabetical contact list and can view a contact's details by touching the contact's name. Touching the device's menu button while viewing a contact's details displays a menu containing **Edit Contact** and **Delete Contact** options (Fig. 10.2). If the user chooses to edit the contact, the app launches an `Activity` that shows the existing information in `EditText`s (Fig. 10.2). If the user chooses to delete the contact, a dialog asks the user to confirm the delete operation (Fig. 10.3). Touching the device's menu button while viewing the contact list displays a menu con-

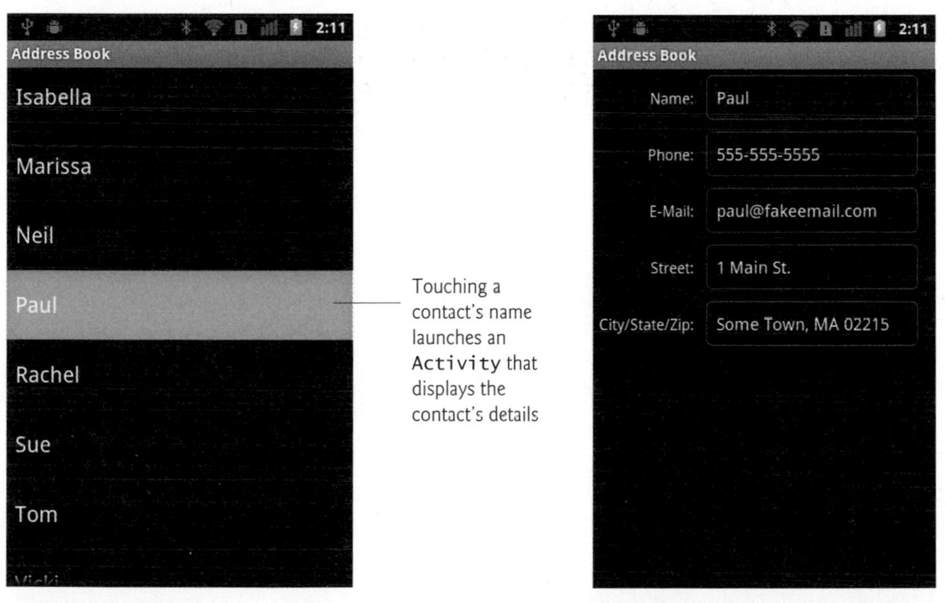

Fig. 10.1 | List of contacts with one item touched and the detailed contact information for the touched contact.

taining an **Add Contact** option—touching that option launches an `Activity` for adding a new contact (Fig. 10.4). Touching the **Save Contact** `Button` adds the new contact and returns the user to the main contact screen.

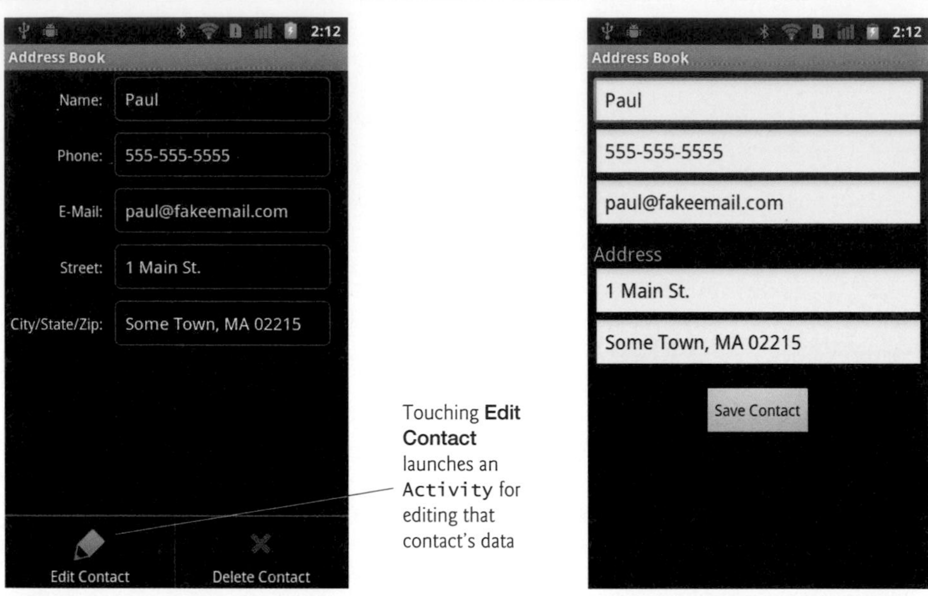

Fig. 10.2 | Editing a contact's data.

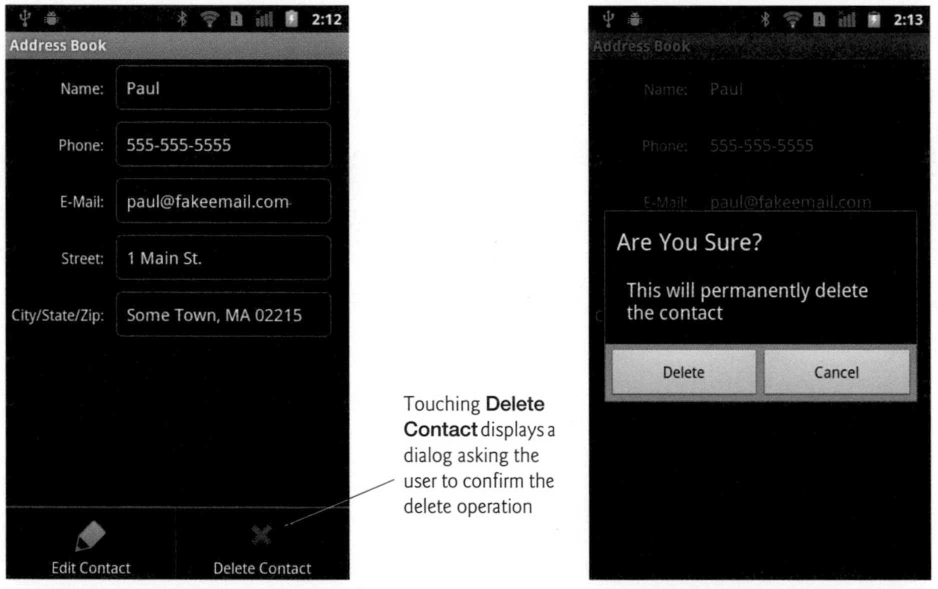

Fig. 10.3 | Deleting a contact from the database.

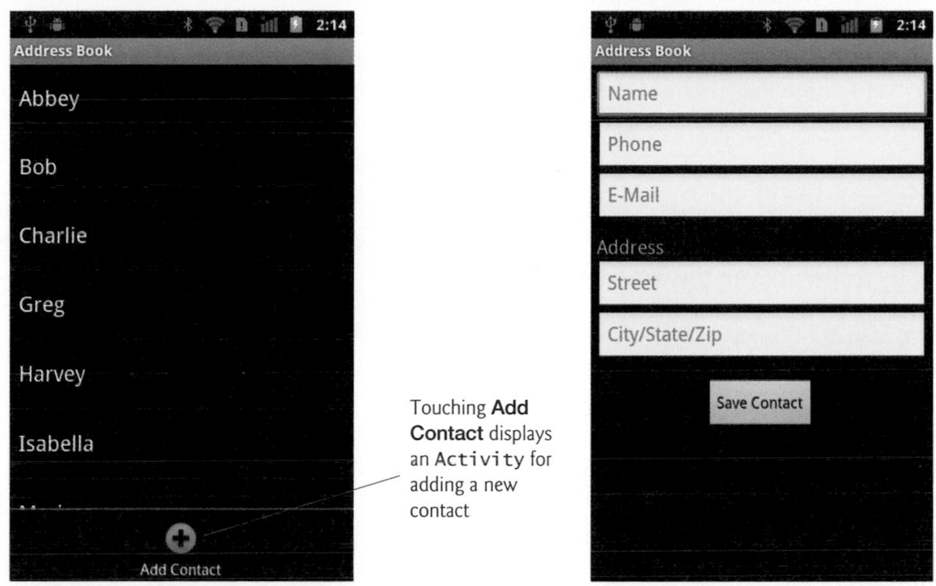

Fig. 10.4 | Adding a contact to the database.

10.2 Test-Driving the Address Book App

Opening and Running the App

Open Eclipse and import the **Address Book** app project. To import the project:

1. Select **File > Import...** to display the **Import** dialog.
2. Expand the **General** node and select **Existing Projects into Workspace**, then click **Next >**.
3. To the right of the **Select root directory:** text field, click **Browse...**, then locate and select the `AddressBook` folder.
4. Click **Finish** to import the project.

Right click the app's project in the **Package Explorer** window, then select **Run As > Android Application** from the menu that appears.

Adding a Contact

The first time you run the app, the contact list will be empty. Touch the device's menu button, then touch **Add Contact** to display the screen for adding a new entry. After adding the contact's information, touch the **Save Contact** `Button` to store the contact in the database and return to the app's main screen. If you choose not to add the contact, you can simply touch the device's back button to return to the main screen. Add more contacts if you wish.

Viewing a Contact

Touch the name of the contact you just added in the contacts list to view that contact's details.

Editing a Contact
While viewing the contact's details, touch the device's menu button then touch **Edit Contact** to display a screen of `EditTexts` that are prepopulated with the contact's data. Edit the data as necessary then touch the **Save Contact** `Button` to store the updated contact information in the database and return to the app's main screen.

Deleting a Contact
While viewing the contact's details, touch the device's menu button, then touch **Delete Contact**. If you wish to delete the contact, confirm this action in the dialog. The contact will be removed from the database and the app will return to the main screen.

Android 2.3 Overscroll
As of Android 2.3, lists like the one used to display the contacts in this app support **overscroll**—a visual effect (orange highlight) that indicates when you've reached the top or bottom of the list while scrolling through its contents. You can see the orange highlight effect by attempting to scroll past the beginning or end of the list.

10.3 Technologies Overview

This section presents the new technologies that we use in the **Address Book** app in the order in which they're encountered throughout the chapter.

Specifying Additional **`activity`** *Elements in the App's Manifest*
The `AndroidManifest.xml` file describes an app's components. In the prior apps, we had only one `Activity` per app. In this app, we have three. Each `Activity` must be described in the app's manifest (Section 10.4.2).

Defining Styles and Applying Them to GUI Components
You can define common GUI component attribute–value pairs as XML **`style`** **resources** (Section 10.4.3). You can then apply the styles to all components that share those values (Section 10.4.6) by using the **`style`** **attribute**. Any subsequent changes you make to a `style` are automatically applied to all GUI components that use the `style`.

Specifying a Background for a **`TextView`**
By default `TextViews` do not have a border. To define one, you can specify a `Drawable` as the value for the `TextView`'s `android:background` attribute. The `Drawable` could be an image, but in this app we'll define a new type of `Drawable` using an XML representation of a `shape` (Section 10.4.4). The XML file for such a `Drawable` is placed in the app's `drawable` folder, which you must create in the app's `res` folder.

Specifying the Format of a **`ListView`***'s Items*
This app uses a **`ListView`** (package `android.widget`) to display the contact list as a list of items that is *scrollable* if the complete list cannot be displayed on the screen. You can specify the layout resource (Section 10.4.5) that will be used to display each `ListView` item.

Creating **`menu`** *Resources in XML and Inflating Them with a* **`MenuInflater`**
In previous apps that used menus, we programmatically created the `MenuItems`. In this app, we'll use **`menu`** **resources** in XML to define the `MenuItems`, then we'll programmati-

cally inflate them (Sections 10.5.1 and 10.5.2) using an `Activity`'s **`MenuInflater`** (package `android.view`), which is similar to a `LayoutInflater`. In addition, we'll use some of Android's standard icons to enhance the visual appearance of the menu items.

Extending Class `ListActivity` to Create an `Activity` That Contains a `ListView`

When an `Activity`'s primary task is to display a scrollable list of items, you can extend class **`ListActivity`** (package `android.app`, Section 10.5.1), which uses a `ListView` that occupies the entire screen as its default layout. `ListView` is a subclass of **`AdapterView`** (package `android.widget`)—a GUI component is bound to a data source via an **`Adapter`** object (package `android.widget`). In this app, we'll use a **`CursorAdapter`** (package `android.widget`) to display the results of a database query in the `ListView`.

Several types of `AdapterViews` can be bound to data using an `Adapter`. For more details on data binding in Android and several tutorials, visit

```
developer.android.com/guide/topics/ui/binding.html
```

Using an Explicit `Intent` to Launch Another `Activity` in the Same App and Passing Data to That `Activity`

This app allows the user to view an existing contact, add a new contact or edit an existing contact. In each case, we launch a new `Activity` to handle the specified task. In Chapter 5, we showed how to use an *implicit* `Intent` to display a URL in the device's web browser. Sections 10.5.1 and 10.5.2 show how to use **explicit `Intents`** to launch another `Activity` in the same app and how to pass data from one `Activity` to another. Section 10.5.3 shows how to return to the `Activity` that launched a particular `Activity`.

Manipulating a SQLite Database

This app's contact information is stored in a SQLite database. SQLite (`www.sqlite.org`) is the world's most widely deployed database engine. Each `Activity` in this app interacts with the SQLite database via our utility class `DatabaseConnector` (Section 10.5.4). Within that class, we use a nested subclass of **`SQLiteOpenHelper`** (package **`android.database.sqlite`**), which simplifies creating the database and enables you to obtain a **`SQLiteDatabase`** object (package `android.database.sqlite`) for manipulating a database's contents. Database query results are managed via a **`Cursor`** (package **`android.database`**).

Using Multithreading to Perform Database Operations Outside the GUI Thread

It's good practice to perform long running operations or operations that block execution until they complete (e.g., file and database access) outside the GUI thread. This helps maintain application responsiveness and avoid *Activity Not Responding (ANR) dialogs* that appear when Android thinks the GUI is not responsive. When we need a database operation's results in the GUI thread, we'll use an **`AsyncTask`** (package `android.os`) to perform the operation in one thread and receive the results in the GUI thread. The details of creating and manipulating threads are handled for you by class `AsyncTask`, as are communicating the results from the `AsyncTask` to the GUI thread.

10.4 Building the GUI and Resource Files

In this section, you'll create the **Address Book** app's resource files and GUI layout files. To save space, we do not show this app's `strings.xml` resource file or the layout files for the

ViewContact Activity (view_contact.xml) and AddEditContact (add_contact.xml). You can view the contents of these files by opening them from the project in Eclipse.

10.4.1 Creating the Project

Begin by creating a new Android project named AddressBook. Specify the following values in the **New Android Project** dialog, then press **Finish**:

- **Build Target:** Ensure that **Android 2.3.3** is checked
- **Application name:** Address Book
- **Package name:** com.deitel.addressbook
- **Create Activity:** AddressBook
- **Min SDK Version:** 8

10.4.2 AndroidManifest.xml

Figure 10.5 shows this app's AndroidManifest.xml file, which contains an activity element for each Activity in the app. Lines 14–15 specify AddEditContact's activity element. Lines 16–17 specify ViewContact's activity element.

```
1  <?xml version="1.0" encoding="utf-8"?>
2  <manifest xmlns:android="http://schemas.android.com/apk/res/android"
3     package="com.deitel.addressbook" android:versionCode="1"
4     android:versionName="1.0">
5     <application android:icon="@drawable/icon"
6        android:label="@string/app_name">
7        <activity android:name=".AddressBook"
8           android:label="@string/app_name">
9           <intent-filter>
10             <action android:name="android.intent.action.MAIN" />
11             <category android:name="android.intent.category.LAUNCHER" />
12          </intent-filter>
13       </activity>
14       <activity android:name=".AddEditContact"
15          android:label="@string/app_name"></activity>
16       <activity android:name=".ViewContact"
17          android:label="@string/app_name"></activity>
18    </application>
19    <uses-sdk android:minSdkVersion="8" />
20 </manifest>
```

Fig. 10.5 | AndroidManifest.xml.

10.4.3 styles.xml

Figure 10.6 defines the style resources used in the layout file view_contact.xml (Section 10.4.6). Like XML documents representing other values, an XML document containing style elements is placed in the app's res/values folder. Each style specifies a name (e.g., line 3), which is used to apply that style to one or more GUI components, and to one or more item elements (e.g., line 4), each specifying an attribute's XML name and a value to apply.

```
1  <?xml version="1.0" encoding="utf-8"?>
2  <resources>
3     <style name="ContactLabelTextView">
4        <item name="android:layout_width">wrap_content</item>
5        <item name="android:layout_height">wrap_content</item>
6        <item name="android:gravity">right</item>
7        <item name="android:textSize">14sp</item>
8        <item name="android:textColor">@android:color/white</item>
9        <item name="android:layout_marginLeft">5dp</item>
10       <item name="android:layout_marginRight">5dp</item>
11       <item name="android:layout_marginTop">5dp</item>
12    </style>
13    <style name="ContactTextView">
14       <item name="android:layout_width">wrap_content</item>
15       <item name="android:layout_height">wrap_content</item>
16       <item name="android:textSize">16sp</item>
17       <item name="android:textColor">@android:color/white</item>
18       <item name="android:layout_margin">5dp</item>
19       <item name="android:background">@drawable/textview_border</item>
20    </style>
21 </resources>
```

Fig. 10.6 | Styles defined in `styles.xml` and placed in the app's `res/values` folder.

10.4.4 `textview_border.xml`

The `style` `ContactTextView` in Fig. 10.6 (lines 13–20) defines the appearance of the `TextView`s that are used to display a contact's details in the `ViewContact` `Activity`. Line 19 specifies a `Drawable` as the value for the `TextView`'s `android:background` attribute. The `Drawable` (`textview_border`) used here is defined in XML as a **`shape` element** (Fig. 10.7) and stored in the app's `res/drawable` folder. The `shape` element's `android:shape` attribute (line 3) can have the value `"rectangle"` (used in this example), `"oval"`, `"line"` or `"ring"`. The **`corners` element** (line 4) specifies the rectangle's corner radius, which rounds the corners. The **`stroke` element** (line 5) defines the rectangle's line width and line color. The **`padding` element** (lines 6–7) specifies the spacing around the content in the element to which this `Drawable` is applied. You must specify the top, left, right and bottom padding amounts separately. The complete specification for defining a shape in XML can be viewed at:

```
developer.android.com/guide/topics/resources/
   drawable-resource.html#Shape
```

```
1  <?xml version="1.0" encoding="utf-8"?>
2  <shape xmlns:android="http://schemas.android.com/apk/res/android"
3     android:shape="rectangle" >
4     <corners android:radius="5dp"/>
5     <stroke android:width="1dp" android:color="#555"/>
6     <padding android:top="10dp" android:left="10dp" android:bottom="10dp"
7        android:right="10dp"/>
8  </shape>
```

Fig. 10.7 | XML representation of a `Drawable` that's used to place a border on a `TextView`.

10.4.5 AddressBook Activity's Layout: contact_list_item.xml

The AddressBook Activity extends ListActivity rather than Activity. A ListActivity's default GUI consists of a ListView that occupies the entire screen, so we do not need to define a separate layout for this Activity. If you wish to customize a ListActivity's GUI, you can define a layout XML file that must contain a ListView with its android:id attribute set to "@android:id/list", which we discuss in Chapter 12's **Slideshow** app.

When populating a ListView with data, you must specify the format that's applied to each list item, which is the purpose of the contact_list_item.xml layout in Fig. 10.8. Each list item contains one contact's name, so the layout defines just a TextView for displaying a name. A ListView's default background color is black, so we set the text color to white (line 5). The android:id attribute will be used to associate data with the TextView. Line 6 sets the list item's minimum height to listPreferredItemHeight—a built in Android attribute constant. Line 7 sets the list item's gravity to center_vertical. If a list item should consist of multiple pieces of data, you may need multiple elements in your list-item layout and each will need an android:id attribute. You'll learn how to use these android:id attributes in Section 10.5.1. Figure 10.1 showed the list-items' appearance.

```
1  <?xml version="1.0" encoding="utf-8"?>
2  <TextView xmlns:android="http://schemas.android.com/apk/res/android"
3     android:id="@+id/contactTextView" android:layout_width="match_parent"
4     android:layout_height="wrap_content" android:padding="8dp"
5     android:textSize="20sp" android:textColor="@android:color/white">
6     android:minHeight="?android:attr/listPreferredItemHeight"
7     android:gravity="center_vertical"></TextView>
```

Fig. 10.8 | Layout for each item in the AddressBook ListActivity's built-in ListView.

10.4.6 ViewContact Activity's Layout: view_contact.xml

When the user selects a contact in the AddressBook Activity, the app launches the ViewContact Activity (Fig. 10.9). This Activity's layout (view_contact.xml) uses a ScrollView containing a TableLayout in which each TableRow contains two TextViews.

The only new feature in this layout is that all of its TextViews have styles from Fig. 10.6 applied to them. For example, lines 11–15 in the layout file:

```
<TextView android:id="@+id/nameLabelTextView"
   style="@style/ContactLabelTextView"
   android:text="@string/label_name"></TextView>
<TextView android:id="@+id/nameTextView"
   style="@style/ContactTextView"></TextView>
```

represent the TextViews in the first TableRow. Each TextView uses the style attribute to specify the style to apply using the syntax @style/*styleName*.

10.4.7 AddEditContact Activity's Layout: add_contact.xml

When the user touches the AddressBook Activity's **Add Contact** menu item or the ViewContact Activity's **Edit Contact** menu item, the app launches the AddEditContact Activity (Fig. 10.10). This Activity's layout uses a ScrollView containing a vertical LinearLayout. If the Activity is launched from the AddressBook Activity, the Edit-

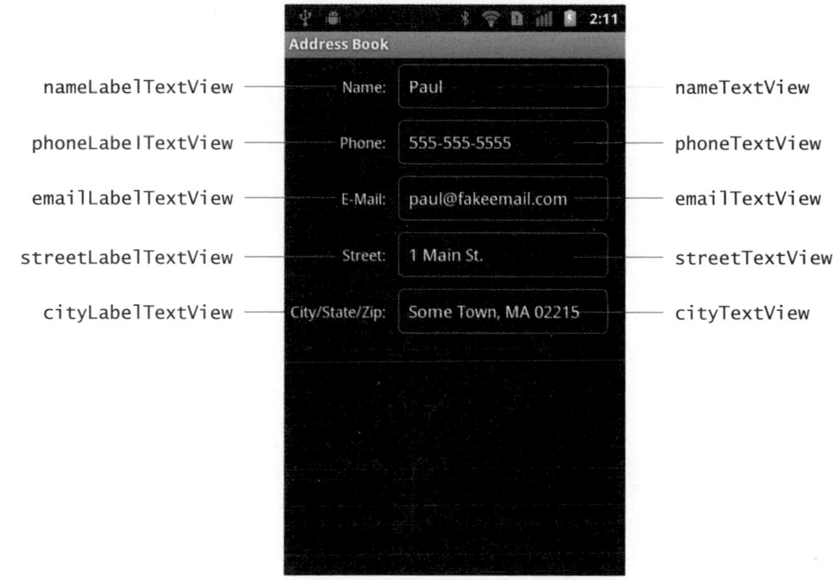

Fig. 10.9 | `ViewContact` `Activity`'s GUI components labeled with their `id` property values. This GUI's root component is a `ScrollView` containing a `TableLayout` with five `TableRows`.

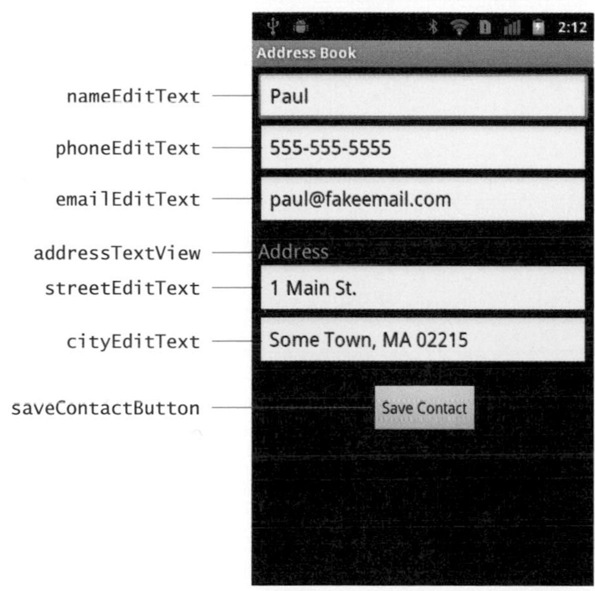

Fig. 10.10 | `AddEditContact` `Activity`'s GUI components labeled with their `id` property values. This GUI's root component is a `ScrollView` that contains a vertical `LinearLayout`.

`Texts` will be empty and will display hints (specified in lines 12, 17, 22, 33 and 38 of the layout's XML file). Otherwise, the `EditTexts` will display the contact's data that was passed to the AddEditContact Activity from the ViewContact Activity. Each EditText specifies the android:inputType and android:imeOptions attributes. For devices that display a soft keyboard, the android:inputType attribute (at lines 13, 18, 23, 34 and 39 in the layout's XML file) specifies which keyboard to display when the user touches the corresponding EditText. This enables us to *customize the keyboard* to the specific type of data the user must enter in a given EditText. As in Chapter 5, we use the android:imeOptions attribute to display a **Next** button on the soft keyboards for the nameEditText, emailEditText, phoneEditText or streetEditText. When one of these has the focus, touching this Button transfers the focus to the next EditText. If the cityEditText has the focus, you can hide the soft keyboard by touching the keyboard's **Done** Button.

10.4.8 Defining the App's MenuItems with menu Resources in XML

Figures 10.11 and 10.12 define the menu resources for the AddressBook Activity and the ViewContact Activity, respectively. Resource files that define menus are placed in the app's res/menu folder (which you must create) and are added to the project like other resource files (originally described in Section 3.5), but in the **New Android XML File** dialog you select **Menu** as the resource type. Each menu resource XML file contains a root **menu element** with nested **item elements** that represent each MenuItem. We show how to inflate the menus in Sections 10.5.1 and 10.5.2.

```
<?xml version="1.0" encoding="utf-8"?>
<menu xmlns:android="http://schemas.android.com/apk/res/android">
   <item android:id="@+id/addContactItem"
      android:title="@string/menuitem_add_contact"
      android:icon="@android:drawable/ic_menu_add"
      android:titleCondensed="@string/menuitem_add_contact"
      android:alphabeticShortcut="e"></item>
</menu>
```

Fig. 10.11 | AddressBook Activity's menu resource.

```
<?xml version="1.0" encoding="utf-8"?>
<menu xmlns:android="http://schemas.android.com/apk/res/android">
   <item android:id="@+id/editItem"
      android:title="@string/menuitem_edit_contact"
      android:orderInCategory="1" android:alphabeticShortcut="e"
      android:titleCondensed="@string/menuitem_edit_contact"
      android:icon="@android:drawable/ic_menu_edit"></item>
   <item android:id="@+id/deleteItem"
      android:title="@string/menuitem_delete_contact"
      android:orderInCategory="2" android:alphabeticShortcut="d"
      android:titleCondensed="@string/menuitem_delete_contact"
      android:icon="@android:drawable/ic_delete"></item>
</menu>
```

Fig. 10.12 | ViewContact Activity's menu resource.

You specify an android:id attribute for each item so that you can interact with the corresponding MenuItem programmatically. Other item attributes we use here include:

- **android:title** and **android:titleCondensed**—these specify the text to display on the MenuItem. The condensed title is used if the regular title text is too long to display properly.
- **android:icon**—specifies a Drawable to display on the MenuItem above the title text. In this example's MenuItems, we use three of the standard icons that are provided with the Android SDK. They're located in the SDK's platforms folder under each platform version's data/res/drawable-hdpi folder. To refer to these icons in your XML layouts, prefix them with @android:drawable/*icon_name* as in Fig. 10.11, line 5 and Fig. 10.12, lines 7 and 12.
- **android:alphabeticShortcut**—specifies a letter that the user can press on a hard keyboard to select the menu item.
- **android:orderInCategory**—determines the order in which the MenuItems appear. We did not use it in Fig. 10.11, as there's only one MenuItem.

For complete details on menu resources, visit:

```
developer.android.com/guide/topics/resources/menu-resource.html
```

10.5 Building the App

This app consists of four classes—class AddressBook (the ListActivity subclass, Figs. 10.13–10.18), class ViewContact (Figs. 10.19–10.23), class AddEditContact (Figs. 10.24–10.27) and class DatabaseConnector (Figs. 10.28–10.31). As in prior apps, this app's main Activity—AddressBook—is created when you create the project, but you'll need to modify it to extend class ListActivity. You must add the other Activity classes and the DatabaseConnector class to the project's src/com.deitel.addressbook folder.

10.5.1 AddressBook Subclass of ListActivity

Class AddressBook (Figs. 10.13–10.18) provides the functionality for the first Activity displayed by this app. As discussed earlier in this chapter, the class extends ListActivity rather than Activity, because this Activity's primary purpose is to display a ListView containing the user's contacts.

package Statement, import Statements and Instance Variables

Figure 10.13 lists AddressBook's package statement, import statements and instance variables. We've highlighted the imports for the new classes discussed in Section 10.3. The constant ROW_ID is used as a key in a key–value pair that's passed between activities (Fig. 10.18). Instance variable contactListView will refer to the AddressBook's built-in ListView, so we can interact with it programmatically. Instance variable contactAdapter will refer to the CursorAdapter that populates the AddressBook's ListView.

```
// AddressBook.java
// Main activity for the Address Book app.
package com.deitel.addressbook;
```

Fig. 10.13 | package statement, import statements and instance variables of class AddressBook. (Part 1 of 2.)

```java

import android.app.ListActivity;
import android.content.Intent;
import android.database.Cursor;
import android.os.AsyncTask;
import android.os.Bundle;
import android.view.Menu;
import android.view.MenuInflater;
import android.view.MenuItem;
import android.view.View;
import android.widget.AdapterView;
import android.widget.AdapterView.OnItemClickListener;
import android.widget.CursorAdapter;
import android.widget.ListView;
import android.widget.SimpleCursorAdapter;

public class AddressBook extends ListActivity
{
   public static final String ROW_ID = "row_id"; // Intent extra key
   private ListView contactListView; // the ListActivity's ListView
   private CursorAdapter contactAdapter; // adapter for ListView

```

Fig. 10.13 | `package` statement, `import` statements and instance variables of class `AddressBook`. (Part 2 of 2.)

Overriding `Activity` *Method* `onCreate`

Method `onCreate` (Fig. 10.14, lines 26–32) initializes the `Activity`. Recall that class `ListActivity` already contains a `ListView` that occupies the entire `Activity`, we don't need to inflate the GUI using method `setContentView` as in previous apps. Line 31 uses the inherited `ListActivity` method **`getListView`** to obtain a reference to the built-in `ListView`. Line 32 then sets the `ListView`'s `OnItemClickListener` to `viewContactListener` (Fig. 10.18), which responds to the user's touching one of the `ListView`'s items.

```java
26    // called when the activity is first created
27    @Override
28    public void onCreate(Bundle savedInstanceState)
29    {
30       super.onCreate(savedInstanceState); // call super's onCreate
31       contactListView = getListView(); // get the built-in ListView
32       contactListView.setOnItemClickListener(viewContactListener);
33
34       // map each contact's name to a TextView in the ListView layout
35       String[] from = new String[] { "name" };
36       int[] to = new int[] { R.id.contactTextView };
37       CursorAdapter contactAdapter = new SimpleCursorAdapter(
38          AddressBook.this, R.layout.contact_list_item, null, from, to);
39       setListAdapter(contactAdapter); // set contactView's adapter
40    } // end method onCreate
41
```

Fig. 10.14 | Overriding `Activity` method `onCreate`.

To display the Cursor's results in a ListView we create a new CursorAdapter object (lines 35–38) which exposes the Cursor's data in a manner that can be used by a ListView. **SimpleCursorAdapter** is a subclass of CursorAdapter that's designed to simplify mapping Cursor columns directly to TextViews or ImagesViews defined in your XML layouts. To create a SimpleCursorAdapter, you must first define arrays containing the column names to map to GUI components and the resource IDs of the GUI components that will display the data from the named columns. Line 35 creates a String array indicating that only the column named name will be displayed, and line 36 creates a parallel int array containing corresponding GUI components' resource IDs (in this case, R.id.contactTextView). Lines 37–38 create the SimpleCursorAdapter. Its constructor receives:

- the Context in which the ListView is running (i.e., the AddressBook Activity)
- the resource ID of the layout that's used to display each item in the ListView
- the Cursor that provides access to the data—we supply null for this argument because we'll specify the Cursor later
- the String array containing the column names to display
- the int array containing the corresponding GUI resource IDs

Line 39 uses inherited ListActivity method **setListAdapter** to bind the ListView to the CursorAdapter, so that the ListView can display the data.

Overriding Activity *Methods* onResume *and* onStop

As you learned in Section 8.5.1, method onResume (Fig. 10.15, lines 42–49) is called each time an Activity returns to the foreground, including when the Activity is first created. In this app, onResume creates and executes an AsyncTask (line 48) of type GetContactsTask (defined in Fig. 10.16) that gets the complete list of contacts from the database and sets the contactAdapter's Cursor for populating the AddressBook's ListView. AsyncTask method **execute** performs the task in a separate thread. Method execute's argument in this case indicates that the task does not receive any arguments— this method can receive a variable number of arguments that are, in turn, passed as arguments to the task's doInBackground method. Every time line 48 executes, it creates a new GetContactsTask object—this is required because each AsyncTask can be executed *only once.*

```
42     @Override
43     protected void onResume()
44     {
45        super.onResume(); // call super's onResume method
46
47        // create new GetContactsTask and execute it
48        new GetContactsTask().execute((Object[]) null);
49     } // end method onResume
50
51     @Override
52     protected void onStop()
53     {
54        Cursor cursor = contactAdapter.getCursor(); // get current Cursor
```

Fig. 10.15 | Overriding Activity methods onResume and onStop. (Part 1 of 2.)

```
55
56         if (cursor != null)
57            cursor.deactivate(); // deactivate it
58
59         contactAdapter.changeCursor(null); // adapted now has no Cursor
60         super.onStop();
61      } // end method onStop
62
```

Fig. 10.15 | Overriding `Activity` methods `onResume` and `onStop`. (Part 2 of 2.)

`Activity` method **`onStop`** (Fig. 10.15, lines 51–61) is called when the `Activity` is no longer visible to the user—typically because another `Activity` has started or returned to the foreground. In this case, the `Cursor` that allows us to populate the `ListView` is not needed, so line 54 calls `CursorAdapter` method **`getCursor`** to get the current `Cursor` from the `contactAdapter`, then line 57 calls `Cursor` method **`deactivate`** to release resources used by the `Cursor`. Line 59 then calls `CursorAdapter` method **`changeCursor`** with the argument `null` to remove the `Cursor` from the `CursorAdapter`.

`GetContactsTask` Subclass of `AsyncTask`

Nested class `GetContactsTask` (Fig. 10.16) extends class `AsyncTask`. The class defines how to interact with the database to get the names of all the contacts and return the results to this `Activity`'s GUI thread for display in the `ListView`. `AsyncTask` is a generic type that requires three type parameters:

- The first is the type of the variable length parameter list for the `AsyncTask`'s **`doInBackground`** method (lines 50–57). When an `AsyncTask`'s `execute` method is called, the task's `doInBackground` method performs the task in a separate thread of execution. In this case, `doInBackground` does not require additional data to perform its task, so we specify `Object` as the type parameter and pass `null` as the argument to the `AsyncTask`'s `execute` method, which calls `doInBackground`.
- The second is the type of the variable length parameter list for the `AsyncTask`'s **`onProgressUpdate`** method. This method executes in the GUI thread and is used to receive intermediate updates of the specified type from a long-running task. We don't use this feature in this example, so we specify type `Object` here and ignore this type parameter.
- The third is the type of the task's result, which is passed to the `AsyncTask`'s **`onPostExecute`** method (lines 80–85). This method executes in the GUI thread and enables the `Activity` to use the `AsyncTask`'s results.

A key benefit of using an `AsyncTask` is that it handles the details of creating threads and executing its methods on the appropriate threads for you, so that you do not have to interact with the threading mechanism directly.

Lines 66–67 create a new object of our utility class `DatabaseConnector`, passing the `Context` (`AddressBook.this`) as an argument to the class's constructor. (We discuss class `DatabaseConnector` in Section 10.5.4.)

Method `doInBackground` (lines 70–77) uses `databaseConnector` to open the database connection, then gets all the contacts from the database. The `Cursor` returned by

```
63     // performs database query outside GUI thread
64     private class GetContactsTask extends AsyncTask<Object, Object, Cursor>
65     {
66        DatabaseConnector databaseConnector =
67           new DatabaseConnector(AddressBook.this);
68
69        // perform the database access
70        @Override
71        protected Cursor doInBackground(Object... params)
72        {
73           databaseConnector.open();
74
75           // get a cursor containing call contacts
76           return databaseConnector.getAllContacts();
77        } // end method doInBackground
78
79        // use the Cursor returned from the doInBackground method
80        @Override
81        protected void onPostExecute(Cursor result)
82        {
83           contactAdapter.changeCursor(result); // set the adapter's Cursor
84           databaseConnector.close();
85        } // end method onPostExecute
86     } // end class GetContactsTask
87
```

Fig. 10.16 | `GetContactsTask` subclass of `AsyncTask`

`getAllContacts` is passed to method `onPostExecute` (lines 80–86). That method receives the `Cursor` containing the results, and passes it to `CursorAdapter` method `changeCursor`, so the `Activity`'s `ListView` can populate itself.

Managing `Cursors`

In this `Activity`, we're managing the `Cursors` with various `Cursor` and `CursorAdapter` methods. Class `Activity` can also manage `Cursors` for you. `Activity` method **`startManagingCursor`** tells the `Activity` to manage the `Cursor`'s lifecycle based on the `Activity`'s lifecycle. When the `Activity` is stopped, it will call `deactivate` on any `Cursors` it's currently managing. When the `Activity` resumes, it will call **`requery`** on its `Cursors`. When the `Activity` is destroyed, it will automatically call `close` to *release all resources* held by any managed `Cursors`. A deactivated `Cursor` consumes less resources than an active one, so it's good practice to align your `Cursor`'s lifecycle with its parent `Activity` if the `Cursor` is not shared among multiple `Activity` objects. Allowing your `Activity` to manage the `Cursor`'s lifecycle also ensures that the `Cursor` will be closed when it's no longer needed.

Overriding `Activity` *Methods* `onCreateOptionsMenu` *and* `onOptionsItemSelected`

When the user opens this `Activity`'s menu, method `onCreateOptionsMenu` (Fig. 10.17, lines 89–96) uses a **`MenuInflater`** to create the menu from `addressbook_menu.xml`, which contains an **Add Contact** `MenuItem`. We obtain the `MenuInflater` by calling `Activity`'s **`getMenuInflater`** **method**. If the user touches that `MenuItem`, method `onOptionsItemSelected` (lines 99–107) launches the `AddEditContact Activity` (Section 10.5.3). Lines

103–104 create a new *explicit* Intent to launch that Activity. The Intent constructor used here receives the Context from which the Activity will be launched and the class representing the Activity to launch (AddEditContact.class). We then pass this Intent to the inherited Activity method startActivity to launch the Activity.

```
88      // create the Activity's menu from a menu resource XML file
89      @Override
90      public boolean onCreateOptionsMenu(Menu menu)
91      {
92         super.onCreateOptionsMenu(menu);
93         MenuInflater inflater = getMenuInflater();
94         inflater.inflate(R.menu.addressbook_menu, menu);
95         return true;
96      } // end method onCreateOptionsMenu
97
98      // handle choice from options menu
99      @Override
100     public boolean onOptionsItemSelected(MenuItem item)
101     {
102        // create a new Intent to launch the AddEditContact Activity
103        Intent addNewContact =
104           new Intent(AddressBook.this, AddEditContact.class);
105        startActivity(addNewContact); // start the AddEditContact Activity
106        return super.onOptionsItemSelected(item); // call super's method
107     } // end method onOptionsItemSelected
108
```

Fig. 10.17 | Overriding Activity methods onCreateOptionsMenu and onOptionsItem-Selected.

Anonymous Inner Class That Implements Interface **OnItemClickListener** *to Process* **ListView** *Events*

The viewContactListener OnItemClickListener (Fig. 10.18) launches the ViewContact Activity to display the user's selected contact. Method **onItemClick** receives:

- a reference to the AdapterView that the user interacted with (i.e., the ListView),
- a reference to the root View of the touched list item,
- the index of the touched list item in the ListView and
- the unique long ID of the selected item—in this case, the row ID in the Cursor.

```
   // event listener that responds to the user touching a contact's name
   // in the ListView
   OnItemClickListener viewContactListener = new OnItemClickListener()
   {
      @Override
      public void onItemClick(AdapterView<?> arg0, View arg1, int arg2,
         long arg3)
      {
```

Fig. 10.18 | OnItemClickListener viewContactListener that responds to ListView touch events. (Part 1 of 2.)

```
117            // create an Intent to launch the ViewContact Activity
118            Intent viewContact =
119               new Intent(AddressBook.this, ViewContact.class);
120
121            // pass the selected contact's row ID as an extra with the Intent
122            viewContact.putExtra(ROW_ID, arg3);
123            startActivity(viewContact); // start the ViewContact Activity
124         } // end method onItemClick
125      }; // end viewContactListener
126   } // end class AddressBook
```

Fig. 10.18 | `OnItemClickListener` `viewContactListener` that responds to `ListView` touch events. (Part 2 of 2.)

Lines 118–119 create an explicit `Intent` to launch the `ViewContact Activity`. To display the appropriate contact, the `ViewContact Activity` needs to know which record to retrieve. You can pass data between activities by adding *extras* to the `Intent` using `Intent`'s **`putExtra`** method (line 122), which adds the data as a key–value pair to a `Bundle` associated with the `Intent`. In this case, the key–value pair represents the unique row ID of the contact the user touched.

10.5.2 `ViewContact` Subclass of `Activity`

The `ViewContact Activity` (Figs. 10.19–10.23) displays one contact's information and provides a menu that enables the user to edit or delete that contact.

`package` Statement, `import` Statements and Instance Variables

Figure 10.19 lists the `package` statement, the `import` statements and the instance variables for class `ViewContact`. We've highlighted the `import` statements for the new classes discussed in Section 10.3. The instance variable `rowID` represents the current contact's unique row ID in the database. The `TextView` instance variables (lines 20–24) are used to display the contact's data on the screen.

```
1   // ViewContact.java
2   // Activity for viewing a single contact.
3   package com.deitel.addressbook;
4
5   import android.app.Activity;
6   import android.app.AlertDialog;
7   import android.content.DialogInterface;
8   import android.content.Intent;
9   import android.database.Cursor;
10  import android.os.AsyncTask;
11  import android.os.Bundle;
12  import android.view.Menu;
13  import android.view.MenuInflater;
14  import android.view.MenuItem;
```

Fig. 10.19 | `package` statement, `import` statements and instance variables of class `ViewContact`. (Part 1 of 2.)

```
import android.widget.TextView;

public class ViewContact extends Activity
{
   private long rowID; // selected contact's name
   private TextView nameTextView; // displays contact's name
   private TextView phoneTextView; // displays contact's phone
   private TextView emailTextView; // displays contact's email
   private TextView streetTextView; // displays contact's street
   private TextView cityTextView; // displays contact's city/state/zip

```

Fig. 10.19 | package statement, import statements and instance variables of class ViewContact. (Part 2 of 2.)

Overriding **Activity** *Methods* **onCreate** *and* **onResume**

The onCreate method (Fig. 10.20, lines 27–43) first gets references to the Activity's TextViews, then obtains the selected contact's row ID. Activity method **getIntent** returns the Intent that launched the Activity. We use that to call Intent method **getExtras**, which returns a Bundle that contains any key–value pairs that were added to the Intent as extras. This method returns null if no extras were added. Next, we use the Bundle's **getLong** method to obtain the long integer representing the selected contact's row ID. [*Note:* We did not test whether the value of extras (line 41) was null, because there will always be a Bundle returned in this app. Testing for null is considered good practice, so you can decide how to handle the problem. For example, you could log the error and return from the Activity by calling finish.] Method onResume (lines 46–53) simply creates a new AsyncTask of type LoadContactTask (Fig. 10.21) and executes it to get and display contact's information.

```
26      // called when the activity is first created
27      @Override
28      public void onCreate(Bundle savedInstanceState)
29      {
30         super.onCreate(savedInstanceState);
31         setContentView(R.layout.view_contact);
32
33         // get the EditTexts
34         nameTextView = (TextView) findViewById(R.id.nameTextView);
35         phoneTextView = (TextView) findViewById(R.id.phoneTextView);
36         emailTextView = (TextView) findViewById(R.id.emailTextView);
37         streetTextView = (TextView) findViewById(R.id.streetTextView);
38         cityTextView = (TextView) findViewById(R.id.cityTextView);
39
40         // get the selected contact's row ID
41         Bundle extras = getIntent().getExtras();
42         rowID = extras.getLong("row_id");
43      } // end method onCreate
44
```

Fig. 10.20 | Overriding Activity method onCreate. (Part 1 of 2.)

```
   // called when the activity is first created
   @Override
   protected void onResume()
   {
      super.onResume();

      // create new LoadContactTask and execute it
      new LoadContactTask().execute(rowID);
   } // end method onResume

```

Fig. 10.20 | Overriding `Activity` method `onCreate`. (Part 2 of 2.)

`GetContactsTask` Subclass of `AsyncTask`

Nested class `GetContactsTask` (Fig. 10.21) extends class `AsyncTask` and defines how to interact with the database and get one contact's information for display. In this case the three generic type parameters are:

- `Long` for the variable-length argument list passed to `AsyncTask`'s `doInBackground` method. This will contain the row ID needed to locate one contact.
- `Object` for the variable-length argument list passed to `AsyncTask`'s `onProgress-Update` method, which we don't use in this example.
- `Cursor` for the type of the task's result, which is passed to the `AsyncTask`'s `on-PostExecute` method.

```
   // performs database query outside GUI thread
   private class LoadContactTask extends AsyncTask<Long, Object, Cursor>
   {
      DatabaseConnector databaseConnector =
         new DatabaseConnector(ViewContact.this);

      // perform the database access
      @Override
      protected Cursor doInBackground(Long... params)
      {
         databaseConnector.open();

         // get a cursor containing all data on given entry
         return databaseConnector.getOneContact(params[0]);
      } // end method doInBackground

      // use the Cursor returned from the doInBackground method
      @Override
      protected void onPostExecute(Cursor result)
      {
         super.onPostExecute(result);

         result.moveToFirst(); // move to the first item

```

Fig. 10.21 | `loadContact` method of class `ViewContact`. (Part 1 of 2.)

```
79          // get the column index for each data item
80          int nameIndex = result.getColumnIndex("name");
81          int phoneIndex = result.getColumnIndex("phone");
82          int emailIndex = result.getColumnIndex("email");
83          int streetIndex = result.getColumnIndex("street");
84          int cityIndex = result.getColumnIndex("city");
85
86          // fill TextViews with the retrieved data
87          nameTextView.setText(result.getString(nameIndex));
88          phoneTextView.setText(result.getString(phoneIndex));
89          emailTextView.setText(result.getString(emailIndex));
90          streetTextView.setText(result.getString(streetIndex));
91          cityTextView.setText(result.getString(cityIndex));
92
93          result.close(); // close the result cursor
94          databaseConnector.close(); // close database connection
95       } // end method onPostExecute
96    } // end class LoadContactTask
97
```

Fig. 10.21 | `loadContact` method of class `ViewContact`. (Part 2 of 2.)

Lines 58–59 create a new object of our `DatabaseConnector` class (Section 10.5.4). Method `doInBackground` (lines 62–69) opens the connection to the database and calls the `DatabaseConnector`'s `getOneContact` method, which queries the database to get the contact with the specified `rowID` that was passed as the only argument to this `AsyncTask`'s `execute` method. In `doInBackground`, the `rowID` is stored in `params[0]`.

The resulting `Cursor` is passed to method `onPostExecute` (lines 72–95). The `Cursor` is positioned *before* the first row of the result set. In this case, the result set will contain only one record, so `Cursor` method **`moveToFirst`** (line 77) can be used to move the `Cursor` to the first row in the result set. [*Note:* It's considered good practice to ensure that `Cursor` method `moveToFirst` returns `true` before attempting to get data from the `Cursor`. In this app, there will always be a row in the `Cursor`.]

We use `Cursor`'s **`getColumnIndex` method** to get the column indices for the columns in the database's `contacts` table. (We hard coded the column names in this app, but these could be implemented as `String` constants as we did for `ROW_ID` in class `AddressBook`.) This method returns `-1` if the column is not in the query result. Class `Cursor` also provides method **`getColumnIndexOrThrow`** if you prefer to get an exception when the specified column name does not exist. Lines 87–91 use `Cursor`'s **`getString` method** to retrieve the `String` values from the `Cursor`'s columns, then display these values in the corresponding `TextView`s. Lines 93–94 close the `Cursor` and this `Activity`'s connection to the database, as they're no longer needed. It's good practice to release resources like database connections when they are not being used so that other activities can use the resources.

Overriding `Activity` *Methods* `onCreateOptionsMenu` *and* `onOptionsItemSelected`

The `ViewContact` `Activity`'s menu provides options for editing the current contact and for deleting it. Method `onCreateOptionsMenu` (Fig. 10.22, lines 99–106) uses a `MenuInflater` to create the menu from the `view_contact.xml` menu resource file, which contains the **Edit Contact** and **Delete Contact** `MenuItem`s. Method `onOptionsItemSelected` (lines 109–134) uses the selected `MenuItem`'s resource ID to determine which one was selected. If it was **Edit Contact**, lines 116–126 create a new *explicit* `Intent` for the `AddEditContact` `Activity` (Section 10.5.3), add extras to the `Intent` representing this contact's information for display in the `AddEditContact` `Activity`'s `EditText`s and launch the `Activity`. If it was **Delete Contact**, line 129 calls the utility method `deleteContact` (Fig. 10.23).

```
98      // create the Activity's menu from a menu resource XML file
99      @Override
100     public boolean onCreateOptionsMenu(Menu menu)
101     {
102        super.onCreateOptionsMenu(menu);
103        MenuInflater inflater = getMenuInflater();
104        inflater.inflate(R.menu.view_contact_menu, menu);
105        return true;
106     } // end method onCreateOptionsMenu
107
108     // handle choice from options menu
109     @Override
110     public boolean onOptionsItemSelected(MenuItem item)
111     {
112        switch (item.getItemId()) // switch based on selected MenuItem's ID
113        {
114           case R.id.editItem:
115              // create an Intent to launch the AddEditContact Activity
116              Intent addEditContact =
117                 new Intent(this, AddEditContact.class);
118
119              // pass the selected contact's data as extras with the Intent
120              addEditContact.putExtra("row_id", rowID);
121              addEditContact.putExtra("name", nameTextView.getText());
122              addEditContact.putExtra("phone", phoneTextView.getText());
123              addEditContact.putExtra("email", emailTextView.getText());
124              addEditContact.putExtra("street", streetTextView.getText());
125              addEditContact.putExtra("city", cityTextView.getText());
126              startActivity(addEditContact); // start the Activity
127              return true;
128           case R.id.deleteItem:
129              deleteContact(); // delete the displayed contact
130              return true;
131           default:
132              return super.onOptionsItemSelected(item);
133        } // end switch
134     } // end method onOptionsItemSelected
135
```

Fig. 10.22 | Overriding methods `onCreateOptionsMenu` and `onOptionsItemSelected`.

Method `deleteContact`

Method `deleteContact` (Fig. 10.23) displays an `AlertDialog` asking the user to confirm that the currently displayed contact should be deleted, and, if so, uses an `AsyncTask` to delete it from the SQLite database. If the user clicks the **Delete** `Button` in the dialog, lines

153–154 create a new `DatabaseConnector`. Lines 158–173 create an `AsyncTask` that, when executed (line 176), passes a `Long` value representing the contact's row ID to the `doInBackground`, which then deletes the contact. Line 164 calls the `DatabaseConnector`'s `deleteContact` method to perform the actual deletion. When the `doInBackground` completes execution, line 171 calls this `Activity`'s `finish` method to return to the `Activity` that launched the `ViewContact Activity`—that is, the `AddressBook Activity`.

```
136    // delete a contact
137    private void deleteContact()
138    {
139       // create a new AlertDialog Builder
140       AlertDialog.Builder builder =
141          new AlertDialog.Builder(ViewContact.this);
142
143       builder.setTitle(R.string.confirmTitle); // title bar string
144       builder.setMessage(R.string.confirmMessage); // message to display
145
146       // provide an OK button that simply dismisses the dialog
147       builder.setPositiveButton(R.string.button_delete,
148          new DialogInterface.OnClickListener()
149          {
150             @Override
151             public void onClick(DialogInterface dialog, int button)
152             {
153                final DatabaseConnector databaseConnector =
154                   new DatabaseConnector(ViewContact.this);
155
156                // create an AsyncTask that deletes the contact in another
157                // thread, then calls finish after the deletion
158                AsyncTask<Long, Object, Object> deleteTask =
159                   new AsyncTask<Long, Object, Object>()
160                   {
161                      @Override
162                      protected Object doInBackground(Long... params)
163                      {
164                         databaseConnector.deleteContact(params[0]);
165                         return null;
166                      } // end method doInBackground
167
168                      @Override
169                      protected void onPostExecute(Object result)
170                      {
171                         finish(); // return to the AddressBook Activity
172                      } // end method onPostExecute
173                   }; // end new AsyncTask
174
175                // execute the AsyncTask to delete contact at rowID
176                deleteTask.execute(new Long[] { rowID });
177             } // end method onClick
178          } // end anonymous inner class
179       ); // end call to method setPositiveButton
```

Fig. 10.23 | `deleteContact` method of class `ViewContact`. (Part 1 of 2.)

```

         builder.setNegativeButton(R.string.button_cancel, null);
         builder.show(); // display the Dialog
      } // end method deleteContact
   } // end class ViewContact
```

Fig. 10.23 | `deleteContact` method of class `ViewContact`. (Part 2 of 2.)

10.5.3 `AddEditContact` Subclass of `Activity`

The `AddEditContact` `Activity` (Figs. 10.24–10.27) enables the user to add a new contact or to edit an existing contact's information.

`package` *Statement,* `import` *Statements and Instance Variables*

Figure 10.24 lists the `package` statement, the `import` statements and the instance variables for class `AddEditContact`. No new classes are used in this `Activity`. Instance variable `databaseConnector` allows this `Activity` to interact with the database. Instance variable `rowID` represents the current contact being manipulated if this `Activity` was launched to allow the user to edit an existing contact. The instance variables at lines 20–24 enable us to manipulate the text in the `Activity`'s `EditText`s.

```
1  // AddEditContact.java
2  // Activity for adding a new entry to or
3  // editing an existing entry in the address book.
4  package com.deitel.addressbook;
5
6  import android.app.Activity;
7  import android.app.AlertDialog;
8  import android.os.AsyncTask;
9  import android.os.Bundle;
10 import android.view.View;
11 import android.view.View.OnClickListener;
12 import android.widget.Button;
13 import android.widget.EditText;
14
15 public class AddEditContact extends Activity
16 {
17    private long rowID; // id of contact being edited, if any
18
19    // EditTexts for contact information
20    private EditText nameEditText;
21    private EditText phoneEditText;
22    private EditText emailEditText;
23    private EditText streetEditText;
24    private EditText cityEditText;
25
```

Fig. 10.24 | `package` statement, `import` statements and instance variables of class `AddEditContact`.

Overriding `Activity` *Method* `onCreate`

Method `onCreate` (Fig. 10.25) initializes the `AddEditContact Activity`. Lines 33–37 get the `Activity`'s `EditText`s. Next, we use `Activity` method `getIntent` to get the `Intent` that launched the `Activity` and call the `Intent`'s `getExtras` method to get the `Intent`'s `Bundle` of extras. When we launch the `AddEditContact Activity` from the `AddressBook Activity`, we don't add any extras to the `Intent`, because the user is about to specify a new contact's information. In this case, `getExtras` will return `null`. If it returns a `Bundle` (line 42) then the `Activity` was launched from the `ViewContact Activity` and the user has chosen to edit an existing contact. Lines 44–49 read the extras out of the `Bundle` by calling methods `getLong` (line 44) and `getString`, and the `String` data is displayed in the `EditText`s for editing. Lines 53–55 register a listener for the `Activity`'s **Save Contact** `Button`.

```
26      // called when the Activity is first started
27      @Override
28      public void onCreate(Bundle savedInstanceState)
29      {
30         super.onCreate(savedInstanceState); // call super's onCreate
31         setContentView(R.layout.add_contact); // inflate the UI
32
33         nameEditText = (EditText) findViewById(R.id.nameEditText);
34         emailEditText = (EditText) findViewById(R.id.emailEditText);
35         phoneEditText = (EditText) findViewById(R.id.phoneEditText);
36         streetEditText = (EditText) findViewById(R.id.streetEditText);
37         cityEditText = (EditText) findViewById(R.id.cityEditText);
38
39         Bundle extras = getIntent().getExtras(); // get Bundle of extras
40
41         // if there are extras, use them to populate the EditTexts
42         if (extras != null)
43         {
44            rowID = extras.getLong("row_id");
45            nameEditText.setText(extras.getString("name"));
46            emailEditText.setText(extras.getString("email"));
47            phoneEditText.setText(extras.getString("phone"));
48            streetEditText.setText(extras.getString("street"));
49            cityEditText.setText(extras.getString("city"));
50         } // end if
51
52         // set event listener for the Save Contact Button
53         Button saveContactButton =
54            (Button) findViewById(R.id.saveContactButton);
55         saveContactButton.setOnClickListener(saveContactButtonClicked);
56      } // end method onCreate
57
```

Fig. 10.25 | Overriding `Activity` methods `onCreate` and `onPause`.

`OnClickListener` *to Process* **Save Contact** `Button` *Events*

When the user touches the **Save Contact** `Button` in the `AddEditContact Activity`, the `saveContactButtonClicked OnClickListener` (Fig. 10.26) executes. To save a contact, the user must enter at least the contact's name. Method `onClick` ensures that the length of the name is greater than 0 characters (line 64) and, if so, creates and executes an AsyncTask to perform the save operation. Method doInBackground (lines 69–74) calls saveContact (Fig. 10.27) to save the contact into the database. Method onPostExecute (lines 76–80) calls finish to terminate this Activity and return to the launching Activity (either AddressBook or ViewContact). If the nameEditText is empty, lines 89–96 show an AlertDialog telling the user that a contact name must be provided to save the contact.

```
58     // responds to event generated when user clicks the Done Button
59     OnClickListener saveContactButtonClicked = new OnClickListener()
60     {
61        @Override
62        public void onClick(View v)
63        {
64           if (nameEditText.getText().length() != 0)
65           {
66              AsyncTask<Object, Object, Object> saveContactTask =
67                 new AsyncTask<Object, Object, Object>()
68                 {
69                    @Override
70                    protected Object doInBackground(Object... params)
71                    {
72                       saveContact(); // save contact to the database
73                       return null;
74                    } // end method doInBackground
75
76                    @Override
77                    protected void onPostExecute(Object result)
78                    {
79                       finish(); // return to the previous Activity
80                    } // end method onPostExecute
81                 }; // end AsyncTask
82
83              // save the contact to the database using a separate thread
84              saveContactTask.execute((Object[]) null);
85           } // end if
86           else
87           {
88              // create a new AlertDialog Builder
89              AlertDialog.Builder builder =
90                 new AlertDialog.Builder(AddEditContact.this);
91
92              // set dialog title & message, and provide Button to dismiss
93              builder.setTitle(R.string.errorTitle);
94              builder.setMessage(R.string.errorMessage);
95              builder.setPositiveButton(R.string.errorButton, null);
96              builder.show(); // display the Dialog
97           } // end else
98        } // end method onClick
99     }; // end OnClickListener saveContactButtonClicked
100
```

Fig. 10.26 | OnClickListener doneButtonClicked responds to the events of the doneButton.

saveContact Method

The saveContact method (Fig. 10.27) saves the information in this Activity's EditTexts. First, line 105 creates the DatabaseConnector object, then we check whether the Intent that launched this Activity had any extras. If not, this is a new contact, so lines 110–115 get the Strings from the Activity's EditTexts and pass them to the DatabaseConnector object's insertContact method to create the new contacts. If there are extras for the Intent that launched this Activity, then an existing contact is being updated. In this case, we get the Strings from the Activity's EditTexts and pass them to the DatabaseConnector object's updateContact method, using the rowID to indicate which record to update. DatabaseConnector methods insertContact and updateContact each handle the opening and closing of the database,

```
101      // saves contact information to the database
102      private void saveContact()
103      {
104         // get DatabaseConnector to interact with the SQLite database
105         DatabaseConnector databaseConnector = new DatabaseConnector(this);
106
107         if (getIntent().getExtras() == null)
108         {
109            // insert the contact information into the database
110            databaseConnector.insertContact(
111               nameEditText.getText().toString(),
112               emailEditText.getText().toString(),
113               phoneEditText.getText().toString(),
114               streetEditText.getText().toString(),
115               cityEditText.getText().toString());
116         } // end if
117         else
118         {
119            databaseConnector.updateContact(rowID,
120               nameEditText.getText().toString(),
121               emailEditText.getText().toString(),
122               phoneEditText.getText().toString(),
123               streetEditText.getText().toString(),
124               cityEditText.getText().toString());
125         } // end else
126      } // end class saveContact
127   } // end class AddEditContact
```

Fig. 10.27 | saveContact method of class AddEditContact.

10.5.4 DatabaseConnector Utility Class

The DatabaseConnector utility class (Figs. 10.28–10.31) manages this app's interactions with SQLite for creating and manipulating the UserContacts database, which contains one table named contacts.

package Statement, import Statements and Fields

Figure 10.28 lists class DatabaseConnector's package statement, import statements and fields. We've highlighted the import statements for the new classes and interfaces discussed in Section 10.3. The `String` constant `DATABASE_NAME` (line 16) specifies the name of the database that will be created or opened. *Database names must be unique within a specific app but need not be unique across apps.* A `SQLiteDatabase` object (line 17) provides read/write access to a SQLite database. The `DatabaseOpenHelper` (line 18) is a `private` nested class that extends abstract class `SQLiteOpenHelper`—such a class is used to manage creating, opening and upgrading databases (perhaps to modify a database's structure). We discuss `SQLOpenHelper` in more detail in Fig. 10.31.

```
1   // DatabaseConnector.java
2   // Provides easy connection and creation of UserContacts database.
3   package com.deitel.addressbook;
4
5   import android.content.ContentValues;
6   import android.content.Context;
7   import android.database.Cursor;
8   import android.database.SQLException;
9   import android.database.sqlite.SQLiteDatabase;
10  import android.database.sqlite.SQLiteOpenHelper;
11  import android.database.sqlite.SQLiteDatabase.CursorFactory;
12
13  public class DatabaseConnector
14  {
15     // database name
16     private static final String DATABASE_NAME = "UserContacts";
17     private SQLiteDatabase database; // database object
18     private DatabaseOpenHelper databaseOpenHelper; // database helper
19
```

Fig. 10.28 | `package` statement, `import` statements and instance variables of utility class `DatabaseConnector`.

Constructor and Methods `open` *and* `close` *for Class* `DatabaseConnector`

`DatabaseConnection`'s constructor (Fig. 10.29, lines 21–26) creates a new object of class `DatabaseOpenHelper` (Fig. 10.31), which will be used to open or create the database. We discuss the details of the `DatabaseOpenHelper` constructor in Fig. 10.31. The `open` method (lines 29–33) attempts to establish a connection to the database and throws a `SQLException` if the connection attempt fails. Method **`getWritableDatabase`** (line 32), which is inherited from `SQLiteOpenHelper`, returns a `SQLiteDatabase` object. If the database has not yet been created, this method will create it; otherwise, the method will open it. Once the database is opened successfully, it will be *cached* by the operating system to improve the performance of future database interactions. The `close` method (lines 36–40) closes the database connection by calling the inherited `SQLiteOpenHelper` method **`close`**.

```
20     // public constructor for DatabaseConnector
21     public DatabaseConnector(Context context)
22     {
```

Fig. 10.29 | Constructor, `open` method and `close` method. (Part 1 of 2.)

```java
      // create a new DatabaseOpenHelper
      databaseOpenHelper =
         new DatabaseOpenHelper(context, DATABASE_NAME, null, 1);
   } // end DatabaseConnector constructor

   // open the database connection
   public void open() throws SQLException
   {
      // create or open a database for reading/writing
      database = databaseOpenHelper.getWritableDatabase();
   } // end method open

   // close the database connection
   public void close()
   {
      if (database != null)
         database.close(); // close the database connection
   } // end method close

```

Fig. 10.29 | Constructor, `open` method and `close` method. (Part 2 of 2.)

Methods `insertContact`, `updateContact`, `getAllContacts`, `getOneContact` *and* `deleteContact`

Method `insertContact` (Fig. 10.30, lines 43–56) inserts a new contact with the given information into the database. We first put each piece of contact information into a new **`ContentValues`** object (lines 46–51), which maintains a map of key–value pairs—the database's column names are the keys. Lines 53–55 open the database, insert the new contact and close the database. `SQLiteDatabase`'s **`insert` method** (line 54) inserts the values from the given `ContentValues` into the table specified as the first argument—the `"contacts"` table in this case. The second parameter of this method, which is not used in this app, is named `nullColumnHack` and is needed because *SQLite does not support inserting a completely empty row into table*—this would be the equivalent of passing an empty `ContentValues` object to `insert`. Instead of making it illegal to pass an empty `ContentValues` to the method, the `nullColumnHack` parameter is used to identify a column that accepts `NULL` values.

```java
42    // inserts a new contact in the database
43    public void insertContact(String name, String email, String phone,
44       String state, String city)
45    {
46       ContentValues newContact = new ContentValues();
47       newContact.put("name", name);
48       newContact.put("email", email);
49       newContact.put("phone", phone);
50       newContact.put("street", state);
51       newContact.put("city", city);
52
```

Fig. 10.30 | Methods `insertContact`, `updateContact`, `getAllContacts`, `getOneContact` and `deleteContact`. (Part 1 of 2.)

```
53        open(); // open the database
54        database.insert("contacts", null, newContact);
55        close(); // close the database
56     } // end method insertContact
57
58     // inserts a new contact in the database
59     public void updateContact(long id, String name, String email,
60        String phone, String state, String city)
61     {
62        ContentValues editContact = new ContentValues();
63        editContact.put("name", name);
64        editContact.put("email", email);
65        editContact.put("phone", phone);
66        editContact.put("street", state);
67        editContact.put("city", city);
68
69        open(); // open the database
70        database.update("contacts", editContact, "_id=" + id, null);
71        close(); // close the database
72     } // end method updateContact
73
74     // return a Cursor with all contact information in the database
75     public Cursor getAllContacts()
76     {
77        return database.query("contacts", new String[] {"_id", "name"},
78           null, null, null, null, "name");
79     } // end method getAllContacts
80
81     // get a Cursor containing all information about the contact specified
82     // by the given id
83     public Cursor getOneContact(long id)
84     {
85        return database.query(
86           "contacts", null, "_id='" + id, null, null, null, null);
87     } // end method getOnContact
88
89     // delete the contact specified by the given String name
90     public void deleteContact(long id)
91     {
92        open(); // open the database
93        database.delete("contacts", "_id=" + id, null);
94        close(); // close the database
95     } // end method deleteContact
96
```

Fig. 10.30 | Methods `insertContact`, `updateContact`, `getAllContacts`, `getOneContact` and `deleteContact`. (Part 2 of 2.)

Method `updateContact` (lines 59–72) is similar to method `insertContact`, except that it calls `SQLiteDatabase`'s **`update` method** (line 70) to update an existing contact. The `update` method's third argument represents a SQL `WHERE` clause (without the keyword `WHERE`) that specifies which record(s) to update. In this case, we use the record's row ID to update a specific contact.

Method `getAllContacts` (lines 75–79) uses `SqLiteDatabase`'s **`query` method** (lines 77–78) to retrieve a `Cursor` that provides access to the IDs and names of all the contacts in the database. The arguments are:

- the name of the table to query
- a `String` array of the column names to return (the `_id` and `name` columns here)—`null` returns all columns in the table, which is generally a poor programming practice, because to conserve memory, processor time and battery power, you should obtain only the data you need
- a SQL `WHERE` clause (without the keyword `WHERE`), or `null` to return all rows
- a `String` array of arguments to be substituted into the `WHERE` clause wherever `?` is used as a placeholder for an argument value, or `null` if there are no arguments in the `WHERE` clause
- a SQL `GROUP BY` clause (without the keywords `GROUP BY`), or `null` if you don't want to group the results
- a SQL `HAVING` clause (without the keyword `HAVING`) to specify which groups from the `GROUP BY` clause to include in the results—`null` is required if the `GROUP BY` clause is `null`
- a SQL `ORDER BY` clause (without the keywords `ORDER BY`) to specify the order of the results, or `null` if you don't wish to specify the order.

The `Cursor` returned by method `query` contains all the table rows that match the method's arguments—the so-called *result set*. The `Cursor` is positioned *before* the first row of the result set—`Cursor`'s various `move` methods can be used to move the `Cursor` through the result set for processing.

Method `getOneContact` (lines 83–87) also uses `SqLiteDatabase`'s `query` method to query the database. In this case, we retrieve all the columns in the database for the contact with the specified ID.

Method `deleteContact` (lines 90–95) uses `SqLiteDatabase`'s **`delete` method** (line 93) to delete a contact from the database. In this case, we retrieve all the columns in the database for the contact with the specified ID. The three arguments are the database table from which to delete the record, the `WHERE` clause (without the keyword `WHERE`) and, if the `WHERE` clause has arguments, a `String` array of values to substitute into the `WHERE` clause (`null` in our case).

`private` Nested Class `DatabaseOpenHelper` That Extends `SQLiteOpenHelper`

The `private` nested class `DatabaseOpenHelper` (Fig. 10.31) extends abstract class `SQLiteOpenHelper`, which helps apps create databases and manage version changes. The constructor (lines 100–104) simply calls the superclass constructor, which requires four arguments:

- the `Context` in which the database is being created or opened,
- the database name—this can be `null` if you wish to use an in-memory database,
- the `CursorFactory` to use—`null` indicates that you wish to use the default SQLite `CursorFactory` (typically for most apps) and
- the database version number (starting from 1).

You must override this class's abstract methods onCreate and onUpgrade. If the database does not yet exist, the DatabaseOpenHelper's **onCreate method** will be called to create it. If you supply a newer version number than the database version currently stored on the device, the DatabaseOpenHelper's **onUpgrade method** will be called to upgrade the database to the new version (perhaps to add tables or to add columns to an existing table).

```
97      private class DatabaseOpenHelper extends SQLiteOpenHelper
98      {
99         // public constructor
100        public DatabaseOpenHelper(Context context, String name,
101           CursorFactory factory, int version)
102        {
103           super(context, name, factory, version);
104        } // end DatabaseOpenHelper constructor
105
106        // creates the contacts table when the database is created
107        @Override
108        public void onCreate(SQLiteDatabase db)
109        {
110           // query to create a new table named contacts
111           String createQuery = "CREATE TABLE contacts" +
112              "(_id integer primary key autoincrement," +
113              "name TEXT, email TEXT, phone TEXT," +
114              "street TEXT, city TEXT);";
115
116           db.execSQL(createQuery); // execute the query
117        } // end method onCreate
118
119        @Override
120        public void onUpgrade(SQLiteDatabase db, int oldVersion,
121           int newVersion)
122        {
123        } // end method onUpgrade
124     } // end class DatabaseOpenHelper
125  } // end class DatabaseConnector
```

Fig. 10.31 | SQLiteOpenHelper class DatabaseOpenHelper.

The onCreate method (lines 107–117) specifies the table to create with the SQL CREATE TABLE command, which is defined as a String (lines 111–114). In this case, the contacts table contains an integer primary key field (_id) that is auto-incremented, and text fields for all the other columns. Line 116 uses SQLiteDatabase's **execSQL** method to execute the CREATE TABLE command. Since we don't need to upgrade the database, we simply override method onUpgrade with an empty body. As of Android 3.0, class SQLiteOpenHelper also provides an **onDowngrade method** that can be used to downgrade a database when the currently stored version has a higher version number than the one requested in the call to class SQLiteOpenHelper's constructor. Downgrading might be used to revert the database back to a prior version with fewer columns in a table or fewer tables in the database—perhaps to fix a bug in the app.

All the SQLiteDatabase methods we used in class DatabaseConnector have corresponding methods which perform the same operations but throw exceptions on failure, as opposed to simply returning -1 (e.g., insertOrThrow vs. insert). These methods are interchangeable, allowing you to decide how to deal with database read and write errors.

10.6 Wrap-Up

In this chapter, you created an **Address Book** app that enables users to add, view, edit and delete contact information that's stored in a SQLite database. You learned that every Activity in an app must be described in the app's AndroidManifest.xml file.

You defined common GUI component attribute–value pairs as XML style resources, then applied the styles to all components that share those values by using the components' style attribute. You added a border to a TextView by specifying a Drawable as the value for the TextView's android:background attribute and you created a custom Drawable using an XML representation of a shape.

You used XML menu resources to define the app's MenuItems and programmatically inflated them using an Activity's MenuInflater. You also used Android standard icons to enhance the visual appearance of the menu items.

When an Activity's primary task is to display a scrollable list of items, you learned that you can extend class ListActivity to create an Activity that displays a ListView in its default layout. You used this to display the contacts stored in the app's database. You also saw that a ListView is a subclass of AdapterView, which allows a component to be bound to a data source, and you used a CursorAdapter to display the results of a database query in main Activity's ListView.

You used explicit Intents to launch new activities that handled tasks such as adding a contact, editing an existing contact and deleting an existing contact. You also learned how to terminate a launched activity to return to the prior one using the Activity's finish method.

You used a subclass of SQLiteOpenHelper to simplify creating the database and to obtain a SQLiteDatabase object for manipulating a database's contents. You processed query results via a Cursor. You used subclasses of AsyncTask to perform database tasks outside the GUI thread and return results to the GUI thread. This allowed you to take advantage of Android's threading capabilities without directly creating and manipulating threads.

In Chapter 11, we present the **Route Tracker** app, which uses GPS technology to track the user's location and draws that location on a street map overlaid on a satellite image. The app uses a MapView to interact with the Google Maps web services and display the maps, and uses an Overlay to display the user's location. The app also receives GPS data and direction information from the Android location services and sensors.

Route Tracker App

Google Maps API, GPS, `LocationManager`, `MapActivity`, `MapView` and `Overlay`

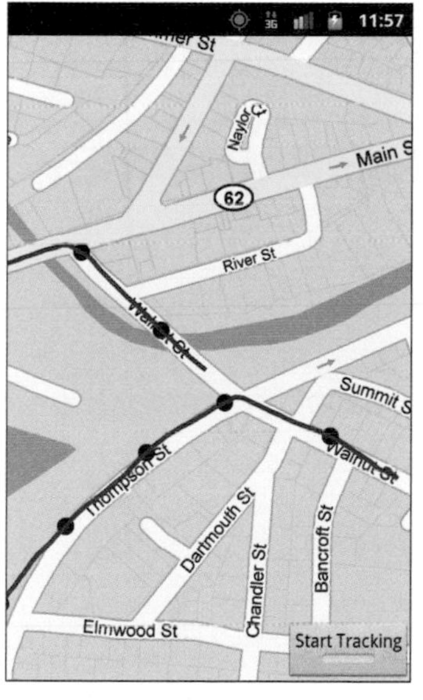

Objectives

In this chapter you'll:

- Test an app that uses GPS location data in the Android Emulator and use the Eclipse DDMS perspective to send sample GPS data to the emulator.
- Use the external Maps API framework and the `MapActivity` and `MapView` classes to display Google Maps™ generated by Google web services.
- Get a Google Maps™ API key unique to your development computer.
- Use location services and the `LocationManager` class to receive information on the device's position and bearing (direction).
- Display the user's route using an `Overlay` on a `MapView` and GPS location data received in the form of `Location` objects.
- Orient a map to the user's current bearing.
- Use the `PowerManager` to keep the device awake.

Outline

11.1 Introduction

As the user travels with an Android device, the **Route Tracker** app monitors the user's *location* and *bearing* (i.e., *direction*), visually displaying a route on a map. The user touches the **Start Tracking** `ToggleButton` (a button that maintains *on–off* state) to begin tracking a route (Fig. 11.1(a)). This also changes the `ToggleButton`'s text to **Stop Tracking** and displays a green bar to indicate that the app is tracking a route. The map shifts as the user moves, keeping the user's current location centered on the screen (Fig. 11.1(b)). The route is a red line with black dots appearing after every 10 GPS data points received by the app (Fig. 11.1(b)). When you use this app on an Android device, the map is oriented such that the route tracking line is pointed in the direction the user is traveling (known as the user's bearing), and that direction points to the *top* of the device. The sample outputs in this chapter show the app running in the Android emulator, which *does not* emulate bearing data. The user can choose the **Map** or **Satellite** options in the app's menu (Fig. 11.2(a)) to change the map styles. Touching **Map** displays a Google™ Maps *street map*—the app's *default*. Touching **Satellite** displays a *satellite image* of the area around the user (Fig. 11.2(b)). The user touches the **Stop Tracking** `ToggleButton` to stop tracking the current route. The app then displays

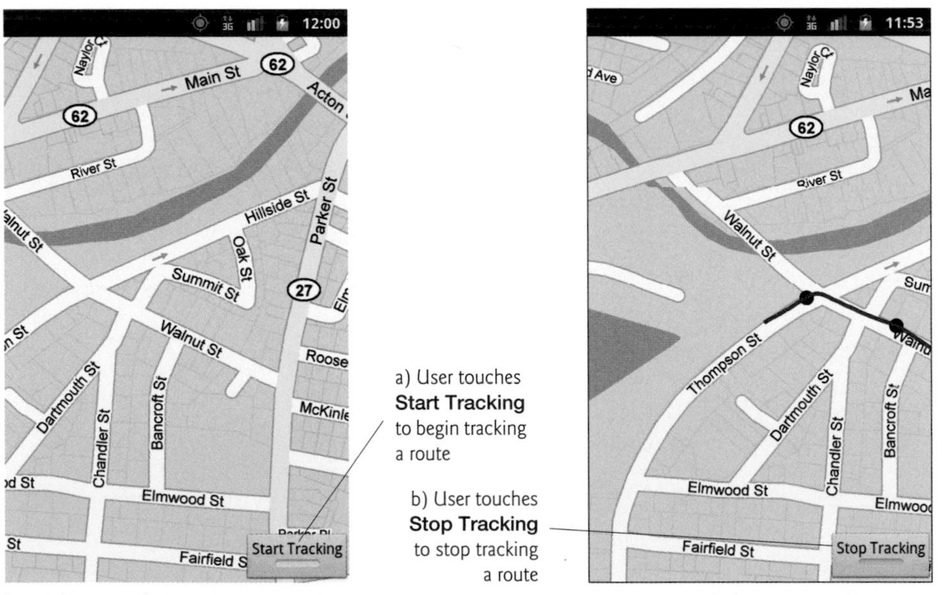

Fig. 11.1 | **Route Tracker** app before and after the user touches **Start Tracking**.

a dialog containing the total distance traveled (in kilometers and miles) and the average speed (in KPH and MPH) over the entire route (Fig. 11.3).

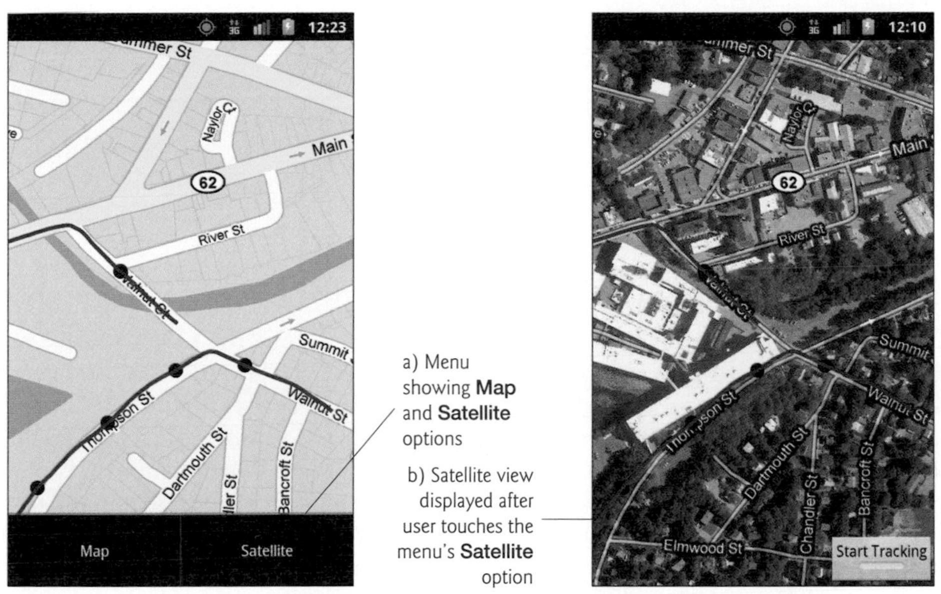

Fig. 11.2 | Menu allowing the user to select between map and satellite views and the app showing the satellite view after the user touches **Satellite**.

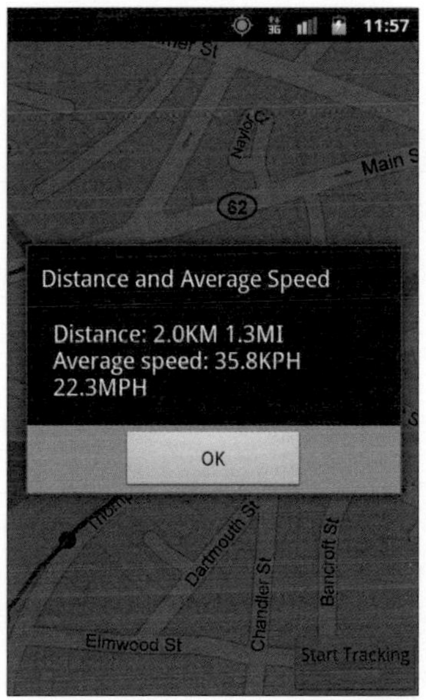

Fig. 11.3 | After the user touches **Stop Tracking**, the route statistics are displayed.

11.2 Test-Driving the Route Tracker App

Importing the App

Open Eclipse and import the **Route Tracker** app project. To import the project:

1. Select **File > Import...** to display the **Import** dialog.
2. Expand the **General** node and select **Existing Projects into Workspace**, then click **Next >**.
3. To the right of the **Select root directory:** text field, click **Browse...**, then locate and select the **Route Tracker** folder.
4. Click **Finish** to import the project.

Obtaining a Google Maps API Key

To run this **Route Tracker** app or to create your own app using the Google Maps API, you'll need to obtain a unique *API key* from Google. Before giving you a key, Google requires a "fingerprint" that uniquely identifies your development computer. Recall from Section 2.7 that apps must be signed with a digital certificate before they can be installed on a device. When you're building and testing apps, the ADT Plugin handles this automatically by creating a *debug certificate* and using it to sign your apps. The fingerprint Google requires (known formally as an *MD5 Fingerprint*) can be generated from this *debug certificate*. The API key you get with this fingerprint can be used only for testing and debugging apps. If you'd like to learn more about MD5 encryption and MD5 fingerprints, visit:

```
en.wikipedia.org/wiki/Md5
en.wikipedia.org/wiki/Public_key_fingerprint
```

Be sure to carefully follow the instructions at:

```
code.google.com/android/add-ons/google-apis/mapkey.html
```

in the section called **Getting the MD5 Fingerprint of the SDK Debug Certificate.** Then, use the fingerprint value that's produced at:

```
code.google.com/android/maps-api-signup.html
```

to get your unique Google Maps API key. If you intend to create an app for distribution, you'll need to follow the instructions in the section **Getting the MD5 Fingerprint of Your Signing Certificate** on the first website above and get a separate Google Maps API key.

[*Note:* To test-drive this app, you must replace the value of the `String` resource named `google_maps_api_key` in the `strings.xml` file with your own Google Maps API key; otherwise, the app will run but won't display maps or satellite images—known as map tiles.]

Running and Test-Driving the App on an Android Device

If you have an Android device with Internet access (which is required to receive the map images), ensure that it's set up correctly for testing and debugging apps (as discussed in the Before You Begin section of the book) and connect the device to your computer. Right click the app's project in the Eclipse **Package Explorer** window, then select **Run As > Android Application** from the menu that appears. If the **Android Device Chooser** window appears, select your device and click **OK** to install the app and run it on that device.

To acquire a GPS signal, your device must have *line-of-sight* with the GPS satellites—typically you must be outside to get this signal and acquiring the signal can take several minutes. Once the **Route Tracker** app is running on your device, go outside. When the device receives a GPS signal, you'll see a `Toast` appear on the screen saying that the GPS signal has been acquired. At this point, touch **Start Tracking** and take a walk for a few minutes.

As you move, your route is marked with a red line. If your device supports bearing data, the app orients the map with the direction you're facing aimed toward the top of the device—*this will not be the case on devices that don't support bearing data.* Open the app's menu and touch the **Satellite** item to display a satellite image rather than a standard street map. You can switch back to a street map by selecting the menu's **Map** item. When you've finished your route, touch **Stop Tracking.** An `AlertDialog` displays your distance traveled and average speed. Touch the **OK** `Button` to close the alert and return to the map. You can browse the route you just completed by panning (dragging your finger on the map) and using pinch gestures to zoom in and out on the map. Touching **Start Tracking** again erases your route from the map and starts tracking a new route.

Running the App in an AVD

To run this app in an AVD, you'll need to ensure that the AVD is configured to use the **Google APIs** for your Android platform version. To do so:

1. Open the **Android SDK and AVD Manager.**
2. Select one of your Android AVDs that you configured in the Before You Begin section (we used the one called NexusS) and click **Edit....**
3. In the **Edit Android Virtual Device (AVD)** window, select the **Google APIs (Google Inc.) - API Level #** from the **Target** drop-down list (where # represents the API level you're targeting), then click **Edit AVD.** This indicates that the AVD should use both the Android APIs *and* the Google APIs for the selected API Level (e.g., API level 10 represents Android 2.3.3). If you prefer not to modify an existing AVD, you can create a separate AVD using the techniques in the Before You Begin section.
4. In the **Android SDK and AVD Manager** window, select the AVD and start it.

Next, right click the app's project in the Eclipse **Package Explorer** window, then select **Run As > Android Application** from the menu that appears. If the **Android Device Chooser** window appears, select your AVD and click **OK** to install the app and run it on that AVD.

Sending GPS Data to an AVD with GPX Files

The Android emulator enables you to send GPS data to an AVD, so you can test your location-based apps without an actual Android device. To do so, you use a file containing GPS data in **GPS Exchange Format**. Such files typically end with the `.gpx` extension and are called GPX files. With the book's examples, we've provided several GPX files (in the `GPXfiles` folder) that you can load and "play" from the ADT Plugin's DDMS perspective. Doing so sends the GPS data to the selected AVD. These GPX files were recorded using a free app called GPSLogger, which can be found in the Android Market at:

```
market.android.com/details?id=com.mendhak.gpslogger
```

The GPS data in the GPX files represent short driving trips in Massachusetts. The GPSLogger tool produces files in GPX version 1.0 format, but the Android emulator uses

GPX version 1.1 format data. There are many tools online for converting between these and other GPS data formats. We used the tool at:

```
www.gpsbabel.org
```

which allowed us to open each file and save it in GPX 1.1 format.

To send GPS data from a GPX file to an AVD, perform the following steps:

1. Once the app is running in the AVD, in Eclipse select **Window > Open Perspective > DDMS** to switch to the DDMS perspective.
2. In the **Devices** tab, select your AVD.
3. In the **Emulator Control** tab, click the **GPX** tab.
4. Click the **Load GPX...** button, then locate and select one of the GPX files in the `GPXFiles` folder located with the book's examples and click **Open**.
5. In the bottom half of the **GPX** tab, select the file you just opened and click the play (▶) button to begin sending the file's GPS data to the selected AVD.

In the AVD, touch **Start Tracking** then watch the route get updated as the app receives the sample GPS data. When you touch **Stop Tracking**, the app displays an alert showing the distance traveled and average speed for the sample data the app received.

11.3 Technologies Overview

This section presents the new technologies that we use in the **Route Tracker** app in the order in which they're encountered in the chapter.

New Features in `AndroidManifest.xml`

This app uses several new features in the app's manifest file (discussed in Section 11.4):

- To access a nonstandard library—that is, one that's not included with the core Android APIs, such as the Google Maps API—you must indicate the library's name in the app's manifest with a **`uses-library`** element nested in the `application` element.
- We'd like the app to use most of the screen to display maps, so we chose to hide the title bar by using one of the standard Android *themes*, which can be specified with the attribute **`android:theme`** in the `activity` element. A theme changes the look-and-feel of an app's GUI. The predefined Android styles and themes are listed at:

```
developer.android.com/reference/android/R.style.html
```

- By default, shared Android services are not accessible to an app. Such services include those that allow an app to change power settings, obtain location data, control whether a device is allowed to sleep, and more. To access these services, you must request permission to use them in the manifest file with **`uses-permission`** elements nested in the root `manifest` element. When a user prepares to install an app, the operating system tells the user which permissions are being requested and asks the user to confirm whether they should be granted. If not, the app will not be installed. The complete list of permissions can be found at:

```
developer.android.com/reference/android/Manifest.permission.html
```

Class **ToggleButton**

A **ToggleButton** (package android.widget) maintains an *on–off* state. Initially, this app's ToggleButton displays the text **Start Tracking** with a gray bar below it to indicate that the button is in the *off* state. The user can touch the button to start tracking a route. At that point, the ToggleButton's text changes to **Stop Tracking**, the button shows a green bar below the text indicating that the button is in the *on* state and the app starts tracking a route. When the user touches the button again, it toggles back to the *off* state (changing its text back to **Start Tracking**), and the app stops tracking and displays a dialog showing the tracking results. ToggleButton is a subclass of CompoundButton. You handle CompoundButton events by implementing interface **CompoundButton.OnCheckedChangeListener**.

Classes **MapActivity**, **MapView** *and* **Overlay**

Package **com.google.android.maps** contains the classes that we used to interact with the Google Maps API. Class RouteTracker (Section 11.5.1) is a subclass of **MapActivity**—an Activity that manages a **MapView** (Section 11.5.2) for displaying maps obtained via the Google Maps API. MapViews support gestures to *zoom* and *pan* the map—any additional functionality must be added programmatically. To display data on a MapView, such as the line representing the route in this app, you create a subclass of **Overlay** (Section 11.5.3) and override its draw method. We use **GeoPoint**s (Sections 11.5.1 and 11.5.3) to translate GPS data into points that can be used to re-center the map based on the user's location and to draw the route.

Location Data

Package **android.location** (Section 11.5.1) contains the classes and interfaces for acquiring and using location data. Class **LocationManager** provides access to the device's location services. These are hardware dependent and can be used to periodically get updates on the device's location or launch an Intent should the user travel with the device to a certain geographic region. Depending on your device, several **location providers** may be supported—LocationManager provides capabilities for choosing the best one based on your app's requirements, which you specify in a **Criteria** object. The settings that can be specified in a Criteria are *accuracy*, *battery usage*, *bearing*, *speed*, *altitude* and the *monetary cost of the provider*. Once you have a location provider, you can request updates from it and have them delivered to a **LocationListener**. The updates are delivered to the listener as **Location** objects that represent the device's *geographic location*—these include *latitude* and *longitude* data, the *time* they were recorded and, depending on the *location provider*, may also include *altitude* and *speed* data (some devices don't have sensors for these). To determine when the device has a *GPS fix*—that is, the device has "locked onto" enough GPS satellites to receive GPS data for tracking—we implement the **GpsStatus.Listener** interface.

Classes **PowerManager** *and* **WakeLock**

Class **PowerManager** (package android.os) enables an app to control the *power state* of an Android device. *An app that changes the power settings can negatively affect the device's battery life when the app is executing, so class* PowerManager *should be used sparingly.* Once the user starts tracking a route, we want the app to record location data even if the screen is off. We use the PowerManager to acquire a **WakeLock** that prevents the device from sleeping so that the app can continue receiving GPS data (Section 11.5.1).

Programmatically Determining the Device's Display Size

Class **`Display`** (package `android.view`) provide's access to the device's screen dimensions. We use these dimensions (Section 11.5.2) to help scale the maps so that they fill the screen as we rotate them to match the user's current bearing.

11.4 Building the GUI and Resource Files

In this section, you'll create the **Route Tracker** app's resource files and GUI layout files. To save space, we do not show this app's `strings.xml` resource file or the layout file for the app's menu. You can view the contents of these files by opening them from the project in Eclipse.

11.4.1 Creating the Project

Begin by creating a new Android project named `RouteTracker`. Specify the following values in the **New Android Project** dialog, then press **Finish**:

- **Build Target:** Ensure that **Google APIs** for platform **2.3.3** (or later) is checked—this tells the ADT Plugin to include in the project both the Android APIs and the Google APIs for Android 2.3.3 (or the version you selected). The Google APIs include those for Google Maps.
- **Application name:** `Route Tracker`
- **Package name:** `com.deitel.routetracker`
- **Create Activity:** `RouteTracker`
- **Min SDK Version:** 8

11.4.2 `AndroidManifest.xml`

Figure 11.4 shows this app's `AndroidManifest.xml` file. We've highlighted several new features in this manifest.

```
<?xml version="1.0" encoding="utf-8"?>
<manifest xmlns:android="http://schemas.android.com/apk/res/android"
   package="com.deitel.routetracker" android:versionCode="1"
   android:versionName="1.0">
   <application android:icon="@drawable/icon"
      android:label="@string/app_name" android:debuggable="true">
      <uses-library android:name="com.google.android.maps" />
      <activity android:name=".RouteTracker"
         android:label="@string/app_name"
         android:theme="@android:style/Theme.Black.NoTitleBar"
         android:screenOrientation="portrait">
         <intent-filter>
            <action android:name="android.intent.action.MAIN" />
            <category android:name="android.intent.category.LAUNCHER" />
         </intent-filter>
      </activity>

```

Fig. 11.4 | `AndroidManifest.xml`. (Part 1 of 2.)

```
18       </application>
19       <uses-sdk android:minSdkVersion="8" android:targetSdkVersion="10"/>
20
21       <uses-permission android:name="android.permission.INTERNET" />
22       <uses-permission
23          android:name="android.permission.ACCESS_FINE_LOCATION" />
24       <uses-permission
25          android:name="android.permission.ACCESS_MOCK_LOCATION" />
26       <uses-permission android:name="android.permission.WAKE_LOCK" />
27    </manifest>
```

Fig. 11.4 | AndroidManifest.xml. (Part 2 of 2.)

Using an External Library

Line 7 declares that this app uses the Google Maps API library with a `uses-library` element nested in the `application` element.

Hiding the App's Title Bar

Line 10 uses the attribute `android:theme` in the `activity` element to change the `Activity`'s theme to `Theme.Black.NoTitleBar`—a variation of the standard Android theme that simply hide's the `Activity`'s title bar.

Requesting App Permissions

The `uses-permission` elements in lines 21–26 indicate that this app will work correctly only with the following permissions granted:

- **`android.permission.INTERNET`**: This app requires Internet access to download map and satellite images.
- **`android.permission.ACCESS_FINE_LOCATION`**: This app requires precise location data to show the user's route on the map.
- **`android.permission.ACCESS_MOCK_LOCATION`**: This app should be able to receive mock data for testing purposes (as shown Section 11.2)—this is necessary only during app development, not in production apps.
- **`android.permission.WAKE_LOCK`**: This app needs access to the `PowerManager` to prevent the device from sleeping while the app is tracking a route.

For more information on Android's permissions and security model, visit:

```
developer.android.com/guide/topics/security/security.html
```

11.4.3 Route Tracker Layout: `main.xml`

The **Route Tracker** app's XML layout (Fig. 11.4) contains a **`FrameLayout`** (package `android.widget`), which by default *stacks* (that is, *layers*) its components with the most recently added component on top. Components are positioned in the `FrameLayout`'s upper-left corner, unless the `gravity` property is used to position them. This layout contains a `ToggleButton` in the bottom-right corner. We programmatically add to this layout an object of our `BearingFrameLayout` class, which contains the `MapView` on which we'll display the route. The `ToggleButton` attributes **`android:textOn`** and **`android:textOff`** (lines 9–10) enable you to specify the text to display on the button in the *on* and *off* states, respectively.

```
<?xml version="1.0" encoding="utf-8"?>
<FrameLayout xmlns:android="http://schemas.android.com/apk/res/android"
   android:id="@+id/mainLayout"
   android:layout_width="match_parent"
   android:layout_height="match_parent">
   <ToggleButton android:id="@+id/trackingToggleButton"
      android:layout_width="wrap_content"
      android:layout_height="wrap_content"
      android:textOn="@string/button_stop_tracking"
      android:textOff="@string/button_start_tracking"
      android:layout_gravity="bottom|right"></ToggleButton>
</FrameLayout>
```

Fig. 11.5 | Layout for the `RouteTracker` subclass of `MapActivity`.

11.5 Building the App

This app consists of classes `RouteTracker` (the `MapActivity` subclass; Figs. 11.6–11.14), `BearingFrameLayout` (Figs. 11.15–11.19) and `RouteOverlay` (Figs. 11.20–11.23). As in prior apps, this app's main `Activity`—`RouteTracker`—is created when you create the project, but you must change its superclass to `MapActivity` in the source code. You must add the other classes to the `src/com.deitel.routetracker` folder of the project.

11.5.1 RouteTracker Subclass of MapActivity

Class `RouteTracker` (Figs. 11.6–11.14) is the app's `Activity` class. As discussed previously, the class extends `MapActivity`, because this `Activity`'s primary purpose is to display a `MapView` showing a Google Map. Like a `ListActivity`, a `MapActivity` provides support for its `View`'s lifecycle. *Only one `MapActivity` per process is currently supported.*

`package` and `import` Statements, and Fields of class `RouteTracker`

Figure 11.6 lists the `package` and `import` statements, and the fields of class `RouteTracker`. We've highlighted the `import` statements for the new classes and interfaces discussed in Section 11.3 and throughout Section 11.5.1. We'll discuss the class's instance variables and constants as we use them.

```
// RouteTracker.java
// Main MapActivity for the RouteTracker app.
package com.deitel.routetracker;

import android.app.AlertDialog;
import android.content.Context;
import android.location.Criteria;
import android.location.GpsStatus;
import android.location.Location;
import android.location.LocationListener;
import android.location.LocationManager;
```

Fig. 11.6 | `package` and `import` statements, and instance variables of the `RouteTracker` `MapActivity` class. (Part 1 of 2.)

```
import android.os.Bundle;
import android.os.PowerManager;
import android.view.Gravity;
import android.view.Menu;
import android.view.MenuInflater;
import android.view.MenuItem;
import android.widget.CompoundButton;
import android.widget.CompoundButton.OnCheckedChangeListener;
import android.widget.FrameLayout;
import android.widget.Toast;
import android.widget.ToggleButton;

import com.google.android.maps.GeoPoint;
import com.google.android.maps.MapActivity;
import com.google.android.maps.MapController;
import com.google.android.maps.MapView;

public class RouteTracker extends MapActivity
{
   private LocationManager locationManager; // gives location data
   private MapView mapView; // displays a Google map
   private MapController mapController; // manages map pan/zoom
   private Location previousLocation; // previous reported location
   private RouteOverlay routeOverlay; // Overlay that shows route on map
   private long distanceTraveled; // total distance the user traveled
   private BearingFrameLayout bearingFrameLayout; // rotates the MapView
   private boolean tracking; // whether app is currently tracking
   private long startTime; // time (in milliseconds) when tracking starts
   private PowerManager.WakeLock wakeLock; // used to prevent device sleep
   private boolean gpsFix; // whether we have a GPS fix for accurate data

   private static final double MILLISECONDS_PER_HOUR = 1000 * 60 * 60;
   private static final double MILES_PER_KILOMETER = 0.621371192;
   private static final int MAP_ZOOM = 18; // Google Maps supports 1-21

```

Fig. 11.6 | `package` and `import` statements, and instance variables of the `RouteTracker` `MapActivity` class. (Part 2 of 2.)

Overriding `Activity` *Method* `onCreate`

Figure 11.7 overrides `Activity` method `onCreate`. Lines 55–56 assign to instance variable `bearingFrameLayout` a new object of our `BearingFrameLayout` class (Section 11.5.2), which creates the `MapView` and rotates it to match the user's bearing (direction). This allows the map to be pointed in the direction the user is moving—the bearing is not supported in the Android emulator. Line 64 gets the `MapView` from the `BearingFrameLayout` and assigns it to instance variable `mapView`. Line 65 gets `mapView`'s `MapController` using its **`getController` method**. You use a `MapController` to programmatically zoom in and out of the map and to change the geographic location appearing centered in the `MapView`. Line 66 uses `MapController`'s **`setZoom` method** to set the map's *zoom level* (i.e., level of detail). Zoom levels can be in the range 1 (maximum zoom out) to 21 (maximum zoom in). As you zoom in, each successive zoom level decreases the amount of area shown on the map by a factor of two. Depending on your location, as you zoom in to see more details, Google may not have map images representing the most detailed maps—in this case, no map or satellite image will be displayed.

```
47     // Called when the activity is first created
48     @Override
49     public void onCreate(Bundle savedInstanceState)
50     {
51        super.onCreate(savedInstanceState);
52        setContentView(R.layout.main);
53
54        // create new MapView using your Google Maps API key
55        bearingFrameLayout = new BearingFrameLayout(this,
56           getResources().getString(R.string.google_maps_api_key));
57
58        // add bearingFrameLayout to mainLayout
59        FrameLayout mainLayout =
60           (FrameLayout) findViewById(R.id.mainLayout);
61        mainLayout.addView(bearingFrameLayout, 0);
62
63        // get the MapView and MapController
64        mapView = bearingFrameLayout.getMapview();
65        mapController = mapView.getController(); // get MapController
66        mapController.setZoom(MAP_ZOOM); // zoom in the map
67
68        // create map Overlay
69        routeOverlay = new RouteOverlay();
70
71        // add the RouteOverlay overlay
72        mapView.getOverlays().add(routeOverlay);
73
74        distanceTraveled = 0; // initialize distanceTraveled to 0
75
76        // register listener for trackingToggleButton
77        ToggleButton trackingToggleButton =
78           (ToggleButton) findViewById(R.id.trackingToggleButton);
79        trackingToggleButton.setOnCheckedChangeListener(
80           trackingToggleButtonListener);
81     } // end onCreate
82
```

Fig. 11.7 | Overriding `Activity` method `onCreate`.

Line 69 assigns to instance variable `routeOverlay` a new object of our `Overlay` subclass `RouteOverlay` (Section 11.5.3), which is used to display the user's route over a `MapView`. Next, line 72 gets `mapView`'s collection of `Overlays` and adds our `routeOverlay` to it. Each `Overlay` is displayed in the same orientation and scale as the map.

Line 74 sets instance variable `distanceTraveled` to `0`. While tracking the route, the app updates `distanceTraveled` when each new GPS data point is received. Finally, lines 77–80 get the `trackingToggleButton` and register the `trackingToggleButtonListener` (Fig. 11.14) as its `OnCheckedChangeListener`.

Overriding Activity Methods **onStart** *and* **onStop**

Figure 11.8 overrides Activity methods onStart and onStop. Method onStart (lines 84–121) begins by configuring the Criteria object that represents an app's requested features and settings for a *location provider*. Lines 91–95 call Criteria methods to specify the following settings:

- **setAccuracy**—the constant Criteria.ACCURACY_FINE indicates that the app requires precise GPS data so that it can report tracking data as close to the user's actual location as possible. High-accuracy GPS data uses more power. If your app doesn't require such accuracy, you can choose Criteria.ACCURACY_COARSE. As of Android 2.3, you can now select from three accuracy levels—Criteria.ACCURACY_HIGH, Criteria.ACCURACY_MEDIUM or Criteria.ACCURACY_LOW.
- **setBearingRequired**—the argument true indicates that bearing (direction) data is required. We use this data to orient the map such that the direction in which the user is moving points toward the top of the device.
- **setCostAllowed**—the argument true indicates that it's OK for the app to use data services (such as the device's Internet connection) that might incur costs to the user. Before doing this in an app that you'll distribute, you should get the user's permission to incur data costs.
- **setPowerRequirement**—location providers require different amounts of power to provide location data to your app. The argument Criteria.POWER_LOW indicates that the app should return a location provider that uses the least amount of power possible to provide the data the app requires. Other options are Criteria.NO_REQUIREMENT, Criteria.POWER_HIGH and Criteria.POWER_MEDIUM.
- **setAltitudeRequired**—the argument false indicates that this app does not require altitude data.

```
83     // called when Activity becoming visible to the user
84     @Override
85     public void onStart()
86     {
87        super.onStart(); // call super's onStart method
88
89        // create Criteria object to specify location provider's settings
90        Criteria criteria = new Criteria();
91        criteria.setAccuracy(Criteria.ACCURACY_FINE); // fine location data
92        criteria.setBearingRequired(true); // need bearing to rotate map
93        criteria.setCostAllowed(true); // OK to incur monetary cost
94        criteria.setPowerRequirement(Criteria.POWER_LOW); // try to conserve
95        criteria.setAltitudeRequired(false); // don't need altitude data
96
97        // get the LocationManager
98        locationManager =
99           (LocationManager) getSystemService(LOCATION_SERVICE);
100
101       // register listener to determine whether we have a GPS fix
102       locationManager.addGpsStatusListener(gpsStatusListener);
```

Fig. 11.8 | Overriding Activity methods onStart and onStop. (Part 1 of 2.)

```
103
104       // get the best provider based on our Criteria
105       String provider = locationManager.getBestProvider(criteria, true);
106
107       // listen for changes in location as often as possible
108       locationManager.requestLocationUpdates(provider, 0, 0,
109          locationListener);
110
111       // get the app's power manager
112       PowerManager powerManager =
113          (PowerManager) getSystemService(Context.POWER_SERVICE);
114
115       // get a wakelock preventing the device from sleeping
116       wakeLock = powerManager.newWakeLock(
117          PowerManager.PARTIAL_WAKE_LOCK, "No sleep");
118       wakeLock.acquire(); // acquire the wake lock
119
120       bearingFrameLayout.invalidate(); // redraw the BearingFrameLayout
121    } // end method onStart
122
123    // called when Activity is no longer visible to the user
124    @Override
125    public void onStop()
126    {
127       super.onStop(); // call the super method
128       wakeLock.release(); // release the wakelock
129    } // end method onStop
130
```

Fig. 11.8 | Overriding `Activity` methods `onStart` and `onStop`. (Part 2 of 2.)

Lines 98–99 get the `LocationManager` system service and assign it to instance variable `locationManager`. Line 102 registers `gpsStatusListener` (Fig. 11.11) as the `LocationManager`'s `GpsStatus.Lisener`. We use this listener to determine when the device has a *GPS fix*—that is, the device has "locked onto" enough GPS satellites to receive GPS data for tracking.

`LocationManager`'s **`getBestProvider` method** (line 105) returns a `String` representing the name of the *location provider* that best meets the given `Criteria`. The `true` argument indicates that only an enabled provider should be returned.

We call `LocationManager`'s **`requestLocationUpdates` method** to register `locationListener` (Fig. 11.10) to listen for location changes from the specified `provider`. Passing `0` as the second argument (minimum time in milliseconds between location updates) and third argument (minimum distance in meters traveled between location updates) indicates that we'd like updates as often as possible, which we do only for demonstrations purposes. *You typically should use positive values for each of these arguments to conserve battery power.* It can take several minutes to acquire a GPS lock. For this reason, many GPS-based apps use `LocationManager`'s **`getLastKnownLocation` method** to get the location that was last reported when the device previously had a GPS fix (such as during a previous execution of the app). Most people spend their time in a relatively small geographical area, so this can be used to display a map that's in relatively close proximity to the user's actual location.

Lines 112–113 get the system's `PowerManager` service. `PowerManager`'s **`newWakeLock` method** returns a new `WakeLock` object (lines 116–117). `WakeLock`'s **`acquire`** method (line 118) ensures that the device remains at the `WakeLock`'s required power level (at least) until its `release` method is called, at which time normal power operation is restored. This app uses the constant `PowerManager.PARTIAL_WAKE_LOCK` to indicate that this app should continue to use the CPU even if the user presses the power button on the device. It also allows the screen to dim and turn off l. This allows the app to continue tracking the route until the user presses the **Stop Tracking** `ToggleButton`. Information on the different available `WakeLock`s and their effects on battery consumption can be found at

```
developer.android.com/reference/android/os/PowerManager.html
```

Method `onStop` (lines 124–130) calls `WakeLock`'s **`release` method** to release the `wakelock`, indicating that we no longer need to prevent the device from sleeping and the device can return to its normal power level.

Method `updateLocation`

Method `updateLocation` (Fig. 11.9), which is called by our `LocationListener` (Fig. 11.10), receives a `Location` and updates the map and overlay accordingly. If the given `location` is not `null` and we have a GPS fix, we do all of the following:

- Call `routeOverlay`'s `addPoint` to add the given `location` to the route.
- If there's a `previousLocation`, we use `Location`'s **`distanceTo` method** (line 143) to calculate the distance between the current `location` and the `previousLocation` and add this to the total `distanceTraveled`, which will be reported when the user stops tracking the route.

```
131    // update location on map
132    public void updateLocation(Location location)
133    {
134       if (location != null && gpsFix) // location not null; have GPS fix
135       {
136          // add the given Location to the route
137          routeOverlay.addPoint(location);
138
139          // if there is a previous location
140          if (previousLocation != null)
141          {
142             // add to the total distanceTraveled
143             distanceTraveled += location.distanceTo(previousLocation);
144          } // end if
145
146          // get the latitude and longitude
147          Double latitude = location.getLatitude() * 1E6;
148          Double longitude = location.getLongitude() * 1E6;
149
150          // create GeoPoint representing the given Locations
151          GeoPoint point =
152             new GeoPoint(latitude.intValue(), longitude.intValue());
```

Fig. 11.9 | `updateLocation` method of class `RouteTracker`. (Part 1 of 2.)

```
153
154            // move the map to the current location
155            mapController.animateTo(point);
156
157            // update the compass bearing
158            bearingFrameLayout.setBearing(location.getBearing());
159            bearingFrameLayout.invalidate(); // redraw based on bearing
160         } // end if
161
162         previousLocation = location;
163      } // end method updateLocation
164
```

Fig. 11.9 | `updateLocation` method of class `RouteTracker`. (Part 2 of 2.)

- Get the latitude and longitude of the `location` and convert it to a `GeoPoint` (lines 147–152). A `GeoPoint` consists of a *latitude* and *longitude* measured in *microdegrees* (millionths of a degree). We use `Location`'s **`getLatitude`** and **`getLongitude`** methods to obtain these readings in degrees, multiplying each by `1E6` to convert them to microdegrees—we assign the results to `latitude` and `longitude`, respectively, then use these new values to create a `GeoPoint` with integer coordinates.
- `MapController`'s **`animateTo` method** (line 155) moves the center of the map to the given `GeoPoint` using a *smooth animation*. If you need to be notified when the animation is finished, you also can pass a `Message` or `Runnable` to this method.
- We use `Location` method **`getBearing`** (line 158) to obtain the bearing from the latest `location`. The bearing is returned as the number of degrees to the east of true north. Next, we use the `bearingFrameLayout`'s `setBearing` method to update the bearing so the map can be rotated accordingly and call the `bearingFrameLayout`'s `invalidate` method to redraw the map. [*Note:* It's also possible to obtain the bearing by calling method **`bearingTo`** on the previous `Location` and passing the current `Location` as an argument. This would enable us to rotate the maps even when testing in an AVD.]

Regardless of whether `location` was `null` we save `location` as `previousLocation` to prepare to process the next location reading.

Anonymous `LocationListener` *Class to Respond to* `LocationManager` *Events*

Figure 11.10 defines our `LocationListener`. `LocationListeners` receive events from the `LocationManager` when the *device's physical location changes* and when the *location provider's status changes*. We enabled this capability with the call to `requestLocationUpdates` (Fig. 11.8, lines 108–109). Method **`onLocationChanged`** (lines 170–176) is called when the device receives an updated `Location`. We set `gpsFix` to `true`—if we're receiving `Locations`, then the device has locked onto enough GPS satellites to get the user's location. If the app is currently tracking a route, we call method `updateLocation` (Fig. 11.9) to add the new `Location` to the route. We provide empty methods that respond to changes in the location provider's status (i.e., `onProviderDisabled`, `onProviderEnabled` and `onStatusChanged`) for the purpose of this app. If your app needs to respond to these events, you should define the methods accordingly.

```
165      // responds to events from the LocationManager
166      private final LocationListener locationListener =
167         new LocationListener()
168      {
169         // when the location is changed
170         public void onLocationChanged(Location location)
171         {
172            gpsFix = true; // if getting Locations, then we have a GPS fix
173
174            if (tracking) // if we're currently tracking
175               updateLocation(location); // update the location
176         } // end onLocationChanged
177
178         public void onProviderDisabled(String provider)
179         {
180         } // end onProviderDisabled
181
182         public void onProviderEnabled(String provider)
183         {
184         } // end onProviderEnabled
185
186         public void onStatusChanged(String provider,
187            int status, Bundle extras)
188         {
189         } // end onStatusChanged
190      }; // end locationListener
191
```

Fig. 11.10 | `LocationListener` responds to `LocationManager` events.

Anonymous Inner Class That Implements `GpsStatus.Listener` to Respond to `GpsStatus` Events

Figure 11.11 defines an anonymous inner class that implements interface `GpsStatus.Listener` so we can determine when the device receive the first GPS fix. We don't start tracking the route until this happens to ensure that our tracking is as accurate as possible. Line 197 determines whether the event was `GpsStatus.GPS_EVENT_FIRST_FIX`. If so, we set `gpsFix` to `true`, then display a `Toast` indicating that the device has locked onto enough GPS satellites to get the user's location. If there's another app on the device that started the GPS and received the first fix, then this app will *not* receive the first fix event. This is why we also set `gpsFix` to true in line 172.

```
192      // determine whether we have GPS fix
193      GpsStatus.Listener gpsStatusListener = new GpsStatus.Listener()
194      {
195         public void onGpsStatusChanged(int event)
196         {
197            if (event == GpsStatus.GPS_EVENT_FIRST_FIX)
198            {
199               gpsFix = true;
```

Fig. 11.11 | Anonymous inner class that implements `GpsStatus.Listener` to determine when the app is able to get a GPS fix to start receiving accurate GPS data. (Part 1 of 2.)

```
200               Toast results = Toast.makeText(RouteTracker.this,
201                  getResources().getString(R.string.toast_signal_acquired),
202                  Toast.LENGTH_SHORT);
203
204               // center the Toast in the screen
205               results.setGravity(Gravity.CENTER,
206                  results.getXOffset() / 2, results.getYOffset() / 2);
207               results.show(); // display the results
208            } // end if
209         } // end method on GpsStatusChanged
210      }; // end anonymous inner class
211
```

Fig. 11.11 | Anonymous inner class that implements `GpsStatus.Listener` to determine when the app is able to get a GPS fix to start receiving accurate GPS data. (Part 2 of 2.)

Overriding `MapActivity` *Method* `isRouteDisplayed`

Figure 11.12 overrides `MapActivity` method **`isRouteDisplayed`** to return `false`. If your app displays route information such as driving directions, *Google's Terms of Use require that this method return* `true`. *You'll be asked to agree to these terms when you register for your API key (*`code.google.com/android/add-ons/google-apis/mapkey.html`*).*

```
212      // Google terms of use require this method to return
213      // true if you're displaying route information like driving directions
214      @Override
215      protected boolean isRouteDisplayed()
216      {
217         return false; // we aren't displaying route information
218      } // end method isRouteDisplayed
219
```

Fig. 11.12 | Overriding `MapActivity` method `isRouteDisplayed`.

Overriding Activity Methods `onCreateOptionsMenu` *and* `onOptionsItemSelected`

Figure 11.13 overrides `Activity` methods `onCreateOptionsMenu` and `onOptionsItemSelected`. Method `onCreateOptionsMenu` uses a `MenuInflater` to create the app's menu from the `route_tracker_menu.xml` menu-resource file. When the user touches either menu item, method `onOptionsItemSelected` responds to the event. If the user chooses the **Map** `MenuItem`, line 238 calls `MapView` method `setSatellite` with the argument `false` to indicate that a standard map should be displayed. If the user chooses the **Satellite** `MenuItem`, line 241 calls `setSatellite` with the argument `true` to indicate that a satellite map should be displayed.

```
220      // create the Activity's menu from a menu resource XML file
221      @Override
222      public boolean onCreateOptionsMenu(Menu menu)
223      {
```

Fig. 11.13 | Overriding `Activity` methods `onCreateOptionsMenu` and `onOptionsItemSelected`. (Part 1 of 2.)

```
        super.onCreateOptionsMenu(menu);
        MenuInflater inflater = getMenuInflater();
        inflater.inflate(R.menu.route_tracker_menu, menu);
        return true;
    } // end method onCreateOptionsMenu

    // handle choice from options menu
    @Override
    public boolean onOptionsItemSelected(MenuItem item)
    {
        // perform appropriate task based on
        switch (item.getItemId())
        {
            case R.id.mapItem: // the user selected "Map"
                mapView.setSatellite(false); // display map image
                return true;
            case R.id.satelliteItem: // the user selected "Satellite"
                mapView.setSatellite(true); // display satellite image
                return true;
            default:
                return super.onOptionsItemSelected(item);
        } // end switch
    } // end method onOptionsItemSelected

```

Fig. 11.13 | Overriding `Activity` methods `onCreateOptionsMenu` and `onOptionsItemSelected`. (Part 2 of 2.)

Anonymous Inner Class That Implements `OnCheckedChangeListener` *to Respond to* `trackingToggleButton`*'s Events*

Figure 11.14 defines the `OnCheckedChangeListener` `trackingToggleButtonListener`, which responds to the events of the `trackingToggleButton` to either display the results for a finished route or start tracking a new route.

```
    // listener for trackingToggleButton's events
    OnCheckedChangeListener trackingToggleButtonListener =
        new OnCheckedChangeListener()
        {
            // called when user toggles tracking state
            @Override
            public void onCheckedChanged(CompoundButton buttonView,
                boolean isChecked)
            {
                // if app is currently tracking
                if (!isChecked)
                {
                    tracking = false; // just stopped tracking locations

```

Fig. 11.14 | `trackingToggleButtonListener` responds to `trackingToggleButton`'s events. (Part 1 of 2.)

```
262                 // compute the total time we were tracking
263                 long milliseconds = System.currentTimeMillis() - startTime;
264                 double totalHours = milliseconds / MILLISECONDS_PER_HOUR;
265
266                 // create a dialog displaying the results
267                 AlertDialog.Builder dialogBuilder =
268                    new AlertDialog.Builder(RouteTracker.this);
269                 dialogBuilder.setTitle(R.string.results);
270
271                 double distanceKM = distanceTraveled / 1000.0;
272                 double speedKM = distanceKM / totalHours;
273                 double distanceMI = distanceKM * MILES_PER_KILOMETER;
274                 double speedMI = distanceMI / totalHours;
275
276                 // display distanceTraveled traveled and average speed
277                 dialogBuilder.setMessage(String.format(
278                    getResources().getString(R.string.results_format),
279                    distanceKM, distanceMI, speedKM, speedMI));
280                 dialogBuilder.setPositiveButton(
281                    R.string.button_ok, null);
282                 dialogBuilder.show(); // display the dialog
283              } // end if
284              else
285              {
286                 tracking = true; // app is now tracking
287                 startTime = System.currentTimeMillis(); // get current time
288                 routeOverlay.reset(); // reset for new route
289                 bearingFrameLayout.invalidate(); // clear the route
290                 previousLocation = null; // starting a new route
291              } // end else
292           } // end method onCheckChanged
293        }; // end anonymous inner class
294  } // end class RouteTracker
```

Fig. 11.14 | `trackingToggleButtonListener` responds to `trackingToggleButton`'s events. (Part 2 of 2.)

When the user touches the `trackingToggleButton`, the **onCheckedChanged method** is called with the current state of the button as the second argument. If it's not checked (line 258), the app is not tracking, so lines 260–282 calculate and display the results. Lines 263–264 determine the `totalHours` the user was tracking the route, so we can use this to determine the user's speed. Variable `distanceTraveled` represents the distance in meters. We divide this by `1000.0` (line 271) to determine the kilometers traveled. Line 272 then calculates kilometers/hour. Lines 273–274 calculate the distance in miles and miles/hour.

If `trackingToggleButton` is checked when the event occurs, the user has just started tracking a route. In this case, lines 286–290 indicate that the app is now tracking, get the start time for this route, reset the `routeOverlay`, invalidate the `bearingFrameLayout` (to clear the prior route, if any) and set `previousLocation` to `null`. When the user touches **Stop Tracking**, we toggle `tracking` back to `false` (line 282) to indicate that we're no longer tracking. We compute the elapsed time `totalMilliseconds` by subtracting `startTime` from the value returned by `System.currentMillis`.

11.5.2 BearingFrameLayout Subclass of FrameLayout

Class BearingFrameLayout (Figs. 11.15–11.19) maintains the app's MapView and orients it such that the user's current bearing is always toward the top of the device.

package and import Statements, and Instance Variables

Figure 11.15 lists class BearingFrameLayout's package statement, import statements and instance variables. Instance variable scale will be used to increase the MapView's width and height to match the diagonal of the device's screen. This ensures that the map fills the entire screen as it is rotated.

```
// BearingFrameLayout.java
// Rotates MapView according to device's bearing.
package com.deitel.routetracker;

import com.google.android.maps.MapView;

import android.app.Activity;
import android.content.Context;
import android.graphics.Canvas;
import android.view.Display;
import android.widget.FrameLayout;

public class BearingFrameLayout extends FrameLayout
{
   private int scale = 0; // amount to scale layout
   private MapView mapView; // displays Google maps
   private float bearing = 0f; // compass bearing

```

Fig. 11.15 | package and import statements, and instance variables of class BearingFrameLayout.

Method getChildLayoutParams

Figure 11.16 defines method getChildLayoutParams, which returns a **LayoutParams** object that represents how a child View should be laid out in a parent layout. LayoutParams are specific to Views and ViewGroups. For example, LinearLayouts use a different subclass of LayoutParams than do RelativeLayouts. Custom Views can define their own LayoutParams, should they need custom parameters. You've set various layout parameters using XML by specifying values such as match_parent or wrap_content for a GUI View's width and/or height.

```
   // returns layout parameters for MapView
   public LayoutParams getChildLayoutParams()
   {
      Display display =
         ((Activity) getContext()).getWindowManager().getDefaultDisplay();
      int w = display.getWidth();
      int h = display.getHeight();
```

Fig. 11.16 | getChildLayoutParams method of class BearingFrameLayout. (Part 1 of 2.)

```
26          scale = (int) Math.sqrt((w * w) + (h * h));
27
28          return new LayoutParams(scale, scale);
29       } // end method getChildLayoutParams
30
```

Fig. 11.16 | `getChildLayoutParams` method of class `BearingFrameLayout`. (Part 2 of 2.)

Lines 22–23 get the system's default `Display` object, which represents the device's screen. Class `Display` provides the *size* of the screen as well as its *refresh rate* and *current orientation*. Its `getWidth` and `getHeight` methods return the *dimensions of the screen*. We want our `BearingMapView` to be large enough to fill the screen as we rotate the `MapView` to match the current bearing. To ensure this, we scale the `MapView` so that its width and height match the screen's diagonal, which is calculated at line 26. Otherwise, as we rotate the `MapView`, there would be black areas at the device's corners, because the map tiles are rectangular.

Constructor

Figure 11.17 defines class `BearingFrameLayout`'s constructor. We call `super`'s constructor, passing it the `context`. We create a new `MapView`, passing it the Google Maps `apiKey`. Lines 37–43 configure the `MapView` as follows:

- **`setClickable`**—the argument `true` indicates that the user can interact with the `MapView` for zooming and panning. You must also enable the `MapView`.
- **`setEnabled`**—the argument `true` enables the `MapView`. If it's not enabled, the user cannot interact with the map by touching it.
- **`setSatellite`**—the argument `false` initially displays the map using standard Google maps, not satellite images.
- **`setBuiltInZoomControls`**—the argument `true` enables the built-in `MapView` zoom controls.
- **`setLayoutParams`**—the `LayoutParams` argument specifies how the `MapView` should be configured in its parent layout; in this case, we use it to specify the dimensions of the `MapView`.

Line 44 adds `mapView` as a child of the `BearingFrameLayout`.

```
31       // public constructor for BearingFrameLayout
32       public BearingFrameLayout(Context context, String apiKey)
33       {
34          super(context); // call super constructor
35
36          mapView = new MapView(context, apiKey); // create new MapView
37          mapView.setClickable(true); // allow user interactions with the map
38          mapView.setEnabled(true); // enables the MapView to generate events
39          mapView.setSatellite(false); // display map image
40          mapView.setBuiltInZoomControls(true); // enable zoom controls
41
```

Fig. 11.17 | Constructor for class `BearingFrameLayout`. (Part 1 of 2.)

```
        // set MapView's layout
        mapView.setLayoutParams(getChildLayoutParams());
        addView(mapView); // add MapView to this layout
    } // end BearingFrameLayout constructor

```

Fig. 11.17 | Constructor for class `BearingFrameLayout`. (Part 2 of 2.)

Overriding `View` *Method* `dispatchDraw`

Figure 11.18 overrides `View` method **`dispatchDraw`**, which is called by a parent `View`'s `draw` method to display its child `View`s. You override this method to control how child `View`s should be displayed. It's here that we *rotate* the `View` to match the current *compass bearing.*

```
47      // rotates the map according to bearing
48      @Override
49      protected void dispatchDraw(Canvas canvas)
50      {
51         if (bearing >= 0) // if the bearing is greater than 0
52         {
53            // get canvas dimensions
54            int canvasWidth = canvas.getWidth();
55            int canvasHeight = canvas.getHeight();
56
57            // dimensions of the scaled canvas
58            int width = scale;
59            int height = scale;
60
61            // center of scaled canvas
62            int centerXScaled = width / 2;
63            int centerYScaled = height / 2;
64
65            // center of screen canvas
66            int centerX = canvasWidth / 2;
67            int centerY = canvasHeight / 2;
68
69            // move center of scaled area to center of actual screen
70            canvas.translate(-(centerXScaled - centerX),
71               -(centerYScaled - centerY));
72
73            // rotate around center of screen
74            canvas.rotate(-bearing, centerXScaled, centerYScaled);
75         } // end if
76
77         super.dispatchDraw(canvas); // draw child Views of this layout
78      } // end method dispatchDraw
79
```

Fig. 11.18 | Overriding `View` method `dispatchDraw`.

Lines 54–55 get the dimensions of the available drawing surface (which is the size of the given `Canvas`). We then scale the dimensions by the number calculated in method `getLayoutParams` and calculate the center points of the original and scaled dimensions (lines 58–67). [*Note:* Scaling the maps is *not allowed* per Google's terms of service—we do this here only for demonstration purposes. There are other mapping APIs available that may have different terms of service.]

Next we move canvas's centerpoint by the difference between the two points, since we are using the scaled dimensions for this `View`'s layout parameters (lines 70–71). Next, we rotate the `Canvas` around the new centerpoint by `-bearing` degrees (line 74). Recall that `bearing` represents the user's direction in degrees to the east of true north. So if true north is toward the top of the device and you start moving northeast, the bearing will be a positive number of degrees toward the device's upper-right corner. In this case, we want the map to rotate to the *left* by that number of degrees—this is why we get the negative of the rotation angle. Rotating the `Canvas` in `dispatchDraw` causes everything drawn to this `View`—including the `Overlay` that represents the route—to rotate based on the user's bearing. Line 77 ensures that any other child `View`s are then drawn.

`setBearing` and `getMapView`

Figure 11.19 defines methods `setBearing` and `getMapView` of class `BearingFrameLayout`. Method `setBearing` sets the object's `bearing` to its argument, and method `getMapView` returns the `MapView`. These are used from the `RouteTracker` class.

```
   // set the compass bearing
   public void setBearing(float bearing)
   {
      this.bearing = bearing;
   } // end method setBearing

   // return the MapView
   public MapView getMapView()
   {
      return mapView;
   } // end method getMapView
} // end class BearingFrameLayout
```

Fig. 11.19 | `setBearing` and `MapView` methods of class `BearingFrameLayout`.

11.5.3 `RouteOverlay` Subclass of `Overlay`

`Overlay` subclass `RouteOverlay` (Figs. 11.20–11.23) maintains the tracked `Location` data and draws the route.

`package` and `import` Statements, and Instance Variables

Figure 11.20 lists class `RouteOverlay`'s `package` statement, `import` statements and instance variables. The constant `POSITION_MARKER` indicates how often a black dot will be displayed along the user's route.

```
// RouteOverlay.java
// Draws route on MapView.
package com.deitel.routetracker;
```

Fig. 11.20 | `package` and `import` statements, and instance variables. (Part 1 of 2.)

```

import java.util.ArrayList;
import java.util.List;

import android.graphics.Canvas;
import android.graphics.Color;
import android.graphics.Paint;
import android.graphics.Path;
import android.graphics.Point;
import android.location.Location;

import com.google.android.maps.GeoPoint;
import com.google.android.maps.MapView;
import com.google.android.maps.Overlay;

public class RouteOverlay extends Overlay
{
   private List<Location> locations; // stores Location tracking data
   private Paint pathPaint; // Paint information for the Path
   private Paint positionPaint; // Paint information for current position
   private final int POSITION_MARKER = 10; // marker frequency

```

Fig. 11.20 | package and `import` statements, and instance variables. (Part 2 of 2.)

Constructor for Class `RouteOverlay`

Figure 11.21 defines class `RouteOverlay`'s constructor. Lines 29–33 define a `Paint` object that specifies the settings for drawing the line that represents the route. The call to `Paint`'s `setAntiAlias` method turns on *antialiasing* to smooth the line's edges. We set the color to red, set the style to `STROKE` and set the line width to 5. The `ArrayList<Location>` called `locations` (line 34) holds the `Locations` along the tracked route. Lines 37–39 configure a second `Paint` object that's used to display black circles every `POSITION_MARKER` number of locations.

```
26     public RouteOverlay()
27     {
28        // Paint for drawing Path as a red line with a width of 5
29        pathPaint = new Paint();
30        pathPaint.setAntiAlias(true);
31        pathPaint.setColor(Color.RED);
32        pathPaint.setStyle(Paint.Style.STROKE);
33        pathPaint.setStrokeWidth(5);
34        locations = new ArrayList<Location>(); // initialize points
35
36        // Paint for drawing black circle every POSITION_MARKER Locations
37        positionPaint = new Paint();
38        positionPaint.setAntiAlias(true);
39        positionPaint.setStyle(Paint.Style.FILL);
40     } // end RouteOverlay constructor
41
```

Fig. 11.21 | Constructor for class `RouteOverlay`.

Methods `addPoint` *and* `reset`

Figure 11.22 defines methods `addPoint` and `reset`. Each time the `RouteTracker` receives a new location event, it passes the `Location` to `addPoint`, which adds it to the `ArrayList<Location>`. Method `reset` is called by `RouteTracker` to clear the previous list of `Locations` when the user starts tracking a new route.

```
   // add new Location to List of Locations
   public void addPoint(Location location)
   {
      locations.add(location);
   } // end method addPoint

   // reset the Overlay for tracking a new route
   public void reset()
   {
      locations.clear(); // delete all prior Locations
   } // end method reset

```

Fig. 11.22 | `addPoint` and `reset` methods of class `RouteOverlay`.

Overriding `Overlay` *Method* `draw`

Figure 11.23 overrides `Overlay` method **`draw`** to display the tracked route on the `MapView`. The method receives a `Canvas` (`canvas`), a `MapView` (`mapView`) and a `boolean` `shadow` and immediately calls the superclass's `draw` method. This method is called first with `true` passed as the last argument, so the `Overlay` draws its shadow layer, then the method is called again with `false` to draw the overlay itself. The shadow layer typically shows shadows for items like the map markers that Google displays when you search using Google Maps.

```
   // draw this Overlay on top of the given MapView
   @Override
   public void draw(Canvas canvas, MapView mapView, boolean shadow)
   {
      super.draw(canvas, mapView, shadow); // call super's draw method
      Path newPath = new Path(); // get a new Path
      Location previous = null; // initialize previous Location to null

      // for each Location
      for (int i = 0; i < locations.size(); ++i)
      {
         Location location = locations.get(i);

         // convert Location to GeoPoint
         Double newLatitude = location.getLatitude() * 1E6;
         Double newLongitude = location.getLongitude() * 1E6;
         GeoPoint newPoint = new GeoPoint(newLatitude.intValue(),
            newLongitude.intValue());

```

Fig. 11.23 | Overriding `View` method `draw`. (Part 1 of 2.)

```
73          // convert the GeoPoint to point on the screen
74          Point newScreenPoints = new Point();
75          mapView.getProjection().toPixels(newPoint, newScreenPoints);
76
77          if (previous != null) // if this is not the first Location
78          {
79             // get GeoPoint for the previous Location
80             Double oldLatitude = previous.getLatitude() * 1E6;
81             Double oldLongitude = previous.getLongitude() * 1E6;
82             GeoPoint oldPoint = new GeoPoint(oldLatitude.intValue(),
83                oldLongitude.intValue());
84
85             // convert the GeoPoint to point on the screen
86             Point oldScreenPoints = new Point();
87             mapView.getProjection().toPixels(oldPoint, oldScreenPoints);
88
89             // add the new point to the Path
90             newPath.quadTo(oldScreenPoints.x, oldScreenPoints.y,
91                (newScreenPoints.x + oldScreenPoints.x) / 2,
92                (newScreenPoints.y + oldScreenPoints.y) / 2);
93
94             // possibly draw a black dot for current position
95             if ((i % POSITION_MARKER) == 0)
96               canvas.drawCircle(newScreenPoints.x, newScreenPoints.y, 10,
97                   positionPaint);
98          } // end if
99          else
100         {
101            // move to the first Location
102            newPath.moveTo(newScreenPoints.x, newScreenPoints.y);
103         } // end else
104
105         previous = location; // store location
106      } // end for
107
108      canvas.drawPath(newPath, pathPaint); // draw the path
109   } // end method draw
110 } // end class RouteOverlay
```

Fig. 11.23 | Overriding `View` method `draw`. (Part 2 of 2.)

We draw the route as a `Path`, so line 59 first creates a new `Path` object. Next we set the `previous Location` to `null`, because we rebuild the `Path` each time `draw` is called. Then, for every `Location` in the `points ArrayList<Location>`, we perform the following tasks:

- Get the next `Location` from `locations` (line 65).
- Create the `GeoPoint` for that `Location` (lines 68–71), using the same technique as in Fig. 11.9.
- Convert the `GeoPoint` for the `Location` to a point on the screen (lines 74–75). `MapView`'s **`getProjection` method** provides a **`Projection`** that converts between *pixel coordinates* and *geographic coordinates*. It's important to use this method to get the updated `Projection` because each time the `MapView` redraws, the `Projection` may change. `Projection`'s **`toPixels` method** takes a `GeoPoint` and a `Point`.

The pixel coordinates matching the screen location where the GeoPoint's *latitude* and *longitude* are displayed are inserted into the Point.

If the Location previous is not null, we prepare the next line segment of the route:

- Lines 80–87 get the GeoPoint for the previous Location and convert it to a point on the screen.
- Lines 90–92 use Path method quadTo to add (as a quadratic Bezier curve) the next line segment to the Path.
- Lines 95–97 draw a circle if the current Location index (i) is divisible by the constant POSITION_MARKER.

If previous is null, we're processing the first Location in the list, so line 102 simply uses the Path's moveTo method to move to the Point specified by newScreenPoints. At the end of the for statement, lines 105 stores the current location in variable previous for the next iteration of the loop. After processing all the Locations, we draw the newPath to the canvas.

11.6 Wrap-Up

In this chapter, you created the **Route Tracker** app that enabled users to track their movements and see them displayed as a line on a Google Map. The app used several new features in the manifest file. To access the Google Maps API library you indicated the library's name in the app's manifest with a uses-library element. You removed the Activity's title bar by changing the Activity's theme with the attribute android:theme in the activity element. You also specified uses-permission elements to request permission to use various system services required for this app to work correctly.

You used a ToggleButton to maintain an *on–off* state representing whether the app was currently tracking the user's route. You handled the ToggleButton's events by implementing interface CompoundButton.OnCheckedChangeListener.

You used various classes from package com.google.android.maps to interact with the Google Maps API. You extended class MapActivity to create an Activity that managed a MapView. To display data on the MapView, you created a subclass of Overlay and overrode its draw method. You used GeoPoints to translate GPS data into points for re-centering the map based on the user's location and for drawing the user's route.

For location data, you used features of package android.location. Class LocationManager provided access to the device's location services and chose the best location provider based on the requirements you specified in a Criteria object. You then requested updates from that provider and had them delivered to a LocationListener. That object received the updates as Locations representing the device's geographic location. To determine when the device had a GPS fix, you implemented the GpsStatus.Listener interface.

Class PowerManager enabled the app to control a device's power state so that the app could record location data even if the screen was off. You used class Display to obtain the device's screen dimensions, then scaled the maps so that they filled the screen as they were rotated to match the user's bearing.

In Chapter 12, we build the **Slideshow** app, which allows the user to create and display slideshows using images and music. The app will allow the user to access the Android device's music and photo libraries. The user can add new photos to the slideshow and choose a song to play during the slideshow.

12

Slideshow App

Gallery and Media Library Access, Built-In Content Providers, MediaPlayer, Image Transitions, Custom ListActivity Layouts and the View-Holder Pattern

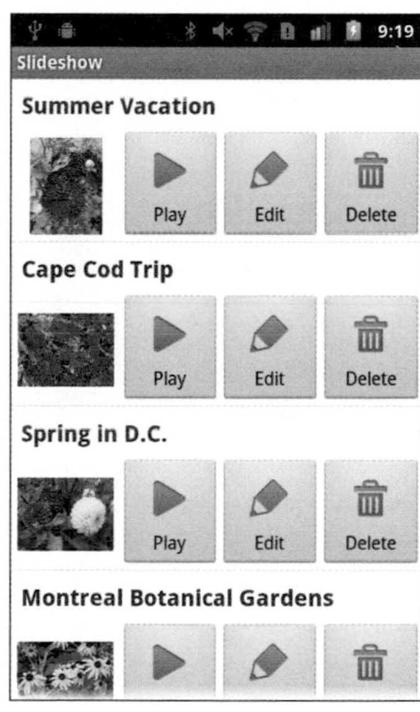

Objectives

In this chapter you'll:

- Use `Intents` and content providers to allow the user to select pictures and music from a device's **Gallery** and media library, respectively.
- Launch `Intents` that return results.
- Use a `MediaPlayer` to play music from the device's media library during the slideshow.
- Customize a `ListActivity`'s layout.
- Use the view holder pattern to improve performance when using complex `ListView`-item layouts.
- Create a custom GUI for an `AlertDialog` to allow a user to enter information.
- Load images as `Bitmaps` using a `BitmapFactory`.
- Use a `TransitionDrawable` to gradually transition between two `BitmapDrawables` that contain images.

Outline

12.1 Introduction

The **Slideshow** app allows the user to create and manage slideshows using pictures and music from the phone's **Gallery** and music library. Figure 12.1 shows the app after the user added several slideshows. Each slideshow's title and first image are displayed in a `ListView` along with three `Buttons`. Touching a slideshow's **Play** `Button` plays that slideshow. Each image displays for five seconds, while a user-chosen song (if any) plays in the background. The images *transition* by *cross fading* to the next image. Touching a slideshow's **Edit** `Button` displays an `Activity` for selecting images and music. Touching the **Delete** `Button` removes the corresponding slideshow. This version of the app *does not save* slideshows when the user closes the app—we add this capability in Chapter 13's **Enhanced Slideshow** app.

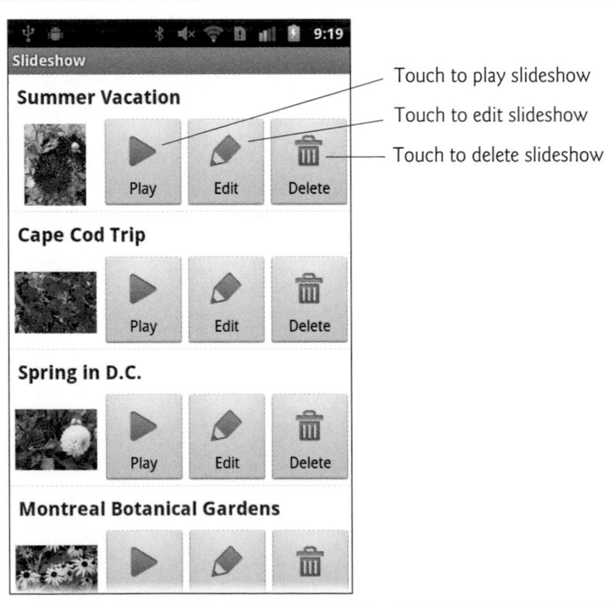

Fig. 12.1 | List of slideshows that the user has created.

When the app first loads, the list of slideshows is empty. Touching the device's menu button displays the **New Slideshow** menu item (Fig. 12.2(a)) and touching that menu item displays the **Set Slideshow Name** dialog (Fig. 12.2(b)) for naming the new slideshow. If the user touches the dialog's **Set Name** button, a new slideshow is created and the **Slideshow Editor** `Activity` is displayed (Fig. 12.3).

a) Touching the device's menu button displays the **New Slideshow** menu item

b) After the user touches **New Slideshow** in the app's menu, the **Set Slideshow Name** dialog appears (shown here after the user enters a name and is touching the **Set Name** button)

Fig. 12.2 | Adding and naming a new slideshow.

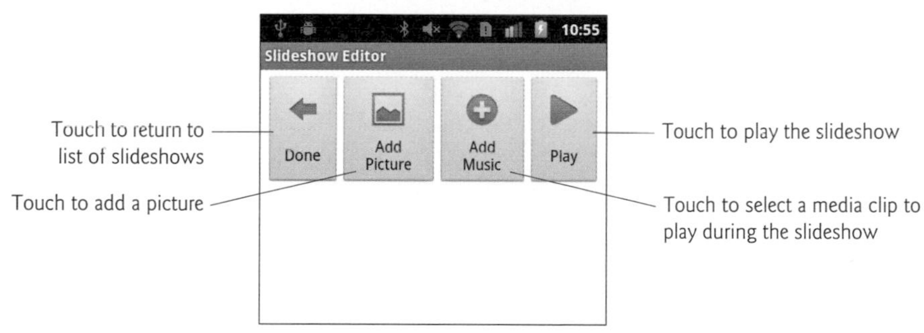

Fig. 12.3 | **Slideshow Editor** `Activity` before any images are added to the slideshow.

When the user touches **Add Picture**, the device's **Gallery** app is displayed (Fig. 12.4(a)) so that the user can select an existing image or take a new picture with the device's camera. Touching a photo adds that photo to the slideshow. Figure 12.4(b) shows the **Slideshow**

a) When the user touches **Add Picture**, the device's **Gallery** is displayed so the user can select an image from the device or take a new picture with the camera

b) The **Slideshow Editor** `Activity` after the user adds several images to the slideshow

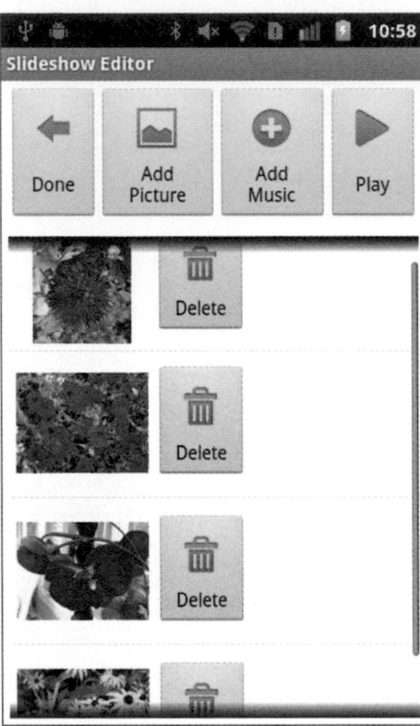

Fig. 12.4 | **Gallery** for selecting images and **Slideshow Editor** `Activity` after several images are selected.

Editor `Activity` after several images have been added to the slideshow. The dark bars at the `ListView`'s top and bottom indicate that there are more items than can be displayed and the user can scroll up and down to see the others. The **Delete** `Button` next to each image allows the user to remove that image from the slideshow.

When the user touches the **Add Music** button, Android displays the list of apps from which the user can select music. On a typical device, the user sees the options **Select music track** and **Sound Recorder** (Fig. 12.5) in a dialog. Choosing **Select music track** displays a list of the music on the device. Choosing **Sound Recorder** launches the **Sound Recorder** app and allows the user to make a new recording to use during slideshow playback. If the

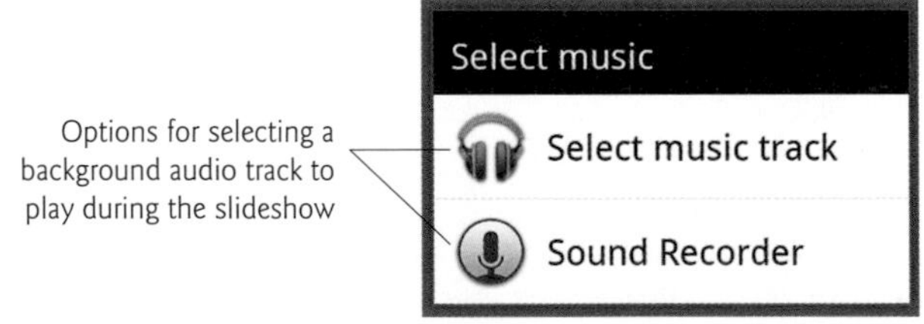

Fig. 12.5 | `Activity`-chooser dialog displayed by Android to let the user select where the media clip will come from—on this device, the user can **Select music track** or use the **Sound Recorder** to record a new track.

user makes a new recording, it will also appear in the device's music list the next time the list is displayed. The user can view the slideshow being edited by pressing the **Play** button in the **Slideshow Editor** (or in the main slideshow list). Figure 12.6 shows one image in a slideshow that's currently playing.

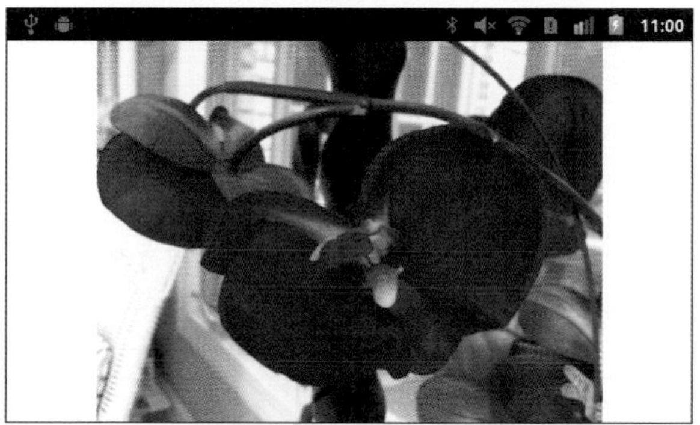

Fig. 12.6 | An image displayed during slideshow playback.

12.2 Test-Driving the Slideshow App

Opening and Running the App

Open Eclipse and import the **Slideshow** app project. To import the project:

1. Select **File > Import...** to display the **Import** dialog.
2. Expand the **General** node and select **Existing Projects into Workspace**, then click **Next >**.
3. To the right of the **Select root directory:** textfield, click **Browse...**, then locate and select the `Slideshow` folder.
4. Click **Finish** to import the project.

Right click the app's project in the **Package Explorer** window, then select **Run As > Android Application** from the menu that appears.

Transferring Music and Photos to an AVD

You can add images and music to an AVD for testing the **Slideshow** app by placing them on the AVD's SD card, which you configured when you set up the AVD. To do so:

1. Launch your AVD using the **Android SDK and AVD Manager**.
2. In Eclipse, use **Window > Open Perspective** to open the **DDMS** perspective.
3. In the **DDMS** perspective, select your AVD in the **Devices** list.
4. At the right side of the **DDMS** perspective, select the **File Explorer** tab to display the AVD's file system.
5. Navigate to `/mnt/sdcard`, then drag your images and music into that folder.
6. Shut down your AVD and restart it without **Launch from snapshot** checked. This will enable AVD to scan the SD card for the new images and/or music.

We provided several sample flower images in the `images` folder with the book's example code. Many online sites provide downloadable music files that you can use for testing—any MP3 file will suffice.

Adding a New Slideshow

Touch the device's menu button, then touch the **New Slideshow** `Button` to view the **Set Slideshow Name** dialog. Name the slideshow, then touch **Set Name** to create the new slideshow and display the **Slideshow Editor.**

Editing the New Slideshow

Touch the **Add Picture** `Button` to view the device's **Gallery**. Touch a photo in the **Gallery** to add it to the slideshow. Repeat this process for each image you wish to add. If you touch the device's back button before touching a photo, you'll be returned to the **Slideshow Editor** without adding a photo. If you wish, touch the **Delete** `Button` next to a picture to remove it from the slideshow.

Touch the **Add Music** `Button` to select background music. When presented with the options **Select music track** and **Sound Recorder**, choose **Select music track** to select an existing music file or **Sound Recorder** to record your own sound. After selecting your music, you'll be returned to the **Slideshow Editor.**

Playing a Slideshow

There are two ways to play a slideshow:

1. In the **Slideshow Editor**, you can touch the **Play** `Button`.
1. You can touch the **Done** `Button` in the **Slideshow Editor** to return to the list of slideshows, then press the **Play** `Button` next to the slideshow you wish to play.

In either case, the slideshow's images are displayed on the screen, with each image cross fading into the next after five seconds. Your chosen music plays in the background. If the music is too short to play for the slideshow's duration, the music loops. You can rotate the phone to view the slideshow in either landscape or portrait orientations. (In the emulator, you can do this by typing *Ctrl* + *F11* and *Ctrl* + *F12* to toggle the rotation.) When the slideshow completes execution, or if you touch the device's back button during playback, you'll be returned to the screen from which you played the slideshow.

Editing and Deleting a Slideshow

To edit an existing slideshow, touch its **Edit** `Button`. You can then add or delete photos as you did previously. Choosing a new song replaces the previous one. Touch a slideshow's **Delete** `Button` to erase it from the app.

12.3 Technologies Overview

This section presents the new technologies that we use in the **Slideshow** app.

Launching `Intent`s That Use Built-In Content Providers

Android does *not* provide storage that can be shared by all applications. Instead, it uses **content providers** that enable apps to save and retrieve data and to make data accessible across applications. You used this in Chapter 9 to save your drawings from the **Doodlz** app into the device's **Gallery**.

Several content providers are built into Android for access to data such as images, audio, video, contact information and more. See the list of classes in the package **android.provider** for a complete list of built-in content providers:

```
developer.android.com/reference/android/provider/
    package-summary.html
```

In this app, we'll use built-in content providers to allow the user to select images and audio stored on the device for use in the slideshow. To do this, we'll launch Intents for which we specify the MIME type of the data from which the user should be able to select (Section 12.5.3). Android will then launch an Activity that shows the specified type of data to the user or will display an Activity-chooser dialog from which the user can select the Activity to use. For example, Fig. 12.4(a) shows the Activity that allows the user to select an image from the device's **Gallery**, and Fig. 12.5 shows the Activity-chooser dialog that allows the user to decide whether to select existing music from the device or to record a new audio using the **Sound Recorder**. For more information on content providers, visit:

```
developer.android.com/guide/topics/providers/content-providers.html
```

Specifying the GUI for an AlertDialog

You can use an AlertDialog to obtain input from the user by specifying your own View for the dialog. The **Slideshow** app obtains a slideshow's name from the user by displaying an AlertDialog that contains an EditText (discussed in Sections 12.4.6 and 12.5.2).

Customizing the Layout for a ListActivity

The **Address Book** app in Chapter 10 introduced ListActivity and ListView. In that app, we used the ListActivity's default layout and built-in ListView. This app's SlideshowEditor ListActivity uses a *custom layout* (Section 12.4.7). When replacing a ListActivity's default layout, you *must* define a ListView in the layout and you *must* assign its android:id attribute the value "@android:id/list".

Launch an Intent *That Returns a Result*

In earlier apps, we've used Intents to launch the device's **Browser** (**Favorite Twitter® Searches**, Chapter 5) and to launch another Activity in the same app (**Address Book**, Chapter 10). In both cases, we used Activity method startActivity to launch the Activity associated with each Intent. In the **Favorite Twitter® Searches** app, the user could return to the app from the **Browser** by pressing the device's back button. In the **Address Book** app, when the launched Activity completed, the user was automatically returned to the app's main Activity. In this app, we introduce Activity method **startActivityForResult**, which enables an Activity to be notified when another Activity completes execution and to receive results back from the completed Activity. We use this to:

- refresh the Slideshow Activity's ListView after the user edits a slideshow,
- refresh the SlideshowEditor Activity's ListView after the user adds a new image to the slideshow and
- get the location of an image or music track the user added to a slideshow.

ArrayAdapter *for a* ListView

As you learned in Chapter 10, you use an adapter to populate a ListView. You used a SimpleCursorAdapter to populate a ListView from data in a database. In this app, we extend

ArrayAdapter (package android.widget) to create objects that populate ListViews with custom layouts using data from collection objects (Sections 12.5.2 and 12.5.3).

View-Holder Pattern

Creating custom ListView items is an expensive runtime operation, especially for large lists with complex list-item layouts. When you scroll in a ListView, as items scroll off the screen, Android reuses those list items for the new ones that are scrolling onto the screen. You can take advantage of the existing GUI components in the reused list items to increase a ListView's performance of your ListViews. To do this, we introduce the **view-holder pattern**. You can use a View's **setTag** method to add any Object to a View. This Object is then available to you via the View's **getTag** method. We'll specify as the tag an object that holds (i.e., contains references to) the list item's Views (i.e., GUI components). Using a View's tag in this manner is a convenient way to provide extra information that can be used in the view-holder pattern or in event handlers (as we'll also demonstrate in this app).

As a new ListView item scrolls onto the screen, the ListView checks whether a reusable list item is available. If not, we'll inflate the new list item's GUI from scratch, then store references to the GUI components in an object of a class that we'll call ViewHolder. Then we'll use setTag to set that ViewHolder object as the tag for the ListView item. If there is a reusable item available, we'll get that item's tag with getTag, which will return the ViewHolder object that was previously created for that ListView item. Regardless of how we obtain the ViewHolder object, we'll then configure the various GUI components that the ViewHolder references.

Notifying a **ListView** *When Its Data Source Changes*

When the ArrayAdapter's data set changes, you can call its **notifyDataSetChanged** method (Sections 12.5.2 and 12.5.3) to indicate that the Adapter's underlying data set has changed and that the corresponding ListView should be updated.

Adding Data to a GUI Component for Use in an Event Handler

The Slideshow and SlideshowEditor classes (Sections 12.5.2 and 12.5.3) use setTag and getTag to add extra information to GUI components for use in their event handlers. In class Slideshow, we add a String to the **Play** and **Edit** Buttons to specify the name of the slideshow to play or edit. We add a SlideshowInfo object to the **Delete** Button to specify which one to remove from the List of SlideshowInfo objects that represents all the slideshows.

Playing Music with a **MediaPlayer**

A **MediaPlayer** (package **android.media**, Section 12.5.4) enables an app to play audio or video from files stored on the device or from streams over a network. We'll use a MediaPlayer to play the music file (if any) that the user selects for a given slideshow.

Loading Images with **BitmapFactory**

A **BitmapFactory** (package android.graphics) creates Bitmap objects. We use one in this app to load images from the device for use as thumbnail images (Sections 12.5.2 and 12.5.3) and for display during slideshow playback (Section 12.5.4). We use an object of the nested static class **BitmapFactory.Options** to configure the Bitmaps created using BitmapFactory. In particular, we use this to downsample the images to save memory. This helps prevent out-of-memory errors, which can be common when manipulating many Bitmaps.

***Cross Fading Between Images with* `TransitionDrawable` *and* `BitmapDrawable`**
When a slideshow is playing, every five seconds the current image fades out and the next image fades in. This transition is performed by displaying a **`TransitionDrawable`** (Section 12.5.4), which provides a *built-in animation* that *transitions* between two `Drawable` objects. `TransitionDrawable` is a subclass of `Drawable` and, like other `Drawables`, can be displayed on an `ImageView`. In this app, we load the images as `Bitmaps`, so we create **`BitmapDrawables`** for use in the transition. `TransitionDrawable` and `BitmapDrawable` are located in the **`android.graphics.drawable`** package.

12.4 Building the GUI and Resource Files

In this section, we discuss the **Slideshow** app's resources and GUI layouts. You've already seen the GUI components and layouts used in this app and you've defined `String` resources in every app, so we do not show most of the layout files or the `strings.xml` resource file. Instead, we provide diagrams that show the names of GUI components, because the components and layouts used have been presented in earlier chapters. You can review the contents of the resource and layout files by opening them in Eclipse.

12.4.1 Creating the Project

Begin by creating a new Android project named `Slideshow`. Specify the following values in the **New Android Project** dialog, then press **Finish**:

- **Build Target:** Ensure that **Android 2.3.3** is checked
- **Application name:** `Slideshow`
- **Package name:** `com.deitel.slideshow`
- **Create Activity:** `Slideshow`
- **Min SDK Version:** 8

12.4.2 Using Standard Android Icons in the App's GUI

You learned in Chapter 10 that Android comes with standard icons that you can use in your own apps. Again, these are located in the SDK's `platforms` folder under each platform version's `data/res/drawable-hdpi` folder. Some of the icons we chose to use in this app are not publicly accessible—this means that they're not guaranteed to be available on every Android device. For this reason, we copied the icons that we use into this app's `res/drawable-hdpi` folder. Expand that folder in Eclipse to see the specific icons we chose.

12.4.3 `AndroidManifest.xml`

Figure 12.7 shows this app's `AndroidManifest.xml` file. There are several key features in this manifest that we've highlighted. In particular, the `Slideshow` and `SlideshowEditor` `activity` elements indicate that each `Activity` is always displayed in portrait mode (lines 10 and 20). Also, we've set the `Slideshow` and `SlideshowPlayer` themes (lines 11 and 24), with the latter using one that does not show a title bar. This provides more room for displaying the slideshow's images.

```
<?xml version="1.0" encoding="utf-8"?>
<manifest xmlns:android="http://schemas.android.com/apk/res/android"
   package="com.deitel.slideshow" android:versionCode="1"
   android:versionName="1.0">
   <application android:icon="@drawable/icon"
      android:label="@string/app_name"
      android:debuggable="true">
      <activity android:name=".Slideshow"
         android:label="@string/app_name"
         android:screenOrientation="portrait"
         android:theme="@android:style/Theme.Light">
         <intent-filter>
            <action android:name="android.intent.action.MAIN" />
            <category android:name="android.intent.category.LAUNCHER" />
         </intent-filter>
      </activity>

      <activity android:name=".SlideshowEditor"
         android:label="@string/slideshow_editor"
         android:screenOrientation="portrait"></activity>

      <activity android:name=".SlideshowPlayer"
         android:label="@string/app_name"
         android:theme="@android:style/Theme.Light.NoTitleBar"></activity>
   </application>
   <uses-sdk android:minSdkVersion="8" />
</manifest>
```

Fig. 12.7 | `AndroidManifest.xml`.

12.4.4 Layout for `ListView` Items in the `Slideshow` `ListActivity`

Figure 12.8 diagrams the layout for the `ListView` items that are displayed in the `Slideshow` `ListActivity`. The layout—defined in `slideshow_list_item.xml`—is a vertical `LinearLayout` that contains a `TextView` and a nested horizontal `LinearLayout`. The horizontal `LinearLayout` contains an `ImageView` and three `Buttons`. Each `Button` uses one new feature—the **`android:drawableTop` attribute** displays a `Drawable` above the `Button`'s text. In each case, we use one of the standard Android icons. For example, in the XML layout file, the `playButton` specifies:

```
android:drawableTop="@drawable/ic_menu_play_clip"
```

which indicates that the image in the file `ic_menu_play_clip.png` should be displayed above the `Button`'s text. There are also **`android:drawableLeft`**, **`android:drawableRight`** and **`android:drawableBottom`** attributes for positioning the icon to left of the text, right of the text or below the text, respectively.

12.4.5 `Slideshow` `ListActivity`'s Menu

Figure 12.9 shows the layout for the `Slideshow` `ListActivity`'s menu. We use the standard `ic_menu_slideshow.png` image as the menu item's icon (line 5).

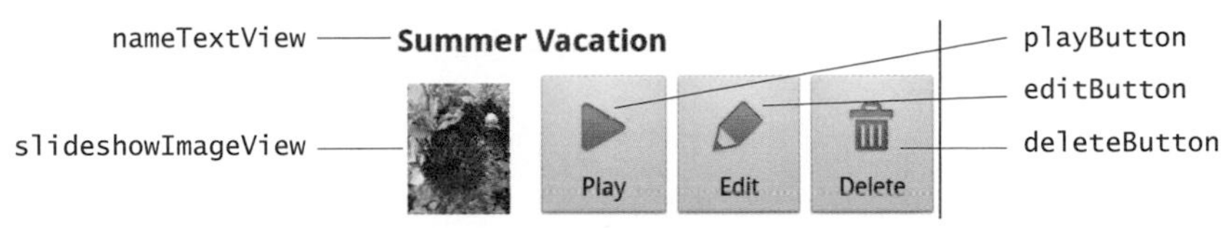

Fig. 12.8 | Layout for `ListView` Items in the `Slideshow` `ListActivity`—`slideshow_list_item.xml`.

```
<?xml version="1.0" encoding="utf-8"?>
<menu xmlns:android="http://schemas.android.com/apk/res/android">
   <item android:id="@+id/newSlideshowItem"
      android:title="@string/menuitem_new_slideshow"
      android:icon="@drawable/ic_menu_slideshow"
      android:titleCondensed="@string/menuitem_new_slideshow"
      android:alphabeticShortcut="n"></item>
</menu>
```

Fig. 12.9 | `Slideshow` `ListActivity`'s menu—`slideshow_menu.xml`.

12.4.6 Layout for the `EditText` in the Set Slideshow Name Dialog

Figure 12.10 shows the **Set Slideshow Name** dialog that enables the user to enter the slideshow's name in an `EditText`. We nested the `nameEditText` in a `LinearLayout` so we could set its left and right margins with the attributes `android:layout_marginLeft` and `android:layout_marginRight`, respectively. We also set the `android:singleLine` attribute to `true` to allow only a single line of text for the slideshow name.

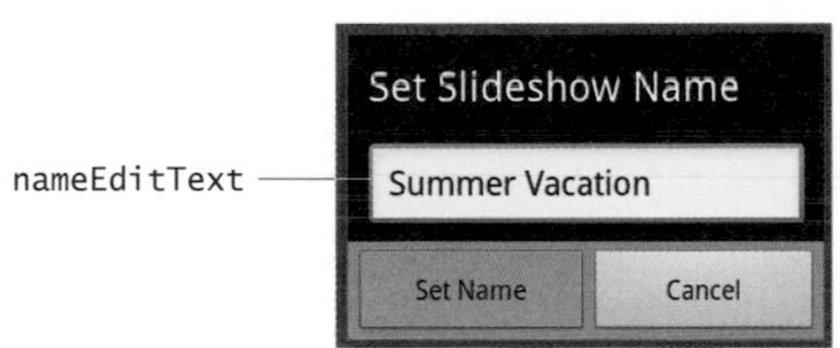

Fig. 12.10 | **Set Slideshow Name** `AlertDialog` with custom GUI for user input—shown after the user has entered a slideshow name and with the **Set Name** `Button` touched.

12.4.7 Layout for the `SlideshowEditor` `ListActivity`

Figure 12.11 diagrams the layout for the `SlideshowEditor` `ListActivity`. Because this `ListActivity` uses a custom layout (defined in `slideshow_list_item.xml`), we must define a `ListView` in the layout with the `android:id` set to `"@android:id/list"`. This is the `ListView` that will be returned by the `ListActivity`'s `getListView` method. The layout defined in `slideshow_editor.xml` is a vertical `LinearLayout` that contains a nested horizontal `LinearLayout` and a `ListView`. The horizontal `LinearLayout` contains the four `Buttons`.

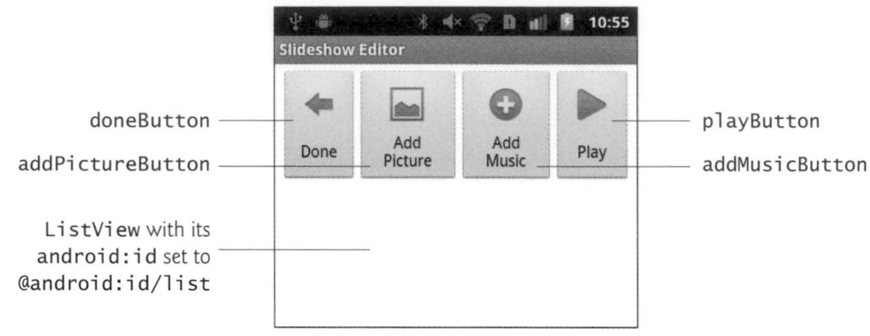

Fig. 12.11 | Layout for the SlideshowEditor ListActivity—slideshow_editor.xml.

12.4.8 Layout for ListView Items in the SlideshowEditor ListActivity

Figure 12.10 diagrams the layout for the ListView items that are displayed in the SlideshowEditor ListActivity. The layout defined in slideshow_edit_item.xml consists of a horizontal LinearLayout that contains an ImageView and a Button.

Fig. 12.12 | Layout for ListView Items in the SlideshowEditor ListActivity—slideshow_edit_item.xml.

12.4.9 Layout for the SlideshowPlayer Activity

Figure 12.13 diagrams the layout for the SlideshowPlayer Activity. The layout defined in slideshow_edit_item.xml is a horizontal LinearLayout containing an ImageView that fills the entire LinearLayout.

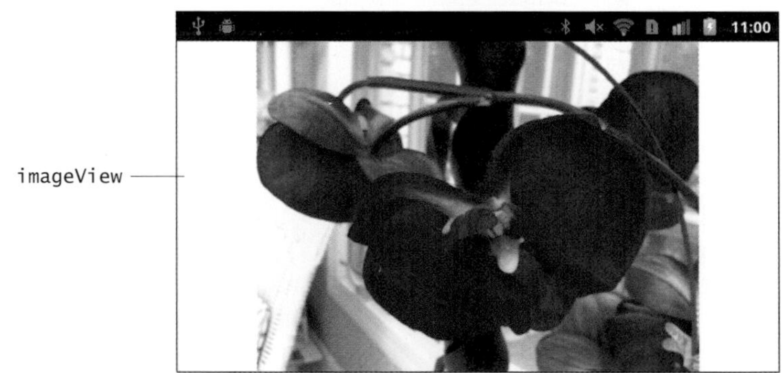

Fig. 12.13 | Layout for the SlideshowPlayer ListActivity—slideshow_player.xml.

12.5 Building the App

This app consists of classes SlideshowInfo (Fig. 12.14), Slideshow (a ListActivity subclass, Figs. 12.15–12.24), SlideshowEditor (a ListActivity subclass, Figs. 12.25–12.33) and SlideshowPlayer (Figs. 12.35–12.39). This app's main Activity, Slideshow, is created when you create the project, but you must change its superclass to ListActivity, then add the other classes to the project's src/com.deitel.slideshow folder.

12.5.1 SlideshowInfo Class

Class SlideshowInfo (Fig. 12.14) stores the data for a single slideshow, which consists of:

- name (line 10)—the slideshow name, which is displayed in the app's slideshow list
- imageList (line 11)—a List of Strings representing the image locations
- musicPath (line 12)—a String representing the location of the music, if any, that should play in the background during the slideshow

The constructor creates imageList as an ArrayList<String>.

```
1  // SlideshowInfo.java
2  // Stores the data for a single slideshow.
3  package com.deitel.slideshow;
4
5  import java.util.ArrayList;
6  import java.util.List;
7
8  public class SlideshowInfo
9  {
10    private String name; // name of this slideshow
11    private List<String> imageList; // this slideshow's images
12    private String musicPath; // location of music to play
13
14    // constructor
15    public SlideshowInfo(String slideshowName)
16    {
17       name = slideshowName; // set the slideshow name
18       imageList = new ArrayList<String>();
19       musicPath = null; // currently there is no music for the slideshow
20    } // end SlideshowInfo constructor
21
22    // return this slideshow's name
23    public String getName()
24    {
25       return name;
26    } // end method getName
27
28    // return List of Strings pointing to the slideshow's images
29    public List<String> getImageList()
30    {
31       return imageList;
32    } // end method getImageList
```

Fig. 12.14 | Stores the data for a single slideshow. (Part 1 of 2.)

```java

   // add a new image path
   public void addImage(String path)
   {
      imageList.add(path);
   } // end method addImage

   // return String at position index
   public String getImageAt(int index)
   {
      if (index >= 0 && index < imageList.size())
         return imageList.get(index);
      else
         return null;
   } // end method getImageAt

   // return this slideshow's music
   public String getMusicPath()
   {
      return musicPath;
   } // end method getMusicPath

   // set this slideshow's music
   public void setMusicPath(String path)
   {
      musicPath = path;
   } // end method setMusicPath

   // return number of images/videos in the slideshow
   public int size()
   {
      return imageList.size();
   } // end method size
} // end class SlideshowInfo
```

Fig. 12.14 | Stores the data for a single slideshow. (Part 2 of 2.)

12.5.2 `Slideshow` Subclass of ListActivity

Class `Slideshow` (Figs. 12.15–12.23) is the app's main `Activity` class. The class extends `ListActivity`, because this `Activity`'s primary purpose is to display a `ListView`.

`package` *and* `import` *Statements, and Fields*

The `Slideshow` subclass of `ListActivity` (Fig. 12.15) is the app's main `Activity`. It displays a `ListView` of all previously created slideshows. We've highlighted the `import` statements for the new classes and interfaces discussed in Section 12.3 and throughout this section. The `List` of `SlideshowInfo` objects (line 41) contains the information for all of the user-created slideshows. This `List` is declared `static` so that it can be shared among the app's activities. The `SlideshowAdapter` (line 43) is a custom `ArrayAdapter` that displays `SlideshowInfo` objects as items in the `ListView`.

```
// Slideshow.java
// Main Activity for the Slideshow class.
package com.deitel.slideshow;

import java.util.ArrayList;
import java.util.List;

import android.app.AlertDialog;
import android.app.ListActivity;
import android.content.ContentResolver;
import android.content.Context;
import android.content.DialogInterface;
import android.content.Intent;
import android.graphics.Bitmap;
import android.graphics.BitmapFactory;
import android.net.Uri;
import android.os.AsyncTask;
import android.os.Bundle;
import android.provider.MediaStore;
import android.view.Gravity;
import android.view.LayoutInflater;
import android.view.Menu;
import android.view.MenuInflater;
import android.view.MenuItem;
import android.view.View;
import android.view.View.OnClickListener;
import android.view.ViewGroup;
import android.widget.ArrayAdapter;
import android.widget.Button;
import android.widget.EditText;
import android.widget.ImageView;
import android.widget.ListView;
import android.widget.TextView;
import android.widget.Toast;

public class Slideshow extends ListActivity
{
   // used when adding slideshow name as an extra to an Intent
   public static final String NAME_EXTRA = "NAME";

   static List<SlideshowInfo> slideshowList; // List of slideshows
   private ListView slideshowListView; // this ListActivity's ListView
   private SlideshowAdapter slideshowAdapter; // adapter for the ListView

```

Fig. 12.15 | `package` and `import` statements, and instance variables for class `Slideshow`.

Overriding `Activity` *Method* `onCreate`

`Slideshow`'s `onCreate` method (Fig. 12.16) gets the `ListView` that displays the user-created slideshows (line 50), then creates the `slideshowList` and `slideshowAdapter`, and sets the `slideshowListView`'s adapter to `slideshowAdapter`. This allows the `slideshowListView` to display each slideshow's name, first thumbnail and **Play**, **Edit** and **Delete** Buttons using the layout defined in `slideshow_list_item.xml` (Section 12.4.4). Lines 58–62 create and display an `AlertDialog` telling the user how to get started with the app.

```
45     // called when the activity is first created
46     @Override
47     public void onCreate(Bundle savedInstanceState)
48     {
49        super.onCreate(savedInstanceState);
50        slideshowListView = getListView(); // get the built-in ListView
51 
52        // create and set the ListView's adapter
53        slideshowList = new ArrayList<SlideshowInfo>();
54        slideshowAdapter = new SlideshowAdapter(this, slideshowList);
55        slideshowListView.setAdapter(slideshowAdapter);
56 
57        // create a new AlertDialog Builder
58        AlertDialog.Builder builder = new AlertDialog.Builder(this);
59        builder.setTitle(R.string.welcome_message_title);
60        builder.setMessage(R.string.welcome_message);
61        builder.setPositiveButton(R.string.button_ok, null);
62        builder.show();
63     } // end method onCreate
64 
```

Fig. 12.16 | Overriding `Activity` method `onCreate` in class `Slideshow`.

Overriding `Activity` *Methods* `onCreateOptionsMenu`*,* `onOptionsItemSelected` *and* `onActivityResult`

Method `onCreateOptionsMenu` (Fig. 12.17, lines 66–73) inflates the `Activity`'s menu from the file `slideshow_menu.xml` (Section 12.4.5). When the user touches the **New Slideshow** menu item, method `onOptionsItemSelected` (lines 79–132) displays a dialog with a custom GUI in which the user can enter the slideshow's name. To display an `EditText` in the dialog, we inflate the layout in `slideshow_name_edittext.xml` (line 87) and set it as the `View` for the dialog (line 93). If the user touches the **OK** button in the dialog, method `onClick` (lines 99–124) gets the name from the `EditText`, then creates a new `SlideshowInfo` object for the slideshow and adds it to the `slideshowList`. Lines 110–112 configure an `Intent` to launch the `SlideshowEditor` `Activity`. Then, line 113 launches the `Intent` using the `startActivityForResult` method. The first argument is the `Intent` representing the sub-`Activity` to launch. The second is a non-negative request code that identifies which `Activity` is returning a result. This value is received as the first parameter in method **`onActivityResult`** (lines 135–141), which is called when the sub-`Activity` returns so that this `Activity` can process the result. If your `Activity` can launch multiple other ones, the request code can be used in `onActivityResult` to determine which sub-`Activity` returned so that you can properly handle the result. Since we launch only one sub-`Activity` from this `Activity`, we used the value 0 (defined as the constant `EDIT_ID` in line 76) for the second argument. Using a negative result code causes `startActivityForResult` to operate identically to `startActivity`. If the system cannot find an `Activity` to handle the `Intent`, then method `startActivityForResult` throws an `ActivityNotFoundException`. [*Note:* In general, you should wrap calls to `startActivity` and `startActivityForResult` in a try statement, so you can catch the exception if there is no Activity to handle the Intent.]

```
    // create the Activity's menu from a menu resource XML file
    @Override
    public boolean onCreateOptionsMenu(Menu menu)
    {
       super.onCreateOptionsMenu(menu);
       MenuInflater inflater = getMenuInflater();
       inflater.inflate(R.menu.slideshow_menu, menu);
       return true;
    } // end method onCreateOptionsMenu

    // SlideshowEditor request code passed to startActivityForResult
    private static final int EDIT_ID = 0;

    // handle choice from options menu
    @Override
    public boolean onOptionsItemSelected(MenuItem item)
    {
       // get a reference to the LayoutInflater service
       LayoutInflater inflater = (LayoutInflater) getSystemService(
          Context.LAYOUT_INFLATER_SERVICE);

       // inflate slideshow_name_edittext.xml to create an EditText
       View view = inflater.inflate(R.layout.slideshow_name_edittext, null);
       final EditText nameEditText =
          (EditText) view.findViewById(R.id.nameEditText);

       // create an input dialog to get slideshow name from user
       AlertDialog.Builder inputDialog = new AlertDialog.Builder(this);
       inputDialog.setView(view); // set the dialog's custom View
       inputDialog.setTitle(R.string.dialog_set_name_title);

       inputDialog.setPositiveButton(R.string.button_set_slideshow_name,
          new DialogInterface.OnClickListener()
          {
             public void onClick(DialogInterface dialog, int whichButton)
             {
                // create a SlideshowInfo for a new slideshow
                String name = nameEditText.getText().toString().trim();

                if (name.length() != 0)
                {
                   slideshowList.add(new SlideshowInfo(name));

                   // create Intent to launch the SlideshowEditor Activity,
                   // add slideshow name as an extra and start the Activity
                   Intent editSlideshowIntent =
                      new Intent(Slideshow.this, SlideshowEditor.class);
                   editSlideshowIntent.putExtra("NAME_EXTRA", name);
```

Fig. 12.17 | Overriding Activity methods onCreateOptionsMenu, onOptionsItemSelected and onActivityResult. (Part 1 of 2.)

```
113                      startActivityForResult(editSlideshowIntent, 0);
114                   } // end if
115                   else
116                   {
117                      // display message that slideshow must have a name
118                      Toast message = Toast.makeText(Slideshow.this,
119                         R.string.message_name, Toast.LENGTH_SHORT);
120                      message.setGravity(Gravity.CENTER,
121                         message.getXOffset() / 2, message.getYOffset() / 2);
122                      message.show(); // display the Toast
123                   } // end else
124                } // end method onClick
125             } // end anonymous inner class
126          ); // end call to setPositiveButton
127
128          inputDialog.setNegativeButton(R.string.button_cancel, null);
129          inputDialog.show();
130
131          return super.onOptionsItemSelected(item); // call super's method
132       } // end method onOptionsItemSelected
133
134       // refresh ListView after slideshow editing is complete
135       @Override
136       protected void onActivityResult(int requestCode, int resultCode,
137          Intent data)
138       {
139          super.onActivityResult(requestCode, resultCode, data);
140          slideshowAdapter.notifyDataSetChanged(); // refresh the adapter
141       } // end method onActivityResult
142
```

Fig. 12.17 | Overriding `Activity` methods `onCreateOptionsMenu`, `onOptionsItemSelected` and `onActivityResult`. (Part 2 of 2.)

Overridden `Activity` method `onActivityResult` (lines 135–141) is called when another `Activity` returns a result to this one. The `requestCode` parameter is the value that was passed as the second argument to `startActivityForResult` when the other `Activity` was started. The `resultCode` parameter's value is:

- `RESULT_OK` if the `Activity` completed successfully
- `RESULT_CANCELED` if the `Activity` did not return a result or crashed, or if the `Activity` explicitly calls method `setResult` with the argument `RESULT_CANCELED`

The third parameter is an `Intent` containing data (as extras) returned to this `Activity`. In this example, we need to know simply that the `SlideshowEditor` `Activity` completed so that we can refresh the `ListView` with the new slideshow. We call `SlideshowAdapter`'s `notifyDataSetChanged` method to indicate that the adapter's underlying data set changed and refresh the `ListView`.

`SlideshowAdapter`: Using the View-Holder Pattern to Populate a `ListView`

Figure 12.18 defines the `private` nested classes `ViewHolder` and `SlideshowAdapter`. Class `ViewHolder` simply defines package-access instance variables that class `SlideshowAdapter` will be able to access directly when manipulating `ViewHolder` objects. When a `ListView` item is created, we'll create an object of class `ViewHolder` and associate it with that `ListView` item. If there is an existing `ListView` item that's being reused, we'll simply obtain the `ViewHolder` object that was previously associated with that item.

```
   // Class for implementing the "ViewHolder pattern"
   // for better ListView performance
   private static class ViewHolder
   {
      TextView nameTextView; // refers to ListView item's TextView
      ImageView imageView; // refers to ListView item's ImageView
      Button playButton; // refers to ListView item's Play Button
      Button editButton; // refers to ListView item's Edit Button
      Button deleteButton; // refers to ListView item's Delete Button
   } // end class ViewHolder

   // ArrayAdapter subclass that displays a slideshow's name, first image
   // and "Play", "Edit" and "Delete" Buttons
   private class SlideshowAdapter extends ArrayAdapter<SlideshowInfo>
   {
      private List<SlideshowInfo> items;
      private LayoutInflater inflater;

      // public constructor for SlideshowAdapter
      public SlideshowAdapter(Context context, List<SlideshowInfo> items)
      {
         // call super constructor
         super(context, -1, items);
         this.items = items;
         inflater = (LayoutInflater)
            getSystemService(Context.LAYOUT_INFLATER_SERVICE);
      } // end SlideshowAdapter constructor

      // returns the View to display at the given position
      @Override
      public View getView(int position, View convertView,
         ViewGroup parent)
      {
         ViewHolder viewHolder; // holds references to current item's GUI

         // if convertView is null, inflate GUI and create ViewHolder;
         // otherwise, get existing ViewHolder
         if (convertView == null)
         {
            convertView =
               inflater.inflate(R.layout.slideshow_list_item, null);

            // set up ViewHolder for this ListView item
            viewHolder = new ViewHolder();
            viewHolder.nameTextView = (TextView)
               convertView.findViewById(R.id.nameTextView);
```

Fig. 12.18 | `SlideshowAdapter` class for populating the `ListView`. (Part 1 of 2.)

```
189                viewHolder.imageView = (ImageView)
190                   convertView.findViewById(R.id.slideshowImageView);
191                viewHolder.playButton =
192                   (Button) convertView.findViewById(R.id.playButton);
193                viewHolder.editButton =
194                   (Button) convertView.findViewById(R.id.editButton);
195                viewHolder.deleteButton =
196                   (Button) convertView.findViewById(R.id.deleteButton);
197                convertView.setTag(viewHolder); // store as View's tag
198             } // end if
199             else // get the ViewHolder from the convertView's tag
200                viewHolder = (ViewHolder) convertView.getTag();
201
202             // get the slideshow the display its name in nameTextView
203             SlideshowInfo slideshowInfo = items.get(position);
204             viewHolder.nameTextView.setText(slideshowInfo.getName());
205
206             // if there is at least one image in this slideshow
207             if (slideshowInfo.size() > a)
208             {
209                // create a bitmap using the slideshow's first image or video
210                String firstItem = slideshowInfo.getImageAt(0);
211                new LoadThumbnailTask().execute(viewHolder.imageView,
212                   Uri.parse(firstItem));
213             } // end if
214
215             // set tage and OnClickListener for the "Play" Button
216             viewHolder.playButton.setTag(slideshowInfo);
217             viewHolder.playButton.setOnClickListener(playButtonListener);
218
219             // create and set OnClickListener for the "Edit" Button
220             viewHolder.editButton.setTag(slideshowInfo);
221             viewHolder.editButton.setOnClickListener(editButtonListener);
222
223             // create and set OnClickListener for the "Delete" Button
224             viewHolder.deleteButton.setTag(slideshowInfo);
225             viewHolder.deleteButton.setOnClickListener(deleteButtonListener);
226
227             return convertView; // return the View for this position
228          } // end getView
229       } // end class SlideshowAdapter
230
```

Fig. 12.18 | `SlideshowAdapter` class for populating the `ListView`. (Part 2 of 2.)

In the `AddressBook` app, we created a `SimpleCursorAdapter` to display `Strings` (contact names) from a database. Recall that such an adapter is designed specifically to map `Strings` and images to `TextViews` and `ImageViews`, respectively. This app's `ListView` items are more complicated. Each contains text (the slideshow name), an image (the first image in the slideshow) and `Buttons` (**Play**, **Edit** and **Delete**). To map slideshow data to these `ListView` items, we extend class `ArrayAdapter` so that we can override method `getView` to configure a custom layout for each `ListView` item. The constructor (lines 162–169) calls the superclass's constructor, then stores the `List` of `SlideshowInfo` objects and the

LayoutInflater for use in the getView method. The second superclass constructor argument represents the resource ID of a layout that contains a TextView for displaying data in a ListView item. In this case, we'll set this ourselves later, so we supply -1 for that argument.

Method **getView** (lines 172–228) performs custom mapping of data to a ListView item. It receives the ListView item's position, the View (convertView) representing that ListView item and that ListView item's parent as arguments. By manipulating convertView, you can customize the ListView item's contents. If convertView is null, lines 182–196 inflate the ListView-item layout slideshow_list_item.xml and assign it to convertView, then create a ViewHolder object and assign the GUI components that were just inflated to the ViewHolder's instance variables. Line 197 sets this ViewHolder object as the ListView item's tag. If convertView is not null, the ListView is reusing a ListView item that has scrolled off the screen. In this case, line 200 gets the tag of the ListView item and simply reuses that ViewHolder object. Line 203 gets the SlideshowInfo object that corresponds to the ListView item's position.

Line 204 sets the viewHolder's nameTextView to the slideshow's name. If there are any images in the slideshow, lines 210–212 get the path to the first image then create and execute a new LoadThumbnailTask AsyncTask (Fig. 12.19) to load and display the image's thumbnail on the viewHolder's imageView.

Lines 216–225 configure the listeners for the **Play**, **Edit** and **Delete** Buttons in this ListView item. In each case, the Button's setTag method is used to provide some extra information (in the form of an Object) that's needed in the corresponding event handler—specifically, the SlideshowInfo object representing the slideshow. For the playButton and editButton event handlers, this object is used as an extra in an Intent so that the SlideshowPlayer and SlideshowEditor know which slideshow to play or edit, respectively. For the deleteButton, we provide the SlideshowInfo object, so that it can be removed from the List of SlideshowInfo objects.

Nested Class ***LoadThumbnailTask***

Class LoadThumbnailTask (Fig. 12.19) loads an image thumbnail in a separate thread of execution to ensure that the GUI thread remains responsive. Method doInBackground uses Slideshow's static utility method getThumbnail to load the thumbnail. When that completes, method onPostExecute receives the thumbnail Bitmap and displays it on the specified ImageView.

```
   // task to load thumbnails in a separate thread
   private class LoadThumbnailTask extends AsyncTask<Object,Object,Bitmap>
   {
      ImageView imageView; // displays the thumbnail

      // load thumbnail: ImageView and Uri as args
      @Override
      protected Bitmap doInBackground(Object... params)
      {
         imageView = (ImageView) params[0];

```

Fig. 12.19 | Class LoadThumbnailTask loads a thumbnail in a separate thread. (Part 1 of 2.)

```
         return Slideshow.getThumbnail((Uri) params[1],
            getContentResolver(), new BitmapFactory.Options());
      } // end method doInBackground

      // set thumbnail on ListView
      @Override
      protected void onPostExecute(Bitmap result)
      {
         super.onPostExecute(result);
         imageView.setImageBitmap(result);
      } // end method onPostExecute
   } // end class LoadThumbnailTask

```

Fig. 12.19 | Class `LoadThumbnailTask` loads a thumbnail in a separate thread. (Part 2 of 2.)

***`OnClickListener playButtonListener`* Responds to the Events of the *`playButton`* of a Specific Slideshow**

The `OnClickListener` `playButtonLIstener` (Fig. 12.20) responds to the `playButton`'s events. We create an `Intent` to launch the `SlideshowPlayer` `Activity`, then add the slideshow's name as an `Intent` extra (lines 262–265). The arguments are a `String` to tag the extra data and the tagged value (the slideshow name). Line 265 uses the `View` argument's `getTag` method to get the value that was set with `setTag` (i.e., the slideshow name) in line 216. Line 266 launches the `Intent`.

```
255    // respond to events generated by the "Play" Button
256    OnClickListener playButtonListener = new OnClickListener()
257    {
258       @Override
259       public void onClick(View v)
260       {
261          // create an intent to launch the SlideshowPlayer Activity
262          Intent playSlideshow =
263             new Intent(Slideshow.this, SlideshowPlayer.class);
264          playSlideshow.putExtra(
265             NAME_EXTRA, ((SlideshowInfo) v.getTag()).getName());
266          startActivity(playSlideshow); // launch SlideshowPlayer Activity
267       } // end method onClick
268    }; // end playButtonListener
269
```

Fig. 12.20 | Event listener for the `playButton`'s click event.

***`OnClickListener editButtonListener`* Responds to the Events of the *`editButton`* of a Specific Slideshow**

The `OnClickListener` `editButtonLIstener` (Fig. 12.21) responds to the `editButton`'s events. We create an `Intent` to launch the `SlideshowEditor` `Activity`, then add the slideshow's name as an `Intent` extra (lines 277–280). Line 280 uses the `View` argument's `getTag` method to get the value that was set with `setTag` (i.e., the slideshow name) in line 220. Line 281 launches the `Intent` with `startActivityForResult`, so this `Activity`'s `List-`

View can be updated by onActivityResult—in case the user changes the first image in the slideshow while editing.

```
270    // respond to events generated by the "Edit" Button
271    private OnClickListener editButtonListener = new OnClickListener()
272    {
273       @Override
274       public void onClick(View v)
275       {
276          // create an intent to launch the SlideshowEditor Activity
277          Intent editSlideshow =
278             new Intent(Slideshow.this, SlideshowEditor.class);
279          editSlideshow.putExtra(
280             NAME_EXTRA, ((SlideshowInfo) v.getTag()).getName());
281          startActivityForResult(editSlideshow, 0);
282       } // end method onClick
283    }; // end playButtonListener
284
```

Fig. 12.21 | Event listener for the editButton's click event.

OnClickListener deleteButtonListener Responds to the Events of the deleteButton of a Specific Slideshow

The OnClickListener deleteButtonLIstener (Fig. 12.22) responds to the deleteButton's events. We confirm that the user wants to delete the slideshow. If so, we use the View argument's getTag method to get the SlideshowInfo object that was set with setTag in line 224, then remove that object from slideshowList. Line 304 refreshes the ListView by calling the slideshowAdapter's notifyDataSetChanged method.

```
285    // respond to events generated by the "Delete" Button
286    private OnClickListener deleteButtonListener = new OnClickListener()
287    {
288       @Override
289       public void onClick(final View v)
290       {
291          // create a new AlertDialog Builder
292          AlertDialog.Builder builder =
293             new AlertDialog.Builder(Slideshow.this);
294          builder.setTitle(R.string.dialog_confirm_delete);
295          builder.setMessage(R.string.dialog_confirm_delete_message);
296          builder.setPositiveButton(R.string.button_ok,
297             new DialogInterface.OnClickListener()
298             {
299                @Override
300                public void onClick(DialogInterface dialog, int which)
301                {
302                   Slideshow.slideshowList.remove(
303                      (SlideshowInfo) v.getTag());
304                   slideshowAdapter.notifyDataSetChanged(); // refresh
305                } // end method onClick
```

Fig. 12.22 | Event listener for the deleteButton's click event. (Part 1 of 2.)

```
            } // end anonymous inner class
         ); // end call to setPositiveButton
         builder.setNegativeButton(R.string.button_cancel, null);
         builder.show();
      } // end method onClick
   }; // end playButtonListener

```

Fig. 12.22 | Event listener for the `deleteButton`'s click event. (Part 2 of 2.)

`getSlideshowInfo` *Method*

Figure 12.23 defines utility method `getSlideshowInfo`, which returns a specified `SlideshowInfo` object. This method simply iterates through the `List` of `SlideshowInfo` objects and compares `name` with the name stored in each. If the corresponding `SlideshowInfo` object is found, line 319 returns it; otherwise, line 321 returns `null`.

```
313    // utility method to locate SlideshowInfo object by slideshow name
314    public static SlideshowInfo getSlideshowInfo(String name)
315    {
316       // for each SlideshowInfo
317       for (SlideshowInfo slideshowInfo : slideshowList)
318          if (slideshowInfo.getName().equals(name))
319             return slideshowInfo;
320
321       return null; // no matching object
322    } // end method getSlideshowInfo
323
```

Fig. 12.23 | Utility method `getSlideshowInfo` returns a `SlideshowInfo` object for the slideshow with the specified name.

`getThumbnail` *Method*

Figure 12.24 defines our utility method `getThumbnail`, which receives three arguments—a `Uri` representing the location of an image, a `ContentResolver` for interacting with the device's file system and a `BitmapFactory.Options` object specifying the `Bitmap` configuration. Line 328 extracts from the `Uri` the `id` of the image for which we'd like to load a thumbnail. Lines 330–331 then use the Android `MediaStore` to get the corresponding thumbnail image. Class **`MediaStore.Images.Thumbnails`** provides its own utility method `getThumbnail` for this purpose. You provide as arguments the `ContentResolver` for interacting with the device's file system, the image's `id`, the type of thumbnail you wish to load and the `BitmapFactory.Options` specifying the `Bitmap` configuration. Line 333 then returns the `Bitmap`.

```
324    // utility method to get a thumbnail image Bitmap
325    public static Bitmap getThumbnail(Uri uri, ContentResolver cr,
326       BitmapFactory.Options options)
327    {
```

Fig. 12.24 | Utility method `getThumbnail` loads an image's thumbnail `Bitmap` from a specified `Uri`. (Part 1 of 2.)

```
        int id = Integer.parseInt(uri.getLastPathSegment());

        Bitmap bitmap = MediaStore.Images.Thumbnails.getThumbnail(cr, id,
           MediaStore.Images.Thumbnails.MICRO_KIND, options);

        return bitmap;
     } // end method getThumbnail
  } // end class Slideshow
```

Fig. 12.24 | Utility method `getThumbnail` loads an image's thumbnail `Bitmap` from a specified `Uri`. (Part 2 of 2.)

12.5.3 `SlideshowEditor` Subclass of `ListActivity`

Class `SlideshowEditor` (Figs. 12.25–12.33) allows the user to add images and a background audio clip to a slideshow. The class extends `ListActivity`, because this `Activity`'s primary purpose is to display a `ListView` of the images in the slideshow. As we discussed in Section 12.4.7, this `ListActivity` uses a custom layout.

`package` and `import` Statements, and Instance Variables of Class `SlideshowEditor`

Figure 12.25 begins the definition of class `SlideShowEditor`. We've highlighted the `import` statements for the new classes and interfaces discussed in Section 12.3 and throughout this section. `SlideshowEditorAdapter` (line 26) is a custom `ArrayAdapter` subclass used to display the images of the slideshow being edited in this `Activity`'s `ListView`. Each photo in the slideshow is displayed as a `ListView` item with a **Delete** `Button` that can be used to remove the image from the slideshow. The slideshow we're editing is represented by the `SlideshowInfo` object declared in line 27.

```
1  // SlideshowEditor.java
2  // Activity for building and Editing a slideshow.
3  package com.deitel.slideshow;
4
5  import java.util.List;
6
7  import android.app.ListActivity;
8  import android.content.Context;
9  import android.content.Intent;
10 import android.graphics.Bitmap;
11 import android.graphics.BitmapFactory;
12 import android.net.Uri;
13 import android.os.AsyncTask;
14 import android.os.Bundle;
15 import android.view.LayoutInflater;
16 import android.view.View;
17 import android.view.View.OnClickListener;
18 import android.view.ViewGroup;
19 import android.widget.ArrayAdapter;
20 import android.widget.Button;
```

Fig. 12.25 | `package` statement, `import` statements and instance variables for class `SlideshowEditor`. (Part 1 of 2.)

```
import android.widget.ImageView;

public class SlideshowEditor extends ListActivity
{
   // slideshowEditorAdapter to display slideshow in ListView
   private SlideshowEditorAdapter slideshowEditorAdapter;
   private SlideshowInfo slideshow; // slideshow data

```

Fig. 12.25 | package statement, import statements and instance variables for class SlideshowEditor. (Part 2 of 2.)

Overriding Activity *Method* onCreate

Figure 12.26 overrides method onCreate which configures this Activity user interface. Line 34 sets this ListActivity's layout to the one specified in slideshow_editor.xml. Line 37 gets the Intent that launched this Activity, then gets the String extra called Slideshow.NAME_EXTRA that was stored in the Intent's Bundle. Line 38 uses class Slideshow's static getSlideshowInfo method (Fig. 12.23) to get the SlideshowInfo object for the slideshow that's being created for the first time or being edited. Lines 41–52 get references to the Buttons in the GUI and register their event handlers. Lines 55–56 create a new SlideshowEditorAdapter (Fig. 12.33) to display each item in this slideshow using the list-item layout defined in slideshow_edit_item.xml. We then set that SlideshowEditorAdapter as the ListView's adapter.

```
29      // called when the activity is first created
30      @Override
31      public void onCreate(Bundle savedInstanceState)
32      {
33         super.onCreate(savedInstanceState);
34         setContentView(R.layout.slideshow_editor);
35
36         // retrieve the slideshow
37         String name = getIntent().getStringExtra(Slideshow.NAME_EXTRA);
38         slideshow = Slideshow.getSlideshowInfo(name);
39
40         // set appropriate OnClickListeners for each Button
41         Button doneButton = (Button) findViewById(R.id.doneButton);
42         doneButton.setOnClickListener(doneButtonListener);
43
44         Button addPictureButton =
45            (Button) findViewById(R.id.addPictureButton);
46         addPictureButton.setOnClickListener(addPictureButtonListener);
47
48         Button addMusicButton = (Button) findViewById(R.id.addMusicButton);
49         addMusicButton.setOnClickListener(addMusicButtonListener);
50
51         Button playButton = (Button) findViewById(R.id.playButton);
52         playButton.setOnClickListener(playButtonListener);
53
```

Fig. 12.26 | Overriding Activity method onCreate in class SlideshowEditor. (Part 1 of 2.)

```
        // get ListView and set its adapter for displaying list of images
        slideshowEditorAdapter =
           new SlideshowEditorAdapter(this, slideshow.getImageList());
        getListView().setAdapter(slideshowEditorAdapter);
     } // end method onCreate

```

Fig. 12.26 | Overriding `Activity` method `onCreate` in class `SlideshowEditor`. (Part 2 of 2.)

Overriding `Activity` *Method* `onActivityResult`

As you learned in Section 12.5.2, method `onActivityResult` (Fig. 12.27) is called when a sub-`Activity` started by the `startActivityForResult` method finishes executing. As you'll see shortly, the `SlideshowEditor` launches one `Activity` that allows the user to select an image from the device and another that allows the user to select music. Because we launch more than one sub-`Activity`, we use the constants at lines 61–62 as request codes to determine which sub-`Activity` is returning results to `onActivityResult`—the request code used to launch an `Activity` with `startActivityForResult` is passed to `onActivityResult` as the first argument. The parameter `resultCode` receives `RESULT_OK` (line 69) if the returning `Activity` executed successfully. We process the result only if there has not been an error. The `Intent` parameter `data` contains the `Activity`'s result. Line 71 uses the `Intent`'s `getData` method to get the `Uri` representing the image or music the user selected. If `onActivityResult` was called after selecting an image (line 74), line 77 adds that image's path to the slideshow's list of image paths, and line 80 indicates that the `SlideshowEditorAdapter`'s data set has changed so the `SlideshowEditor`'s `ListView` can be updated. If `onActivityResult` was called after selecting music (line 82), then line 83 sets the slideshow's music path.

```
60     // set IDs for each type of media result
61     private static final int PICTURE_ID = 1;
62     private static final int MUSIC_ID = 2;
63
64     // called when an Activity launched from this Activity returns
65     @Override
66     protected void onActivityResult(int requestCode, int resultCode,
67        Intent data)
68     {
69        if (resultCode == RESULT_OK) // if there was no error
70        {
71           Uri selectedUri = data.getData();
72
73           // if the Activity returns an image
74           if (requestCode == PICTURE_ID)
75           {
76              // add new image path to the slideshow
77              slideshow.addImage(selectedUri.toString());
78
79              // refresh the ListView
80              slideshowEditorAdapter.notifyDataSetChanged();
81           } // end if
```

Fig. 12.27 | Overriding `Activity` method `onActivityResult`. (Part 1 of 2.)

```
82          else if (requestCode == MUSIC_ID) // Activity returns music
83             slideshow.setMusicPath(selectedUri.toString());
84       } // end if
85    } // end method onActivityResult
86
```

Fig. 12.27 | Overriding `Activity` method `onActivityResult`. (Part 2 of 2.)

`OnClickListener` `doneButtonListener` for `doneButton`'s Click Event

When the user touches the `doneButton`, the `doneButtonListener` (Fig. 12.28) calls `Activity` method `finish` (line 94) to terminate this `Activity` and return to the launching one.

```
87    // called when the user touches the "Done" Button
88    private OnClickListener doneButtonListener = new OnClickListener()
89    {
90       // return to the previous Activity
91       @Override
92       public void onClick(View v)
93       {
94          finish();
95       } // end method onClick
96    }; // end OnClickListener doneButtonListener
97
```

Fig. 12.28 | `OnClickListener` `backButtonListener` responds to the events of the `backButton`.

`OnClickListener` `addPictureButtonListener` for `addPictureButton`'s Click Event

The `addPictureButtonListener` (Fig. 12.29) launches an external image-choosing `Activity` (such as **Gallery**) when the `addPictureButton` is clicked. Line 105 creates a new `Intent` with `Intent`'s `ACTION_GET_CONTENT` constant, indicating that the `Intent` allows the user to select content that's stored on the device. `Intent`'s **`setType` method** is passed a `String` representing the image MIME type, indicating that the user should be able to select an image. The asterisk (*) in the MIME type indicates that *any* type of image can be selected. `Intent` method **`createChooser`** returns the specified `Intent` as one of type `android.intent.action.CHOOSER`, which displays an `Activity` chooser that allows the user to select which `Activity` to use for choosing an image (if more than one `Activity` on the device supports this). If there's only one such `Activity`, it's launched—for example, our test device allows us to choose images *only* from the **Gallery** app. The second argument to `createChooser` is a title that will be displayed on the `Activity` chooser.

```
98    // called when the user touches the "Add Picture" Button
99    private OnClickListener addPictureButtonListener = new OnClickListener()
100   {
```

Fig. 12.29 | `OnClickListener` `addPictureButtonListener` responds to the events of the `addPictureButton`. (Part 1 of 2.)

```
        // launch image choosing activity
        @Override
        public void onClick(View v)
        {
           Intent intent = new Intent(Intent.ACTION_GET_CONTENT);
           intent.setType("image/*");
           startActivityForResult(Intent.createChooser(intent,
              getResources().getText(R.string.chooser_image)), PICTURE_ID);
        } // end method onClick
     }; // end OnClickListener addPictureButtonListener

```

Fig. 12.29 | `OnClickListener` `addPictureButtonListener` responds to the events of the `addPictureButton`. (Part 2 of 2.)

`OnClickListener addMusicButtonListener` for `addMusicButton`'s Click Event

The `addMusicButtonListener` `OnClickListener` (Fig. 12.30) launches an external music-choosing `Activity` to select the sound track for the slideshow. This event handler works just like the one in Fig. 12.29, except that the `Intent` uses the MIME type `"audio/*"` to allow the user to select any type of audio on the device. On a typical device, launching this `Intent` displays the chooser shown in Fig. 12.30, allowing the user to **Select music track** or record a new audio clip with the **Sound Recorder**.

```
     // called when the user touches the "Add Music" Button
     private OnClickListener addMusicButtonListener = new OnClickListener()
     {
        // launch music choosing activity
        @Override
        public void onClick(View v)
        {
           Intent intent = new Intent(Intent.ACTION_GET_CONTENT);
           intent.setType("audio/*");
           startActivityForResult(Intent.createChooser(intent,
              getResources().getText(R.string.chooser_music)), MUSIC_ID);
        } // end method onClick
     }; // end OnClickListener addMusicButtonListener

```

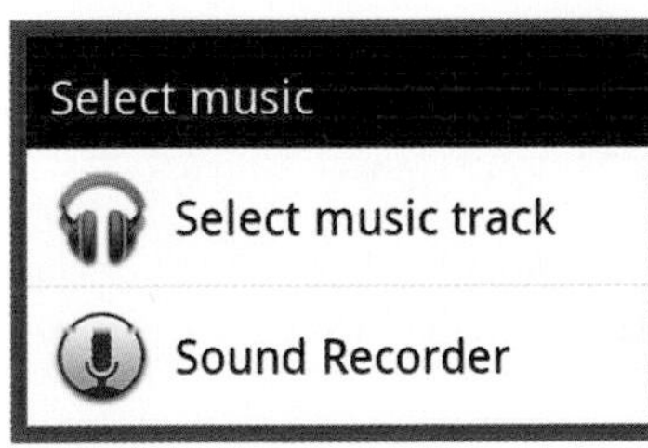

Fig. 12.30 | `OnClickListener` `addMusicButtonListener` responds to the events of the `addMusicButton`.

`OnClickListener playButtonListener` for `PlayButton`'s Click Event

The `playButtonListener OnClickListener` (Fig. 12.31) launches the `SlideshowPlayer` `Activity` when the user touches the **Play** `Button`. Lines 137–142 create a new `Intent` for the `SlideshowPlayer` class, include the slideshow's name as an `Intent` extra and launch the `Intent`.

```
126    // called when the user touches the "Play" Button
127    private OnClickListener playButtonListener = new OnClickListener()
128    {
129       // plays the current slideshow
130       @Override
131       public void onClick(View v)
132       {
133          // create new Intent to launch the SlideshowPlayer Activity
134          Intent playSlideshow =
135             new Intent(SlideshowEditor.this, SlideshowPlayer.class);
136
137          // include the slideshow's name as an extra
138          playSlideshow.putExtra(
139             Slideshow.NAME_EXTRA, slideshow.getName());
140          startActivity(playSlideshow); // launch the Activity
141       } // end method onClick
142    }; // end playButtonListener
143
```

Fig. 12.31 | `OnClickListener playButtonListener` responds to the events of the `playButton`.

`OnClickListener deleteButtonListener` for `deleteButton`'s Click Event

The `deleteImage OnClickListener` (Fig. 12.32) deletes the image corresponding to the **Delete** `Button` that was touched. Each **Delete** `Button` stores the path of its associated image as its tag. Line 152 gets the tag and passes it to the `slideshowEditorAdapter`'s **`remove` method**, which also updates the `SlideshowEditor`'s `ListView` because the data set has changed.

```
144    // called when the user touches the "Delete" Button next
145    // to an ImageView
146    private OnClickListener deleteButtonListener = new OnClickListener()
147    {
148       // removes the image
149       @Override
150       public void onClick(View v)
151       {
152          slideshowEditorAdapter.remove((String) v.getTag());
153       } // end method onClick
154    }; // end OnClickListener deleteButtonListener
155
```

Fig. 12.32 | `OnClickListener deleteButtonListener` responds to the events of the `deleteButton` next to a specific image.

`private` Classes `ViewHolder` and `SlideshowEditorAdaptor`: Displaying Slideshow Images Using the View-Holder Pattern

As in Fig. 12.18, we used the view-holder pattern when displaying items in the `SlideshowEditor`'s `ListView`. Class `ViewHolder` (Fig. 12.33, lines 158–162) defines the two GUI components used in each `ListView` item. Class `SlideshowEditorAdapter` (lines 165–212) extends `ArrayAdapter` to display each image in the slideshow as an item in `SlideshowEditor`'s `ListView`. The `items List`, which is initialized in the constructor, holds `Strings` representing the locations of the slideshow's images. The code for `SlideshowEditorAdapter` is similar to the `SlideshowAdapter` in Fig. 12.18, but this adapter uses the layout `slideshow_edit_item.xml` for the `ListView`'s items. For details on how we display each image, see the discussion for Fig. 12.18.

```
156    // Class for implementing the "ViewHolder pattern"
157    // for better ListView performance
158    private static class ViewHolder
159    {
160       ImageView slideImageView; // refers to ListView item's ImageView
161       Button deleteButton; // refers to ListView item's Button
162    } // end class ViewHolder
163
164    // ArrayAdapter displaying Slideshow images
165    private class SlideshowEditorAdapter extends ArrayAdapter<String>
166    {
167       private List<String> items; // list of image Uris
168       private LayoutInflater inflater;
169
170       public SlideshowEditorAdapter(Context context, List<String> items)
171       {
172          super(context, -1, items);
173          this.items = items;
174          inflater = (LayoutInflater)
175             getSystemService(Context.LAYOUT_INFLATER_SERVICE);
176       } // end SlideshoweditorAdapter constructor
177
178       @Override
179       public View getView(int position, View convertView, ViewGroup parent)
180       {
181          ViewHolder viewHolder; // holds references to current item's GUI
182
183          // if convertView is null, inflate GUI and create ViewHolder;
184          // otherwise, get existing ViewHolder
185          if (convertView == null)
186          {
187             convertView =
188                inflater.inflate(R.layout.slideshow_edit_item, null);
189
190             // set up ViewHolder for this ListView item
191             viewHolder = new ViewHolder();
```

Fig. 12.33 | `private` nested class `SlideshowEditorAdapter` displays the slideshow images in the `SlideshowEditor`'s `ListView`. (Part 1 of 2.)

```
            viewHolder.slideImageView = (ImageView)
               convertView.findViewById(R.id.slideshowImageView);
            viewHolder.deleteButton =
               (Button) convertView.findViewById(R.id.deleteButton);
            convertView.setTag(viewHolder); // store as View's tag
         } // end if
         else // get the ViewHolder from the convertView's tag
            viewHolder = (ViewHolder) convertView.getTag();

         // get and display a thumbnail Bitmap image
         String item = items.get(position); // get current image
         new LoadThumbnailTask().execute(viewHolder.slideImageView,
            Uri.parse(item));

         // configure the "Delete" Button
         viewHolder.deleteButton.setTag(item);
         viewHolder.deleteButton.setOnClickListener(deleteButtonListener);

         return convertView;
      } // end method getView
   } // end class SlideshowEditorAdapter
```

Fig. 12.33 | `private` nested class `SlideshowEditorAdapter` displays the slideshow images in the `SlideshowEditor`'s `ListView`. (Part 2 of 2.)

Nested Class **LoadThumbnailTask**

Class `LoadThumbnailTask` (Fig. 12.34) loads an image thumbnail in a separate thread of execution to ensure that the GUI thread remains responsive. Method `doInBackground` uses `Slideshow`'s `static` utility method `getThumbnail` to load the thumbnail. When that completes, method `onPostExecute` receives the thumbnail `Bitmap` and displays it on the specified `ImageView`.

```
   // task to load thumbnails in a separate thread
   private class LoadThumbnailTask extends AsyncTask<Object,Object,Bitmap>
   {
      ImageView imageView; // displays the thumbnail

      // load thumbnail: ImageView, MediaType and Uri as args
      @Override
      protected Bitmap doInBackground(Object... params)
      {
         imageView = (ImageView) params[0];

         return Slideshow.getThumbnail((Uri) params[1],
            getContentResolver(), new BitmapFactory.Options());
      } // end method doInBackground
```

Fig. 12.34 | Class `LoadThumbnailTask` loads an image thumbnail in a separate thread. (Part 1 of 2.)

```
        // set thumbnail on ListView
        @Override
        protected void onPostExecute(Bitmap result)
        {
           super.onPostExecute(result);
           imageView.setImageBitmap(result);
        } // end method onPostExecute
     } // end class LoadThumbnailTask
  } // end class SlideshowEditor
```

Fig. 12.34 | Class `LoadThumbnailTask` loads an image thumbnail in a separate thread. (Part 2 of 2.)

12.5.4 `SlideshowPlayer` Subclass of `ListActivity`

`Activity` class `SlideshowPlayer` (Figs. 12.35–12.39) plays a slideshow specified as an extra of the `Intent` that launches this `Activity`.

`package` *and* `import` *Statements, and Fields of Class* `SlideshowPlayer`

Figure 12.35 begins the definition of class `SlideShowPlayer`. We've highlighted the `import` statements for the new classes and interfaces discussed in Section 12.3 and throughout this section. The `String` constant at line 25 is used for logging error messages that occur when attempting to play music in the background of the slideshow. The `String` constants in lines 28–30 are used to save state information in `onSaveInstanceState` and to load that information in `onCreate` in cases when the `Activity` goes to the background and returns to the foreground, respectively. The `int` constant at line 32 specifies the duration for which each slide is shown. Lines 33–40 declare the instance variables that are used to manage the slideshow.

```
 1  // SlideshowPlayer.java
 2  // Plays the selected slideshow that's passed as an Intent extra
 3  package com.deitel.slideshow;
 4
 5  import java.io.FileNotFoundException;
 6  import java.io.InputStream;
 7
 8  import android.app.Activity;
 9  import android.content.ContentResolver;
10  import android.graphics.Bitmap;
11  import android.graphics.BitmapFactory;
12  import android.graphics.drawable.BitmapDrawable;
13  import android.graphics.drawable.Drawable;
14  import android.graphics.drawable.TransitionDrawable;
15  import android.media.MediaPlayer;
16  import android.net.Uri;
17  import android.os.AsyncTask;
18  import android.os.Bundle;
19  import android.os.Handler;
20  import android.util.Log;
```

Fig. 12.35 | `package` and `import` statements, and fields of class `SlideshowPlayer`. (Part 1 of 2.)

```
import android.widget.ImageView;

public class SlideshowPlayer extends Activity
{
   private static final String TAG = "SLIDESHOW"; // error logging tag

   // constants for saving slideshow state when config changes
   private static final String MEDIA_TIME = "MEDIA_TIME";
   private static final String IMAGE_INDEX = "IMAGE_INDEX";
   private static final String SLIDESHOW_NAME = "SLIDESHOW_NAME";

   private static final int DURATION = 5000; // 5 seconds per slide
   private ImageView imageView; // displays the current image
   private String slideshowName; // name of current slideshow
   private SlideshowInfo slideshow; // slideshow being played
   private BitmapFactory.Options options; // options for loading images
   private Handler handler; // used to update the slideshow
   private int nextItemIndex; // index of the next image to display
   private int mediaTime; // time in ms from which media should play
   private MediaPlayer mediaPlayer; // plays the background music, if any

```

Fig. 12.35 | package and import statements, and fields of class SlideshowPlayer. (Part 2 of 2.)

Overriding Activity *Method* onCreate

Figure 12.36 overrides Activity method onCreate to configure the SlideshowPlayer. Line 49 gets SlideshowPlayer's ImageView. Lines 51–68 determine whether the Activity is starting from scratch, in which case the savedInstanceState Bundle will be null (line 51), or the Activity is restarting (perhaps due to a configuration change). If the Activity is starting from scratch, line 54 gets the slideshow's name from the Intent that launched this Activity, line 55 sets mediaTime to 0 to indicate that the music should play from its beginning, and line 56 sets nextItemIndex to 0 to indicate that the slideshow should start from the beginning. If the Activity is restarting, lines 61–67 set these instance variables with values that were stored in the savedInstanceState Bundle.

```
42      // initializes the SlideshowPlayer Activity
43      @Override
44      public void onCreate(Bundle savedInstanceState)
45      {
46         super.onCreate(savedInstanceState);
47         setContentView(R.layout.slideshow_player);
48
49         imageView = (ImageView) findViewById(R.id.imageView);
50
51         if (savedInstanceState == null)
52         {
53            // get slideshow name from Intent's extras
54            slideshowName = getIntent().getStringExtra(Slideshow.NAME_EXTRA);
55            mediaTime = 0; // position in media clip
```

Fig. 12.36 | Overriding Activity method onCreate in class SlideshowPlayer. (Part 1 of 2.)

```
56            nextItemIndex = 0; // start from first image
57         } // end if
58         else // Activity resuming
59         {
60            // get the play position that was saved when config changed
61            mediaTime = savedInstanceState.getInt(MEDIA_TIME);
62
63            // get index of image that was displayed when config changed
64            nextItemIndex = savedInstanceState.getInt(IMAGE_INDEX);
65
66            // get name of slideshow that was playing when config changed
67            slideshowName = savedInstanceState.getString(SLIDESHOW_NAME);
68         } // end else
69
70         // get SlideshowInfo for slideshow to play
71         slideshow = Slideshow.getSlideshowInfo(slideshowName);
72
73         // configure BitmapFactory.Options for loading images
74         options = new BitmapFactory.Options();
75         options.inSampleSize = 4; // sample at 1/4 original width/height
76
77         // if there is music to play
78         if (slideshow.getMusicPath() != null)
79         {
80            // try to create a MediaPlayer to play the music
81            try
82            {
83               mediaPlayer = new MediaPlayer();
84               mediaPlayer.setDataSource(
85                  this, Uri.parse(slideshow.getMusicPath()));
86               mediaPlayer.prepare(); // prepare the MediaPlayer to play
87               mediaPlayer.setLooping(true); // loop the music
88               mediaPlayer.seekTo(mediaTime); // seek to mediaTime
89            } // end try
90            catch (Exception e)
91            {
92               Log.v(TAG, e.toString());
93            } // end catch
94         } // end if
95
96         handler = new Handler(); // create handler to control slideshow
97      } // end method onCreate
98
```

Fig. 12.36 | Overriding `Activity` method `onCreate` in class `SlideshowPlayer`. (Part 2 of 2.)

Next, line 71 gets the `SlideshowInfo` object for the slideshow to play, and lines 74–75 configure the `BitmapFactory.Options` used for downsampling the images that are displayed in the slideshow.

If music is associated with the slideshow, line 83 creates a `MediaPlayer` object to play the music. We call `MediaPlayer`'s **`setDataSource` method** (lines 84–85) with a `Uri` representing the location of the music to play. `MediaPlayer`'s **`prepare` method** (line 86) prepares the `MediaPlayer` for playback. This method blocks the current thread until the

MediaPlayer is ready for playback. This method should be used only for music stored on the device. If playing a streaming media file, it's recommended that you use the **prepareAsync method**, which returns immediately, instead; otherwise, prepare will block the current thread until the stream has been buffered. Method prepare will throw an exception if the MediaPlayer cannot be prepared—for example, if it's currently playing a media clip. If an exception occurs, we log the error message (line 92). A detailed state-diagram for the MediaPlayer class can be found at

```
developer.android.com/reference/android/media/MediaPlayer.html
```

Line 87 calls MediaPlayer's **setLooping method** with the argument true to loop playback if the music's duration is shorter than the total slideshow duration. Line 88 calls MediaPlayer's **seekTo method** to move the audio playback to the specified time in milliseconds—the argument will be 0 if this Activity is starting from scratch; otherwise, the argument will represent where playback last paused. Finally, line 96 creates the Handler that controls the slideshow.

Overriding Activity *Methods* onStart, onPause, onResume, onStop *and* onDestroy

Figure 12.37 overrides Activity methods onStart, onPause, onResume, onStop and onDestroy. Method onStart (lines 100–105) immediately posts the updateSlideshow Runnable (Fig. 12.39) for execution. Method onPause (lines 108–115) pauses the background audio by calling MediaPlayer's **pause method**—this prevents the music from playing when the Activity is *not* in the foreground. Method onResume (lines 118–125) calls MediaPlayer's **start method**, which starts the music, or restarts it if it was paused. Method onStop (lines 128–135) calls the handler's removeCallbacks to prevent previously scheduled updateSlideshow Runnables from executing when the Activity is stopped. Method onDestroy (lines 138–145) calls MediaPlayer's **release method**, which releases the resources used by the MediaPlayer.

```
99     // called after onCreate and sometimes onStop
100    @Override
101    protected void onStart()
102    {
103       super.onStart();
104       handler.post(updateSlideshow); // post updateSlideshow to execute
105    } // end method onStart
106
107    // called when the Activity is paused
108    @Override
109    protected void onPause()
110    {
111       super.onPause();
112
113       if (mediaPlayer != null)
114          mediaPlayer.pause(); // pause playback
115    } // end method onPause
```

Fig. 12.37 | Overriding Activity methods onStart, onPause, onResume and onStop. (Part 1 of 2.)

```

    // called after onStart or onPause
    @Override
    protected void onResume()
    {
       super.onResume();

       if (mediaPlayer != null)
          mediaPlayer.start(); // resume playback
    } // end method onResume

    // called when the Activity stops
    @Override
    protected void onStop()
    {
       super.onStop();

       // prevent slideshow from operating when in background
       handler.removeCallbacks(updateSlideshow);
    } // end method onStop

    // called when the Activity is destroyed
    @Override
    protected void onDestroy()
    {
       super.onDestroy();

       if (mediaPlayer != null)
          mediaPlayer.release(); // release MediaPlayer resources
    } // end method onDestroy

```

Fig. 12.37 | Overriding `Activity` methods `onStart`, `onPause`, `onResume` and `onStop`. (Part 2 of 2.)

Overriding `Activity` *Method* `onSaveInstanceState`

Figure 12.38 overrides the `onSaveInstanceState` to allow the `Activity` to save the slideshow's music playback position, current image index (minus one, because `nextItemIndex` actually represents the next image to display) and slideshow name in the `outState` `Bundle` when the device's configuration changes. This information can be restored in `onCreate` to allow the slideshow to continue from the point at which the configuration change occurred.

```
    // save slideshow state so it can be restored in onCreate
    @Override
    protected void onSaveInstanceState(Bundle outState)
    {
       super.onSaveInstanceState(outState);

```

Fig. 12.38 | Overriding `Activity` method `onSaveInstanceState`. (Part 1 of 2.)

```
      // if there is a mediaPlayer, store media's current position
      if (mediaPlayer != null)
         outState.putInt(MEDIA_TIME, mediaPlayer.getCurrentPosition());

      // save nextItemIndex and slideshowName
      outState.putInt(IMAGE_INDEX, nextItemIndex - 1);
      outState.putString(SLIDESHOW_NAME, slideshowName);
   } // end method onSaveInstanceState

```

Fig. 12.38 | Overriding `Activity` method `onSaveInstanceState`. (Part 2 of 2.)

private Runnable updateSlideshow

Figure 12.39 defines the `Runnable` that displays the slideshow's images. If the last slideshow image has already been displayed (line 168), lines 171–172 **`reset`** the `MediaPlayer` to release its resources and line 173 calls the `Activity`'s `finish` method to terminate this `Activity` and return to the one that launched the `SlideshowPlayer`.

```
162    // anonymous inner class that implements Runnable to control slideshow
163    private Runnable updateSlideshow = new Runnable()
164    {
165       @Override
166       public void run()
167       {
168          if (nextItemIndex >= slideshow.size())
169          {
170             // if there is music playing
171             if (mediaPlayer != null && mediaPlayer.isPlaying())
172                mediaPlayer.reset(); // slideshow done, reset mediaPlayer
173             finish(); // return to launching Activity
174          } // end if
175          else
176          {
177             String item = slideshow.getImageAt(nextItemIndex);
178             new LoadImageTask().execute(Uri.parse(item));
179             ++nextItemIndex;
180          } // end else
181       } // end method run
182
183       // task to load thumbnails in a separate thread
184       class LoadImageTask extends AsyncTask<Uri, Object, Bitmap>
185       {
186          // load iamges
187          @Override
188          protected Bitmap doInBackground(Uri... params)
189          {
190             return getBitmap(params[0], getContentResolver(), options);
191          } // end method doInBackground
192
```

Fig. 12.39 | `Runnable updateSlideshow` displays the next image in the slideshow and schedules itself to run again in five seconds. (Part 1 of 2.)

```
            // set thumbnail on ListView
            @Override
            protected void onPostExecute(Bitmap result)
            {
               super.onPostExecute(result);
               BitmapDrawable next = new BitmapDrawable(result);
               next.setGravity(android.view.Gravity.CENTER);
               Drawable previous = imageView.getDrawable();

               // if previous is a TransitionDrawable,
               // get its second Drawable item
               if (previous instanceof TransitionDrawable)
                  previous = ((TransitionDrawable) previous).getDrawable(1);

               if (previous == null)
                  imageView.setImageDrawable(next);
               else
               {
                  Drawable[] drawables = { previous, next };
                  TransitionDrawable transition =
                     new TransitionDrawable(drawables);
                  imageView.setImageDrawable(transition);
                  transition.startTransition(1000);
               } // end else

               handler.postDelayed(updateSlideshow, DURATION);
            } // end method onPostExecute
         } // end class LoadImageTask

         // utility method to get a Bitmap from a Uri
         public Bitmap getBitmap(Uri uri, ContentResolver cr,
            BitmapFactory.Options options)
         {
            Bitmap bitmap = null;

            // get the image
            try
            {
               InputStream input = cr.openInputStream(uri);
               bitmap = BitmapFactory.decodeStream(input, null, options);
            } // end try
            catch (FileNotFoundException e)
            {
               Log.v(TAG, e.toString());
            } // end catch

            return bitmap;
         } // end method getBitmap
      }; // end Runnable updateSlideshow
   } // end class SlieshowPlayer
```

Fig. 12.39 | `Runnable` `updateSlideshow` displays the next image in the slideshow and schedules itself to run again in five seconds. (Part 2 of 2.)

If there are more images to display, line 177 gets the next image's path and line 178 launches a `LoadImageTask` to load and display the image. Class `LoadImageTask` (lines 184–220) loads the next image and transitions from the last image to the next one. First `doInBackground` calls `getBitmap` (defined in lines 223–240) to get the image. When the image is returned, `onPostExecute` handles the image transition. Lines 198–199 create a `BitmapDrawable` from the returned `Bitmap` (`result`) and set its gravity to center so the image is displayed in the center of the `ImageView`. Line 200 gets a reference to the preceding `Drawable`. If it's a `TransitionDrawable`, we get the second `BitmapDrawable` out of the `TransitionDrawable` (so we don't create a chain of `TransitionDrawables` and run out of memory). If there is no previous `Drawable`, line 208 simply displays the new `BitmapDrawable`. Otherwise, lines 211–215 use a `TransitionDrawable` to transition between two `Drawable` objects in an `ImageView`. Line 214 passes the `TransitionDrawable` to `ImageView`'s `setImageDrawable` method to display it on `currentImageView`. We create the `TransitionDrawable` programmatically, since we need to dynamically determine the previous and next images. `TransitionDrawable`'s **`startTransition` method** (line 215) performs the transition over the course of one second (`1000` milliseconds). The transition automatically cross fades from the first to the second `Drawable` in the `drawables` array. Line 218 schedules `updateSlideshow` for execution five seconds in the future so we can display the next image.

Function `getBitmap` (lines 223–240) uses a `ContentResolver` to get an `InputSteam` for a specified image. Then, line 232 uses `BitmapFactory`'s `static` **`decodeStream` method** to create a `Bitmap` from that stream. The arguments to this method are the `InputStream` from which to read the image, a `Rect` for padding around the image (`null` for no padding) and a `BitmapFactory.Options` object indicating how to downsample the image.

12.6 Wrap-Up

In this chapter, you created the **Slideshow** app that enables users to create and manage slideshows. You learned that Android uses content providers to enable apps to save data, retrieve data and make data accessible across apps. In addition, you used built-in content providers to enable the user to select images and audio stored on a device. To take advantage of these built-in content providers, you launched `Intents` and specified the MIME type of the data required. Android then launched an `Activity` that showed the specified type of data to the user or displayed an `Activity`-chooser dialog from which the user could select the `Activity` to use.

You used an `AlertDialog` with a custom `View` to obtain input from the user. You also customized a `ListActivity`'s layout by replacing its default layout with one that contained a `ListView` with its `android:id` attribute set to the value `"@android:id/list"`. You also used subclasses of `ArrayAdapter` to create objects that populate `ListViews` using data from collection objects. When an `ArrayAdapter`'s data set changed, you called its `notifyDataSetChanged` method to refresh the corresponding `ListView`. You learned how to use the view-holder pattern to boost the performance of `ListViews` with complex list-item layouts.

You learned how to use an `Intent` to launch an `Activity` that returns a result and how to process that result when the `Activity` returned. You used a `View`'s `setTag` method to add an `Object` to a `View` so that `Object` could be used later in an event handler.

You used a `MediaPlayer` to play audio from files stored on the device. You also used a `BitmapFactory` to create `Bitmap` objects using settings specified in a `BitmapFactory.Options` object. Finally, you transitioned between images with a `TransitionDrawable` displayed on an `ImageView`.

In Chapter 13, you'll build the **Enhanced Slideshow** app, which lets you use the camera to take pictures, lets you select video to include in the slideshow and lets you save slideshows to the device.

Enhanced Slideshow App

Serializing Data, Taking Pictures with the Camera and Playing Video in a VideoView

Objectives

In this chapter you'll:

- Use an `Intent` and content resolvers to allow the user to select videos from the device's media library.
- Use the device's rear-facing camera to take new pictures to add to the slideshow.
- Use `SurfaceView`, `SurfaceHolder` and `Camera` objects to display a photo preview with various color effects.
- Use an `VideoView` to play videos.
- Use `Serializable` objects to save and load slideshows.
- Save slideshows to the device with `ObjectOutputStream` and `FileOutputStream`.
- Load slideshows from the device with `ObjectInputStream` and `FileInputStream`.

Outline

13.1 Introduction

The **Enhanced Slideshow** app adds several capabilities to Chapter 12's **Slideshow** app. With this version, the user can *save* the slideshows' contents on the device using *file processing* and *object serialization*, so the slideshows are available for playback when the app executes in the future. In addition, when editing a slideshow, the user can *take a new picture* using the device's *camera* (rear facing, by default; Fig. 13.1) and *select videos* from the device to include in the slideshow (Fig. 13.2(a)). As with images, after the user selects a video, a thumbnail is displayed (Fig. 13.2(b)) in the list of items included in the slideshow. When the `SlideshowPlayer Activity` encounters a video (Fig. 13.2), it plays the video in a `VideoView` while the slideshow's music continues to play in the background. [*Note: This app's picture taking and video features require an actual Android device for testing purposes.* At the time of this writing, the Android emulator does not support camera functionality and its video playback capabilities are buggy.]

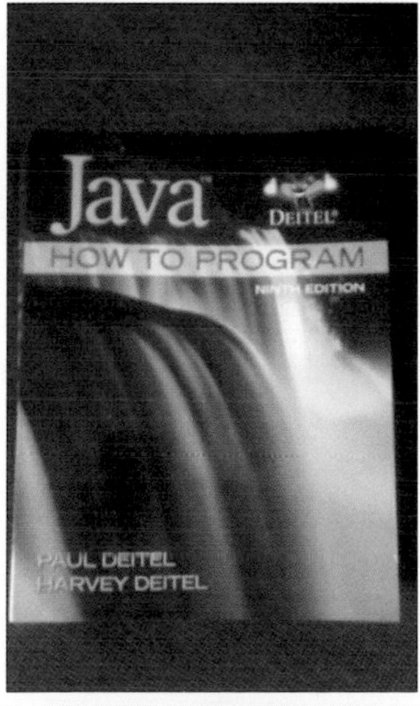

Fig. 13.1 | Previewing a new picture with the camera.

a) Selecting a video from the device

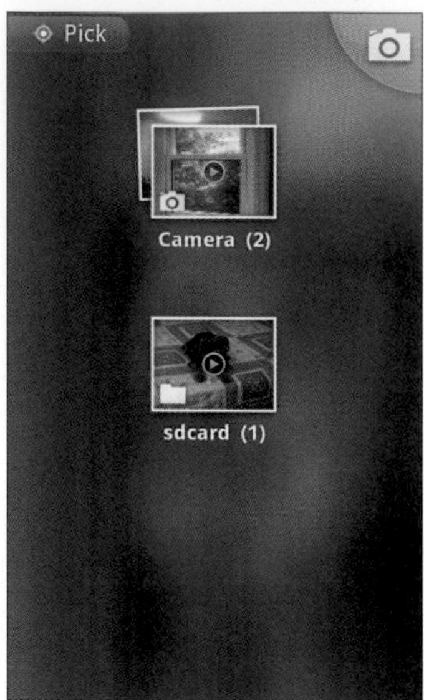

b) Video thumbnail after selection

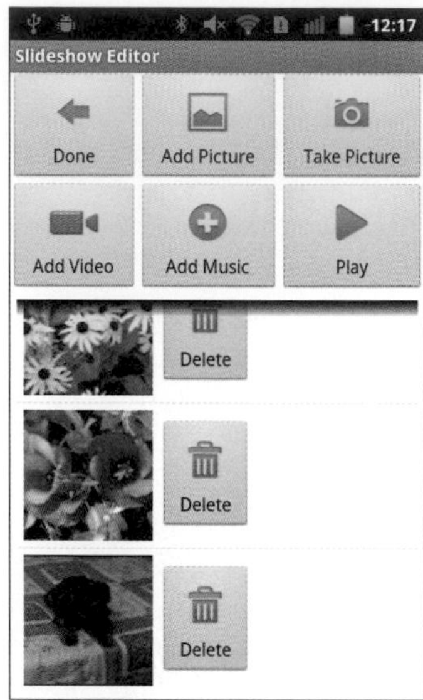

Fig. 13.2 | Selecting a video and displaying the video's thumbnail after selection.

Fig. 13.3 | Video playing in a `VideoView` with the device in landscape mode.

13.2 Test-Driving the Enhanced Slideshow App

Opening and Running the App

Open Eclipse and import the **Enhanced Slideshow** app project. To import the project:

1. Select **File > Import...** to display the **Import** dialog.
2. Expand the **General** node and select **Existing Projects into Workspace**, then click **Next >**.
3. To the right of the **Select root directory:** textfield, click **Browse...** then locate and select the `EnhancedSlideshow` folder.
4. Click **Finish** to import the project.

Right click the app's project in the **Package Explorer** window, then select **Run As > Android Application** from the menu that appears.

Adding Video to Your AVD

Follow the steps in Section 12.2 for adding images and audio to your AVD to add the sample video that we provide in the `video` folder with the book's examples. [*Note:* Again, the emulator does not support video well, so it's best to test this app on a device if possible.]

Adding and Editing a New Slideshow

As in Chapter 12, touch the device's menu button then the **New Slideshow** menu item to display the **Set Slideshow Name** dialog. Name the slideshow, then touch **Set Name** to create the new slideshow and display the **Slideshow Editor**.

Edit the slideshow as you did in Chapter 12. In this version of the app, be sure to test adding a video and taking a new picture. When you finish editing the slideshow and touch the **Done** button, the app returns to the main `Slideshow Activity`, which *saves* the slideshow to the device. [*Note:* This app saves the slideshow when the user returns to the app's main screen after editing the slideshow. The app could certainly be configured to save as changes are made to a slideshow in the **Slideshow Editor**.]

Playing a Slideshow

During playback, when the `SlideshowPlayer Activity` encounters a video, it plays the video in a `VideoView` while the slideshow's music continues to play in the background.

13.3 Technologies Overview

This section presents the new technologies that we use in the **Enhanced Slideshow** app.

File Processing and Object Serialization

The app stores slideshows on the device for viewing later. Earlier apps showed techniques for saving text data in key–value pairs. This app stores entire `SlideshowInfo` objects using **object serialization** (Section 13.5.3). A serialized object is represented as a sequence of bytes that includes the object's data and information about the object's type.

The serialization capabilities are located in package `java.io`. To use an object with the serialization mechanism, the object's class must implement the **`Serializable`** interface, which is a **tagging interface**. Such an interface does not contain methods. Objects of a class that implements `Serializable` are *tagged* as being `Serializable` objects—that is, any object of a class that implements `Serializable` *is a* `Serializable` object. An **`ObjectOutputStream`** serializes `Serializable` objects to a specified `OutputSteam`—in this app, a **`FileOutputStream`**. Tagging objects as `Serializable` is important, because an `ObjectOutputStream` output *only* `Serializable` objects.

This app serializes the entire `List` of `SlideshowInfo` objects by passing the `List` to `ObjectOutputStream`'s **`writeObject` method**. This method creates an **object graph** that contains the `List` object, all of the `SlideshowInfo` objects referenced by the `List`, all of the objects that those `SlideshowInfo` objects reference, and so on. If any object in the graph is not `Serializable`, a **`NotSerializableException`** occurs, so it's important to check the class descriptions for library classes in the online documentation to determine whether the objects you're trying to serialize implement `Serializable` directly or by inheriting that relationship from a superclass in the hierarchy.

A serialized object can be read from a file and **deserialized**—that is, the type information and bytes that represent the object and its data can be used to recreate the object graph in memory. This is accomplished with an **ObjectInputStream** that reads the bytes from a specified InputStream—a **FileInputStream** in this app. ObjectOutputStream's **readObject method** returns the deserialized object as type Object. To use it in the app, you must cast the object to the appropriate type—in this app, List<SlideshowInfo>.

Using a Rear Facing Camera to Take Pictures and Store Them in the Device's Gallery

The **Enhanced Slideshow** app allows the user to take a new picture using the device's rear facing camera, store that picture in the device's **Gallery** and add the new picture to the slideshow. In Section 13.5.5, we use class **Camera** (package android.hardware) and a SurfaceView (package android.view) to display a preview of the picture the user is about to take. When the user touches the screen, our PictureTaker Activity tells the Camera to *take the picture*, then a **Camera.PictureCallback** object is notified that the picture was taken. We capture the image data, store it in the **Gallery** and return its Uri to the SlideshowEditor Activity, which adds the new image to the slideshow. The PictureTaker Activity also provides a menu in which the user can select from the Camera's list of supported *color effects*. The default is to take a color picture, but the cameras in today's devices support color effects, such as *black and white*, *sepia* and *photo negative*. You obtain the list of supported effects from a **Camera.Parameters** object associated with the Camera. Note that we could have launched the built-in camera Activity to allow the user to take pictures, but we wanted to demonstrate how to use camera features directly. You can use the built-in camera Activity, as follows:

```
Intent intent = new Intent(MediaStore.ACTION_IMAGE_CAPTURE);
intput.putExtra(MediaStore.EXTRA_OUTPUT, storageURI);
startActivityForResult(intent, requestCode);
```

in which *storageURI* indicates where to save the photo. Then, you can override onActivityResult to check for *requestCode* and process the results returned from the built-in camera Activity.

Selecting Videos to Play in the Slideshow

The **Slideshow** app used an Intent to launch an Activity for choosing an image from the **Gallery**. We use the same technique in this app (Section 13.5.4) to allow the user to select videos, but specify a different MIME type for the data so that only videos are displayed.

Playing Videos with a VideoView

The **Enhanced Slideshow** app's SlideshowPlayer Activity (Section 13.5.6) uses a **VideoView** to play a slideshow's videos. We'll specify the VideoView's video URI to indicate the location of the video to play and **MediaController** (package android.widget) to provide video playback controls. The VideoView maintains its own MediaPlayer to play the video. We'll use a **MediaPlayer.OnCompletionListener** to determine when the video finishes playing so we can continue playing the slideshow with the next image or video.

13.4 Building the GUI and Resource Files

In this section, we discuss the **Enhanced Slideshow** app's changes to the resources and GUI layouts from Chapter 12's **Slideshow** app. Once again, you can view the complete contents of the resource files by opening them in Eclipse.

13.4.1 Creating the Project

Rather than creating this app from scratch, you can copy Chapter 12's **Slideshow** app and rename it as follows:

1. Copy the `Slideshow` folder and name the new folder `EnhancedSlideshow`.
2. Import the project from the `EnhancedSlideshow` folder into Eclipse.
3. Expand the project's `src` node
4. Right click the package `com.deitel.slideshow` and select **Refactor > Rename...**.
5. In the **Rename Package** dialog, enter `com.deitel.enhancedslideshow`, then click **Preview >**.
6. Click **OK** to change the package name throughout the project.
7. In the `strings.xml` resource file, change the value of the `app_name` `String` resource `"Enhanced Slideshow"`.

13.4.2 AndroidManifest.xml

Figure 13.4 shows this app's `AndroidManifest.xml` file. We've added an `activity` element for the new `PictureTaker` `Activity` (lines 26–29) and indicated that this app requires the `WRITE_EXTERNAL_STORAGE` and `CAMERA` permissions.

```
1  <?xml version="1.0" encoding="utf-8"?>
2  <manifest xmlns:android="http://schemas.android.com/apk/res/android"
3     package="com.deitel.enhancedslideshow" android:versionCode="1"
4     android:versionName="1.0">
5     <application android:icon="@drawable/icon"
6        android:label="@string/app_name"
7        android:debuggable="true">
8        <activity android:name=".Slideshow"
9           android:label="@string/app_name"
10          android:screenOrientation="portrait"
11          android:theme="@android:style/Theme.Light">
12          <intent-filter>
13             <action android:name="android.intent.action.MAIN" />
14             <category android:name="android.intent.category.LAUNCHER" />
15          </intent-filter>
16       </activity>
17
18       <activity android:name=".SlideshowEditor"
19          android:label="@string/slideshow_editor"
20          android:screenOrientation="portrait"></activity>
21
22       <activity android:name=".SlideshowPlayer"
23          android:label="@string/app_name"
24          android:theme="@android:style/Theme.NoTitleBar"></activity>
25
26       <activity android:name=".PictureTaker"
27          android:label="@string/app_name"
```

Fig. 13.4 | `AndroidManifest.xml`. (Part 1 of 2.)

```
            android:theme="@android:style/Theme.NoTitleBar.Fullscreen"
            android:screenOrientation="landscape"></activity>
      </application>
      <uses-sdk android:minSdkVersion="8" />
      <uses-permission
         android:name="android.permission.WRITE_EXTERNAL_STORAGE">
      </uses-permission>
      <uses-permission android:name="android.permission.CAMERA">
      </uses-permission>
   </manifest>
```

Fig. 13.4 | AndroidManifest.xml. (Part 2 of 2.)

13.4.3 SlideshowEditor ListActivity's Modified Layout

Figure 13.5 diagrams the modified layout for the SlideshowEditor ListActivity, which now contains two rows of Buttons in a TableLayout at the top of the GUI.

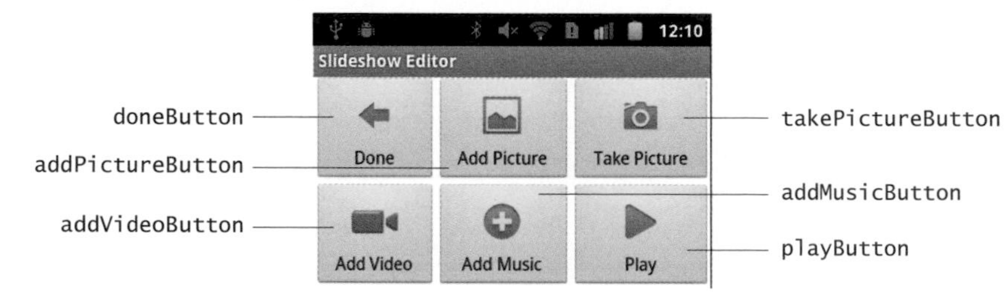

Fig. 13.5 | Modified layout for the SlideshowEditor ListActivity—defined in slideshow_editor.xml.

13.4.4 PictureTaker Activity's Layout

Figure 13.5 shows the PictureTaker Activity's XML layout (camera_preview.xml), which consists of a SurfaceView that fills the screen. The SurfaceView will display the camera's preview image when the user is preparing to take a picture.

```
<?xml version="1.0" encoding="utf-8"?>
<SurfaceView xmlns:android="http://schemas.android.com/apk/res/android"
   android:id="@+id/cameraSurfaceView" android:layout_width="match_parent"
   android:layout_height="match_parent">
</SurfaceView>
```

Fig. 13.6 | PictureTaker Activity's layout—camera_preview.xml.

13.4.5 SlideshowPlayer Activity's Modified Layout

Figure 13.7 shows slideshow_player.xml—the SlideshowPlayer Activity's modified XML layout. In this app, we display an ImageView or a VideoView, depending on whether the current item in the slideshow is an image or a video, respectively. For this reason, we chose a FrameLayout with both the ImageView and the VideoView occupying the entire screen. We programmatically show and hide these Views based on what needs to be displayed at a given time.

```
<?xml version="1.0" encoding="utf-8"?>
<FrameLayout xmlns:android="http://schemas.android.com/apk/res/android"
   android:layout_width="match_parent"
   android:layout_height="match_parent">
   <ImageView android:id="@+id/imageView" android:scaleType="centerInside"
      android:layout_width="match_parent"
      android:layout_height="match_parent"
      android:layout_gravity="center"></ImageView>
   <VideoView android:id="@+id/videoView" android:layout_gravity="center"
      android:layout_width="match_parent"
      android:layout_height="match_parent"></VideoView>
</FrameLayout>
```

Fig. 13.7 | Modified layout for the SlideshowPlayer Activity—defined in slideshow_editor.xml.

13.5 Building the App

This app consists of classes MediaItem (Fig. 13.8), SlideshowInfo (Fig. 13.9), Slideshow (Figs. 13.10–13.15), SlideshowEditor (Figs. 13.16–13.18), PictureTaker (Figs. 13.19–13.24) and SlideshowPlayer (Figs. 13.25–13.27). For the classes that are modified from Chapter 12, we show only what has changed.

13.5.1 MediaItem Class

In the **Slideshow** app, we stored each image's location in a List<String> that was maintained by the Slideshow ListActivity. This app allows the user to include images and video in the app, so we created class MediaItem (Fig. 13.8), which stores a MediaType and a String. The enum MediaType (line 12) contains constants for specifying whether the MediaItem represents an image or a video. Class SlideshowInfo (Section 13.5.2) maintains a List of MediaItems representing all the images and video in a slideshow. Because the **Enhanced Slideshow** app serializes SlideshowInfo objects so the user can play them in the future, class MediaItem implements interface Serializable.

```
1  // MediaItem.java
2  // Represents an image or video in a slideshow.
3  package com.deitel.enhancedslideshow;
4
5  import java.io.Serializable;
6
7  public class MediaItem implements Serializable
8  {
9     private static final long serialVersionUID = 1L; // class's version #
10
```

Fig. 13.8 | MediaItem class used to represent images and videos in a slideshow. (Part 1 of 2.)

```
   // constants for media types
   public static enum MediaType { IMAGE, VIDEO }

   private final MediaType type; // this MediaItem is an IMAGE or VIDEO
   private final String path; // location of this MediaItem

   // constructor
   public MediaItem(MediaType mediaType, String location)
   {
      type = mediaType;
      path = location;
   } // end constructor

   // get the MediaType of this image or video
   public MediaType getType()
   {
      return type;
   } // end method MediaType

   // return the description of this image or video
   public String getPath()
   {
      return path;
   } // end method getDescription
} // end class MediaItem
```

Fig. 13.8 | `MediaItem` class used to represent images and videos in a slideshow. (Part 2 of 2.)

13.5.2 `SlideshowInfo` Class

The `SlideshowInfo` class in this app (Fig. 13.9) has been modified to store a `List<MediaItem>` (line 13) representing image and video locations and the type of each item, rather than a `List<String>` representing just image locations. In addition, methods `getImageList`, `addImage` and `getImageAt` have been renamed as `getMediaItemList` (line 31), `addMediaItem` (line 37) and `getMediaItemAt` (line 43), respectively. Each method now manipulates `MediaItem`s rather than `String`s. To support serialization, class `SlideshowInfo` implements `Serializable` (line 9).

```
1  // SlideshowInfo.java
2  // Stores the data for a single slideshow.
3  package com.deitel.enhancedslideshow;
4
5  import java.io.Serializable;
6  import java.util.ArrayList;
7  import java.util.List;
8
9  public class SlideshowInfo implements Serializable
10 {
11    private static final long serialVersionUID = 1L; // class's version #
12    private String name; // name of this slideshow
```

Fig. 13.9 | Modified `SlideshowInfo` class stores a `List` of `MediaItem`s. (Part 1 of 3.)

```
   private List<MediaItem> mediaItemList; // this slideshow's images
   private String musicPath; // location of music to play

   // constructor
   public SlideshowInfo(String slideshowName)
   {
      name = slideshowName; // set the slideshow name
      mediaItemList = new ArrayList<MediaItem>();
      musicPath = null; // currently there is no music for the slideshow
   } // end SlideshowInfo constructor

   // return this slideshow's name
   public String getName()
   {
      return name;
   } // end method getName

   // return List of MediaItems pointing to the slideshow's images
   public List<MediaItem> getMediaItemList()
   {
      return mediaItemList;
   } // end method getMediaItemList

   // add a new MediaItem
   public void addMediaItem(MediaItem.MediaType type, String path)
   {
      mediaItemList.add(new MediaItem(type, path));
   } // end method addMediaItem

   // return MediaItem at position index
   public MediaItem getMediaItemAt(int index)
   {
      if (index >= 0 && index < mediaItemList.size())
         return mediaItemList.get(index);
      else
         return null;
   } // end method getMediaItemAt

   // return this slideshow's music
   public String getMusicPath()
   {
      return musicPath;
   } // end method getMusicPath

   // set this slideshow's music
   public void setMusicPath(String path)
   {
      musicPath = path;
   } // end method setMusicPath

   // return number of images/videos in the slideshow
   public int size()
   {
```

Fig. 13.9 | Modified `SlideshowInfo` class stores a `List` of `MediaItems`. (Part 2 of 3.)

```
        return mediaItemList.size();
    } // end method size
} // end class SlideshowInfo
```

Fig. 13.9 | Modified `SlideshowInfo` class stores a `List` of `MediaItems`. (Part 3 of 3.)

13.5.3 `Slideshow` Class

In this app, we save the slideshows to the device for future playback. As discussed in Section 13.3, we use object serialization to save the slideshow information. Class `Slideshow` (Figs. 13.10–13.15)—the app's main `Activity`—has been modified to support saving and loading the `List<SlideshowInfo>` object. This section presents only the changes to class `Slideshow`.

`package` and `import` Statements, and Fields

The `Slideshow` subclass of `ListActivity` (Fig. 13.10) has several new `import` statements and a new instance variable. The new features are highlighted. Lines 5–9 and 24 import classes that are used for the file processing and serialization in this app. The instance variable `slideshowFile` (line 53) represents the location of the app's file on the device.

```
1  // Slideshow.java
2  // Main Activity for the Slideshow class.
3  package com.deitel.enhancedslideshow;
4
5  import java.io.File;
6  import java.io.FileInputStream;
7  import java.io.FileOutputStream;
8  import java.io.ObjectInputStream;
9  import java.io.ObjectOutputStream;
10 import java.util.ArrayList;
11 import java.util.List;
12
13 import android.app.AlertDialog;
14 import android.app.ListActivity;
15 import android.content.ContentResolver;
16 import android.content.Context;
17 import android.content.DialogInterface;
18 import android.content.Intent;
19 import android.graphics.Bitmap;
20 import android.graphics.BitmapFactory;
21 import android.net.Uri;
22 import android.os.AsyncTask;
23 import android.os.Bundle;
24 import android.provider.MediaStore;
25 import android.util.Log;
26 import android.view.Gravity;
27 import android.view.LayoutInflater;
28 import android.view.Menu;
```

Fig. 13.10 | `package` and `import` statements, and instance variables for class `Slideshow`. (Part 1 of 2.)

```
import android.view.MenuInflater;
import android.view.MenuItem;
import android.view.View;
import android.view.View.OnClickListener;
import android.view.ViewGroup;
import android.widget.ArrayAdapter;
import android.widget.Button;
import android.widget.EditText;
import android.widget.ImageView;
import android.widget.ListView;
import android.widget.TextView;
import android.widget.Toast;


public class Slideshow extends ListActivity
{
   private static final String TAG = "SLIDESHOW"; // error logging tag

   // used when adding slideshow name as an extra to an Intent
   public static final String NAME_EXTRA = "NAME";

   static List<SlideshowInfo> slideshowList; // List of slideshows
   private ListView slideshowListView; // this ListActivity's ListView
   private SlideshowAdapter slideshowAdapter; // adapter for the ListView
   private File slideshowFile; // File representing location of slideshows

```

Fig. 13.10 | package and import statements, and instance variables for class Slideshow. (Part 2 of 2.)

Overriding Activity *Method* onCreate

Slideshow's onCreate method (Fig. 13.11) creates a File object (lines 63–65) representing the location where this app stores slideshows in the Android file system. The Context class provides methods for accessing the file system. Its method **getExternalFilesDir** returns a File representing an application-specific external storage directory on the device—typically an SD card, but it could be on the device itself if it does not support SD cards. Files you create in this location are automatically managed by the system—if you delete your app, its files are deleted as well. We call getAbsolutePath on the File object, then append /EnhancedSlideshowData.ser to create a path to the file in which this app will store the slideshows. (Keep in mind that a device's external directory may not be available for many reasons that are outside of the control of your app—for example, the user could have removed the SD card.) Line 66 creates an object of our AsyncTask subclass LoadSlideshowsTask (Fig. 13.12) and calls its execute method to load previously saved slideshows (if any). The task does not require any arguments, so we pass null to execute.

```
55      // called when the activity is first created
56      @Override
57      public void onCreate(Bundle savedInstanceState)
58      {
```

Fig. 13.11 | Overriding Activity method onCreate in class Slideshow. (Part 1 of 2.)

```
      super.onCreate(savedInstanceState);
      slideshowListView = getListView(); // get the built-in ListView

      // get File location and start task to load slideshows
      slideshowFile = new File(
         getExternalFilesDir(null).getAbsolutePath() +
            "/EnhancedSlideshowData.ser");
      new LoadSlideshowsTask().execute((Object[]) null);

      // create a new AlertDialog Builder
      AlertDialog.Builder builder = new AlertDialog.Builder(this);
      builder.setTitle(R.string.welcome_message_title);
      builder.setMessage(R.string.welcome_message);
      builder.setPositiveButton(R.string.button_ok, null);
      builder.show();
   } // end method onCreate

```

Fig. 13.11 | Overriding `Activity` method `onCreate` in class `Slideshow`. (Part 2 of 2.)

`LoadSlideshowsTask` Subclass of `AsyncTask`

The `doInBackground` method of class `LoadSlideshowsTask` (Fig. 13.12) checks whether the `EnhancedSlideshowData.ser` file exists (line 84) and, if so, creates an `ObjectInputStream` (lines 88–89). Line 90 calls `ObjectInputStream` method `readObject` to read the `List<SlideshowInfo>` object from the `slideshowFile`. If the file does not exist, or there is an exception when reading from the file, line 115 creates a new `List<SlideshowInfo>` object. If an exception occurs, lines 94–110 use `Activity` method **`runOnUiThread`** to display a `Toast` from the UI thread indicating the problem. When the background task completes, method `onPostExecute` (lines 121–130) is called on the UI thread to set up the `Slideshow`'s `ListView` adapter.

```
76    // Class to load the List<SlideshowInfo> object from the device
77    private class LoadSlideshowsTask extends AsyncTask<Object,Object,Object>
78    {
79       // load from non-GUI thread
80       @Override
81       protected Object doInBackground(Object... arg0)
82       {
83          // if the file exists, read the file; otherwise, create it
84          if (slideshowFile.exists())
85          {
86             try
87             {
88                ObjectInputStream input = new ObjectInputStream(
89                   new FileInputStream(slideshowFile));
90                slideshowList = (List<SlideshowInfo>) input.readObject();
91             } // end try
```

Fig. 13.12 | Class `LoadSlideshowsTask` deserializes the `List<SlideshowInfo>` object from a file or creates the object if the file does not exist. (Part 1 of 2.)

```
            catch (final Exception e)
            {
               runOnUiThread(
                  new Runnable()
                  {
                     public void run()
                     {
                        // display error reading message
                        Toast message = Toast.makeText(Slideshow.this,
                           R.string.message_error_reading,
                           Toast.LENGTH_LONG);
                        message.setGravity(Gravity.CENTER,
                           message.getXOffset() / 2,
                           message.getYOffset() / 2);
                        message.show(); // display the Toast
                        Log.v(TAG, e.toString());
                     } // end method run
                  } // end Runnable
               ); // end call to runOnUiThread
            } // end catch
         } // end if

         if (slideshowList == null) // if null, create it
            slideshowList = new ArrayList<SlideshowInfo>();

         return (Object) null; // method must satisfy the return type
      } // end method doInBackground

      // create the ListView's adapter on the GUI thread
      @Override
      protected void onPostExecute(Object result)
      {
         super.onPostExecute(result);

         // create and set the ListView's adapter
         slideshowAdapter =
            new SlideshowAdapter(Slideshow.this, slideshowList);
         slideshowListView.setAdapter(slideshowAdapter);
      } // end method onPostEecute
   } // end class LoadSlideshowsTask

```

Fig. 13.12 | Class `LoadSlideshowsTask` deserializes the `List<SlideshowInfo>` object from a file or creates the object if the file does not exist. (Part 2 of 2.)

`SaveSlideshowsTask` Subclass of `AsyncTask`

The `doInBackground` method of class `SaveSlideshowsTask` (Fig. 13.13) checks whether the `EnhancedSlideshowData.ser` file exists (line 143) and, if not, creates the file. Next, lines 147–148 create an `ObjectOutputStream`. Line 149 calls `ObjectOutputStream` method `writeObject` to write the `List<SlideshowInfo>` object into `slideshowFile`. If an exception occurs, lines 154–169 use `Activity` method `runOnUiThread` to display a `Toast` from the UI thread indicating the problem.

```
   // Class to save the List<SlideshowInfo> object to the device
   private class SaveSlideshowsTask extends AsyncTask<Object,Object,Object>
   {
      // save from non-GUI thread
      @Override
      protected Object doInBackground(Object... arg0)
      {
         try
         {
            // if the file doesn't exist, create it
            if (!slideshowFile.exists())
               slideshowFile.createNewFile();

            // create ObjectOutputStream, then write slideshowList to it
            ObjectOutputStream output = new ObjectOutputStream(
               new FileOutputStream(slideshowFile));
            output.writeObject(slideshowList);
            output.close();
         } // end try
         catch (final Exception e)
         {
            runOnUiThread(
               new Runnable()
               {
                  public void run()
                  {
                     // display error reading message
                     Toast message = Toast.makeText(Slideshow.this,
                        R.string.message_error_writing, Toast.LENGTH_LONG);
                     message.setGravity(Gravity.CENTER,
                        message.getXOffset() / 2,
                        message.getYOffset() / 2);
                     message.show(); // display the Toast
                     Log.v(TAG, e.toString());
                  } // end method run
               } // end Runnable
            ); // end call to runOnUiThread
         } // end catch

         return (Object) null; // method must satisfy the return type
      } // end method doInBackground
   } // end class SaveSlideshowsTask

```

Fig. 13.13 | Class `SaveSlideshowsTask` serializes the `List<SlideshowInfo>` object to a file.

Overriding `Activity` *Method* `onActivityResult`

Method `onActivityResult` (Fig. 13.14) has been changed to save the `List<SlideshowInfo>` object once the user returns from editing a slideshow. To do so, line 251 creates an object of the `AsyncTask` subclass `SaveSlideshowsTask` (Fig. 13.13) and invokes its `execute` method.

```
   // refresh ListView after slideshow editing is complete
   @Override
   protected void onActivityResult(int requestCode, int resultCode,
      Intent data)
   {
      super.onActivityResult(requestCode, resultCode, data);
      new SaveSlideshowsTask().execute((Object[]) null); // save slideshows
      slideshowAdapter.notifyDataSetChanged(); // refresh the adapter
   } // end method onActivityResult

```

Fig. 13.14 | Overriding Activity methods onCreateOptionsMenu, onOptionsItemSelected and onActivityResult.

Method getThumbnail

Method getThumbnail (Fig. 13.15) has been updated to support loading thumbnails for both images and videos (lines 439–454).

```
438    // utility method to get a thumbnail image Bitmap
439    public static Bitmap getThumbnail(MediaItem.MediaType type, Uri uri,
440       ContentResolver cr, BitmapFactory.Options options)
441    {
442       Bitmap bitmap = null;
443       int id = Integer.parseInt(uri.getLastPathSegment());
444
445       if (type == MediaItem.MediaType.IMAGE) // if it is an image
446          bitmap = MediaStore.Images.Thumbnails.getThumbnail(cr, id,
447             MediaStore.Images.Thumbnails.MICRO_KIND, options);
448       else if (type == MediaItem.MediaType.VIDEO) // if it is a video
449          bitmap = MediaStore.Video.Thumbnails.getThumbnail(cr, id,
450             MediaStore.Video.Thumbnails.MICRO_KIND, options);
451
452       return bitmap;
453    } // end method getThumbnail
```

Fig. 13.15 | Method getThumbnail updated to return an image thumbnail or a video thumbnail.

13.5.4 SlideshowEditor Class

Class SlideshowEditor (Figs. 13.16–13.18) now supports taking a picture and selecting videos to include in a slideshow. This section shows the changes required to support these new features.

Overriding Activity *Method* onActivityResult

Class SlideshowEditor contains two more Buttons that initiate selecting a video and taking a picture, respectively. For this reason, we've added the constants at lines 71–72 (Fig. 13.16) which are passed to Activity method startActivityForResult then returned to method onActivityResult to identify which Activity returned the result. Method onActivityResult has been modified to use these constants to process the Uri that's returned for the picture or video.

```
   // set IDs for each type of media result
   private static final int PICTURE_ID = 1;
   private static final int MUSIC_ID = 2;
   private static final int VIDEO_ID = 3;
   private static final int TAKE_PICTURE_ID = 4;

   // called when an Activity launched from this Activity returns
   @Override
   protected final void onActivityResult(int requestCode, int resultCode,
      Intent data)
   {
      if (resultCode == RESULT_OK) // if there was no error
      {
         Uri selectedUri = data.getData();

         // if the Activity returns an image
         if (requestCode == PICTURE_ID ||
            requestCode == TAKE_PICTURE_ID || requestCode == VIDEO_ID )
         {
            // determine media type
            MediaItem.MediaType type = (requestCode == VIDEO_ID ?
               MediaItem.MediaType.VIDEO : MediaItem.MediaType.IMAGE);

            // add new MediaItem to the slideshow
            slideshow.addMediaItem(type, selectedUri.toString());

            // refresh the ListView
            slideshowEditorAdapter.notifyDataSetChanged();
         } // end if
         else if (requestCode == MUSIC_ID) // Activity returns music
            slideshow.setMusicPath(selectedUri.toString());
      } // end if
   } // end method onActivityResult
```

Fig. 13.16 | Updated constants and method `onActivityResult`.

Event Listeners for the `takePictureButton` *and* `addVideoButton`

Figure 13.17 presents the event handlers for the `takePictureButton` (lines 128–141) and the `addVideoButton` (lines 144–155). To select a video, the `addVideoButtonListener` uses the same techniques shown in Fig. 12.29, but sets the MIME type to `"video/*"` so that the user can select from the videos stored on the device.

```
127    // called when the user touches the "Take Picture" Button
128    private OnClickListener takePictureButtonListener =
129       new OnClickListener()
130       {
131          // launch image choosing activity
132          @Override
133          public void onClick(View v)
134          {
```

Fig. 13.17 | Event Listeners for the `takePictureButton` and `addVideoButton`. (Part 1 of 2.)

```
            // create new Intent to launch the Slideshowplayer Activity
            Intent takePicture =
               new Intent(SlideshowEditor.this, PictureTaker.class);

            startActivityForResult(takePicture, TAKE_PICTURE_ID);
         } // end method onClick
      }; // end OnClickListener takePictureButtonListener

   // called when the user touches the "Add Picture" Button
   private OnClickListener addVideoButtonListener = new OnClickListener()
   {
      // launch image choosing activity
      @Override
      public void onClick(View v)
      {
         Intent intent = new Intent(Intent.ACTION_GET_CONTENT);
         intent.setType("video/*");
         startActivityForResult(Intent.createChooser(intent,
            getResources().getText(R.string.chooser_video)), VIDEO_ID);
      } // end method onClick
   }; // end OnClickListener addVideoButtonListener
```

Fig. 13.17 | Event Listeners for the `takePictureButton` and `addVideoButton`. (Part 2 of 2.)

Updated `LoadThumbnailTask` *Sublcass of* `AsyncTask`

Class `LoadThumbnailTask` (Fig. 13.18) has been updated to pass the `MediaItem`'s type to `Slideshow` method `getThumbnail`, which returns a thumbnail `Bitmap` for the specified image or video.

```
   // task to load thumbnails in a separate thread
   private class LoadThumbnailTask extends AsyncTask<Object,Object,Bitmap>
   {
      ImageView imageView; // displays the thumbnail

      // load thumbnail: ImageView, MediaType and Uri as args
      @Override
      protected Bitmap doInBackground(Object... params)
      {
         imageView = (ImageView) params[0];

         return Slideshow.getThumbnail((MediaItem.MediaType)params[1],
            (Uri) params[2], getContentResolver(),
            new BitmapFactory.Options());
      } // end method doInBackground

      // set thumbnail on ListView
      @Override
      protected void onPostExecute(Bitmap result)
      {
```

Fig. 13.18 | Class `LoadThumbnailTask` loads image or video thumbnails in a separate thread. (Part 1 of 2.)

```
            super.onPostExecute(result);
            imageView.setImageBitmap(result);
        } // end method onPostExecute
    } // end class LoadThumbnailTask
```

Fig. 13.18 | Class `LoadThumbnailTask` loads image or video thumbnails in a separate thread. (Part 2 of 2.)

13.5.5 `PictureTaker` Subclass of `Activity`

Class `PictureTaker` (Figs. 13.19–13.24) allows the user to take a picture that will be added to the slideshow. While previewing the picture, the user can touch the screen to take the picture.

`package` and `import` Statements, and Instance Variables of Class `SlideshowEditor`

Figure 13.19 begins the definition of class `PictureTaker`. We've highlighted the `import` statements for the new classes and interfaces discussed in Section 13.3 and used in this section. Lines 31–32 declare the `SurfaceView` that displays the live camera-preview image and the `SurfaceHolder` that manages the `SurfaceView`. Line 35 declares a `Camera`, which provides access to the device's camera hardware. The `List<String>` named `effects` (line 36) stores the camera's supported color effects—we'll use this to populate a menu from which the user can select the effect to apply to the picture (such as black and white, sepia, etc.). The `List<Camera.Size>` named `sizes` (line 37) stores the camera's supported image-preview sizes—we'll use the first supported size for the image preview in this app. The `String` `effect` is initialized to `Camera.Parameter`'s `EFFECT_NONE` constant to indicate that no color effect is selected.

```
1   // PictureTaker.java
2   // Activity for taking a picture with the device's camera
3   package com.deitel.enhancedslideshow;
4
5   import java.io.IOException;
6   import java.io.OutputStream;
7   import java.util.List;
8
9   import android.app.Activity;
10  import android.content.ContentValues;
11  import android.content.Intent;
12  import android.hardware.Camera;
13  import android.net.Uri;
14  import android.os.Bundle;
15  import android.provider.MediaStore.Images;
16  import android.util.Log;
17  import android.view.Gravity;
18  import android.view.Menu;
19  import android.view.MenuItem;
20  import android.view.MotionEvent;
21  import android.view.SurfaceHolder;
```

Fig. 13.19 | `PictureTaker` `package` statement, `import` statements and fields. (Part 1 of 2.)

```
import android.view.SurfaceView;
import android.view.View;
import android.view.View.OnTouchListener;
import android.widget.Toast;

public class PictureTaker extends Activity
{
   private static final String TAG = "PICTURE_TAKER"; // for logging errors

   private SurfaceView surfaceView; // used to display camera preview
   private SurfaceHolder surfaceHolder; // manages the SurfaceView changes
   private boolean isPreviewing; // is the preview running?

   private Camera camera; // used to capture image data
   private List<String> effects; // supported color effects for camera
   private List<Camera.Size> sizes; // supported preview sizes for camera
   private String effect = Camera.Parameters.EFFECT_NONE; // default effec

```

Fig. 13.19 | `PictureTaker` package statement, `import` statements and fields. (Part 2 of 2.)

Overriding `Activity` *Method* `onCreate`

Method `onCreate` (Fig. 13.20) prepares the view to display a photo preview, much like Android's actual **Camera** app. First we create the `SurfaceView` and register a listener for its touch events—when the user touches the screen, the `PictureTaker` `Activity` will capture the picture and store it in the device's gallery. Next, we create the `SurfaceHolder` and register an object to handle its `Callbacks`—these occur when the `SurfaceView` being managed is created, changed or destroyed. Finally, prior to Android 3.0 line 56 was required. `SurfaceHolder` method `setType` and its constant argument are now both deprecated and will simply be ignored in Android 3.0 and higher.

```
40       // called when the activity is first created
41       @Override
42       public void onCreate(Bundle bundle)
43       {
44          super.onCreate(bundle);
45          setContentView(R.layout.camera_preview); // set the layout
46
47          // initialize the surfaceView and set its touch listener
48          surfaceView = (SurfaceView) findViewById(R.id.cameraSurfaceView);
49          surfaceView.setOnTouchListener(touchListener);
50
51          // initialize surfaceHolder and set object to handles its callbacks
52          surfaceHolder = surfaceView.getHolder();
53          surfaceHolder.addCallback(surfaceCallback);
54
55          // required before Android 3.0 for camera preview
56          surfaceHolder.setType(SurfaceHolder.SURFACE_TYPE_PUSH_BUFFERS);
57       } // end method onCreate
58
```

Fig. 13.20 | Overriding `Activity` method `onCreate` in class `PictureTaker`.

Overriding `Activity` *Methods* **`onCreateOptionsMenu`** *and* **`onOptionsItemSelected`**

Method `onCreateOptionsMenu` (Fig. 13.21, lines 60–70) displays the list of the camera's supported color effects in a menu. When the user selects one of these options, method `onOptionsItemSelected` gets the camera's `Camera.Parameter` object (line 76) then uses its **`setColorEffect`** method to set the effect. Line 78 uses the camera's **`setParameters`** method to reconfigure the camera. At this point, the selected color effect is applied to the camera preview image on the device's screen.

```
59      // create the Activity's menu from list of supported color effects
60      @Override
61      public boolean onCreateOptionsMenu(Menu menu)
62      {
63         super.onCreateOptionsMenu(menu);
64
65         // create menu items for each supported effect
66         for (String effect : effects)
67            menu.add(effect);
68
69         return true;
70      } // end method onCreateOptionsMenu
71
72      // handle choice from options menu
73      @Override
74      public boolean onOptionsItemSelected(MenuItem item)
75      {
76         Camera.Parameters p = camera.getParameters(); // get parameters
77         p.setColorEffect(item.getTitle().toString()); // set color effect
78         camera.setParameters(p); // apply the new parameters
79         return true;
80      } // end method onOptionsItemSelected
81
```

Fig. 13.21 | Overriding `Activity` methods `onCreateOptionsMenu` and `onOptionsItemSelected`.

Handling the **`SurfaceHolder`***'s* **`Callbacks`**

When the `SurfaceView` is created, changed or destroyed, its `SurfaceHolder`'s `Callback` methods are called. Figure 13.22 presents the anonymous inner class that implements `SurfaceHolder.Callback`.

```
   // handles SurfaceHolder.Callback events
   private SurfaceHolder.Callback surfaceCallback =
      new SurfaceHolder.Callback()
      {
         // release resources after the SurfaceView is destroyed
         @Override
         public void surfaceDestroyed(SurfaceHolder arg0)
         {
```

Fig. 13.22 | `PictureTaker` package statement, `import` statements and fields. (Part 1 of 2.)

```
90             camera.stopPreview(); // stop the Camera preview
91             isPreviewing = false;
92             camera.release(); // release the Camera's Object resources
93          } // end method surfaceDestroyed
94
95          // initialize the camera when the SurfaceView is created
96          @Override
97          public void surfaceCreated(SurfaceHolder arg0)
98          {
99             // get camera and its supported color effects/preview sizes
100            camera = Camera.open(); // defaults to back facing camera
101            effects = camera.getParameters().getSupportedColorEffects();
102            sizes = camera.getParameters().getSupportedPreviewSizes();
103         } // end method surfaceCreated
104
105         @Override
106         public void surfaceChanged(SurfaceHolder holder, int format,
107            int width, int height)
108         {
109            if (isPreviewing) // if there's already a preview running
110               camera.stopPreview(); // stop the preview
111
112            // configure and set the camera parameters
113            Camera.Parameters p = camera.getParameters();
114            p.setPreviewSize(sizes.get(0).width, sizes.get(0).height);
115            p.setColorEffect(effect); // use the current selected effect
116            camera.setParameters(p); // apply the new parameters
117
118            try
119            {
120               camera.setPreviewDisplay(holder); // display using holder
121            } // end try
122            catch (IOException e)
123            {
124               Log.v(TAG, e.toString());
125            } // end catch
126
127            camera.startPreview(); // begin the preview
128            isPreviewing = true;
129         } // end method surfaceChanged
130      }; // end SurfaceHolder.Callback
131
```

Fig. 13.22 | `PictureTaker` package statement, `import` statements and fields. (Part 2 of 2.)

`SurfaceHolder.Callback`'s **`surfaceDestroyed` method** (lines 88–93) stops the photo preview and releases the `Camera`'s resources. We use `SurfaceHolder.Callback`'s **`surfaceCreated` method** (lines 96–103) to get a `Camera` and its supported features. `Camera`'s `static` **`open` method** gets a `Camera` object that allows the app to use the device's rear facing camera. Next, we use the `Camera`'s `Parameters` object to get the `List<String>` representing the camera's supported effects and the `List<Camera.Size>` representing the supported preview image sizes. [*Note:* We did not catch the open method's possible `RuntimeException` that occurs if the camera is not available.]

The `SurfaceHolder.Callback` interface's **`surfaceChanged` method** (lines 105–129) is called each time the size or format of the `SurfaceView` changes—typically when the device is rotated and when the `SurfaceView` is first created and displayed. (In the manifest, we've disabled rotation for this `Activity`.) Line 109 checks if the camera preview is running and if so stops it using `Camera`'s **`stopPreview` method**. Next, we get the `Camera`'s `Parameters` then call the **`setPreviewSize` method** to set the camera's preview size using the width and height of the first object in `sizes` (the `List<Camera.Size>` containing the supported preview sizes). We call `setColorEffect` to apply the current color effect to the preview (and any photos to be taken). We then reconfigure the `Camera` by calling its `setParameters` method to apply the changes. Line 120 passes the `SurfaceHolder` to `Camera`'s **`setPreviewDisplay` method**—this indicates that the preview will be displayed on our `SurfaceView`. Line 127 then starts the preview using `Camera`'s **`startPreview`** method.

Handling the `Camera`'s `PictureCallback`s

Figure 13.23 defines the **`Camera.PictureCallback`** anonymous class that receives the image data after the user takes a picture. Method **`onPictureTaken`** takes a `byte` array containing the picture data and the `Camera` that was used to take the picture. In this example, the `imageData` `byte` array stores the JPEG format version of the picture, so we can simply save the `imageData` array to the device (lines 154–158). Lines 161–163 create a new `Intent` and use its `setData` method to specify the `Uri` of the saved image as the data to return from this `Activity`. `Activity` method **`setResult`** (line 163) is used to indicate that there was no error and set the `returnIntent` as the result. The `SlideshowEditor` `Activity` will use this `Intent`'s data to store the image in the slideshow and load the corresponding thumbnail image.

```
132    // handles Camera callbacks
133    Camera.PictureCallback pictureCallback = new Camera.PictureCallback()
134    {
135       // called when the user takes a picture
136       public void onPictureTaken(byte[] imageData, Camera c)
137       {
138          // use "Slideshow_" + current time in ms as new image file name
139          String fileName = "Slideshow_" + System.currentTimeMillis();
140
141          // create a ContentValues and configure new image's data
142          ContentValues values = new ContentValues();
143          values.put(Images.Media.TITLE, fileName);
144          values.put(Images.Media.DATE_ADDED, System.currentTimeMillis());
145          values.put(Images.Media.MIME_TYPE, "image/jpg");
146
147          // get a Uri for the location to save the file
148          Uri uri = getContentResolver().insert(
149             Images.Media.EXTERNAL_CONTENT_URI, values);
150
```

Fig. 13.23 | Implementing `Camera.PictureCallback` to save a picture. (Part 1 of 2.)

```
         try
         {
            // get an OutputStream to uri
            OutputStream outStream =
               getContentResolver().openOutputStream(uri);
            outStream.write(imageData); // output the image
            outStream.flush(); // empty the buffer
            outStream.close(); // close the stream

            // Intent for returning data to SlideshowEditor
            Intent returnIntent = new Intent();
            returnIntent.setData(uri); // return Uri to SlideshowEditor
            setResult(RESULT_OK, returnIntent); // took pic successfully

            // display a message indicating that the image was saved
            Toast message = Toast.makeText(PictureTaker.this,
               R.string.message_saved, Toast.LENGTH_SHORT);
            message.setGravity(Gravity.CENTER, message.getXOffset() / 2,
               message.getYOffset() / 2);
            message.show(); // display the Toast

            finish(); // finish and return to SlideshowEditor
         } // end try
         catch (IOException ex)
         {
            setResult(RESULT_CANCELED); // error taking picture

            // display a message indicating that the image was saved
            Toast message = Toast.makeText(PictureTaker.this,
               R.string.message_error_saving, Toast.LENGTH_SHORT);
            message.setGravity(Gravity.CENTER, message.getXOffset() / 2,
               message.getYOffset() / 2);
            message.show(); // display the Toast
         } // end catch
      } // end method onPictureTaken
   }; // end pictureCallback

```

Fig. 13.23 | Implementing `Camera.PictureCallback` to save a picture. (Part 2 of 2.)

Handling the **`SurfaceView`***'s Touch Events*

The `onTouch` method (Fig. 13.24) takes a picture when the user touches the screen. `Camera`'s `takePicture` method (line 195) asynchronously takes a picture with the device's camera. This method receives several listeners as arguments. The first is an instance of **`Camera.ShutterCallback`** that's notified just after the image is captured. This is the ideal place to provide visual or audio feedback that the picture was taken. We don't use this callback in the app, so we pass `null` as the first argument. The last two listeners are instances of `Camera.PictureCallback` that enable the app to receive and process the RAW image data (i.e., uncompressed image data) and JPEG image data, respectively. We don't use the RAW data in this app, so `takePicture`'s second argument is also `null`. The third call back uses our `pictureCallback` (Fig. 13.23) to process the JPEG image.

```
   // takes picture when user touches the screen
   private OnTouchListener touchListener = new OnTouchListener()
   {
      @Override
      public boolean onTouch(View v, MotionEvent event)
      {
         // take a picture
         camera.takePicture(null, null, pictureCallback);
         return false;
      } // end method onTouch
   }; // end touchListener
} // end class PictureTaker
```

Fig. 13.24 | Implementing `OnTouchListener` to handle touch events.

13.5.6 `SlideshowPlayer` Class

The `SlideshowPlayer` `Activity` (Figs. 13.25–13.27) plays a slideshow with accompanying background music. We've updated `SlideshowPlayer` to play any videos that are included in the slideshow. This section shows only the parts of the class that have changed.

`package` and `import` Statements, and Instance Variables of Class `SlideshowEditor`

Figure 13.25 begins class `SlideshowPlayer`. We've highlighted the `import` statements for the new classes and interfaces discussed in Section 13.3 and used in this section. Variable `videoView` is used to manipulate the `VideoView` on which videos are played.

```
// SlideshowPlayer.java
// Plays the selected slideshow that's passed as an Intent extra
package com.deitel.enhancedslideshow;

import java.io.FileNotFoundException;
import java.io.InputStream;

import android.app.Activity;
import android.content.ContentResolver;
import android.graphics.Bitmap;
import android.graphics.BitmapFactory;
import android.graphics.drawable.BitmapDrawable;
import android.graphics.drawable.Drawable;
import android.graphics.drawable.TransitionDrawable;
import android.media.MediaPlayer;
import android.media.MediaPlayer.OnCompletionListener;
import android.net.Uri;
import android.os.AsyncTask;
import android.os.Bundle;
import android.os.Handler;
import android.util.Log;
import android.view.View;
import android.widget.ImageView;
import android.widget.MediaController;
import android.widget.VideoView;
```

Fig. 13.25 | `SlideshowPlayer` package statement, `import` statements and fields. (Part 1 of 2.)

```

public class SlideshowPlayer extends Activity
{
   private static final String TAG = "SLIDESHOW"; // error logging tag

   // constants for saving slideshow state when config changes
   private static final String MEDIA_TIME = "MEDIA_TIME";
   private static final String IMAGE_INDEX = "IMAGE_INDEX";
   private static final String SLIDESHOW_NAME = "SLIDESHOW_NAME";

   private static final int DURATION = 5000; // 5 seconds per slide
   private ImageView imageView; // displays the current image
   private VideoView videoView; // displays the current video
   private String slideshowName; // name of current slideshow
   private SlideshowInfo slideshow; // slideshow being played
   private BitmapFactory.Options options; // options for loading images
   private Handler handler; // used to update the slideshow
   private int nextItemIndex; // index of the next image to display
   private int mediaTime; // time in ms from which media should play
   private MediaPlayer mediaPlayer; // plays the background music, if any

```

Fig. 13.25 | `SlideshowPlayer` package statement, `import` statements and fields. (Part 2 of 2.)

Overriding `Activity` *Method* `onCreate`

Lines 55–65 are the only changes in method `onCreate` (Fig. 13.26). Line 55 gets the layout's `VideoView`, then lines 56–65 register its **`OnCompletionListener`**, which is notified when a video in the `VideoView` completes playing. Method **`onCompletion`** calls the `Handler`'s `postUpdate` method and passes the `updateSlideshow` `Runnable` as an argument to process the next image or video in the slideshow.

```
47    // initializes the SlideshowPlayer Activity
48    @Override
49    public void onCreate(Bundle savedInstanceState)
50    {
51       super.onCreate(savedInstanceState);
52       setContentView(R.layout.slideshow_player);
53
54       imageView = (ImageView) findViewById(R.id.imageView);
55       videoView = (VideoView) findViewById(R.id.videoView);
56       videoView.setOnCompletionListener( // set video completion handler
57          new OnCompletionListener()
58          {
59             @Override
60             public void onCompletion(MediaPlayer mp)
61             {
62                handler.post(updateSlideshow); // update the slideshow
63             } // end method onCompletion
64          } // end anonymous inner class
65       ); // end OnCompletionListener
```

Fig. 13.26 | Overriding `Activity` method `onCreate` in class `SlideshowPlayer`. (Part 1 of 2.)

```

      if (savedInstanceState == null) // Activity starting
      {
         // get slideshow name from Intent's extras
         slideshowName = getIntent().getStringExtra(Slideshow.NAME_EXTRA);
         mediaTime = 0; // position in media clip
         nextItemIndex = 0; // start from first image
      } // end if
      else // Activity resuming
      {
         // get the play position that was saved when config changed
         mediaTime = savedInstanceState.getInt(MEDIA_TIME);

         // get index of image that was displayed when config changed
         nextItemIndex = savedInstanceState.getInt(IMAGE_INDEX);

         // get name of slideshow that was playing when config changed
         slideshowName = savedInstanceState.getString(SLIDESHOW_NAME);
      } // end else

      // get SlideshowInfo for slideshow to play
      slideshow = Slideshow.getSlideshowInfo(slideshowName);

      // configure BitmapFactory.Options for loading images
      options = new BitmapFactory.Options();
      options.inSampleSize = 4; // sample at 1/4 original width/height

      // if there is music to play
      if (slideshow.getMusicPath() != null)
      {
         // try to create a MediaPlayer to play the music
         try
         {
            mediaPlayer = new MediaPlayer();
            mediaPlayer.setDataSource(
               this, Uri.parse(slideshow.getMusicPath()));
            mediaPlayer.prepare(); // prepare the MediaPlayer to play
            mediaPlayer.setLooping(true); // loop the music
            mediaPlayer.seekTo(mediaTime); // seek to mediaTime
         } // end try
         catch (Exception e)
         {
            Log.v(TAG, e.toString());
         } // end catch
      } // end if

      handler = new Handler(); // create handler to control slideshow
   } // end method onCreate
```

Fig. 13.26 | Overriding `Activity` method `onCreate` in class `SlideshowPlayer`. (Part 2 of 2.)

Changes to the `updateSlideshow Runnable`

The `updateSlideshow Runnable` (Fig. 13.27) now processes images *and* videos. In method run, if the slideshow hasn't completed, lines 193–208 determine whether the next item in the slideshow is an image or a video. If it's an image, lines 197–198 show the `imageView` and hide the `videoView`, then line 199 creates a `LoadImageTask AsyncTask` (defined in lines 213–249) to load and display the image. Otherwise, lines 203–204 hide the `imageView` and show the `videoView`, then line 205 calls `playVideo` (defined in lines 272–279). The `playVideo` method plays a video file located at the given `Uri`. Line 275 calls `VideoView`'s `setVideoUri` method to specify the location of the video file to play. Lines 276–277 set the `MediaController` for the `VideoView`, which displays video playback controls. Line 278 begins the video playback using `VideoView`'s `start` method.

```
178    // anonymous inner class that implements Runnable to control slideshow
179    private Runnable updateSlideshow = new Runnable()
180    {
181       @Override
182       public void run()
183       {
184          if (nextItemIndex >= slideshow.size())
185          {
186             // if there is music playing
187             if (mediaPlayer != null && mediaPlayer.isPlaying())
188                mediaPlayer.reset(); // slideshow done, reset mediaPlayer
189             finish(); // return to launching Activity
190          } // end if
191          else
192          {
193             MediaItem item = slideshow.getMediaItemAt(nextItemIndex);
194
195             if (item.getType() == MediaItem.MediaType.IMAGE)
196             {
197                imageView.setVisibility(View.VISIBLE); // show imageView
198                videoView.setVisibility(View.INVISIBLE); // hide videoView
199                new LoadImageTask().execute(Uri.parse(item.getPath()));
200             } // end if
201             else
202             {
203                imageView.setVisibility(View.INVISIBLE); // hide imageView
204                videoView.setVisibility(View.VISIBLE); // show videoView
205                playVideo(Uri.parse(item.getPath())); // plays the video
206             } // end else
207
208             ++nextItemIndex;
209          } // end else
210       } // end method run
211
212       // task to load thumbnails in a separate thread
213       class LoadImageTask extends AsyncTask<Uri, Object, Bitmap>
214       {
215          // load iamges
216          @Override
217          protected Bitmap doInBackground(Uri... params)
218          {
```

Fig. 13.27 | `Runnable` that handles the display of an image or playing of a video. (Part 1 of 3.)

```
            return getBitmap(params[0], getContentResolver(), options);
         } // end method doInBackground

         // set thumbnail on ListView
         @Override
         protected void onPostExecute(Bitmap result)
         {
            super.onPostExecute(result);
            BitmapDrawable next = new BitmapDrawable(result);
            next.setGravity(android.view.Gravity.CENTER);
            Drawable previous = imageView.getDrawable();

            // if previous is a TransitionDrawable,
            // get its second Drawable item
            if (previous instanceof TransitionDrawable)
               previous = ((TransitionDrawable) previous).getDrawable(1);

            if (previous == null)
               imageView.setImageDrawable(next);
            else
            {
               Drawable[] drawables = { previous, next };
               TransitionDrawable transition =
                  new TransitionDrawable(drawables);
               imageView.setImageDrawable(transition);
               transition.startTransition(1000);
            } // end else

            handler.postDelayed(updateSlideshow, DURATION);
         } // end method onPostExecute
      } // end class LoadImageTask

      // utility method to get a Bitmap from a Uri
      public Bitmap getBitmap(Uri uri, ContentResolver cr,
         BitmapFactory.Options options)
      {
         Bitmap bitmap = v;

         // get the image
         try
         {
            InputStream input = cr.openInputStream(uri);
            bitmap = BitmapFactory.decodeStream(input, null, options);
         } // end try
         catch (FileNotFoundException e)
         {
            Log.v(TAG, e.toString());
         } // end catch

         return bitmap;
      } // end method getBitmap

```

Fig. 13.27 | `Runnable` that handles the display of an image or playing of a video. (Part 2 of 3.)

```
        // play a video
        private void playVideo(Uri videoUri)
        {
           // configure the video view and play video
           videoView.setVideoURI(videoUri);
           videoView.setMediaController(
              new MediaController(SlideshowPlayer.this));
           videoView.start(); // start the video
        } // end method playVideo
     }; // end Runnable updateSlideshow
  } // end class SlideshowPlayer
```

Fig. 13.27 | `Runnable` that handles the display of an image or playing of a video. (Part 3 of 3.)

13.6 Wrap-Up

In this app, you used the `java.io` package's object serialization capabilities to store slideshows on the device for viewing later. To use an object with the serialization mechanism, you implemented the tagging interface `Serializable`. You used an `ObjectOutputStream`'s `writeObject` method to create an object graph and serialize objects. You read and deserialized objects with an `ObjectInputStream`'s `readObject` method.

You allowed users to take new pictures using a device's rear facing camera, stored that picture in the device's **Gallery** and added the new picture to the slideshow. To do so, you used class `Camera` and a `SurfaceView` to display a preview of the picture. When the user touched the screen, you told the `Camera` to take the picture, then a `Camera.PictureCallback` object was notified that the picture was taken and processed the image data. You also used the `Camera`'s supported color effects.

The **Slideshow** app used an `Intent` to launch an `Activity` for choosing an image from the **Gallery**. You used the same technique here to allow the user to select videos, but specified a different MIME type for the data so that only videos were displayed.

You used a `VideoView` to play videos in a slideshow. To do so, you specified the `VideoView` video URI and `MediaController`. A `MediaPlayer.OnCompletionListener` determined when the video finished playing.

In the next chapter, we'll cover several key features of developing tablet apps with Android 3.x. In addition, we'll use WeatherBug's web services to create the **Weather Viewer** app.

Weather Viewer App

Web Services, JSON, `Fragment`, `ListFragment`, `DialogFragment`, `ActionBar`, Tabbed Navigation, App Widgets, Broadcast `Intents` and `BroadcastReceivers`

Objectives

In this chapter you'll:

- Use WeatherBug® web services to get the current conditions and five-day forecast for a specified city and process that data using an Android 3.x `JsonReader`.
- Use `Fragments` to create reusable components and make better use of the screen real estate in a tablet app.
- Implement tabbed navigation using the Android 3.x `ActionBar`.
- Create a companion app widget that can be installed on the user's home screen.
- Broadcast changes of the app's preferred city to the companion app widget.

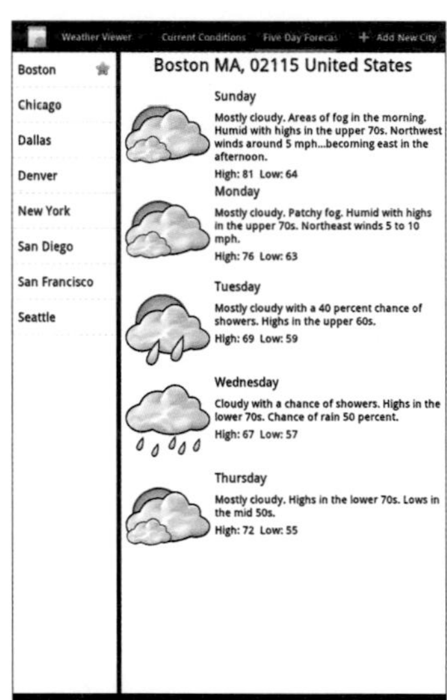

Outline

14.1 Introduction

The **Weather Viewer** app (Fig. 14.1) uses WeatherBug® web services to obtain a city's current weather conditions or its five-day weather forecast. The app is pre-populated with a list of cities in which Boston is set as the preferred city when you first install the app.

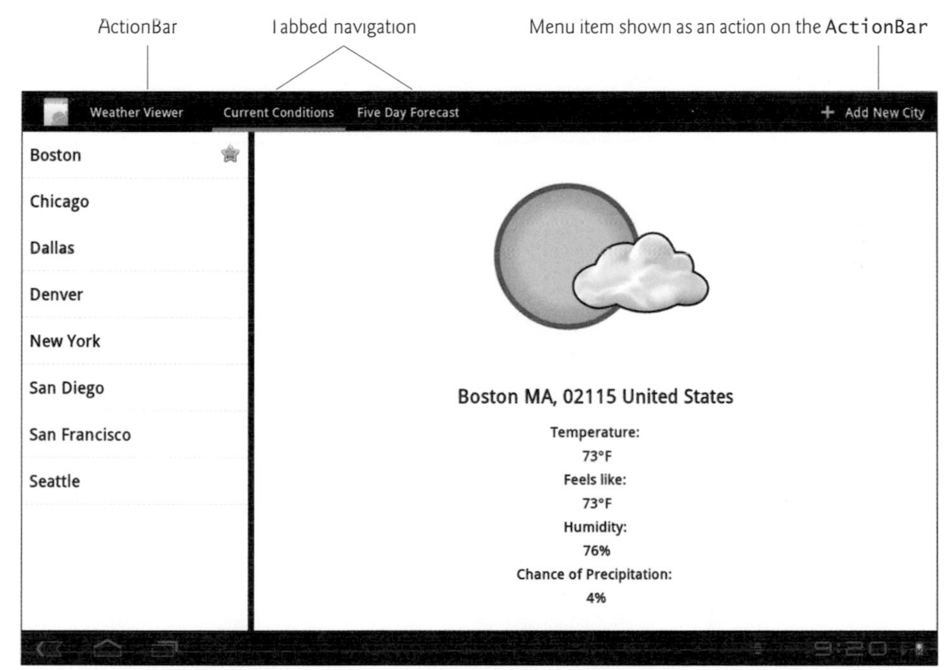

Fig. 14.1 | **Weather Viewer** app displaying the current weather conditions for Boston, MA.

This is an Android tablet app that takes advantage of various features which were introduced in Android 3.x. We use an Android 3.x `JsonReader` to read the weather data returned by the WeatherBug web services, which is returned to the app in *JSON (JavaScript Object Notation)* data format.

We use the Android 3.x action bar at the top of the screen, which is where menus and other app navigation elements are typically placed. You can add a new city by touching the **Add New City** option in the action bar. This displays a dialog (Fig. 14.2) in which you can enter a ZIP code and specify whether that city should be the preferred one. You can also switch between the current conditions and the five-day forecast (Fig. 14.3) by using the action bar's *tabbed navigation* (**Current Conditions** and **Five Day Forecast** to the right of the app name in Fig. 14.1).

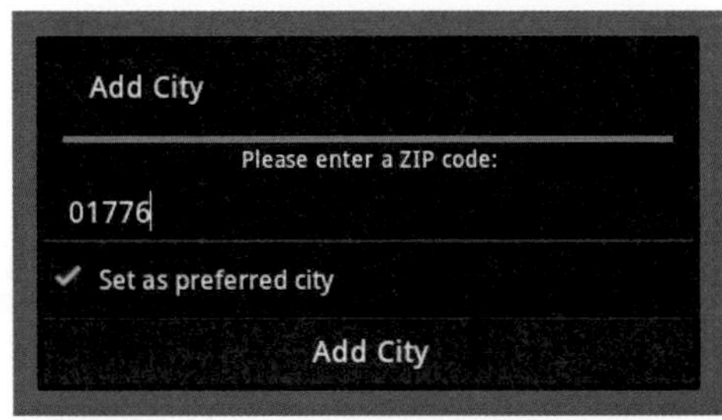

Fig. 14.2 | **Add City** dialog with a ZIP code entered and the **Set as preferred city** CheckBox checked.

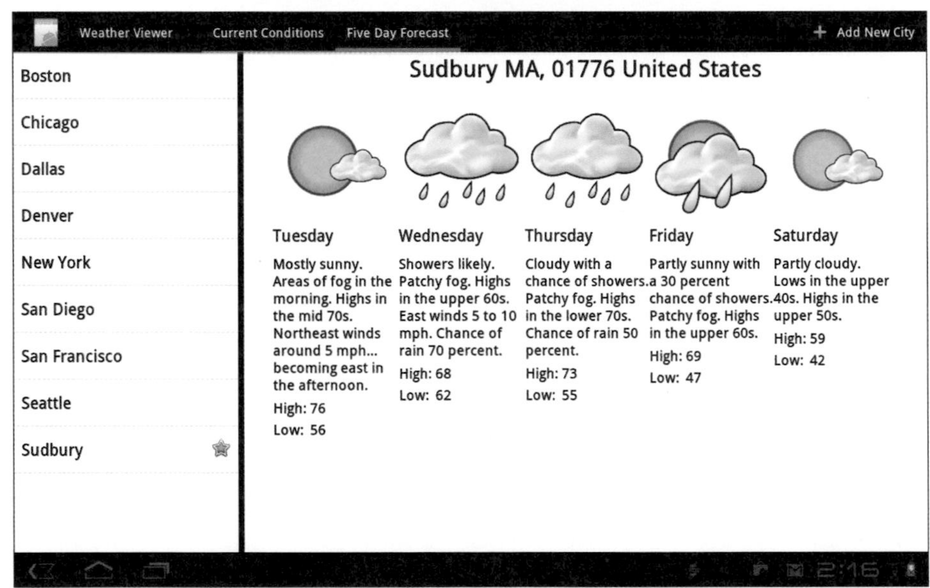

Fig. 14.3 | **Weather Viewer** app displaying the five-day forecast for Sudbury, MA.

The list of cities, the current conditions, the five-day forecast and the dialogs in this app are implemented using Android 3.x *fragments*, which typically represent a reusable portion of an `Activity`'s user interface. An `Activity` can display multiple fragments to take advantage of tablet screen sizes. The list of cities is displayed as a `ListFragment`—a `Fragment` containing a `ListView`. Long pressing a city name in the list of cities displays a `DialogFragment` that allows you to remove that city or set it as the preferred one—the one for which the app displays the current conditions when it first loads. The dialog displayed when you touch **Add New City** in the action bar is also a `DialogFragment`. Touching a city's name displays weather information for that city in a `Fragment` object.

This app also has a companion app widget (Fig. 14.4) that can be installed on one of your home screens. App widgets have been part of Android since its early versions. Android 3.x makes them *resizable*. The **Weather Viewer** app widget allows you to see your preferred city's current weather conditions on the home screen of your choice.

Fig. 14.4 | **Weather Viewer** app's companion app widget showing the current conditions for the preferred city that's set in the app.

14.2 Test-Driving the Weather Viewer App

Opening and Running the App

Open Eclipse and import the **Weather Viewer** app project. To import the project:

1. Select **File > Import...** to display the **Import** dialog.
2. Expand the **General** node and select **Existing Projects into Workspace**, then click **Next >**.
3. To the right of the **Select root directory:** textfield, click **Browse...** then locate and select the `WeatherViewer` folder.
4. Click **Finish** to import the project.

The application receives weather data from the WeatherBug web services. To run this example, you must register for your own WeatherBug API key at

```
weather.weatherbug.com/desktop-weather/api.html
```

Once you've obtained your API key, use it to replace `YOUR_API_KEY` on line 62 of class `ReadLocationTask`, line 66 of class `ReadForecastTask` and line 53 of class `ReadFiveDayForecastTask`. Once you've inserted your API key, you can right-click the app's project in the **Package Explorer** window, then select **Run As > Android Application** from the menu that appears.

Viewing a City's Current Weather Conditions and Five-Day Forecast
Touch a city in the list of cities to see its current weather conditions. Touch **Five Day Forecast** in the action bar at the top of the screen to switch to the five-day forecast view. Rotate your tablet between landscape and portrait modes to see the differences in the layouts for each orientation. You can return to the current weather conditions by touching **Current Conditions** in the action bar.

Adding a New City
Touch **Add New City** in the action bar to display the **Add City** dialog. Enter the ZIP code for the city you'd like to add. If you want this to be the preferred city, check the **Set as preferred city** `CheckBox`. Touch the **Add City** button to add the city to the list.

Removing a City from the City List and Changing the Preferred City
To remove a city from the city list or change the preferred city, long touch a city name to display a dialog with three buttons—**Set as Preferred City**, **Delete** and **Cancel**. Then touch the appropriate button for the task you wish to perform. If you delete the preferred city, the first city in the list is automatically set as the preferred one.

Adding the App Widget to Your Home Screen
To add this app's associated home screen app widget, touch the home button on your device, then long touch in an empty spot on your home screen to display the list of widgets you can install. Scroll to the right until you find the **Weather Viewer** widget. Touch the widget to add it to the currently selected home screen, or drag the widget to one of the five home screens. Once you've added the widget, it automatically displays the current weather conditions for your preferred city. You can remove the widget by long touching it and dragging it over **Remove** in the upper-right corner of the screen. You can also resize the widget. To do so, long touch it then remove your finger from the screen. Android displays resizing handles that you can use to resize the widget.

14.3 Technologies Overview

Android 3.x **`Fragment`**, **`ListFragment`** *and* **`DialogFragment`**
Fragments are a key new feature of Android 3.x. A **fragment** typically represents a reusable portion of an `Activity`'s user interface, but it can also represent reusable logic code. This app focuses on using fragments to create and manage portions of the app's GUI. You can combine several fragments to create robust user interfaces and to better take advantage of tablet screen sizes. You can also easily interchange fragments to make your GUIs more dynamic.

The base class of all fragments is **`Fragment`** (package `android.app`). This app uses several types of fragments. The list of cities is displayed as a **`ListFragment`**—a fragment containing a `ListView`. Dialog boxes are displayed using **`DialogFragments`**. The current weather conditions and the five-day forecast are displayed using subclasses of `Fragment`.

Though fragments were introduced in Android 3.x, there's a *compatibility package* that enables you to use them with earlier versions of Android. You can get the latest version of this package at:

```
http://developer.android.com/sdk/compatibility-library.html
```

Managing Fragments

Like an `Activity`, each `Fragment` has a *life cycle*—we'll discuss the `Fragment` life cycle methods as we encounter them. `Fragments` must be hosted in a parent `Activity`—they cannot be executed independently. The app's main `WeatherViewerActivity` is the parent `Activity` for the app's `Fragments`. The parent `Activity` uses a **`FragmentManager`** (package `android.app`) to manage the `Fragments`. A **`FragmentTransaction`** (package `android.app`) obtained from the `FragmentManager` allows the `Activity` to *add*, *remove* and *transition* between `Fragments`.

Fragment Layouts

Like an `Activity`, each `Fragment` has its own layout that's typically defined as an XML layout resource, but also can be dynamically created. For the five-day forecast `Fragment`, we provide different layouts for landscape and portrait orientations, so we can better use the screen real estate available to the app. We display the five-day forecast from left to right in landscape orientation and from top to bottom in portrait orientation. We use the `Activity`'s `Configuration` (package `android.content.res`) to determine the current orientation, then specify the layout to use accordingly.

Android 3.x Action Bar

Android 3.x replaces the app's title bar that was used in earlier Android versions with an **action bar** at the top of the screen. The app's icon and name are displayed at the left side. In addition, the action bar can display the app's options menu, navigation elements (such as tabbed navigation) and other interactive GUI components. In this app, we use the action bar to implement tabbed navigation between the current weather conditions `Fragment` and the five-day forecast `Fragment` for a particular city. The app also has an options menu with one option for adding a new city to the cities `ListFragment`. You can also designate menu items as actions that should be placed in the action bar if there's room. To do so, you can set the menu item's `android:showAsAction` attribute.

Handling Long Touches

When the user long touches an item in this app's cities `ListFragment`, we'll use an **`AdapterView.OnItemLongClickListener`** (package `android.widget`) to respond to that event and allow the user to set the selected city as the preferred one, delete the city or cancel the operation.

Companion App Widget

This app has a companion app widget that displays the current weather conditions for the user's preferred city, as set in the **Weather Viewer** app. The user can long touch the home screen to select and add the widget. We extend class **`AppWidgetProvider`** (package **`android.appwidget`**), a subclass of **`BroadcastReceiver`** (package `android.content`), to create the app widget and allow it to receive notifications from the system when the app widget is enabled, disabled, deleted or updated.

`PendingIntent` to Launch an `Activity` from an App Widget

It's common practice to allow a user to launch an app by touching the app's companion widget on the device's home screen. We use a **`PendingIntent`** (package `android.app`) to launch the app and display the current weather conditions for the preferred city.

Web Services and JsonReader

This app uses **JsonReader** (package android.util) to read JSON objects containing the weather data. We use a URL object to specify the URL that invokes the WeatherBug RESTful web service that returns JSON objects. We open an InputStream for that URL, which invokes the web service. The JsonReader gets its data from that InputStream.

Broadcast Intents *and Receivers*

The Weather Viewer's companion app widget displays the current conditions for the preferred city, as currently set in the app. The user can change the preferred city at any time. When this occurs, the app uses an Intent to broadcast the change. The app widget uses a **BroadcastReceiver** (package android.content) to listen for this change so that it can display the current conditions for the appropriate city.

14.4 Building the App's GUI and Resource Files

In this section, we review the new features in the GUI and resource files for the **Weather Viewer** app. To save space, we do not show this app's strings.xml resource file, nor do we show most of the layout XML files.

14.4.1 AndroidManifest.xml

Figure 14.5 shows this app's AndroidManifest.xml file. We set the uses-sdk element's android:minSdkVersion attribute to "12" (line 5), which represents the Android 3.1 SDK. This app will run only on Android 3.1+ devices and AVDs. Lines 6–7 indicate that this app requires an Internet connection. The **receiver** element (lines 19–30) registers the WeatherProvider class (which represents the app widget) as a BroadcastReceiver, specifies the XML file for the app widget's metadata and specifies WeatherProvider's Intent filters. Line 32 registers WeatherProvider's nested class WeatherService as a **service**, so that it can be launched to execute in the background. We use this WeatherService to update the weather data in our app widget. Like activities, all services must be registered in the manifest; otherwise, they cannot be executed.

```
1  <?xml version="1.0" encoding="utf-8"?>
2  <manifest xmlns:android="http://schemas.android.com/apk/res/android"
3     package="com.deitel.weatherviewer" android:versionCode="1"
4     android:versionName="1.0">
5     <uses-sdk android:minSdkVersion="12" />
6     <uses-permission android:name="android.permission.INTERNET">
7     </uses-permission>
8
9     <application android:icon="@drawable/icon"
10       android:label="@string/app_name">
11       <activity android:name=".WeatherViewerActivity"
12          android:label="@string/app_name">
13          <intent-filter>
14             <action android:name="android.intent.action.MAIN" />
```

Fig. 14.5 | AndroidManifest.xml. (Part 1 of 2.)

```
            <category android:name="android.intent.category.LAUNCHER" />
         </intent-filter>
      </activity>

      <receiver android:name=".WeatherProvider">
         <meta-data android:name="android.appwidget.provider"
            android:resource="@xml/weather_widget_provider_info" />
         <intent-filter>
            <action android:name=
               "android.appwidget.action.APPWIDGET_UPDATE" />
         </intent-filter>
         <intent-filter>
            <action android:name=
               "com.deitel.weatherviewer.UPDATE_WIDGET" />
         </intent-filter>
      </receiver>

      <service android:name=".WeatherProvider$WeatherService" />
   </application>
</manifest>
```

Fig. 14.5 | `AndroidManifest.xml`. (Part 2 of 2.)

14.4.2 WeatherViewerActivity's main.xml Layout

The `main.xml` resource file (Fig. 14.6) defines the `WeatherViewerActivity`'s layout. We include a `CitiesFragment` as the first child of the root `LinearLayout` with the **`fragment`** element. The `CitiesFragment` will be created automatically when `WeatherViewerActivity` inflates its layout. We use the `forecast_replacer FrameLayout` as a placeholder in which we'll display the `ForecastFragments`. By including this placeholder we define the size and location of the area in which the `ForecastFragments` will appear in the `Activity`. The `WeatherViewerActivity` swaps between `ForecastFragments` in this location using `FragmentTransactions`.

```
<?xml version="1.0" encoding="utf-8"?>
<LinearLayout xmlns:android="http://schemas.android.com/apk/res/android"
   android:orientation="horizontal" android:layout_width="match_parent"
   android:layout_height="match_parent">
   <fragment class="com.deitel.weatherviewer.CitiesFragment"
      android:id="@+id/cities" android:layout_weight="3"
      android:layout_width="wrap_content"
      android:layout_height="match_parent"/>
   <FrameLayout android:layout_width="8dp"
      android:layout_height="match_parent"
      android:background="@android:color/black"/>
   <FrameLayout android:id="@+id/forecast_replacer"
      android:layout_width="match_parent"
      android:layout_height="match_parent"
      android:layout_weight="1" android:background="@android:color/white"/>
</LinearLayout>
```

Fig. 14.6 | `WeatherViewerActivity`'s `main.xml` layout.

14.4.3 Default Cities and ZIP Codes in arrays.xml

The default cities and their respective ZIP codes are stored in the app's `arrays.xml` resource file (Fig. 14.7). This allows us to read lists of `String` resource values directly as opposed to reading each individually. The two `String` arrays are loaded in the `WeatherViewerActivity` by calling `Resources` method `getStringArray`.

```
<?xml version="1.0" encoding="utf-8"?>
<resources>
   <string-array name="default_city_names">
      <item>Boston</item>
      <item>Chicago</item>
      <item>Dallas</item>
      <item>Denver</item>
      <item>New York</item>
      <item>San Diego</item>
      <item>San Francisco</item>
      <item>Seattle</item>
   </string-array>
   <string-array name="default_city_zipcodes">
      <item>02115</item>
      <item>60611</item>
      <item>75254</item>
      <item>80202</item>
      <item>10024</item>
      <item>92104</item>
      <item>94112</item>
      <item>98101</item>
   </string-array>
</resources>
```

Fig. 14.7 | Default cities and ZIP codes in `arrays.xml`.

14.4.4 WeatherViewerActivity's actionmenu.xml Menu Layout

The `actionmenu.xml` resource file (Fig. 14.8) defines the `ActionBar`'s menu items. The menu resource's attributes are the same as those for the standard Android menu. We introduce the new attribute **`android:showAsAction`** which defines how a menu item should appear in the `ActionBar`. The value `ifRoom` specifies that this item should be visible in the `ActionBar` if there's room to lay it out completely. You can force an item to appear in the `ActionBar` by using the `always` value but you risk overlapping menu items by doing so. The `withText` value specifies that the `String` value for the item's `android:title` attribute is displayed with the menu item.

```
<?xml version="1.0" encoding="utf-8"?>
<menu xmlns:android="http://schemas.android.com/apk/res/android">
   <item android:id="@+id/add_city_item"
      android:icon="@android:drawable/ic_input_add"
      android:title="@string/add_new_city"
      android:showAsAction="ifRoom|withText"/>
</menu>
```

Fig. 14.8 | `WeatherViewerActivity`'s `actionmenu.xml` menu layout.

14.4.5 WeatherProvider App Widget Configuration and Layout

The weather_widget_provider_info.xml file (Fig. 14.9) defines the metadata for the WeatherViewer's AppWidgetProvider. The minWidth and minHeight attributes describe the initial size of the app widget. So that home-screen icons and widgets can be sized and arranged uniformly, Android divides the home screen into equally sized cells, as described at:

```
http://developer.android.com/guide/practices/ui_guidelines/
   widget_design.html#sizes
```

There are several standard widget sizes, one of which we've specified with the minWidth and minHeight attributes. The app widget's layout resource is defined using the initialLayout attribute. The updatePeriodMillis attribute defines how often the AppWidgetProvider should receive the ACTION_APPWIDGET_UPDATE broadcast Intent. Each time this Intent is received, class WeatherProvider (Section 14.5.11) starts a new WeatherService to update the app widget's current weather data. Any values for this attribute below 30 minutes are ignored. App widgets that require more frequent updates must do so using an AlarmManager. The **android:resizeMode attribute** is new to Android 3.1 and defines the directions in which the app widget can be resized on the home screen.

```
<?xml version="1.0" encoding="utf-8"?>
<appwidget-provider
   xmlns:android="http://schemas.android.com/apk/res/android"
   android:minWidth="212dp" android:minHeight="148dp"
   android:initialLayout="@layout/weather_app_widget_layout"
   android:updatePeriodMillis="3600000"
   android:resizeMode="horizontal|vertical"/>
```

Fig. 14.9 | WeatherProvider app widget configuration.

The app widget's layout is specified in weather_app_widget_layout.xml, which uses a simple nested LinearLayout. We specified as the main LinearLayout's background one of Google's standard app widget borders, which you can download from

```
http://developer.android.com/guide/practices/ui_guidelines/
   widget_design.html#frames
```

14.5 Building the App

This app consists of 11 classes that are discussed in detail in Sections 14.5.1–14.5.11. Here we provide a brief overview of the classes and how they relate.

- Class WeatherViewerActivity (Section 14.5.1) is the app's only Activity. The Activity uses an AddCityDialogFragment (Section 14.5.3) to allow the user to add new cities to the app. The Activity contains one instance of class CitiesFragment (Section 14.5.2) that's always located at the left side of the screen. WeatherViewerActivity is responsible for swapping in and out the various ForecastFragments (Sections 14.5.4, 14.5.5 and 14.5.8) that are displayed on the right side of the app. This Activity also contains the ActionBar code and loads the default cities and the cities that the user adds to the app.

- Class `ReadLocationTask` (Section 14.5.6) gets location information for a given ZIP code from the WeatherBug web services. It's used in `WeatherViewerActivity`, both subclasses of `ForecastFragment` and the app widget.
- Class `SingleForecastFragment` (Section 14.5.5) is a `Fragment` that displays a single day's forecast. The data that's displayed is read by the `AsyncTask ReadForecastTask` (Section 14.5.7).
- Class `FiveDayForecastFragment` (Section 14.5.8) is similar to `SingleForecastFragment`, but it displays the five-day forecast, which is obtained by the `AsyncTask ReadFiveDayForecastTask` (Section 14.5.9). Class `DailyForecast` (Section 14.5.10) represents a single day's forecast data. We use this class to simplify passing information back from the `ReadFiveDayForecast` task.
- Class `WeatherProvider` (Section 14.5.11) manages and updates the app widget. In addition to standard app widget broadcasts from the system, the widget receives broadcasts from the `WeatherViewerActivity` when the preferred city is changed.

14.5.1 Class `WeatherViewerActivity`

The `WeatherViewerActivity` class (Fig. 14.10) has several new `import` statements—the new features are highlighted. The class implements interface `DialogFinishedListener` (defined in Fig. 14.33) to so it can respond when the user adds a new city. We discuss the class's fields as they're used throughout this section.

```
// WeatherViewerActivity.java
// Main Activity for the Weather Viewer app.
package com.deitel.weatherviewer;

import java.util.HashMap;
import java.util.Map;

import android.app.ActionBar;
import android.app.ActionBar.Tab;
import android.app.ActionBar.TabListener;
import android.app.Activity;
import android.app.FragmentManager;
import android.app.FragmentTransaction;
import android.content.Intent;
import android.content.SharedPreferences;
import android.content.SharedPreferences.Editor;
import android.os.Bundle;
import android.os.Handler;
import android.view.Gravity;
import android.view.Menu;
import android.view.MenuInflater;
import android.view.MenuItem;
import android.widget.Toast;
```

Fig. 14.10 | Class `WeatherViewerActivity` package statement, `import` statements and fields. (Part 1 of 2.)

```

import com.deitel.weatherviewer.AddCityDialogFragment.
     DialogFinishedListener;
import com.deitel.weatherviewer.CitiesFragment.CitiesListChangeListener;
import com.deitel.weatherviewer.ReadLocationTask.LocationLoadedListener;

public class WeatherViewerActivity extends Activity implements
   DialogFinishedListener
{
   public static final String WIDGET_UPDATE_BROADCAST_ACTION =
      "com.deitel.weatherviewer.UPDATE_WIDGET";

   private static final int BROADCAST_DELAY = 10000;

   private static final int CURRENT_CONDITIONS_TAB = 0;

   public static final String PREFERRED_CITY_NAME_KEY =
      "preferred_city_name";
   public static final String PREFERRED_CITY_ZIPCODE_KEY =
      "preferred_city_zipcode";
   public static final String SHARED_PREFERENCES_NAME =
      "weather_viewer_shared_preferences";
   private static final String CURRENT_TAB_KEY = "current_tab";
   private static final String LAST_SELECTED_KEY = "last_selected";

   private int currentTab; // position of the current selected tab
   private String lastSelectedCity; // last city selected from the list
   private SharedPreferences weatherSharedPreferences;

   // stores city names and the corresponding zipcodes
   private Map<String, String> favoriteCitiesMap;
   private CitiesFragment listCitiesFragment;
   private Handler weatherHandler;

```

Fig. 14.10 | Class WeatherViewerActivity package statement, import statements and fields. (Part 2 of 2.)

WeatherViewerActivity method onCreate

Method onCreate (Fig. 14.11) initializes a new WeatherViewerActivity. We call Activity's **getFragmentManager** method (line 66) to get the FragmentManager used to interact with this Activity's Fragments—in this case, we get the CitiesFragment. The FragmentManager is also available to any of the Activity's Fragments. In addition to initializing several other instance variables, we call setupTabs (defined in Fig. 14.26) to initialize the Activity's ActionBar.

```
57    // initializes this Activity and inflates its layout from xml
58    @Override
59    public void onCreate(Bundle savedInstanceState)
60    {
```

Fig. 14.11 | Overriding method onCreate in class WeatherViewerActivity. (Part 1 of 2.)

```
      super.onCreate(savedInstanceState); // pass given Bundle to super
      setContentView(R.layout.main); // inflate layout in main.xml

      // get the CitiesFragment
      listCitiesFragment = (CitiesFragment)
         getFragmentManager().findFragmentById(R.id.cities);

      // set the CitiesListChangeListener
      listCitiesFragment.setCitiesListChangeListener(
         citiesListChangeListener);

      // create HashMap storing city names and corresponding ZIP codes
      favoriteCitiesMap = new HashMap<String, String>();

      weatherHandler = new Handler();

      weatherSharedPreferences = getSharedPreferences(
         SHARED_PREFERENCES_NAME, MODE_PRIVATE);

      setupTabs(); // set up the ActionBar's navigation tabs
   } // end method onCreate

```

Fig. 14.11 | Overriding method `onCreate` in class `WeatherViewerActivity`. (Part 2 of 2.)

`WeatherViewerActivity` methods `onSaveInstanceState` and `onRestoreInstanceState`

Method `onSaveInstanceState` (Fig. 14.12, lines 84–92) saves the current selected tab position and selected list item. The index of the currently selected tab is added to the given `Bundle` using `Bundle`'s `putInt` method. These values are read in the method `onRestoreInstanceState` (lines 95–104), allowing the `Activity` to display the same city and the same selected tab across orientation changes.

```
83    // save this Activity's state
84    @Override
85    public void onSaveInstanceState(Bundle savedInstanceStateBundle)
86    {
87       // save the currently selected tab
88       savedInstanceStateBundle.putInt(CURRENT_TAB_KEY, currentTab);
89       savedInstanceStateBundle.putString(LAST_SELECTED_KEY,
90          lastSelectedCity); // save the currently selected city
91       super.onSaveInstanceState(savedInstanceStateBundle);
92    } // end method onSaveInstanceState
93
94    // restore the saved Activity state
95    @Override
96    public void onRestoreInstanceState(Bundle savedInstanceStateBundle)
97    {
98       super.onRestoreInstanceState(savedInstanceStateBundle);
```

Fig. 14.12 | Overriding methods `onSaveInstanceState` and `onRestoreInstanceState` in class `WeatherViewerActivity`. (Part 1 of 2.)

```
99
100        // get the selected tab
101        currentTab = savedInstanceStateBundle.getInt(CURRENT_TAB_KEY);
102        lastSelectedCity = savedInstanceStateBundle.getString(
103           LAST_SELECTED_KEY); // get the selected city
104     } // end method onRestoreInstanceState
105
```

Fig. 14.12 | Overriding methods `onSaveInstanceState` and `onRestoreInstanceState` in class `WeatherViewerActivity`. (Part 2 of 2.)

`WeatherViewerActivity` method `onResume`

We populate the favorite cities list in the `Activity`'s `onResume` method (Fig. 14.13). If the `favoriteCitiesMap` is empty, we read the saved cities from the app's `SharedPreferences` by calling method `loadSavedCities` (Fig. 14.17). If there's no data in the `SharedPreferences` the `favoriteCitiesMap` will still be empty. In this case, we call `addSampleCities` (Fig. 14.18) to add the pre-configured cities from XML resources. We specify the `ActionBar`'s currently selected tab using its **`selectTab` method** (line 124) then load the selected city's forecast by calling `loadSelectedForecast` (Fig. 14.15).

```
106     // called when this Activity resumes
107     @Override
108     public void onResume()
109     {
110        super.onResume();
111
112        if (favoriteCitiesMap.isEmpty()) // if the city list is empty
113        {
114           loadSavedCities(); // load previously added cities
115        } // end if
116
117        // if there are no cities left
118        if (favoriteCitiesMap.isEmpty())
119        {
120           addSampleCities(); // add sample cities
121        } // end if
122
123        // load previously selected forecast
124        getActionBar().selectTab(getActionBar().getTabAt(currentTab));
125        loadSelectedForecast();
126     } // end method onResume
127
```

Fig. 14.13 | Overriding `WeatherViewerActivity` method `onResume`.

Implementing `CitiesListChangeListener`

The `CitiesListChangeListener` (Fig. 14.14) receives updates from the `CitiesFragment` when the user selects a new city or changes the preferred one. Method `onSelectedCityChanged` (lines 133–138) is called when the user selects a new city. The given city name is passed to `WeatherViewerActivity`'s `selectForecast` method (Fig. 14.20) to display the selected city's forecast in a `ForecastFragment`. Changes to the preferred city are reported to the `onPreferredCityChanged` method (lines 141–146). We pass the given city name to `WeatherViewerActivity`'s `setPreferred` method (Fig. 14.16) to update the app's `SharedPreferences`.

```
128    // listens for changes to the CitiesFragment
129    private CitiesListChangeListener citiesListChangeListener =
130       new CitiesListChangeListener()
131    {
132       // called when the selected city is changed
133       @Override
134       public void onSelectedCityChanged(String cityNameString)
135       {
136          // show the given city's forecast
137          selectForecast(cityNameString);
138       } // end method onSelectedCityChanged
139
140       // called when the preferred city is changed
141       @Override
142       public void onPreferredCityChanged(String cityNameString)
143       {
144          // save the new preferred city to the app's SharedPreferences
145          setPreferred(cityNameString);
146       } // end method onPreferredCityChanged
147    }; // end CitiesListChangeListener
148
```

Fig. 14.14 | Implementing `CitiesListChangeListener`.

`WeatherViewerActivity` Method `loadSelectedForecast`

Method `loadSelectedForecast` (Fig. 14.15) calls method `selectForecast` (Fig. 14.20) to load the forecast of the last city that the user selected in the `CitiesFragment`. If no city is selected the preferred city's forecast is loaded.

```
   // load the previously selected forecast
   private void loadSelectedForecast()
   {
      // if there was a previously selected city
      if (lastSelectedCity != null)
      {
         selectForecast(lastSelectedCity); // select last selected city
      } // end if
      else
      {
         // get the name of the preferred city
         String cityNameString = weatherSharedPreferences.getString(
            PREFERRED_CITY_NAME_KEY, getResources().getString(
            R.string.default_zipcode));
```

Fig. 14.15 | `WeatherViewerActivity` method `loadSelectedForecast`. (Part 1 of 2.)

```
            selectForecast(cityNameString); // load preferred city's forecast
        } // end else
    } // end loadSelectedForecast

```

Fig. 14.15 | `WeatherViewerActivity` method `loadSelectedForecast`. (Part 2 of 2.)

`WeatherViewerActivity` *Method* ***`setPreferred`***

Method `setPreferred` (Fig. 14.16) updates the preferred city entry in the app's `SharedPreferences`. We get the ZIP code matching the given city name then get an `Editor` using `SharedPreferences` method `edit`. The name and ZIP code of the new preferred city are passed to `Editor`'s `putString` method. `SharedPreferences` method **`apply`** saves the changes. We clear the last selected city then call `loadSelectedForecast` (Fig. 14.15) to display the forecast of the new preferred city. Next, we create an `Intent` of type `WIDGET_UPDATE_BROADCAST_ACTION` and broadcast it using `Activity`'s **`sendBroadcast`** method. If the user installed the app widget on a home screen, the `WeatherProvider` (Section 14.5.11) will receive this broadcast and update the app widget to display the new preferred city's forecast. Many web services, including those provided by WeatherBug, limit the number and frequency of calls you can make to the service. For this reason, we use a `Handler` to send the broadcast after a short delay—this prevents the app and the app widget from calling the web service at the same time to load the new forecast.

```
    // set the preferred city
    public void setPreferred(String cityNameString)
    {
        // get the give city's ZIP code
        String cityZipcodeString = favoriteCitiesMap.get(cityNameString);
        Editor preferredCityEditor = weatherSharedPreferences.edit();
        preferredCityEditor.putString(PREFERRED_CITY_NAME_KEY,
            cityNameString);
        preferredCityEditor.putString(PREFERRED_CITY_ZIPCODE_KEY,
            cityZipcodeString);
        preferredCityEditor.apply(); // commit the changes
        lastSelectedCity = null; // remove the last selected forecast
        loadSelectedForecast(); // load the preferred city's forecast

        // update the app widget to display the new preferred city
        final Intent updateWidgetIntent = new Intent(
            WIDGET_UPDATE_BROADCAST_ACTION);

        // send broadcast after short delay
        weatherHandler.postDelayed(new Runnable()
        {
            @Override
            public void run()
            {
                sendBroadcast(updateWidgetIntent); // broadcast the intent
            }
```

Fig. 14.16 | `WeatherViewerActivity` method `setPreferred`. (Part 1 of 2.)

```
      }, BROADCAST_DELAY);
   } // end method setPreferred

```

Fig. 14.16 | WeatherViewerActivity method setPreferred. (Part 2 of 2.)

WeatherViewerActivity *Method* loadSavedCities

Method loadSavedCities (Fig. 14.17) loads the favorite cities list from the app's SharedPreferences. A map of each city and ZIP code pair is obtained via SharedPreferences method getAll. We loop through the pairs and add them to the list using WeatherViewerActivity's addCity method (Fig. 14.19).

```
   // reads previously saved city list from SharedPreferences
   private void loadSavedCities()
   {
      Map<String, ?> citiesMap = weatherSharedPreferences.getAll();

      for (String cityString : citiesMap.keySet())
      {
         // if this value is not the preferred city
         if (!(cityString.equals(PREFERRED_CITY_NAME_KEY) ||
            cityString.equals(PREFERRED_CITY_ZIPCODE_KEY)))
         {
            addCity(cityString, (String) citiesMap.get(cityString), false);
         } // end if
      } // end for
   } // end method loadSavedCities

```

Fig. 14.17 | WeatherViewerActivity method loadSavedCities.

WeatherViewerActivity *Method* addSampleCities

Method addSampleCities (Fig. 14.18) method reads the default favorite cities from the app's arrays.xml resource file. We use class Resource's **getStringArray** method (lines 216–217 and 220–221) to retrieve arrays containing the default city names and ZIP codes. We loop through each city and add it to the list using the addCity method (Fig. 14.19). The first sample city's name is passed to WeatherViewerActivity's setPreferred method to select it as the preferred city (Fig. 14.16).

```
212    // add the sample cities
213    private void addSampleCities()
214    {
215       // load the array of city names from resources
216       String[] sampleCityNamesArray = getResources().getStringArray(
217          R.array.default_city_names);
218
```

Fig. 14.18 | WeatherViewerActivity method addSampleCities. (Part 1 of 2.)

```
      // load the array of ZIP codes from resources
      String[] sampleCityZipcodesArray = getResources().getStringArray(
         R.array.default_city_zipcodes);

      // for each sample city
      for (int i = 0; i < sampleCityNamesArray.length; i++)
      {
         // set the first sample city as the preferred city by default
         if (i == 0)
         {
            setPreferred(sampleCityNamesArray[i]);
         } // end if

         // add city to the list
         addCity(sampleCityNamesArray[i], sampleCityZipcodesArray[i],
            false);
      } // end for
   } // end method addSampleCities

```

Fig. 14.18 | `WeatherViewerActivity` method `addSampleCities`. (Part 2 of 2.)

`WeatherViewerActivity` Method `addCity`

New cities are added to the `CitiesFragment` (Section 14.5.2) using the `addCity` method (Fig. 14.19). The given city name and ZIP code are added to the `favoriteCitiesMap` then passed to `CitiesFragment`'s `addCity` method. We also add the city to the app's `SharedPreferences` and call `apply` to save the new city.

```
   // add a new city to the CitiesFragment ListFragment
   public void addCity(String city, String zipcode, boolean select)
   {
      favoriteCitiesMap.put(city, zipcode); // add to HashMap of cities
      listCitiesFragment.addCity(city, select); // add city to Fragment
      Editor preferenceEditor = weatherSharedPreferences.edit();
      preferenceEditor.putString(city, zipcode);
      preferenceEditor.apply();
   } // end method addCity

```

Fig. 14.19 | `WeatherViewerActivity` method `addCity`.

`WeatherViewerActivity` Method `selectForecast`

Method `selectForecast` (Fig. 14.20) displays the forecast information for the given city. We get the current visible forecast `Fragment` using `FragmentManager`'s **`findFragmentById`** method. We pass to this method the ID of the `FrameLayout` in the `Activity`'s layout. The first time this method executes, the result will be `null`. The `FragmentManager` can access the visible forecast `Fragment` after we replace the `FrameLayout` with a `Fragment` during a `FragmentTransaction`. If the current selected `ActionBar` tab is the **Current Conditions** tab, we create a new `ForecastFragment` using the given ZIP code (lines 270–271). Otherwise, the **Five Day Forecast** `Tab` must be selected, so we create a new `FiveDayForecastFragment` (lines 276–277). We create a new `FragmentTransaction` using `FragmentManager`'s **`beginTransaction`** method (lines 281–282). `FragmentTransactions` are used to add, remove and replace `Fragments`, among other interactions. In this case, we'll replace the `Fragment` on the right half of the `Activity` with the new `Fragment` we just created. We pass `FragmentTransaction`'s **`TRANSIT_FRAGMENT_FADE`** constant to its `setTransition` method (285–286) to visually fade the old `Fragment` into the new one. Next we call `ForecastFragment`'s **`replace` method** (lines 290–291) with the ID of the item to be replaced and the `Fragment` to take its place. `FragmentTransaction`'s **`commit` method** (line 293) executes the transaction.

```
248    // display forecast information for the given city
249    public void selectForecast(String name)
250    {
251       lastSelectedCity = name; // save the city name
252       String zipcodeString = favoriteCitiesMap.get(name);
253       if (zipcodeString == null) // if the ZIP code can't be found
254       {
255          return; // do not attempt to load a forecast
256       } // end if
257
258       // get the current visible ForecastFragment
259       ForecastFragment currentForecastFragment = (ForecastFragment)
260          getFragmentManager().findFragmentById(R.id.forecast_replacer);
261
262       if (currentForecastFragment == null ||
263          !(currentForecastFragment.getZipcode().equals(zipcodeString) &&
264          correctTab(currentForecastFragment)))
265       {
266          // if the selected current tab is "Current Conditions"
267          if (currentTab == CURRENT_CONDITIONS_TAB)
268          {
269             // create a new ForecastFragment using the given ZIP code
270             currentForecastFragment = SingleForecastFragment.newInstance(
271                zipcodeString);
272          } // end if
273          else
274          {
275             // create a new ForecastFragment using the given ZIP code
276             currentForecastFragment = FiveDayForecastFragment.newInstance(
277                zipcodeString);
278          } // end else
279
280          // create a new FragmentTransaction
281          FragmentTransaction forecastFragmentTransaction =
282             getFragmentManager().beginTransaction();
283
284          // set transition animation to fade
285          forecastFragmentTransaction.setTransition(
286             FragmentTransaction.TRANSIT_FRAGMENT_FADE);
```

Fig. 14.20 | `WeatherViewerActivity` method `selectForecast`. (Part 1 of 2.)

```

         // replace the Fragment (or View) at the given id with our
         // new Fragment
         forecastFragmentTransaction.replace(R.id.forecast_replacer,
            currentForecastFragment);

         forecastFragmentTransaction.commit(); // begin the transition
      } // end if
   } // end method selectForecast

```

Fig. 14.20 | `WeatherViewerActivity` method `selectForecast`. (Part 2 of 2.)

`WeatherViewerActivity` Methods `correctTab` and `selectTab`

Method `correctTab` (Fig. 14.21, lines 298–313) returns `true` if the given `ForecastFragment` matches the currently selected tab—in particular, when the **Current Conditions** tab is selected and it's given a `SingleForecastFragment` or when the **Five Day Forecast** tab is selected and it's given a `FiveDayForecastFragment`. The `selectForecast` method uses this information to determine whether it needs to update the visible `ForecastFragment`. Method `selectTab` (lines 316–320) selects the tab at the given index. We save the index to the `currentTab` instance variable then call `loadSelectedForecast` (Fig. 14.15).

```
297    // is this the proper ForecastFragment for the currently selected tab?
298    private boolean correctTab(ForecastFragment forecastFragment)
299    {
300       // if the "Current Conditions" tab is selected
301       if (currentTab == CURRENT_CONDITIONS_TAB)
302       {
303          // return true if the given ForecastFragment
304          // is a SingleForecastFragment
305          return (forecastFragment instanceof SingleForecastFragment);
306       } // end if
307       else // the "Five Day Forecast" tab is selected
308       {
309          // return true if the given ForecastFragment
310          // is a FiveDayForecastFragment
311          return (forecastFragment instanceof FiveDayForecastFragment);
312       } // end else
313    } // end method correctTab
314
315    // select the tab at the given position
316    private void selectTab(int position)
317    {
318       currentTab = position; // save the position tab
319       loadSelectedForecast();
320    } // end method selectTab
321
```

Fig. 14.21 | `WeatherViewerActivity` methods `correctTab` and `selectTab`.

Overriding Activity *Methods* onCreateOptionsMenu *and* onOptionsItemSelected

Method onCreateOptionsMenu (Fig. 14.22, lines 323–332) initializes the **Add New City** button in the ActionBar. We get the global MenuInflator using Activity's getMenuInflator method. We inflate the menu defined in actionmenu.xml and attach it to the given Menu object. Method onOptionsItemSelected (lines 335–346) is called when the user touches the **Add New City** item on the ActionBar. We confirm that the MenuItem matches the expected resource ID then call showAddCityDialog (Fig. 14.23) to display an AddCityDialogFragment (Section 14.5.3). We return true to indicate that the menu item selection was handled in this method.

```
322     // create this Activities Menu
323     @Override
324     public boolean onCreateOptionsMenu(Menu menu)
325     {
326        super.onCreateOptionsMenu(menu);
327        MenuInflater inflater = getMenuInflater(); // global MenuInflator
328
329        // inflate layout defined in actionmenu.xml
330        inflater.inflate(R.menu.actionmenu, menu);
331        return true; // return true since the menu was created
332     } // end method onCreateOptionsMenu
333
334     // when one of the items was clicked
335     @Override
336     public boolean onOptionsItemSelected(MenuItem item)
337     {
338       // if the item selected was the "Add City" item
339        if (item.getItemId() == R.id.add_city_item)
340        {
341           showAddCityDialog(); // show Dialog for user input
342           return true; // return true since we handled the selection
343        } // end if
344
345        return false; // do not handle unexpected menu items
346     } // end method onOptionsItemSelected
347
```

Fig. 14.22 | Overriding Activity methods onCreateOptionsMenu and onOptionsItemSelected.

WeatherViewerActivity *Methods* showAddCityDialog *and* onDialogFinished

Method showAddCityDialog (Fig. 14.23, lines 349–364) displays a DialogFragment allowing the user to enter a ZIP code. After creating a new AddCityDialogFragment, we get the Activity's FragmentManager (line 356). We create a new FragmentTransaction using FragmentManager's beginTransaction method. We pass the FragmentTransaction to DialogFragment's show method to display it over the Activity. Although not demonstrated here, it's also possible to embed a FragmentDialog in the Activity's View hierarchy. Method onDialogFinished (lines 367–372) is called when the AddCityDialog is dismissed. The zipcodeString argument represents the user-entered ZIP code. The boolean argument preferred is true if the user checks the **Set as preferred city** CheckBox. We pass both of these to method getCityNameFromZipcode (Fig. 14.24).

```
   // display FragmentDialog allowing the user to add a new city
   private void showAddCityDialog()
   {
      // create a new AddCityDialogFragment
      AddCityDialogFragment newAddCityDialogFragment =
         new AddCityDialogFragment();

      // get instance of the FragmentManager
      FragmentManager thisFragmentManager = getFragmentManager();

      // begin a FragmentTransaction
      FragmentTransaction addCityFragmentTransition =
         thisFragmentManager.beginTransaction();

      // show the DialogFragment
      newAddCityDialogFragment.show(addCityFragmentTransition, "");
   } // end method showAddCityDialog

   // called when the FragmentDialog is dismissed
   @Override
   public void onDialogFinished(String zipcodeString, boolean preferred)
   {
      // convert ZIP code to city
      getCityNameFromZipcode(zipcodeString, preferred);
   } // end method onDialogFinished

```

Fig. 14.23 | WeatherViewerActivity methods showAddCityDialog and onDialogFinished.

WeatherViewerActivity Methods getCityNameFromZipcode

Method getCityNameFromZipcode (Fig. 14.24) launches a new ReadLocationTask (Section 14.5.6) to retrieve the city name for the given ZIP code. If the ZIP code is already in the favorite cities list, we do not launch the AsyncTask but instead display a Toast indicating that the user cannot add duplicate cities.

```
   // read city name from ZIP code
   private void getCityNameFromZipcode(String zipcodeString,
      boolean preferred)
   {
      // if this ZIP code is already added
      if (favoriteCitiesMap.containsValue(zipcodeString))
      {
         // create a Toast displaying error information
         Toast errorToast = Toast.makeText(WeatherViewerActivity.this,
            WeatherViewerActivity.this.getResources().getString(
            R.string.duplicate_zipcode_error), Toast.LENGTH_LONG);
```

Fig. 14.24 | WeatherViewerActivity methods getCityNameFromZipcode. (Part 1 of 2.)

```
         errorToast.setGravity(Gravity.CENTER, 0, 0);
         errorToast.show(); // show the Toast
      } // end if
      else
      {
         // load the location information in a background thread
         new ReadLocationTask(zipcodeString, this,
            new CityNameLocationLoadedListener(zipcodeString, preferred)).
            execute();
      } // end else
   } // end method getCityNameFromZipcode

```

Fig. 14.24 | `WeatherViewerActivity` methods `getCityNameFromZipcode`. (Part 2 of 2.)

Implementing Interface `LocationLoadedListener`

The `CityNameLocationLoadedListener` (Fig. 14.25) receives information from a completed `ReadLocationTask`. When the `LocationLoadedListener` is constructed we specify whether or not this location is the preferred city using the `boolean` parameter `preferred`. We add the city to the favorite city list by passing the city name and ZIP code to `WeatherViewerActivity`'s `addCity` method. The third argument to this method determines whether or not the new city's forecast is loaded. If the new city is set to be the preferred city we pass the city name to `setPreferred`.

```
   // listens for city information loaded in background task
   private class CityNameLocationLoadedListener implements
      LocationLoadedListener
   {
      private String zipcodeString; // ZIP code to look up
      private boolean preferred;

      // create a new CityNameLocationLoadedListener
      public CityNameLocationLoadedListener(String zipcodeString,
         boolean preferred)
      {
         this.zipcodeString = zipcodeString;
         this.preferred = preferred;
      } // end CityNameLocationLoadedListener

      @Override
      public void onLocationLoaded(String cityString, String stateString,
         String countryString)
      {
         // if a city was found to match the given ZIP code
         if (cityString != null)
         {
            addCity(cityString, zipcodeString, !preferred); // add new city

            if (preferred) // if this location is the preferred city
            {
```

Fig. 14.25 | Implementing interface `LocationLoadedListener`. (Part 1 of 2.)

```
                 // save the preferred city to SharedPreferences
                 setPreferred(cityString);
              } // end if
           } // end if
           else
           {
              // display a text explaining that location information could
              // not be found
              Toast zipcodeToast = Toast.makeText(WeatherViewerActivity.this,
                 WeatherViewerActivity.this.getResources().getString(
                 R.string.invalid_zipcode_error), Toast.LENGTH_LONG);
              zipcodeToast.setGravity(Gravity.CENTER, 0, 0);
              zipcodeToast.show(); // show the Toast
           } // end else
        } // end method onLocationLoaded
     } // end class CityNameLocationLoadedListener

```

Fig. 14.25 | Implementing interface `LocationLoadedListener`. (Part 2 of 2.)

`WeatherViewerActivity` Method `setupTabs`

The `ActionBar`'s *tabbed navigation* is initialized in the `setupTabs` method (Fig. 14.26). We call `Activity`'s `getActionBar` method to get a reference to its `ActionBar`. The `ActionBar` replaces the title bar in all 3.x apps and provides capabilities that allow users to navigate the app with tabs and drop-down menus. Next, we pass `ActionBar`'s **NAVIGATION_MODE_TABS** constant to its `setNavigationMode` method to indicate we'll be using `Tabs`. We create two **`Tab`** objects with `ActionBar`'s **`newTab`** method (lines 449 and 460) to allow the user to select between the current weather conditons and the five-day forecast. For each `Tab`, we set its text and register its **`TabListener`** (`weatherTabListener`, defined in Fig. 14.27). Lines 457 and 464 add the `Tabs` to the `ActionBar` with `ActionBar`'s **addTab** method. We create two `Tabs`, one for the **Current Conditions** and one for the **Five Day Forecast.**

```
440     // set up the ActionBar's tabs
441     private void setupTabs()
442     {
443        ActionBar weatherActionBar = getActionBar(); // get the ActionBar
444
445        // set ActionBar's navigation mode to use tabs
446        weatherActionBar.setNavigationMode(ActionBar.NAVIGATION_MODE_TABS);
447
448        // create the "Current Conditions" Tab
449        Tab currentConditionsTab = weatherActionBar.newTab();
450
451        // set the Tab's title
452        currentConditionsTab.setText(getResources().getString(
453           R.string.current_conditions));
```

Fig. 14.26 | `WeatherViewerActivity` method `setupTabs`. (Part 1 of 2.)

```

      // set the Tab's listener
      currentConditionsTab.setTabListener(weatherTabListener);
      weatherActionBar.addTab(currentConditionsTab); // add the Tab

      // create the "Five Day Forecast" tab
      Tab fiveDayForecastTab = weatherActionBar.newTab();
      fiveDayForecastTab.setText(getResources().getString(
         R.string.five_day_forecast));
      fiveDayForecastTab.setTabListener(weatherTabListener);
      weatherActionBar.addTab(fiveDayForecastTab);

      // select "Current Conditions" Tab by default
      currentTab = CURRENT_CONDITIONS_TAB;
   } // end method setupTabs

```

Fig. 14.26 | `WeatherViewerActivity` method `setupTabs`. (Part 2 of 2.)

Implementing Interface `TabListener`

Figure 14.27 implements `TabListener` to handle the events that occur when the user selects the tabs created in Fig. 14.26. Method `onTabSelected` (lines 480–485) calls function `selectTab` (Fig. 14.21) with the selected `Tab`'s index to display the appropriate weather data.

```
470    // listen for events generated by the ActionBar Tabs
471    TabListener weatherTabListener = new TabListener()
472    {
473       // called when the selected Tab is re-selected
474       @Override
475       public void onTabReselected(Tab arg0, FragmentTransaction arg1)
476       {
477       } // end method onTabReselected
478
479       // called when a previously unselected Tab is selected
480       @Override
481       public void onTabSelected(Tab tab, FragmentTransaction arg1)
482       {
483          // display the information corresponding to the selected Tab
484          selectTab(tab.getPosition());
485       } // end method onTabSelected
486
487       // called when a tab is unselected
488       @Override
489       public void onTabUnselected(Tab arg0, FragmentTransaction arg1)
490       {
491       } // end method onTabSelected
492    }; // end WeatherTabListener
493 } // end Class WeatherViewerActivity
```

Fig. 14.27 | Implementing interface `TabListener`.

14.5.2 Class CitiesFragment

The CitiesFragment defines a ListFragment designed to hold a list of cities. The WeatherViewerActivity's View hierarchy includes one CitiesFragment which remains pinned to the left side of the Activity at all times.

CitiesFragment package Statement, import Statements, Fields and CitiesListChangeListener Nested Interface

Fig. 14.28 begins the definition of class CitiesFragment. This Fragment reports user interactions to its parent Activity, which implements the nested interface CitiesListChangeListener (lines 40–47; implemented in Fig. 14.14). Method onSelectedCityChanged is called when the user touches a city name in the list of cities. Method onPreferredCityChanged reports changes to the preferred city.

```
1  // CitiesFragment.java
2  // Fragment displaying list of favorite cities.
3  package com.deitel.weatherviewer;
4
5  import java.util.ArrayList;
6  import java.util.List;
7
8  import android.app.AlertDialog;
9  import android.app.ListFragment;
10 import android.content.Context;
11 import android.content.DialogInterface;
12 import android.content.SharedPreferences;
13 import android.content.SharedPreferences.Editor;
14 import android.content.res.Resources;
15 import android.graphics.Color;
16 import android.os.Bundle;
17 import android.view.Gravity;
18 import android.view.View;
19 import android.view.ViewGroup;
20 import android.widget.AdapterView;
21 import android.widget.AdapterView.OnItemLongClickListener;
22 import android.widget.ArrayAdapter;
23 import android.widget.ListView;
24 import android.widget.TextView;
25 import android.widget.Toast;
26
27 public class CitiesFragment extends ListFragment
28 {
29    private int currentCityIndex; // the currently selected list position
30
31    // key used to save list selection in a Bundle
32    private static final String CURRENT_CITY_KEY = "current_city";
33
34    public ArrayList<String> citiesArrayList; // list of city names
35    private CitiesListChangeListener citiesListChangeListener;
```

Fig. 14.28 | CitiesFragment package statement, import Statements, fields and CitiesListChangeListener nested interface. (Part 1 of 2.)

```
   private ArrayAdapter<String> citiesArrayAdapter;

   // interface describing listener for changes to selected city and
   // preferred city
   public interface CitiesListChangeListener
   {
      // the selected city is changed
      public void onSelectedCityChanged(String cityNameString);

      // the preferred city is changed
      public void onPreferredCityChanged(String cityNameString);
   } // end interface CitiesListChangeListener

```

Fig. 14.28 | `CitiesFragment` package statement, `import` Statements, fields and `CitiesListChangeListener` nested interface. (Part 2 of 2.)

`CitiesFragment` Methods `onActivityCreated` and `setCitiesListChangeListener`

Method `onActivityCreated` (Fig. 14.29, lines 50–78) initializes this `ListFragment`'s `ListView`. We first check if the given `Bundle` is `null`. If not, the selected city is retrieved using `Bundle`'s `getInt` method. This allows us to persist the selected list item across orientation changes. We then create a new `ListAdapter` of type `CitiesArrayAdapter` (Fig. 14.30) using the `Activity`'s context, the list item layout in `city_list_item.xml` and an empty `ArrayList`. We also indicate that the `ListView` should allow only one choice at a time, and register its `OnLongItemClickListener`, so the user can set the city as the preferred one or delete it.

Method `setCitiesListChangeListener` (lines 81–85) allows the parent `Activity` to set this `CitiesFragment`'s `CitiesListChangeListener`. This listener reports changes in the `CitiesFragment` to the `WeatherViewerActivity`.

```
49    // called when the parent Activity is created
50    @Override
51    public void onActivityCreated(Bundle savedInstanceStateBundle)
52    {
53       super.onActivityCreated(savedInstanceStateBundle);
54 
55       // the the given Bundle has state information
56       if (savedInstanceStateBundle != null)
57       {
58          // get the last selected city from the Bundle
59          currentCityIndex = savedInstanceStateBundle.getInt(
60             CURRENT_CITY_KEY);
61       } // end if
62 
63       // create ArrayList to save city names
64       citiesArrayList = new ArrayList<String>();
```

Fig. 14.29 | `CitiesFragment` methods `onActivityCreated` and `setCitiesListChangeListener`. (Part 1 of 2.)

```

      // set the Fragment's ListView adapter
      setListAdapter(new CitiesArrayAdapter<String>(getActivity(),
         R.layout.city_list_item, citiesArrayList));

      ListView thisListView = getListView(); // get the Fragment's ListView
      citiesArrayAdapter = (ArrayAdapter<String>)getListAdapter();

      // allow only one city to be selected at a time
      thisListView.setChoiceMode(ListView.CHOICE_MODE_SINGLE);
      thisListView.setBackgroundColor(Color.WHITE); // set background color
      thisListView.setOnItemLongClickListener(
          citiesOnItemLongClickListener);
   } // end method onActivityCreated

   // set CitiesListChangeListener
   public void setCitiesListChangeListener(
      CitiesListChangeListener listener)
   {
      citiesListChangeListener = listener;
   } // end method setCitiesChangeListener

```

Fig. 14.29 | `CitiesFragment` methods `onActivityCreated` and `setCitiesListChangeListener`. (Part 2 of 2.)

`CitiesFragment` *Nested Class* `CitiesArrayAdapter`

The `CitiesArrayAdapter` (Fig. 14.30) is a custom `ArrayAdapter` which displays each city name in a list item. A star icon is placed to the left of the preferred city's name. The `getView` method (line 101–122) is called each time the `Fragment`'s `ListView` needs a new list item `View`. We first save the results from the call to the superclass's `getView` method, ensuring that an existing `View` is reused if one is available. We pass the city name for this list item to the `isPreferredCity` method (125–136). If this is the preferred city we display the star icon using `TextView`'s `setCompoundDrawables` method. If not, we use the same method to clear any previous star. Method `isPreferredCity` returns `true` if the given `String` matches the preferred city's name. We use the parent `Activity`'s `Context` to access the app's shared preferences then compare the given `String` to the preferred city name.

```
87    // custom ArrayAdapter for CitiesFragment ListView
88    private class CitiesArrayAdapter<T> extends ArrayAdapter<String>
89    {
90       private Context context; // this Fragment's Activity's Context
91
92       // public constructor for CitiesArrayAdapter
93       public CitiesArrayAdapter(Context context, int textViewResourceId,
94          List<String> objects)
95       {
96          super(context, textViewResourceId, objects);
```

Fig. 14.30 | `CitiesFragment` nested class `CitiesArrayAdapter`. (Part 1 of 2.)

```
         this.context = context;
      } // end CitiesArrayAdapter constructor

      // get ListView item for the given position
      @Override
      public View getView(int position, View convertView, ViewGroup parent)
      {
         // get the TextView generated by ArrayAdapter's getView method
         TextView listItemTextView = (TextView)
            super.getView(position, convertView, parent);

         // if this item is the preferred city
         if (isPreferredCity(listItemTextView.getText().toString()))
         {
            // display a star to the right of the list item TextView
            listItemTextView.setCompoundDrawablesWithIntrinsicBounds(0, 0,
               android.R.drawable.btn_star_big_on, 0);
         } // end if
         else
         {
            // clear any compound drawables on the list item TextView
            listItemTextView.setCompoundDrawablesWithIntrinsicBounds(0, 0,
               0, 0);
         } // end else
         return listItemTextView;
      } // end method getView

      // is the given city the preferred city?
      private boolean isPreferredCity(String cityString)
      {
         // get the app's SharedPreferences
         SharedPreferences preferredCitySharedPreferences =
            context.getSharedPreferences(
            WeatherViewerActivity.SHARED_PREFERENCES_NAME,
            Context.MODE_PRIVATE);

         // return true if the given name matches preferred city's name
         return cityString.equals(preferredCitySharedPreferences.getString(
            WeatherViewerActivity.PREFERRED_CITY_NAME_KEY, null));
      } // end method isPreferredCity
   } // end class CitiesArrayAdapter

```

Fig. 14.30 | `CitiesFragment` nested class `CitiesArrayAdapter`. (Part 2 of 2.)

Implementing Interface **`OnItemLongClickListener`**

The `citiesOnItemLongClickListener` (Fig. 14.31) responds to long presses on the `Fragment`'s `ListView` items. We construct an `AlertDialog` allowing the user to delete the selected item or set it as the preferred city. We use `AlertDialog.Builder`'s `setPositiveButton` method to construct the **Set Preferred** option. The `OnClickListener`'s `onClick` method for this `Button` (lines 172–177) passes the selected city's name to the `CitiesListChangeListener`'s `onPreferredCityChanged` method. `ArrayAdapter`'s `notifyDataSetChanged` method refreshes the `ListView`. We then create a `Button` for the **Delete** option, which removes the selected city from the app. In its `onClick` method, lines 185–233), we first check if the selected item is the only item in the list using `ArrayAdapter`'s `getCount` method, in which case we do not allow it to be deleted and display a `Toast`. Otherwise the item is deleted using `ArrayAdapter`'s `remove` method. We then delete the city name from the app's shared preferences. If the deleted city was previously the preferred city, we select the first city in the list as the new preferred city. Otherwise, we ask the `WeatherViewerActivity` to display the preferred city's forecast by passing its name to the `CitiesListChangeListener`'s `onSelectedCityChanged` method.

```
139    // responds to events generated by long pressing ListView item
140    private OnItemLongClickListener citiesOnItemLongClickListener =
141       new OnItemLongClickListener()
142    {
143       // called when a ListView item is long-pressed
144       @Override
145       public boolean onItemLongClick(AdapterView<?> listView, View view,
146          int arg2, long arg3)
147       {
148          // get the given View's Context
149          final Context context = view.getContext();
150
151          // get Resources to load Strings from xml
152          final Resources resources = context.getResources();
153
154          // get the selected city's name
155          final String cityNameString =
156             ((TextView) view).getText().toString();
157
158          // create a new AlertDialog
159          AlertDialog.Builder builder = new AlertDialog.Builder(context);
160
161          // set the AlertDialog's message
162          builder.setMessage(resources.getString(
163             R.string.city_dialog_message_prefix) + cityNameString +
164             resources.getString(R.string.city_dialog_message_postfix));
165
166          // set the AlertDialog's positive Button
167          builder.setPositiveButton(resources.getString(
168             R.string.city_dialog_preferred),
169             new DialogInterface.OnClickListener()
170             {
171                @Override
172                public void onClick(DialogInterface dialog, int which)
173                {
174                   citiesListChangeListener.onPreferredCityChanged(
175                      cityNameString);
176                   citiesArrayAdapter.notifyDataSetChanged();
177                } // end method onClick
178            }); // end DialogInterface.OnClickListener
```

Fig. 14.31 | Implementing interface `OnItemLongClickListener`. (Part 1 of 3.)

```
         // set the AlertDialog's neutral Button
         builder.setNeutralButton(resources.getString(
            R.string.city_dialog_delete),
            new DialogInterface.OnClickListener()
            {
              // called when the "Delete" Button is clicked
               public void onClick(DialogInterface dialog, int id)
               {
                  // if this is the last city
                  if (citiesArrayAdapter.getCount() == 1)
                  {
                     // inform the user they can't delete the last city
                     Toast lastCityToast =
                        Toast.makeText(context, resources.getString(
                        R.string.last_city_warning), Toast.LENGTH_LONG);
                     lastCityToast.setGravity(Gravity.CENTER, 0, 0);
                     lastCityToast.show(); // show the Toast
                     return; // exit the method
                  } // end if

                  // remove the city
                  citiesArrayAdapter.remove(cityNameString);

                  // get the app's shared preferences
                  SharedPreferences sharedPreferences =
                     context.getSharedPreferences(
                     WeatherViewerActivity.SHARED_PREFERENCES_NAME,
                     Context.MODE_PRIVATE);

                  // remove the deleted city from SharedPreferences
                  Editor preferencesEditor = sharedPreferences.edit();
                  preferencesEditor.remove(cityNameString);
                  preferencesEditor.apply();

                  // get the current preferred city
                  String preferredCityString =
                     sharedPreferences.getString(
                        WeatherViewerActivity.PREFERRED_CITY_NAME_KEY,
                        resources.getString(R.string.default_zipcode));

                  // if the preferred city was deleted
                  if (cityNameString.equals(preferredCityString))
                  {
                    // set a new preferred city
                     citiesListChangeListener.onPreferredCityChanged(
                        citiesArrayList.get(0));
                  } // end if
                  else if (cityNameString.equals(citiesArrayList.get(
                     currentCityIndex)))
                  {
                    // load the preferred city's forecast
                    citiesListChangeListener.onSelectedCityChanged(
                        preferredCityString);
```

Fig. 14.31 | Implementing interface `OnItemLongClickListener`. (Part 2 of 3.)

```
                  } // end else if
               } // end method onClick
            }); // end OnClickListener
         // set the AlertDialog's negative Button
         builder.setNegativeButton(resources.getString(
            R.string.city_dialog_cancel),
            new DialogInterface.OnClickListener()
            {
              // called when the "No" Button is clicked
               public void onClick(DialogInterface dialog, int id)
               {
                  dialog.cancel(); // dismiss the AlertDialog
               } // end method onClick
            }); // end OnClickListener

         builder.create().show(); // display the AlertDialog
         return true;
      } // end citiesOnItemLongClickListener
   }; // end OnItemLongClickListener

```

Fig. 14.31 | Implementing interface `OnItemLongClickListener`. (Part 3 of 3.)

`CitiesFragment` Methods `onSaveInstanceState`, `addCity` and `onListItemClick`

Method `onSaveInstanceState` (Fig. 14.32) saves the position of the `CitiesFragment`'s currently selected item. The `addCity` method (Lines 263–273) is used by the `WeatherViewerActivity` to add new cities to the `ListView`. We add the new `String` to our `ArrayAdapter` then sort the `Adapter`'s items alphabetically. If the `boolean` parameter `select` is `true`, we pass the city name to the `CitiesListChangeListener`'s `onSelectedCityChanged` method so the `WeatherViewerActivity` will display the corresponding forecast.

Method `onListItemClick` (lines 276–283) responds to clicks on the `ListView`'s items. We pass the selected item's city name to our `CitiesListChangeListener`'s `onSelectedCityChanged` method to inform the `WeatherViewerActivity` of the new selection, then store the index of the selected list item in `currentCityIndex`.

```
252    // save the Fragment's state
253    @Override
254    public void onSaveInstanceState(Bundle outStateBundle)
255    {
256       super.onSaveInstanceState(outStateBundle);
257
258       // save current selected city to the Bundle
259       outStateBundle.putInt(CURRENT_CITY_KEY, currentCityIndex);
260    } // end onSaveInstanceState
261
```

Fig. 14.32 | `CitiesFragment` methods `onSaveInstanceState`, `addCity` and `onListItemClick`. (Part 1 of 2.)

```
    // add a new city to the list
    public void addCity(String cityNameString, boolean select)
    {
       citiesArrayAdapter.add(cityNameString);
       citiesArrayAdapter.sort(String.CASE_INSENSITIVE_ORDER);

       if (select) // if we should select the new city
       {
          // inform the CitiesListChangeListener
          citiesListChangeListener.onSelectedCityChanged(cityNameString);
       } // end if
    } // end method addCity

    // responds to a ListView item click
    @Override
    public void onListItemClick(ListView l, View v, int position, long id)
    {
       // tell the Activity to update the ForecastFragment
       citiesListChangeListener.onSelectedCityChanged(((TextView)v).
          getText().toString());
       currentCityIndex = position; // save current selected position
    } // end method onListItemClick
 } // end class CitiesFragment
```

Fig. 14.32 | `CitiesFragment` methods `onSaveInstanceState`, `addCity` and `onListItem-Click`. (Part 2 of 2.)

14.5.3 Class AddCityDialogFragment

Class `AddCityDialogFragment` (Fig. 14.33) allows the user to enter a ZIP code to add a new city to the favorite city list. The `DialogFinishedListener` interface (lines 19–23) is implemented by class `WeatherViewerActivity` (Fig. 14.23) so the `Activity` can receive the information that the user enters in the `AddCityDialogFragment`. Interfaces are commonly used in this manner to communicate information from a `Fragment` to a parent `Activity`. The `DialogFragment` has an `EditText` in which the user can enter a ZIP code, and a `CheckBox` that the user can select to set the new city as the preferred one.

```
1  // AddCityDialogFragment.java
2  // DialogFragment allowing the user to enter a new city's ZIP code.
3  package com.deitel.weatherviewer;
4
5  import android.app.DialogFragment;
6  import android.os.Bundle;
7  import android.view.LayoutInflater;
8  import android.view.View;
9  import android.view.View.OnClickListener;
10 import android.view.ViewGroup;
11 import android.widget.Button;
12 import android.widget.CheckBox;
13 import android.widget.EditText;
```

Fig. 14.33 | Class `AddCityDialogFragment`. (Part 1 of 3.)

```
public class AddCityDialogFragment extends DialogFragment
   implements OnClickListener
{
   // listens for results from the AddCityDialog
   public interface DialogFinishedListener
   {
      // called when the AddCityDialog is dismissed
      void onDialogFinished(String zipcodeString, boolean preferred);
   } // end interface DialogFinishedListener

   EditText addCityEditText; // the DialogFragment's EditText
   CheckBox addCityCheckBox; // the DialogFragment's CheckBox

   // initializes a new DialogFragment
   @Override
   public void onCreate(Bundle bundle)
   {
      super.onCreate(bundle);

      // allow the user to exit using the back key
      this.setCancelable(true);
   } // end method onCreate

   // inflates the DialogFragment's layout
   @Override
   public View onCreateView(LayoutInflater inflater, ViewGroup container,
      Bundle argumentsBundle)
   {
      // inflate the layout defined in add_city_dialog.xml
     View rootView = inflater.inflate(R.layout.add_city_dialog, container,
        false);

      // get the EditText
      addCityEditText = (EditText) rootView.findViewById(
         R.id.add_city_edit_text);

      // get the CheckBox
      addCityCheckBox = (CheckBox) rootView.findViewById(
         R.id.add_city_checkbox);

      if (argumentsBundle != null) // if the arguments Bundle isn't empty
      {
         addCityEditText.setText(argumentsBundle.getString(
            getResources().getString(
               R.string.add_city_dialog_bundle_key)));
      } // end if

      // set the DialogFragment's title
      getDialog().setTitle(R.string.add_city_dialog_title);

```

Fig. 14.33 | Class AddCityDialogFragment. (Part 2 of 3.)

```
65          // initialize the positive Button
66          Button okButton = (Button) rootView.findViewById(
67             R.id.add_city_button);
68          okButton.setOnClickListener(this);
69          return rootView; // return the Fragment's root View
70       } // end method onCreateView
71
72       // save this DialogFragment's state
73       @Override
74       public void onSaveInstanceState(Bundle argumentsBundle)
75       {
76          // add the EditText's text to the arguments Bundle
77          argumentsBundle.putCharSequence(getResources().getString(
78             R.string.add_city_dialog_bundle_key),
79             addCityEditText.getText().toString());
80          super.onSaveInstanceState(argumentsBundle);
81       } // end method onSaveInstanceState
82
83       // called when the Add City Button is clicked
84       @Override
85       public void onClick(View clickedView)
86       {
87          if (clickedView.getId() == R.id.add_city_button)
88          {
89             DialogFinishedListener listener =
90                (DialogFinishedListener) getActivity();
91             listener.onDialogFinished(addCityEditText.getText().toString(),
92                addCityCheckBox.isChecked() );
93             dismiss(); // dismiss the DialogFragment
94          } // end if
95       } // end method onClick
96    } // end class AddCityDialogFragment
```

Fig. 14.33 | Class `AddCityDialogFragment`. (Part 3 of 3.)

Overriding Method `onCreate`

We override `onCreate` (lines 29–36) to call `DialogFragment`'s `setCancelable` method. This allows the user to dismiss the `DialogFragment` using the device's back key.

Overriding Method `onCreateView`

The `DialogFragment`'s layout is inflated in method `onCreateView` (lines 39–70). Lines 44–53 inflate the layout defined in `add_city_dialog.xml` then retrieve the `DialogFragment`'s `EditText` and `Checkbox`. If the user rotates the device while this dialog is displayed, the `argumentsBundle` contains any text the user entered into the `EditText`. This allows the `DialogFragment` to be rotated without clearing the `EditText`.

Overriding Method `onCreate`

Method `onSaveInstanceState` (lines 73–81) saves the current contents of the `EditText` allowing the `Fragment` to be restored with the same text in the future. We call the given `argumentBundle`'s `putCharSequence` method to save the text in the `Bundle`.

Overriding Method **onCreate**

We add the new city to the list and dismiss the `AddCityDialogFragment` in the `onClick` method (lines 84–95), which is called when the user clicks the `Fragment`'s `Button`. We pass the `EditText`'s text and the `CheckBox`'s checked status to our `DialogFinishedListener`'s `onDialogFinished` method. `DialogFragment`'s `dismiss` method is called to remove this `Fragment` from the `Activity`.

14.5.4 Class ForecastFragment

The `ForecastFragment` abstract class (Fig. 14.34) extends `Fragment` and provides the abstract method `getZipcode` that returns a ZIP code `String`. Class `WeatherViewerActivity` uses subclasses of `ForecastFragment` named `SingleForecastFragment` (Section 14.5.5) and `FiveDayForecastFragment` (Section 14.5.8) to display the current weather conditions and five-day forecast, respectively. Class `WeatherViewerActivity` uses `getZipcode` to get the ZIP code for the weather information displayed in each type of `ForecastFragment`.

```
// ForecastFragment.java
// An abstract class defining a Fragment capable of providing a ZIP code.
package com.deitel.weatherviewer;

import android.app.Fragment;

public abstract class ForecastFragment extends Fragment
{
   public abstract String getZipcode();
} // end class ForecastFragment
```

Fig. 14.34 | Class `ForecastFragment`.

14.5.5 Class SingleForecastFragment

The `SingleForecastFragment` is a subclass of `Fragment` designed to display the current conditions for a city.

***SingleForecastFragment* package** *Statement,* **import** *Statements and Fields*

Figure 14.35 begins the definition of class define `SingleForecastFragment` and defines its fields. Lines 25–30 define various `String` constants that are used as keys when we save and restore a `SingleForecastFragment`'s state during orientation changes.

```
1  // SingleForecastFragment.java
2  // Displays forecast information for a single city.
3  package com.deitel.weatherviewer;
4
5  import android.content.Context;
6  import android.content.res.Resources;
7  import android.graphics.Bitmap;
8  import android.os.Bundle;
```

Fig. 14.35 | `SingleForecastFragment` `package` statement, `import` statements and fields. (Part 1 of 2.)

```
import android.view.Gravity;
import android.view.LayoutInflater;
import android.view.View;
import android.view.ViewGroup;
import android.widget.ImageView;
import android.widget.TextView;
import android.widget.Toast;

import com.deitel.weatherviewer.ReadForecastTask.ForecastListener;
import com.deitel.weatherviewer.ReadLocationTask.LocationLoadedListener;

public class SingleForecastFragment extends ForecastFragment
{
   private String zipcodeString; // ZIP code for this forecast

   // lookup keys for the Fragment's saved state
   private static final String LOCATION_KEY = "location";
   private static final String TEMPERATURE_KEY = "temperature";
   private static final String FEELS_LIKE_KEY = "feels_like";
   private static final String HUMIDITY_KEY = "humidity";
   private static final String PRECIPITATION_KEY = "chance_precipitation";
   private static final String IMAGE_KEY = "image";

   // used to retrieve ZIP code from saved Bundle
   private static final String ZIP_CODE_KEY = "id_key";

   private View forecastView; // contains all forecast Views
   private TextView temperatureTextView; // displays actual temperature
   private TextView feelsLikeTextView; // displays "feels like" temperature
   private TextView humidityTextView; // displays humidity

   private TextView locationTextView;

   // displays the percentage chance of precipitation
   private TextView chanceOfPrecipitationTextView;
   private ImageView conditionImageView; // image of current sky condition
   private TextView loadingTextView;
   private Context context;
   private Bitmap conditionBitmap;

```

Fig. 14.35 | `SingleForecastFragment` package statement, `import` statements and fields. (Part 2 of 2.)

`SingleForecastFragment` Overloaded Method `newInstance`

`SingleForecastFragment`'s `static` `newInstance` methods create and return a new `Fragment` for the specified ZIP code. In the first version of the method (Fig. 14.36, lines 50–64), we create a new `SingleForecastFragment`, then insert the ZIP code into a new `Bundle` and pass this to `Fragment`'s `setArguments` method. This information will later be retrieved in the `Fragment`'s overridden `onCreate` method. The `newInstance` method that takes a `Bundle` as an argument (lines 67–72), reads the ZIP code from the given bundle then returns the result of calling the `newInstance` method that takes a `String`.

```
   // creates a new ForecastFragment for the given ZIP code
   public static SingleForecastFragment newInstance(String zipcodeString)
   {
      // create new ForecastFragment
      SingleForecastFragment newForecastFragment =
         new SingleForecastFragment();

      Bundle argumentsBundle = new Bundle(); // create a new Bundle

      // save the given String in the Bundle
      argumentsBundle.putString(ZIP_CODE_KEY, zipcodeString);

      // set the Fragement's arguments
      newForecastFragment.setArguments(argumentsBundle);
      return newForecastFragment; // return the completed ForecastFragment
   } // end method newInstance

   // create a ForecastFragment using the given Bundle
   public static SingleForecastFragment newInstance(Bundle argumentsBundle)
   {
      // get the ZIP code from the given Bundle
      String zipcodeString = argumentsBundle.getString(ZIP_CODE_KEY);
      return newInstance(zipcodeString); // create new ForecastFragment
   } // end method newInstance

```

Fig. 14.36 | `SingleForecastFragment` overloaded method `newInstance`.

`SingleForecastFragment` Methods `onCreate`, `onSaveInstanceState` and `getZipcode`

In method onCreate (Fig. 14.37, lines 75–82), the ZIP code `String` is read from the `Bundle` parameter and saved in `SingleForecastFragment`'s `zipcodeString` instance variable.

Method `onSaveInstanceState` (lines 85–102) saves the forecast information currently displayed by the `Fragment` so we do not need to launch new `AsyncTasks` after each orientation change. The text of each `TextView` is added to the `Bundle` parameter using `Bundle`'s `putString` method. The forecast image `Bitmap` is included using `Bundle`'s `putParcelable` method. `ForecastFragment`'s `getZipcode` method (lines 105–108) returns a `String` representing the ZIP code associated with this `SingleForecastFragment`.

```
74    // create the Fragment from the saved state Bundle
75    @Override
76    public void onCreate(Bundle argumentsBundle)
77    {
78       super.onCreate(argumentsBundle);
79
80       // get the ZIP code from the given Bundle
81       this.zipcodeString = getArguments().getString(ZIP_CODE_KEY);
82    } // end method onCreate
```

Fig. 14.37 | `SingleForecastFragment` methods `onCreate`, `onSaveInstanceState` and `getZipcode`. (Part 1 of 2.)

```

   // save the Fragment's state
   @Override
   public void onSaveInstanceState(Bundle savedInstanceStateBundle)
   {
      super.onSaveInstanceState(savedInstanceStateBundle);

      // store the View's contents into the Bundle
      savedInstanceStateBundle.putString(LOCATION_KEY,
         locationTextView.getText().toString());
      savedInstanceStateBundle.putString(TEMPERATURE_KEY,
         temperatureTextView.getText().toString());
      savedInstanceStateBundle.putString(FEELS_LIKE_KEY,
         feelsLikeTextView.getText().toString());
      savedInstanceStateBundle.putString(HUMIDITY_KEY,
         humidityTextView.getText().toString());
      savedInstanceStateBundle.putString(PRECIPITATION_KEY,
         chanceOfPrecipitationTextView.getText().toString());
      savedInstanceStateBundle.putParcelable(IMAGE_KEY, conditionBitmap);
   } // end method onSaveInstanceState

   // public access for ZIP code of this Fragment's forecast information
   public String getZipcode()
   {
      return zipcodeString; // return the ZIP code String
   } // end method getZIP code

```

Fig. 14.37 | `SingleForecastFragment` methods `onCreate`, `onSaveInstanceState` and `getZipcode`. (Part 2 of 2.)

Overriding Method `onCreateView`

Method `onCreateView` (Fig. 14.38) inflates and initializes `ForecastFragment`'s `View` hierarchy. The layout defined in `forecast_fragment_layout.xml` is inflated with the given `LayoutInflator`. We pass `null` as the second argument to `LayoutInflator`'s `inflate` method. This argument normally specifies a `ViewGroup` to which the newly inflated `View` will be attached. It's important *not* to attach the `Fragment`'s root `View` to any `ViewGroup` in its `onCreateView` method. This happens automatically later in the `Fragment`'s lifecycle. We use `View`'s `findViewById` method to get references to each of the `Fragment`'s `Views` then return the layout's root `View`.

```
   // inflates this Fragement's layout from xml
   @Override
   public View onCreateView(LayoutInflater inflater, ViewGroup container,
      Bundle savedInstanceState)
   {
      // use the given LayoutInflator to inflate layout stored in
      // forecast_fragment_layout.xml
      View rootView = inflater.inflate(R.layout.forecast_fragment_layout,
         null);
```

Fig. 14.38 | Overriding method `onCreateView`. (Part 1 of 2.)

```

      // get the TextView in the Fragment's layout hierarchy
      forecastView = rootView.findViewById(R.id.forecast_layout);
      loadingTextView = (TextView) rootView.findViewById(
         R.id.loading_message);
      locationTextView = (TextView) rootView.findViewById(R.id.location);
      temperatureTextView = (TextView) rootView.findViewById(
         R.id.temperature);
      feelsLikeTextView = (TextView) rootView.findViewById(
         R.id.feels_like);
      humidityTextView = (TextView) rootView.findViewById(
         R.id.humidity);
      chanceOfPrecipitationTextView = (TextView) rootView.findViewById(
         R.id.chance_of_precipitation);
      conditionImageView = (ImageView) rootView.findViewById(
         R.id.forecast_image);

      context = rootView.getContext(); // save the Context

      return rootView; // return the inflated View
   } // end method onCreateView

```

Fig. 14.38 | Overriding method `onCreateView`. (Part 2 of 2.)

Overriding Method **`onActivityCreated`**

Method `onActivityCreated` (Fig. 14.39) is called after the `Fragment`'s parent `Activity` and the `Fragment`'s `View` have been created. We check whether the `Bundle` parameter contains any data. If not, we hide all the `Views` displaying forecast information and display a loading message. Then we launch a new `ReadLocationTask` to begin populating this `Fragment`'s data. If the `Bundle` is not `null`, we retrieve the information stored in the `Bundle` by `onSaveInstanceState` (Fig. 14.37) and display that information in the `Fragment`'s `Views`.

```
   // called when the parent Activity is created
   @Override
   public void onActivityCreated(Bundle savedInstanceStateBundle)
   {
      super.onActivityCreated(savedInstanceStateBundle);

      // if there is no saved information
      if (savedInstanceStateBundle == null)
      {
         // hide the forecast and show the loading message
         forecastView.setVisibility(View.GONE);
         loadingTextView.setVisibility(View.VISIBLE);

         // load the location information in a background thread
         new ReadLocationTask(zipcodeString, context,
            new WeatherLocationLoadedListener(zipcodeString)).execute();
      } // end if
```

Fig. 14.39 | Overriding method `onActivityCreated`. (Part 1 of 2.)

```
      else
      {
         // display information in the saved state Bundle using the
         // Fragment's Views
         conditionImageView.setImageBitmap(
            (Bitmap) savedInstanceStateBundle.getParcelable(IMAGE_KEY));
         locationTextView.setText(savedInstanceStateBundle.getString(
            LOCATION_KEY));
         temperatureTextView.setText(savedInstanceStateBundle.getString(
            TEMPERATURE_KEY));
         feelsLikeTextView.setText(savedInstanceStateBundle.getString(
            FEELS_LIKE_KEY));
         humidityTextView.setText(savedInstanceStateBundle.getString(
            HUMIDITY_KEY));
         chanceOfPrecipitationTextView.setText(
            savedInstanceStateBundle.getString(PRECIPITATION_KEY));
      } // end else
   } // end method onActivityCreated

```

Fig. 14.39 | Overriding method `onActivityCreated`. (Part 2 of 2.)

Implementing Interface `ForecastListener`

The `weatherForecastListener` (Fig. 14.40) receives data from the `ReadForecastTask` (Section 14.5.7). We first check that this `Fragment` is still attached to the `WeatherViewerActivity` using `Fragment`'s `isAdded` method. If not, the user must have navigated away from this `Fragment` while the `ReadForecastTask` was executing, so we exit without doing anything. If data was returned successfully we display that data in the `Fragment`'s `Views`.

```
   // receives weather information from AsyncTask
   ForecastListener weatherForecastListener = new ForecastListener()
   {
      // displays the forecast information
      @Override
      public void onForecastLoaded(Bitmap imageBitmap,
         String temperatureString, String feelsLikeString,
         String humidityString, String precipitationString)
      {
         // if this Fragment was detached while the background process ran
         if (!SingleForecastFragment.this.isAdded())
         {
            return; // leave the method
         } // end if
         else if (imageBitmap == null)
         {
            Toast errorToast = Toast.makeText(context,
               context.getResources().getString(
               R.string.null_data_toast), Toast.LENGTH_LONG);
            errorToast.setGravity(Gravity.CENTER, 0, 0);
```

Fig. 14.40 | Implementing interface `ForecastListener`. (Part 1 of 2.)

```
            errorToast.show(); // show the Toast
            return; // exit before updating the forecast
         } // end if

         Resources resources = SingleForecastFragment.this.getResources();

         // display the loaded information
         conditionImageView.setImageBitmap(imageBitmap);
         conditionBitmap = imageBitmap;
         temperatureTextView.setText(temperatureString + (char)0x00B0 +
            resources.getString(R.string.temperature_unit));
         feelsLikeTextView.setText(feelsLikeString + (char)0x00B0 +
            resources.getString(R.string.temperature_unit));
         humidityTextView.setText(humidityString + (char)0x0025);
         chanceOfPrecipitationTextView.setText(precipitationString +
            (char)0x0025);
         loadingTextView.setVisibility(View.GONE); // hide loading message
         forecastView.setVisibility(View.VISIBLE); // show the forecast
      } // end method onForecastLoaded
   }; // end weatherForecastListener

```

Fig. 14.40 | Implementing interface `ForecastListener`. (Part 2 of 2.)

Implementing Interface `LocationLoadedListener`

The `WeatherLocationLoadedListener` (Fig. 14.41) receives location information from the `ReadLocationTask` (Section 14.5.6) and displays a `String` constructed from that data in the `locationTextView`. We then execute a new `ReadForecastTask` to retrieve the forecast's remaining data.

```
   // receives location information from background task
   private class WeatherLocationLoadedListener implements
      LocationLoadedListener
   {
      private String zipcodeString; // ZIP code to look up

      // create a new WeatherLocationLoadedListener
      public WeatherLocationLoadedListener(String zipcodeString)
      {
         this.zipcodeString = zipcodeString;
      } // end WeatherLocationLoadedListener

      // called when the location information is loaded
      @Override
      public void onLocationLoaded(String cityString, String stateString,
         String countryString)
      {
         if (cityString == null) // if there is no returned data
         {
```

Fig. 14.41 | Implementing interface `LocationLoadedListener`. (Part 1 of 2.)

```
               // display the error message
               Toast errorToast = Toast.makeText(
                  context, context.getResources().getString(
                  R.string.null_data_toast), Toast.LENGTH_LONG);
               errorToast.setGravity(Gravity.CENTER, 0, 0);
               errorToast.show(); // show the Toast
               return; // exit before updating the forecast
            } // end if
            // display the return information in a TextView
            locationTextView.setText(cityString + " " + stateString + ", " +
               zipcodeString + " " + countryString);
            // load the forecast in a background thread
            new ReadForecastTask(zipcodeString, weatherForecastListener,
               locationTextView.getContext()).execute();
         } // end method onLocationLoaded
      } // end class LocationLoadedListener
   } // end class SingleForecastFragment
```

Fig. 14.41 | Implementing interface `LocationLoadedListener`. (Part 2 of 2.)

14.5.6 Class ReadLocationTask

The `ReadLocationTask` retrieves city, state and country names for a given ZIP code. The `LocationLoadedListener` interface describes a listener capable of receiving the location data. `String`s for the city, state and country are passed to the listener's `onLocationLoaded` method when the data is retrieved.

ReadLocationTask* package *Statement,* import *Statements and Fields

Figure 14.42 begins the definition of class `ReadLocationTask` and defines the instance variables used when reading a location from the WeatherBug web services.

```
// ReadLocationTask.java
// Reads location information in a background thread.
package com.deitel.weatherviewer;

import java.io.IOException;
import java.io.InputStreamReader;
import java.io.Reader;
import java.net.MalformedURLException;
import java.net.URL;

import android.content.Context;
import android.content.res.Resources;
import android.os.AsyncTask;
import android.util.JsonReader;
import android.util.Log;
import android.view.Gravity;
import android.widget.Toast;
```

Fig. 14.42 | `ReadLocationTask` package statement, `import` statements and fields. (Part 1 of 2.)

```

// converts ZIP code to city name in a background thread
class ReadLocationTask extends AsyncTask<Object, Object, String>
{
   private static final String TAG = "ReadLocatonTask.java";

   private String zipcodeString; // the ZIP code for the location
   private Context context; // launching Activity's Context
   private Resources resources; // used to look up String from xml

   // Strings for each type of data retrieved
   private String cityString;
   private String stateString;
   private String countryString;

   // listener for retrieved information
   private LocationLoadedListener weatherLocationLoadedListener;

```

Fig. 14.42 | `ReadLocationTask` package statement, `import` statements and fields. (Part 2 of 2.)

Nested Interface LocationLoadedListener and the **`ReadLocationTask`** *Constructor*

Nested interface `LocationLoadedListener` (Fig. 14.43, lines 37–41) defines method `onLocationLoaded` that's implemented by several other classes so they can be notified when the `ReadLocationTask` receives a response from the WeatherBug web services. The `ReadLocationTask` constructor (lines 44–51) takes a ZIP code `String`, the `WeatherViewerActivity`'s `Context` and a `LocationLoadedListener`. We save the given `Context`'s `Resources` object so we can use it later to load `Strings` from the app's XML resources.

```
36    // interface for receiver of location information
37    public interface LocationLoadedListener
38    {
39       public void onLocationLoaded(String cityString, String stateString,
40          String countryString);
41    } // end interface LocationLoadedListener
42
43    // public constructor
44    public ReadLocationTask(String zipCodeString, Context context,
45       LocationLoadedListener listener)
46    {
47       this.zipcodeString = zipCodeString;
48       this.context = context;
49       this.resources = context.getResources();
50       this.weatherLocationLoadedListener = listener;
51    } // end constructor ReadLocationTask
52
```

Fig. 14.43 | Nested interface `LocationLoadedListener` and `ReadLocationTask`'s constructor.

ReadLocationTask Method doInBackground

In method `doInBackground` (Fig. 14.44), we create an `InputStreamReader` accessing the WeatherBug webservice at the location described by the `URL`. We use this to create a `JsonReader` so we can read the JSON data returned by the web service. (You can view the JSON document directly by opening the `weatherServiceURL` in a browser.) **JSON (JavaScript Object Notation)**—a simple way to represent JavaScript objects as strings—is an alternative to XML for passing data between the client and the server. Each object in JSON is represented as a list of property names and values contained in curly braces, in the following format:

```
{ "propertyName1" : value1, "propertyName2": value2 }
```

Arrays are represented in JSON with square brackets in the following format:

```
[ value1, value2, value3 ]
```

Each value can be a string, a number, a JSON representation of an object, `true`, `false` or `null`. JSON is commonly used to communicate in client/server interaction.

```
      // load city name in background thread
      @Override
      protected String doInBackground(Object... params)
      {
         try
         {
            // construct Weatherbug API URL
            URL url = new URL(resources.getString(
               R.string.location_url_pre_zipcode) + zipcodeString +
               "&api_key=YOUR_API_KEY");

            // create an InputStreamReader using the URL
            Reader forecastReader = new InputStreamReader(
               url.openStream());

            // create a JsonReader from the Reader
            JsonReader forecastJsonReader = new JsonReader(forecastReader);
            forecastJsonReader.beginObject(); // read the first Object

            // get the next name
            String name = forecastJsonReader.nextName();

            // if the name indicates that the next item describes the
            // ZIP code's location
            if (name.equals(resources.getString(R.string.location)))
            {
               // start reading the next JSON Object
               forecastJsonReader.beginObject();

               String nextNameString;
```

Fig. 14.44 | `ReadLocationTask` method `doInBackground`. (Part 1 of 2.)

```
83
84             // while there is more information to be read
85             while (forecastJsonReader.hasNext())
86             {
87                nextNameString = forecastJsonReader.nextName();
88                // if the name indicates that the next item describes the
89                // ZIP code's corresponding city name
90                if ((nextNameString).equals(
91                   resources.getString(R.string.city)))
92                {
93                   // read the city name
94                   cityString = forecastJsonReader.nextString();
95                } // end if
96                else if ((nextNameString).equals(resources.
97                   getString(R.string.state)))
98                {
99                   stateString = forecastJsonReader.nextString();
100               } // end else if
101               else if ((nextNameString).equals(resources.
102                  getString(R.string.country)))
103               {
104                  countryString = forecastJsonReader.nextString();
105               } // end else if
106               else
107               {
108                  forecastJsonReader.skipValue(); // skip unexpected value
109               } // end else
110            } // end while
111
112            forecastJsonReader.close(); // close the JsonReader
113         } // end if
114      } // end try
115      catch (MalformedURLException e)
116      {
117         Log.v(TAG, e.toString()); // print the exception to the LogCat
118      } // end catch
119      catch (IOException e)
120      {
121         Log.v(TAG, e.toString()); // print the exception to the LogCat
122      } // end catch
123
124      return null; // return null if the city name couldn't be found
125   } // end method doInBackground
126
```

Fig. 14.44 | ReadLocationTask method doInBackground. (Part 2 of 2.)

JsonReader has methods beginObject and beginArray to begin reading objects and arrays, respectively. Line 70 uses JsonReader' beginObject method to read the first object in the JSON document. We get the name from the first name–value pair in the object with JsonReader's nextName method (line 73), then check that it matches the expected name for a location information document. If so, we move to the next object (line 80), which describes the ZIP code's location information, and read each name–value pair in the object using a loop (lines 85–110). If the name in a name–value pair matches one of the pieces of data we use to display weather information in this app, we save the corresponding value to one of `ReadLocationTask`'s instance variables. Class `JsonReader` provides methods for reading `booleans`, `doubles`, `ints`, `longs` and `Strings`—since we're displaying all the data in `String` format, we use only `JsonReader`'s `getString` method. All unrecognized names are skipped using `JsonReader`'s `skipValue` method. [*Note:* The code for reading the JSON data returned by the WeatherBug web services depends directly on the structure of the JSON document returned. If WeatherBug changes the format of this JSON data in the future, an exception may occur.]

ReadLocationTask *Method* onPostExecute

Method `onPostExecute` (Fig. 14.45) delivers the results to the GUI thread for display. If the retrieved data is not `null` (i.e., the web service call returned data), we pass the location information `Strings` to the stored `LocationLoadedListener`'s `onLocationLoaded` method. Otherwise, we display a `Toast` informing the user that the location information retrieval failed.

```
   // executed back on the UI thread after the city name loads
   protected void onPostExecute(String nameString)
   {
      // if a city was found to match the given ZIP code
      if (cityString != null)
      {
         // pass the information back to the LocationLoadedListener
         weatherLocationLoadedListener.onLocationLoaded(cityString,
            stateString, countryString);
      } // end if
      else
      {
         // display Toast informing that location information
         // couldn't be found
         Toast errorToast = Toast.makeText(context, resources.getString(
            R.string.invalid_zipcode_error), Toast.LENGTH_LONG);
         errorToast.setGravity(Gravity.CENTER, 0, 0); // center the Toast
         errorToast.show(); // show the Toast
      } // end else
   } // end method onPostExecute
} // end class ReadLocationTask
```

Fig. 14.45 | `ReadLocationTask` method `onPostExecute`.

14.5.7 Class ReadForecastTask

The `ReadForecastTask` retrieves the current weather conditions for a given ZIP code.

ReadForecastTask package *Statement,* import *Statements and Fields*

Figure 14.46 begins the definition of class `ReadForecastTask`. The `String` instance variables store the text for the weather conditions. A `Bitmap` stores an image of the current conditions. The `bitmapSampleSize` variable is used to specify how to downsample the image `Bitmap`.

The `ForecastListener` interface (lines 37–41) describes a listener capable of receiving the forecast image `Bitmap` and `String`s representing the current temperature, feels-like temperature, humidity and chance of precipitation.

```
1  // ReadForecastTask.java
2  // Reads weather information off the main thread.
3  package com.deitel.weatherviewer;
4
5  import java.io.IOException;
6  import java.io.InputStreamReader;
7  import java.io.Reader;
8  import java.net.MalformedURLException;
9  import java.net.URL;
10
11 import android.content.Context;
12 import android.content.res.Resources;
13 import android.graphics.Bitmap;
14 import android.graphics.BitmapFactory;
15 import android.os.AsyncTask;
16 import android.util.JsonReader;
17 import android.util.Log;
18
19 class ReadForecastTask extends AsyncTask<Object, Object, String>
20 {
21    private String zipcodeString; // the ZIP code of the forecast's city
22    private Resources resources;
23
24    // receives weather information
25    private ForecastListener weatherForecastListener;
26    private static final String TAG = "ReadForecastTask.java";
27
28    private String temperatureString; // the temperature
29    private String feelsLikeString; // the "feels like" temperature
30    private String humidityString; // the humidity
31    private String chanceOfPrecipitationString; // chance of precipitation
32    private Bitmap iconBitmap; // image of the sky condition
33
34    private int bitmapSampleSize = -1;
35
36    // interface for receiver of weather information
37    public interface ForecastListener
38    {
39       public void onForecastLoaded(Bitmap image, String temperature,
40          String feelsLike, String humidity, String precipitation);
41    } // end interface ForecastListener
42
```

Fig. 14.46 | `ReadForecastTask` package statement, import statements and fields.

`ReadForecastTask` Constructor and `setSampleSize` Methods

The `ReadForecastTask` constructor (Fig. 14.47, lines 44–50) takes a ZIP code `String`, a `ForecastListener` and the `WeatherViewerActivity`'s `Context`.

The `setSampleSize` method (lines 53–56) sets the downsampling rate when loading the forecast's image `Bitmap`. If this method is not called, the `Bitmap` is not downsampled. The `WeatherProvider` uses this method because there is a strict limit on the size of `Bitmaps` that can be passed using a `RemoteViews` object. This is because the `RemoteViews` object communicates with the app widget across processes.

```
43    // creates a new ReadForecastTask
44    public ReadForecastTask(String zipcodeString,
45       ForecastListener listener, Context context)
46    {
47       this.zipcodeString = zipcodeString;
48       this.weatherForecastListener = listener;
49       this.resources = context.getResources();
50    } // end constructor ReadForecastTask
51
52    // set the sample size for the forecast's Bitmap
53    public void setSampleSize(int sampleSize)
54    {
55       this.bitmapSampleSize = sampleSize;
56    } // end method setSampleSize
57
```

Fig. 14.47 | `ReadForecastTask` constructor and `setSampleSize` methods.

`ReadForecastTask` Methods `doInBackground` and `onPostExecute`

The `doInBackground` method (Fig. 14.48, lines 59–101) gets and parses the WeatherBug JSON document representing the current weather conditions in a background thread. We create a `URL` pointing to the web service then use it to construct a `JsonReader`. `JsonReader`'s `beginObject` and `nextName` methods are used to read the first name of the first object in the document (lines 75 and 78). If the name matches the `String` specified in the `String` resource `R.string.hourly_forecast`, we pass the `JsonReader` to the `readForecast` method to parse the forecast. The `onPostExecute` method (lines 104–110) returns the retrieved `Strings` to the `ForecastLoadedListener`'s `onForecastLoaded` method for display.

```
58    // load the forecast in a background thread
59    protected String doInBackground(Object... args)
60    {
61       try
62       {
63          // the url for the WeatherBug JSON service
64          URL webServiceURL = new URL(resources.getString(
65             R.string.pre_zipcode_url) + zipcodeString  + "&ht=t&ht=i&"
66             + "ht=cp&ht=fl&ht=h&api_key=YOUR_API_KEY");
67
68          // create a stream Reader from the WeatherBug url
69          Reader forecastReader = new InputStreamReader(
70             webServiceURL.openStream());
```

Fig. 14.48 | `ReadForecastTask` methods `doInBackground` and `onPostExecute`. (Part 1 of 2.)

```

         // create a JsonReader from the Reader
         JsonReader forecastJsonReader = new JsonReader(forecastReader);

         forecastJsonReader.beginObject(); // read the first Object

         // get the next name
         String name = forecastJsonReader.nextName();

         // if its the name expected for hourly forecast information
         if (name.equals(resources.getString(R.string.hourly_forecast)))
         {
            readForecast(forecastJsonReader); // read the forecast
         } // end if

         forecastJsonReader.close(); // close the JsonReader
      } // end try
      catch (MalformedURLException e)
      {
         Log.v(TAG, e.toString());
      } // end catch
      catch (IOException e)
      {
         Log.v(TAG, e.toString());
      } // end catch
      catch (IllegalStateException e)
      {
        Log.v(TAG, e.toString() + zipcodeString);
      } // end catch
      return null;
   } // end method doInBackground

   // update the UI back on the main thread
   protected void onPostExecute(String forecastString)
   {
      // pass the information to the ForecastListener
      weatherForecastListener.onForecastLoaded(iconBitmap,
         temperatureString, feelsLikeString, humidityString,
         chanceOfPrecipitationString);
   } // end method onPostExecute

```

Fig. 14.48 | ReadForecastTask methods doInBackground and onPostExecute. (Part 2 of 2.)

ReadForecastTask Method getIconBitmap

The static getIconBitmap method (Fig. 14.49) converts a condition String to a Bitmap. The WeatherBug JSON document provides the relative path to the forecast' image on the WeatherBug website. We create a URL pointing to the image's location. We load the image from the WeatherBug server using BitmapFactory's static decodeStream method.

```
112    // get the sky condition image Bitmap
113    public static Bitmap getIconBitmap(String conditionString,
114       Resources resources, int bitmapSampleSize)
115    {
116       Bitmap iconBitmap = null; // create the Bitmap
117       try
118       {
119          // create a URL pointing to the image on WeatherBug's site
120          URL weatherURL = new URL(resources.getString(
121             R.string.pre_condition_url) + conditionString +
122             resources.getString(R.string.post_condition_url));
123
124          BitmapFactory.Options options = new BitmapFactory.Options();
125          if (bitmapSampleSize != -1)
126          {
127             options.inSampleSize = bitmapSampleSize;
128          } // end if
129
130          // save the image as a Bitmap
131          iconBitmap = BitmapFactory.decodeStream(weatherURL.
132             openStream(), null, options);
133       } // end try
134       catch (MalformedURLException e)
135       {
136          Log.e(TAG, e.toString());
137       } // end catch
138       catch (IOException e)
139       {
140          Log.e(TAG, e.toString());
141       } // end catch
142
143       return iconBitmap; // return the image
144    } // end method getIconBitmap
145
```

Fig. 14.49 | `ReadForecastTask` method `getIconBitmap`.

`ReadForecastTask` Method `readForecast`

The `readForecast` method (Fig. 14.50) parses a single current conditions forecast using the `JsonReader` parameter. `JsonReader`'s `beginArray` and `beginObject` methods (lines 151–152) are used to start reading the first object in the next array in the JSON document. We then loop through each name in the object and compare them to the expected names for the information we'd like to display. `JsonReader`'s `skipValue` method is used to skip the information we don't need.

```
146    // read the forecast information using the given JsonReader
147    private String readForecast(JsonReader reader)
148    {
149       try
150       {
```

Fig. 14.50 | `ReadForecastTask` method `readForecast`. (Part 1 of 2.)

```
            reader.beginArray(); // start reading the next array
            reader.beginObject(); // start reading the next object

            // while there is a next element in the current object
            while (reader.hasNext())
            {
               String name = reader.nextName(); // read the next name

               // if this element is the temperature
               if (name.equals(resources.getString(R.string.temperature)))
               {
                  // read the temperature
                  temperatureString = reader.nextString();
               } // end if
               // if this element is the "feels-like" temperature
               else if (name.equals(resources.getString(R.string.feels_like)))
               {
                  // read the "feels-like" temperature
                  feelsLikeString = reader.nextString();
               } // end else if
               // if this element is the humidity
               else if (name.equals(resources.getString(R.string.humidity)))
               {
                  humidityString = reader.nextString(); // read the humidity
               } // end else if
               // if this next element is the chance of precipitation
               else if (name.equals(resources.getString(
                  R.string.chance_of_precipitation)))
               {
                  // read the chance of precipitation
                  chanceOfPrecipitationString = reader.nextString();
               } // end else if
               // if the next item is the icon name
               else if (name.equals(resources.getString(R.string.icon)))
               {
                  // read the icon name
                  iconBitmap = getIconBitmap(reader.nextString(), resources,
                     bitmapSampleSize);
               } // end else if
               else // there is an unexpected element
               {
                  reader.skipValue(); // skip the next element
               } // end else
            } // end while
         } // end try
         catch (IOException e)
         {
            Log.e(TAG, e.toString());
         } // end catch
         return null;
      } // end method readForecast
   } // end ReadForecastTask
```

Fig. 14.50 | ReadForecastTask method readForecast. (Part 2 of 2.)

14.5.8 Class FiveDayForecastFragment

The FiveDayForecastFragment displays the five-day forecast for a single city.

FiveDayForecastFragment package Statement, import Statements and Fields

In Fig. 14.51, we begin class FiveDayForecastFragment and define the fields used throughout the class.

```
// FiveDayForecastFragment.java
// Displays the five day forecast for a single city.
package com.deitel.weatherviewer;

import android.content.Context;
import android.content.res.Configuration;
import android.os.Bundle;
import android.view.Gravity;
import android.view.LayoutInflater;
import android.view.View;
import android.view.ViewGroup;
import android.widget.ImageView;
import android.widget.LinearLayout;
import android.widget.TextView;
import android.widget.Toast;

import com.deitel.weatherviewer.ReadFiveDayForecastTask.
   FiveDayForecastLoadedListener;
import com.deitel.weatherviewer.ReadLocationTask.LocationLoadedListener;

public class FiveDayForecastFragment extends ForecastFragment
{
   // used to retrieve ZIP code from saved Bundle
   private static final String ZIP_CODE_KEY = "id_key";
   private static final int NUMBER_DAILY_FORECASTS = 5;

   private String zipcodeString; // ZIP code for this forecast
   private View[] dailyForecastViews = new View[NUMBER_DAILY_FORECASTS];

   private TextView locationTextView;

```

Fig. 14.51 | FiveDayForecastFragment package statement, import statements and fields.

FiveDayForecastFragment Overloaded newInstance Methods

Similar to the SingleForecastFragment, we provide overloaded newInstance method (Fig. 14.52) to create new FiveDayForecastFragments. The first method (lines 32–46) takes a ZIP code String. The other (lines 49–55) takes a Bundle containing the ZIP code String, extracts the ZIP code and passes it to the first method. Lines 38 and 41 create and configure a Bundle containing the ZIP code String, then pass it to Fragment's setArguments method so it can be used in onCreate (Fig. 14.53).

```
   // creates a new FiveDayForecastFragment for the given ZIP code
   public static FiveDayForecastFragment newInstance(String zipcodeString)
   {
      // create new ForecastFragment
      FiveDayForecastFragment newFiveDayForecastFragment =
         new FiveDayForecastFragment();

      Bundle argumentsBundle = new Bundle(); // create a new Bundle

      // save the given String in the Bundle
      argumentsBundle.putString(ZIP_CODE_KEY, zipcodeString);

      // set the Fragement's arguments
      newFiveDayForecastFragment.setArguments(argumentsBundle);
      return newFiveDayForecastFragment; // return the completed Fragment
   } // end method newInstance

   // create a FiveDayForecastFragment using the given Bundle
   public static FiveDayForecastFragment newInstance(
      Bundle argumentsBundle)
   {
      // get the ZIP code from the given Bundle
      String zipcodeString = argumentsBundle.getString(ZIP_CODE_KEY);
      return newInstance(zipcodeString); // create new Fragment
   } // end method newInstance

```

Fig. 14.52 | FiveDayForecastFragment overloaded newInstance methods.

FiveDayForecastFragment Methods onCreate and getZipCode

The ZIP code is read in the Fragment's onCreate method (Fig. 14.53, lines 58–65). Fragment's getArguments method retrieves the Bundle then Bundle's getString method accesses the ZIP code String. Method getZipcode (lines 68–71) is called by the WeatherViewerActivity to get the FiveDayForecastFragment's ZIP code.

```
57    // create the Fragment from the saved state Bundle
58    @Override
59    public void onCreate(Bundle argumentsBundle)
60    {
61       super.onCreate(argumentsBundle);
62
63       // get the ZIP code from the given Bundle
64       this.zipcodeString = getArguments().getString(ZIP_CODE_KEY);
65    } // end method onCreate
66
67    // public access for ZIP code of this Fragment's forecast information
68    public String getZipcode()
69    {
70       return zipcodeString; // return the ZIP code String
71    } // end method getZipcode
72
```

Fig. 14.53 | FiveDayForecastFragment methods onCreate and getZipCode.

FiveDayForecastFragment Method onCreateView

The Fragment's layout is created in method onCreateView (Fig. 14.54). We inflate the layout defined in five_day_forecast.xml using the given LayoutInflator and pass null as the second argument. We check the orientation of the device here to determine which layout to use for each daily forecast View. We then inflate five of the selected layouts and add each View to the container LinearLayout. Next we execute a ReadLocationTask to retrieve the location information for this Fragment's corresponding city.

```
   // inflates this Fragement's layout from xml
   @Override
   public View onCreateView(LayoutInflater inflater, ViewGroup container,
      Bundle savedInstanceState)
   {
      // inflate the five day forecast layout
      View rootView = inflater.inflate(R.layout.five_day_forecast_layout,
         null);
      // get the TextView to display location information
      locationTextView = (TextView) rootView.findViewById(R.id.location);

      // get the ViewGroup to contain the daily forecast layouts
      LinearLayout containerLinearLayout =
         (LinearLayout) rootView.findViewById(R.id.containerLinearLayout);

      int id; // int identifier for the daily forecast layout

      // if we are in landscape orientation
      if (container.getContext().getResources().getConfiguration().
         orientation == Configuration.ORIENTATION_LANDSCAPE)
      {
         id = R.layout.single_forecast_layout_landscape;
      } // end if
      else // portrait orientation
      {
         id = R.layout.single_forecast_layout_portrait;
         containerLinearLayout.setOrientation(LinearLayout.VERTICAL);
      } // end else

      // load five daily forecasts
      View forecastView;
      for (int i = 0; i < NUMBER_DAILY_FORECASTS; i++)
      {
         forecastView = inflater.inflate(id, null); // inflate new View

         // add the new View to the container LinearLayout
         containerLinearLayout.addView(forecastView);
         dailyForecastViews[i] = forecastView;
      } // end for

      // load the location information in a background thread
      new ReadLocationTask(zipcodeString, rootView.getContext(),
         new WeatherLocationLoadedListener(zipcodeString,
         rootView.getContext())).execute();
```

Fig. 14.54 | FiveDayForecastFragment method onCreateView. (Part 1 of 2.)

```

      return rootView;
   } // end method onCreateView

```

Fig. 14.54 | `FiveDayForecastFragment` method `onCreateView`. (Part 2 of 2.)

Implementing Interface `LocationLoadedListener`

`FiveDayForecastFragment`'s `WeatherLocationLoadedListener` (Fig. 14.55) is similar to the other `LocationLoadedListener`'s in the app. It receives data from a `ReadLocationTask` and displays a formatted `String` of location information using the `locationTextView`.

```
   // receives location information from background task
   private class WeatherLocationLoadedListener implements
      LocationLoadedListener
   {
      private String zipcodeString; // ZIP code to look up
      private Context context;

      // create a new WeatherLocationLoadedListener
      public WeatherLocationLoadedListener(String zipcodeString,
         Context context)
      {
         this.zipcodeString = zipcodeString;
         this.context = context;
      } // end WeatherLocationLoadedListener

      // called when the location information is loaded
      @Override
      public void onLocationLoaded(String cityString, String stateString,
         String countryString)
      {
         if (cityString == null) // if there is no returned data
         {
            // display error message
            Toast errorToast = Toast.makeText(context,
              context.getResources().getString(R.string.null_data_toast),
               Toast.LENGTH_LONG);
            errorToast.setGravity(Gravity.CENTER, 0, 0);
            errorToast.show(); // show the Toast
            return; // exit before updating the forecast
         } // end if

         // display the return information in a TextView
         locationTextView.setText(cityString + " " + stateString + ", " +
            zipcodeString + " " + countryString);

         // load the forecast in a background thread
         new ReadFiveDayForecastTask(
            weatherForecastListener,
```

Fig. 14.55 | `Implementing` interface `LocationLoadedListener`. (Part 1 of 2.)

```
            locationTextView.getContext()).execute();
      } // end method onLocationLoaded
   } // end class WeatherLocationLoadedListener

```

Fig. 14.55 | `Implementing` interface `LocationLoadedListener`. (Part 2 of 2.)

Implementing Interface `FiveDayForecastLoadedListener`

The `FiveDayForecastLoadedListener` (Fig. 14.56) receives an array of five `DailyForecast` `Objects` in its `onForecastLoaded` method. We display the information in the `DailyForecasts` by passing them to method `loadForecastIntoView` (Fig. 14.57).

```
   // receives weather information from AsyncTask
   FiveDayForecastLoadedListener weatherForecastListener =
      new FiveDayForecastLoadedListener()
   {
      // when the background task looking up location information finishes
      @Override
      public void onForecastLoaded(DailyForecast[] forecasts)
      {
         // display five daily forecasts
         for (int i = 0; i < NUMBER_DAILY_FORECASTS; i++)
         {
            // display the forecast information
            loadForecastIntoView(dailyForecastViews[i], forecasts[i]);
         } // end for
      } // end method onForecastLoaded
   }; // end FiveDayForecastLoadedListener

```

Fig. 14.56 | Implementing interface `FiveDayForecastLoadedListener`.

`FiveDayForecastFragment` *Method* `loadForecastIntoView`

The `loadForecastIntoView` method (Fig. 14.57) displays the information in the given `DailyForecast` using the given `View`. After ensuring that this `Fragment` is still attached to the `WeatherViewerActivity` and the given `DailyForecast` is not empty, we get references to each child `View` in the given `ViewGroup`. These child `Views` are used to display each data item in the `DailyForecast`.

```
   // display the given forecast information in the given View
   private void loadForecastIntoView(View view,
      DailyForecast dailyForecast)
   {
      // if this Fragment was detached while the background process ran
      if (!FiveDayForecastFragment.this.isAdded())
      {
         return; // leave the method
      } // end if
```

Fig. 14.57 | `FiveDayForecastFragment` method `loadForecastIntoView`. (Part 1 of 2.)

```
      // if there is no returned data
      else if (dailyForecast == null ||
         dailyForecast.getIconBitmap() == null)
      {
         // display error message
         Toast errorToast = Toast.makeText(view.getContext(),
            view.getContext().getResources().getString(
            R.string.null_data_toast), Toast.LENGTH_LONG);
         errorToast.setGravity(Gravity.CENTER, 0, 0);
         errorToast.show(); // show the Toast
         return; // exit before updating the forecast
      } // end else if

      // get all the child Views
      ImageView forecastImageView = (ImageView) view.findViewById(
         R.id.daily_forecast_bitmap);
      TextView dayOfWeekTextView = (TextView) view.findViewById(
         R.id.day_of_week);
      TextView descriptionTextView = (TextView) view.findViewById(
         R.id.daily_forecast_description);
      TextView highTemperatureTextView = (TextView) view.findViewById(
         R.id.high_temperature);
      TextView lowTemperatureTextView = (TextView) view.findViewById(
         R.id.low_temperature);

      // display the forecast information in the retrieved Views
      forecastImageView.setImageBitmap(dailyForecast.getIconBitmap());
      dayOfWeekTextView.setText(dailyForecast.getDay());
      descriptionTextView.setText(dailyForecast.getDescription());
      highTemperatureTextView.setText(dailyForecast.getHighTemperature());
      lowTemperatureTextView.setText(dailyForecast.getLowTemperature());
   } // end method loadForecastIntoView
} // end class FiveDayForecastFragment
```

Fig. 14.57 | FiveDayForecastFragment method loadForecastIntoView. (Part 2 of 2.)

14.5.9 Class ReadFiveDayForecastTask

The ReadFiveDayForecastTask is an AsyncTask which uses a JsonReader to load five-day forecasts from the WeatherBug web service.

ReadFiveDayForecastTask package Statement, import Statements, Fields and Nested Interface FiveDayForecastLoadedListener

Figure 14.58 begins the definition of class ReadFiveDayForecastTask and defines the fields used throughout the class. The FiveDayForecastLoadedListener interface (lines 30–33) describes a listener capable of receiving five DailyForecasts when the background task returns data to the GUI thread for display.

```
1 // ReadFiveDayForecastTask.java
2 // Read the next five daily forecasts in a background thread.
3 package com.deitel.weatherviewer;
```

Fig. 14.58 | Class ReadFiveDayForecast. (Part 1 of 2.)

```java

import java.io.IOException;
import java.io.InputStreamReader;
import java.io.Reader;
import java.net.MalformedURLException;
import java.net.URL;

import android.content.Context;
import android.content.res.Resources;
import android.content.res.Resources.NotFoundException;
import android.graphics.Bitmap;
import android.os.AsyncTask;
import android.util.JsonReader;
import android.util.Log;

class ReadFiveDayForecastTask extends AsyncTask<Object, Object, String>
{
   private static final String TAG = "ReadFiveDayForecastTask";

   private String zipcodeString;
   private FiveDayForecastLoadedListener weatherFiveDayForecastListener;
   private Resources resources;
   private DailyForecast[] forecasts;
   private static final int NUMBER_OF_DAYS = 5;

   // interface for receiver of weather information
   public interface FiveDayForecastLoadedListener
   {
      public void onForecastLoaded(DailyForecast[] forecasts);
   } // end interface FiveDayForecastLoadedListener

```

Fig. 14.58 | Class `ReadFiveDayForecast`. (Part 2 of 2.)

`ReadFiveDayForecastTask` Constructor

The `ReadFiveDayForecastTask` constructor (Fig. 14.59) receives the selected city's `zipcodeString`, a `FiveDayForecastLoadedListener` and the `WeatherViewerActivity`'s `Context`. We initialize the array to hold the five `DailyForecasts`.

```java
   // creates a new ReadForecastTask
   public ReadFiveDayForecastTask(String zipcodeString,
      FiveDayForecastLoadedListener listener, Context context)
   {
      this.zipcodeString = zipcodeString;
      this.weatherFiveDayForecastListener = listener;
      this.resources = context.getResources();
      this.forecasts = new DailyForecast[NUMBER_OF_DAYS];
   } // end constructor ReadFiveDayForecastTask

```

Fig. 14.59 | `ReadFiveDayForecast` constructor.

ReadFiveDayForecastTask Method doInBackground

Method doInBackground (Fig. 14.60) invokes the web service in a separate thread. We create an InputStreamReader accessing the WeatherBug web service at the location described by the webServiceURL. After accessing the first object in the JSON document (line 62), we read the next name and ensure that it describes a forecast list. We then begin reading the next array (line 70) and call forecastJsonRead's skipValue to skip the next object. This skips all the values in the first object that describes the current weather conditions. Next, we call readDailyForecast for the next five objects, which contain the next five daily forecasts.

```
45      @Override
46      protected String doInBackground(Object... params)
47      {
48         // the url for the WeatherBug JSON service
49         try
50         {
51            URL webServiceURL = new URL("http://i.wxbug.net/REST/Direct/" +
52               "GetForecast.ashx?zip="+ zipcodeString  + "&ht=t&ht=i&"
53               + "nf=7&ht=cp&ht=fl&ht=h&api_key=YOUR_API_KEY");
54
55            // create a stream Reader from the WeatherBug url
56            Reader forecastReader = new InputStreamReader(
57               webServiceURL.openStream());
58
59            // create a JsonReader from the Reader
60            JsonReader forecastJsonReader = new JsonReader(forecastReader);
61
62            forecastJsonReader.beginObject(); // read the next Object
63
64            // get the next name
65            String name = forecastJsonReader.nextName();
66
67            // if its the name expected for hourly forecast information
68            if (name.equals(resources.getString(R.string.forecast_list)))
69            {
70               forecastJsonReader.beginArray(); // start reading first array
71               forecastJsonReader.skipValue(); // skip today's forecast
72
73               // read the next five daily forecasts
74               for (int i = 0; i < NUMBER_OF_DAYS; i++)
75               {
76                  // start reading the next object
77                  forecastJsonReader.beginObject();
78
79                  // if there is more data
80                  if (forecastJsonReader.hasNext())
81                  {
82                     // read the next forecast
83                     forecasts[i] = readDailyForecast(forecastJsonReader);
84                  } // end if
85               } // end for
86            } // end if
```

Fig. 14.60 | ReadFiveDayForecastTask method doInBackground. (Part 1 of 2.)

```
         forecastJsonReader.close(); // close the JsonReader

      } // end try
      catch (MalformedURLException e)
      {
         Log.v(TAG, e.toString());
      } // end catch
      catch (NotFoundException e)
      {
         Log.v(TAG, e.toString());
      } // end catch
      catch (IOException e)
      {
         Log.v(TAG, e.toString());
      } // end catch
      return null;
   } // end method doInBackground
```

Fig. 14.60 | `ReadFiveDayForecastTask` method `doInBackground`. (Part 2 of 2.)

`ReadFiveDayForecastTask` Methods `readDailyForecast` and `onPostExecute`

Each forecast JSON object is read and processed using the `readDailyForecast` method (Fig. 14.61, lines 107–161). We create a new `String` array with four items and a `Bitmap` to store all the forecast information. We check whether there are any unread items in the object using `forecastReader`'s `hasNext` method. If so, we read the next name and check if it matches one of the pieces of data we want to display. If there's a match, we read the value using `JsonReader`'s `nextString` method. We pass the icon's `String` to our `getIconBitmap` method to get a `Bitmap` from the WeatherBug website. We skip the values of unrecognized names using `JsonReader`'s `skipValue` method. `DailyForecast` objects encapsulate the weather information for each day.

The `onPostExecute` method (lines 164–167) returns the results to the GUI thread for display. We pass the array of `DailyForecasts` back to the `FiveDayForecastFragment` using its `FiveDayForecastListener`'s `onForecastLoaded` method.

```
106    // read a single daily forecast
107    private DailyForecast readDailyForecast(JsonReader forecastJsonReader)
108    {
109       // create array to store forecast information
110       String[] dailyForecast = new String[4];
111       Bitmap iconBitmap = null; // store the forecast's image
112
113       try
114       {
115          // while there is a next element in the current object
116          while (forecastJsonReader.hasNext())
117          {
```

Fig. 14.61 | `ReadFiveDayForecastTask` methods `readDailyForecast` and `onPostExecute`. (Part 1 of 2.)

```
            String name = forecastJsonReader.nextName(); // read next name

            if (name.equals(resources.getString(R.string.day_of_week)))
            {
               dailyForecast[DailyForecast.DAY_INDEX] =
                  forecastJsonReader.nextString();
            } // end if
            else if (name.equals(resources.getString(
               R.string.day_prediction)))
            {
               dailyForecast[DailyForecast.PREDICTION_INDEX] =
                  forecastJsonReader.nextString();
            } // end else if
            else if (name.equals(resources.getString(R.string.high)))
            {
               dailyForecast[DailyForecast.HIGH_TEMP_INDEX] =
                  forecastJsonReader.nextString();
            } // end else if
            else if (name.equals(resources.getString(R.string.low)))
            {
               dailyForecast[DailyForecast.LOW_TEMP_INDEX] =
                  forecastJsonReader.nextString();
            } // end else if
            // if the next item is the icon name
            else if (name.equals(resources.getString(R.string.day_icon)))
            {
               // read the icon name
               iconBitmap = ReadForecastTask.getIconBitmap(
                  forecastJsonReader.nextString(), resources, 0);
            } // end else if
            else // there is an unexpected element
            {
               forecastJsonReader.skipValue(); // skip the next element
            } // end else
         } // end while
         forecastJsonReader.endObject();
      } // end try
      catch (IOException e)
      {
         Log.e(TAG, e.toString());
      } // end catch

      return new DailyForecast(dailyForecast, iconBitmap);
   } // end method readDailyForecast

   // update the UI back on the main thread
   protected void onPostExecute(String forecastString)
   {
      weatherFiveDayForecastListener.onForecastLoaded(forecasts);
   } // end method onPostExecute
} // end class ReadFiveDayForecastTask
```

Fig. 14.61 | ReadFiveDayForecastTask methods readDailyForecast and onPostExecute. (Part 2 of 2.)

14.5.10 Class DailyForecast

The DailyForecast (Fig. 14.62) class encapsulates the information of a single day's weather forecast. The class defines four public index constants used to pull information from the String array storing the weather data. Bitmap iconBitmap stores the forecast's image.

The DailyForecast constructor takes a String array assumed to be in the correct order so that the index constants match the correct underlying data. We also provide public accessor methods for each piece of data in a DailyForecast.

```
// DailyForecast.java
// Represents a single day's forecast.
package com.deitel.weatherviewer;

import android.graphics.Bitmap;

public class DailyForecast
{
   // indexes for all the forecast information
   public static final int DAY_INDEX = 0;
   public static final int PREDICTION_INDEX = 1;
   public static final int HIGH_TEMP_INDEX = 2;
   public static final int LOW_TEMP_INDEX = 3;

   final private String[] forecast; // array of all forecast information
   final private Bitmap iconBitmap; // image representation of forecast

   // create a new DailyForecast
   public DailyForecast(String[] forecast, Bitmap iconBitmap)
   {
      this.forecast = forecast;
      this.iconBitmap = iconBitmap;
   } // end DailyForecast constructor

   // get this forecast's image
   public Bitmap getIconBitmap()
   {
      return iconBitmap;
   } // end method getIconBitmap

   // get this forecast's day of the week
   public String getDay()
   {
      return forecast[DAY_INDEX];
   } // end method getDay

   // get short description of this forecast
   public String getDescription()
   {
      return forecast[PREDICTION_INDEX];
   } // end method getDescription

```

Fig. 14.62 | Class DailyForecast. (Part 1 of 2.)

```
    // return this forecast's high temperature
    public String getHighTemperature()
    {
       return forecast[HIGH_TEMP_INDEX];
    } // end method getHighTemperature

    // return this forecast's low temperature
    public String getLowTemperature()
    {
       return forecast[LOW_TEMP_INDEX];
    } // end method getLowTemperature
 } // end class DailyForecast
```

Fig. 14.62 | Class `DailyForecast`. (Part 2 of 2.)

14.5.11 Class WeatherProvider

The `WeatherProvider` class extends `AppWidgetProvider` to update the **Weather Viewer** app widget. `AppWidgetProviders` are special `BroadcastReceivers` which listen for all broadcasts relevant to their app's app widget.

WeatherProvider* package *Statement,* import *Statements and Constant

Figure 14.63 begins the definition of class `ReadFiveDayForecastTask` and defines the fields used throughout the class. The `BITMAP_SAMPLE_SIZE` constant was chosen to downsample the `Bitmap` to a size that can be used with `RemoteViews`—a `View` hierarchy that can be displayed in another process. Android restricts the amount of data that can be passed between processes.

```
// WeatherProvider.java
// Updates the Weather app widget
package com.deitel.weatherviewer;

import android.app.IntentService;
import android.app.PendingIntent;
import android.appwidget.AppWidgetManager;
import android.appwidget.AppWidgetProvider;
import android.content.ComponentName;
import android.content.Context;
import android.content.Intent;
import android.content.SharedPreferences;
import android.content.res.Resources;
import android.graphics.Bitmap;
import android.widget.RemoteViews;
import android.widget.Toast;

import com.deitel.weatherviewer.ReadForecastTask.ForecastListener;
import com.deitel.weatherviewer.ReadLocationTask.LocationLoadedListener;

```

Fig. 14.63 | `WeatherProvider` package statement, `import` statements and constant. (Part 1 of 2.)

```
public class WeatherProvider extends AppWidgetProvider
{
   // sample size for the forecast image Bitmap
   private static final int BITMAP_SAMPLE_SIZE = 4;

```

Fig. 14.63 | `WeatherProvider` package statement, `import` statements and constant. (Part 2 of 2.)

`WeatherProvider` *Methods* `onUpdate`, `getZipcode` *and* `onReceive`

The `onUpdate` method (Fig. 14.64, lines 27–32) responds to broadcasts with actions matching `AppWidgetManager`'s `ACTION_APPWIDGET_UPDATE` constant. In this case, we call our `startUpdateService` method (Fig. 14.64) to update the weather conditions.

Method `getZipcode` (lines 35–48) returns the preferred city's ZIP code from the app's `SharedPreferences`.

Method `onReceive` (lines 51–61) is called when the `WeatherProvider` receives a broadcast. We check whether the given `Intent`'s action matches `WeatherViewerActivity.WIDGET_UPDATE_BROADCAST`. The `WeatherViewerActivity` broadcasts an `Intent` with this action when the preferred city changes, so the app widget can update the weather information accordingly. We call `startUpdateService` to display the new city's forecast.

```
26      // updates all installed Weather App Widgets
27      @Override
28      public void onUpdate(Context context,
29         AppWidgetManager appWidgetManager, int[] appWidgetIds)
30      {
31         startUpdateService(context); // start new WeatherService
32      } // end method onUpdate
33
34      // gets the saved ZIP code for this app widget
35      private String getZipcode(Context context)
36      {
37         // get the app's SharedPreferences
38         SharedPreferences preferredCitySharedPreferences =
39            context.getSharedPreferences(
40            WeatherViewerActivity.SHARED_PREFERENCES_NAME,
41            Context.MODE_PRIVATE);
42
43         // get the ZIP code of the preferred city from SharedPreferences
44         String zipcodeString = preferredCitySharedPreferences.getString(
45            WeatherViewerActivity.PREFERRED_CITY_ZIPCODE_KEY,
46               context.getResources().getString(R.string.default_zipcode));
47         return zipcodeString; // return the ZIP code string
48      } // end method getZipcode
49
50      // called when this AppWidgetProvider receives a broadcast Intent
51      @Override
52      public void onReceive(Context context, Intent intent)
53      {
```

Fig. 14.64 | `WeatherProvider` methods `onUpdate`, `getZipcode` and `onReceive`. (Part 1 of 2.)

```
      // if the preferred city was changed in the app
      if (intent.getAction().equals(
         WeatherViewerActivity.WIDGET_UPDATE_BROADCAST_ACTION))
      {
         startUpdateService(context); // display the new city's forecast
      } // end if
      super.onReceive(context, intent);
   } // end method onReceive

```

Fig. 14.64 | WeatherProvider methods onUpdate, getZipcode and onReceive. (Part 2 of 2.)

WeatherProvider Method startUpdateService

The startUpdateService method (Fig. 14.65) starts a new IntentService of type WeatherService (Fig. 14.66) to update the app widget's forecast in a background thread.

```
   // start new WeatherService to update app widget's forecast information
   private void startUpdateService(Context context)
   {
      // create a new Intent to start the WeatherService
      Intent startServiceIntent;
      startServiceIntent = new Intent(context, WeatherService.class);

      // include the ZIP code as an Intent extra
      startServiceIntent.putExtra(context.getResources().getString(
         R.string.zipcode_extra), getZipcode(context));
      context.startService(startServiceIntent);
   } // end method startUpdateService

```

Fig. 14.65 | WeatherProvider method startUpdateService.

WeatherProvider Nested Class WeatherService

The WeatherService IntentService (Fig. 14.66) retrieves information from the WeatherBug web service and updates the app widget's Views. IntentService's constructor (lines 80–83) takes a String used to name the Service's worker Thread—the String can be used for debugging purposes. Method onHandleIntent (lines 89–101) is called when the WeatherService is started. We get the Resources from our application Context and get the ZIP code from the Intent that started the Service. Then, we launch a ReadLocationTask to read location information for the given ZIP code.

```
76    // updates the Weather Viewer app widget
77    public static class WeatherService extends IntentService
78       implements ForecastListener
79    {
80       public WeatherService()
81       {
```

Fig. 14.66 | WeatherProvider nested class WeatherService. (Part 1 of 2.)

```
         super(WeatherService.class.toString());
      } // end WeatherService constructor

      private Resources resources; // the app's Resources
      private String zipcodeString; // the preferred city's ZIP code
      private String locationString; // the preferred city's location text

      @Override
      protected void onHandleIntent(Intent intent)
      {
         resources = getApplicationContext().getResources();

         zipcodeString = intent.getStringExtra(resources.getString(
            R.string.zipcode_extra));

         // load the location information in a background thread
         new ReadLocationTask(zipcodeString, this,
            new WeatherServiceLocationLoadedListener(
            zipcodeString)).execute();
      } // end method onHandleIntent

```

Fig. 14.66 | `WeatherProvider` nested class `WeatherService`. (Part 2 of 2.)

`WeatherService` Nested Class `onForecastLoaded` Method

Method `onForecastLoaded` (Fig. 14.67) is called when the `AsyncTask` finishes reading weather information from the WeatherBug webservice. We first check if the returned `Bitmap` is `null`. If it is, the `ReadForecastTask` failed to return valid data, so we simply display a `Toast`. Otherwise, we create a new `PendingIntent` (lines 118–120) that will be used to launch the `WeatherViewerActivity` if the user touches the app widget. A `PendingIntent` represents an `Intent` and an action to perform with that `Intent`. A `PendingIntent` can be passed across processes, which is why we use one here.

When updating an app widget from an `AppWidgetProvider`, you do not update the app widget's `Views` directly. The app widget is actually in a separate process from the `AppWidgetProvider`. Communication between the two is achieved through an object of class `RemoteViews`. We create a new `RemoteViews` object for the app widget's layout (lines 123–124). We then pass the `PendingIntent` to `remoteView`'s `setOnClickPendingIntent` (lines 127–128), which registers the app widget's `PendingIntent` that's launched when the user touches the app widget to lauch the **Weather Viewer** app. We specify the layout ID of the root `View` in the app widget's `View` hierarchy. We update the app widget's `TextViews` by passing each `TextView` resource ID and the desired text to `RemoteView`'s `setTextViewText` method. The image is displayed in an `ImageView` using `RemoteView`'s `setImageViewBitmap`. We create a new `ComponentName` (lines 154–155) representing the `WeatherProvider` application component. We get a reference to this app's `AppWidgetManager` using its `static getInstance` method (line 158). We pass the `ComponentName` and `RemoteViews` to `AppWidgetManager`'s `updateAppWidget` method (line 161) to apply the changes made to the `RemoteViews` to the app widget's `Views`.

```
      // receives weather information from the ReadForecastTask
      @Override
      public void onForecastLoaded(Bitmap image, String temperature,
         String feelsLike, String humidity, String precipitation)
      {
         Context context = getApplicationContext();

         if (image == null) // if there is no returned data
         {
            Toast.makeText(context, context.getResources().getString(
               R.string.null_data_toast), Toast.LENGTH_LONG);
            return; // exit before updating the forecast
         } // end if

         // create PendingIntent to launch WeatherViewerActivity
         Intent intent = new Intent(context, WeatherViewerActivity.class);
         PendingIntent pendingIntent = PendingIntent.getActivity(
            getBaseContext(), 0, intent, 0);

         // get the App Widget's RemoteViews
         RemoteViews remoteView = new RemoteViews(getPackageName(),
            R.layout.weather_app_widget_layout);

         // set the PendingIntent to launch when the app widget is clicked
         remoteView.setOnClickPendingIntent(R.id.containerLinearLayout,
            pendingIntent);

         // display the location information
         remoteView.setTextViewText(R.id.location, locationString);

         // display the temperature
         remoteView.setTextViewText(R.id.temperatureTextView,
            temperature + (char)0x00B0 + resources.getString(
            R.string.temperature_unit));

         // display the "feels like" temperature
         remoteView.setTextViewText(R.id.feels_likeTextView, feelsLike +
            (char)0x00B0 + resources.getString(R.string.temperature_unit));

         // display the humidity
         remoteView.setTextViewText(R.id.humidityTextView, humidity +
            (char)0x0025);

         // display the chance of precipitation
         remoteView.setTextViewText(R.id.precipitationTextView,
            precipitation + (char)0x0025);

         // display the forecast image
         remoteView.setImageViewBitmap(R.id.weatherImageView, image);

         // get the Component Name to identify the widget to update
         ComponentName widgetComponentName = new ComponentName(this,
            WeatherProvider.class);
```

Fig. 14.67 | WeatherService nested class onForecastLoaded method. (Part 1 of 2.)

```
        // get the global AppWidgetManager
        AppWidgetManager manager = AppWidgetManager.getInstance(this);

        // update the Weather AppWdiget
        manager.updateAppWidget(widgetComponentName, remoteView);
     } // end method onForecastLoaded

```

Fig. 14.67 | `WeatherService` nested class `onForecastLoaded` method. (Part 2 of 2.)

`WeatherService`'s `WeatherServiceLocationLoadedListener` Class

The `WeatherServiceLocationLoadedListener` (Fig. 14.68) receives location information read from the WeatherBug web service in an `AsyncTask`. In `onLocationLoaded` (lines 177–202), we construct a `String` using the returned data then execute a new `ReadForecastTask` to begin reading the weather information for the current weather conditions of the preferred city. We set the forecast `Bitmap`'s sample size using `ReadForecastTask`'s `setSampleSize` method. There is a size limit on `Bitmaps` that can displayed using `RemoteViews`.

```
164      // receives location information from background task
165      private class WeatherServiceLocationLoadedListener
166         implements LocationLoadedListener
167      {
168         private String zipcodeString; // ZIP code to look up
169
170         // create a new WeatherLocationLoadedListener
171         public WeatherServiceLocationLoadedListener(String zipcodeString)
172         {
173            this.zipcodeString = zipcodeString;
174         } // end WeatherLocationLoadedListener
175
176         // called when the location information is loaded
177         @Override
178         public void onLocationLoaded(String cityString,
179            String stateString, String countryString)
180         {
181            Context context = getApplicationContext();
182
183            if (cityString == null) // if there is no returned data
184            {
185               Toast.makeText(context, context.getResources().getString(
186                  R.string.null_data_toast), Toast.LENGTH_LONG);
187               return; // exit before updating the forecast
188            } // end if
189
190            // display the return information in a TextView
191            locationString = cityString + " " + stateString + ", " +
192               zipcodeString + " " + countryString;
193
```

Fig. 14.68 | `WeatherService`'s `WeatherServiceLocationLoadedListener` class. (Part 1 of 2.)

```
            // launch a new ReadForecastTask
            ReadForecastTask readForecastTask = new ReadForecastTask(
               zipcodeString, (ForecastListener) WeatherService.this,
               WeatherService.this);

            // limit the size of the Bitmap
            readForecastTask.setSampleSize(BITMAP_SAMPLE_SIZE);
            readForecastTask.execute();
         } // end method onLocationLoaded
      } // end class WeatherServiceLocationLoadedListener
   } // end class WeatherService
} // end WeatherProvider
```

Fig. 14.68 | `WeatherService`'s `WeatherServiceLocationLoadedListener` class. (Part 2 of 2.)

14.6 Wrap-Up

In this chapter, we presented the **Weather Viewer** app and its companion app widget. The app used various features new to Android 3.x.

You learned how to use fragments to create and manage portions of the app's GUI. You used subclasses of `Fragment`, `DialogFragment` and `ListFragment` to create a robust user interface and to take advantage of a tablet's screen size. You learned that each `Fragment` has a life cycle and it must be hosted in a parent `Activity`. You used a a `FragmentManager` to manage the `Fragments` and a `FragmentTransaction` to add, remove and transition between `Fragments`.

You used the Android 3.x action bar at the top of the screen to display the app's options menu and tabbed navigation elements. You also used long-touch event handling to allow the user to select a city as the preferred one or to delete the city. The app also used `JsonReader` to read JSON objects containing the weather data from the WeatherBug web services.

You created a a companion app widget (by extending class `AppWidgetProvider`) to display the current weather conditions for the user's preferred city, as set in the app. To launch the app when the user touched the widget, you used a `PendingIntent`. When the user changed preferred cities, the app used an `Intent` to broadcast the change to the app wedget.

Staying in Contact with Deitel & Associates, Inc.

We hope you enjoyed reading *Android for Programmers: An App-Driven Approach* as much as we enjoyed writing it. We'd appreciate your feedback. Please send your questions, comments, suggestions and corrections to `deitel@deitel.com`. Check out our growing list of Android-related Resource Centers at `www.deitel.com/ResourceCenters.html`. To stay up to date with the latest news about Deitel publications and corporate training, sign up for the free weekly *Deitel® Buzz Online* e-mail newsletter at `www.deitel.com/newsletter/subscribe.html`, and follow us on Facebook (`www.deitel.com/deitelfan`) and Twitter (`@deitel`). To learn more about Deitel & Associates' worldwide on-site programming training for your company or organization, visit `www.deitel.com/training` or e-mail `deitel@deitel.com`.

Index

D

G

J

K

N

O

X

Y

Z